Collected Papers on Monetary Theory

Collected Papers on Monetary Theory

Robert E. Lucas, Jr.

Edited by

Max Gillman

Harvard University Press
Cambridge, Massachusetts
London, England
2013

Library of Congress Cataloging-in-Publication Data

Lucas, Robert E., Jr.
Collected papers on monetary theory / Robert E. Lucas, Jr. ; edited by Max Gillman.
p. cm.
Includes bibliographical references and index.
ISBN 978-0-674-06687-8 (alk. paper)
1. Monetary policy. 2. Money. 3. Lucas, Robert E., Jr. I. Gillman, Max. II. Title.
HG230.3.L83 2013
339.5′3—dc23 2012017312

Contents

Preface

MAX GILLMAN

This book collects papers on monetary economics written by Robert E. Lucas, Jr., over the past forty years. Insofar as they can be said to have a common theme, it would be the application of the theory of general equilibrium dynamics to a set of problems that had previously been studied using other, less powerful methods. Lucas built upon the tradition of his teacher Milton Friedman: questioning the Phillips curve as a long-term phenomenon, analyzing real money within consumer demand theory, connecting money printing to inflation, and exploring how unexpected money printing can cause inefficient short-run output fluctuations. Lucas's derivation of the Phillips curve as a temporary phenomenon in general equilibrium is the direct subject of four chapters in this collection, starting with his 1972 article (Chapter 1) and including a previously unpublished manuscript from 1989 (Chapter 12), his Nobel address of 1996 (Chapter 16), and his 2007 article with Golosov on menu costs (Chapter 20). These chapters show how money can cause temporary real effects, a theme going back to Hume but poised within the recursive dynamic methodology, or DSGE (dynamic stochastic general equilibrium) framework, as it is often called today. Chapter 15 explicitly discusses the Friedman and Schwartz money-to-output thesis of the famous *Monetary History*, a thesis related to the Phillips curve debate (see also Friedman 1971).

Carrying on the work of our teachers is an adventure in life and science. Rarely, leaders such as Lucas arise, who raise the stakes to heights that transmit the quest to the next generation and more. Many would agree that Lucas is among the great teachers, researchers, and writers of the past several generations. This makes it a privilege to edit this collection. The aim is to enable the reader to tie together the strands more easily, to see the man and his work more as a whole, and to develop a stronger platform from which to teach and do research.

My perspective comes from being a Lucas student during the 1980s. One defining feature of the tradition Lucas propounded was that there is no fire wall between microeconomics and macroeconomics. The Chicago way of developing macroeconomics was by developing microeconomics so that a certain macroeconomic story could be told. The tradition of using price theory in this way included T. W. Schultz, George Stigler, Gary Becker, Friedman, and Lucas. Agricultural economics classes included T. W. Schultz's explanation of growth through human capital investment. Stigler, Becker, and Friedman all had price theory textbooks that included some fundamental macroeconomics. Classes from Stigler, Becker, Rosen, and Lucas, field exams by Schultz and Stigler, the Lucas "Money and Banking" workshop with presenters such as Sargent, and guest visitors such as Friedman all made Chicago an engaging atmosphere.

Lucas added to the idea explosion by extending the Friedman tradition in monetary theory and macroeconomics.[1] Lucas's teaching formalized Friedman's quantity-theoretic idea that real money had a well-defined demand function just like other goods. He taught us quantity-theoretic relations from his 1980 "Two Illustrations" article (Chapter 4). He presented the 1980 cash-in-advance (CIA) money demand model with leisure added (Chapter 3). And he showed how the CIA inflation tax induced substitution from goods toward leisure, caused employment and output to fall, and lowered welfare. This gave a general equilibrium view of money demand that related to Cagan, Bailey, and Friedman and the welfare cost of inflation. In a 1981 paper (Chapter 5) and a later, 2000 paper (Chapter 17), Lucas expanded on this. He also taught us his cash-goods and credit-goods model (Chapter 7). This gave us a theoretical basis for inflation targeting to achieve optimal monetary and fiscal policy.[2]

1. See Lucas (2001) for his views on Friedman, such as his being a "moral example" to follow.

2. Classes were rather relaxed. Lucas would always bring an ashtray with him and smoke cigarettes throughout the class (he could not get away with that today!). He would throw out occasional questions and just wait patiently for someone eventually to offer an answer. He also changed what he taught every time he taught a course, such as "Topics in Monetary Economics," basically by teaching whatever he was working on at the time. Most important, he would always carefully set out the model on the board and derive the equilibrium conditions so that we could follow him. This produced generations of cohorts, each following some aspect of his continuous stream of output.

Lucas offered us a way to move forward without losing traditional elements. Friedman's and Meltzer's permanent income hypothesis applications to money demand (see Chapter 11) could be seen within the context of Lucas's 1976 analysis of consumption demand. His 1978 asset pricing paper (Chapter 2) plus his monetary theory enabled an integration of money, macroeconomics, and finance.

After poring over Lucas's 1976 critique, I finally realized the extent to which textbook general equilibrium monetary theory and macroeconomics was not well based in microeconomic theory.[3] This confused me: IS-LM "stabilization policy" involved no real dynamics and did not arise from consumer optimization. Monetary theory in the IS-LM world was a story of how a onetime increase in the money supply increases output. It did not use marginal analysis to explain inflation, money demand, or its velocity. Lucas's monetary approach was holistic, solid, and revolutionary: the price-theoretic approach became reformulated as a dynamic general equilibrium based on key technology and utility parameters.

Lucas's 1982, 1984, and 1987 papers (Chapters 6, 8, and 10) extended the CIA approach. We also could read Friedman and Schwartz's 1982 book and Friedman on velocity using a permanent income approach to money demand. I eventually latched on to a concluding discussion by Lucas in his 1980 paper (Chapter 3) on how velocity could be endogenized through an explicit, separate "credit mechanism" that coexisted with cash: "a hybrid system left for future research."

A separate credit mechanism seemed a good way to explain velocity. As my dissertation supervisor, Lucas helped me to endogenize velocity in Prescott's 1987 model with money and exchange credit. This meant adding a condition that set the marginal exchange cost of money equal to that of credit (related to Baumol 1952). The ad hoc part was a non-micro-based transactions cost of using credit. This became my PhD dissertation model. Lucas also showed me several applications: formulating the welfare cost of inflation in general equilibrium with a compensating variation approach (see Gillman 1993) and comparing partial with general equilibrium welfare cost estimates (see Gillman 1995). The dissertation also included the effect on welfare of taxes on credit (Gillman 2000).

Several students in my cohort also pursued cash-in-advance research.

3. Alan Meltzer once mentioned to me that he had asked Lucas to write up this 1976 critique for a conference so that people could try to understand his radically new views. The critique was published in the first issue of the *Carnegie-Rochester Conference Series*, now part of the *Journal of Monetary Economics*.

Narayana Kocherlakota and Deborah Lucas concluded that the Lucas-Stokey model could not explain velocity movements well (Hodrick et al. 1991). Deborah Lucas also evaluated CIA models in a separate review (D. Lucas 1991). Pamela Labadie used a stochastic CIA model combined with Lucas asset pricing to account for the equity premium (Labadie 1989). Her related CIA paper found insufficient stochastic inflation effects on stock returns as compared to the data (Giovannini and Labadie 1991). Wilbur John Coleman II used a Lucas and Stokey CIA extension to explain the equity premium, low risk-free returns, and the term structure of interest rates (Bansal and Coleman 1996). They used a transactions cost function for exchange credit.

Most of my colleagues subsequently followed different directions. For example, Kocherlakota focused on search theory that uses a design mechanism with bonds as the main substitute for money. Recently he reviewed contrasting neoclassical and search-theoretic monetary literatures (2005). John Heaton, another 1980s classmate, and Deborah Lucas collaborated in asset pricing theory (Heaton and Lucas 2000).

My coauthors and I thought a continued CIA velocity focus offered promise if we could make it endogenous without an hoc transaction cost function. Lucas sets an exogenous fraction "*a*" of purchases made with money (Chapter 11, equation 4).[4] We endogenized this *a* by producing exchange credit to buy the remaining $1 - a$ of consumption. This employed the financial intermediation production function of Clark (1984) such that $1 - a$ is the credit per unit of consumption, and deposits are a factor of production. This results in endogenous velocity, a Cagan-type money demand, and integration of a price-theoretic form of financial intermediation. By adding deposits as a third factor of production, this gives an upward-sloping marginal cost per unit of credit that overcomes the King and Plosser (1984) puzzle of there being no unique equilibrium with both money and exchange credit as produced with a standard Cobb-Douglas function. Hancock (1985) found empirical support for this Clark (1984) production function, and it has been used continuously in the banking literature. This approach can then be placed within the Lucas (1988) endogenous growth framework as extended to include monetary volatility across different cyclic frequencies. For example, endogenous velocity helps

4. Lucas writes: "a(i)ε[0, 1] is the fraction of purchases of good i that must be covered by money."

explain the negative inflation-growth relation found in the literature (Gillman and Kejak 2005), one that in the mid-1990s was controversial (see Kocherlakota 1996). It also can explain the inflation-investment negative relation found in evidence by extending the Lucas (1980) CIA constraint to include investment (Gillman and Kejak 2011). Velocity with credit shocks extends Cooley and Hansen (1989) to enable plausible explanations of velocity and output cyclic properties (Benk et al. 2005, 2010).

Money (cash or non-interest-bearing accounts accessed by debit cards) and its exchange credit substitute (credit cards paid off at the end of the period) coexist and perhaps always will, since no one can magically get goods without exchange. Exchange is a friction. Insurance agents, real estate agents, lawyers, doctors, and bankers all exist because frictions are everywhere that Coase implies. Banking exists as a market that prices the "transactions costs" of intermediation. Exchange can be viewed as an intermediate good produced in order to ultimately consume goods: a view from Becker's household production approach to consumer theory. The combination of Beckerian consumer theory and Lucasian monetary theory provides a basis for quantity-theoretic monetary economics to address policy.

Research into monetary policy has been reinvigorated in the wake of the recent banking crisis. Is re-regulation of the banking sector causing a decline in banking productivity that is prolonging unemployment? Could an international risk-based, "universal" deposit insurance system do better? Does velocity and traditional monetary theory matter for monetary policy? Will researchers continue using Lucas's foundations to give insight into such issues? I think the answer to these questions is yes.

Monetary theory appears well equipped to be developed from foundations Lucas has established to frame current policy debates. Extensions of his work show how researchers have followed directions signposted by Lucas. Some have remarked that we are all Keynesians, or all Friedmanians, but perhaps all monetary economists are indebted to Lucas. This is why I have worked to put together this monetary-based collection of Lucas's work. It represents a historic advancement in monetary, macroeconomic, and finance theory.

I am grateful to Bob Lucas and Mike Aronson for extensive comments on my preface and for helping to select the collection of papers, and I am especially grateful to Bob for his introduction and for offering the unpublished manuscript that is Chapter 12. I also am grateful to Michal Kejak for comments.

References

Bansal, Ravi, and Wilbur John Coleman II. 1996. "A Monetary Explanation of the Equity Premium, Term Premium, and Risk-Free Rate Puzzles." *Journal of Political Economy* 104, no. 6 (December): 1135–71.

Baumol, William J. 1952. "The Transactions Demand for Cash: An Inventory Theoretic Approach." *Quarterly Journal of Economics* 66 (November): 545–556.

Benk, Szilard, Max Gillman, and Michal Kejak. 2005. "Credit Shocks in the Financial Deregulatory Era: Not the Usual Suspects." *Review of Economic Dynamics* 8, no. 3 (July): 668–687.

———. 2010. "A Banking Explanation of the U.S. Velocity of Money: 1919–2004." *Journal of Economic Dynamics and Control* 34, no. 4 (April): 765—779.

Clark, J. A. 1984. "Estimation of Economies of Scale in Banking Using a Generalized Functional Form." *Journal of Money, Credit, and Banking* 16, no. 1 (February): 53–68.

Cooley, Thomas F., and Gary D. Hanson. 1989. "The Inflation Tax in a Real Business Cycle Model." *American Economic Review* 79, no. 4 (September): 733–748.

Friedman, Milton. 1971. "A Monetary Theory of Nominal Income." *Journal of Political Economy* 79, no. 2 (March-April): 323–337.

———. 1976. *Price Theory.* Chicago: Aldine.

Friedman, Milton and Anna J. Schwartz. 1982. *Monetary Trends in the United States and the United Kingdom: Their Relation to Income, Prices, and Interest Rates, 1867–1975.* Chicago: University of Chicago Press.

Gillman, Max. 1993. "The Welfare Costs of Inflation in a Cash-in-Advance Model with Costly Credit." *Journal of Monetary Economics* 31, no. 1 (February): 97–116.

———. 1995. "Comparing Partial and General Equilibrium Estimates of the Welfare Cost of Inflation." *Contemporary Economic Policy* 13, no. 4 (October): 60–71.

———. 2000. "On the Optimality of Restricting Credit: Inflation-Avoidance and Productivity." *Japanese Economic Review* 51, no. 3 (September): 375–390.

Gillman, Max, and Michal Kejak. 2005. "Inflation and Balanced-Path Growth with Alternative Payment Mechanisms." *Economic Journal* 115, no. 500 (January): 247–270.

———. 2011. "Inflation, Investment and Growth: A Banking Approach." *Economica* 78, no. 310 (April): 260—282.

Giovannini, Alberto, and Pamela Labadie. 1991. "Asset Prices and Interest Rates in Cash-in-Advance Models." *Journal of Political Economy* 99, no. 6 (December): 1215–1251.

Hancock, Diana. 1985. "The Financial Firm: Production with Monetary and Nonmonetary Goods." *Journal of Political Economy* 93, no. 5 (October): 859–880.

Heaton, John. and Deborah Lucas. 2000. "Portfolio Choice and Asset Prices: The Importance of Entrepreneurial Risk." *Journal of Finance* 55, no. 3: 1163–1198.

Hodrick, Robert J., Narayana R. Kocherlakota, and Deborah Lucas. 1991. "The Variability of Velocity in Cash-in-Advance Models." *Journal of Political Economy* 99, no. 2 (April): 358–384.

King, Robert G., and Charles I. Plosser. 1984. "Money, Credit, and Prices in a Real Business Cycle." *American Economic Review* 74, no. 3 (June): 363–380.

Kocherlakota, Narayana. 1996. "Inflation and Growth—Commentary." *Proceedings, Federal Reserve Bank of St. Louis* (May): 170–172.

———. 2005. "Optimal Monetary Policy: What We Know and What We Don't Know." *International Economic Review* 46, no. 2: 715–729.

Labadie, Pamela. 1989. "Stochastic Inflation and the Equity Premium." *Journal of Monetary Economics* 24, no. 2 (September): 277–298.

Lucas, Deborah J. 1991. "Foundations of the Cash-in-Advance Model: A Review Essay." *Journal of Monetary Economics* 27, no. 3 (June): 487–493.

Lucas, Robert E., Jr. 1976. "Econometric Policy Evaluation: A Critique." *Carnegie-Rochester Conference Series on Public Policy* 1, no. 1 (January): 19–46.

———. 1988. "On the Mechanics of Economic Development." *Journal of Monetary Economics* 22, no. 1 (July): 3–42.

———. 2001. "Professional Memoir." Unpublished manuscript.

Prescott, Edward C. 1987. "A Multiple Means-of-Payment Model." Pp. 42–51, in *New Approaches to Monetary Economics*, edited by W. A. Barnett and K. J. Singleton. Cambridge: Cambridge University Press.

Introduction

ROBERT E. LUCAS, JR.

When I started out in economics, I thought of a collection of papers as something to be assembled after a set of problems had been satisfactorily resolved. The purpose of the collection would be to announce the solutions. I may even have had something like this in mind in my 1981 collection, *Studies in Business Cycle Theory*, though I at least had the good sense not to say so. Soon after that book came out many of its basic premises were swept away in the great tide of research that followed Kydland and Prescott's 1982 paper, and more recently the events of 2008 swept away still more. Obsolescence is a necessary—indeed, welcome—feature of a scientific career.

Even so, when Max Gillman proposed collecting my work on monetary theory in a book, my first reaction was that I hadn't solved enough problems to warrant a book, and anyway that economists were not as interested in monetary theory as they used to be. Both reactions are true enough, but as Max and I went over all these papers I found that I liked most of them at least as much as I did when they were written. Soon I began to think of others to add to the list.

The twenty papers collected in this volume are presented in the order in which they were written, but with a few overlaps they fall naturally into three groups. I will label these *core monetary theory and public finance* (Chapters 3, 4, 5, 7, 9, 10, 11, 14, and 17), *asset pricing* (Chapters 2, 6, 8, 13, and 18), and *real effects of monetary instability* (Chapters 1, 12, 15, 16, 19, and 20). What follows are memories and afterthoughts on each of the areas.

Core Monetary Theory and Public Finance

When I moved from Carnegie-Mellon to Chicago in 1975, I began to teach in the first-year sequence in macroeconomics, a practice I maintained for more than twenty-five years. For the core (as we called it) I thought I needed a coherent approach to the basics of monetary theory, which I thought of as the quantity theory of money and the evidence that supported that theory. I wanted to do this in a way that made maximum use of modern general equilibrium theory. I'm sure I began with Samuelson's 1958 overlapping generations model and the developments of that theory due to David Cass, Menahem Yaari, and others, but I became dissatisfied with the abstractness of that framework and sought a view in which money is an asset that we hold to pay bills with, a factor in a *payments system*.

I began to develop a set of class notes based on the cash-in-advance payment convention that Robert Clower had introduced. In this model, households could only consume the endowment of someone else and it was the responsibility of one member of the household to deliver cash payments physically to sellers of the good they wanted to consume. The first set of notes, in which a continuum of households faced idiosyncratic preference shocks, became "Equilibrium in a Pure Currency Economy," Chapter 3 in this volume. It developed into a paper that I gave at a 1978 Minneapolis Fed conference that Jack Kareken and Neil Wallace had organized. Clower was there, liked my paper, and it was published soon in the journal he edited.

A second set of notes was circulated, called "Equilibrium in a Pure Credit Economy," in which people pay their bills with interest-bearing debt. I had planned to combine these two models by assuming a fixed cost for credit use but not for cash use so both assets would be held. I had thought that my pure credit allocation was economically efficient and could therefore serve as an ideal benchmark, but Ed Prescott and Rob Townsend convinced me that this could not be right: efficiency would require at least partial insurance of the idiosyncratic risk that everyone had to bear. But I knew nothing about mechanism design then and had no idea how such insurance could be provided. This was discouraging, since I couldn't very well center my core course on a model that I didn't understand. Many years later, Andy Atkeson showed me how this efficient insurance problem could be solved, and we wrote two papers together, but by then my planned sequence of models was ancient history.

In this same core course I also felt responsible for familiarizing students with the "mountain of evidence" (in Milton Friedman's words) that supported the quantity theory of money's implications for money growth, inflation, and interest rates. Unlike the still-speculative theories on the effects of transient monetary shocks, this long-run and cross-country evidence is easy to interpret with models of balanced growth and perfect foresight and is overwhelmingly supportive of the theory. It is still astonishing to me how many generally well trained economists are unfamiliar with this evidence, which should be a main feature of the empirical basis for monetary economics. How can we talk about liquidity if we can't say what it is and think about how it might be measured?

I also tried to reconcile these long-run facts with the fact that these regularities break down at higher frequencies, making the time-series evidence harder to read than the cross-sections. My "Two Illustrations" (Chapter 4) was an attempt to deal with this, using a "filter" to separate low-frequency and high-frequency movements. I used postwar U.S. data, so the paper is basically a study of the inflation of the 1970s. Recent, very useful work by Luca Benati goes over similar issues with more and better data and much more sophisticated time-series methods.

In 1981 I was asked to be a discussant of Stanley Fischer's Carnegie-Rochester paper on the costs of inflation, which by the end of the 1970s had become a headline topic. Fischer's starting point was the same one I had learned as a student: Martin Bailey's use of Hotelling-Harberger welfare triangles to assess the welfare cost of inflation, viewed as a distorting tax. The problem Fischer faced, one I was initially in sympathy with, was that the cost of inflation, measured this way, seemed much too small. A permanent 10 percent inflation was estimated as about the equivalent of less than a 1 percent reduction of consumption. Fischer sought other costs and ended up focusing on uncertainty about inflation. But as I went through the details of the argument, I became more and more convinced that Bailey's approach had got pretty much everything: adding even generous estimates of the cost of year-to-year fluctuations in the inflation tax was a third- or fourth-decimal-place issue. At a later conference, where, as I remember it, Fischer discussed a paper of mine, Milton Friedman came down solidly on Stan's side on this. I can only say that I think they were both wrong.

Soon after the discussion of Fischer's paper I was asked to contribute a paper on the gold standard for another Carnegie-Rochester conference. Nancy Stokey and I had just completed a very sharp theoretical paper on recursive utility and I asked her to work with me on this one too. Neither one of us had any real knowledge or enthusiasm about a gold standard, but it seemed like an occasion to go over some of the general equilibrium questions of monetary policy that Fischer and I (and many others) had discussed but had not really modeled. Nancy proposed that we use a full-dress Arrow-Debreu contingent claims formulation, with a cash-in-advance constraint added. We introduced a new feature to these models by distinguishing between "cash goods" that must be paid for with cash at the time of purchase and "credit goods" that could be paid for a period later. This device introduced substitution possibilities that mirrored the substitutability assumed and estimated in empirical money demand functions. These were the first steps on a path since followed by many others. Our substantive objective was to consider the inflation tax as part of a conventional tax system, motivated by an exogenous need for public goods and an obligation to honor existing debt.

Dynamic models of taxation invariably run into problems of time consistency: a tax authority acting in the best interests of the public will always want to issue promises about future tax rates that it does not honor when the time comes. This is clearest in the tax treatment of capital goods, which, once built, are inelastically supplied and so form an ideal tax base. To avoid this particular complication we simply kept capital out of our model. But the same issue came up in the maturity structure of the nominal government debt. It will always appear to be attractive to default on initial debt and promise never to do so in the future. If direct default is not an option, as we assumed, the government may still be able to engineer an effective, partial default by using its market power over interest rates. In our model, though, we discovered that a government can always find a maturity structure for the debt it leaves to its successor, which will remove this incentive for partial default. This was a completely unexpected result, a perfect illustration of the way in which a tightly formulated theoretical model can take you into new, interesting substantive territory.

Chapter 9, "Principles of Fiscal and Monetary Policy," was a political economy lecture given at Harvard in 1984. I thought it was a useful exposition of Nancy's and my paper, as a unified treatment of the aggregative aspects of fiscal and monetary policy.

Our *Econometrica* paper, here Chapter 10, was another development from Chapter 7, a recursive formulation of a purely monetary policy with fiscal aspects set aside. These simplifications let us construct the dynamic equilibrium, which we had done only in a linear-quadratic example in the earlier paper, and do so under a variety of assumptions on the assumed information structure. The paper illustrated some of the problems involved in inferring causal relations among monetary actions, interest rates, and inflation rates on the basis of leads and lags in the data. The chapter also includes a correction to an error in the original paper, identified by Teh-Ming Huo.

The monetary models that Nancy and I had developed were well designed to match up with empirical work on money demand pioneered by Milton Friedman and Allan Meltzer, but in that pre-calibration era we ourselves had not done anything quantitative with this connection. When I was asked to give a paper at a Carnegie-Rochester Conference honoring Allan, I thought immediately of a replication of his 1963 paper. In carrying this out, I was amazed at how well Meltzer's estimates of the income and interest elasticities of money demand had stood up to thirty years of additional data. At that time there was concern about the failure of some money demand functions to track quarter-to-quarter changes, and this shows up in my replication too. But what impressed me, and what is entirely consistent with the other implications of the quantity theory of money, is the stability of these estimates over the entire twentieth century and the ability of the quantitative model to trace medium-frequency comovements in interest rates and velocity.

I came back to money demand estimation in my presidential address to the Econometric Society, Chapter 17, shifting the focus to measuring the welfare cost of inflation. My modeling approach and my welfare estimates were considerably refined compared to my discussion of Fischer twenty years earlier, owing in part to the help of Esteban Rossi-Hansberg. But the underlying logic and the conclusions were about the same.

Chapter 14, "Supply-Side Economics: An Analytical Review," is a favorite of mine, even though it is basically a survey of work done by others. During the 1980s many economists had applied dynamic general equilibrium modeling to the analysis of taxation, just as Nancy and I had done, but with carefully calibrated models and closer attention to matching features of the actual tax system. I had paid little attention to these developments and had not thought to associate them with the "supply-side economics" that I was reading about in the newspapers. I suppose I had absorbed the attitude of contempt for this phrase that was then standard in the economics establishment. I remember a seminar lunch in Chicago where Larry Kotlikoff treated me to a summary of results that he and Alan Auerbach and others were finding on the effects of capital taxation on capital accumulation and real output. This was not crackpot stuff. I began to work through this literature, and when I was invited to give the Hicks Lecture at Oxford, I used the occasion to organize what I had learned.

Asset Pricing

The particular asset pricing model studied in Chapter 2 was described to me by Pentti Kouri when he visited Chicago for a job interview. According to Stanley Fischer, Kouri had got it from Paul Samuelson, who had proposed the problem to classes at MIT. This and my subsequent asset pricing papers are all fairly straightforward applications of general equilibrium theory.

When I arrived at Chicago, Jacob Frenkel was on the faculty (soon joined by Michael Mussa) and there was enormous student interest in international monetary issues. I wrote "Interest Rates and Currency Prices in a Two-Country World" (Chapter 6) in order to be a part of this and to learn something about international economics from Jacob. The model introduced money in each of two symmetric economies and assumed that residents of both economies valued goods produced in the other. Mechanical cash-in-advance restrictions were imposed (this was before Nancy's and my work on money) and nominal prices and interest rates were solved for. But without the Keynesian features that Mundell had introduced, there wasn't much to this exercise. It was mostly just a matter of keeping the units straight.

The title of Chapter 8, "Money in a Theory of Finance," is taken from a classic book by Gurley and Shaw, which stated and tried to face the problems raised by two coexisting payment mediums: government-issued fiat money ("outside money") and privately issued or "inside" money. This remains a central issue of monetary theory today, I think, but neither Gurley and Shaw nor anyone since has resolved it. My paper does introduce money into an asset pricing model—a step in the right direction—but it does not address the questions raised by inside money.

Chapter 13, "Liquidity and Interest Rates," was inspired by innovative work on "segmented markets" by Sandy Grossman and Julio Rotemberg. I introduced an assumption that vastly simplified the analysis (without losing much, I would say) and made it possible—easy, in fact—to introduce some genuine asset pricing dynamics.

Chapter 18, "Interest Rates and Inflation," is another segmented market model, jointly written with Fernando Alvarez (who was developing segmented market ideas in other directions in his own work) and Warren Weber. The paper is a nice reconciliation of inflation targeting using interest rate setting as the tool with a monetarist view where the money supply (or the base) is the tool and interest rates are market-determined. In our setup, these are just two different ways of describing the same policy.

Real Effects of Monetary Instability

All of the papers I have discussed so far deal with economic models in which changes in the quantity of money are either ignored or assumed to affect only nominal prices and interest rates but (except for the inflation tax) not real quantities and relative prices. It is this quantity theory of money and the evidence that bears on it that I viewed and taught as core macroeconomics.

My thinking on the real effects of monetary instability began with Keynesian IS/LM models as developed by Hicks, Modigliani, and others. Martin Bailey's class notes—and later a textbook—were the version I took with me when I began teaching at Carnegie Tech. This was the theoretical background with which I read Milton Friedman and Anna Schwartz's 1963 monograph, *A Monetary History of the United States.* The book attributes the 1929–1933 downturn to monetary factors and centers the analysis of all other U.S. depressions/recessions on monetary factors as well.

Chapter 15 is my retrospective review of this book, part of a special issue of the *Journal of Monetary Economics* that Tom Cooley organized and to which Jeffrey Miron and Bruce Smith also contributed. By the time that review was written, research by Kydland and Prescott, Gary Hansen, Cooley, and others had shown that purely real factors could account for much of the fluctuations in the postwar United States, and certainly this research required a rethinking of Friedman and Schwartz's accounts of prewar fluctuations as well. I held, then and now, to the view that the 1929–1933 downturn was due mainly to a banking crisis that the Federal Reserve could and should have tried to offset by monetary expansion, but this Great Contraction now seems to me more like a remarkable and exceptional event than a useful template for depressions generally.

In my 2002 presidential address to the American Economic Association, here Chapter 19, I reviewed the postwar evidence from as many angles as I could think of and concluded that this evidence was consistent with only a minor role for monetary factors over the postwar period. Of course, this conclusion was that monetary factors had not been a major source of real instability over this period, not that they *could* not be important or that they never had been. I shared Friedman and Schwartz's views on the contraction phase, 1929–1933, of the Great Depression, and this is also the way I now see the post-Lehman 2008–2009 phase of the current recession. Obviously, the latter possibility was far from my mind in 2002.

Beliefs aside, a successful policy to deal with a monetary or liquidity crisis will need to be based on some understanding of how real effects of monetary shocks come about, some kind of theory. This has been a central unresolved issue for economists at least since David Hume addressed it in the eighteenth century. This is the theme of my Nobel Lecture, Chapter 16 here, but no resolution is offered in that essay.

My first attempt at this question of monetary non-neutrality was "Expectations and the Neutrality of Money," the first chapter in this volume. (It was also included in my earlier collection, *Studies in Business Cycle Theory.*) The paper's contribution was to propose one way that nominal prices might be "sticky," or "rigid," or non-neutral, something other than an across-the-board units change. I took the general equilibrium perspective from Edmund Phelps, who had outlined an "islands" model explicitly focused on price rigidity at the conference that turned into the "Phelps volume." Leonard Rapping's and my contribution to that volume was a partial equilibrium model of the labor market only. The idea was that agents had to base production and employment decisions on partial information and that this could lead them to decisions that to an omniscient observer would appear pathological. The new elements in my paper, relative to Phelps's outline, were its mathematical explicitness and its use of rational expectations. The example developed in the paper made it clear that the possibility of using monetary policy to stimulate production would depend on the information people have and could not be reliably described by a stable Phillips curve. But attempts to construct quantitative models of recessions based on this feature alone have not succeeded.

Over the years I have kept my eyes open for other resolutions to the price rigidity problem. Ed Prescott devised one of these (for an entirely different purpose) with an example of hotel rooms priced in advance. In his example, before it is known how many visitors will arrive in town, hotels all set different prices on rooms. Customers arrive, filling up the low-cost rooms first and as more arrive filling up rooms with higher prices.

Sales of high-priced rooms are rare, but lucrative when they occur. *Expected* returns are equalized over the whole range of prices. My paper in Chapter 12 introduces money into a dynamic version of Prescott's model and shows how an unexpected increase in nominal spending can result in an increase in both production (hotel rooms occupied) and the price level: a kind of non-neutrality.

That paper was never published. My analysis relied on the assumption that prices are fixed in advance and cannot be altered once customers begin to arrive: if I see that my hotel room is unsold, I cannot put it on sale. Mike Woodford, then a Chicago colleague, saw that this assumption could be weakened as long as sellers got no direct information on demand during a period, and we collaborated on a version using this weaker assumption. Our efforts, which got very complicated, were reported in the 1993 NBER working paper no. 4250. Another, similarly motivated version can be found in Eden (1994).

It has long been noticed that prices for individual goods and services, as posted by sellers, tend to be unchanged for long periods (many days, weeks, months, even years in some cases) and then jump to new values. Since new information of all kinds flows in continuously, this observation suggests the existence of fixed costs associated with changing prices. In macroeconomic discussions these are usually referred to as "menu costs." I had not contributed to menu cost modeling, but at a conference held in honor of Edmund Phelps in 2001 I commented on a paper on price stickiness that, I thought, had some unfortunate implications that a menu cost model would not have had. I teased the authors and other "new Keynesians" in the audience about what I saw as an unwillingness to take on menu cost models because of their notorious technical difficulties. This commentary was so convincing (to me) that I decided to try a menu cost model myself. For this I recruited Mikhail Golosov, who was then a Minnesota graduate student and an RA at the Minneapolis Fed, and together we wrote the paper that is Chapter 20 in this volume. Mike suggested that we make use of a new data set on individual prices that Pete Klenow and Oleksiy Kryvstov had put together from Bureau of Labor Statistics survey data. This elevated the ambitions of our modeling from a qualitative example to a serious empirical project with well-calibrated parameters. The model's predictions for the relation between inflation rates and the frequency of individual price changes were consistent with evidence from both high-inflation and low-inflation countries. But I was again disappointed to find that menu costs as we formulated them could not take us far from monetary neutrality.

Occasional Pieces and Conclusion

The final chapter in the volume contains several occasional pieces. Each of them illustrates my views on monetary or macroeconomic issues, although none of them can be seen as a research contribution. There is a transcript of a luncheon talk that I gave to some MBA alumni soon after coming to Chicago. A written version, entitled "The Death of Keynesian Economics," was then worked up from my notes for an alumni publication that is apparently no longer available. A friend of mine, the historian of economic thought Michel Devroey, came across my original notes in an archive of some of my papers that had been moved to Duke University years before. I edited the notes—added articles, punctuation, etc.—to get the version printed here. Brief excerpts from this talk have been cited, apparently to make a case that I am a dangerous character, but the talk itself is pretty reasonable, and my sociological forecast there came out better than my economic forecasts usually do. Years later I gave a talk to members of the History of Political Economy Society, later published, called "My Keynesian Education." This too was worked up from notes. Also included is my review of the first two volumes of Robert Sidelsky's biography of Keynes, published in the *Journal of Modern History.* The last selection in this chapter is a brief talk I gave at a retirement party for Otmar Issing, the European Central Bank's first chief economist. Issing was perhaps the last central banker to advocate the use of monetary aggregates, in addition to short-term interest rates, to measure the ease or tightness of monetary policy, a position that I fully agree with. In my talk I tried to explain why.

Now, toward the end of my career as at the beginning, I see myself as a monetarist, as a student of Milton Friedman and Allan Meltzer. My contributions to monetary theory have been in incorporating the quantity theory of money into modern, explicitly dynamic modeling, continuing on the path initiated by Miguel Sidrauski in the 1960s and pursued by many others since. For the empirically well established predictions of the quantity theory—the long-run links between money growth, inflation, and nominal interest rates, and the stable relation between the money/nominal GDP ratio over the last century—this has been mostly accomplished. On the harder questions of monetary economics—the real effects of monetary instability, the roles of outside and inside money, the instability of fractional reserve banks—this volume may contribute some useful theoretical examples but little in the way of empirically successful models. It is understandable that in the leading operational macroeconomic models today—real business cycle models and new Keynesian models—money as a measurable magnitude plays no role at all, but I hope we can do better than this in the models of the future.

For the most part my many debts to others are reasonably well documented in the individual papers in this volume, but there are exceptions. Of all the papers included here, the ones that Nancy Stokey and I wrote together on taxation and monetary dynamics have had by far the largest influence on later theorists. Applied theory is always a mix of rigor and compromise, and we managed to hit on one that works under a wide variety of circumstances. My joint efforts with Mike Woodford, Fernando Alvarez, Warren Weber, and Mike Golosov were also learning experiences for me.

I thank Max Gillman for reminding me how much I have enjoyed the stimulus of trying to teach monetary economics to so many generations of Chicago PhD students and for conceiving and carrying out this project. Finally, and for the third time, I thank Mike Aronson for his editorial skills and his friendship.

References

Eden, Benjamin. 1994. "The Adjustment of Prices to Monetary Shocks When Trade Is Uncertain and Sequential." *Journal of Political Economy* 102, no. 3 (June): 493–509.

Kydland, Finn E., and Edward C. Prescott. 1982. "Time to Build and Aggregate Fluctuations." *Econometrica* 50, no. 6 (November): 1345–1370.

Collected Papers on
Monetary Theory

— 1 —

Expectations and the Neutrality of Money

1. Introduction*

This paper provides a simple example of an economy in which equilibrium prices and quantities exhibit what may be the central feature of the modern business cycle: a systematic relation between the rate of change in nominal prices and the level of real output. The relationship, essentially a variant of the well-known Phillips curve, is derived within a framework from which all forms of "money illusion" are rigorously excluded: all prices are market clearing, all agents behave optimally in light of their objectives and expectations, and expectations are formed optimally (in a sense to be made precise below).

Exchange in the economy studied takes place in two physically separated markets. The allocation of traders across markets in each period is in part stochastic, introducing fluctuations in relative prices between the two markets. A second source of disturbance arises from stochastic changes in the quantity of money, which in itself introduces fluctuations in the nominal price level (the average rate of exchange between money and goods). Information on the current state of these real and monetary disturbances is transmitted to agents only through prices in the market where each agent happens to be. In the particular framework presented below, prices convey this information only imperfectly, forcing agents to hedge on whether a particular price movement results from a relative demand shift or a nominal (monetary) one. This hedging behavior results in a nonneu-

Journal of Economic Theory 4, no. 2 (April 1972): 103–124.

* I would like to thank James Scott for his helpful comments.

trality of money, or broadly speaking a Phillips curve, similar in nature to that which we observe in reality. At the same time, classical results on the long-run neutrality of money, or independence of real and nominal magnitudes, continue to hold.

These features of aggregate economic behavior, derived below within a particular, abstract framework, bear more than a surface resemblance to many of the characteristics attributed to the U.S. economy by Friedman [3 and elsewhere]. This paper provides an explicitly elaborated example, to my knowledge the first, of an economy in which some of these propositions can be formulated rigorously and shown to be valid.

A second, in many respects closer, forerunner of the approach taken here is provided by Phelps. Phelps [8] foresees a new inflation and employment theory in which Phillips curves are obtained within a framework which is neoclassical except for "the removal of the postulate that all transactions are made under complete information." This is precisely what is attempted here.

The substantive results developed below are based on a concept of equilibrium which is, I believe, new (although closely related to the principles underlying dynamic programming) and which may be of independent interest. In this paper, equilibrium prices and quantities will be characterized mathematically as *functions* defined on the space of possible states of the economy, which are in turn characterized as finite dimensional vectors. This characterization permits a treatment of the relation of information to expectations which is in some ways much more satisfactory than is possible with conventional adaptive expectations hypotheses.

The physical structure of the model economy to be studied is set out in the following section. Section 3 deals with preference and demand functions; and in section 4, an exact definition of equilibrium is provided and motivated. The characteristics of this equilibrium are obtained in section 5, with certain existence and uniqueness arguments deferred to the appendix. The paper concludes with the discussion of some of the implications of the theory, in sections 6, 7, and 8.

2. The Structure of the Economy

In order to exhibit the phenomena described in the introduction, we shall utilize an abstract model economy, due in many of its essentials to Samuelson [10].[1] Each period, N identical individuals are born, each of whom lives for two periods (the current one and the next). In each period, then, there is a constant population of $2N$: N of age 0 and N of age 1. During the first period of life, each person supplies, at this discretion n, units of labor which yield the same n units of output. Denote the output consumed by a member of the younger generation (its producer) by c^0, and that consumed by the old by c^1. Output cannot be stored but can be freely disposed of, so that the aggregate production-consumption possibilities for any period are completely described (in per capita terms) by:

$$c^0 + c^1 \leq n, \qquad c^0, c^1, \geq 0. \tag{2.1}$$

Since n may vary, it is physically possible for this economy to experience fluctuations in real output.

In addition to labor-output, there is one other good: fiat money, issued by a government which has no other function. This money enters the economy by means of a beginning-of-period transfer to the members of the older generation, in a quantity proportional to the pretransfer holdings of each. No inheritance is possible, so that unspent cash balances revert, at the death of the holder, to the monetary authority.

Within this framework, the only exchange which can occur will involve a surrender of output by the young, in exchange for money held over from the preceding period, and altered by transfer, by the old.[2] We shall assume that such exchange occurs in two physically separate markets. To keep matters as simple as possible, we assume that the older generation is allocated across these two markets so as to equate total monetary demand between them. The young are allocated stochastically, fraction $\theta/2$ going to one and $1 - (\theta/2)$ to the other. Once the assignment of persons to markets is made, no switching or communication between markets is possible. Within each market, trading by auction occurs, with all trades transcated at a single, market clearing price.[3]

1. The usefulness of this model as a framework for considering problems in monetary theory is indicated by the work of Cass and Yaari [1, 2].

2. This is not quite right. If members of the younger generation were risk preferrers, they could and would exchange claims on future consumption among themselves so as to increase variance. This possibility will be ruled out in the next section.

3. This device of viewing traders as randomly allocated over distinct markets serves two purposes. First, it provides a setting in which information is imperfect in a specific (and

The pretransfer money supply, per member of the older generation, is known to all agents.[4] Denote this quantity by m. Posttransfer balances, denoted by m', are not generally known (until next period) except to the extent that they are "revealed" to traders by the current period price level. Similarly, the allocation variable θ is unknown, except indirectly via price. The development through time of the nominal money supply is governed by

$$m' = mx, \tag{2.2}$$

where x is a random variable. Let x' denote next period's value of this transfer variable, and let θ' be next period's allocation variable. It is assumed that x and x' are independent, with the common, continuous density function f on $(0, \infty)$. Similarly, θ and θ' are independent, with the common, continuous symmetric density g on $(0, 2)$.

To summarize, the state of the economy in any period is entirely described by three variables m, x, and θ. The motion of the economy from state to state is independent of decisions made by individuals in the economy, and is given by (2.2) and the densities f and g of x and θ.

3. Preferences and Demand Functions

We shall assume that the members of the older generation prefer more consumption to less, other things equal, and attach no utility to the holding of money. As a result, they will supply their cash holdings, as augmented by transfers, inelastically. (Equivalently, they have a unit elastic demand for goods.) The young, in contrast, have a nontrivial decision problem, to which we now turn.

The objects of choice for a person of age 0 are his current consumption c, current labor supplied, n, and future consumption, denoted by c'. All individuals evaluate these goods according to the common utility function:

---

hence analyzable) way. Second, random variation in the allocation of traders provides a source of *relative* price variation. This could as well have been achieved by postulating random taste or technology shifts, with little effect on the structure of the model.

4. This somewhat artificial assumption, like the absence of capital goods and the serial independence of shocks, is part of an effort to keep the laws governing the transition of the economy from state to state as simple as possible. In general, I have tried to abstract from all sources of *persistence* of fluctuations, in order to focus on the nature of the initial disturbances.

$$U(c, n) + E\{V(c')\}. \tag{3.1}$$

(The distribution with respect to which the expectation in (3.1) is taken will be specified later.) The function U is increasing in c, decreasing in n, strictly concave, and continuously twice differentiable. In addition, current consumption and leisure are not inferior goods, or:

$$U_{cn} + U_{nn} < 0 \quad \text{and} \quad U_{cc} + U_{cn} < 0. \tag{3.2}$$

The function V is increasing, strictly concave and continuously twice differentiable. The function $V'(c')c'$ is increasing, with an elasticity bounded away from unity, or:

$$V''(c')c' + V'(c') > 0, \tag{3.3}$$

$$\frac{c'V''(c')}{V'(c')} \leq -a < 0. \tag{3.4}$$

Condition (3.3) essentially insures that a rise in the price of future goods will, ceteris paribus, induce an increase in current consumption or that the substitution effect of such a price change will dominate its income effect.[5] The strict concavity requirement imposed on V implies that the left term of (3.4) be negative, so that (3.4) is a slight strengthening of concavity. Finally, we require that the marginal utility of future consumption be high enough to justify at least the first unit of labor expended, and ultimately tend to zero:

$$\lim_{c' \to 0} V'(c') = +\infty, \tag{3.5}$$

$$\lim_{c' \to \infty} V'(c') = 0. \tag{3.6}$$

Future consumption, c', cannot be purchased directly by an age 0 individual. Instead, a known quantity of nominal balances λ is acquired in exchange for goods. If next period's price level (dollars per unit of output) is p' and if next period's transfer is x', these balances will then purchase $x'\lambda/p'$ units of future consumption.[6] Although it is purely formal at this

5. The restrictions (3.2) and (3.3) are similar to those utilized in an econometric study of the labor market conducted by Rapping and myself, [5]. Their function here is the same as it was in [5]: to assure that the Phillips curve slopes the "right way."

6. There is a question as to whether cash balances in this scheme are "transactions balances" or a "store of value." I think it is clear that the model under discussion is not rich enough to permit an interesting discussion of the distinctions between these, or other, motives for holding money. On the other hand, *all* motives for holding money require that it

point, it is convenient to have some notation for the distribution function of (x', p'), conditioned on the information currently available to the age-0 person: denote it by $F(x', p' \mid m, p)$, where p is the current price level. Then the decision problem facing an age-0 person is:

$$\max_{c,n,\lambda \geq 0} \left\{ U(c,n) + \int V\left(\frac{x'\lambda}{p'}\right) dF(x', p' \mid m, p) \right\} \tag{3.7}$$

subject to:

$$p(n - c) - \lambda \geq 0. \tag{3.8}$$

Provided the distribution F is so specified that the objective function is continuously differentiable, the Kuhn-Tucker conditions apply to this problem and are both necessary and sufficient. These are:

$$U_c(c, n) - p\mu \leq 0, \qquad \text{with equality if} \quad c > 0, \tag{3.9}$$

$$U_n(c, n) + p\mu \leq 0, \qquad \text{with equality if} \quad n > 0, \tag{3.10}$$

$$p(n - c) - \lambda \geq 0, \qquad \text{with equality if} \quad \mu > 0, \tag{3.11}$$

$$\int V'\left(\frac{x'\lambda}{p'}\right)\frac{x'}{p'} dF(x', p' \mid m, p) - \mu \leq 0, \quad \text{with equality if} \quad \lambda > 0, \tag{3.12}$$

where μ is a nonnegative multiplier.

We first solve (3.9)–(3.11) for c, n, and $p\mu$ as functions of λ/p. This is equivalent to finding the optimal consumption and labor supply for a fixed acquisition of money balances. The solution for $p\mu$ will have the interpretation as the *marginal cost* (in units of foregone utility from consumption and leisure) of holding money. This solution is diagrammed in Fig. 1.

It is not difficult to show that, as Fig. 1 suggests, for any $\lambda/p > 0$ (3.9)–

be held for a positive time interval before being spent: there is no reason to use money (as opposed to barter) if it is to be received for goods and then *instantaneously* exchanged for other goods. There is also the question of whether money "yields utility." Certainly the answer in this context is *yes*, in the sense that if one imposes on an individual the constraint that he cannot hold cash, his utility under an optimal policy is lower than it will be if this constraint is removed. It should be equally clear, however, that this argument does *not* imply that real or nominal balances should be included as an argument in the individual preference functions. The distinction is the familiar one between the utility function and the *value* of this function under a particular set of choices.

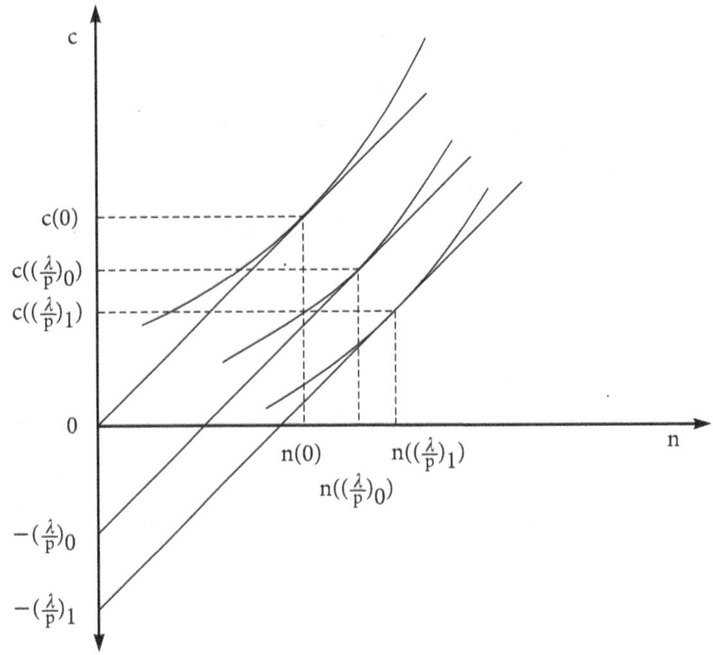

Figure 1

(3.11) may be solved for unique values of c, n, and $p\mu$. As λ/p varies, these solution values vary in a continuous and (almost everywhere) continuously differentiable manner. From the noninferiority assumptions (3.2), it follows that as λ/p increases, n increases and c decreases. The solution value for $p\mu$, which we denote by $h(\lambda/p)$ is, positive, increasing, and continuously differentiable. As λ/p tends to zero, $h(\lambda/p)$ tends to a positive limit, $h(0)$.

Substituting the function h into (3.12), one obtains

$$h\left(\frac{\lambda}{p}\right)\frac{1}{p} \geq \int V'\left(\frac{x'\lambda}{p'}\right)\frac{x'}{p'}\,dF(x',\ p' \mid m,\ p), \tag{3.13}$$

with equality if $\lambda > 0$. After multiplying through by p, (3.13) equates the marginal cost of acquiring cash (in units of current utility foregone) to the marginal benefit (in units of expected future utility gained). Implicitly, (3.13) is a demand function for money, relating current nominal quantity demanded, λ, to the current and expected future price levels.

4. Expectations and a Definition of Equilibrium

Since the two markets in this economy are structurally identical, and since within a trading period there is no communication between them, the economy's general (current period) equilibrium may be determined by determining equilibrium in each market separately. We shall do so by equating nominal money demand (as determined in section 3) and nominal money supply in the market which receives a fraction $\theta/2$ of the young. Equilibrium in the other market is then determined in the same way, with θ replaced by $2 - \theta$, and aggregate values of output and prices are determined in the usual way by adding over markets. This will be carried out explicitly in section 6.

At the beginning of the last section, we observed that money be supplied inelastically in each market. The total money supply, after transfer, is Nmx. Following the convention adopted in section 1, $Nmx/2$ is supplied in each market. Thus in the market receiving a fraction $\theta/2$ of the young, the quantity supplied per demander is $(Nmx/2)/(\theta N/2) = mx/\theta$. Equilibrium requires that $\lambda = mx/\theta$, where λ is quantity demanded per age-0 person. Since $mx/\theta > 0$, substitution into (3.13) gives the equilibrium condition

$$h\left(\frac{mx}{\theta p}\right)\frac{1}{p} = \int V'\left(\frac{mxx'}{\theta p'}\right)\frac{x'}{p'}\,dF(x', p' \mid m, p). \tag{4.1}$$

Equation (4.1) relates the current period price level to the (unknown) future price level, p'. To "solve" for the market clearing price p (and hence to obtain the current equilibrium values of employment, output, and consumption) p and p' must be linked. This connection is provided in the definition of equilibrium stated below, which is motivated by the following considerations.

First, it was remarked earlier that in some (not very well defined) sense the *state* of the economy is fully described by the three variables (m, x, θ). That is, if at two different points in calendar time the economy arrives at a particular state (m, x, θ) it is reasonable to expect it to behave the same way both times, regardless of the route by which the state was attained each time. If this is so, one can express the equilibrium price as a function $p(m, x, \theta)$ on the space of possible states and similarly for the equilibrium values of employment, output, and consumption.

Second, if price can be expressed as a function of (m, x, θ), the *true* probability distribution of next period's price, $p' = p(m', x', \theta') = p(mx, x', \theta')$ is known, conditional on m, from the known distributions of x, x', and θ'. Further information is also available to traders, however, since the current price, $p(m, x, \theta)$, yields information on x. Hence, on the basis of information available to him, an age-0 trader should take the expectation in (4.1) [or (3.13)] with respect to the joint distribution of (m, x, x', θ') conditional on the values of m and $p(m, x, \theta)$, or treating m as a parameter, the joint distribution of (x, x', θ') conditional on the value of $p(m, x, \theta)$.[7] Denote this latter distribution by $G(x, x', \theta | p(m, x, \theta))$.

We are thus led to the following

DEFINITION. An equilibrium price is a continuous, nonnegative function $p(\cdot)$ of (m, x, θ), with $mx/\theta p(m, x, \theta)$ bounded and bounded away from zero, which satisfies:

$$h\left[\frac{mx}{\theta p(m, x, \theta)}\right]\frac{1}{p(m, x, \theta)} = \int V'\left[\frac{mxx'}{\theta p(m\xi, x', \theta')}\right]\frac{x'}{p(m\xi, x', \theta')}\, dG(\xi, x', \theta' \mid p(m, x, \theta)). \tag{4.2}$$

Equation (4.2) is, of course, simply (4.1) with p replaced by the value of the function $p(\cdot)$ under the current state, (m, x, θ), and p' replaced by the value of the *same* function under next period's state (mx, x', θ). In addition, we have dispensed with unspecified distribution F, taking the expectation instead with respect to the well-defined distribution G.[8]

In the next section, we show that (4.2) has a unique solution and develop the important characteristics of this solution. The more difficult mathematical issues will be relegated to the appendix.

7. The assumption that traders use the correct conditional distribution in forming expectations, together with the assumption that all exchanges take place at the market clearing price, implies that markets in this economy are *efficient,* as this term is defined by Roll [9]. It will also be true that price expectations are *rational* in the sense of Muth [7].

8. The restriction, embodied in this definition, that price may be expressed as a function of the state of the economy appears innocuous but in fact is very strong. For example, in the models of Cass and Yaari without storage, the state of the economy never changes, so the only sequences satisfying the definition used here are constant sequences (or stationary schemes, in the terminology of [1]).

5. Characteristics of the Equilibrium Price Function

We proceed by showing the existence of a solution to (4.2) of a particular form, then showing that there are no other solutions, and finally by characterizing the unique solution. As a useful preliminary step, we show:

LEMMA 1. *If $p(\cdot)$ is any solution to (4.2), it is monotonic in x/θ in the sense that for any fixed m, $x_0/\theta_0 > \chi_1/\theta_1$ implies $p(m, x_0, \theta_0) \neq p(m, x_1, \theta_1)$.*

PROOF. Suppose to the contrary that $x_0/\theta_0 > x_1/\theta_1$ and $p(m, x_0, \theta_0) = p(m, x_1, \theta_1) = p_0$ (say). Then from (4.2),

$$h\left(\frac{mx_0}{\theta_0 p_0}\right)\frac{1}{p_0} = \int V'\left[\frac{mx_0 x'}{\theta_0 p(m\xi, x', \theta')}\right]\frac{x'}{p(m\xi, x', \theta')}\, dG(\xi, x', \theta' \mid p_0),$$

and

$$h\left(\frac{mx_1}{\theta_1 p_0}\right)\frac{1}{p_0} = \int V'\left[\frac{mx_1 x'}{\theta_1 p(m\xi, x', \theta')}\right]\frac{x'}{p(m\xi, x', \theta')}\, dG(\xi, x', \theta' \mid p_0).$$

Since h is strictly increasing while V' is strictly decreasing, these equalities are contradictory. This completes the proof.

In view of this Lemma, the distribution of (x, x', θ') conditional on $p(m, x, \theta)$ is the same as the distribution conditional on x/θ for *all* solution functions $p(\cdot)$, a fact which vastly simplifies the study of (4.2).

It is a plausible conjecture that solutions to (4.2) assume the form $p(m, x, \theta) = m\phi(x/\theta)$, where ϕ is a continuous, nonnegative function.[9] If this is true, the function ϕ satisfies (multiplying (4.2) through by mx/θ and substituting):

$$\begin{aligned} & h\left[\frac{x}{\theta\phi(x/\theta)}\right]\frac{x}{\theta\phi(x/\theta)} \\ & = \int V'\left[\frac{xx'}{\theta\xi\phi(x'/\theta')}\right]\frac{xx'}{\theta\xi\phi(x'/\theta')}\, dG\left(\xi, x', \theta' \mid \frac{x}{\theta}\right). \end{aligned} \tag{5.1}$$

9. To decide whether it is plausible that m should factor out of the equilibrium price function, the reader should ask himself: what are the consequences of a *fully announced* change in the quantity of money which does not alter the distribution of money over persons? To see why only the *ratio* of x to θ affects price, recall that x/θ *alone* determines the demand for goods facing each individual producer.

Let us make the change of variable $z = x/\theta$, and $z' = x'/\theta'$, and let $H(z, \theta)$ be the joint density function of z and θ and let $\tilde{H}(z, \theta)(z, \theta)$ be the density of θ conditional on z. Then (5.1) is equivalent to:

$$h\left[\frac{z}{\phi(z)}\right]\frac{z}{\phi(z)} = \int V'\left[\frac{\theta'}{\theta}\frac{z'}{\phi(z')}\right]\frac{\theta'}{\theta}\frac{z'}{\phi(z')}\,\tilde{H}(z, \theta)\,H(z', \theta')\,d\theta\,dz'\,d\theta'. \tag{5.2}$$

Equations (4.2) and (5.2) are studied in the appendix. The result of interest is:

THEOREM 1. *Equation* (5.2) *has exactly one continuous solution* $\phi(z)$ *on* $(0, \infty)$ *with* $z/\phi(z)$ *bounded. The function* $\phi(z)$ *is strictly positive and continuously differentiable. Further,* $m\phi(x/\theta)$ *is the unique equilibrium price function.*

PROOF. See the appendix.

We turn next to the characteristics of the solution function ϕ. It is convenient to begin this study by first examining two polar cases, one in which $\theta = 1$ with probability one, and a second in which $x = 1$ with probability one.

The first of these two cases may be interpreted as applying to an economy in which all trading place in a single market, and no nonmonetary disturbances are present. Then z is simply equal to x and, in view of Lemma 1, the current value of x is fully revealed to traders by the equilibrium price. It should not be surprising that the following classical neutrality of money theorem holds.

THEOREM 2. *Suppose* $\theta = 1$ *with probability one. Let* y^* *be the unique solution to*

$$h(y) = V'(y). \tag{5.3}$$

Then $p(m, x, \theta) = mx/y^*$ *is the unique solution to* (4.2).

PROOF. We have observed that h is increasing and V' is decreasing, tending to 0 as y tends to infinity by (3.6). By (3.5), $h(0) < V'(0)$. Hence (5.3) does have a unique solution, y^*. It is clear that $\phi(z) = z/y^*$ satisfies (5.2). By Theorem 1, it is the only solution and mx/y^* is the unique solution to (4.2).

The second polar case, where x is identically 1, may be interpreted as applying to an economy with real disturbances but with a perfectly stable monetary policy. In this case, $z = 1/\theta$, so that the current market price reveals θ to all traders. It is convenient to let $\Psi(\theta) = [\theta\phi(1/\theta)]^{-1}$ so that (5.2) becomes:

$$h[\Psi(\theta)]\ \Psi(\theta) = \int V'\left[\frac{\theta'}{\theta}\ \Psi(\theta')\right]\frac{\theta'}{\theta}\ \Psi(\theta')\ d\theta'. \tag{5.4}$$

Denote the right side of (5.4) by $m(\theta)$. Then

$$m'(\theta) = \int\left[V''\frac{\theta'}{\theta}\ \Psi(\theta') + V'\right]\left[\frac{-\theta'\Psi(\theta')}{\theta^2}\right]g(\theta')\ d\theta'$$

(suppressing the arguments of V'' and V'). The *elasticity* of $m(\theta)$ is therefore

$$\frac{\theta m'(\theta)}{m(\theta)} = -\int w(\theta,\theta')(V')^{-1}\left[V''\frac{\theta'}{\theta}\ \Psi(\theta') + V'\right]d\theta'$$

where

$$w(\theta,\theta') = \left[\int V'\frac{\theta'}{\theta}\ \Psi(\theta')\ g(\theta')\ d\theta'\right]^{-1}\left[V'\frac{\theta'}{\theta}\ \Psi(\theta')\ g(\theta)'\right].$$

Clearly, $w(\theta,\theta') \geq 0$ and $\int w(\theta,\theta')\ d\theta' = 1$. From (3.3) and (3.4)

$$0 < (V')^{-1}\left[V''\frac{\theta'}{\theta}\ \Psi(\theta') + V'\right] < 1.$$

Hence $-[\theta m'(\theta)/m(\theta)]$ is a mean value of terms between 0 and 1, so that

$$-1 < \frac{\theta m'(\theta)}{m(\theta)} < 0. \tag{5.5}$$

Now differentiating both sides of (5.4), we have

$$[h'(\Psi)\Psi + h]\ \Psi'(\theta) = m'(\theta),$$

which using (5.5) and the fact that h is increasing implies

$$-1 < \frac{\theta\Psi(\theta)}{\Psi(\theta)} < 0. \tag{5.6}$$

Recalling the definition of $\Psi(\theta)$ in terms of $\phi(\theta)$, it is readily seen that (5.6) implies

$$0 < \frac{z\phi'(z)}{\phi(z)} < 1.$$

We summarize the discussion of this case in

THEOREM 3. *Suppose* $x = 1$ *with probability one. Then* (4.2) *has a unique solution* $p(m, x, \theta) = m\phi(1/\theta)$, *where* ϕ *is a continuously differentiable function, with an elasticity between zero and one.*

If the factor disturbing the economy is exclusively monetary, then current price will adjust *proportionally* to changes in the money supply. Money is neutral in the short run, in the classical sense that the equilibrium level of real cash balances, employment, and consumption will remain unchanged in the face even of unanticipated monetary changes. These, in words, are the implications of Theorem 2. If, on the other hand, the forces disturbing the economy are exclusively real, the money supply being held fixed, disturbances will have real consequences. Those of the young generation who find themselves in a market with few of their cohorts (in a market with a low θ, or a high z-value) obtain what is in effect a lower price of future consumption. Theorem 3, resting on the assumptions of income and substitution effects set out in section 3, indicates that they will distribute all of this gain to the future, holding higher real balances. This attempt is partially frustrated by a rise in the current price level.

Returning to the general case, in which both x and θ fluctuate, it is clear that the current price informs agents only of the *ratio* x/θ of these two variables. Agents cannot discriminate with certainty between real and monetary changes in demand for the good they offer, but must instead make inferences on the basis of the known distributions $f(x)$ and $g(\theta)$ and the value of x/θ revealed by the current price level. It seems reasonable that their behavior will somehow mix the strategies described in Theorems 2 and 3, since a high x/θ value indicates a high x *and* a low θ.

Unfortunately this last statement, aside from being imprecise, is not true, as one can easily show by example.[10] Hence we wish to impose addi-

10. For example, let x take only the values 1 and 1.05 and let θ be either 0.5 or 1.5. Then a *decrease* of x/θ from 2.0 to 0.7 implies (with certainty) an increase in x from 1 to 1.05. It is not difficult to construct continuous densities f and g which exhibit this sort of behavior.

tional restrictions on the densities f and g, with the aim of assuring that, first, for any fixed $\bar{\theta}$, $\Pr\{\theta \leq \bar{\theta} \mid x/\theta = z\}$ is an increasing function of z, and, second, that for any fixed $\bar{x}$, $\Pr\{x \leq \bar{x} \mid x/\theta = z\}$ is a decreasing function of z. Using $\tilde{H}(z, \theta)$ as above to denote the density of θ conditional on $x/\theta = z$ the first of these probabilities is

$$F(z, \bar{\theta}) = \int_0^{\bar{\theta}} \tilde{H}(z, \theta)\, d\theta,$$

while the second, in terms of the same function F, is $F(z, \bar{x}/z)$. The desired restriction is then found (by differentiating with respect to z) to be:

$$0 < F_z(z, \theta) < \frac{\theta \tilde{H}(z, \theta)}{z} \tag{5.7}$$

for all (z, θ). We proceed, under (5.7), with a discussion analogous to that which precedes Theorem 3.

Let

$$m(\theta) = \int V'\left[\frac{\theta'}{\theta}\frac{z'}{\phi(z')}\right]\frac{\theta'}{\theta}\frac{z'}{\phi(z')}\, H(z', \theta')\, dz'\, d\theta',$$

where, as in the proof of Theorem 3, $m(\theta)$ is positive with an elasticity between -1 and 0.

Then (5.2) may be written

$$h\left[\frac{z}{\phi(z)}\right]\frac{z}{\phi(z)} = \int m(\theta)\, \tilde{H}(z, \theta)\, d\theta. \tag{5.8}$$

Denote the right side of (5.8) by $G(z)$. Then integrating by parts,

$$G(z) = m(2) - \int m'(\theta) F(z, \theta)\theta$$

where it will be recalled that 2 is the upper limit of the range of θ. Then

$$G'(z) = -\int m'(\theta) F_z(z'\theta) d\theta > 0,$$

by the first inequality of (5.7). Continuing,

$$\frac{zG'(z)}{G(z)} = -\frac{z\int m'(\theta)\, F_z(z, \theta)\, d\theta}{\int m(\theta)\, \tilde{H}(z, \theta)\, d\theta}$$

$$= \int w(z, \theta)\left[-\frac{\theta m'(\theta)}{m(\theta)}\right]\left[\frac{zF_z(z, \theta)}{\theta \tilde{H}(z, \theta)}\right] d\theta,$$

where $w(z, \theta) = [\int m(\theta)\, \tilde{H}(z, \theta)\, d\theta]^{-1}\, m(\theta)\, \tilde{H}(z, \theta)$. Hence, applying (5.7) again,

$$0 < \frac{z\phi'(z)}{\phi(z)} < 1. \tag{5.9}$$

We summarize the discussion of this case in

THEOREM 4. *Suppose the function $F\{z, \theta)$, obtained from the densities $f(x)$ and $g(\theta)$, satisfies the restriction* (5.7). *Then* (4.2) *has a unique solution $p(m, x, \theta) = m\phi(x/\theta)$, where ϕ is a continuously differentiable function, with an elasticity between zero and one.*

Theorems 2–4 indicate that, within this framework, monetary changes have real consequences only because agents cannot discriminate perfectly between real and monetary demand shifts. Since their ability to discriminate should not be altered by a proportional change in the *scale* of monetary policy, intuition suggests that such scale changes should have no real consequences. We formalize this as a corollary to Theorem 4:

COROLLARY. *Let the hypotheses of Theorem* 4 *hold, but let the transfer variable be $y = \lambda x$, where λ is a positive constant. Then the equilibrium price is $p(m, y, \theta) = m\phi(y/\lambda\theta) = m\phi(x/\theta)$, where ϕ is as in Theorem* 4.

PROOF. In the derivation of (5.2), let $z = y/\lambda\theta = x/\theta$.

6. Positive Implications of the Theory

In the previous section we have studied the determination of price in one of the markets in this two market economy: the one which received a fraction $\theta/2$ of producers. Excluding the limiting case in which the disturbance is purely monetary, this price function was found to take the form $m\phi(x/\theta)$, where $\phi(x/\theta)$ is positive with an elasticity between zero and one. Recalling the study of the individual producer-consumer in section 3, this price function implies an equilibrium employment function $n(x/\theta)$, where $n'(x/\theta) > 0$.[11] That is, increases in demand induce increases in real output.

11. The analysis of section 3 showed that if age-0 consumers wish to accumulate more real balances, they will finance this accumulation in part by supplying more labor. In section 5 it was shown that equilibrium per capita real balances, $[\theta\phi(x/\theta)]^{-1}x$, rise with x/θ. These two facts together imply $n'(x/\theta) > 0$.

Since the two markets are identical in structure, equilibrium price in the other market will be $m\phi(x/(2-\theta))$ and employment will be $n(x/(2-\theta))$. In short, we have characterized behavior in all markets in the economy under all possible states.

With this accomplished, it is in order to ask whether this behavior does in fact resemble certain aspects of the observed business cycle. One way of phrasing this question is: how would citizens of this economy describe the ups and downs they experience?[12]

Certainly casual observers would describe periods of higher than average x-values (monetary expansions) as "good times" even, or perhaps especially, in retrospect. The older generation will do so with good reason: they receive the transfer, and it raises their real consumption levels to higher than average levels. The younger generation will similarly approve a monetary expansion as it occurs: they perceive it only through a higher-than-average price of the goods they are selling which, on average, means an increase in their real wealth. In the future, they will, of course, be disappointed (on average) in the real consumption their accumulated balances provide. Yet there is no reason for them to attribute this disappointment to the previous expansion; it would be much more natural to criticize the current inflation. This criticism could be expected to be particularly severe during periods, which will regularly arise, when inflation continues at a higher than average rate while real output declines.[13] To summarize, in spite of the symmetry between ups and downs built into this simple model, *all* participants will agree in viewing periods of high real output as better than other periods.[14]

Less casual observers will similarly be misled. To see why, we consider the results of fitting a variant of an econometric Phillips curve on realiza-

12. The following discussion, while I hope it is suggestive, is not intended to be a substitute for econometric evidence.

13. The term "regularly arise" is appropriate. The *current* real output level, relative to "normal," depends only on the current monetary expansion. The current inflation rate, however, depends on the current *and* previous period's monetary expansion. Thus a large expansion followed by a modest contraction will occur (though perhaps infrequently) and will result in the situation described in the text.

14. This unanimity rests, of course, on the assumption that new money is introduced so as *never* to subject cash holders to a real capital loss. If transfers were, say, randomly distributed over young and old, there would be a group among the old which perceives monetary expansion as harmful.

tions generated by the economy described above. Let Y_t denote real GNP (or employment) in period t, and let P_t be the implicit GNP deflator for t. Consider the regression hypothesis

$$\ln Y_t = \beta_0 + \beta_1 (\ln P_t - \ln P_{t-1}) + \varepsilon_t, \tag{6.1}$$

where $\varepsilon_1, \varepsilon_2, \ldots$ is a sequence of independent, identically distributed random variables with 0 mean. Certainly a positive estimate for β_1 would, provided the estimated residuals do not violate the hypothesis, be interpreted as evidence for the existence of a "trade-off" between inflation and real output. By this point, it should be clear intuitively that there is no such trade-off in the model under study, yet β_1 will turn out to be positive. We next develop the latter point more explicitly.

We have:

$$Y_t = \frac{1}{2}\theta_t Nn\left(\frac{x_t}{\theta_t}\right) + \frac{1}{2}(2-\theta_t)\, Nn\left(\frac{x_t}{2-\theta_t}\right) \tag{6.2}$$

and

$$P_tY_t = \frac{1}{2}\theta_t Nn\left(\frac{x_t}{\theta_t}\right) m_t\phi\left(\frac{x_t}{\theta_t}\right) + \frac{1}{2}(2-\theta_t)\, Nn\left(\frac{x_t}{2-\theta_t}\right) m_t\phi\left(\frac{x_t}{2-\theta_t}\right). \tag{6.3}$$

Let $\mu = E[\ln(x)] = \int \ln(x)\, f(x)\, dx$. Regarding the logs of the right sides of (6.2) and (6.3) as functions of $\ln(x_t)$ and θ_t, expanding these about $(\mu, 1)$ and discarding terms of the second order and higher we obtain the approximations:

$$\ln(Y_t) = \ln(N) + \ln(n(\mu)) + \eta_n[\ln x_t - \mu], \tag{6.4}$$

and

$$\ln(P_t) - \ln(P_{t-1}) = \eta_\phi \ln x_t + (1-\eta_\phi) \ln x_{t-1},$$

where η_n and η_ϕ are the elasticities of the functions n and ϕ, respectively, evaluated at μ.

Using (6.4) and (6.5), one can compute the approximate[15] probability limit of the estimated coefficient β_1 of (6.1). It is the covariance of $\ln(Y_t)$ and $\ln(P_t/P_{t-1})$, divided by the variance of the latter, or

15. Because (6.4) and (6.5) are approximations.

$$\frac{\eta_n \eta_\phi}{1 - 2\eta_\phi + 2\eta_\phi^2} > 0.$$

The estimated residuals from this regression will exhibit negative serial correlation. By adding $\ln(Y_{t-1})$ as an additional variable, however, this problem is eliminated and a near perfect fit is obtained [cf. (6.4) and (6.5)]. The coefficient on the inflation rate remains positive.[16]

To summarize this section, we have deliberately constructed an economy in which there is *no* usable trade-off between inflation and real output. Yet the econometric evidence for the existence of such trade-offs is much more convincing here than is the comparable evidence from the real world.

7. Policy Considerations

Within the framework developed and studied in the preceding sections, the choice of a monetary policy is equivalent to the choice of a density function f governing the stochastic rate of monetary expansion. Densities f which are concentrated on a single point correspond to fixing the rate of monetary growth at a constant percentage rate k. Following Friedman, we shall call such a policy a *k-percent rule.* Any other policy implies random fluctuations about a constant mean. Since (as far as I know) no critic of a k-percent rule consciously advocates a randomized policy in its stead, there is little interest pursuing a study of monetary policies within the restricted class available to us in this context. We can, however, show that *if* a k-percent rule is followed the competitive allocation will be Pareto-optimal. This demonstration will occupy the remainder of this section.

For the case of a constant money supply ($x = 1$) there is an equilibrium price function $m\phi(1/\theta)$, the properties of which are given in Theorem 3. Corresponding to this price function are functions $\bar{c}(\theta)$, $\bar{n}(\theta)$ which give the equilibrium values of consumption and labor supply of the young for each possible state of the world, θ. Since product is exhausted, these imply an average per capita consumption level for the old in the same market:[17]

16. It is interesting to note that if one formulates a distributed lag version of the Phillips curve, as Rapping and I have done in [6], one will obtain a positive estimated *long-run* real output-inflation trade-off *even if* a model of the above sort is valid.

17. The unequal distribution of money acquired during the first year of life (due to varying θ values) creates two classes among the old. In general, then, no one will actually obtain

$$\bar{c}'(\theta) = \theta[\bar{n}(\theta) - \bar{c}(\theta)].$$

By the Corollary to Theorem 4, this allocation rule $\{\bar{c}(\theta), \bar{n}(\theta), \bar{c}'(\theta)\}$ will be followed if monetary policy follows any *k*-percent rule. We wish to compare the efficiency of this rule to alternative (nonmarket) allocation rules $\{c(\theta), n(\theta), c'(\theta)\}$.

The individuals whose tastes are to be taken into account are the successive generations inhabiting the model economy. If we continue to ignore calendar time (to treat present and future generations symmetrically) each generation can be indexed by the states of nature (θ, θ') which prevail during its lifetime. This leads to the notion that one allocation is superior to another in a Pareto sense if it is preferred *uniformly* over all possible states, or to the following

DEFINITION. An allocation rule $\{\bar{c}(\theta), \bar{n}(\theta), \bar{c}'(\theta)\}$ is Pareto-optimal if it satisfies

$$c(\theta) + \frac{1}{\theta}c'(\theta) \leq n(\theta), \qquad c(\theta),\ n(\theta),\ c'(\theta) \geq 0 \tag{7.1}$$

(is feasible) for all $0 < \theta < 2$, and if there is no feasible allocation rule $\{c(\theta), n(\theta), c'(\theta)\}$ such that

$$U[c(\theta), n(\theta)] \geq U[\bar{c}(\theta)\ \bar{n}(\theta)], \tag{7.2}$$

$$c'(\theta) \geq \bar{c}'(\theta), \tag{7.3}$$

for all θ, with strict inequality in either (7.2) or (7.3) over some subset of (0, 2) assigned positive probability by $g(\theta)$.

We then have:

THEOREM 5. *The equilibrium* $\{\bar{c}(\theta), \bar{n}(\theta), \bar{c}'(\theta)\}$, *which arises under a k-percent rule, is Pareto-optimal.*

PROOF. Suppose, to the contrary, that an allocation $\{c(\theta), n(\theta), c'(\theta)\}$ satisfying (7.1)–(7.3) exists. Recall from sections 3 and 5 that the problem

the average consumption $\bar{c}'(\theta)$. But a reallocation which receives the unanimous consent of the old in the market receiving a fraction θ of producers is possible if and only if average consumption is increased. For our purposes, then, we can ignore the distribution of actual consumption about this average.

$$\max_{c,\,n,\,\lambda}\left\{U(c,n)+\int V\left[\frac{\lambda}{m\phi(1/\theta')}\right]g(\theta')\,d\theta'\right\},$$

subject to

$$m\phi\left(\frac{1}{\theta}\right)[n-c]-\lambda\geq 0$$

is uniquely solved by $\bar{c}(\theta)$, $\bar{n}(\theta)$ and $\lambda = m/\theta$. Hence $\bar{c}'(\theta) = [\phi(1/\theta)]^{-1}$. Now using (7.1), if

$$\lambda(\theta)=[n(\theta)-c(\theta)]\,m\phi\left(\frac{1}{\theta}\right)=\frac{m}{\theta}\,\phi\left(\frac{1}{\theta}\right)c'(\theta),$$

then $c(\theta)$, $n(\theta)$, $\lambda(\theta)$ is feasible for this problem. Since (if it differs from the equilibrium) it cannot be optimal for this problem.

$$U[\bar{c}(\theta),\bar{n}(\theta)]+\int V\left[\frac{1}{\theta\phi(1/\theta')}\right]g(\theta')\,d\theta'$$

$$>U[c(\theta),n(\theta)]+\int V\left[\frac{(1/\theta)\,\phi(1/\theta)\,c'(\theta)}{\phi(1/\theta')}\right]g(\theta')\,d\theta'.$$

By (7.2), this implies

$$\int\left\{V\left[\frac{1}{\theta\phi(1/\theta')}\right]-V\left[\frac{(1/\theta)\,\phi(1/\theta)\,c'(\theta)}{\phi(1/\theta')}\right]\right\}g(\theta')\,g\theta'>0. \qquad (7.4)$$

But by (7.3), $c'(\theta) \geq \bar{c}'(\theta)$, so that

$$V\left[\frac{(1/\theta)\,\phi(1/\theta)\,c'(\theta)}{\phi(1/\theta')}\right]\geq V\left[\frac{\phi(1/\theta)\,\bar{c}'(\theta)}{\theta\phi(1/\theta')}\right]=V\left[\frac{1}{\theta\phi(1/\theta')}\right].$$

This contradicts (7.4), contradicting the assuming superiority of $\{c(\theta), n(\theta), c'(\theta)\}$, and completes the proof.

Two features of this discussion should perhaps be reemphasized. First, Theorem 5 does *not* compare resource allocation under a *k*-percent rule to allocations which result from other monetary policies. In general, the latter allocations will be randomized, in the sense that allocation for given θ will be stochastic. It *does* compare allocation under a *k*-percent rule to other nonrandomized (and thus nonmarket) allocation rules. Second, our discussion of optimality takes the market and information structure of the economy as a physical *datum*. Obviously, if the two markets can costlessly be merged, superior resource allocation can be obtained.

8. Conclusion

This paper has been an attempt to resolve the paradox posed by Gurley [4], in his mild but accurate parody of Friedmanian monetary theory: "Money is a veil, but when the veil flutters, real output sputters." The resolution has been effected by postulating economic agents free of money illusion, so that the Ricardian hypothetical experiment of a fully announced, proportional monetary expansion will have no real consequences (that is, so that money *is* a veil). These rational agents are then placed in a setting in which the information conveyed to traders by market prices is inadequate to permit them to distinguish real from monetary disturbances. In this setting, monetary fluctuations lead to real output movements in the same direction.

In order for this resolution to carry any conviction, it has been necessary to adopt a framework simple enough to permit a precise specification of the information available to each trader at each point in time, and to facilitate verification of the rationality of each trader's behavior. To obtain this simplicity, most of the interesting features of the observed business cycle have been abstracted from, with one notable exception: the Phillips curve emerges not as an unexplained empirical fact, but as a central feature of the solution to a general equilibrium system.

Appendix: Proof of Theorem 1

We first show the existence of a unique solution to (5.2). Define $\Psi(z)$ by

$$\Psi(z) = h\left[\frac{z}{\phi(z)}\right]\frac{z}{\phi(z)}.$$

Let G_1 be the inverse of the function $h(x)x$, so that $z/\phi(z) = G_1[\Psi(z)]$. The function $G_1(x)$ is positive for all $x > 0$, and satisfies

$$\lim_{x\to 0} G_1(x) = 0, \tag{A.1}$$

and

$$0 < \frac{xG_1'(x)}{G_1(x)} < 1. \tag{A.2}$$

Let $G_2(x) = V'(x)x$. $G_2(x) > 0$ for all $x > 0$ and, repeating (3.3) and (3.4),

$$0 < \frac{xG_2'(x)}{G_2(x)} \leq 1 - a < 1. \tag{A.3}$$

In terms of the functions Ψ, G_1, and G_2 (5.2) becomes

$$\Psi(z) = \int G_2\left[G_1\left(\Psi(x')\right)\frac{\theta'}{\theta}\right] \tilde{H}(z,\theta)\, H(z',\theta')\, d\theta\, d\theta'\, dz'. \tag{A.4}$$

Let S denote the space of bounded, continuous functions on $(-\infty, \infty)$, normed by

$$\|f\| = \sup_z |f(z)|.$$

Define the operator T on S by

$$Tf = \ln \int G_2\left[G_1(e^{f(z')})\frac{\theta'}{\theta}\right] \tilde{H}(z,\theta)\, H(z',\theta')\, d\theta\, d\theta'\, dz'.$$

In terms of T, (A.4) is

$$\text{In}\,\Psi = T \ln \Psi. \tag{A.5}$$

We have:

LEMMA 2. *T is a contraction mapping: for any $f, g \in S$,*

$$\|Tf - Tg\| \leq (1-a)\|f - g\|.$$

PROOF.

$$\|Tf - Tg\| = \sup_z \left| \ln \int w(\theta, z, \theta', z') \frac{G_2[G_1(e^{f(z')})(\theta'/\theta)]}{G_2[G_1(e^{g(z')})(\theta'/\theta)]} d\theta\, d\theta'\, dz' \right|,$$

where

$$w(\theta, z, \theta', z') = \left[\int G_2\tilde{H}(z,\theta)\, H(z',\theta')\, d\theta\, d\theta'\, dz'\right]^{-1} [G_2\tilde{H}(z,\theta)\, H(z',\theta')].$$

Since $w(\theta, z, \theta', z') > 0$ and $\int w\, d\theta\, d\theta'\, dz' = 1$ we have, continuing,

$$\|Tf - Tg\| \leq \sup_{z,\theta',\theta} \left| \ln G_2\left[G_1(e^{f(z)})\frac{\theta'}{\theta}\right] - \ln G_2\left[G_1(e^{g(z)})\frac{\theta'}{\theta}\right]\right|. \quad \text{(A.6)}$$

Now

$$\frac{\partial}{\partial x} \ln G_2\left[G_1(e^x)\frac{\theta'}{\theta}\right] = \left[\frac{G_1(e^x)(\theta'/\theta)\; G_2'[G_1(e^x)(\theta'/\theta)]}{G_2[G_1(e^x)(\theta'/\theta)]}\right]\left[\frac{e^x G_1'(e^x)}{G_1(e^x)}\right].$$

By (A.3), the first of these factors is between 0 and $1 - a$. By (A.2), the second factor is between 0 and 1. Since these observations are valid for all (x, θ, θ'), application of the mean value theorem to the right side of (A.6) gives

$$\|Tf - Tg\| = (1 - a)\|f - g\|,$$

which completes the proof.

It follows from Lemma 2 and the Banach fixed point theorem that the equation $Tf = f$ has a unique bounded, continuous solution f^*. Then $\Psi(z) = e^{f^*(z)}$ is the unique solution to (A.4). Clearly $\Psi(z)$ is positive, bounded, and bounded away from zero. It follows that $G_1[\Psi(z)]$ has these properties, and hence that $\phi(z) = z/(G_1[\Psi(z)])$ is the function referred to in Theorem 1.

Clearly $m\phi(x/\theta)$ is an equilibrium price function [satisfies (4.2)]. In view of Lemma 1, any solution $p(m, x, \theta)$ must satisfy:

$$h\left[\frac{mx}{\theta p(m, x, \theta)}\right]\frac{mx}{\theta p(m, x, \theta)}$$
$$= \int V'\left[\frac{m\xi x'}{\theta' p(m\xi, x', \theta')}\frac{\theta' x}{\theta \xi}\right]\frac{m\xi x'}{\theta' p(m\xi, x', \theta')}\, dG\left(\xi, x', \theta' \,\middle|\, \frac{\xi}{\theta}\right).$$

Now let $\Psi(m, x, \theta) = h[mx/\theta p(m, x, \theta)]\; mx/[\theta p(m, x, \theta)]$. Proceeding as before, one finds that there is only one bounded solution $\Psi(m, x, \theta)$. This proves Theorem 1.

References

1. D. Cass and M. E. Yaari, A Re-examination of the Pure Consumption Loans Model, *J. Polit. Econ.* 74 (1966).
2. D. Cass and M. E. Yaari, "A Note on the role of Money in Providing Sufficient Intermediation," Cowles Foundation Discussion Paper No. 215, 1966.
3. M. Friedman, The role of monetary policy, *Amer. Econ. Rev.* 58 (1968).
4. J. G. Gurley, review of M. Friedman, "A Program for Monetary Stability," *Rev. Econ. Stat.* 43 (1961), 307–308.
5. R. E. Lucas, Jr., and L. A. Rapping, Real wages, employment and inflation, *J. Polit. Econ.* 77 (1969).
6. R. E. Lucas, Jr., and L. A. Rapping, Price Expectations and the Phillips Curve, *Amer. Econ. Rev.* 59 (1969).
7. J. F. Muth, Rational expectations and the theory of price movements, *Econometrica* 29 (1961).
8. E. S. Phelps, introductory chapter *in* E. S. Phelps, *et al.*, "Microeconomic Foundations of Employment and Inflation Theory," Norton, New York, 1969.
9. R. Roll, The efficient market model applied to U. S. Treasury bill rates, University of Chicago doctoral dissertation, 1968.
10. P. A. Samuelson, An exact consumption-loan model of interest with or without the contrivance of money, *J. Polit. Econ.* 66 (1958).

— 2 —

Asset Prices in an Exchange Economy

1. Introduction[1]

This paper is a theoretical examination of the stochastic behavior of equilibrium asset prices in a one-good, pure exchange economy with identical consumers. The single good in this economy is (costlessly) produced in a number of different productive units; an *asset* is a claim to all or part of the output of one of these units. Productivity in each unit fluctuates stochastically through time, so that equilibrium asset prices will fluctuate as well. Our objective will be to understand the relationship between these exogenously determined productivity changes and market determined movements in asset prices.

Most of our attention will be focused on the derivation and application of a functional equation in the vector of equilibrium asset prices, which is solved for price as a function of the physical state of the economy. This equation is a generalization of the Martingale property of stochastic price sequences, which serves in practice as the defining characteristic of market "efficiency," as that term is used by Fama [7] and others. The model thus serves as a simple context for examining the conditions under which a price series' failure to possess the Martingale property can be viewed as evidence of non-competitive or "irrational" behavior.

Econometrica 46, no. 6 (November 1978): 1429–1445.

1. This paper originated in a conversation with Pentti Kouri, who posed to me the problem studied below. I would also like to thank Yehuda Freidenberg, Jose Scheinkman, and Joseph Williams for many helpful comments.

The analysis is conducted under the assumption that, in Fama's terms, prices "fully reflect all available information," an hypothesis which Muth [13] had earlier termed "rationality of expectations." As Muth made clear, this hypothesis (like utility maximization) is not "behavioral": it does not describe the way agents think about their environment, how they learn, process information, and so forth. It is rather a property likely to be (approximately) possessed by the *outcome* of this unspecified process of learning and adapting. One would feel more comfortable, then, with rational expectations equilibria if these equilibria were accompanied by some form of "stability theory" which illuminated the forces which move an economy toward equilibrium. The present paper also offers a convenient context for discussing this issue.

The conclusions of this paper with respect to the Martingale property precisely replicate those reached earlier by LeRoy (in [10] and [11]), and not surprisingly, since the economic reasoning in [10] and the present paper is the same. The context used here differs somewhat from LeRoy's, however, and the analytical methods used differ considerably.

The economy is informally described in the next section, and equilibrium is formally defined in Section 3. In Section 4, the basic functional equation for prices is derived and studied. Section 5 develops a certain "duality" property, on which is based the discussion of stability in Section 6. Section 7 deals with examples which are simple enough to permit either explicit solution or some "comparative static" exercises. The role of the Martingale property is discussed in Section 8. Section 9 concludes the paper.

2. Description of the Economy

Consider an economy with a single consumer, interpreted as a representative "stand in" for a large number of identical consumers. He wishes to maximize the quantity

$$E\left\{\sum_{t=0}^{\infty} \beta^t U(c_t)\right\} \tag{1}$$

where c_t is a stochastic process representing consumption of a single good, β is a discount factor, $U(\cdot)$ is a current period utility function, and $E\{\cdot\}$ is an expectations operator.

The consumption good is produced on n distinct productive units. Let y_{it} be the output of unit i in period t, $i = 1, \ldots, n$, and let $y_t = (y_{1t}, \ldots, y_{nt})$ be the output vector in t. Output is perishable, so that feasible consumption levels are those which satisfy

$$0 \leq c_t \leq \sum_{i=1}^{n} y_{it}.$$

Production is entirely "exogenous": no resources are utilized, and there is no possibility of affecting the output of any unit at any time. The motion of y_t will be taken to follow a Markov process, defined by its transition function

$$F(y', y) = \text{pr}\{y_{t+1} \leq y' | y_t = y\}.$$

Ownership in these productive units is determined each period in a competitive stock market. Each unit has outstanding one perfectly divisible equity share. A share entitles its owner as of the beginning of t to all of the unit's output in period t. Shares are traded, after payment of real dividends, at a competitively determined price vector $p_t = (p_{1t}, \ldots, p_{nt})$. Let $z_t = (z_{1t}, \ldots, z_{nt})$ denote a consumer's beginning-of-period share holdings.

In this economy, it is easy to determine equilibrium *quantities* of consumption and asset holdings. All output will be consumed ($c_t = \Sigma_i y_{it}$) and all shares will be held ($z_t = (1, 1, \ldots, 1) = \underline{1}$ for all t). The main analytical issue, then, will be the determination of equilibrium price behavior.

Our attack on this problem begins from the observation that *all* relevant information on the current and future physical state of the economy is summarized in the current output vector y. Since, given recursive preferences, the asset market "solves" a problem of the same form each period, equilibrium prices should (if they behave in a systematic way at all) be expressible as some fixed function $p(\cdot)$ of the state of the economy, or $p_t = p(y_t)$ where the ith coordinate $p_i(y_t)$ is the price of a share of unit i when the economy is in the state y_t. If so, knowledge of the transition function $F(y', y)$ and this function $p(y)$ will suffice to determine the stochastic character of the price process $\{p_t\}$.

Similarly, one would expect a consumer's current consumption and portfolio decisions, c_t and z_{t+1}, to depend on his beginning of period portfolio, z_t, the prices he faces, p_t, and the relevant information he possesses on current and future states of the economy, y_t. If so, his behavior can be described by fixed decision rules $c(\cdot)$ and $g(\cdot)$: $c_t = c(z_t, y_t, p_t)$ and $z_{t+1} = g(z_t, y_t, p_t)$.

Now *given* perceived, future price behavior $F(y', y)$ and $p(y)$, consumers will be able to determine these decision rules $c(\cdot)$ and $g(\cdot)$ optimally. In this sense, a price function p determines consumer behavior. On the other hand, *given* decision rules $c(\cdot)$ and $g(\cdot)$, the current period market clearing conditions determine a price function $p(\cdot)$. In this sense, consumer behavior determines the equilibrium price function. We close the system with the assumption of *rational expectations:* the market clearing price function p implied by consumer behavior is assumed to be the same as the price function p on which consumer decisions are based.

3. Definition of Equilibrium

The economy described in the preceding section is specified by the functions U and F and the number β. Assume $0 < \beta < 1$. $U: R^+ \rightarrow R^+$ is continuously differentiable, bounded, increasing, and strictly concave, with $U(0) = 0$.[2] $F: E^{n+} \times E^{n+} \rightarrow R$ is continuous; $F(\cdot, y)$ is a distribution function for each fixed y, with $F(0, y) = 0$. Assume that the process defined by F has a stationary distribution $\phi(\cdot)$, the unique solution to

$$\phi(y') = \int F(y', y)\, d\phi(y),$$

and that for any continuous function $g(y)$,

$$\int g(y')\, dF(y', y)$$

is a continuous function of y.

An equilibrium will be a *pair* of functions: a price function $p(y)$, as discussed above, and an optimum value function $v(z, y)$. The value $v(z, y)$ will be interpreted as the value of the objective (1) for a consumer who begins in state y with holdings z, and follows an optimum consumption-portfolio policy thereafter.

2. R^+ is the set of nonnegative real numbers. E^n is n-dimensional space. E^{n+} is the subset of E^n with all components nonnegative ($x \in E^n$ and $x \geq 0$). L^n is the set of continuous, bounded functions with domain E^n. and so on.

DEFINITION: An *equilibrium* is a continuous function $p(y) : E^{n+} \to E^{n+}$ and a continuous, bounded function $v(z, y) : E^{n+} \times E^{n+} \to R^{+}$ such that

$$v(z, y) = \max_{c, x} \left\{U(c) + \beta \int v(x, y')\, dF(y', y)\right\} \qquad \text{(i)}$$

subject to

$$c + p(y) \cdot x \leq y \cdot z + p(y) \cdot z, \quad c \geq 0, \quad 0 \leq x \leq \bar{z},$$

where $\bar{z}$ is a vector with components exceeding one;

$$\text{for each y, } v(\underline{1}, y) \text{ is attained by } c = \Sigma_i y_i \text{ and } x = \underline{1}. \qquad \text{(ii)}$$

Condition (i) says that, given the behavior of prices, a consumer allocates his resources $y \cdot z + p(y) \cdot z$ optimally among current consumption c and end-of-period share holdings x.[3] Condition (ii) requires that these consumption and portfolio decisions be market clearing. Since the market is always cleared, the consumer will never be observed except in the state $z = \underline{1}$. On the other hand, the consumer has (though he always rejects it) the option to choose security holdings $x \neq \underline{1}$. To evaluate these options, he needs to know $v(z, y)$ for *all* z.[4]

4. Construction of the Equilibrium

We begin by studying the consumer's maximum problem (i) for given price behavior $p(y)$. We have the following proposition.

PROPOSITION 1: *For each continuous price function $p(\cdot)$ there is a unique, bounded, continuous, nonnegative function $v(z, y; p)$ satisfying (i). For each y, $v(z, y; p)$ is an increasing, concave function of z.*

PROOF: Define the operator T_p on functions $v(z, y)$ such that (i) is equivalent to $T_p v = v$. The domain of T_p is the nonnegative orthant L^{2n+} of

3. The bound $\bar{z}$ on x is to assure that the maximization in (i) is always over a compact set, even if some components of $p(y)$ are zero.

4. This is not a "new" concept of equilibrium. It is (though no proof is offered) a standard, Arrow-Debreu equilibrium where the commodity space is the space of all possible realizations of the process $\Sigma_i y_{it}$. See [12] for a full development of this relationship in a closely related context.

the space L^{2n} of continuous, bounded functions $u : E^{n+} \times E^{n+} \rightarrow R$, normed by

$$\|u\| = \sup_{z,y} |u(z, y)|.$$

Since applying T_p involves maximizing a continuous function over a compact set, $T_p u$ is well defined for any $u \in L^{2n+}$. Since $U(c)$ is bounded, $T_p u$ is bounded, and by [2, p. 116] $T_p u$ is continuous. Hence $T_p : L^{2n+} \rightarrow L^{2n+}$. T_p is monotone ($u \geq v$ implies $T_p u \geq T_p v$) and for any constant A, $T_p(u + A) = T_p u + \beta A$. Then from [3, Theorem 5] T_p is a contraction mapping. It follows that $T_p v = v$ has a unique solution v in L^{2n+}, as was to be shown. Further, $\lim_{n\rightarrow\infty} T_p^n u = v$ for any $u \in L^{2n+}$.

To prove that v is increasing in z, observe that $T_p u$ is an increasing function of z for *any* u. Since $v = T_p v$, this implies that v is increasing in z.

To prove that v is concave in z, we first show that if $u(z, y)$ is concave in z, so is $(T_p u)(z, y)$. Let z_0, z_1 be chosen, let $0 \leq \theta \leq 1$, and let $z^\theta = \theta z^0 + (1 - \theta)z^1$. Let (c_i, x_i) attain $(T_p u)(z^i, y)$, $i = 0, 1$. Now $(c^\theta, x^\theta) = (\theta c^0 + (1 - \theta)c^1, \theta x^0 + (1 - \theta)x^1)$ satisfies $c^\theta + p(y) \cdot x^\theta \leq y \cdot z^\theta + p(y) \cdot z^\theta$, so that

$$\begin{aligned}(T_p u)(z^\theta, y) &\geq U(c^\theta) + \beta \int u(x^\theta, y')\, dF(y', y) \\ &\geq \theta(T_p u)(z^0, y) + (1 - \theta)(T_p u)(z^1, y)\end{aligned}$$

using the concavity of U and u. Hence $(T_p u)(z, y)$ is concave in z. It follows by an induction that $T_p^n u$ is concave in z for all $n = 1, 2, \ldots$. Then, since $\lim_{n\rightarrow\infty} = v$, v is concave.

The derivatives of v with respect to z are described in the following proposition.

PROPOSITION 2: *If $v(z, y; p)$ is attained at (c, x) with $c > 0$, then v is differentiable with respect to z at (z, y) and*

$$\frac{\partial v(z, y; p)}{\partial z_i} = U'(c)[y_i + p_i(y)] \qquad (i = 1, \ldots, n). \tag{2}$$

PROOF: Define $f : R^+ \rightarrow R^+$ by

$$f(A) = \max_{c,x} \left\{U(c) + \beta \int v(x, y')\, dF(y', y)\right\}$$

subject to

$$c + p(y) \cdot x \leq A, \quad c, x \geq 0.$$

For each A, $f(A)$ is attained at $c(A)$, $x(A)$ say, and since the maximand is strictly concave in c, $c(A)$ is unique and varies continuously with A [2, p. 116]. If $c(A) > 0$ and if h is sufficiently small, $c(A)+h$ is feasible at "income" $A + h$, and $c(A + h) - h$ is feasible at income A. Thus

$$\begin{aligned} f(A+h) &\geq u\big(c(A)+h\big) + \beta \textstyle\int v\big(x(A), y'\big)\, dF(y', y) \\ &= u\big(c(A)+h\big) - u\big(c(A)\big) + f(A) \end{aligned}$$

and

$$\begin{aligned} f(A) &\geq u\big(c(A+h)-h\big) + \beta \textstyle\int v\big(x(A+h), y', y\big) \\ &= u\big(c(A+h)-h\big) - u\big(c(A+h)\big) + f(A+h). \end{aligned}$$

Combining these inequalities gives

$$\begin{aligned} U\big(c(A)+h\big) - U\big(c(A)\big) &\leq f(A+h) - f(A) \\ &\leq U\big(c(A+h)\big) - U\big(c(A+h)-h\big). \end{aligned}$$

Dividing by h, letting $h \to 0$, and utilizing the continuity of $c(\cdot)$ gives

$$f'(A) = U'(c(A)).$$

Now letting $A = y \cdot z + p(y) \cdot z$, so that $v(z, y; p) = f(A)$, we obtain $(\partial v / \partial z_i) = f'(A)(\partial A / \partial z_i)$, as was to be shown.

With the main features of $v(z, y; p)$ thus established, we proceed to the study of the maximum problem (i), still taking asset prices p to be described by an arbitrary continuous function. The first order conditions, necessary and sufficient in this instance, are:

$$U'(c)p_i(y) = \beta \int \frac{\partial v(x, y')}{\partial x_i}\, dF(y', y) \qquad (i = 1, \ldots, n), \tag{3}$$

$$c + p(y) \cdot x = y \cdot z + p(y) \cdot z, \tag{4}$$

provided $c, x > 0$. If next period's optimum consumption c' is also positive, Proposition 2 implies in addition

$$\frac{\partial v(x, y')}{\partial x_i} = U'(c')[y_i' + p_i(y')] \qquad (i = 1, \ldots, n). \tag{5}$$

Now in equilibrium (condition (ii)) $z = x = \underline{1}$, $c = \Sigma_j y_j$, and $c' = \Sigma_j y'_j$. Combining (3) and (5) and using these facts gives

$$U'\left(\sum_j y_j\right)p_i(y) = \beta \int U'\left(\sum_j y'_j\right)(y'_i + p_i(y'))\,dF(y', y), \tag{6}$$

for $i = 1, \ldots, n$. One may think of (6), loosely, as equating the marginal rate of substitution of current for future consumption to the market rate of transformation, as given in the market rate of return on security i. Mathematically, (6) is a stochastic Euler equation. It is conceptually the same as equations (8) in [10].

Since equation (6) does not involve the particular value function $(z, y; p)$ used in its derivation, it must hold for *any* equilibrium price function. Conversely, if $p^*(y)$ solves (6) and $v(z, y; p^*)$ is as constructed in Proposition 1, then the pair $(p^*(y), v(z, y; p^*))$ is an equilibrium. Thus solutions to (6) and equilibrium price functions are coincident.

To study (6), define

$$g_i(y) = \beta \int U'\left(\sum_j y'_j\right) y'_i\, dF(y', y) \qquad (i = 1, \ldots, n).$$

Then if the n independent functional equations

$$f(y) = g_i(y) + \beta \int f(y')\,dF(y', y) \qquad (i = 1, \ldots, n) \tag{7}$$

have solutions $(f_1(y), \ldots, f_n(y))$, the price functions

$$p_i(y) = \frac{f_i(y)}{U'\left(\sum_j y_j\right)} \qquad (i = 1, \ldots, n), \tag{8}$$

will solve (6), and $p(y) = (p_1(y), \ldots, p_n(y))$ will be the equilibrium price function.

If f is any continuous, bounded, nonnegative function on E^{n+}, the function $T_i f: E^{n+} \to R^+$ given by

$$(T_i f)(y) = g_i(y) + \beta \int f(y')\,dF(y', y) \tag{9}$$

is well-defined and continuous in y. Since U is concave and bounded (by B, say) we have for any c:

$$0 = U(0) \leq U(c) + U'(c)(-c) \leq B - cU'(c)$$

so that $cU'(c) \leq B$ for all c. It follows that the functions $g_i(y)$ are bounded, since they are nonnegative and their sum is bounded by βB. Then the operators T_i defined by (9) take elements of the space L^{n+} of continuous, bounded functions into the same space. Evidently, solutions to $T_i f = f$

are solutions to (7), and conversely. We have, then, the following proposition.

PROPOSITION 3: *There is exactly one continuous, bounded solution f_i to (7) (or to $T_i f = f$). For any $f_0 \in L^{n+}$, $\lim_{n\to\infty} T^n f_0 = f_i$.*

The *proof* follows from the fact that T_i is a contraction, verified as in the proof of Proposition 1.

In summary, we have learned that there is exactly one equilibrium price function for this economy, and we have in (6) (equivalently in (7) and (8)) an equation useful in characterizing it. In the next two sections, we develop further results at this "general" level, and then turn to the study of the nature of equilibrium prices in special cases.

5. A "Duality Theorem"

There is a second way to construct the equilibrium price function, as will be shown in this section. Since the preceding section already provides one way, this method appears somewhat redundant in the present context. The second method is slightly more general however (since it does not require differentiability of U); it is also suggestive for stability theory.

Consider the functional equation

$$r(z, y) = \inf_{q\in E^{n+}} \left[\sup_{c,x} \left\{ U(c) + \beta \int r(x, y)' dF(y', y) \right\} \right] \tag{10}$$
$$\text{subject to } c + q \cdot x \leq y \cdot z + q \cdot z.$$

It will turn out that optimal policy functions $q(z, y)$ for this dynamic program are, when evaluated at $(\underline{1}, y)$, equivalent to the equilibrium price functions found in Section 4.

To study (10), let B be the space of bounded integrable functions on $E^{n+} \times E^{n+}$, and let $M : B \to B$ be the operator such that (10) is equivalent to: $r = Mr$. For the record, we have the following proposition.

PROPOSITION 4: *There is exactly one bounded integrable function r satisfying $r = Mr$, and for any $u \in B$, $\lim_{n\to\infty} M^n u = r$.*

The *proof* parallels that of Proposition 1, and will be omitted. In fact, much more can be said about the function r.

PROPOSITION 5: *The solution r to* (10) *satisfies*

$$r(z, y) = U(y \cdot z) + \beta \int r(z, y')\, dF(y', y). \tag{11}$$

Further, r is continuous, and nondecreasing and concave in z for each fixed y.

PROOF: Define $R: L^{2n+} \to L^{2n+}$ by

$$(Rw)(z, y) = U(y \cdot z) + \beta \int w(z, y')\, dF(y', y)$$

so that (11) reads: $r = Rr$. We show that if w is continuous, and nondecreasing and concave in z for each y, then (i) Rw has these properties, (ii) $Mw = Rw$.

The proof of (i) parallels arguments in the proof of Proposition 1, and can be omitted.

To prove (ii), observe that the point $(c, x) = (y \cdot z, z)$ satisfies $c + q \cdot x \leq y \cdot z + q \cdot z$ for all q, so that $Mw \geq Rw$. Since w is concave, for any (z, y) the set

$$A = \left\{(c, x): U(c) + \beta \int w(x, y')\, dF(y', y) \geq (Rw)(z, y)\right\}$$

is convex. From the separation theorem for convex sets, there is a number a_0 and a vector $a \in E^n$ (not both zero) such that $(c, x) \in A$ implies $a_0 c + a \cdot x \geq a_0 y \cdot z + a \cdot z$. Since $U(c)$ is strictly increasing, it follows that $a_0 > 0$ and a $a \geq 0$, so we can define $q = (a/a_0)$ and write

$$(c, x) \in \text{A implies } c + q \cdot x \geq y \cdot z + q \cdot z. \tag{12}$$

Now for this vector q, suppose there is a (c, x) in the interior of A with $c + q \cdot x = y \cdot z + q \cdot z$. Then by reducing c slightly, we obtain a point (c', x) in A such that $c' + q \cdot x < y \cdot z + q \cdot z$: a contradiction to (12). This proves that q attains Mw, or that $Mw = Rw$.

Finally, the properties listed for r follow easily from the fact that r solves (11), using the methods applied to the proof of Proposition 1. This completes the proof.

As immediate corollaries, we have the following propositions.

PROPOSITION 6: *For all* y, $r(\underline{1}, y) = v(\underline{1}, y)$.

PROOF: From the definition of equilibrium v is the solution to (11) with $z = \underline{1}$.

PROPOSITION 7: *If* $p(y)$ *is an equilibrium price function, then* $q(\underline{1}, y) = p(y)$ *attains* $r(\underline{1}, y)$.

The converse to Proposition 7 is the following.

PROPOSITION 8: *If $q(\underline{1}, y)$ attains $r(\underline{1}, y)$ then $p(y) = q(\underline{1}, y)$ is an equilibrium price function.*

PROOF: Let $q(\underline{1}, y)$ attain $r(\underline{1}, y)$ and suppose that (c^0, x^0) uniquely attains

$$\max_{c,x} \left\{ U(c) + \beta \int r(x, y')\, dF(y', y) \right\} \tag{13}$$

subject to

$$c + q(\underline{1}, y) \cdot x \leq y \cdot \underline{1} + q(\underline{1}, y) \cdot 1.$$

If $(c^0, x^0) = (\Sigma_i y_i, \underline{1})$, then the assertion follows from Proposition 6 and the definition of equilibrium. If $(c^0, x^0) \neq (\Sigma_i y_i, \underline{1})$, then a convex combination of these two points is feasible for problem (13) and yields a higher value to the objective function (since r is concave in z and U is strictly concave) contradicting the assumption that (c^0, x^0) solves problem (13).

6. Stability of Equilibrium

The preceding sections showed that there is only one way for the economy under study to be in competitive equilibrium: when all output is consumed, all asset shares are held, and asset prices follow (6), or equivalently, solve the dynamic program (10). As always, there are innumerable ways for the economy to be *out of* equilibrium, so we must expect any treatment of out-of-equilibrium behavior to have considerable arbitrariness, not resolvable by economic reasoning. On the other hand, the model described above "assumes" that agents know a great deal about the structure of the economy, and perform some non-routine computations. It is in order to ask, then: will an economy with agents armed with "sensible" rules-of-thumb, revising these rules from time to time so as to claim observed rents, tend as time passes to behave as described in Sections 4 and 5?

To sharpen this loosely posed question somewhat, let us recognize at least three different stability questions raised by this model, and dispose of two of them at once. First, in each period an ordinary "static" market clearing occurs, in which current asset prices are set. Since stability in this sense is well understood, we need add nothing here except the assumption that it always obtains. Second, agents may be in ignorance of the distribution $F(y', y)$ of the exogenous production shocks, and learn its characteristics only gradually. Stability in this sense, too, is a well understood problem in Bayesian decision theory [5, Ch. 10] and need not be discussed here. Finally, consumers may be in error as to the price function, or equivalently, about the distribution of future prices conditional on the current state, or again equivalently, about the way they wish to evaluate their end-of-period portfolio, x. We focus here on this last kind of disequilibrium.

The "correct" way, given preferences, to evaluate an end-of-period portfolio x is to use the equilibrium value function v: $\int v(x, y')\, dF(y', y)$, but agents must know this, and the economy must be in equilibrium for this valuation to be correct. Suppose instead that agents use some other function $u(z, y)$, say, where u is continuous, concave, and increasing in z, but otherwise arbitrary, so that an end-of-period portfolio x is valued at $\int u(x, y')\, dF(y', y)$. (To retain the conveniences of the representative consumer device, we are forced to treat all agents as being wrong in the same way.) Suppose on the basis of this arbitrary portfolio evaluation formula, asset demands are drawn and a current period market clearing asset price vector q is established, at which $c = \Sigma_i y_i$ and $x = \underline{1}$. Now if prices are established in this fashion, what will be the *realized* utility yields experienced by agents?

The answer is given by the function $(Mu)(z, y)$, where M is the operator defined in association with equation (10). That this is so is the content of Proposition 5: the price q which attains the right side of (10) is precisely that price which clears markets, given the portfolio valuation function u.

If this experience is utilized by agents, they will replace the initial valuation u with the value Mu actually experienced, then new prices will be established, and utilities M^2u experienced, and so on.[5] Since, as shown in the preceding section, $M^n u \rightarrow v$, where v is the equilibrium value function, prices will converge to the equilibrium price function. In short, the successive approximations used in Section 5 constitute a kind of stability theory.

It is worth emphasizing that the adjustment toward equilibrium described by these successive approximations does not presuppose that agents are familiar with the theory of Markov processes or of dynamic programming; nor need agents in equilibrium be particularly skilled at responding to survey questions about future price movements. All that is required is they have consistent preferences for consumption and asset holdings

5. As one of the referees for this paper emphasized, the process by which u is "replaced" by Mu, Mu by M^2u, and so forth, might well be quite complicated to spell out. It involves "learning" a function over time by experiencing discrete values of the function Mu at arguments partly selected by the household (z) and partly by nature (y). There are many ways to formulate learning of this sort; for our purposes here, it seems simpler just to assume that households are good at it.

(which would seem necessary for dealing in asset markets at all) *and* that they revise these preferences in the direction of the consumption utility actually yielded by their asset holdings.

The point of this section, it should also be said, is *not* that one would use any of the successive approximations $M^n u$ as a description of observed behavior. (This suggestion is not even operational, since u was arbitrarily chosen.) It is rather to argue that there is a theoretical reason for expecting the *equilibrium* to be a good approximation to behavior. Certainly one would not expect to capture the creativity which is devoted to discovering and gaining from disequilibria in actual economies in *any* mechanical approximation routine.

7. Examples

7.1. *Linear Utility*

The case of constant marginal utility of consumption does not exactly fit the assumptions of Section 3 (it violates boundedness) but is easily handled separately, and is a useful point of departure. In this case, equation (6) reduces to

$$P_i(y) = \beta E(y_i' \mid y) + \beta E(p_i(y') \mid y) \tag{14}$$

which may be solved for

$$p_i(y) = \sum_{s=1}^{\infty} \beta^s E(y_{i,t+s} \mid y_{it} = y).$$

That is, the price of the *i*th asset is the expected, discounted present value of its real dividend stream, conditioned on current information y.

7.2. *One Asset*

It is easy to use equation (6) (or (7)) to characterize the function $p(y)$, as can be illustrated for the case of a one-asset economy. The crucial issues are the information content of the current state y (that is, the way $F(y', y)$ varies with y) and the degree of "risk aversion" (the curvature of U). Suppose, as a first case, that $\{y_t\}$ is a sequence of independent random variables: $F(y', y) = \phi(y')$. Then $g(y)$ is the constant

$$\bar{g} = \beta \int y' U'(y')\, d\phi(y') = \beta E[yU'(y)]$$

and calculating f from (9) as $\lim_{n\to\infty} T^n 0$, say, we get

$$f(y) = \frac{\bar{g}}{1-\beta}, \quad f'(y) = 0.$$

Then differentiating (8) gives

$$p'(y) = -\frac{\beta E[yU'(y)]U''(y)}{(1-\beta)[U'(y)]^2} = p(y)\frac{-U''(y)}{U'(y)} > 0.$$

Rearranging,

$$\frac{yp'(y)}{p(y)} = -\frac{yU''(y)}{U'(y)}.$$

That is, the elasticity of price with respect to income is equal to the Arrow-Pratt [1] measure of relative risk aversion.

In a period of high transitory income, then, agents attempt to distribute part of the windfall over future periods, via securities purchases. This attempt is frustrated (since storage is precluded) by an increase in asset prices.

Next, we consider autocorrelated production disturbances, under a restriction which amounts to requiring that the stochastic difference equation governing y_t have its root between zero and one: assume that F is differentiable, and that its derivatives F_1 and F_2 satisfy

$$0 < -F_2 < F_1. \tag{15}$$

We will repeatedly apply the following lemma.

LEMMA 1: *Let F satisfy* (15), *and let $h(y)$ have a derivative bounded between* 0 *and* $h'_M > 0$. *Then*

$$0 \le \frac{d}{dy}\int h(y')\,dF(y',y) \le h'_M. \tag{16}$$

PROOF: Use the change of variable $u = F(y', y)$, and invert to get $y' = G(u, y)$, so that $G_2 = (-F_2)/F_1$. Then the derivative in question is

$$\frac{d}{dy}\int_0^1 h\big(G(u,y)\big)\,du = \int_0^1 h'(G)G_2(u,y)\,du$$

and the result follows from (15).

Now from (9), for any differentiable f,

$$\frac{d}{dy}(Tf)(y) = g'(y) + \beta \frac{d}{dy} \int f(y')\, dF(y', y) \tag{17}$$

and from the definition of $g(y)$,

$$g'(y) = \beta \frac{d}{dy} \int U'(y')y'\, dF(y', y). \tag{18}$$

To get any information on the slope of the solution $f(y)$ to (7), then, we must begin with bounds on the derivative of $U'(y)y$, or on $U''(y)y + U'(y)$. (This derivative is $U'(y)[1 - R(y)]$, where R is the Arrow-Pratt measure of relative risk aversion, so its magnitude has received some consideration.) For the sake of discussion, take 0 and $\bar{a}$ as lower and upper bounds on $U''(y)y + U'(y)$. Then applying Lemma 1 to (18),

$$0 \leq g'(y) \leq \beta\bar{a}.$$

Then repeated application of (17), using Lemma 1 at each step, yields

$$0 \leq f'(y) \leq \frac{\beta\bar{a}}{1-\beta} \tag{19}$$

where $f(y)$ is the solution to (8) in this one asset case.[6] From (8), the elasticity of the equilibrium price function is

$$\frac{yp'(y)}{p(y)} = \frac{yf'(y)}{f(y)} - \frac{yU''(y)}{U'(y)} \tag{20}$$

The second term on the right of (20) is the "income effect" we have seen above; it is positive. The first term might be called the "information effect";[7] it has the sign of $f'(y)$. Evidently, the use one can make of these formulas depends on our knowledge of the curvature of U; (19) and (20) show how to translate such knowledge into knowledge about asset prices.

In the present case of relative risk aversion[8] less than unity, we have

6. Differentiability of the approximations T^nF does not imply the differentiability of f, and in fact, there is no easy way to verify this. For "$f'(y) \leq c$" read: "$f(y_1) - f(y_0) \leq c(y_1 - y_0)$."

7. This follows Grossman [8].

8. In this multiperiod context, the term "risk aversion" is perhaps misleading, since the curvature of U also governs the intertemporal substitutability of consumption. With time-additive utility, there is no way to disentangle these conceptually distinct aspects of preferences.

found in (19) that $f'(y) > 0$, so that the information effect is positive. Thus as one might expect, new optimistic information on future dividends leads to increased asset prices. (Of course, one might also expect that this information will lead to an attempted consumption binge now, lowering asset prices!)

Observationally, the derivative $p'(y)$ is the change in the ratio of a comprehensive stock price index to the CPI, as real output varies. Even in the simplified economy under study, then, the relationship of asset prices to real output is far from simple and possibly not even monotonic. Perhaps it has been good judgment, not merely timidity, which has led aggregate theorists to steer clear of any attempt to "understand the market."

7.3. *Many, Independent Assets*

If the number of productive units is large, and if there is sufficient independence across units, one would expect that replacing the term $U'(\Sigma_j y_j)$ in (6) with $U'(\mu)$, where

$$\mu = \sum_j \mu_j = \sum_j \int y_j \phi(y)\, dy$$

in mean total output, would yield a good approximation to the equilibrium price function. Let us pursue this idea, and the question of approximation generally, with the aid of the next lemma.

LEMMA 2: *Let S, T : L → L be contractions with modulus β and fixed points $f_S, f_T \in L$. Suppose that*

$$\|Sf - Tf\| \leq A \quad \textit{for all } f \in L.$$

Then

$$\|f_S - f_T\| \leq \frac{A}{1-\beta}.$$

PROOF: For any f,

$$\begin{aligned} \|S^2 f - T^2 f\| &\leq \|S^2 f - TSf\| + \|TSf - T^2 f\| \\ &\leq \|S(Sf) - T(Sf)\| + \beta\|Sf - Tf\| \\ &\leq A + \beta A, \end{aligned}$$

and, in general,

$$\|S^n f - T^n f\| \leq A(1 + \beta + \ldots + \beta^{n-1}).$$

Letting $n \to \infty$ gives the result.

Now if $\tilde{g}_i(y)$ is an approximation to $g_i(y)$, and $\tilde{T}_i$ is defined by

$$\tilde{T}_i f = \tilde{g}_i(y) + \beta \int f(y') \, dF(y', y),$$

we have

$$\left\|\tilde{T}_i f - T_i f\right\| = \left\|\tilde{g}_i(y) - g_i(y)\right\|.$$

Then if f_i and $\tilde{f}_i$ are the fixed points of T_i and $\tilde{T}_i$, respectively, Lemma 2 gives the bound

$$\left\|\tilde{f}_i - f_i\right\| \leq (1 - \beta)^{-1} \left\|\tilde{g}_i - g_i\right\|. \tag{21}$$

Returning to the specific approximation proposed above, let

$$\tilde{g}_i(y) = U'(\mu) \int y_i \, dF(y', y),$$

define $\tilde{T}_i$ as above, and let $\tilde{f}_i$ be the fixed point of $\tilde{T}_i$. Then the approximate price function

$$\tilde{p}_i(y) = \frac{\tilde{f}_i(y)}{U'(\mu)}$$

is just the solution calculated in 7.1 above.

To evaluate this approximation, we need bounds on $\|\tilde{g}_i - g_i\|$. To this end, let us bound $U''(y)$: $\|U''\| \leq M$. Then

$$\begin{aligned} \left\|g_i(y) - \tilde{g}_i(y)\right\| &= \beta \left\| \int \left[U'\left(\sum_j y'_j\right) - U'(\mu) \right] y'_i \, dF(y', y) \right\|. \\ &\leq \beta M \left\| \int \left(\sum_j y'_j - \mu \right) y'_i \, dF(y', y) \right\| \end{aligned}$$

using the mean value theorem. If the y_i's are independent, or if $F(y', y) = \Pi_k F_k(y'_k, y_k)$, then

$$\int\left(\sum_j y'_j - \mu\right) y'_i \, dF(y', y) = \int\left(\sum_j (y'_j - \mu_j)\right)(y'_i - \mu_i)\, dF(y', y)$$

$$+ \mu_i \int \sum_j (y'_j - \mu_j)\, dF(y', y)$$

$$= \text{var}(y'_i \mid y_i) + \mu_i \sum_j E(y'_j - \mu_j y_j).$$

Combining gives

$$\|g_i(y) - (\tilde{g}_i)\| \le \sup_y [\text{var}(y'_i \mid y_i) + \mu_i \sum_j E(y'_j - \mu_j \mid y_j)].$$

If we think of a sequence of economies of the same total size, but with more and more independent productive units of roughly equal size, $\text{var}(y'_i \mid y_i)$ and $\mu_i \, \Sigma_j \, E(y'_i - \mu_j \mid y_j)$ will tend to zero, and the approximations $\tilde{f}_i$ will become close.

8. The Martingale Property

We have shown that equation (6) exhausts the implications of the assumption that, in this model economy, prices are in equilibrium and "reflect all available information." Evidently, asset prices themselves do not possess the Martingale property. The series that does have this property (*something* has to, in this time-additive set up) is the series $w_{it}(i = 1, \ldots, n)$ defined by

$$w_{i,t+1} - w_{it} = \beta U'\left(\sum_j y_{j,t+1}\right)(y_{i,t+1} + p_{i,t+1}) - U'\left(\sum_j y_{jt}\right) p_{it},$$

since from (6), the expectation of the right side of (22), conditioned on all available information (in this case, y_t) is zero.

If the terms $U'(\Sigma_j y_{jt})$ do not vary much, either because agents are indifferent to risk (example 7.1) or because there is little aggregate risk (example 7.3), then securities prices properly "corrected" for dividends y_{it} *almost* have the property but not without another "correction" for the discount factor β. In any case, neither rationale for a constant $U'(\Sigma_j y_{jt})$ seems likely to closely approximate reality.

It should be added that the importance of the requirement that "the conditions of market equilibrium can be stated in terms of expected returns" has been repeatedly emphasized by Fama and other efficient market theorists; it is not a new result from this paper. What *is* new, I think, is an explicit framework within which one can judge what this requirement means and whether or not it is satisfied, or which in other words can lend some insight into the conditions under which the Martingale property is likely to approximately describe a price series. Within this framework, it is clear that the presence of a diminishing marginal rate of substitution of future for current consumption is inconsistent with this property.[9]

9. Conclusions

What can be concluded from this exercise (beyond the observation that a little knowledge of geometric series goes a long way, or perhaps, is a dangerous thing)? Substantively, the discussion of stability of Section 6 indicates that the applicability of the hypothesis that agents "know" the "true" probability distributions of future prices has little to do with the question of whether agents (ourselves included) think of, or describe, their behavior in these terms. A relatively crude use of hindsight, applied in a reasonably stationary physical environment, will lead to behavior well-approximated by rational expectations.

With respect to the random character of stock prices, it is evident that one can construct rigorous economic models in which price series have this characteristic[10] and ones with equally rational and well-informed agents in which they do not. This would suggest that the outcomes of tests as to whether *actual* price series have the Martingale property do not in themselves shed light on the generally posed issue of market "efficiency."

In the main, however, this paper is primarily methodological: an illustration of the use of some methods which may help to bring financial and economic theories closer together. It may help, then, to close with some guesses as to the fronts on which further progress can be expected.

The time-additive preference structure is, as remarked earlier, a nuisance, and it has no rationale beyond tractability. It would not be difficult (with the aid of [6]) to use recursive, but non-additive preferences of the Koopmans-Diamond-Williamson [9] type, provided sufficient "impatience" is assumed.

Second, one would like to introduce capital accumulation. In this re-

9. This complements Danthine's [4] finding that a diminishing marginal rate of *transformation* over time, in a model with storage, has the same effect.

10. Samuelson did this in [14].

gard, the marginal analysis of Section 4 is probably a dead-end: equation (6) is a kind of Euler condition, and will necessarily involve capital provided capital enters the model in a non-trivial way. Aside from special cases (such as the one studied in Section 4) stochastic Euler equations are not likely to be of value in constructing solutions. Equation (10) in Section 5 appears more promising; perhaps it has useful analogues in more generally formulated models.

References

[1] Arrow, Kenneth J.: *Aspects of the Theory of Risk Bearing.* Helsinki: Yrjo Jahnsson Lectures, 1965.

[2] Berge, Claude: *Topological Spaces.* New York: Macmillan, 1963.

[3] Blackwell, David: "Discounted Dynamic Programming," *Annals of Mathematical Statistics,* 36 (1965), 226–235.

[4] Danthine, Jean-Pierre: "On the Relevance of the Efficient Market Model," Carnegie-Mellon University Working Paper, 1974.

[5] De Groot, Morris H.: *Optical Statistical Decisions.* New York: McGraw-Hill, 1969.

[6] Denardo, Eric V.: "Contraction Mappings in the Theory Underlying Dynamic Programming," *SIAM Review,* 9 (1967), 165–177.

[7] Fama, Eugene F.: "Efficient Capital Markets: A Review of Theory and Empirical Work," *Journal of Finance,* 25 (1970), 387–417.

[8] Grossman, Sandford: "The Existence of Futures Markets, Noisy Expectations, and Informational Externalities," unpublished University of Chicago Working Paper, 1975.

[9] Koopmans, Tjalling C., Peter A. Diamond, and Richard E. Williamson: "Stationary Utility and Time Perspective," *Econometrica,* 32 (1964), 82–100.

[10] LeRoy, Stephen F.: "Risk Aversion and the Martingale Property of Stock Prices," *International Economic Review,* 14 (1973), 436–446.

[11] ———: "The Determination of Stock Prices," unpublished University of Pennsylvania Doctoral Dissertation, 1971.

[12] Lucas, Robert E., Jr., and Edward C. Prescott: "Investment under Uncertainty," *Econometrica,* 39 (1971), 659–681.

[13] Muth, John F.: "Rational Expectations and the Theory of Price Movements," *Econometrica,* 29 (1961), 1–23.

[14] Samuelson, Paul A.: "Proof that Properly Anticipated Prices Fluctuate Randomly," *Industrial Management Review,* 6 (1965), 41–49.

— 3 —

Equilibrium in a Pure Currency Economy*

This paper studies the determination of the equilibrium price level in a stationary economy in which all exchange involves the trade of fiat money for goods. The use of money in exchange is guaranteed by the imposition of a constraint, as suggested by Clower in (1967), which requires that purchases of goods must necessarily be paid for by currency held over from the preceding period. The models examined also resemble closely that studied by Friedman in the first part of (1959). Individual behavior resembles that captured in inventory-theoretic models of money demand, as studied by Baumol (1952) and Tobin (1956), so that another way to think of the paper is as an attempt to study the transactions demand for money in as simple as possible a general equilibrium setting.

In the next section, an example with perfect certainty is analyzed, with a digression to motivate the cash-in-advance constraint. In this example, which is a special case of the much more general set-up treated by Grandmont and Younes (1972, 1973), equilibrium velocity is determined in an entirely mechanical way by the assumed payments period. In Section II, individual uncertainty is introduced, giving rise to a precautionary motive for holding currency and a non-trivial problem of equilibrium determination, in which velocity depends on the kinds of economic factors long thought to be important in reality. The analysis of this latter case is continued in Sections III–V.

Economic Inquiry 18, no. 2 (April 1980): 203–220.

* University of Chicago. This paper was prepared for the Minneapolis Fed Conference on Models of Monetary Economies, December 7–8, 1978. I want to thank Milton Harris for his helpful criticism.

I think of this exercise not so much as an end in itself, but as an analytical step toward models which capture more and more features which monetary economists believe to be important in understanding actual monetary systems. In the concluding section, then, I will go well beyond the results developed in the paper to venture some opinions on some of these other issues.

I. An Economy with Certainty

Throughout the paper, I will study an economy with a continuum of identical traders. Each trader is endowed with one unit of labor each period, to which no disutility is attached, which yields y units of a non-storable consumption good. In the present section, preferences over consumption sequences $\{c_t\}$, $c_t \geq 0$, are

$$\sum_{t=0}^{\infty} \beta^t U(c_t) \tag{1.1}$$

where $0 < \beta < 1$, and $U : R^+ \rightarrow R$ is bounded, twice differentiable, with $U'(\cdot) > 0$ and $U''(\cdot) < 0$.

Considering only allocations in which identical traders are identically treated, it is clear that an optimal allocation is $c_t = y$ for all t. Nothing more will be done in this section than to propose a monetary arrangement which will bring this allocation about and to determine the money price of goods under this arrangement.

In order to motivate the need for *any* monetary arrangement (indeed for any arrangement other than autarchy, in which each agent consumes his own produce y), I will first re-interpret this model economy as one involving many goods, as follows. Let the goods come in n colors, where items of each color are produced under the technology assumed above: one unit of labor yields y units of any color. Consumption is now a vector $(c_{1t}, \ldots, c_{nt})$, where c_{it} is consumption of color i in period t. Let current period utility be

$$V(c_1, \ldots, c_n) = U\left[\prod_{i=1}^{n}\left(\frac{c_i}{\alpha_i}\right)^{\alpha_i}\right]$$

where U is as above and $\Sigma_i \alpha_i = 1$, $\alpha_i > 0$, all i. Let $c = \Sigma_i c_i$. Now given the assumed constant returns to scale technology, equilibrium requires relative prices of unity among all goods.[1] With these prices, consumers will select color proportions c_i/c equal to α_i for all i, and given this mix, $V(c_i, \ldots, c_n) = U(c)$. Without altering the example, one can think of all agents having the same α-weights, of agents distributed by a fixed c.d.f. $F(\alpha)$ of weights, or of each agent drawing a period-t weight α from F in a way which is unpredictable even to himself. In each of these cases, the equilibrium output mix (per capita) is $(\bar{\alpha}_i y_i, \ldots, \bar{\alpha}_n y_n)$ each period, where $\bar{\alpha}_i = \int \alpha_i \, dF(\alpha)$. I imagine this sort of elaboration is what we always have in mind when we work with aggregative models.

Next, imagine each "agent" as consisting of a husband-wife pair, one of whom spends each day shopping (call him or her the "shopper") and the other of whom works at the production of a single color (call him the "worker"). Production and sale occur at spatially distinct stores. Each day, the worker goes to his store, while the shopper moves from store to store purchasing the mix dictated by the current drawing of α. Equilibrium dictates that the value of the worker's labor y should equal the total expenditures by the shopper over all n (at least) stores.

What will assure that this equilibrium is, in fact, executed? What, for example, prevents a shopper from collecting $2y$ in various goods in the course of a day? To get an idea of the importance of this question, let us suppose that each store keeps an exact record of each shopper's purchases, and continuously informs all other stores throughout the day as to how many "credits" (it is almost impossible even to discuss this matter without using language suggesting securities) have been used up. Then for each shopper, each of the first $n - 1$ stops necessitates $n - 1$ messages, or $(n - 1)^2$ per household per day. Let the work day be eight hours, and let each message require six seconds of a worker's time to send. Then with 101 stores, this information transmission activity utilizes $(100)^2 \cdot 6/(60)^2 = 16\frac{2}{3}$ hours, or more than twice national product!

This issue could be pursued further by spelling out in more detail a technology for information storage, transmission and processing, and the

1. Technically, this remark is premature (since *equilibrium* has yet to be defined) and perhaps substantively questionable as well. This scenario depends on prices being set in a spatially decentralized manner, as opposed to in a single, centralized auction, so that it may not be clear how a constant-returns technology is manifested in the structure of equilibrium prices. In the present paper, the discussion will be confined to stationary examples in which one can easily imagine a constant relative price structure arising from "custom." In a situation in which market equilibrium were subject to shocks it would, I think, be necessary to treat this issue with more care.

available methods for enforcing against fraud, after the fact. An easier route is suggested by the observation that the adoption of paper currency can reduce these costs essentially to *zero.* Let each shopper, at the beginning of a period, be issued claims to y units of consumption. Proceeding from store to store, these claims are exhausted, and redistributed to workers at the end of each day. This system (except for resources used to print currency and prevent counterfeiting) economizes *perfectly* on informational costs. Note that nothing has been said as to how this monetary solution to the information problem might come into being, nor is it at all clear how an individual agent, or a collection of agents, could act so as to bring this system into existence. The monetary solution involves a *social convention,* with the property that if (for some reason) everyone else adopts it, then it is in one's own interest to adopt it as well.

A formal definition of a monetary equilibrium with a constant money supply M which embodies this convention is developed by means of the optimal value function $v(m)$, interpreted as the value of the objective function (1.1) for a consumer who begins the current period with nominal balances m and behaves optimally. This function v must satisfy:

$$v(m) = \max_{c,\, m' \geq 0} \{U(c) + \beta v(m')\} \tag{1.2}$$

subject to

$$m' = m - pc + py \tag{1.3}$$

$$m \geq pc. \tag{1.4}$$

Here p is the constant equilibrium price level, c is current goods consumption and m' is end-of-period balances. (1.3) is the standard budget constraint, and (1.4) is the cash-in-advance constraint discussed above. Then in terms of v, equilibrium is defined as follows.[2]

DEFINITION. An *equilibrium* in the certainty economy is a number $p \geq 0$ and a continuous, bounded function $v : R^{+} \rightarrow R$ such that

2. An alternative to this definition would be to define an equilibrium as an element of a space of infinite sequences $\{c_t, p_t, m_t\}$ of consumptions, prices and money demands, satisfying feasibility, utility maximization and market clearing. In this alternative set-up, the equilibrium specified below (a constant sequence) is the only one, but this must (and can) be argued using a "transversality condition." The "stationarity" built into the definition used here will prove convenient in the section following. Whether it rules out any behavior of economic interest is not known, though my own opinion is that, in the present context, it does not.

(i) given p, v satisfies (1.2) – (1.4)
(ii) $(c, m') = (y, M)$ attains $v(M)$.

That is, consumers behave optimally (condition (i)) and money demand equals money supply (condition (ii)).

Enough has been said already to make it clear that the unique equilibrium on this definition involves $p = M/y$ and $v(M) = u(y)/(1 - \beta)$. That is, each household spends all of its current money balances M on goods each period, replenishing these holdings with the workers' end of period pay. Since this example is a special case of the one analyzed in the next section, a formal substantiation of this claim is omitted.

II. An Economy with Individual Uncertainty

In this section, the technology and trading arrangements will be assumed the same as in Section I, but individual preferences will be taken to be subject to uncertainty, unpredictable even to the household itself. (Think of an unanticipated medical "need," or the unexpected discovery of an item of a particularly attractive "color.") Formally, let the shock to preferences be a drawing, independent over time and over persons at a point in time, of a random variable θ from the fixed c.d.f. F(θ). Take F to be strictly increasing on the interval $I = [\underline{\theta}, \overline{\theta}] \subset R$ with $F(\underline{\theta}) = 0$ and $F(\overline{\theta}) = 1$. Then with a continuum of agents, there is no aggregative uncertainty: the state of the *economy* will not change from period to period.

Let preferences be given by

$$E\left\{\sum_{t=0}^{\infty} \beta^t\, U(c_t, \theta_t)\right\} \tag{2.1}$$

where $0 < \beta < 1$, $U: R^{+} x\, I \rightarrow R$ is bounded, twice differentiable, with $U_c > 0$, $U_\theta > 0$, $U_{cc} < 0$, and $U_{c\theta} > 0$. Require also that for all $c \geq y$

$$\lim_{\theta \rightarrow \overline{\theta}} U_c(c, \theta) = \infty \tag{2.2}$$

or that consumption may be "arbitrarily urgent."[3] At the time the t-th period decision is taken, regard θ_t as known, so that the expectation in (2.1) is taken with respect to the distribution of $(\theta_1, \theta_2, \ldots)$, with θ_0 given.

3. Condition (2.2) is used only in the proof of Lemma 1, Section III, where it is clear from the context that it could be replaced, with appropriate modification in the argument, with a much weaker condition.

As in the preceding section, I will study an economy with the constant money supply M, and seek an equilibrium in which the price level is constant at p. The situation of any *individual*, however, cannot be expected to "settle down," since he is continually shocked by new drawings of θ. I will first develop the problem faced by a representative trader, then discuss what is meant by market clearing in this context, and then summarize these in a formal definition of equilibrium. With this accomplished, I will turn to the analytical issues involved in constructing and characterizing the equilibrium.

The budget constraints facing an agent are as in the preceding section, but in this case it is convenient to let m denote an individual's *real* balances (nominal balances divided by the constant price level p). Let $v(m, \theta)$ be the optimum value function for a consumer who begins the current period with real balances m, draws an "urgency to consume" θ, and behaves optimally. Then his current period decision problem is

$$v(m, \theta) = \max_{c, m' \geq 0} \left\{U(c, \theta) + \beta \int_I v(m', \theta')\, dF(\theta')\right\} \tag{2.3}$$

subject to

$$c + m' \leq m + y, \tag{2.4}$$

$$c \leq m. \tag{2.5}$$

The opportunity set defined by (2.4) and (2.5) is as drawn in Figure 1 (for given m and y). If the derived preference function for c and m', $U(c, \theta) + \beta \int v(m', \theta')dF(\theta')$ has indifference curves of the usual shape, then the household will either locate at a tangency point to the line given when (2.4) holds with equality, spending less than his initial balances, or he will spend all he has, choosing $c = m$ and $m' = y$. Assuming this problem has a solution, denote the individual demand functions for goods and end-of-period balances by $c = c(m, \theta)$, and $m' = g(m, \theta)$. This individual decision problem will receive more detailed attention in the next section.

In *market* equilibrium in this economy, it must be true that per capita demand for real balances (averaged over agents) equals per capita balances supplied M/p at the given nominal quantity supplied M and the assumed constant equilibrium price level p. To calculate per-capita end-of-period demand one needs to know the distribution of agents by beginning of period balances, $\psi(m)$, say. *Given* ψ, per capita demand is

$$\int\int g(m, \theta)\, d\psi(m)\, dF(\theta)$$

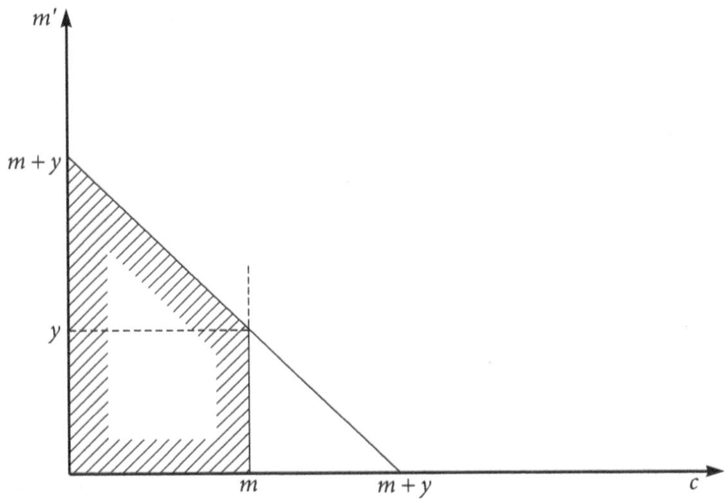

Figure 1

so the equilibrium condition is

$$\int\int g(m, \theta)\, d\psi(m)\, dF(\theta) = M/p. \tag{2.6}$$

In general, the p-value satisfying (2.6) will depend on the distribution $\psi(m)$ of real balances over persons. In order, then, for consumers' expectations that p be constant over time to be rational (or correct) we require also that $\psi(m)$ replicate itself over time, or that it be a stationary distribution for the stochastic difference equation

$$m_{t+1} = g(m_t, \theta_t).$$

This requirement is just that ψ solve:[4]

$$\psi(m') = \int\int_{A(m')} d\psi(m)\, dF(\theta) \tag{2.7}$$

where $A(m')$ is the region of the (m, θ) plane defined by

$$A(m') = \left\{(m, \theta): m \geq 0, \quad \theta \in I, g(m, \theta) \leq m'\right\}. \tag{2.8}$$

The foregoing considerations can be summarized in the following.

4. Notice that if (2.7) holds, (2.6) is equivalent to

$$\int\int m\, d\psi(m)\, dF(\theta) = M/P.$$

DEFINITION. An *equilibrium* in the economy with individual uncertainty is a number $p > 0$, a continuous bounded function $v : R^{+} x I \rightarrow R$, a pair of continuous functions $c, g : R^{+} x I \rightarrow R^{+}$ and a c.d.f. $\psi : R^{+} \rightarrow [0, 1]$ such that

(i) $v(m, \theta)$ solves (2.3),
(ii) (c, g) solves the maximum problem (2.3) for each (m, θ),
(iii) g, ψ and p satisfy (2.6),
(iv) g and ψ satisfy (2.7).

III. Construction of the Equilibrium

Equilibrium was defined as four unknown functions together with a positive number. This simultaneous system may be solved sequentially, first by finding a function v which satisfies (i), then finding the policy functions c and g satisfying (ii), then finding the c.d.f. ψ satisfying (iv), and finally finding the price p which satisfies condition (iii).

The relevant facts about the value function $v(m, \theta)$ are given in

PROPOSITION 1. There is exactly one continuous bounded function $v(m, \theta)$ satisfying (2.3). This solution v is strictly increasing and strictly concave with respect to m.

The *proof* is standard (see, e.g., Lucas, 1978), involving the following formulation and facts. Let L be the Banach space of continuous, bounded functions $u : R^{+} x I \rightarrow R$, normed by

$$\|u\| = \sup_{m,\theta} |u(m, \theta)|.$$

Define T as the operator on L such that (2.3) reads: $v = Tv$. Using [2; p. 116], $T : L \rightarrow L$. Using [3; Thm. 5] T is a contraction, so that $Tv = v$ has a unique solution $v^{*} \in L$ and $\| T^{n}u - v^{*} \| \rightarrow 0$ as $n \rightarrow \infty$ for all $u \in L$.

It is easy to verify that T takes non-decreasing, concave functions of m into strictly increasing, strictly concave functions of m. It follows that $v^{*} = \lim_{n \rightarrow \infty} T^{n} \cdot 0$ is non-decreasing and concave, and then, since $v^{*} = Tv^{*}$ that these properties hold strictly.

PROPOSITION 2. There exist unique, continuous functions $c(m, \theta)$, $g(m, \theta) : R^{+} x I \rightarrow R^{+}$ such that $c = c(m, \theta)$ and $m' = g(m, \theta)$ attain the r.h.s. of (2.3) for each (m, θ).

PROOF. The maximum problem (2.3) involves maximizing a continuous strictly concave function over a compact convex set. Hence $c(m, \theta)$, $g(m, \theta)$ are uniquely defined. Their continuity follows from [2; p. 116].

PROPOSITION 3. The solution v to (2.3) is continuously differentiable with respect to m, for each fixed θ, and, if $c(m, \theta) > 0$,

$$v_m(m, \theta) = U_c[c(m, \theta), \theta]. \tag{3.1}$$

PROOF. In the interior of the region of the (m, θ) plane on which (2.5) is not binding, the proof follows that in [13; prop. 2]. In the interior of the region on which (2.5) is binding,

$$v(m, \theta) = U(m, \theta) + \beta \int v(y, \theta')\, dF(\theta')$$

and (3.1) follows since $c(m, \theta) \equiv m$ in this region. Since the one-sided derivatives agree on the boundary of these two regions, the result follows.

Now the function $g(m, \theta)$ and the c.d.f. F of θ together define a Markov process

$$m_{t+1} = g(m_t, \theta_t) \tag{3.2}$$

with state space R^+. That is, given an initial distribution of persons by cash balances $\psi_0(m)$, say, where $\psi_0(m)$ is the fraction of consumers beginning period 0 with initial balances less than or equal to m, the distribution $F(\theta)$ and the difference equation (3.2) together determine the *sequence* of distributions $\psi_1(m), \psi_2(m) \ldots$ which prevail at times 1, 2, . . . Our interest will be in the limiting behavior of this sequence.

The behavior of this sequence of distributions can be studied by examining the characteristics of the transition probabilities of the process defined by (3.2) and F. For $m \geq 0$ and any measurable $A \subseteq R^+$, these are given by:

$$P(m, A) = \int_{B(m)} dF(\theta)$$

where

$$B(m) = \{\theta \in I : g(m, \theta) \in A\}.$$

Then if ρ is the set of probability measures μ on R^+ define $S : \rho \rightarrow \rho$ by

$$(S\mu)(A) = \int_0^\infty P(m, A)\, \mu(dm).$$

Then if $\psi_o(m) = \int_0^m \mu_o(du)$ is the initial distribution mentioned above, the t-th term in the sequence is

$$\psi_t(m) = \int_0^m (S^t \mu_o)(du).$$

A solution μ^* to $S\mu = \mu$ corresponds to a solution $\psi^*(m) = \int_0^m \mu^*(du)$ to (3.7): a stationary distribution of agents by real balances. The process (3.2) will be studied here via S using results from Doob (1953, pp. 190–218)[5] and the implications of the maximum problem (2.3).

The first-order condition for the maximum problem (2.3) when (2.5) is ignored and (2.4) is used to eliminate the variable c is, in view of proposition 3,

$$U_c(m + y - m', \theta) = \beta \int v_m(m', \theta')\, dF(\theta'). \tag{3.3}$$

It then follows from the strict concavity of U and v in their first arguments that the m' value, call it $\tilde{g}(m, \theta)$, satisfying (3.3) is increasing in m and decreasing in θ. Then, clearly, the money demand function $g(m, \theta) = \max[y, \tilde{g}(m, \theta)]$ so that $g(m, \theta)$ is as drawn in Figure 2, for θ fixed. The ergodic set for the process (3.2) is included in $[y, \infty)$, since $g(m, \theta) \geq y$ for all (m, θ). An upper bound on m can be obtained from examination of

$$U_c(y, \underline{\theta}) = \beta \int v_m(m, \theta')\, dF(\theta') \tag{3.4}$$

which is the form (3.3) takes if $(c, m') = (y, m)$ is optimal at $(m, \underline{\theta})$, where $\underline{\theta}$ is the lower bound on θ. The r.h.s. of (3.4) is a decreasing function of m. Since $v(m, \theta)$ is, for θ fixed, an increasing, concave, bounded and differentiable function of m, we have

$$v(0, \theta) \leq v(m, \theta) + v_m(m, \theta)(-m)$$

or

$$0 \leq m\, v_m(m, \theta) \leq v(m, \theta) - v(0, \theta) \leq B - v(0, \theta)$$

where B is a bound for v. Hence $v_m(m, \theta) \to 0$ as $m \to \infty$. It follows that (3.4) is solved for a unique $m = \bar{m} \geq y$ if

$$\beta \int v_m(y, \theta')\, dF(\theta) \geq U_c(y, \underline{\theta})$$

5. A very useful recent treatment of the same issues is given in Futia (undated).

and has no solution otherwise. In the latter case, the ergodic set for the process (3.2) is just $E = \{y\}$. In the case where $\bar{m} > y$ satisfies (3.4) $g(\bar{m}, \underline{\theta}) = \bar{m}$, so that initial balances are just maintained. For $\theta > \underline{\theta}$, $g(\bar{m}, \theta) < \bar{m}$, and also for $m > \bar{m}$, $g(m, \theta) < m$, for all θ. Thus the ergodic set of the process (3.2) is $E = [y, \bar{m}]$. There are no cyclically moving subsets.

The next result verifies that the Doeblin condition (Doob, condition D, p. 192) holds on $[y, \bar{m}] = E$.

LEMMA 1. There is a finite measure λ on E and an $\varepsilon > 0$ such that $\lambda(A) \leq \varepsilon$ implies $P(m, A) \leq 1 - \varepsilon$, for all $m \in E$.

PROOF. For the case $\bar{m} = y$ the result is trivial. For the case $\bar{m} > y$, assign measure $\lambda_0 \in (0, 1)$ to the point y and let $\lambda([m_1, m_2]) = (1 - \lambda_0)\frac{m_2 - m_1}{\bar{m} - y}$ for $y < m_1 \leq m_2 \leq \bar{m}$, so that $\lambda(E) = 1$. Now using (3.3), $g(m, \theta) = y$ whenever

$$U_c(m, \theta) > \beta \int v_m(y, \theta')\, dF(\theta')$$

so that

$$P(m, \{y\}) = \Pr\{U_c(m, \theta) > \beta \int v_m(y, \theta')\, dF(\theta')\}.$$

Then for $m \in E$,

$$P(m, \{y\}) \geq \Pr\left\{U_c(\bar{m}, \theta) > \beta \int v_m(y, \theta')\, dF(\theta')\right\}.$$

By condition (2.2) $\theta^o < \bar{\theta}$ can be chosen such that $\theta \geq \theta^o$ implies $U_c(\bar{m}, \theta) > \beta \int U_c(y, \theta')\, dF(\theta')$, so that if $\Pr\{\theta^o \leq \theta \leq \bar{\theta}\} = b$,

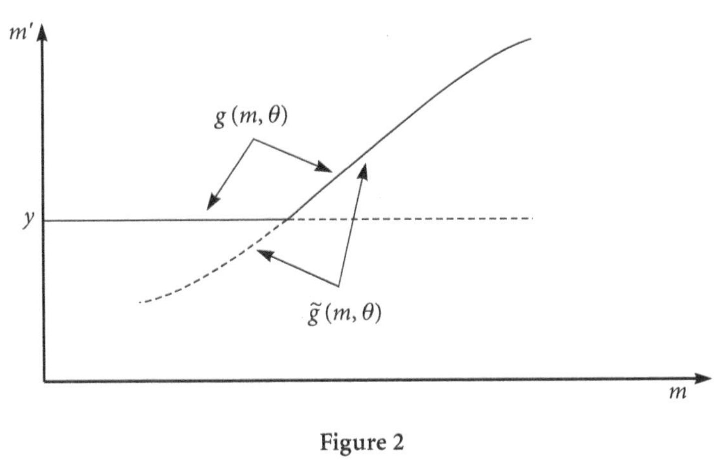

Figure 2

$$P(m, \{y\}) \geq b.$$

Choose $\varepsilon > 0$ with $\varepsilon < \lambda_o$ and $\varepsilon < b$. Then $\lambda(A) \leq \varepsilon$ implies $y \notin A$ so that for all m,

$$P(m, A) \leq 1 - P(m, \{y\}) \leq 1 - b \leq 1 - \varepsilon.$$

This proves Lemma 1.

It then follows from (Doob, p. 214) that

PROPOSITION 4. Given g as in proposition 2, there is exactly one solution ψ to (2.7) (or solution μ to $S\mu = \mu$), and $\psi(m) = 0$ for $m < y$, $\psi(y) > 0$ and $\psi(\bar{m}) = 1$.

The final step in establishing the existence of a unique equilibrium is taken by observing that (2.6) can be solved, given M, for a unique, positive price p.

IV. Discussion of the Equilibrium

In constructing the equilibrium distribution of persons by real balance holdings, $\psi(m)$, we began with an *arbitrary* distribution $\psi_o(m)$ and then studied the limit of the *sequence* of distributions $\psi_t(m)$ (that is, measures $S^t\mu_o$). This was merely a technical device for arriving at a solution ψ to (2.7), but the sequence $\psi_t(m)$ has an economic interpretation. It is the sequence of distributions which *would* prevail, in an economy starting at ψ_o, if all agents believed that the current price level will prevail into the next period (that the nominal yield on money is always zero). In fact, if $\psi_o \neq \psi$, prices will *not* be constant, so that these consumer beliefs will be confirmed only in the limit. In the vocabulary of growth theory, this equilibrium is a stationary point of an economy with static expectations, where the distributions ψ_t play the role of capital. This equilibrium is *not* a "golden rule" (a stationary state with discount factor $\beta = 1$). In contrast to optimal growth paths, however, *only* the stationary state can be interpreted as an equilibrium: along any approach path, an agent taking prices as given can increase his utility. This seems to me to mirror exactly Friedman's statement, in a very similar context, that while "it is easy to see what the final position [following a change in M] will be . . . it is much harder to say anything about the transition" (1969, p. 6).

The shape of the equilibrium distribution of real balances is shown in

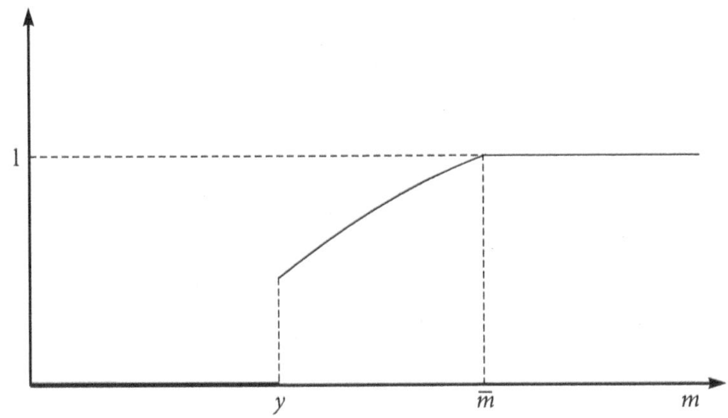

Figure 3

Figure 3. There is a mass point at the institutional minimum holding y, and then a smooth distribution on $(y, \bar{m})$. The existence of a mass point clearly follows from the economics of the situation: if individuals did not occasionally spend all available cash (return to y) they would be holding too much money. Money is an inventory, held against a particular contingency, and one never has an optimal inventory bounded away from zero. There is, however, no presumption that the lower bound y is visited "frequently" or, which comes to the same thing, that a "large" fraction of consumers will be at $m = y$ at any point in time.

The determinants of the demand for money, or of velocity, in this model are a mix of "institutional" and "economic" factors. Clearly, the length of a "day" will affect the equilibrium; indeed, there are economists to whom a constraint of the form $pc \leq M$ (in units, \$/t ≤ \$) must appear unthinkable. As long as one remembers not to vary the length of a "day" in mid-argument, this raises no problems, however. Moreover, the rate at which the earth rotates *does* have important economic implications and there is nothing to be gained in insisting on an economic explanation for *this* phenomenon.

The economic factors affecting money demand are preferences U, the discount factor β, the volatility F of the shocks θ and income y. Thus the amount of risk and people's attitude toward it (U and F) will affect money demand, as is appropriate in a model stressing the precautionary motive; so too will the rate of time preference. One's intuition as to the direction of effect of changes in these forces is fairly strong, but rigorous verification is somewhat complicated. The next section, a treatment of the income effect on real balance demand, illustrates a useful method for answering questions of this type, and also addresses a question of substantive interest.

V. Engel Curves for Real Balances

The relationship of the demand for real balances to the level of real income has received a great deal of attention, both theoretically and empirically. Early inventory-theoretic treatments suggested an income elasticity less than unity, a prediction which has never found any empirical confirmation. Friedman's early empirical work (1959) led to estimated income elasticities of around 1.8, which he rationalized in terms of conventional consumer demand theory by concluding that real balances, as a consumer durable, are a "luxury" good. I think it is now recognized that any empirically estimated Engel curve can be rationalized theoretically as well as any other, so that the issue is purely an empirical one. The model studied in this paper does not suggest modifications to this open conclusion, but it can be utilized to isolate the contributions of the several determinants of the income elasticity of money demand somewhat more satisfactorily than can be done with theories at the level of individual behavior only.

Real output (per capita productivity) was taken as a constant in Sections I–III. This assumption will be maintained here for each *individual* agent, but it will be assumed that each agent's constant income y is taken from a distribution $\Lambda(y \mid \bar{y})$ where $\bar{y}$ is mean income:

$$\bar{y} \equiv \int y \Lambda(dy \mid \bar{y}).$$

One may then consider the *individual* Engel curve, describing the way average real balances vary with y for *given* $\bar{y}$, and the *market* Engel curve describing the way average balances vary across economies with different average income levels $\bar{y}$.

In these seemingly more complex economies, individuals continue to solve (2.3). Denote the resulting value and policy functions, constructed exactly as in Section III, by $v(m, \theta, y)$ $c(m, \theta, y)$, $g(m, \theta, y)$. Similarly, (2.7) and (2.8) continue to define the stationary distribution of real balances, *conditioned* on y, as constructed in Section III. Call this c.d.f. $\psi(m|y)$. This is the fraction of time an agent with income y will hold balances less than or equal to m, *independent* of the average income $\bar{y}$ in his society. The individual Engel curve is then

$$h(y) = \int_{y}^{\bar{m}(y)} m \, d\psi(m \mid y). \tag{5.1}$$

The market Engel curve requires averaging over $\Lambda(y \mid \bar{y})$. It is:

$$k(\bar{y}) = \int_{0}^{\infty} \int_{y}^{\bar{m}(y)} m \, d\psi(m \mid y) d\Lambda(y \mid \bar{y}) = \int_{0}^{\infty} h(y) d\Lambda(y \mid \bar{y}). \tag{5.2}$$

Market equilibrium (price level determination) is obtained by replacing (2.6) with

$$k(\bar{y}) = M/p. \tag{5.3}$$

I shall turn, then, to methods for learning about the function $h(y)$, with the reader forewarned by the introduction to this section that sharp predictions are not likely to be forthcoming.

The function $h(y)$, evaluated at a particular y-value, is the mean value of the function $f(m) \equiv m$ with respect to the stationary distribution $\psi(m|y)$. This function is continuous, and therefore bounded on the interval $[y, \bar{m}(y)]$. I shall utilize well known facts about mean values of continuous bounded functions with respect to stationary distributions. First:

LEMMA 2. If $\mu^* = S\mu^*$ and for all measurable $A \subset R^*$

$$\lim_{t \to \infty} (S^t \mu_0)(A) = \mu^*(A),$$

independent of μ_0, then for all continuous, bounded f_0

$$\lim_{t \to \infty} \int_{0}^{\infty} f_0(m)(S^t \mu_0)(dm) = \int_{0}^{\infty} f_0(m) \mu^*(dm). \tag{5.4}$$

PROOF. [6; p. 243].

Second, using (3.2), one notices that

$$\int_{0}^{\infty} f_0(m)(S^{t+1} \mu_0)(dm) = \int_{0}^{\infty} \int_{I} f_0 \left[g(m,\theta) \right] dF(\theta)(S^t \mu_0)(dm) \tag{5.5}$$

since both sides of (5.5) express the mean value of $f_0(m_{t+1})$ given the initial distribution μ_0. Then if the sequence $\{f_t\}$ is defined recursively from f_0 by

$$f_{t+1}(m) = \int_{I} f_t \left[g(m,\theta) \right] dF(\theta) \tag{5.6}$$

repeated application of (5.5) gives (c.f. [6; p. 266])

$$\int_0^\infty f_t(m)\mu_o(dm) = \int_0^\infty f_o(m)(S^t\mu_o)(dm), \qquad t = 0, 1, 2, \ldots \tag{5.7}$$

Thus (5.4) may be replaced by

$$\lim_{t\to\infty} \int_0^\infty f_t(m)\mu_o(dm) = \int_0^\infty f_o(m)\mu^*(dm). \tag{5.8}$$

Moreover, since the choice of μ_o was arbitrary, $\{f_t\}$ must converge (almost everywhere) to a constant function, so that (5.8) [or (5.4)] can be replaced by

$$\lim_{t\to\infty} f_t(m) = \int_0^\infty f_o(m)\mu^*(dm) \qquad \text{for all} \qquad m \geq 0. \tag{5.9}$$

We know from proposition 4, Section III, that the hypotheses of Lemma 2 are satisfied for each fixed y. Then Lemma 2, with (5.4) replaced by (5.9) provides an inductive method for verifying statements about mean values of functions of m with respect to the stationary distribution.

Returning to the particular function $f_o(m) \equiv m$ of interest here, we have

LEMMA 3. Suppose $g(m, \theta, y)$ is a non-decreasing function of m and y. Then $h(y)$ as defined in (5.1) is a non-decreasing function of y.

The *proof* is an induction on the sequence $\{f_t\}$ defined by (5.6) and $f_o(m) \equiv m$. Clearly $f_o(\text{m}) = m$ is non-decreasing in m and y. Then if f_t has these properties, so does f_{t+1}, from (5.6) and the hypotheses on $g(m, \theta, y)$. The result then follows from Lemma 2, the fact that (5.4) implies (5.9), and (5.9).

To verify the hypotheses of Lemma 3, we need to go back to the maximum problem (2.3). In Section III (c.f. Figure 2) we found that $g(m, \theta, y)$ is non-decreasing in m. In the (m, θ) region on which $g(m, \theta, y) = y$, g is clearly increasing in y. From (3.3), one can see that this is also true when $g(m, \theta, y) > y$. This proves, applying Lemma 3,

PROPOSITION 5. $h(y)$ is a non-decreasing function of y. From (5.2), it also follows that if increases in mean income $\bar{y}$ shift the entire distribution $\Lambda(y \mid \bar{y})$ to the right, then $k(\bar{y})$ is also an increasing function.

It has been established, then, that both the individual and market Engel curves for real balances are upward-sloping (really, only that they are never downward-sloping) or that real balances are a "normal" good. The methods used to establish this fact make it fairly clear, I think, that no sharper predictions on the magnitude of the slope of this curve will be obtained without much stronger restrictions on preferences (on U and F). Put backwards, any empirically found slope would be consistent with the theory.

Since the model of this paper is inventory-theoretic, one might wonder why the "scale economies" which played such a prominent role in earlier theory do not seem to arise here. One way to answer this is by suggesting a modification of the model which would, or might, re-introduce them. In Section I, I suggested that the cash-in-advance constraint facing households be motivated as imposed on a household in which one member spends a "day" spending the cash earned by the other member on the preceding day. No provision was made for the shopper to make visits *during* a day to the "store" of the worker, picking up currency earned there in the first hour, the second hour, and so on. That is, I have taken the payments period to be *institutionally* rather than *economically* determined. Were this convention relaxed, it might be the case that increases in y would induce the number of intra-day currency "re-orders" to rise, so that real balances demanded would rise less than proportionally with income y. This modification would introduce no new *possibilities* for the shape of $h(y)$ into the theory. It is possible, though not a conjecture I would expend much effort to verify, that it would rule out some $h(y)$ possibilities. The cross-section results obtained by Meltzer (1963) suggest that this role of "scale economies" may safely be abstracted from.

VI. Concluding Comments

One of many issues not touched upon above is that of the economic *efficiency* of the monetary equilibrium found in Sections II and III. Clearly, the equilibrium in the economy with certainty (Section I) is efficient.[6] With individual uncertainty introduced, even to *define* efficiency in a satisfactory way is a problem of some complexity. If one thinks of each individual's current θ as observable to all, a marginal condition expressing the

6. The assumption in Section I that no disutility is attached to labor supply is crucial to this conclusion. See Locay and Palmon (1978), where in a context very similar to that of this paper, but with disutility attached to labor, it is shown that a Friedman-like deflationary policy is required for the monetary allocation to be efficient. An earlier, more general treatment of this efficiency question is given in Grandmont and Younes (1973).

idea "from each according to his ability; to each according to his need" can be derived. Presumably, however, one is interested in the case in which each agent "observes" *his own* θ, but not anyone else's, in which case issues of incentive compatibility of allocative arrangements become central.

Without exploring this difficult matter further one can, I think, see that on *any* efficiency criterion which takes these issues into account, the monetary equilibrium of Sections II and III will *not* be efficient. In any period, there will be some households in a run of low θ's, with large real balances accumulated but no particular urgency to spend them. There will be others in a run of high θ's, with balances of y and a high marginal utility of current consumption. Here, then, are two sides to a nonexistent *credit* market on which some would gladly lend at positive interest rather than the zero yield provided by currency and others would gladly pay this premium to consume today at the expense of future consumption.

Can this gap be filled by a government-engineered deflation, in which currency is withdrawn from the system via lump-sum taxes and a positive real yield thereby created? Clearly not, though by some efficiency criteria this policy may be utility-increasing. The problem here is not one involving the attractiveness of currency *on average*, but one of permitting the benefits of gains from trade between *differently* situated agents.

The introduction of a credit market into this economy would, with impatient agents ($\beta < 1$), be associated with a positive interest rate and hence with real balance holdings at the institutionally-fixed minimum level (as in Section I). (With arbitrarily short periods, this would imply arbitrarily high, or "infinite" velocity.) With the introduction of some real cost associated with dealing in a credit market (say, the time involved for one's credit worthiness to be established) one can imagine a model in which currency demand is governed by a mechanism such as that studied above, co-existing with a credit mechanism for larger transactions. The analysis of such a hybrid system must be left for future research.

In the present model, as in more complex elaborations which one may imagine, there is a clear sense in which money is a "second-rate" asset. It serves a role, and commands resources, *only* insofar as it enables the economy to economize on some sort of record-keeping or other "transactions cost." At best, then, money is viewed as a means of *approximating* some idealized "real" resource allocation. This feature may be contrasted with the role of money in the intergenerational models introduced by Samuelson (1958). There, money converts an economy which is allocating resources inefficiently into an efficient one. It does not provide a cheap approximation to an idealized and efficient real allocation which one can at least imagine being achieved in a decentralized, non-monetary way; it is the *only* device short of centralized planning by which an efficient real allocation may be attained.

This theoretical second-rate-ness of money seems to me a *virtue* of models in which its use is motivated by a cash-in-advance constraint, and therefore a reason for attempting to pursue the analysis of models of this type more deeply. In the first place, money (or currency, certainly) *really is* a second rate asset: if any of us were to have free overnight access to Federal Funds, we would take advantage of it. In the second place, this view of money as an aid in *approximately* attaining real general equilibrium is consistent with the way economists use real general equilibrium or relative price theory. When we apply theories of "barter" economies to problems in, say, public finance or labor economics, it is not our intent to obtain results applicable only to primitive or pre-historic societies. We apply this body of theory to money-using economies such as our own because we believe that, for many problems, the fact that money is used in attaining equilibrium can be abstracted from, or that the theoretical "barter" economy is a tractable idealized model which approximates well (is well approximated by) the actual, monetary economy. If this practice is sound, then we want monetary theories which rationalize it or at least which do not radically conflict with it.

References

Baumol, William J., "The Transactions Demand for Cash: An Inventory Theoretic Approach." *Quarterly Journal of Economics, 66*, 1952, 545–56.

Berge, Claude, *Topological Spaces*. New York: Macmillan, 1963.

Blackwell, David, "Discounted Dynamic Programming." *Annals of Mathematical Statistics, 36*, 1965, 226–35.

Clower, Robert W., "A Reconsideration of the Microfoundations of Money." *Western Economic Journal, 6*, 1967, 1–9.

Doob, J. L., *Stochastic Processes*. New York: Wiley, 1953.

Feller, William, An *Introduction to Probability Theory and Its Applications*, Vol. 2, New York: Wiley, 1966.

Friedman, Milton, "The Demand for Money—Some Theoretical and Empirical Results." *Journal of Political Economy, 67*, 1959, 327–51.

———, *The Optimum Quantity of Money and Other Essays.* Chicago: Aldine, 1969.

Futia, Carl, "A Stochastic Approach to Economic Dynamics." Bell Laboratories Working Paper, undated.

Grandmont, Jean-Michel and Yves Younes, "On the Role of Money and the Existence of a Monetary Equilibrium." *Review of Economic Studies, 39,* July 1972, 355–72.

———, "On the Efficiency of a Monetary Equilibrium." *Review of Economic Studies, 40,* April 1973, 149–65.

Locay, Luis and Oded Palmon, "The Optimum Quantity of Money in a Perfect Foresight Monetary Model." University of Chicago, working paper, 1978.

Lucas, Robert E., Jr., "Asset Prices in an Exchange Economy," *Econometrica, 46,* 1978, 1429–46.

Meltzer, Allan H., "The Demand for Money: A Cross-section Study of Business Firms." *Quarterly Journal of Economics, 77,* 1963, 405–22.

Samuelson, Paul A., "An Exact Consumption-Loan Model of Interest With or Without the Contrivance of Money." *Journal of Political Economy, 66,* 1958, 467–82.

Tobin, James, "The Interest-Elasticity of the Transactions Demand for Cash." *Review of Economics and Statistics, 38,* 1956, 241–47.

— 4 —

Two Illustrations of the Quantity Theory of Money

This paper presents empirical illustrations of two central implications of the quantity theory of money: that a given change in the rate of change in the quantity of money induces (i) an equal change in the rate of price inflation; and (ii) an equal change in nominal rates of interest.* The illustrations were obtained by comparing moving averages of the three variables in question, using quarterly *U.S.* time-series for the period 1953–77. Readers may find the results of interest as additional confirmation of the quantity theory, as an example of one way in which the quantity-theoretic relationships can be uncovered via atheoretical methods from time-series which are subject to a variety of other forces, or as a measure of the extent to which the inflation and interest rate experience of the postwar period can be understood in terms of purely classical, monetary forces.

The theoretical background of the study is reviewed, very briefly as it is familiar material, in the next section. The data processing methods are described and rationalized in Section II. The illustrations resulting from the application of these methods are in Section III. Section IV contains some decompositions of postwar time-series and concluding comments.

I. Theoretical and Empirical Background

The two quantity-theoretic propositions stated in the introduction possess a combination of theoretical coherence and empirical verification shared

---

American Economic Review, 70, no. 5 (December 1980): 1005–1014.

*I have benefited from discussions with Jacob Frenkel, Sherwin Rosen, Thomas Sargent, Gary Skoog, and William Wecker. I would also like to thank Frederick Miller and Christopher Flinn for their assistance, and the National Science Foundation for its support.

by no other propositions in monetary economics. By "theoretical coherence," I mean that each of these laws appears as a characteristic of solutions to explicit theoretical models of idealized economies, models which give some guidance as to why one might expect them to obtain in reality, also as to conditions under which one might expect them to break down. For present purposes, Miguel Sidrauski's monetary version of the Solow-Swan one-sector model of economic growth (1967a, b) is perhaps the most useful, single theoretical illustration. In that model, both laws appear as explicit, necessary characteristics of the stationary solution of the differential equations which describe equilibrium in the system. To restate this in a way which is more suggestive empirically, they appear as characteristics of long-run average behavior in the model economy.

Both of these laws are, as is clear from the Sidrauski example, propositions about the consequences of a unit's change. Thus neither appears to depend crucially on particular features of the preferences and technology postulated by Sidrauski. It is not difficult to construct other examples to illustrate the insensitivity of these laws to variations in the structure of the economy. In particular, if stochastic elements are introduced, the laws are reinterpreted to apply to means of theoretical stationary distributions or, as before, to long-run average behavior.[1]

Sidrauski's example, together with variations appearing in the literature both before and since he wrote, also suggests some qualifications or limitations to these laws. First, Sidrauski's version of the neoclassical model does not exhibit the Mundell-Tobin effect of a monetary expansion: the possibility that an inflation, by reducing the real yield on money, will shift saving to real capital accumulation. If this effect is important, it would force us to modify the second law to predict interest rate increases by *less* than the increase in the monetary growth rate (due to the decline in the real return on capital, offsetting the inflation premium).[2] Theoretically, I think it is clear from related work (see, for example, David Levhari and Don

1. This interpretation of the quantity theory of money as a set of predictions about the long-run average behavior of a general equilibrium system is different from, though not inconsistent with, Milton Friedman. There, Friedman stresses the stability of the market demand function for money, a property which is neither necessary nor sufficient for the quantity theory to obtain in the sense used here.

2. Since interest payments are taxable, the maintenance of a given real yield on bonds would require interest rates to rise by more than the inflation rate. This effect will offset, and perhaps even reverse, the Mundell-Tobin effect.

Patinkin, Stanley Fischer, and Ronald Michener) that only a very coincidental combination of assumptions produces an absence of a Mundell-Tobin effect in Sidrauski's example and that, in general, one does not want to view this effect as ruled out on prior, logical grounds. This conclusion, of course, leaves us free to hope that the required modifications are minor enough to be neglected in some applications.

Second, and perhaps more fundamental, theory at this level gives no guidance as to the measurement of the quantity of money, or as to which (if any) of the available time-series on monetary aggregates corresponds to the variable theoretically termed "money." (Of course, it also gives no guidance as to the empirical definition of "the price level," but there is a good deal of other economic theory which does.) As recent theoretical work of John Bryant and Neil Wallace and Marco Martins has emphasized, this question of which monetary aggregate one would theoretically *expect* to move in proportion to prices is much more open than has traditionally been recognized. In the experiments reported below, money means *M*1, but the arbitrariness of this measurement choice should be emphasized at the outset, particularly as it is likely that very similar results would have been obtained under a variety of other choices.

In summary, then, we have specific theoretical examples exhibiting both quantity-theoretic laws in clear, exact form, and others which suggest possibly important qualifications. This is all we can ever hope for from our theory: some strong clues as to what to look for in the data; some warnings as to potential sources of error in these predictions. This is the theoretical coherence of the neoclassical laws.

Since the two quantity-theoretic laws are obtained as characteristics of steady states, or limiting distributions, of theoretical models, the ideal experiment for testing them would be a comparison of long-term average behavior across economies with different monetary policies but similar in other respects. Many such tests of the first law are available;[3] a particularly clean example is shown in Figure 1. These data are taken from Robert Vogel's study of inflation in sixteen Latin American economies, using annual data for the period 1950–69.[4] Vogel does not report the interest rate data which would have permitted a comparable test of the Fisherian interest-

3. See in particular Anna Schwartz.

4. The countries included in Vogel's study are Argentina, Bolivia, Brazil, Chile, Colombia, Costa Rica, Ecuador, El Salvador, Guatemala, Honduras, Mexico, Nicaragua, Paraguay, Peru, Uruguay, and Venezuela.

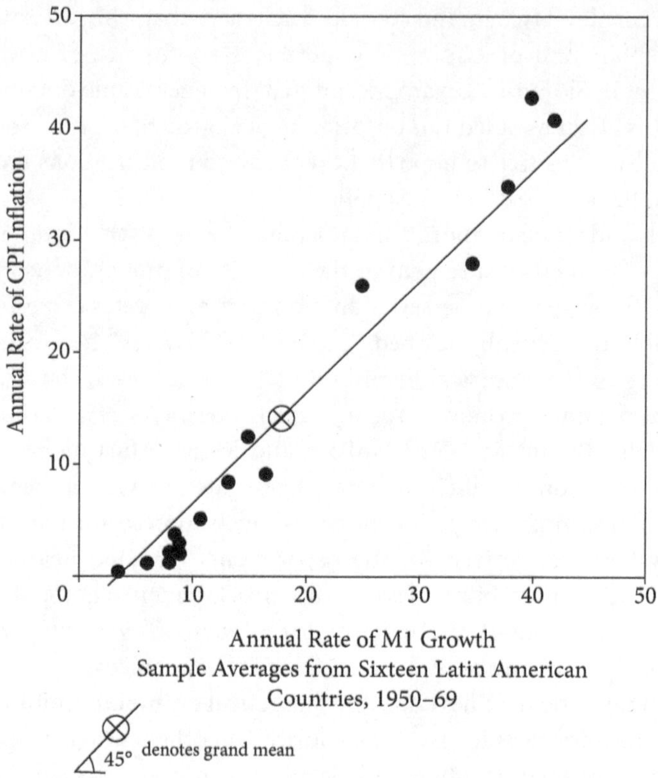

Figure 1

inflation relationship. In general, such evidence is difficult to obtain, no doubt due to the fact that in inflationary economies published interest rates are rarely left free to reach their equilibrium levels.

The line in Figure 1 is drawn through the grand mean of the 16 × 20 = 320 annual money growth rate inflation pairs in Vogel's sample. This is the one "free parameter" permitted by the theory. Its slope is 45°, as specified theoretically: it is not fit to the data. It is hard to imagine a nonvacuous economic prediction obtaining stronger confirmation than that shown in Figure 1. This is the kind of "empirical verification" of the quantity theory on which economists who assign it a central theoretical role base most of their confidence.

In the absence of the kind of decisive natural experiment used by Vogel, one could in principle test the neoclassical laws by deriving their implications for the parameters of a structural econometric model. This course, while attractive in theory (since it broadens considerably the class of data which might shed light on the laws), is in practice a difficult one, since it involves nesting the two hypotheses in question within a complex maintained hypothesis, which must be accepted as valid in order to carry out the test. The virtue of relatively atheoretical tests, such as carried out by Vogel, is that they correspond to our theoretically based intuition that the quantity theoretic laws are consistent with a wide variety of possible structures. If so, it would be desirable to test them independently and then, if confirmed, to *impose* them in constructing particular structural models, rather than to proceed in the reverse direction. It would be of value, then, to have measurement techniques which are atheoretical in the sense of Vogel's but which can be applied to continuous time-series for a single economy. The use of one such technique is illustrated below.

II. Data and Data Processing Methods

The time-series used in this study are the money supply ($M1_t$), the consumer price level (P_t) and the ninety-day Treasury bill rate (r_t). The value of $M1_t$ for quarter t is demand deposits plus currency outside banks, for the first month of the quarter, seasonally adjusted, taken from successive issues of the *Federal Reserve Bulletin.* The *CPI* is similarly timed, not seasonally adjusted, from the Consumer Price Index. The bill rate is that used and described by Eugene Fama.

I shall work with the following transformed variables:

$$X_{0t} = ln(M1_{t+1}) - ln(M1_t)$$

$$X_{1t} = ln(P_{t+1}) - ln(P_t)$$

$$X_{2t} = r_t$$

Scatter diagrams of X_{1t} and X_{2t} against X_{0t} are given in Figures 2 and 3, in the next section. These figures seem to capture fairly well what people mean when they say that the quantity theory of money is not a "short-run" relationship.

The general idea of what follows will be to examine scatter diagrams of

$X_{it}(\beta)$, $i = 1, 2$, against $X_{0t}(\beta)$ where for $i = 0, 1, 2$, $X_{it}(\beta)$ is the two-sided exponentially weighted moving average given by[5]

$$X_{it}(\beta) = \alpha \sum_{k=-\infty}^{\infty} \beta^{|k|} x_{i,t+k} \tag{1}$$

where
$$\alpha = \frac{1-\beta}{1+\beta}, \; 0 \leq \beta < 1$$

The effect of the filter (1) is to smooth the original series; indeed, as β approaches unity, the filtered observations $X_{it}(\beta)$ approach the sample average values of the original series. In the latter case, plots of $X_{1t}(\beta)$ and $X_{2t}(\beta)$ against $X_{0t}(\beta)$ will degenerate to a point, vacuously lying on a line with slope 45°. Our interest will be in seeing whether the points $(X_{0t}(\beta), X_{it}(\beta))$, $i = 1, 2$, fall on a 45° line for β-values less than unity, providing a time-series confirmation of the cross-country results obtained by Vogel and others. Viewed as a measurement procedure, the test of this method will be the quality of the pictures it yields. It may be useful first, however, to look in more detail into what the filter (1) does to a time-series, and what statistical and economic rationales may underlie its use.

The Fourier transform of the filter given in (1), with α free, is for $0 \leq \omega \leq \pi$,

$$\begin{aligned} f(\omega; \alpha, \beta) &= \alpha \sum_{k=-\infty}^{\infty} \beta^{|k|} e^{-i\omega k} \\ &= \frac{\alpha(1-\beta^2)}{1+\beta^2 - 2\beta\cos(\omega)} \end{aligned} \tag{2}$$

5. Here and below I write as though the entire doubly infinite record were available for each variable. In the calculations, the algorithm described by Thomas Cooley, Barr Rosenberg, and Kent Wall was used. This algorithm permits the assignment of a diffuse prior on x_{it} values outside the sample period which appear in the doubly infinite sum (1). With beliefs about points prior to 1953 and after 1977 so described, it calculates posterior means of the slowly moving "signal," called s_t below. Except for points near the beginning and the end of the sample period, virtually identical results were obtained simply by replacing missing observations in (1) by zeros. So as not to present results which are unduly dependent on the way out-of-sample X_{it} values are treated, numbers for 1953–54 and 1976–77 are not plotted.

One verifies that $f(0) = 1$ if $\alpha = (1 - \beta)/(1 + \beta)$, that $f(\pi)>0$ and that $f'(\omega) < 0$ for all $0 \leq \omega \leq \pi$. Also $f''(0) < 0$ and $f''(\pi) > 0$; $f''(\omega)$ changes sign once, at the unique ω value at which $X = \cos(\omega)$ is a positive root of

$$X^2 + \frac{1+\beta^2}{2\beta} X - 2 = 0$$

For high β-values (for example, near 0.9) this root occurs very near $\omega = 0$. Since the spectral density of the filtered series $X_{it}(\beta)$ is just the spectral density of X_{it} multiplied by $f(\omega; \alpha_i \beta)$, one sees that the filter (1) retains power at very low frequencies, while sharply reducing power at higher frequencies.

Filters of the form (1) are solutions to a well-known signal-extraction problem, the form of which may also be instructive.[6] Let $\{v_t, w_t\}$ be a white noise process with mean (0, 0) and covariance matrix $\sigma^2 \begin{bmatrix} \theta & 0 \\ 0 & 1 \end{bmatrix}$.

Define the processes u_t and s_t by

$$u_t = s_t + v_t$$

$$s_t = \rho s_{t-1} + w_t$$

$$0 < \rho < 1$$

Imagine that this structure, including the values of the parameters θ, σ^2, and ρ, is known and that one has observations on the u_t, $t = -\infty, \ldots, \infty$. It is desired to obtain minimum variance unbiased estimators $\hat{s}_t$ of the sequence of signals s_t. Projecting s_t on u_t, $t = -\infty, \ldots, \infty$

$$\begin{aligned} s_t &= \hat{s}_t + \eta_t \\ &= \sum_{k=-\infty}^{\infty} \gamma_k u_{t+k} + \eta_t \end{aligned}$$

where $E(u_t \eta_s) = 0$, all s, t. The coefficients γ_k must satisfy the normal equations:

$$E(u_{t+j} s_t) = \sum_{k=-\infty}^{\infty} \gamma_k E(u_{t+j} u_{t+k})$$

$$j = -\infty, \ldots, \infty$$

6. See Peter Whittle (ch. 5) for a discussion of this and other examples.

Taking the Fourier transform of both sides:[7]

$$f_{us}(\omega) = f_{uu}(\omega) f_{\gamma}(\omega), 0 \leq \omega \leq \pi$$

or, exploiting the particular structure of the process assumed here,

$$f_{ss}(\omega) = \left[f_{ss}(\omega) + f_{vv}(\omega) \right] f_{\gamma}(\omega)$$

Solving for $f_{\gamma}(\omega)$ gives

$$f_{\gamma}(\omega) = \frac{1}{1 + \theta\left[1 + \rho^2 - 2\rho\cos(\omega)\right]} \tag{3}$$

since $f_{vv}(\omega) = \theta\sigma^2$ and $f_{ss}(\omega) = [1 + \rho^2 - 2\rho\cos(\omega)]^{-1}\sigma^2$.

For the functions $f(\omega; \alpha, \beta)$ in (2) and $f_{\gamma}(\omega)$ in (3) to be the transforms of the same filter, it is necessary that the right-hand sides of these equations be identically equal in ω on $[0, \pi]$. This requires that β in (2) be that root of

$$0 = 1 - \beta\left[\frac{1 + \theta(1 + \rho^2)}{\theta\rho}\right] + \beta^2$$

which lies in (0, 1). Given β, α must satisfy

$$\alpha = \frac{\beta}{\theta\rho(1 - \beta^2)}$$

The particular filter given in (1) is a one-parameter family in which α and β are constrained by $\alpha = (1 - \beta)(1 + \beta)^{-1}$. This case is seen to correspond to the limiting situation where $\rho = 1$ and β solves[8]

$$0 = 1 - \left[\frac{1 + 2\theta}{\theta}\right]\beta + \beta^2 \tag{4}$$

7. For two time-series $\{x_t\}$ and $\{y_t\}$, the notation $f_{xy}(\omega)$ means

$$f_{xy}(\omega) = \sum_{k=-\infty}^{\infty} e^{-i\omega k} Cov(x_{t+k}, y_t)$$

8. This is the quadratic John Muth arrived at, for the same reasons, in his study of the permanent income hypothesis.

Hence if the variance of the "noise" v_t is small relative to the variance of w_t ($\theta \cong 0$), the root β of (4) in (0, 1) will be near 0. This means that the current observation u_t is a good estimate of the true signal s_t. In our economic application, where s_t is taken to be that part of a time-series which is dominated by quantity-theoretic forces, this would correspond to a situation in which other "real" forces play a negligible role. At the other extreme, when the noise variance is high (θ large), β will be near one, and the best estimate of the true signal at t will be a very long moving average of the observed u_t.[9]

This purely statistical rationale for experimenting with the filter (1) has no basis in economic theory, and a little reflection suggests that none will be forthcoming: a *good* economic theory accounting for both quantity-theoretic and other forces on interest rate and price series would surely suggest the use of a "sharper" filter than (1). Nevertheless, the following scenario may be helpful. Imagine an economy in which the rate of monetary growth is a constant, known to agents, plus noise. The known, constant component is incorporated exactly into inflation and interest rates, with a negligible Mundell-Tobin effect. The monetary noise induces noise in interest and prices. In this example, the signal s_t represents the "constant" known, common component in monetary growth, price inflation, and interest rates. The noise v_t will be different for the different series.

Next, imagine that s_t, while constant for long stretches of time, infrequently changes to a new value from time to time. That is, model s_t by

$$s_t = \begin{cases} s_{t-1} & \text{with} \quad prob\ \lambda \\ \tilde{s}_t & \text{with} \quad prob\ 1 - \lambda \end{cases}$$

where $\tilde{s}_t$ is serially independent with mean 0, and variance τ^2, and where $1 - \lambda$ is "small." This process has the same covariance structure as the "signal" used in the statistical example above, with $\rho = \lambda$ and $\sigma^2 = (1 - \lambda)\tau^2$.

For an econometrician to treat this economy as posing a signal processing problem of the above type, one assumes that the "structural changes" in s_t are perfectly understood by agents as they occur, but cannot be ob-

9. In the application below, the noise component is not serially uncorrelated as assumed in the example just discussed. For a more general discussion of the rationales for the use of a filter such as that described by (1), see Christopher Sims.

served by the econometrician. Hence the use of a *two-sided* moving average filter.[10]

The hope in applying this filter is not, of course, that an economic model of this type holds *exactly.* It is rather the general idea that the actual series may be generated by a *very* slowly changing structure of monetary policy, with business cycle activity occurring at higher frequencies superimposed. One can construct examples of economies fitting this description rather well, and one can construct other examples deviating very sharply from this description.

III. Illustrations

Figures 2 and 3 present scatter diagrams of inflation and interest rates, respectively, against rates of *M*1 growth. As remarked earlier, no relationship is evident.

Figures 4 and 5 are plots of moving averages with weights (on all series) equal to 0.5. That is, Figure 4 plots $X_{1t}(0.5)$ against $X_{0t}(0.5)$ and Figure 5 plots $X_{2t}(0.5)$ against $X_{0t}(0.5)$. Figures 6 and 7 utilize $\beta = 0.8$; 8 and 9, $\beta = 0.9$; and 10 and 11, $\beta = 0.95$. All figures are drawn to the same scale. To avoid clutter, only points for the second quarter of each year are plotted. For high β-values, it is clear that this choice, while arbitrary, is of no consequence. Points for the first two years (1953–54) and last two (1967–77) are not plotted, though they were used in calculating the 1955–75 observations.

Given the preparatory discussion in Section II, little need be said about these figures. It is evident that a filter with $\beta = 0.5$ does not quite extract the quantity-theoretic signal. A β-value of 0.9 reveals a clear 45° line, as predicted by the quantity theory and produces a picture about as clear as Vogel's cross-country estimates (Figure 1); $\beta = 0.95$ is clearer still. If a Mundell-Tobin effect were present, and if it dominated tax effects, this would show up in the odd-numbered figures as a line with slope less than 45°. Perhaps this may be seen, for example, in Figure 9. Since deviations of

10. This is not, of course, a compelling reason for using a two-sided filter. It is simply the condition under which it would be optimal to do so. In general, agents *know* only the past (arguing for a one-sided backward filter) but they *care* only about the future, and probably process much more information in forecasting that part of the future relevant to their own decisions than we econometricians can observe (arguing for a one-sided forward filter).

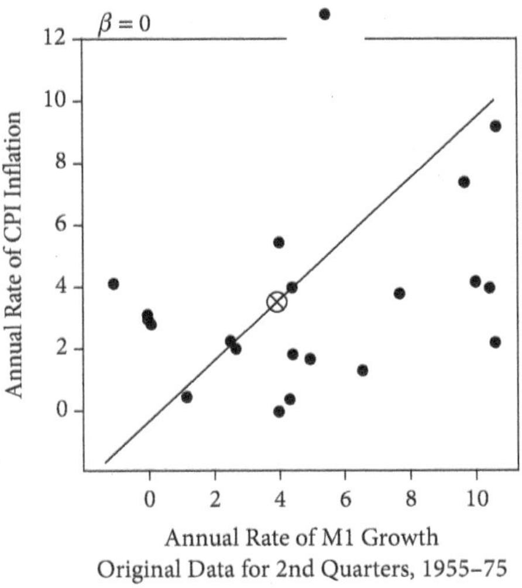

Figure 2

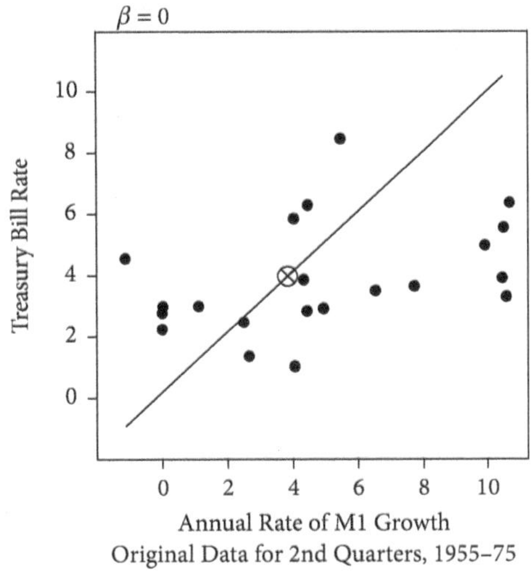

Figure 3

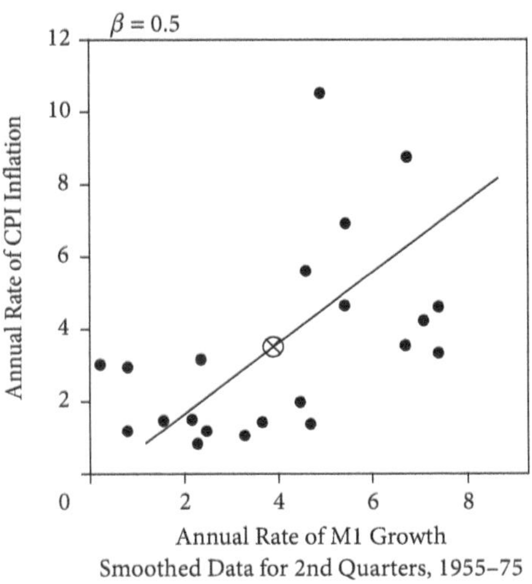

Figure 4

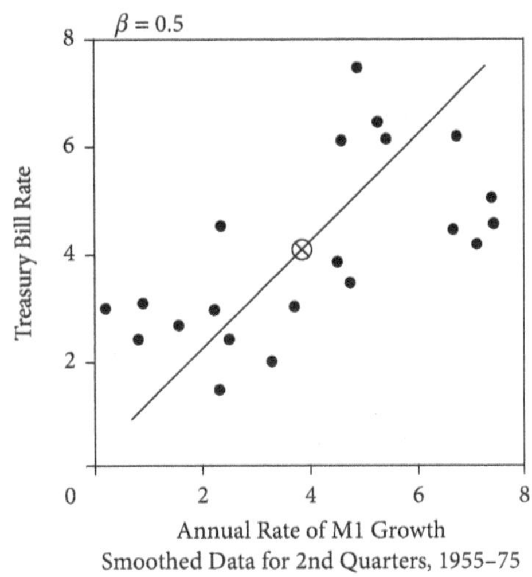

Figure 5

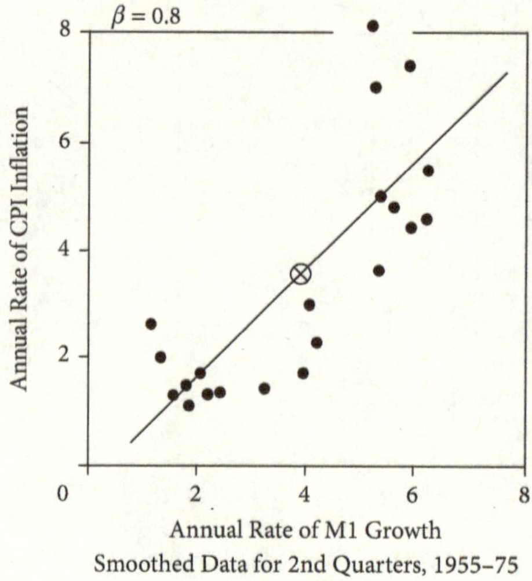

Figure 6

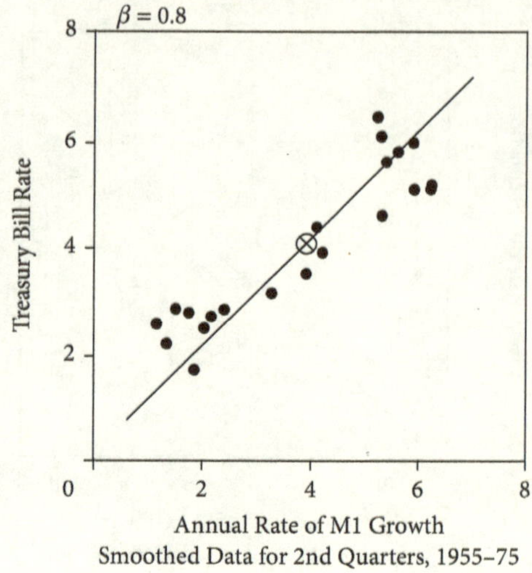

Figure 7

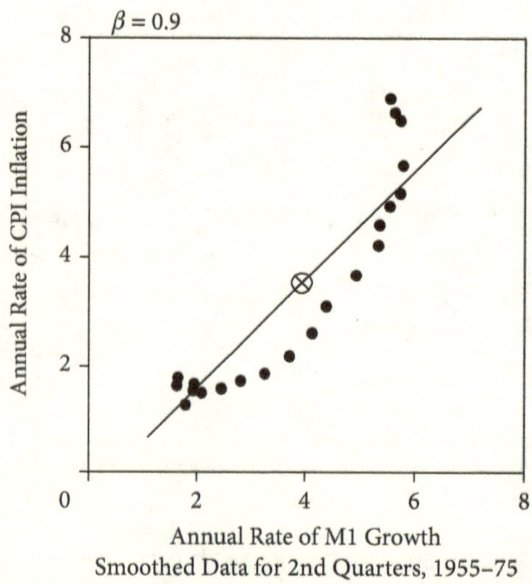

Figure 8

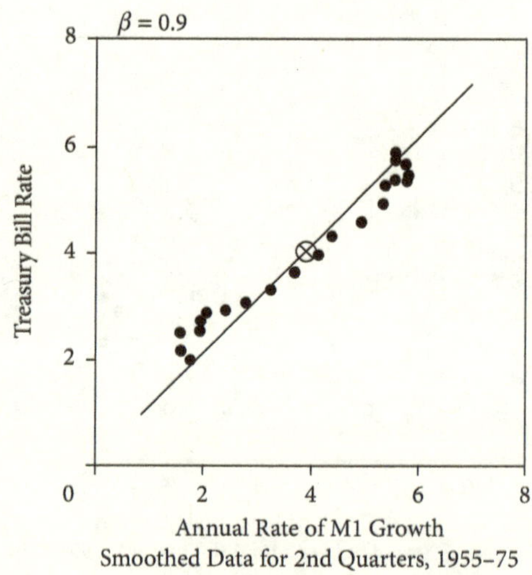

Figure 9

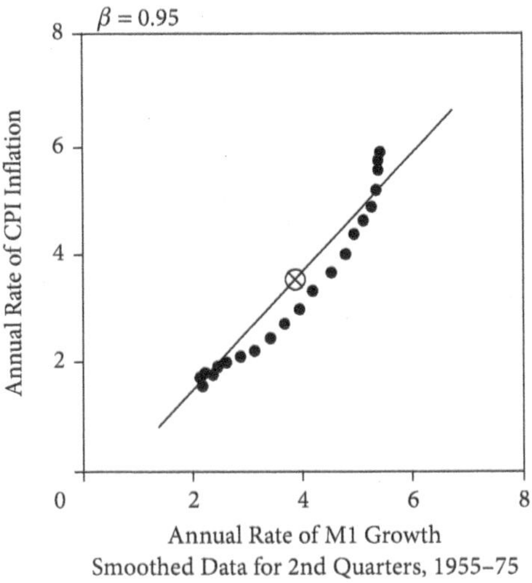

Figure 10

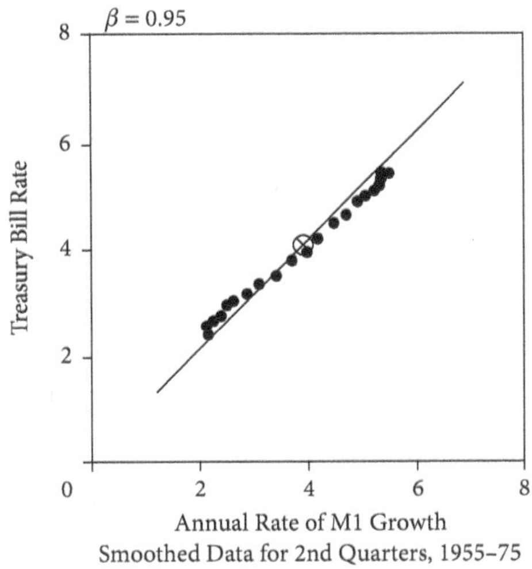

Figure 11

the moving averages from the 45° line are sure to exhibit patterns, the temptation to read Figure 9 (or 11) this way should probably be resisted.

It should be added that subjecting any two series to moving-average filtering of the type used here will cause a "pattern" of some kind to emerge. To illustrate, Figure 13 plots a two-sided moving average of the unemployment rate,[11] with $\beta = 0.9$, against the smoothed monetary change $X_{0t}(0.9)$, while Figure 12 plots one raw variable against the other. Again, one sees order of a sort emerging from confusion but it is an order that makes no sense economically. The difference between this order and that displayed in Figures 8 and 9 is that the latter is an implication of a coherent economic theory.

Since the comparison of $X_{it}(.9)$, $i = 1, 2$, to $X_{0t}(.9)$ in Figures 8 and 9 utilizes only low-frequency components of the original series, these figures will illustrate the quantity theory well only if the time-series used convey information on low-frequency movements in X_{0t}. In the absence of such information, the method applied above will produce merely a "blob" at the sample means of $X_{it}(\beta)$, $i = 1, 2$, and $X_{0t}(\beta)$ as β approaches unity, even if the quantity theory is valid. This is the time-series equivalent of the observation that if the countries studied by Vogel had had similar rates of mon-

11. Last month of quarter, not seasonally adjusted, from *Employment and Earnings*.

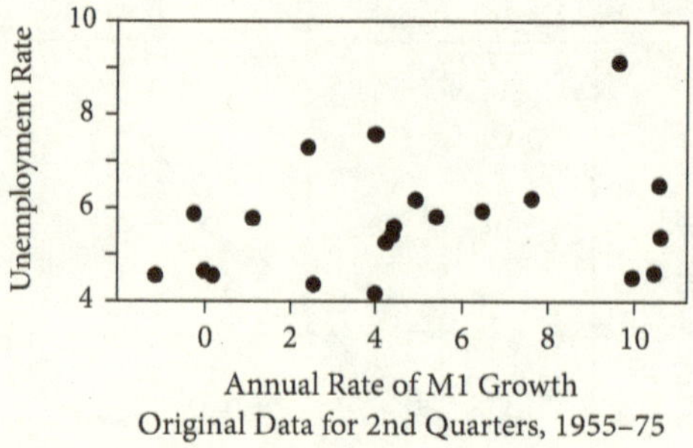

Figure 12

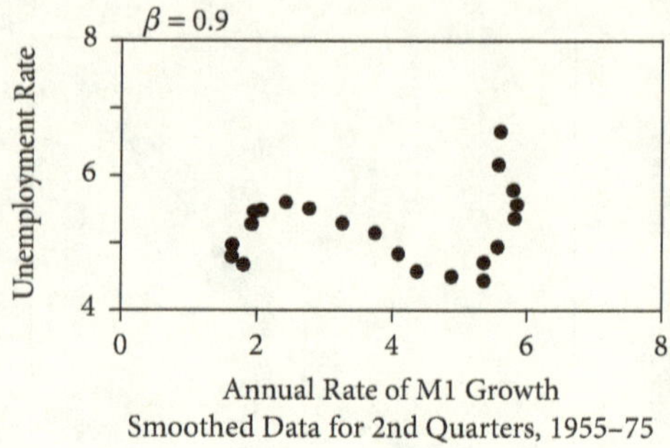

Figure 13

etary growth over his sample period, his method would not have produced a clear 45° line. That is, these methods will yield clear results only if a good enough "experiment" has been run by "nature" over the sample period used.

IV. Concluding Remarks

The filtering techniques described and applied in Sections II and III represent what might be called a "minimal" use of the quantity theory of money, in the sense that they utilize only the widely agreed-upon "long-run" implications of that theory. To this was added the hunch that identifying long-run with "very low frequency" might isolate those movements in postwar inflation and interest rates which can be accounted for on purely quantity-theoretic grounds. Figures 8 and 9 (or 10 and 11) confirm both the hunch and the underlying theory.

Figures 14 and 15 plot actual postwar inflation and interest rates, respectively, against time (i.e., X_{1t} and X_{2t}). On each diagram is also plotted the corresponding series with the smoothed portion subtracted (that is, $X_{1t} - X_{1t}(0.9)$ and $X_{2t} - X_{2t}\ (0.9)$). Evidently, both the inflation and the high interest rates of the 1970's are well accounted for by the quantity theory or, to put the same point backwards, any nonmonetary explanation of these trends would lead to large, unexplained deviations from the relationships depicted so clearly in Figures 8–11.

The method applied in this paper involves decomposing movements in money and other nominal variables into two components, one of which I have called quantity theoretic and the other of which has been left unla-

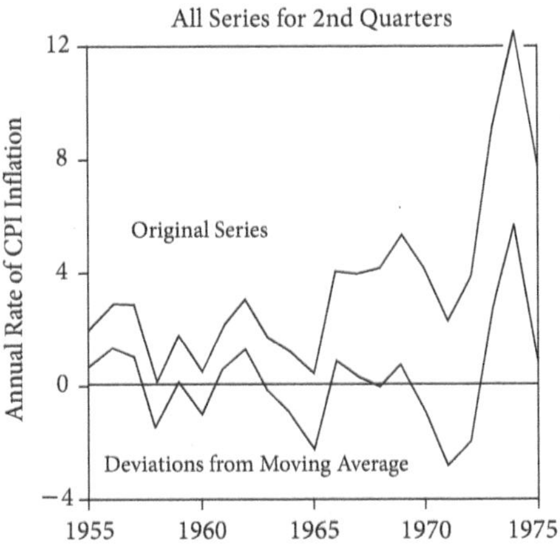

Figure 14

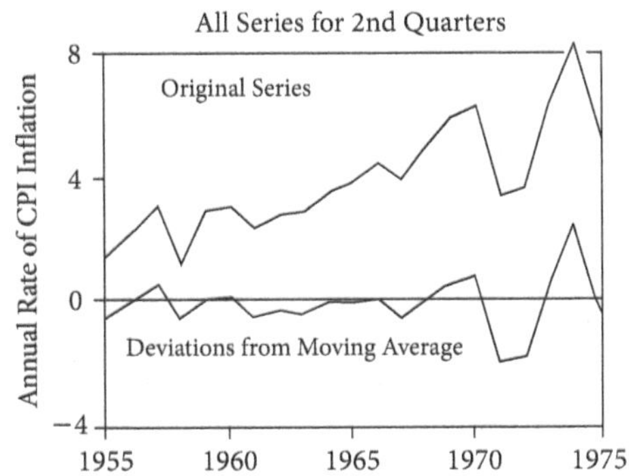

Figure 15

beled. This raises the question of the relationship of this decomposition to the clearly related decompositions of Thomas Sargent, and Robert Barro, among others, of monetary movements into "anticipated" and "unanticipated" components. Though it would be hard to spell out the details, my opinion would be that *all* of what I have called $X_{0t}(0.9)$ should be identified as anticipated in the Sargent-Barro sense, and *in addition,* that much of my $X_{0t} - X_{0t}$ (0.9) should also be thought of as anticipated. Indeed, this is what I mean by referring to the methods above as a *minimal* use of the quantity theory.

Putting the matter in this way should make it clear that no one decomposition method can dominate the other. By using weaker theory, one is more confident that his filter has not incorrectly labeled noise as signal; on the other side, there is no doubt that the methods used in this paper have not fully extracted from the series all that the quantity theory can account for.

References

R. J. Barro, "Unanticipated Money Growth and Unemployment in the United States," *Amer. Econ. Rev.,* Mar. 1977, *67,* 101–15.

J. Bryant and N. Wallace, "The Inefficiency of Interest-Bearing National Debt," *J. Polit. Econ.,* Apr. 1979, *87,* 365–81.

T. F. Cooley, B. Rosenberg, and K. D. Wall, "A Note on Optimal Smoothing for

Time-Varying Coefficient Problems," *Annals Econ. Soc. Measure.*, Fall 1977, *6*, 453–56.

E. Fama, "Short-Term Interest Rates as Predictors of Inflation," *Amer. Econ. Rev.*, June 1975, *65*, 269–82.

S. Fischer, "Capital Accumulation on the Transition Path in a Monetary Optimizing Model," work. paper, M.I.T., Feb. 1978.

Milton Friedman, "The Quantity Theory of Money—A Restatement," in his *Studies in the Quantity Theory of Money*, Chicago 1956.

D. Levhari and D. Patinkin, "The Role of Money in a Simple Growth Model," *Amer. Econ. Rev.*, Sept. 1968, *58*, 713–53.

M. A. C. Martins, "A Nominal Theory of the Nominal Rate of Interest and the Price Level," *J. Polit. Econ.*, Feb. 1980, *88*, 174–85.

R. Michener, "An Application of Non-Additive Preferences to a Problem in Money and Growth," work. paper, Univ. Chicago, Nov. 1977.

R. A. Mundell, "Inflation and Real Interest," *J. Polit. Econ.*, June 1963, *71*, 280–83.

J. F. Muth, "Optimal Properties of Exponentially Weighted Forecasts," *J. Amer. Statist. Assn.*, June 1960, *55*, 299–306.

T. J. Sargent, "A Classical Macroeconometric Model of the United States," *J. Polit. Econ.*, Apr. 1976, *84*, 207–38.

A. J. Schwartz, "Secular Price Change in Historical Perspective," *J. Money, Credit, Banking*, Feb. 1973, *5*, 243–69.

M. Sidrauski, (1967a) "Rational Choice and Patterns of Growth in a Monetary Economy," *Amer Econ. Rev. Proc.*, May 1967, *57*, 534–44.

———, (1967b) "Inflation and Economic Growth," *J. Polit. Econ.*, Dec. 1967, *75*, 796–810.

C. A. Sims, "The Role of Approximate Prior Restrictions in Distributed Lag Estimation," *J. Amer. Statist. Assn.*, Mar. 1972, *67*, 169–75.

J. Tobin, "Money and Economic Growth," *Econometrica*, Oct. 1965, *33*, 671–84.

R. C. Vogel, "The Dynamics of Inflation in Latin America, 1950–1969," *Amer. Econ. Rev.*, Mar. 1974, *64*, 102–14.

Peter Whittle, *Prediction and Regulation by Linear Least-Square Methods*, London 1963.

Board of Governors of the Federal Reserve System, *Fed. Res. Bull.*, Washington various issues.

U.S. Bureau of Labor Statistics, *Employment and Earnings*, various issues.

— 5 —

Discussion of Stanley Fischer, "Towards an Understanding of the Costs of Inflation: II"

The great disciplining virtue of applied welfare economics is that it forces one to take a position on all of the issues involved in constructing a quantitatively serious general equilibrium model of the entire economy.* Unless one cheats, and in his paper Stanley Fischer tries very conscientiously not to, *everything* must be faced. In a monetary application especially, this can be a humbling experience because it lays bare the many really basic issues on which we are far from a solidly-based understanding.

Fischer's starting point is the solution to the problem of measuring the welfare cost of inflation that Bailey (1956) and Cagan (1956) arrived at in the 1950s, in one of the happiest marriages of good theory and imaginative empirical work our profession has seen. Bailey used the area under a demand function for money to measure the annual real income supplement that would be needed to make the citizens of an economy undergoing a smooth inflation of π percent per year as well off as they would be in the same economy but with stable prices. Implicitly, the stable price economy is financing its government expenditures with some nondistorting tax. This leads to a formula for the welfare cost expressed as a fraction C of real national income of:

$$C = \frac{1}{b \cdot v}\left[1 - (1 + b\pi)e^{-b\pi}\right] \simeq \frac{1}{2}\frac{b}{v}\pi^2 \tag{1}$$

Carnegie-Rochester Conference Series on Public Policy 15, no. 1 (January 1981): 43–52.

* I want to thank Stanley Fischer for discovering an error in an earlier draft.

where v is velocity at zero inflation and b is the semi-elasticity of a Cagan-type money demand function.[1] The approximation on the right of (1) is the second-order Taylor approximation about $\pi = 0$, the area of the welfare "triangle." Once one has decided what "money" is, v is observable. Cagan proposed estimating b by making use of the "experiments" provided by the postwar European hyperinflations, arriving at estimates ranging from 3 to 10.

As a critic of such a courageously quantitative paper as Fischer's I feel under a collegial obligation to pick a number myself even though I feel somewhat foolish doing so. I'll take "money" to be $M1$, v to be 4, b to be 5. Then $C(.05) = .0013$, $C(.10) = .0045$ and $C(.15) = .0086$. As deadweight losses go, 0.9 percent of national income is a sizable number. This seems to me about right as an indication of the annual cost of inflation in the United States today.

In arriving at these numbers, or at the similar numbers Fischer obtains, positions have to be taken on a number of crucial and ill-understood questions. A useful way for me to organize my reactions to the Fischer paper will be to list what seem to me the most central of these issues, and to consider both how he resolves them and how I would prefer to resolve them. I will discuss briefly and incompletely, in turn, the questions of (a) what money is, (b) what modifications one needs to make in Bailey's analysis if the alternatives to the inflation tax are also distorting, and (c) what modifications are required to adapt the formula (1) to permit it to assess erratic or uncertain inflation paths.

1. What Is Money?

The easiest way to answer this question for present purposes is to observe that formula (1) applies only to noninterest-bearing assets or to assets the interest on which is restricted to below-market rates. In the United States at present, currency and demand deposits are "money" and savings deposits are "money" insofar as their rates are restricted. But as Fischer rightly observes, unless these interest rate restrictions have some rationale, that part of C that is due solely to their existence is more properly called a welfare cost due to inappropriate restrictions and could be eliminated by simply removing these restrictions. Accordingly, in section II.1, Fischer calcu-

1. See Frenkel (1976) for further discussion of this formula and several variations.

lates *C* with money defined as "high powered money" only, obtaining a cost of 0.3% of GNP.[2] With interest paid on bank reserves (as feasible a "reform" as the elimination of interest rate ceilings) one would define "money" as currency only, obtaining a still smaller estimate. The question "What is Money?" becomes, then, the question of what we want to *make into* money via government restrictions of various kinds on the operation of the private banking system.

This much harder question has a traditional but rather arbitrary "monetarist" answer, forcefully challenged once again in recent papers by Fama (1980) and Sargent and Wallace (1981). I will try to summarize the traditional answer, not with the intent of providing a "deep" defense but rather a reminder of what an effective challenge needs to contain. The answer requires acceptance of the idea that there is some activity, describable in everyday English as "effecting transactions," that at least hand-to-hand currency serves. We believe in the importance of this activity not because we have tight theoretical models enabling us to see its exact nature clearly (for we obviously do not) but because of experience casually and formally recorded.[3] If this activity is identified as motivating people's holding and exchanging currency, then one cannot help but see it as motivating the holding and exchange of other assets that appear to be used in very similar ways to the way currency is used. This identification is easiest for assets, like demand deposits, the return on which is restricted by law to equal the return on currency, but obviously this identification does not justify such restrictions in a welfare-economic sense. Nor does the fact that demand deposits carry a zero return in our present legal environment prevent other, interest-bearing, assets from serving the same, or very similar, transactions purposes.

These observations help us to imagine a society in which currency is, by its nature, noninterest-bearing, but in which other assets, perhaps defined in terms of currency, perhaps not, are entirely unrestricted legally. In such a society, one would not be tempted to add up the amount of currency in circulation and the amount of some subset of the liabilities of various firms, and call the total "money." The fact that models with these charac-

2. Several alternative estimates are also offered.

3. In the U.S. about 5% of total employment is in the sector "Finance, Insurance and Real Estate," or is, in other words, engaged in matching people with contingent claims of various kinds. If one hour of each intermediary's time is matched with an hour of one of his clients' time, this means about ten percent of total labor is devoted to this activity.

teristics can be constructed does not, it seems to me, even *suggest*, in the welfare-economic sense, moving from our present, heavily regulated banking system to one more closely resembling the hypothetical examples of Fama, and Sargent and Wallace. Such a case must at some point deal with the poor business cycle experience of those economies with relatively unregulated banking, compared to those economies preceding the invention of modern banking, those in which modern banking has been effectively outlawed (the centrally planned economies), and those (such as ours) in which institutions providing transactions-effecting services are fairly sharply differentiated by legal restrictions that necessarily oppose the competitive forces working to blur these restrictions.

This is the traditional case for attaching special importance to *M*1. Obviously the usefulness of aggregates like this depends on manmade institutional arrangements, and in the face of our current inflation it is equally obvious that this particular aggregate has lost much of the meaning it once had. The question we face now is not whether there is some "natural" reason to treat *M*1 as an interesting number but whether we want to enforce an "unnatural" situation that will *make* it interesting.

2. What Are Taxes?

Following Phelps (1973), Fischer recognizes that the importance of the assumption of the availability of nondistorting taxes is central to strict application of the Bailey formula and is also remote from reality. Perhaps the "inflation tax" should be assessed as part of a comprehensive tax package. This sounds pretty hard, but Fischer does not flinch, and does a good job of trying to bring up-to-date ideas from the theory of public finance to bear on this problem. I will not criticize this attempt in any detail, but rather confine myself to two peripheral remarks.

Fischer refers to distortions resulting from the combination of inflation and the current United States tax structure as "almost entirely avoidable," meaning that one can conceive of a fully indexed tax structure under which these distortions would be much alleviated. There is a clear sense in which this is right (although "full indexation" is not as easy as it sounds); and if one were to take literally the Bailey abstraction of a society *permanently* undergoing an inflation of ten percent per year, indexing would be desirable and would, I imagine, be adopted (as it has been in most countries where inflationary finance is accepted as a way of life). If one views inflation as a *transient* phenomenon, however, it seems to me that there is much to be said for the old-fashioned view that the "automatic stabilizer" effects of progressive taxation in an unindexed system are virtues. Sustained, serious inflations are always fiscal phenomena, so that deficit reduction necessarily plays a role in the termination of inflations that ever terminate.

Second, Fischer raises the question of whether we *want* to terminate inflations, or whether an inflation tax has a part in a well-designed tax structure. I would prefer to see this issue settled on noneconomic grounds. Politically, in the United States, a *tax* has referred to a decision taken by the elected representatives of the citizens to collect revenues from citizens in a particular way.[4] It has not referred to actions taken by "independent" agencies associated with government which are not required to consult with anyone and which have the incidental effect of transferring resources from the private to the government sector. Thus we do not, politically, speak of the bribing of police officers as a form of taxation of criminal activity, although economically that is exactly what it is and although it can, for some purposes, be fruitfully analyzed as being just that.

Fischer's observation (this is only a minor aside in his paper) that the "inflation tax" may be a good way to tax the illegal "underground economy" seems to be a *reductio ad absurdum* of the purely economic view of this matter. Would one rationalize air pollution on the ground that, it being so costly to apprehend and incarcerate criminals, it is more cost-effective to foul up their lungs?

If our attempt to find laws that best serve society, the working hypothesis that those laws will be well-enforced is, to be sure, utopian. But welfare economics is a utopian business. Let us recognize this and try to do it right.

3. What is Inflation?

Bailey's formula was obtained by a theoretical comparison of two hypothetical societies, differing only in their smooth, predictable inflation rates. How do we want to adapt this formula to assess actual inflations? A primary intent of Fischer's paper was to force re-thinking on this issue, and

4. This echoes Prescott (1975).

for me, it worked. I think the answer best approximating the truth is: Not at all.

I take it that by an inflation we mean a fairly long-term average of rates of price change, and we take this to be determined by similarly long-term average rates of "money" growth. But the actual policies we try to evaluate are generally erratic in various systematic or unsystematic ways and have effects on variables other than prices. Comparing the effects of the monetary-fiscal policies pursued in the United States in the 1970s with the effects of, say, budget balance and smooth money growth consistent with price stability involves a much more complicated comparison than the hypothetical comparison Bailey used. What does one make of this?

There is a slightly new-fashioned Keynesian way of dealing with this question, which I will sketch as follows. Interpret Bailey's comparison as referring to the comparison of two societies on the same path of "full employment" or "potential output" (a comparison incorporating a "long run" neutrality of money). Now the economy will in general not be expected to follow its potential output path, due to shocks of various kinds, unless monetary and fiscal measures are carefully selected on a year-to-year basis to make it do so. Hence welfare costs will be assigned not to year-to-year movements in money or prices, but to the "gap" between actual and potential output. In the older applications of this view, the "gap" was simply taken as a deadweight loss itself, dwarfing not only Bailey's triangle but the sum of all the triangles associated with every inefficiency the profession could imagine! Even among unreconstructed Keynesians it is now widely recognized that this is a large overstatement (Gordon (1973)). Anyway, this way of looking at the question enables one to compare societies with erratic as well as smooth paths of money and prices in a fairly coherent way

There is a second way of facing this same issue, which seems to me more promising though much needs to be done before it is fully operational. This route begins by distinguishing between anticipated and unanticipated monetary-fiscal shocks, and working with structures in which the anticipated part has price effects only. Then Bailey's analysis is applied to this anticipated effect only, which in practice means something very close to inserting *average* inflation rates into (1). So far, the resulting estimates are very close to those I have called Keynesian, above, though the story is a little different. The unanticipated parts of these shocks (in practice, fluctuations about a slow-moving trend) will, in these structures, induce fluctuations in prices *and* quantities. Insofar as these latter movements are viewed as avoidable mistakes, each has a triangle associated with it. To obtain the *average* cost of this avoidable variability, then, one would average the areas of these triangles over time. This is the way one would obtain an answer to the question, *exactly* analogous to Bailey's: What is the annual real income supplement that would be needed to make citizens of an economy with a given level of avoidable monetary-fiscal variability (variance) as well off as they would be in an identical economy with the same average inflation rate but with *no* variability?

This is a question that could be put exactly to the economy modeled by me in (1972). Barro (1976) and Taylor (1979) offer frameworks for assessing variability costs, but their models do not connect this cost to preferences. Kydland and Prescott (1980) have an operational model capable of giving an exact answer (although the relevant variability in their model is technological, not monetary). None of these models quite suits the purposes of the paragraph above, but all would lend strong support to the conjecture that: The costs of variability at a 1970s level, assessed in this way, would be *trivial* compared to the costs of an expected 10% inflation rate, measured Bailey's way.[5]

Fischer, too, is concerned with "inflation uncertainty," but takes neither of the approaches outlined above, nor does he offer a third. He nods toward "gaps" by citing some regressions relating "the Livingston estimates of inflation uncertainty" to unemployment and industrial production. Why even *mention* this sort of "evidence," especially when, as Fischer obviously recognizes, it needs to be so heavily qualified that the reader is effectively told to pay it no attention?

More seriously, Fischer attempts, in the first part of his paper, to formulate a framework capable of assessing for a typical household the utility consequences of changes in the variability of general and relative prices. This is an effort in the spirit of Bailey's work, and with the same intent as

5. The point is not that serious depressions raise trivial costs, but that postwar depressions have been so modest. To a user of "gaps" as measures of welfare costs, a 7% unemployment rate is about .28 times as "bad" as was the 25% rate in the Great Depression. Even deducting a 5% natural rate from both, it is .09 times as bad. Using the ratio of these deviations squared as a measure, which is very roughly what any serious welfare analysis involves, it is .008 times as bad. If the "crisis" rhetoric associated with postwar recessions could be reduced to .008 times its 1932 level, our discussion of these events would be much more productive.

the second approach I have sketched above, of trying to deal with erratic as well as smooth inflations. As Fischer says in his opening paragraph, however, we do not want to talk about the welfare cost of *price* movements, but rather of the cost of suboptimum *policies*. In Bailey's application, price inflation and monetary growth are so tightly linked that there is little cost to using these terms interchangeably. For erratic inflations, by contrast, Fischer's partial equilibrium approach and his failure to identify the *sources* of the price movements his representative household faces lead to ambiguities that make it impossible to know how to apply his results to observed series. Is this a framework for estimating the social cost of business cycles? Is it for estimating the cost of price variability only? If the latter, is there to be a second framework for estimating the cost of *quantity* variability? If so, what will be the relationship between these frameworks? I am here just repeating in different ways the objections that any partial equilibrium framework for assessing welfare costs is subject to. I suspect I am also explaining why Fischer makes so little use of this framework when he turns to the evidence.

In summary, I agree with Fischer that price variability has costs, but I think they can be analyzed only if viewed as symptoms of something else. If monetary and fiscal instability is a main source of business cycles, as I believe to be the case, then we want to estimate the cost of (avoidable) business cycles, not price variability. If, as in Taylor (1979), some monetary (and price) instability is useful in eliminating business cycles, again one doesn't want to treat price variability as an unoffset cost. However these difficult issues may be resolved, it seems to me clearest and closest to common usage to restrict the term "costs of inflation" to those captured in Bailey's triangle, treating variability in some other way.

4. Conclusions

In reviewing these comments I am struck, in the first place, by how frequently I have taken issue with Fischer's paper and, in the second place, by the way each of my reactions was so clearly set up by Fischer's presentation of the issues. In his paper with Modigliani (1978), Fischer catalogued the remarkable variety of ways in which inflation affects our lives and our decisions. In the present paper, he gives a challenging presentation of what would be required to incorporate these various factors into a welfare analysis at the level of Bailey's work.

In my comments, I have tried to be constructive and helpful, offering suggestions that I am sure Fischer will have no difficulty in utilizing in the third paper in this series. To do so, he need only (a) straighten out the foundations of monetary theory, so that we have a clear idea of what "money" is, and what it ought to be, (b) provide a theoretically rigorous and empirically substantiated explanation for business cycles, and (c) integrate all of this with the general theory of optimum taxation.

References

Bailey, M. J. (1956) The Welfare Cost of Inflationary Finance. *Journal of Political Economy*, 64:93–110.

Barro, R. J. (1976) Rational Expectations and the Role of Monetary Policy. *Journal of Monetary Economics*, 2:1–32.

Cagan, P. (1956) The Monetary Dynamics of Hyperinflation. *Studies in the Quantity Theory of Money*. Ed. M. Friedman, Chicago: University of Chicago Press.

Fama, E. F. (1980) Banking in the Theory of Finance. *Journal of Monetary Economics*, 6: 39–58.

Fischer, S. and Modigliani, F. (1978) Towards an Understanding of the Real Effects and Costs of Inflation. *Weltwirtschaftliches Archiv*, 114: 810–833.

Frenkel, J. A. (1976) Some Dynamic Aspects of the Welfare Costs of Inflationary Finance. *Money and Finance in Economic Growth and Development*. Ed. R. McKinnon. Essays in Honor of Edward S. Shaw. Dekker, Inc., N. Y.

Gordon, R. J. (1973) The Welfare Cost of Higher Unemployment. *Brookings Papers on Economic Activity*, 1: 133–205.

Kydland, F. E. and Prescott, E. C. (1980) Time to Build and the Persistency of Unemployment. Carnegie-Mellon University Working Paper.

Lucas, R. E., Jr. (1972) Expectations and the Neutrality of Money. *Journal of Economic Theory*, 4: 103–24.

Phelps, E. S. (1973) Inflation in the Theory of Public Finance. *Swedish Journal of Economics*, 75: 67–82.

Prescott, E. C. (1975) Efficiency of the Natural Rate. *Journal of Political Economy*, 83: 1229–36.

Sargent, T. J. and Wallace, N. (1981) The Real Bills Doctrine vs. the Quantity Theory. Federal Reserve Bank of Minneapolis, Research Department Staff Report 64.

Taylor, J. B. (1979) Estimation and Control of a Macroeconomic Model with Rational Expectations. *Econometrica*, 47: 1267–86.

— 6 —

Interest Rates and Currency Prices in a Two-Country World

1. Introduction

This paper is a theoretical study of the determination of prices, interest rates and currency exchange rates, set in an infinitely-lived two-country world which is subject both to stochastic endowment shocks and to monetary instability.* The objectives of the study, or more exactly, the limits to the study's objectives, are in large measure dictated by the nature of the model's simplifying assumptions. In this introduction, then, I will first describe the common features of the models themselves, and then consider the range of substantive questions on which these models seem likely to shed some light.

In its real aspects, the model is a variation on that developed in Lucas (1978).[1] Traders of both countries are identical, with preferences defined over the infinite stream of consumption goods. Goods are non-storable, arriving as unproduced endowments, following a Markov process. Agents are risk averse, so they will be interested in pooling these endowment risks,

---

Journal of Monetary Economics 10, no. 3 (1982): 335–359.

*I wish to thank my colleagues Jacob Frenkel and Nasser Saidi for many detailed discussions which materially influenced the direction this inquiry took and Sanford Grossman and David Hsieh, who corrected errors in an earlier version of this paper. I am also grateful for criticism of an earlier draft received at seminars at New York University, Northwestern University, the Board of Governors of the Federal Reserve System, Harvard University, and The University of Chicago. I also thank the National Science Foundation for its support.

1. See also Breeden (1979), Brock (1979), Cox et al. (1978), Danthine (1977) and LeRoy (1973). Much of this literature can be traced back to Merton (1973), to which the reader with deeper genealogical interests is referred.

and since they have identical preferences, an equilibrium in which all agents hold the same portfolio will, if ever attained, be indefinitely maintained. This perfectly pooled equilibrium is the one studied, in various forms, below. Since equilibrium quantities consumed are, in this exchange system, dictated by nature, the analysis of the real system involves simply reading the Arrow–Debreu securities prices off the appropriate marginal rates of substitution. This is carried out in section 2.

In section 3, a single 'world' currency is introduced, with its use motivated by a 'finance constraint' of the form proposed by Clower (1967) and Tsiang (1956), to the effect that goods must be purchased with currency accumulated in advance of the period in which trading takes place.[2] With a constant supply of money, or currency, the real aspects of equilibrium replicate exactly those of the barter equilibrium of section 2. When the money supply is stochastic, the formulas for securities prices require modification.

Section 4 introduces national currencies, together with a free market or 'flexible exchange rate' system under which currencies may be traded, along with other securities, prior to shopping for goods. In section 5, the consequences of imposing a specific form of exchange rate fixing are examined. The normative conclusion reached from comparing these two regimes is a reproduction of the equivalence result reached earlier, and for basically identical reasons, by Helpman (1979). Concluding comments are contained in sections 6 and 7.

The aspirations of this study are difficult to assess, for it is in some respects highly ambitious and, in others, very modest. The framework here proposed provides one way of integrating monetary theory, domestic and international, with the powerful apparatus of modern financial economics. It is capable of replicating all of the classical results of monetary theory as well as the main formulas for securities pricing that the theory of finance produces, and of suggesting modifications to the latter theory suited to an unstable monetary environment. There is little doubt that the main task of monetary economics now is to catch up with our colleagues in fi-

2. I take the term 'finance constraint' from Kohn (1980), who traces the history of what I had been calling the 'Clower constraint' back to important earlier contributions by Robertson (1940) and Tsiang (1956), as well as forward to Tsiang's (1980) recent paper. Kohn's paper, which does not in any way detract from Clower's (1967) contribution also deals decisively with some common criticisms of this point of departure in monetary theory.

nance, though the question of how this may best be done must be regarded as considerably more open.

On the side of modesty, it must be conceded that when this integration is carried out as is done here, many, perhaps most, of the central substantive questions of monetary economics are left unanswered. These failings will appear below more nakedly than is customary in the monetary literature, so much so that they may well appear to be failings of the particular approach taken here as opposed to those of this literature in general. I do not believe this to be the case.

2. A Barter Model

Though the main concern of this paper is with alternative monetary arrangements, it is convenient to begin with an analysis of a barter equilibrium. The demography, technology and preferences of this barter economy will remain unchanged in the monetary variations discussed later.

Consider a world economy with two countries. These countries have identical constant populations; all variables will then be expressed in per (own country) capita terms. Each citizen of country 0 is endowed each period with ξ units of a freely transportable, non-storable consumption good, x. Each citizen of country 1 is endowed with η units of a second good, y. These endowments ξ and η are stochastic, following a Markov process with transitions given by

$$\Pr\{\xi_{t+1} \le \xi', \eta_{t+1} \le \eta' \mid \xi_t = \xi, \eta_t = \eta\} = F(\xi', \eta', \xi, \eta).$$

Assume that the process $\{\xi_t, \eta_t\}$ has a unique stationary distribution $\phi(\xi, \eta)$. The realizations ξ, η are taken to be known at the beginning of the period, prior to any trading, but no information (other than full knowledge of F) is available earlier.

Each agent in country i wishes to maximize

$$E\left\{\sum_{t=0}^{\infty} \beta^t U\left(x_{it}, y_{it}\right)\right\}, \quad 0 < \beta < 1, \tag{2.1}$$

where x_{it} is consumption in country i in period t of the good x, and y_{it} is consumption of the good y. The function U and the discount factor β are common to both countries. U is assumed to be bounded, continuously differentiable, increasing in both arguments, and strictly concave. The remainder of the paper will be concerned with resource allocation in this abstract world under alternative market arrangements.

The arrangement considered in this section is one of complete markets in the sense of Arrow (1964) and Debreu (1959), under which agents trade in both goods, spot and in advance, contingent on all possible realizations of the shock process $\{\xi_t, \eta_t\}$. In setting out the notation for such an equilibrium, I will exploit the simplicity of the present set-up to the full.

The preferences of agents have been assumed independent of their nationalities, so that agents differ, if at all, only in their endowments. Moreover, agents are risk-averse so that in the face of stochastically varying endowments, one would expect them to use available securities markets to pool these risks. In this context, pooling must come down to an exchange of claims on 'home' endowment for claims on 'foreign' endowment in return. Perfect pooling, in this sense would involve agents of each country owning half the claims to 'home' endowment and half of the foreign endowment. The equilibrium constructed below is one in which agents begin perfectly pooled in this sense and remained so pooled under all realized paths of the dusturbances.[3] Under these circumstances, the world economy becomes virtually identical to that studied in Lucas (1978), with a single representative consumer consuming half of the endowments of both goods, or $\left(\frac{1}{2}\xi, \frac{1}{2}\eta\right)$ each period, and holding the 'market portfolio' of such securities as are traded. Our analytical task will be to price these securities.

Let $s = (\xi, \eta)$ be the current state of the system. Take the price of all goods, current and future, to be functions of the current state s, with the understanding that prices are assumed stationary in the sense that the same set of prices is established at s independent of the calendar time at which s may be realized. Then knowledge of the equilibrium price functions together with knowledge of the transition function $F(s', s) = F(\xi', \eta', \xi, \eta)$ amounts to knowledge of the probability distribution of all future prices, or rational expectations. In what follows, agents are assumed to have such knowledge.

3. This restriction of the analysis to a particular stationary equilibrium obviously must leave open questions involving the stability of equilibrium, or of whether a system beginning with agents imperfectly pooled would tend over time to approach the perfectly pooled equilibrium studied below. For reasons given in Lucas and Stokey (1982) and Nairay (1981), time-additive preferences of the form (2.1) probably imply a negative answer to this stability question.

In view of the simplicity of the model under study, it is evident that although all Arrow–Debreu contingent claim securities can be priced, only a very limited set of securities is needed to represent the 'market portfolio' that traders will hold in equilibrium. I will proceed under the following, wholly arbitrary, conventions as to which goods and securities will be traded, indicating at various points below how other securities may easily be priced as well.

For a system in any current state s, let the current spot price of good x be unity, so that all other prices will be in terms of current x-units. Let $p_y(s)$ be the spot price of good y, in x-units, if the system is in state s. Let $q_x(s)$ be the current x-unit price of a claim to the entire future (from tomorrow on) stream $\{\xi_t\}$ of the endowment of good x, and $q_y(s)$ the current price of a claim to the future stream $\{\eta_t\}$.

With these conventions set, consider an individual trader entering a period endowed with θ units of wealth, in the form of claims to current and future goods, valued in current x-units. His objects of choice are current consumptions (x, y), at spot prices $(1, p_y(s))$, equity shares θ_x in future endowments $\{\xi_t\}$ at the price per share $q_x(s)$, and shares θ_y in future $\{\eta_t\}$, priced at $q_y(s)$. His budget constraint is thus

$$x + p_y(s)y + q_x(s)\theta_x + q_y(s)\theta_y \leq \theta. \tag{2.2}$$

For a given portfolio choice (θ_x, θ_y), his wealth in x-units as of the beginning of the next period will, if next period's state is s', be given by

$$\theta' = \theta_x[\xi' + q_x(s')] + \theta_y[p_y(s')\eta' + q_y(s')]. \tag{2.3}$$

With this investment in notation, one can write out a functional equation for the value $v(\theta, s)$ of the objective (2.1) for a consumer (of either nationality) who finds himself in state s with wealth θ and proceeds optimally. It is

$$v(\theta, s) = \max_{x, y, \theta_x, \theta_y} \left\{U(x, y) + \beta \int v(\theta', s') f(s', s)\, ds'\right\}, \tag{2.4}$$

subject to the constraint (2.2), where θ' is given by (2.3) and where f is the transition density for the transition function F.[4]

The first order conditions for this problem are (2.2), with equality, and

$$U_x(x, y) = \lambda, \tag{2.5}$$

4. For a rigorous treatment of an equation essentially identical to (2.4), see Lucas (1978). I am proceeding here at a much less formal level.

$$U_y(x, y) = \lambda p_y(s), \tag{2.6}$$

$$\beta \int v_\theta(\theta', s')[\xi' + q_x(s')]f(s', s)ds' = \lambda q_x(s), \tag{2.7}$$

$$\beta \int v_\theta(\theta', s')[p_y(s')\eta' + q_y(s')]f(s', s)ds' = \lambda q_y(s). \tag{2.8}$$

Moreover, we know that the multiplier λ is the derivative of the maximized objective function $v(\theta, s)$ with respect to the right-hand side of (2.2), or that

$$v_\theta(\theta, s) = \lambda. \tag{2.9}$$

In a perfectly-pooled equilibrium, we know that each trader consumes his share of both endowments, so that $(x, y) = \left(\frac{1}{2}\xi, \frac{1}{2}\eta\right)$. Hence from (2.5) and (2.6), the equilibrium spot prices of y in terms of x is

$$P_y(s) = U_y\left(\tfrac{1}{2}\xi, \tfrac{1}{2}\eta\right)/U_x\left(\tfrac{1}{2}\xi, \tfrac{1}{2}\eta\right) = U_y(s)/U_x(s), \tag{2.10}$$

where the second equality defines a shorthand that will be used frequently below.

Also in equilibrium, each trader begins and ends a period with the identical portfolio of equity claims $\theta_x = \theta_y = \frac{1}{2}$. Then from (2.3), (2.5), (2.7) and (2.9), shares in the $\{\xi_t\}$ process are priced by

$$q_x(s) = \beta[U_x(s)]^{-1} \int U_x(s')[\xi' + q_x(s')]f(s', s)ds'. \tag{2.11}$$

Symmetrically (almost) from (2.3), (2.5), (2.8) and (2.9) shares in the $\{\eta_t\}$ process are priced by

$$q_y(s) = \beta[U_x(s)]^{-1} \int U_x(s')[p_y(s')\eta' + q_y(s')]f(s', s)ds'. \tag{2.12}$$

These formulas may be compared to their counterpart (6) in Lucas (1978). Either may be solved 'forward' to give the current price in terms of future dividends only. Thus from (2.11)

$$q_x(s) = \left[U_x(s)\right]^{-1} \sum_{t=1}^{\infty} \beta^t E\left\{\xi_t U_x(s_t) \middle| s_0 = s\right\}. \tag{2.13}$$

Eq. (2.2) may similarly be solved for $q_y(s)$. If $U_x(s)$ were constant, (2.11) and (2.13) would be entirely familiar theoretical relationships between equity prices and dividends.

In addition to pricing equities, this theory can price any one-period Arrow–Debreu security. Thus let A be any s'-set to which $F(s', s)$ assigns probability, let $\chi_A(s')$ be the characteristic function of this set ($\chi_A(s') = 1$ if $s' \in A$ and 0 otherwise) and let $q^{(1)}(A, s)$ be the price today, if today's state is s, of a claim to one unit of good x tomorrow if $s' \in A$ and 0 otherwise. If it is possible to purchase z units of such a security (or sell $-z$ units) the consumer's problem (2.4) becomes

$$v(\theta, s) = \max_{x, y, \theta_x, \theta_y, z} \{u(x, y) + \beta \int v(\theta', s') f(s', s) ds'\}, \tag{2.14}$$

subject to, in place of (2.2),

$$x + p_s(y)y + q_x(s)\theta_x + q_y(s)\theta_y + q^{(1)}(A, s)z \leq \theta \tag{2.15}$$

and with tomorrow's wealth θ' given by

$$\theta' = \theta_x[\xi' + q_x(s')] + \theta_y[p_y(s')\eta' + q_y(s')] + z\chi_A(s'), \tag{2.16}$$

in place of (2.3). The first-order condition for z for this problem is

$$\beta \int v_\theta(\theta', s')\chi_A(s')f(s', s)ds' = \lambda q^{(1)}(A, s). \tag{2.17}$$

Now the *equilibrium* level of z must be zero, since all x-units are already claimed by equity holders, so all other equilibrium prices are as determined above. Hence applying the facts $\lambda = v_\theta(\theta, s) = U_x(s)$ to (2.17) gives

$$q^{(1)}(A, s) = \beta[U_x(s)]^{-1} \int_A U_x(s')f(s', s)ds'. \tag{2.18}$$

It will be convenient below to have a notation for the 'density function' $q(s', s)$ corresponding to the function $q^{(1)}(A, s)$. Let

$$q(s', s) = \beta[u_x(s)]^{-1}u_x(s')f(s', s), \qquad \text{so that} \tag{2.19}$$

$$q^{(1)}(A, s) = \int_A q(s's)ds'. \tag{2.20}$$

Loosely, $q(s', s)$ prices a claim to one unit of x contingent on next period's state being s', today's state being s.

Having priced one-period securities in (2.18), the recursive character of the model can be used to price n-period securities via the Markovian formula

$$q^{(n)}(A, s) = \int q^{(n-1)}(A, u)q^{(1)}(du, s), \qquad n = 2, 3, \ldots, \tag{2.21}$$

or, in terms of the density $q(s', s)$,

$$q^{(n)}(A, s) = \int q^{(n-1)}(A, u)q(u, s)du, \qquad n = 2, 3, \ldots, \tag{2.22}$$

Here $q^{(n)}(A, s)$ is the price, if today's state is s, of a unit of good x n periods hence contingent on the system's being in a state in A at that date.

In addition to pricing all claims to returns made risky by nature, the theory can price arbitrary, man-made lotteries. Thus let $g(u, s', s)$ be a probability density for u, conditioned on (s', s), and let it be possible to purchase or sell at the price $r(s)$ per unit, z units of a claim to u units of x delivered tomorrow, where u is drawn from $g(u, s', s)$. Then by reasoning identical to that leading to the formula (2.18) one arrives at the lottery ticket price formula:

$$r(s) = \beta[U_x(s)]^{-1}\int U_x(s')ug(u, s', s)f(s', s)du\, ds'. \tag{2.23}$$

Notice that if u and s' are independent the integral on the right-hand side of (2.23) factors and, recalling (2.19) one obtains

$$r(s) = \int q(s', s)f(s', s)ds' \cdot \int ug(u, s)du. \tag{2.24}$$

That is, the price of a lottery ticket is the price of one unit of future x, with certainty, times the mean return (in units of x) per lottery ticket. Where is the risk premium associated with the variability of u? It is absent, as it should be, since in a competitive market no one is in a position to *impose* risk on anyone else, and no premium need be charged for risks not borne.

3. Monetary Models

The preceding section provides a complete theory of equilibrium goods and securities pricing for a two-good, barter exchange economy. The remainder of the paper considers a variety of alternative monetary arrangements for this same world economy. In all models studied, the use of 'money' or 'currency' will be motivated by a constraint imposed on all traders to the effect that goods can be purchased only with currency accumulated in advance. The idea, as sketched in Lucas (1980), is that under certain circumstances currency can serve as an inexpensive record-keeping device for decentralized transactions, enabling a decentralized system to imitate closely a centralized Arrow–Debreu system. I will not elaborate on these features of the technology that make 'decentralized' exchange economical, relative to 'centralized'.[5]

The timing of trading is taken to be the following. At the beginning of a period, traders from both countries meet in a centralized marketplace,

5. See Howitt (1974) and Lucas (1980) for scenarios which try to make this reference to a decentralized exchange of money and goods more concrete and hence better motivated for present purposes.

bringing securities and currency holdings previously accumulated, and engage in perfectly competitive securities trading. Before the trading opens, the current period's real state, $s = (\xi, \eta)$, is known to all, as are any current monetary shocks. At the conclusion of securities trading, agents disperse to trade in goods and currencies. I find it helpful to think of each trader as a two-person household, in which one partner harvests the endowment and sells it for currency to various strangers while the other uses the household's currency holdings to purchase goods from other strangers, with no possibility of intra-day communication between them, but this little story plays no formal role in the analysis. At the end of a period, agents consume their goods and add cash receipts from endowment sales to their securities holdings.

Given this timing of trading, *and* given the presence of any securities earning a positive nominal return in some currency, it is evident that agents will hold non-interest-bearing units of that currency in exactly the amount needed to cover their perfectly predictable current-period goods purchases. This extremely sharp distinction between 'transactions' and 'store of value' motives for holding various assets is, for some purposes, much overdrawn, but for other purposes it is extremely convenient, as it collapses current period 'goods demand' and 'currency demand' into a single decision problem.

In the economy under study, let M_t nominal dollars per capita (of each country, or $2M_t$ in total) be in circulation, so that there is a single 'world' money, and the world economy behaves, as in section 2, as a single two-good system. Prior to any trading in period t, let each trader's money holdings be augmented by a lump-sum dollar transfer of $w_t M_{t-1}$, so that the money supply evolves according to

$$M_{t+1} = (1 + w_{t+1})M_t. \tag{3.1}$$

That is, M_t denotes the *post*-transfer, *pre*-trading per capita supply of money for period t. Let $\{w_t\}$ follow a Markov process, possibly related to the real process $\{s_t\}$, with the transition function

$$H(w', w, s', s) = \Pr\{w_{t+1} \leq w' \mid w_t = w, s_{t+1} = s', s_t = s\}$$

and a corresponding transition density $h(w', w, s', s)$. Think of w_t as being known, along with s_t prior to any period t trading.

Now let $p_x(s, M)$ be the dollar price of a unit of good x, when the real state of the economy is s and when post-transfer dollar balances are M, and let $p_y(s)$ be the relative price of y in terms of x-units. Since all currency is, by hypothesis, spent on current goods, we have

$$2M = p_x(s, M)[\xi + p_y(s)\eta]$$

so that nominal prices follow:

$$p_x(s, M) = \frac{2M}{\xi + p_y(s)\eta}. \tag{3.2}$$

This is the unit-velocity version of the quantity theory of money to which the Clower constraint leads in the absence of a 'precautionary motive' for money holding.

To determine the behavior of equilibrium goods and securities prices, I will seek an equilibrium, analogous to that constructed in section 2, in which agents from both countries begin in a situation of equal wealth and maintain this situation over time. Let there be two securities traded, in addition to currency: a perfectly divisible claim to all of the dollar receipts from the current and future sale of the process ξ_t, priced (in x-units) at $q_x(s, w)$, and a claim to the η_t process, priced at $q_y(s, w)$.

Now consider a resident of either country, beginning a period with post-transfer claims of x-unit value θ. Let the world be in state (s, w, M) and denote the agent's optimum value function by $v(s, w, M, \theta)$. His initial decision, as he engages in securities trading, is to divide θ among a portfolio (θ_x, θ_y) of equity claims, at the prices $q_x(s, w)$ and $q_y(s, w)$, and dollars of currency m at the price $[p_x(s, M)]^{-1}$ given in (3.2). In this choice, he faces the constraint

$$\frac{m}{p_x(s, M)} + q_x(s, w)\theta_x + q_y(s, w)\theta_y \leq \theta. \tag{3.3}$$

After completing securities trading, he uses currency to finance goods purchases (x, y) at the x-unit prices $(1, p_y(s))$. Thus his finance constraint is

$$x + p_y(s)y \leq \frac{m}{p_x(s, M)}. \tag{3.4}$$

A given set of choices m, θ_x, θ_y, x and y will dictate a beginning-of-next-period asset position θ' as follows. His sources of funds *in dollars* are unspent currency carried over from the current period, $m - p_x(s, M)(x +$

$p_y(s)y$), dividends and the new market value of his $\{\xi_t\}$ holdings θ_x, $\theta_x[p(s, M)\xi + p_x(s', M')q_x(s', w')]$, dividends and the market value of his $\{\eta_t\}$ holdings, $\theta_y[p_x(s, M)p_y(s)\eta + p_x(s', M')q_y(s', w')]$, and his next-period money transfer $w'M$. Since θ' is measured in x-units, each of these terms must be deflated by $p_x(s', M')$. Then

$$\theta' = \frac{1}{p_x(s', M')}[m - p_x(s, M)(x + p_y(s)y)] + \frac{p_x(s, M)}{p_x(s', M')}[\xi_t\theta_x + p_s(y)\eta_t\theta_y] + q_x(s', w')\theta_x + q_y(s', w')\theta_y + \frac{w'm}{p_x(s', M')}. \tag{3.5}$$

The monetary analogue to (2.4) is then

$$v(s, w, M, \theta) = \max_{x, y, m, \theta_x, \theta_y} \left\{U(x, y) + \beta \int v(s', w', M', \theta')dF\, dH\right\}, \tag{3.6}$$

subject to (3.3) and (3.4), where θ' is given by (3.5) and where dF and dH abbreviate $f(s', s)ds'$ and $h(s', s, w', w)dw'$, respectively.

Now m can be eliminated between (3.3) and (3.4) to give

$$x + p_y(s)y + q_x(s, w)\theta_x + q_y(s, w)\theta_y \leq \theta. \tag{3.7}$$

If the finance constraint (3.4) is binding in all states, the first term on the right-hand side of (3.5) will be zero. Replacing $p_x(\cdot,\cdot)$ with the values given at (s, M) and $(s', M') = (s', M(1 + w'))$ by (3.2), (3.5) can be replaced by

$$\theta' = \frac{\xi' + p_y(s')\eta'}{(1 + w')(\xi + p_y(s)\eta)}[\xi\theta_x + p_y(s)\eta\theta_y] + q_x(s', w')\theta_x + q_y(s', w')\theta_y + \tfrac{1}{2}\frac{w'}{1 + w'}(\xi' + p_y(s')\eta'). \tag{3.8}$$

With these simplifications, it is clear that $v(s, w, M, \theta)$ does not depend on M, and (3.6) can be replaced by

$$v(s, w, \theta) = \max_{x, y, \theta_x, \theta_y} \left\{U(x, y) + \beta \int v(s', w', \theta')dF\, dH\right\} \tag{3.9}$$

subject to (3.7) and with θ' given by (3.8).

The first-order conditions for this problem are

$$U_x(x, y) = \lambda, \tag{3.10}$$

$$U_y(x, y) = \lambda p_y(s), \tag{3.11}$$

$$\beta \int v_\theta(s', w', \theta') \left[q_x(s', w') + \frac{\xi' + p_y(s')\eta'}{1 + w'} \cdot \frac{\xi}{\xi + p_y(s)\eta} \right] dF\, dH \\ = \lambda q_x(s, w), \tag{3.12}$$

$$\beta \int v_\theta(s', w', \theta') \left[q_y(s', w') + \frac{\xi' + p_y(s')\eta'}{1 + w'} \cdot \frac{\xi}{\xi + p_y(s)\eta} \right] dF\, dH \\ = \lambda q_y(s, w). \tag{3.13}$$

In addition

$$v(s, w, \theta) = \lambda \tag{3.14}$$

holds. These are analogues to (2.5)–(2.9).

In the equilibrium here conjectured, quantities of current goods are $(x, y) = (\frac{1}{2}\xi, \frac{1}{2}\eta)$ and a trader beginning a period with the equity holdings $(\frac{1}{2}, \frac{1}{2})$ will choose to end with $(\theta_x, \theta_y) = (\frac{1}{2}, \frac{1}{2})$. At these consumption levels, (3.10) and (3.11) are satisfied with the same relative price $p_y(s)$ given in (2.10) and $\lambda = U_x(\frac{1}{2}\xi, \frac{1}{2}\eta) = U_x(s)$. Then (3.12) and (3.13) become

$$U_x(s) q_x(s, w) = \\ \beta \int U_x(s') \left[q_x(s', w') + \frac{\xi' + p_y(s')\eta'}{1 + w'} \cdot \frac{\xi}{\xi + p_y(s)\eta} \right] dF\, dH, \tag{3.15}$$

$$U_x(s) q_y(s, w) = \\ \beta \int U_x(s') \left[q_y(s', w') + \frac{\xi' + p_y(s')\eta'}{1 + w'} \cdot \frac{p_y(s)\eta}{\xi + p_y(s)\eta} \right] dF\, dH. \tag{3.16}$$

Evidently, the portfolio $(\theta_x, \theta_y) = (\frac{1}{2}, \frac{1}{2})$ is feasible for an agent beginning a period with a θ-value equal to one-half the world's money supply and one-half the outstanding equity shares. [See (3.3).] Evaluating the right-hand side of (3.8) at $(\theta_x, \theta_y) = (\frac{1}{2}, \frac{1}{2})$ gives

$$\theta' = \tfrac{1}{2}[q_x(s', w') + q_y(s', w') + \xi' + p_y(s')\eta']$$

so that this portfolio choice maintains the perfectly pooled equilibrium. Hence (3.15) and (3.16) are, as conjectured, equilibrium equity prices and (2.11) continues to describe equilibrium goods prices.

It is necessary also to verify that equilibrium nominal interest rates are strictly positive under all states, since this equilibrium has been obtained under the provisional hypothesis that the finance constraint is always binding. To do so, it is necessary to price dollar-denominated one-period bonds, which can be done as follows. A claim to one dollar next period is a claim to $[p_x(s', M')]^{-1}$ units of x next period, where $M' = M(1 + w')$ is next period's post-transfer money supply. From (3.2), then, a claim to a dollar one period hence is a claim to $[2M(1 + w')]^{-1}[\xi' + p_y(s')\eta']$ units of x, one period hence. Using the 'density' $q(s', s)$ defined in (2.19), the equilibrium price today, in x-units, of the claim is

$$\frac{\beta}{2M}[U_x(s)]^{-1}\int U_x(s')[\xi' + p_y(s')\eta'](1 + w')^{-1}f(s', s') \cdot h(w', w, s', s)ds'\,dw'.$$

Its price in dollars is then $p_x(s, M)$ times this quantity, or applying (3.2) again

$$b(s, w) = \beta \int \frac{U_x(s')\xi' + U_y(s')\eta'}{U_y(s)\xi + U_y(s)\eta} \cdot \frac{h(w', w, s', s)}{1 + w'} f(s', s)ds'\,dw', \tag{3.17}$$

where $b(s, w)$ is the dollar price today of a claim on one dollar tomorrow.

Eq. (3.17) is a version of the familiar decomposition of the nominal interest rate $(b^{-1} - 1)$ into a 'real rate of interest' and an 'expected inflation premium', but in a context in which these terms have a definite meaning and in which agents' attitudes toward risk are taken fully into account. The term 'real rate' is inherently ambiguous in a multi-good economy, but the factor

$$\beta \int \frac{U_x(s')\xi' + U_y(s')\eta'}{U_x(s)\xi + U_y(s)\eta} f(s', s)ds' \tag{3.18}$$

is a decent enough index number of the 'own rates' of interest on goods x and y, and describes how nominal interest rates would behave under a regime of perfectly stable money, or $w_t = 0$ with probability one, for all t. If money is not perfectly stable, the integrand of the term (3.4), will in equilibrium be divided by $1 + w'$, integrated with respect to the distribution $H(w', w, s', s)$ of the next monetary injection w', and the resulting function of next period's real state s' will be integrated with respect to s'. This is the way rational risk-averse agents will assign an 'inflation premium' onto the nominal interest rate in situations where current conditions, real and monetary, convey information on future money growth.

Now, as already observed, (3.2) will hold in equilibrium in all states only if nominal interest rates are positive in all states. Hence the restriction

$$b(s, w) < 1 \qquad \text{for all } (s, w) \tag{3.19}$$

must be added in what follows. Eq. (3.17) displays the requirements imposed by (3.19): A high subjective discount rate (low β), low s variability, and high average inflation all work to make (3.19) more likely to hold.

It is illuminating to compare the equity price formulas (3.15) and (3.16) to the equity prices $q_x(s)$ and $q_y(s)$ given in (2.11) and (2.12). In the barter economy of section 2, the price $q(s) = q_x(s) + q_y(s)$ of a claim to the entire world's output sequence satisfies, adding (2.11) and (2.12)

$$q(s) = \beta[U_x(s)]^{-1} \int U_x(s')[q(s') + \xi' + p_y(s')\eta']dF. \tag{3.20}$$

In the monetary economy, the price $q(s, w) = q_x(s, w) + q_y(s, w)$ obtained by adding (3.15) and (3.16) satisfies

$$q(s, w) = \beta[U_x(s)]^{-1} \int U_x(s')\left[q(s', w') + \frac{\xi' + p_y(s')\eta'}{1 + w'}\right] dF\, dH. \tag{3.21}$$

[Both (3.20) and (3.21) may be solved forward to obtain analogues to (2.13).]

The formulas (3.20) and (3.21) differ by the factor $(1 + w')^{-1}$ that deflates the real 'dividend' in (3.21). The point is that in a monetary economy an equity claim is a claim to *dollar* receipts, and this claim may be diluted (or enhanced) by monetary transfers. Agents in a monetary economy are free to exchange all of the 'real' securities available to them in section 2 [so that, for example, $q(s)$ as given by (3.20) continues to price total world output correctly in the monetary economy], but it is no longer possible for all private portfolios together to claim all real output. The 'inflation tax' must be paid by someone.

Notice also that, depending on the *joint* distribution $H(w', w, s', s)$, monetary transfers may well have a *differential* effect on equity prices. The integrands on the right-hand side of (3.15) and (3.16) permit arbitrary correlations between monetary transfers w' and real shocks ξ' and η'. In the present context of an exchange system with identical agents, *nothing* can affect consumption patterns and welfare, but relative prices are clearly not invariant to the nature of monetary-fiscal policy. Not only is money not 'neutral' but there is a variety of possibilities for non-neutral effects.

Finally, notice that under a perfectly stable monetary policy, with the transfer shock w' identically zero, a one-period nominal bond is the exact equivalent to an equity claim on next period's output. From (3.17), the x-unit price of a claim to all of tomorrow's money is, under the policy $w' \equiv 0$,

$$2M \cdot [p_x(s, M)]^{-1} \beta \int \frac{U_x(s')\xi' + U_y(s')\eta'}{U_x(s)\xi + U_y(s)\eta} dF$$

which, using (3.2) and (2.10), equals

$$\beta [U_x(s)]^{-1} \int U_x(s')[\xi' + p_y(s')\eta'] dF.$$

This expression is identical to the 'dividend' term in the equity price formula (3.21), when $w' \equiv 0$.

In this model, nothing is gained by economizing on the number of securities traded, but it is of some interest, I think, that with stable monetary policy, a single dollar-denominated bond is the equivalent of a fully diversified equity claim to 'world output' one period hence. As soon as money becomes variable this simplicity is lost and additional securities are needed. It may be the case that in situations in which costs are associated with multiplying the number of distinct securities held, this loss of simplicity is one of the welfare costs of monetary instability.

4. A National Currency, Flexible Exchange Rate Model

In this section, the timing and monetary conventions of section 3 will be retained but instead of a single world currency, two national currencies will circulate.[6] These currencies will be exchanged freely at a centralized securities market, along with any other securities people wish to trade,

6. Karaken and Wallace (1978) study equilibrium with multiple currencies, but in a setting in which traders are free to use any currency in any transaction (provided it is acceptable to both parties in the exchange). In the present paper, the question of which sellers will accept which currency is settled at the outset, by convention [see (4.3) and (4.4)]. This starting point obviously precludes making progress on some of the fundamental questions posed in Karaken and Wallace (1978).

prior to trading in goods. As in section 3, it will be assumed that nominal interest rates for bonds denominated in either currency are positive in all states, so that the finance constraints for both currencies are always binding.

Let there be M_t 'dollars' in circulation after any transfers have occurred in period t, and N_t 'pounds'. These currency supplies are assumed to evolve according to

$$M_{t+1} = (1 + w_{0,\,t+1})M_t, \tag{4.1}$$

$$N_{t+1} = (1 + w_{1,\,t+1})N_t, \tag{4.2}$$

where the transitions for the process $\{w_t\} = \{w_{0t}, w_{1t}\}$ are given by

$$K(w', w, s', s) =$$

$$\Pr\{w_{0,\,t+1} \leq w'_0, w_{1,\,t+1} \leq w'_1 \mid w_{0t} = w_0, w_{1t} = w_1, s_{t+1} = s', s_t = s\}.$$

Each citizen of country 0 receives a lump-sum dollar transfer of $w_{0t}M_{t-1}$ at the beginning of t; each citizen of 1 receives the pound transfer $w_{1t}N_{t-1}$.

With the finance constraint binding, equilibrium nominal goods prices are simply

$$p_x(s, M) = M/\xi, \tag{4.3}$$

$$p_y(s, N) = N/\eta, \tag{4.4}$$

analogous to (3.2). Letting $p_y(s)$ denote, as before, the price of y in x-units, the equilibrium exchange rate (\$/£) is given by the purchasing-power-parity (i.e., arbitrage) formula

$$e(s, M, N) = p_x(s, M)p_y(s)[p_y(s, N)]^{-1} = \frac{M\,\eta}{N\,\xi}\,p_y(s). \tag{4.5}$$

Notice that this formula for the exchange rate depends on the relative currency supplies in exactly the way one would expect on quantity-theoretic grounds. It will also vary with real endowments, in a manner that depends on the derivatives of

$$\frac{\eta}{\xi}\,p_y(s) = \frac{\eta\,U_y(\frac{1}{2}\xi, \frac{1}{2}\eta)}{\xi\,U_x(\frac{1}{2}\xi, \frac{1}{2}\eta)}.$$

To see what is involved, consider the case where U is homothetic, so that the marginal rate of substitution is a positive, negatively-sloped function $g(r)$, say, of the endowment ratio $r = \eta/\xi$ only. Then the dollar price of pounds will increase with an increase in British output relative to the U.S. if

$$\frac{d}{dr} rg(r) = g(r)[1 + rg'(r)/g(r)] > 0.$$

The reverse sign would occur in the case where relative prices are so sensitive to relative quantity changes that the terms of trade 'turn against' a high output country: the case Bhagwati (1958) and Johnson (1956) called 'immiserizing growth'.

This discussion of the relationship of exchange rate behavior to the curvature of indifference curves has an 'elasticities approach' flavor to it. Yet the formula (4.5) is also consistent with the 'monetary approach' to exchange rate determination, being based on relative money supplies and demands. The reason these two approaches are so compatible in the present context is that the extreme 'transactions demand' emphasis implicit in the use of the finance constraint makes the 'stock' demand for money and the 'flow' demand for goods equivalent.[7]

As in section 3, securities pricing will be studied under the provisional hypothesis that agents of both countries hold identical portfolios. Having obtained prices under this hypothesis, it will then be verified that this is in fact equilibrium behavior. As always, there is a great deal of latitude as to which limited set of specific securities is assumed to be traded in equilibrium. I will select a set that facilitates comparison with the analysis of sections 2 and 3.

Let $q_x(s, w)$ be the price, in x-units, of claim to all of the dollar receipts of the ξ_t process and let $q_y(s, w)$ be the x-unit price of the pound receipts of the η_t process. Agents hold these two securities in a portfolio (θ_x, θ_y). In addition, since monetary transfers accrue (by assumption) to nationals of each country, agents will want to pool this monetary form of endowment risk. Let $r_x(s, w)$ be the price, in x-units, of an equity claim to all future periods' dollar transfers, $w_0' M$, and let $r_y(s, w)$ be the x-unit price of all future periods' pound transfers $w_1' N$. Let (ψ_x, ψ_y) denote an agent's holding of these two instruments. Then the portfolio constraint for an agent beginning a period with x-unit holdings of amount θ is, analogous to (3.3),

7. See Stockman (1980) for a closely related, earlier discussion.

$$\frac{m}{p_x(s,M)} + \frac{e(s,M,N)n}{p_x(s,M)} \\ + r_x(s,w)\psi_x + r_y(s,w)\psi_y + q_x(s,w)\theta_x + q_y(s,w)\theta_y \leq \theta. \tag{4.6}$$

His finance constraints, analogous to (3.4), are

$$p_x(s, M)x \leq m, \tag{4.7}$$

$$p_y(s, M)y \leq n. \tag{4.8}$$

Consolidating these constraints and using (4.5) gives the analogue to (3.7):

$$x + p_y(s)y + r_x(s, w)\psi_x + r_y(s, w)\psi_y + q_x(s, w)\theta_x + q_y(s, w)\theta_y \leq \theta. \tag{4.9}$$

For a citizen of country 0, the beginning-of-next-period wealth (in x-units) θ' resulting from the spending-portfolio decisions (x, y, m, n, ψ_x, ψ_y, θ_x, θ_y) is analogous to (3.8):

$$\begin{aligned}\theta' = {} & \frac{1}{p_x(s',M')}[m - p_x(s,M)x + e(s',M',N')(n - p_y(s,M)y)] \\ & + \frac{p_x(s,M)}{p_x(s',M')}\xi\theta_x + \frac{e(s',M',N')p_y(s,N)}{p_x(s',M')}\eta\theta_y \\ & + q_x(s',w')\theta_x + q_y(s',w')\theta_y \\ & + \frac{w_0'M}{p_x(s',M')}\psi_x + \frac{e(s',M',N')w_1'N}{p_x(s',M')}\psi_y \\ & + r_x(s',w')\psi_x + r_y(s',w')\psi_y \\ & + \frac{w_0'M}{p_x(s',M')}.\end{aligned} \tag{4.10}$$

For a citizen of country 1, the last term on the right-hand side of (4.10) is $[p_x(s', M')]^{-1}e(s', M', N')w_1' N$ and (4.10) is otherwise the same for him as for the country 0 citizen.

With the constraints (4.7) and (4.8) binding, the first term on the right-hand side of (4.10) is zero. The remaining terms can be simplified using the nominal price formulas (4.3)–(4.5), so that (4.10) reduces to the analogue of (3.8):

$$\theta' = \frac{\xi'}{1+w_0'}\theta_x + \frac{\eta'}{1+w_1'}p_y(s')\theta_y + q_x(s',w')\theta_x$$
$$+ q_y(s',w')\theta_y + \frac{w_0'}{1+w_0'}\xi'(1+\psi_x) + \frac{w_1'}{1+w_1'}p_y(s')\eta'\psi_y \quad (4.11)$$
$$+ r_x(s',w')\psi_x + r_y(s',w')\psi_y.$$

(This is for country 0. The modification for country 1 is obvious.) The problem facing the agent is then given by

$$v(s,w,\theta) = \max_{x,y,\theta_x,\theta_y,\psi_x,\psi_y} \{U(x,y) + \beta \int v(s',w',\theta')dF\,dK\}, \quad (4.12)$$

subject to (4.9), with θ' given by (4.11).

The development of the first-order conditions for this problem is sufficiently close to the preceding section that it need not be repeated. In a symmetric equilibrium, the agent must buy $(x,y) = (\frac{1}{2}\xi, \frac{1}{2}\eta)$, $(\theta_x,\theta_y) = (\frac{1}{2},\frac{1}{2})$, and $(\psi_x,\psi_y) = (-\frac{1}{2},\frac{1}{2})$. A country 1 agent holds $(\psi_x,\psi_y) = (\frac{1}{2},-\frac{1}{2})$ and otherwise behaves identically. In such an equilibrium equity prices are given by the analogues to (3.15)–(3.16):

$$U_x(s)q_x(s,w) = \beta\int U_x(s')\left[q_x(s',w') + \frac{\xi'}{1+w_0'}\right]dF\,dK, \quad (4.13)$$

$$U_x(s)q_y(s,w) = \beta\int U_x(s')\left[q_y(s',w') + \frac{\eta'}{1+w_1'}p_y(s')\right]dF\,dK. \quad (4.14)$$

The prices of the claims to future monetary transfers are similarly given by

$$U_x(s)r_x(s,w) = \beta\int U_x(s')\left[r_x(s',w') + \frac{w_0'}{1+w_0'}\xi'\right]dF\,dK, \quad (4.15)$$

$$U_x(s)r_y(s,w) = \beta\int U_x(s')\left[r_y(s',w') + \frac{w_1'}{1+w_0'}p_y(s')\eta'\right]dF\,dK. \quad (4.16)$$

As in section 3, it is necessary to determine the conditions under which nominal interest rates will be strictly positive. A claim to one dollar one period hence is a claim to $M^{-1}(1+w_0')^{-1}\xi'$ x-units and hence has a current x-unit price of

$$\beta[U_x(s)]^{-1}M^{-1}\int U_x(s')(1+w_0')^{-1}\xi'\, dF\, dK.$$

Its dollar price is therefore

$$b_x(s,w) = \beta \int \frac{U_x(s')\xi'}{U_x(s)\xi} \frac{1}{1+w_0'}\, dF\, dK. \tag{4.17}$$

Similarly, a claim to a pound one period hence has the current pound value:

$$b_y(s,w) = \beta \int \frac{U_y(s')\eta'}{U_y(s)\eta} \frac{1}{1+w_1'}\, dF\, dK. \tag{4.18}$$

The discussion following eq. (3.17) is applicable to (4.17)–(4.18) as well.

5. A National Currency, Fixed Exchange Rate Model

In this section, the timing, monetary conventions, and market structure of section 4 will be maintained without change. The objective of the analysis will be to find a symmetric, perfectly pooled equilibrium in which the exchange rate is maintained at a constant level through central bank intervention in the currency market.

Not infrequently, fixed exchange rate regimes are discussed as though they were equivalent to a single currency regime such as that analyzed in section 3. Thus if there are $\$M$ and $£N$ in circulation, and if the exchange rate is fixed at $\bar{e}$ then one could call $M + \bar{e}N$ the 'world money supply' and let this magnitude play the role of M in section 3. This is where the analysis of this section is headed, too, but in order to gain some insight into the conditions under which this simplifying device is legitimate, it is best to begin at a prior level. Accordingly, the existence of differentiated national currencies in the sense of section 4, and a currency-and-securities market operating under the same rules, are both assumed here. Hence, if the exchange rate is to be fixed, someone or some agency has to do something to make it fixed. I will assign this role to a single, central authority, holding reserves of both currencies, trading in spot currency markets so as to maintain the exchange rate e at some constant value $\bar{e}$.[8]

To analyze such a regime under rational expectations, it is necessary ei-

8. This model of an exchange rate fixing institution is taken from Helpman (1979), where national central banks are also considered.

ther to assume that the behavior of this central authority, in combination with the behavior of monetary policy and real shocks in the two countries, is consistent with the *permanent* maintenance of the rate $\bar{e}$, or to incorporate into the analysis the possibility of devaluations and the consequent speculative activity this possibility would necessarily involve. I will take the former, much simpler, course.

Let the authority begin (and also end) a given period with total reserves of dollar value D, possibly after receiving new currency transfers from one or both countries. Let its holdings after all securities trading is completed be \$$R$ and £S so that at the conclusion of trading

$$D - R + \bar{e}S \tag{5.1}$$

must hold. Under the hypothesis, provisionally maintained here, that nominal interest rates are uniformly positive, eqs. (4.3) and (4.4) will continue to hold, but with M and N replaced by the quantities $M - R$ and $N - S$ of these currencies remaining in private circulation. Then the formula (4.5) for the equilibrium exchange rate becomes

$$\bar{e} = \frac{M - R}{N - S}\frac{\eta}{\xi}p_y(s). \tag{5.2}$$

Given $\bar{e}$, given the value of $s = (\xi, \eta)$ selected by nature, and given the two national money supplies M and N, (5.1) and (5.2) are two equations in the end-of-period reserve levels R and S. Viability of the fixed rate regime, then, requires that $R > 0$ and $S > 0$ for all possible states (s, M, N). It is readily seen that these two inequalities are equivalent to

$$D > N\bar{e} - M\frac{\eta}{\xi}p_y(s), \quad \text{and} \tag{5.3}$$

$$D > M - N\bar{e}\Big/\left[\frac{\eta}{\xi}p_y(s)\right]. \tag{5.4}$$

To interpret these conditions, suppose that the positive random variable $(\eta/\xi)p_y(s)$ ranges in value from zero to infinity. Then for (5.3) and (5.4) to hold for all states of nature s the stabilizing authority must hold reserves of dollar value D exceeding *both* the dollar value of pounds outstanding $N\bar{e}$ [inequality (5.3)] *and* all outstanding dollars M [inequality (5.4)]. Tighter bounds on the range of $(\eta/\xi)p_y(s)$ would permit smaller reserves. With constant money supplies M and N (or with $w_{0t} = w_{1t} = 0$ for all t) it is clear that a sufficiently large reserve level D can always be selected.

With M_t and N_t drifting over time, even if the drifts w_{0t} and w_{1t} are perfectly correlated, it is clear that no constant reserve level D can maintain (5.3) and (5.4) forever. Surely this cannot be surprising. It is equally clear that by augmenting reserves appropriately from time to time the inequalities (5.3) and (5.4) can be indefinitely maintained. In this rather weak and obvious sense, then, the maintenance of fixed exchange rate requires coordination in the monetary policies of the two countries and of the stabilizing authority. At the same time, there may remain a good deal of latitude for independent monetary policies on a period-to-period basis. Indeed, over a sample period in which no devaluations occur, the inequalities (5.3) and (5.4) should probably be viewed as placing no econometrically useful restrictions on the joint distribution of the process w_{0t}, w_{1t}.

With (5.3) and (5.4) maintained, then, the rest of the analysis is precisely that of the single-money world economy studied in section 3. Now $M_t - R_t + \bar{e}(N_t - S_t)$, or 'world money' plays the role of M_t in section 3. The Markov processes governing the motion of world money would have to be derived from the behavior of the two monetary policies and the stabilizing authority, and might not be first-order. Modifying the analysis of section 3 to incorporate higher-order processes on the monetary shock is not a difficult exercise. Of course, the requirement (3.19) that nominal interest rates be positive is presupposed in this adaptation, too.

In summary, then, it is possible to devise a pegged exchange rate regime under which the Pareto-optimal resource allocation obtained under a flexible rate system is replicated exactly, provided only that the authority responsible for maintaining the fixed rate is armed with sufficient reserves. This conclusion does not, of course, rest on the notion that price fixing is innocuous in any general sense, but rather on the function served by the particular prices that appear in this model. In the barter allocation of section 2, a full list of Arrow–Debreu contingent claim securities is available. In the monetary model of section 3 money is introduced *in addition to* these contingent claim securities, motivated by the idea that current goods purchases are carried out in a decentralized, anonymous fashion. With stable money, this monetary modification does not disturb the relative price configuration of section 2.

In section 4, a second money was introduced and trade in the two currencies was permitted. Again, with stable money supplies, relative prices and quantities are not altered. This redundant security does no harm. It also does no good, however, and thus when it is effectively removed, as in the present section, the efficiency properties of the real resource allocation are left undisturbed. The price-fixing involved does not (or need not) alter the relative price of any pair of goods, as it does in the classic case for flexible rates constructed by analogy to ordinary commodity price pegging. Neither does it introduce any new options, as it does in Mundell's (1973) defense of a 'common currency'.

One frequently sees exchange rate regimes compared in terms of where it is that certain shocks get 'absorbed'. In the present model, with perfectly flexible prices in all markets, 'shock absorption' is easy and the issue of which prices respond to which shocks is of no welfare consequence. However, the two regimes do differ radically in their implications for the volatility of domestic nominal prices, and a comparison may be suggestive in thinking about extensions of the model to cover situations in which nominal price instability is associated with real pain.

Consider only regimes with perfectly stable money supplies, M and N, so that the only shocks are to ξ and η. In the flexible rate regime, nominal prices in country 0 are given in (4.3). Here $p_x(s, M)$ responds to changes in home endowment with an elasticity of minus one, and to changes in the foreign endowment not at all. In the fixed rate regime, $p_x(s, M)$ is given by $(M - R)/\xi$, where reserves R also fluctuate stochastically. Solving for $M - R$ from (5.1) and (5.2), one obtains

$$M - R = \left[1 + \frac{\eta}{\xi} p_y(s)\right]^{-1} [M + \bar{e}N - D],$$

so that the domestic price level is just

$$p_x(s, M) = [\xi + \eta p_y(s)]^{-1}[M - \bar{e}N - D]$$

or world money in private circulation divided by world output, valued in x-units. Now if world output fluctuates less than output in each individual country, domestic price levels have less 'shock absorbing' to do under fixed than flexible rates. This observation is very much in the spirit of Mundell's argument in Mundell (1973).

To what extent these results, and those of Helpman (1979) and Helpman and Razin's (1981) earlier work should be taken to bear on the controversy over which set of international monetary institutions are to be preferred in practice is difficult to determine. I suspect that the central issue in this debate is whether one takes a nationalist or an internationalist point of view toward relations among countries. If so, economic analysis cannot be expected to resolve the question directly, but it may contribute indirectly to its resolution by making it more difficult for contestants to defend essentially political conclusions on the basis of what seem to be 'purely' economic arguments.

6. Possible Relaxations

Of the many ways in which the models in this paper differ from reality, four seem to me likely to be the most crucial in applications: the assumed absence of production, the implication that the velocity of circulation is fixed, independent of interest rates and income, the implication that all agents hold identical portfolios, and the absence of business cycle effects. The purpose of this section is to discuss briefly the likely causes and/or consequences of these presumed deficiencies in the model.

Production can be introduced into the barter model of section 2, so long as the one consumer device is retained. Using the connection between competitive equilibria and Pareto-optima, one can obtain the optimum (and equilibrium) quantities produced and consumed, and insert these quantities into the marginal-rate-of-substitution formulas used in section 2 to price securities. See Brock (1979).

In the monetary economics of sections 3–5, matters are not so simple. As in Grandmont and Younes (1973), the Clower constraint sets up a 'wedge' between the private and social returns to capital and labor. Factors of production utilized today produce goods consumed today, but since factors are paid at the end of the period, the private trade-off involves exchanging effort today for consumption tomorrow. With a positive discount rate, this difference matters. These observations are valid even under a perfectly stable monetary policy; with stochastic variability in the latter, still more complications are involved. These are not difficulties of formulating a coherent *definition* of an equilibrium with production, but they are barriers to applying the solution methods used in Brock (1979) or Lucas (1978) and hence challenges to future research.

The unit-velocity prediction (really, assumption) of Clower-based monetary models is a great convenience theoretically, as we have seen earlier in this paper, but a serious liability in any empirical application one can imagine. It arises because of the way information is assumed to flow in the model: *first,* people learn exactly how much they will buy in the current 'period' and at what price, *second,* they execute these purchases using currency balances finely tuned for this purpose. By reversing this sequence by, for example, making people commit themselves to money holdings prior to learning the current value of the shocks ξ and η, or by introducing non-insurable, personal shocks as in Lucas (1980), one can introduce a precautionary motive to money demand that leads to a richer and more conventional treatment of velocity. These modifications lead to complications of their own, however, and I thought it best to abstract from them in this first pass at a set of problems which is complicated enough in its own right.

Of course, even if modified to incorporate a precautionary motive, any Clower-based model assigns a heavy burden to the idea of a 'period', and one is definitely not supposed to let the length of a period tend to zero and hope that the predictions of such a model will be unchanged. This observation is sometimes raised as a criticism of models of this class. If such criticism were accompanied by examples of serious monetary theory which does *not* have this property, it would have considerably more force.[9]

The fact that, in equilibrium, all traders in the world hold the identical market portfolio is a simplification that is absolutely crucial to the model of analysis used above. It is also grossly at variance with what we know about the spatial distribution of portfolios: Americans hold a disproportionately high fraction of claims to American earnings in their portfolios, Japanese a high fraction of Japanese assets, and so on. For that matter, neighborhood savings-and-loan banks attract local savings, mostly, and invest it in local assets, mostly, even within a single city in a single country.

Why is this? Much of conventional trade theory 'explains' this simply by forgetting the existence of international capital markets, in certain selective ways.[10] A real answer must have something to do with the local nature of the information people have, but it is difficult to think of models that even make a beginning on understanding this issue. It is encouraging that

9. The finance constraint idea can be adapted to continuous time models [see Frenkel and Helpman (1980)], in which case the relevant 'period' becomes a fixed lag between the date of sale and the date of receipt of payment.

10. An exception is Weiss's (1980) analysis.

the theory of finance has obtained theories of securities price behavior that do very well empirically based on this common portfolio assumption, even though their predictions on portfolio composition are as badly off as those of this paper.

Finally, these models contain nothing that I would call a 'business cycle'. There is real variability, due to endowment fluctuations, and monetary variability, due to unstable fiscal policy, but the only connection between these two kinds of shocks arises because policies may react to endowment movements. There is no sense in which real movements are *induced* by monetary instability. There is no doubt that the absence of such effects must limit the ability of models of this general class to fit time series, though the seriousness of this limitation for relatively smooth episodes such as the post-World War II period is not well-established.

7. Conclusion

This paper has been devoted to the development of a simple prototype model capturing certain real and monetary aspects of the theory of international trade. Its results consist mainly of the re-derivation within a unified framework of a number of familiar formulas (or close analogues thereto) from the theories of finance, money and trade. Perhaps the best way to sum up, then, is simply to provide a compact index of these formulas.

The formula for equity pricing in an 'efficient market' in a real system is given in (2.11) [or (2.13)] in a form that reflects agents' aversion to risk; (2.23) adapts this formula to any arbitrary, related security. Modifications of these formulas suited to an erratic, monetary environment are given in (3.15)–(3.16) (for the one-money cases) and (4.13)–(4.14) (for the two-money case).

The 'equation of exchange' for determining domestic prices appears as (3.2) and (4.3)–(4.4). A version of the Fisherian formula for expressing the nominal interest rate in terms of its real and nominal determinants is given in (3.17) and again in (4.17)–(4.18). The purchasing-power-parity law of exchange rate determination is given in (4.5).

I found it striking that all of these formulas—really, every main result in classical monetary theory and the theory of finance—fall out so easily, once an investment in notation is made. This seems to me an encouraging feature of models based on the finance constraint. It remains to be seen, however, whether models of this type can be pushed into genuinely new substantive territory.

References

Arrow, Kenneth J., 1964, The role of securities in the optimal allocation of risk-bearing, Review of Economic Studies 31, April, 91–96.

Bhagwati, Jagdish, 1958, Immiserizing growth: A geometric note, Review of Economic Studies 25, 201–205.

Breeden, Douglas T., 1979, An intertemporal asset pricing model with stochastic consumption and investment opportunities, Journal of Financial Economics 7, 265–296.

Brock, William A., 1979, Asset prices in a production economy, Caltech working paper.

Clower, Robert W., 1967, A reconsideration of the microfoundations of monetary theory, Western Economic Journal 6, 1–9.

Cox, J., J. W. Ingersoll, Jr. and S. Ross, 1978, A theory of the term structure of interest rates, Working paper (Stanford University, Stanford, CA).

Danthine, Jean-Pierre, 1977, Martingales, market efficiency and Commodity prices, European Economic Review 10, 1–17.

Debreu, Gerard, 1959, Theory of value (Yale University Press, New Haven, CT).

Frenkel, Jacob A. and Elhanan Helpman, 1980, Private notes.

Grandmont, Jean-Michel and Yves Younes, 1973, On the efficiency of a monetary equilibrium, Review of Economic Studies 40, April, 149–165.

Helpman, Elhanan, 1979, An exploration in the theory of exchange rate regimes, Working paper (University of Rochester, Rochester, NY).

Helpman, Elhanan and Assaf Razin, 1981, Comparative dynamics of monetary policy in a floating exchange rate regime, Working paper (Tel-Aviv University, Tel-Aviv).

Howitt, Peter W., 1974, Stability and the quantity theory, Journal of Political Economy 82, 133–151.

Johnson, Harry G., 1956, A mathematical note on immiserizing growth, Unpublished working paper.

Karaken, John H. and Neil Wallace, 1978, Samuelson's consumption-loan model with country specific fiat monies, Federal Reserve Bank of Minneapolis staff paper.

Kohn, Meir, 1980, In defense of the finance constraint, Working paper (Dartmouth College, Hanover, NH).

LeRoy, Stephen F., 1973, Risk aversion and the Martingale property of stock prices, International Economic Review 14, 436–446.

Lucas, Robert E., Jr., 1978, Asset prices in an exchange economy, Econometrica 46, 1429–1445.

Lucas, Robert E., Jr., 1980, Equilibrium in a pure currency economy, Economic Inquiry 18, 203–220.

Lucas, Robert E., Jr. and Nancy L. Stokey, 1982, Optimal growth with many consumers, Working paper (Northwestern University, Evanston, IL).

Merton, Robert C., 1973, An intertemporal capital asset pricing model, Econometrica 41, Sept., 867–888.

Mundell, Robert A., 1973, Uncommon arguments for common currencies, in: H. G Johnson and A. K. Swoboda, eds., The economics of common currencies (Allen and Unwin, London).

Nairay, Alain E., 1981, Consumption-investment decisions under uncertainty and variable time preference, Unpublished Yale University doctoral dissertation.

Robertson, D. H., 1940, Saving and hoarding, Reprinted in Essays in Monetary Theory (London).

Stockman, Alan C., 1980, A theory of exchange rate determination, Journal of Political Economy 88, 673–698.

Tsiang, S. C., 1956, Liquidity preference and loanable funds theories, multiplier and velocity analyses: A synthesis, American Economic Review 46, 540–564.

Tsiang, S. C., 1980, Keynes's 'finance demand for liquidity,' Robertson's loanable funds theory, and Friedman's monetarism, Quarterly Journal of Economics 14, 467–491.

Weiss, Lawrence, 1980, A model of international trade and finance, Quarterly Journal of Economics 14, 277–292.

— 7 —

Optimal Fiscal and Monetary Policy in an Economy without Capital*

ROBERT E. LUCAS, JR.

NANCY L. STOKEY

1. Introduction

This paper is an application of the theory of optimal taxation to the study of aggregative fiscal and monetary policy. Our analysis is squarely in the neoclassical, welfare-economic tradition stemming from Ramsey's (1927) contribution, so it will be useful to begin by reviewing the leading applications of this theory to aggregative questions of public finance, and by situating our approach and results within this tradition.

Ramsey studied a static, one ('representative') consumer economy with many goods. A government requires fixed amounts of each of these goods, which are purchased at market prices, financed through the levy of flat-rate excise taxes on the consumption goods. It is assumed that for any given pattern of excise taxes, prices and quantities are established competitively. In this setting, Ramsey sought to characterize the excise tax pattern(s) that would maximize the utility of the consumer (or minimize the 'excess burden' or 'welfare cost' of taxation). He thus abstracted from distributional questions and from issues of possible conflict between the objectives of 'government' and those governed, abstractions that will be maintained in this paper, as they were in those cited below.

Pigou (1947) and later Kydland and Prescott (1977), Barro (1979). Turnovsky and Brock (1980), and others noted that Ramsey's formulation could

---

Journal of Monetary Economics 12, no. 1 (1983): 55–93.

*We wish to thank Robert Barro, Stanley Fischer, Sanford Grossman. Kenneth Judd, Finn Kydland, Roger Myerson and Edward Prescott for helpful discussions. Support from the National Science Foundation and from the Center for Advanced Study in Economics and Management Science at Northwestern University is gratefully acknowledged.

be applied to the study of fiscal policy over time if the many goods being taxed were interpreted as dated deliveries of a single, aggregate consumption good. In this reinterpretation, the excise tax on 'good t' is interpreted as the general level of taxes in period t. Since tax receipts in a given period will not, in general, be optimally set equal to government consumption in that period, the theory of optimal taxation becomes, in this reinterpretation, a theory of the optimal use of public debt as well. Roughly concurrently, Bailey (1956), Friedman (1969), Phelps (1973), Calvo (1978) and others developed the observation that if one could interpret the holding of cash balances as consumption, at each date, of a second 'good' then the Ramsey formulation could be applied to the study of monetary as well as fiscal policy, with the 'inflation tax' induced by monetary expansions playing the formal role of an ordinary excise tax.

In all of these applications of the Ramsey theory, tax rates on various goods are thought of as being simultaneously chosen. In Ramsey's original static setting this assumption seems a natural one, but in a dynamic application it is more realistic to think of tax rates as being set sequentially through time by a succession of governments, each with essentially no ability to bind the tax decisions of its successor governments. Kydland and Prescott (1977) showed, through a series of graphic examples, how fundamental a difference this reinterpretation makes. If government at each date is free to rethink the optimal tax problem from the current date on, it will not, in general, find it best to continue with the policy initially found to be optimal. In the terminology of Strotz (1955–1956), tax policies optimal in the Ramsey sense are, in general, *time-inconsistent.* Since the normative advice to a society to follow a specific 'optimal' policy is operational only if that policy might conceivably be carried out over time under the political institutions within which that society operates, the Kydland-Prescott paper calls into serious question the applicability of all dynamic adaptations of the Ramsey framework.

One 'reason' for the time-inconsistency of optimal policies is the classical issue of the 'capital levy'. In the Ramsey framework, with lump-sum (and hence non-distorting) taxes assumed unavailable, it is best to focus excise taxes on goods that are inelastically supplied or demanded, to tax 'pure rents'. In a dynamic setting, goods produced in the past, capital, always have this quality and the returns to such goods are thus 'optimally' taxed away. Yet it will clearly not induce an optimal pattern of capital accumulation if such confiscatory taxes are announced for the future. Such a discrepancy between the best future tax policies to announce today and the best policy actually to execute when the future arrives is precisely what is meant by time-inconsistency.

In the present paper, we consider only economies without capital of any form, so that the difficult issues raised by capital levies are simply set aside. Private and government consumption goods are assumed to be produced under constant returns to scale using labor as the only input, and government consumption is taken to follow an exogenously given stochastic process. Moreover, the analysis is conducted in a neoclassical framework, thus precluding any countercyclical role for fiscal or monetary policy.

In section 2 we consider a barter economy. We assume that in each period the current government has full control over current tax rates, the issue of new debt, and the refinancing (at market prices) of old debt. However, it takes as fully binding the debt commitments made by its predecessors. We ask whether debt commitments (fully honored) are sufficient to induce successor governments to continue—*as if* they were bound to do so—tax policies that are optimal initially or sufficient, in short, to enforce the time-consistency of optimal tax policies. Our main finding is that with debt commitments of a sufficiently rich maturity structure an optimal policy, if one exists, can be made time consistent. That is, given an optimal tax policy, there exists a unique debt policy that makes it time-consistent. Section 3 consists of a series of examples, in which optimal tax-debt policies are characterized for a variety of specific assumptions about government consumption.

In section 4, money is introduced, its use motivated by a Clower (1967)-type transactions demand, modified to permit velocity to be responsive to variations in interest rates. Within this framework, familiar results on the optimal 'inflation tax' are readily replicated by exploiting the analogies between this monetary economy and the barter economy studied in section 2. With respect to the time-consistency of optimal policies, however, these analogies turn out, perhaps not surprisingly, to be more misleading than helpful. An optimal 'inflation tax' requires commitment by 'rules' in a sense that does not seem to have a counterpart in the dynamic theory of ordinary excise taxes.

Section 5 contains an informal discussion of the likely consequences of relaxing some of the simplifying assumptions of our necessarily abstract treatment of these issues, and of some directions on which further progress might be made. Section 6 is a compact summary of the main findings.

2. A Barter Economy

Though the issues raised in the introduction have mainly to do with monetary economies, it is convenient to begin with the study of fiscal policies in a simple barter economy. In this section, we describe one such economy, and characterize the equilibrium behavior of prices and quantities in the economy for a *given* fiscal policy. With this as a background, alternative ways of formulating the problem faced by the government will then be discussed.

There is one produced good, and government consumption of this good is taken to follow a given stochastic process, the realizations $g \equiv (g_0, g_1, g_2, \ldots)$ of which have the joint distribution F.[1] Let F^t denote the marginal distribution of the history $g^t \equiv (g_0, g_1, \ldots, g_t)$ of these shocks from 0 through t, for $t = 0, 1, 2, \ldots$. Assume that F has a density f, and let f^t denote the density for F^t. Finally, define $g_s^t \equiv (g_s, g_{s+1}, \ldots, g_t)$, for $0 \leq s \leq t$, and let $F_s^t\left(\cdot \mid g^{s-1}\right)$, with density $f_s^t\left(\cdot \mid g^{s-1}\right)$, denote the conditional distribution of g_s^t given g^{s-1}. (Evidently, these distributions will need to be restricted to assure that feasible patterns of government consumption exist. We postpone the question of how this might best be done.)

There is no other source of uncertainty in the economy, so that the basic commodity space will be the space of infinite sequences $(c, x) = \left\{(c_t, x_t)\right\}_{t=0}^{\infty}$, where c_t, private consumption of the produced good in period t, and x_t, private consumption of 'leisure' in period t, are both (contingent-claim) functions of g^t, the history of government shocks between 0 and t. Prices, tax rates, and government obligations, all to be introduced below, will lie in this same space. The endowment of labor in each period is unity, the produced good is non-storable, and the technology is such that one unit of labor yields one unit of output, so that feasible allocations are those satisfying

$$c_t + x_t + g_t \leq 1. \qquad t = 0, 1, 2, \ldots. \qquad \text{all } g^t. \tag{2.1}$$

1. Many, perhaps most, of the main points made below could as well have been developed in a context of perfect certainty [as in Turnovsky and Brock (1980)] so there is something to be said for the strategy of simply reading 'z' wherever we write '$\int z \, dF^t(g^t)$' or '$\int z \, dg^t$'. The reader for whom this simplification is helpful is invited to do this. When we turn, in section 3, to characterizing optimal fiscal policies under erratic government expenditure paths, however, the stochastic examples seem easier to interpret than the deterministic ones.

The preferences of the single, 'representative' consumer are then given by the von Neumann-Morgenstern utility function

$$E\left\{\sum_{t=0}^{\infty}\beta^t U\left(c_t, x_t\right)\right\} = \sum_{t=0}^{\infty}\beta^t \int U\left(c_t(g^t), x_t(g^t)\right) dF^t(g^t). \qquad (2.2)$$

The discount factor β is between 0 and 1, and the current period utility function, $U : R_+^2 \to R$, is strictly increasing in both arguments and strictly concave, with goods and leisure both normal (non-inferior).

Since there is no capital in this system, it is clear that *efficient* allocations (c, x) are fully characterized by (2.1) and the condition

$$U_c(c_t, x_t) = U_x(c_t, x_t), \quad t = 0, 1, 2, \ldots, \quad \text{all } g^t, \qquad (2.3)$$

to the effect that the marginal rate of substitution between goods and leisure is equal to the marginal rate of transformation, unity. If lump-sum taxes were available, the optimal policy would be to set the tax in period t equal to g_t, so that (2.3) would always hold. We will assume, to the contrary, that the *only* tax available to the government is a flat-rate tax τ_t levied against labor income $1 - x_t$. Under a continuously balanced government budget, then, the equality $g_t = \tau_t(1 - x_t)$ would hold each period, under all realizations of g^t.

To admit other possibilities, we will introduce government debt (possibly negative), in the form of sequences ${}_tb = \{{}_tb_s\}_{s=t}^{\infty}$, $t = 0, 1, 2, \ldots,$ where ${}_tb_s(g^{t-1}, g_t^s)$ is the claim held by the consumer at the beginning of period t, given that the event g^{t-1} occurred, to consumption goods in period $s \geq t$, contingent on the event g_t^s. The idea of a government issuing contingent claims may seem an odd one, but it is easy to introduce into the formalism we are using and it permits us, as will be seen below, to consider fiscal policies of practical interest that could not be analyzed if government debt were assumed at the outset to represent a certain claim on future goods.

The market structure throughout will be as follows. In each period $t = 0, 1, 2, \ldots,$ from the point of view of both the government and the representative consumer, current and past government expenditures, g^t, are known: future government expenditures g_{t+1}^{∞} are given by 'nature', with known conditional distribution $F_{t+1}^{\infty}(\cdot \mid g^t)$; and the consumer's contingent claims to current and future goods, ${}_tb$, are given by history. Given g^t, there are markets for the current consumption good $c_t(g^t)$ and current labor

$x_t(g^t)$, and a complete set of securities markets for future contingent claims, ${}_{t+1}b_s(g^t, g^s_{t+1})$, $s = t+1, t+2, \ldots$, all g^s_{t+1}. Given these market arrangements, we examine in turn the optimal behavior of consumers for given prices and taxes, the determination of competitive equilibrium, given taxes and government spending, and finally the optimal behavior of the fiscal authority. All questions of characterizing optimal fiscal policies under various assumptions on the shocks g will be deferred to the next section.

2.1. Consumer Behavior

First, consider the behavior of the representative consumer. Assume that he takes as given the sequence $\tau = \{\tau_t\}_{t=0}^{\infty}$ of contingent tax rates, and the price sequence $p = \{p_t\}_{t=0}^{\infty}$, where $p_t(g^t)$ is interpreted as follows. The consumer (correctly) expects that in each period $t = 0, 1, 2, \ldots$, given g^t, the market price of a claim to a unit of current goods or labor will be $p_t(g^t)$ and the market price of a contingent claim to a unit of goods in period s, contingent on the event g^s_{t+1}, will be $p_s(g^t, g^s_{t+1})$, $s = t+1, t+2, \ldots$, all g^s_{t+1}.

The consumer's behavior is described in two stages. In period $t = 0$, given τ, p, F, and g_0, the consumer solves his optimization problem by *planning* a sequence of (contingent) consumptions of goods and leisure, (c, x). However, in the market in each period $t = 0, 1, 2, \ldots$, he *trades* only current goods and labor (c_t, x_t), and assets, $\{{}_{t+1}b_s\}_{s=t+1}^{\infty}$. Consequently he must be careful to carry out these trades in such a way that he will in fact be able to afford to purchase his planned allocation in every period t, for every realization of g^t.

The consumer's planning problem, then, is to maximize (2.2), with τ, p, F, and g_0 given, subject to the budget constraint

$$p_0\left[c_0 - (1-\tau_0)(1-x_0) - {}_0b_0\right] + \sum_{t=1}^{\infty} \int p_t\left[c_t - (1-\tau_t)(1-x_t) - {}_0b_t\right]dg_1^t \leq 0. \tag{2.4}$$

The first-order conditions for this concave program are (2.4), with equality, and (if the solution is interior) the marginal conditions

$$\frac{U_x(c_t, x_t)}{U_c(c_t, x_t)} = 1 - \tau_t, \qquad t = 0, 1, 2, \ldots, \quad \text{all } g_1^t, \quad \text{and} \tag{2.5}$$

$$\beta^t \frac{U_c(c_t, x_t)}{U_c(c_0, x_0)} f_1^t(g_1^t | g_0) = \frac{p_t}{p_0}, \qquad t = 0, 1, 2, \ldots, \quad \text{all } g_1^t. \quad (2.6)$$

Let (c, x) be the solution of (2.4)–(2.6), given (τ, p). (Since U is strictly concave, the solution will be unique.)

The transactions required to attain this allocation are carried out as follows. When the market meets in period t, with g^t known, the consumer *purchases* his current allocation $(c_t(g^t), x_t(g^t))$, and any bond holdings ${}_{t+1}b$ satisfying

$$\begin{aligned} p_{t+1}\ {}_{t+1}b_{t+1} &+ \sum_{s=t+2}^{\infty} \int p_s\ {}_{t+1}b_s\, dg_{t+2}^s \\ &= p_{t+1}\left[c_{t+1} - (1 - \tau_{t+1})(1 - x_{t+1})\right] \\ &\quad + \sum_{s=t+2}^{\infty} \int p_s\left[c_s - (1 - \tau_s)(1 - x_s)\right] dg_{t+2}^s, \end{aligned} \quad (2.7)$$

all g_{t+1}, g^t given.

This ensures that his budget constraint in the following period will be satisfied, for any realization of g_{t+1}. The consumer is indifferent among all bond holdings ${}_{t+1}b$ satisfying (2.7). To see that the required bond holdings are always in the consumer's budget set, suppose that (2.7) holds for some particular g_t, g^{t-1} given. Then choose any ${}_{t+1}b$ satisfying (2.7) for (g^t, g_{t+1}), all g_{t+1}, g^t given. Integrating the second set of equations with respect to g_{t+1} and subtracting the first from it one obtains

$$p_t[c_t - (1 - \tau_t)(1 - x_t) - {}_tb_t] + \sum_{s=t+1}^{\infty} \int p_s[{}_{t+1}b_s - {}_tb_s]\, dg_{t+1}^s = 0,$$

so that the chosen bond holdings ${}_{t+1}b$ are in the consumer's budget set at g^t. Thus, by induction, if (2.7) holds at g^t, the required debt holdings of the consumer are affordable at all later dates. Since (2.7) holds for $t = -1$ [cf. (2.4)], the argument is complete.

2.2. *Competitive Equilibrium*

With consumer behavior thus described, given τ and F an *equilibrium* resource allocation plan (c, x)—if one exists—is uniquely determined from (2.1) and (2.5), with supporting prices (interest factors), p, given in (2.6).

Substituting from (2.5) and (2.6) into (2.4) and simplifying, one sees that the following condition must hold in a competitive equilibrium:

$$(c_0 - {}_0b_0)U_c(c_0, x_0) - (1 - x_0)U_x(c_0, x_0) \tag{2.8}$$
$$+ \sum_{t=1}^{\infty} \beta^t \int \left[(c_t - {}_0b_t)U_c(c_t, x_t) - (1 - x_t)U_x(c_t, x_t)\right] dF_1^t(g_1^t \mid g_0) = 0.$$

From the government's point of view in period 0, given current government consumption, g_0, given the conditional distribution of future government consumption, F_1^∞, and given the existing (contingent) government obligations, ${}_0b$, any allocation (c, x) that can be implemented by some tax policy τ must thus satisfy (2.1) and (2.8). Conversely, any allocation that satisfies (2.1) and (2.8) can be implemented by setting tax rates according to (2.5). Equilibrium prices, given those tax rates, are described by (2.6), and the required debt restructurings $\{{}_tb\}_{t=1}^{\infty}$ are any sequence satisfying (2.7) for $t = 0, 1, 2, \ldots$. Eqs. (2.1) and (2.8) then provide a complete description of the set of competitive equilibrium allocations attainable through feasible government policies.

Note that by Walras' law, if eq. (2.4) holds then the government budget constraint is also satisfied. Substituting from (2.1), one finds that (2.4) is simply a statement to the effect that the present value of outstanding government obligations must equal the present value of the excesses of tax revenues over government expenditures on goods. Writing this familiar condition in the form (2.8) emphasizes the facts that the choice of a tax policy in effect dictates the private sector equilibrium resource allocation and, in particular, dictates the interest rates to be used in carrying out this present value calculation. It is for the latter reason that one cannot take the initial *value* of government debt as historically given to the current government. One needs to know the entire schedule of (contingent) coupon payments due.

2.3. Optimal Fiscal Policy with Commitment

With the behavior of the private sector, given a fiscal policy, spelled out in (2.5)–(2.8), we turn to the problem faced by government in choosing a fiscal policy. Here and throughout the paper we take the *objective* of government to be to maximize consumer welfare as given in expression (2.2). As is well known, this hypothesis is consistent with a variety of equilibria, depending on what is assumed about the government's ability to bind itself (or its successors) at time 0 to state-contingent decisions that will actually be carried out at times $t > 0$. We will initially consider the problem faced by a government with the ability to bind itself at time 0 to a tax policy for the entire future. Later on, we will ask whether such a policy might actually be carried out under a more realistic view of government institutional arrangements.

Define, then, an *optimal* (tax-induced) allocation $(c, x) = \{(c_t, x_t)\}$ as one that maximizes (2.2) subject to (2.1) and (2.8). Letting λ_0 be the multiplier associated with the constraint (2.8), and $\mu_{0t}(g^t) \geq 0$ be the multiplier associated with (2.1) for g^t, the first-order conditions for this problem are (2.1), (2.8) and

$$(1+\lambda_0)U_c + \lambda_0[(c_t - {}_0b_t)U_{cc} + (x_t - 1)U_{cx}] - \mu_{0t} = 0, \quad (2.9a)$$

$$t = 0, 1, 2, \ldots, \text{ all } g^t,$$

$$(1+\lambda_0)U_x + \lambda_0[(c_t - {}_0b_t)U_{cx} + (x_t - 1)U_{xx}] - \mu_{0t} = 0, \quad (2.9b)$$

where the derivatives of U are evaluated at (c_t, x_t). Since the second-order conditions for this maximization problem involve third derivatives of U, solutions to (2.1), (2.8)–(2.9) may represent local maxima, minima, or saddle points. Or, (2.1), (2.8)–(2.9) may have no solution. Clearly, if g and/or ${}_0b$ are 'too large', there will be no feasible policy (no policy satisfying the government's budget constraint), and hence no optimal policy. However, assuming—as we will—that an optimal policy exists and that the solution is interior, it will satisfy (2.1), (2.8)–(2.9). Our analysis applies to these situations only. Appendix A treats the issues of existence and uniqueness of an optimal policy for an example with quadratic utility.

To construct a solution to (2.1), (2.8)–(2.9), one would solve (2.1) and (2.9) for c_t and x_t as functions of g^t, ${}_0b_t$, and λ_0, and then substitute these functions into (2.8) to obtain an equation in the unknown λ_0. Having so obtained the optimal allocation (c, x), the tax policy τ that will implement it is given in (2.5) and the resulting equilibrium prices p in (2.6).

In each period $t = 0, 1, 2, \ldots$, debt issues or retirements will be required to make up the difference between current tax revenue, $\tau_t(1 - x_t)$, and the sum of current government consumption and current debt payments due, $g_t + {}_tb_t$. Thus, the government must in each period buy or sell bonds at market prices, and do this in such a way that the end-of-period debt, ${}_{t+1}b$, satisfies (2.7). However, it is clear that once the government is committed to a particular tax policy for all time, relative prices of traded commodities and securities at each date are determined, so that within the constraint imposed by (2.7), only the *total* value of the debt at these prices matters. That is, *given* current and future tax rates, the maturity structure of the debt is of no consequence, provided that (2.7) holds.

2.4. Time Consistency of the Optimal Fiscal Policy

The optimal tax policy given implicitly in (2.1), (2.8)–(2.9) is of interest as a benchmark, but the decision problem it solves has no clear counterpart in actual democratic societies. In practice, a government in office at time t is free to re-assess the tax policy selected earlier, continuing it or not as it sees fit. To study fiscal policies that might actually be carried out under institutional arrangements bearing some resemblance to those that now exist, we need to face up to the problem of time-inconsistency. There are many ways to do this; we choose the following.

Imagine the government at $t = 0$ as choosing the current tax rate, τ_0, announcing a future tax policy $\{\tau_t\}_{t=1}^{\infty}$, and restructuring the outstanding debt, leaving the government at $t = 1$ with the maturity structure ${}_1b$. Take this debt-restructuring to be carried out at prices consistent with the announcements of future tax policies being perfectly credible. Imagine the government at $t = 1$ to be fully bound to honor the debt ${}_1b$, but to be free to select any current tax rate τ'_1 it wishes, announce any future taxes $\{\tau'_t\}_{t=2}^{\infty}$ it wishes, and to restructure the debt as it wishes. The debt restructuring at $t = 1$ is carried out at prices consistent with the *new* announcements $\{\tau'_t\}_{t=2}^{\infty}$ being perfectly credible. Suppose that the (contingent) tax rates announced at $t = 0$ are always chosen at $t = 1, \tau_1 \equiv \tau'_1$, all g^1, and that the (contingent) tax rates for subsequent periods announced at $t = 0$ are announced again at $t = 1, \tau_t \equiv \tau'_t, t = 2, 3, \ldots$, all g^t. Suppose, moreover, that this is true for all later periods as well. Then we will call the optimal policy *time-consistent.*

As shown in appendix B, if the optimal policy is time-consistent in this sense, it is also time-consistent in the following (weaker) sense: The policy (current tax rate and debt restructuring as functions of current government consumption and inherited debt) of each dated government, maximizes that government's objective function (the total discounted expected utility of the consumer from the current period on), taking as given the (maximizing) policies to be adopted by its successors. This holds for every possible value of the state variables (current government consumption and inherited debt), for every dated government. Viewing the dated governments as players in a game, a time-consistent optimal policy corresponds to a set of subgame perfect Nash equilibrium strategies (one for each player).

Somewhat surprisingly, we will show that *the optimal policy is time-consistent.*[2] More exactly, we show that if an allocation (c, x) together with a multiplier λ_0 satisfy (2.1), (2.8)–(2.9), then it is always possible to choose a restructured debt $\{{}_1b_t\}_{t=1}^{\infty}$, at market prices given by (2.6), such that the continuation $\{(c_t, x_t)\}_{t=1}^{\infty}$ of this same allocation satisfies (2.1), (2.8)–(2.9), given ${}_1b$, for all realizations g^1. By induction, then, the same is true in all later periods.

If such a ${}_1b$ can be chosen, there must be functions $\lambda_1(g^1)$ and $\mu_{1t}(g^t)$ such that

$$\sum_{t=1}^{\infty} \beta^t \int [(c_t - {}_1b_t)U_c - (1 - x_t)U_x]\, dF^t(g^t \mid g^1) = 0, \quad \text{all } g^1, \quad (2.8')$$

$$(1 + \lambda_1)U_c + \lambda_1[(c_t - {}_1b_t)U_{cc} + (x_t - 1)U_{cx}] - \mu_{1t} = 0, \quad (2.9a')$$
$$t = 1, 2, 3, \ldots, \text{all } g^t,$$

$$(1 + \lambda_1)U_x + \lambda_1[(c_t - {}_1b_t)U_{cx} + (x_t - 1)U_{xx}] - \mu_{1t} = 0, \quad (2.9b')$$

hold at $\{(c_t, x_t)\}_{t=1}^{\infty}$. Since by assumption leisure is a normal good, $U_{cc} - U_{cx} < 0$. Therefore, adding (2.9a) minus (2.9b) minus (2.9a′) plus (2.9b′), and solving for ${}_1b_t$ for each fixed $t \geq 1$ and g^t gives

$$\lambda_1\, {}_1b_t = \lambda_0\, {}_0b_t + (\lambda_1 - \lambda_0)a_t, \quad t = 1, 2, 3, \ldots, \text{all } g^t, \text{ where} \quad (2.10)$$

$$a_t(g^t) \equiv [(U_c - U_x) + (U_{cc} - U_{cx})c_t$$
$$+ (U_{xx} - U_{cx})(1 - x_t)]/(U_{cc} - U_{cx}), \quad t = 1, 2, 3, \ldots, \text{all } g^t. \quad (2.11)$$

If $\lambda_0 = 0$, then from (2.9) and (2.9′) we see that $\lambda_1 = 0$. If $\lambda_0 \neq 0$, then $\lambda_1 \neq 0$, and substituting for ${}_1b$ from (2.10) into (2.7) yields an equation in λ_1 that has a unique solution for each g^1; the resulting values for ${}_1b$ satisfy (2.8′).

The following example illustrates why the maturity structure of the debt is important. Let the utility function be quadratic:

2. This conclusion differs from that reached by Turnovsky and Brock (1980), in a context very similar to this one. The key difference is that our formulation involves debt issues at all maturities, while theirs restricts attention to one-period debt only. It is easy to see that the time-consistency proof below fails if the restriction ${}_1b_s = 0$ for $s > t$ is added.

$$U(c, x) = c + x - \tfrac{1}{2}(c^2 + x^2), \quad \text{so that}$$

$$U_c = 1 - c, \quad U_x = 1 - x, \quad U_{cc} = U_{xx} = -1, \quad U_{cx} = 0.$$

Then combining (2.9a) and (2.9b) to eliminate μ_{0t}, at an optimum:

$$(1 + \lambda_0)(x_t - c_t) - \lambda_0[c_t - {}_0b_t + (1 - x_t)] = 0, \quad t = 0, 1, 2.$$

Let there be three periods, $t = 0, 1, 2$, and let $\beta = 1$. Suppose that there is no government consumption, $g_0 = g_1 = g_2 = 0$, and that there is a constant amount of debt due in each period, ${}_0b_0 = {}_0b_1 = {}_0b_2 = \frac{1}{6}$. Therefore, substituting from (1), necessary conditions for an optimum are

$$(1 + \lambda_0)(1 - 2c_t) - \lambda_0[2c_t - \tfrac{1}{6}] = 0, \qquad t = 0, 1, 2.$$

Thus, $c_0 = c_1 = c_2$, so that (2.8) requires

$$(c_t - \tfrac{1}{6})(1 - c_t) - c_t^2 = 0, \qquad t = 0, 1, 2.$$

The relevant solution (see appendix A) is

$$\tau_t = \tfrac{1}{2}, \quad c_t = \tfrac{1}{3}, \quad x_t = \tfrac{2}{3}, \quad p_t = 1, \quad t = 0, 1, 2.$$

Taxing at the optimal rate at $t = 0$ generates exactly enough revenue to redeem the currently maturing debt, and the optimal debt policy is to leave the existing (flat) maturity structure in place: ${}_1b_1 = {}_1b_2 = \frac{1}{6}$. Clearly the optimal plan is time-consistent under this restructuring: when the government at $t = 1$ optimizes it will choose $\tau_1 = \frac{1}{2}$, the revenue collected will exactly cover debt currently due, and the debt due at $t = 2$ will be left in place. The government at $t = 2$ will set $\tau_2 = \frac{1}{2}$, and redeem the remaining debt.

Now suppose instead that the government at $t = 0$ were to restructure the debt, at the prices $p_1 = p_2 = 1$, so that it was all long term. ${}_1b_1' = 0$ and ${}_1b_2' = \frac{1}{3}$. Then in period $t = 1$, necessary conditions for an optimum would be

$$(1 + \lambda_1)(1 - 2c_1) - \lambda_1[2c_1] = 0, \qquad (1 + \lambda_1)(1 - 2c_2) - \lambda_1[2c_2 - \tfrac{1}{3}] = 0.$$

Clearly these will not be satisfied with $c_1 = c_2$. Instead the optimum is (approximately)

$$c_1' \approx 0.38, \quad \tau_1' \approx 0.53, \quad c_2' \approx 0.32, \quad \tau_2' \approx 0.39, \quad p_2'/p_1' \approx 0.91.$$

Note that by raising the current tax rate and lowering the future tax rate, the government at $t = 1$ induces an increase in current goods consumption and a fall in future goods consumption. This is accompanied by a fall in the price of future goods relative to current goods, i.e., a rise in the interest rate. Thus, the value of the outstanding debt, measured in goods at $t = 1$, falls. It is this 'devaluing' of the debt that provides an incentive for the (benevolent) government at $t = 1$ to deviate from the optimal (at $t = 0$) tax policy. (Note that if consumers foresee this, they will not exchange short-term for long-term debt on a one-for-one basis at $t = 0$.)

2.5. Extension to Many Consumer Goods

It is not difficult to extend this formulation, the calculation of the optimal open-loop allocation, and the above time-consistency conclusion, to the case of many non-storable consumption goods. Since this extension turns out to be useful in the analysis (section 4) of a monetary economy, we will develop it briefly here. Let there be n produced goods, so that period t's consumption is the vector $c_t = (c_{1t}, \ldots, c_{nt})$, and the description (2.1) of the technology is replaced by

$$\sum_{i=1}^{n} c_{it} + x_t + g_t \leq 1. \tag{2.12}$$

Preferences are given by (2.2), but with c_t reinterpreted as an n-vector so that $U : R_+^{n+1} \rightarrow R$. The consumer's budget constraint (2.4) is replaced by

$$p_0\left[1 - x_0 - \sum_{i=1}^{n}(1 + \theta_{i0})(c_{i0} - b_{i0})\right]$$

$$+ \sum_{t=1}^{\infty}\int p_t\left[1 - x_t - \sum_{i=1}^{n}(1 + \theta_{it})(c_{it} - b_{it})\right]dg_1^t = 0, \tag{2.13}$$

where $\theta_{it}(g^t)$ is a state-contingent excise tax levied on good i in state g^t.

Notice that in (2.13), in contrast to (2.4), goods purchases, not labor sales, are taxed. The one good case studied above corresponds here to the case $n = 1$, with $1 + \theta_{it} \equiv (1 - \tau_t)^{-1}$. This is a notational modification only. Notice also that there are n types of contingent bonds in (2.13), one for each good, and that the coupon payments b_{it} on these bonds are not subject to tax.[3] Notice finally that if 'leisure' could be taxed symmetrically with the other n goods in the system, then taxing the $n + 1$ 'goods' $c_{1t}, \ldots, c_{nt}$ and x_t at a common rate would be the equivalent of a direct tax on the endowment, or of a lump-sum tax. Eq. (2.13) is written in a way that rules out this possibility. These last two remarks point up substantive features of this formulation that are crucial to the conclusions that follow.

The first-order conditions for the problem: maximize (2.2) subject to (2.13), are (2.13),

$$\beta^t \frac{U_x(c_t, x_t)}{U_x(c_0, x_0)} f^t(g^t) = \frac{p_t}{p_0}, \qquad t = 0, 1, 2, \ldots, \text{ all } g^t, \text{ and} \tag{2.14}$$

$$\frac{U_i(c_t, x_t)}{U_x(c_t, x_t)} = 1 + \theta_{it}, \quad i = 1, 2, \ldots, n, \quad t = 0, 1, 2, \ldots, \text{ all } g^t, \tag{2.15}$$

where $U_i(c_t, x_t) = (\partial/\partial c_{it}) U(c_t, x_t)$. Letting $U' \equiv (U_1, U_2, \ldots, U_n, U_x)^T$, any allocation (c, x) satisfying (2.12) and

$$\sum_{t=0}^{\infty} \beta^t \int \begin{bmatrix} c_t - {}_0b_t \\ x_t - 1 \end{bmatrix}^T \cdot U' \, dF^t(g^t \mid g_0) = 0, \tag{2.16}$$

can be implemented using taxes only on goods $i = 1, \ldots, n$. Prices are then given in (2.14), tax rates in (2.15).

An optimal open-loop tax policy, then, corresponds to an allocation (c, x) that maximizes (2.2) subject to (2.12) and (2.16). The first-order conditions for this problem, written with the arguments of U and its derivatives suppressed, are (2.12), (2.16) and

$$(1 + \lambda_0)U' + \lambda_0 U'' \begin{bmatrix} c_t - {}_0b_t \\ x_t - 1 \end{bmatrix} - \mu_{0t} 1 = 0, \; t = 0, 1, 2, \ldots, \text{ all } g^t, \tag{2.17}$$

where λ_0 is the multiplier associated with (2.16), $\mu_{0t}(g^t) \geq 0$ is the multiplier associated with (2.12) for state g^t, and U'' is the matrix

3. This argument for making interest payments on government debt non-taxable was anticipated, in an early recognition of the importance of time-consistency, by Hamilton (1795).

$$U'' \equiv \frac{\partial^2 U}{\partial (c_t, x_t)^2} = \begin{bmatrix} U_{11} & U_{12} & \cdots & U_{1n} & U_{1x} \\ \vdots & \vdots & \ddots & \vdots & \vdots \\ U_{n1} & U_{n2} & \cdots & U_{nn} & U_{nx} \\ U_{x1} & U_{x2} & \cdots & U_{xn} & U_{xx} \end{bmatrix}.$$

The $n + 2$ equations in (2.17) and (2.12) correspond to (2.9) and (2.1) for the one-good case. Note that within each period, in each state, the optimal allocation satisfies the Ramsey tax rule, modified only for the existence of outstanding debt, ${}_0b_t \neq 0$. If ${}_0b_t(g^t) = 0$, the optimal tax rates $0_i\ (g^t)$, $i = 1, 2, \ldots, n$, are the usual Ramsey taxes.[4]

Constructing an optimal tax policy involves, then, the following steps. First, solve (2.17) and (2.12) for the allocations (c_t, x_t) as functions of g^t, ${}_0b_t$, and λ_0. Insert these functions into (2.16) to obtain λ_0, and hence the optimal allocation. Finally, use (2.15) to obtain the excise tax structure that implements this allocation.

The definition of time-consistency used in the one-good case serves as well for the many-goods case under examination here, and the proof that the optimal open-loop policy is time-consistent involves no new elements. Premultiplying (2.17) by the $n \times (n + 1)$ matrix $[I_n \mid -1]$ to eliminate μ_{0t}, and subtracting the analogous system of equations for period 1, we find that

4. The connection with standard Ramsey taxes is most clearly seen as follows. Define (c^*, x^*) by

$$U_1(c^*, x^*) = U_2(c^*, x^*) = \cdots = U_n(c^*, x^*) = U_x(c^*, x^*), \quad \sum{}_j c_j^* + x^* - 1 = 0,$$

and let δ be the common value of $U_i(c^*, x^*)$. Then for g_t and ${}_0b_t$ small, or whenever U is a quadratic form, we can write

$$U' \approx \delta 1 + U''^* \begin{bmatrix} c_t - c^* \\ \hdashline x_t - x^* \end{bmatrix},$$

where U''^* is the matrix U'' evaluated at (c^*, x^*) Note that since U is strictly concave, U''^* is an $(n + 1) \times (n + 1)$ matrix of full rank. Substituting into (2.17) and approximating U'' by U''^*, we find that

$$(1 + \lambda_0)U''^* \begin{bmatrix} c_t - c^* \\ \hdashline x_t - x^* \end{bmatrix} + \lambda_0 U''^* \begin{bmatrix} c_t - {}_0b_t \\ \hdashline x_t - 1 \end{bmatrix} + \big(\delta(1 + \lambda_0) - \mu_{0t}\big)1 = 0.$$

The solution $(c_t, x_t)^T \in R_+^{n+1}$ is unique, given μ_{0t}. The required value for μ_{0t} yields a satisfying (2.12).

$$
\begin{aligned}
&(\lambda_0 - \lambda_1)[I_n \mid -1]\left[U' + U''\left[\frac{c_t}{x_t - 1}\right]\right] \\
&- [I_n \mid -1]U''\left[\frac{\lambda_0\,{}_0b_t - \lambda_1\,{}_1b_t}{0}\right] = 0.
\end{aligned}
\tag{2.18}
$$

Since by assumption leisure is a normal good, the $n \times (n + 1)$ matrix $[I_n|-1]U''$ has rank n, so that ${}_1b_t$ is uniquely given by

$$
\lambda_1\,{}_1b_t = \lambda_0\,{}_0b_t + (\lambda_1 - \lambda_0)a_t, \quad t = 1, 2, \ldots, \text{all } g^t, \tag{2.19}
$$

where a_t is the (unique) solution of

$$
[I_n \mid -1]U''\left[\frac{a_t}{0}\right] = [I_n \mid -1]\left[U' + U''\left[\frac{c_t}{x_t - 1}\right]\right], \; t = 1, 2, \ldots, \text{ all } g^t. \tag{2.20}
$$

2.6. *Summary*

It is worth re-emphasizing the *central* importance in this analysis of optimal fiscal policy over time of the nature of a government's ability to bind its successors. One sees from (2.1), (2.5) and (2.6) [or from (2.12), (2.14) and (2.15)] that *if* the government could commit itself at $t = 0$ to a complete set of current and future contingent tax rates, this commitment would fully determine the equilibrium resource allocation and the associated equilibrium prices. If such a commitment were possible, the maturity and risk structure of the debt would be immaterial. This case of complete commitment lies at one extreme of the range of possibilities.

At the other extreme, one might imagine a government with *no* ability to commit its successors, so that any debt it issued would be honored by its successors if they found it in their interest to do so, and repudiated otherwise. In this case, it is evident from (2.7) or (2.16) that debt commitments reduce the set of feasible allocations, so that at time 0, a government with the ability simply to repudiate debt will always choose to do so. In this situation, of course, no debt could ever be sold to the public in the first place, so that in fact all government consumption would have to be financed out of contemporaneous taxes. In general, this allocation will be inferior to the optimal policy with debt available (in the sense of yielding lower expected utility).

Our analysis has been focused on a situation intermediate between these two, in which there are no binding commitments on future taxes but in which debt commitments are fully binding. Our interest in this case does not arise from features that are intrinsic to the theory, since the theory sheds no light on why certain commitments can be made binding and others not, but because this combination of binding debts and transient tax policies seems to come closest to the institutional arrangements we observe in stable, democratically governed countries. It would be interesting to know why this is so, but pursuit of this issue would take us too far afield.

Our main finding, for this intermediate situation, is that being unable to make commitments about future tax rates is not a constraint. In the absence of any ability to bind choices about tax rates directly, each government restructures the debt in a way that *induces* its successors to continue with the optimal tax policy. For this to be possible, a rich enough mix of debt instruments must be available, where 'rich enough' means, roughly, one security for each dated, state-contingent good being traded ('leisure' expected).

3. Characteristics of Optimal Fiscal Policies

In the preceding section we obtained the necessary conditions for optimal fiscal policies, and showed that optimal policies are time-consistent. This analysis was carried out with the path of government expenditures and the initial pattern of inherited government debt permitted to take essentially any form. In this section we present several examples, in each restricting government expenditures and initial debt to a specific form, so that we can characterize more sharply the optimal resource allocation and associated tax and debt policies. The idea in the simpler examples is to build up confidence that what we are calling 'optimal policies' accord with common sense, and in the more complicated ones to learn something about how fiscal policy ought ideally to be conducted.

The following preliminary calculations will be useful in the examples. First, substitute from (2.1), (2.5) and (2.6) into (2.8) to get

$$\sum_{t=0}^{\infty} \beta^t \int U_c \left[\tau_t(1-x_t) - g_t - {}_0b_t\right] dF^t(g^t \mid g_0) = 0. \tag{3.1}$$

Then multiplying (2.9a) by $(c_t - {}_0b_t)$ and (2.9b) by $(x_t - 1)$ and summing, we find that

$$
\begin{aligned}
&(1+\lambda_0)[(c_t - {}_0b_t)U_c + (x_t - 1)U_x] \\
&\quad + \lambda_0[(c_t - {}_0b_t)^2 U_{cc} + 2(c_t - {}_0b_t)(x_t - 1)U_{cx} + (x_t - 1)^2\, U_{xx}] \qquad (3.2) \\
&\quad - (c_t + x_t - 1 - {}_0b_t)\,\mu_{0t} = 0.
\end{aligned}
$$

Note that since U is strictly concave, the quadratic term in (3.2) is negative. Finally, integrating (3.2) with respect to $dF^t(g^t)$, multiplying the tth equation by β^t, summing over t, and using (2.1) and (2.8), we find that

$$\lambda_0 Q + \sum_{t=0}^{\infty} \beta^t \int (g_t + {}_0b_t)\mu_{0t} dF^t(g^t \mid g_0) = 0, \tag{3.3}$$

where Q is the sum of negative terms. Since $Q < 0$, and $\mu_{0t} > 0$, $t = 0, 1, 2, \ldots$, all g^t, it follows from (3.3) that if $(g_t + {}_0b_t) > 0$, $t = 0, 1, 2, \ldots$, all g^t, then $\lambda_0 > 0$.

In all of the examples that follow, we assume that g_0, F_1^∞, and ${}_0b$ are such that an optimal policy exists.

EXAMPLE 1. Let $g \equiv 0$ and ${}_0b \equiv 0$. Since $Q < 0$, it follows from (3.3) that $\lambda_0 = 0$. Hence (2.9) implies that the optimal allocation is constant over time, $(c_t, x_t) = (\bar{c}, \bar{x}), t = 0, 1, 2, \ldots$, where $(\bar{c}, \bar{x})$ satisfies (2.1) and the efficiency condition $U_e(\bar{c}, \bar{x}) = U_x(\bar{c}, \bar{x})$. From (2.5) it then follows that the optimal tax rates are identically zero, $\tau \equiv 0$.

Since the optimal policy is time-consistent, the analog of (2.9) must hold when the government re-solves its optimization problem in later periods. Letting λ_t denote the multiplier associated with the analog of (2.8) in period t, this implies that $\lambda_t = \lambda_0 = 0$, $t = 1, 2, 3, \ldots$. Hence from (2.10), debt issues are indeterminate except that—from the government budget constraint—the *net* value of debt issues must be zero in each period.

EXAMPLE 2. Let $g_t + {}_0b_t = 0$, $t = 0, 1, 2, \ldots$, all g^t. As in the previous example, it follows from (3.3) that $\lambda_0 = 0$. Hence, using (2.9), we find that the optimal allocation (c_t, x_t) is given by (2.1) and

$$U_c(c_t, x_t) = U_x(c_t, x_t), \quad t = 0, 1, 2, \ldots, \quad \text{all } g^t.$$

The optimal tax and debt policies are exactly as in Example 1.

In Example 1 there is no government activity. In Example 2, the private sector initially holds a pattern of lump-sum obligations to government that precisely offset government consumption demand. In neither case is there any need to resort to distorting taxes, so that the multiplier λ_0 associated with the government budget constraint in each case is zero.

EXAMPLE 3. Let $g_t = G$ and ${}_0b_t = B$, be constants for $t = 0, 1, 2, \ldots$, with $G + B > 0$. Then from (2.9), the optimal allocation is constant over time: $(c_t, x_t) = (\bar{c}, \bar{x})$, $t = 0, 1, 2, \ldots$, and from (2.5), the tax rate required to implement the optimal allocation is also constant over time: $\tau_t = \bar{\tau}, t = 0$, 1, 2, ... Consequently, (3.1) implies that the government budget is balanced in each period, or that tax revenue in each period is just sufficient to cover current government consumption and redeem the currently maturing debt:

$$\bar{\tau}(1 - \bar{x}) - G - B = 0.$$

Since $G + B > 0$, it follows from (3.3) that $\lambda_0 > 0$. Since the analog of (2.9) must hold in all later periods, it follows that $\lambda_t = \lambda_0 > 0$, $t = 0, 1, 2, \ldots$. From (2.10) it then follows that no new debt is ever issued, and in each period only the currently maturing debt is redeemed, ${}_sb_t = B$, all s, t.

The function of government debt issues is to smooth distortions over time. If expenditures and debt obligations are smooth, as in this example, they are optimally financed from contemporaneous taxes. Nothing is gained either by issuing new debt or retiring existing debt.

Our remaining examples exploit the following simplification of (2.10). If the system begins with no debt outstanding, new issues of debt under the optimal policy have a particular form. Recall that if $\lambda_0 \neq 0$, then $\lambda_t \neq 0$, t = 1, 2, . . . , all g^t. Assume that $\lambda_0 \neq 0$. If ${}_0b \equiv 0_s$, $s = 1, 2, 3, \ldots$, all g^s, then from (2.10), in period 0 debt issues will be

$${}_1b_s = (1 - \lambda_0/\lambda_1)a_s, \quad s = 1, 2, \ldots, \quad \text{all } g^s,$$

where a_s is as defined in (2.11). In period 1 debt issues will be

$${}_2b_s = \frac{\lambda_1}{\lambda_2}\,{}_1b_s + \left(1 - \frac{\lambda_1}{\lambda_2}\right)a_s = \left(\frac{\lambda_1}{\lambda_2}\left(1 - \frac{\lambda_0}{\lambda_1}\right) + \left(1 - \frac{\lambda_1}{\lambda_2}\right)\right)a_s$$

$$= \left(1 - \frac{\lambda_0}{\lambda_2}\right)a_s, \qquad s = 2, 3, \ldots, \quad \text{all } g^s.$$

Continuing by induction, one finds that if an optimal policy is followed from the beginning, then at any date t, the outstanding debt obligations satisfy

$$ {}_tb_s = (1 - \lambda_0/\lambda_t)a_s, \quad s = t, t+1, t+2, \ldots, \quad t = 1, 2, \ldots. \quad (3.4) $$

Thus, at the beginning of any period t, in any state g^t, there is in effect only one security outstanding—a bond of infinite maturity. The current coupon payment on this bond is $a_t(g^t)$, and the coupon payment in any period $s > t$, contingent on the event g^s_{t+1}, is $a_s(g^t, g^s_{t+1})$. The quantity of this security outstanding is $(1 - \lambda_0/\lambda_t(g^t))$.

Therefore, in period $t-1$, an array of such securities—indexed by g_t—must be traded. Since the government in period $t-1$ inherits $(1 - \lambda_0/\lambda_{t-1}(g^{t-1}))$ outstanding bonds (of infinite maturity), its securities trades must be as follows.

It meets the current coupon payments $(1 - \lambda_0/\lambda_{t-1})a_{t-1}$ on the (single type of) outstanding bonds, and then buys all of those bonds back from consumers. At the same time it issues a new *set* of (contingent) bonds, each of which is contingent on the single event g_t, government consumption in the next period. For each possible value for g_t, it issues the quantity $(1 - \lambda_0/\lambda_t(g^{t-1}, g_t))$ of an infinite-maturity bond with the following coupon payments: $a_t(g^{t-1}, g_t)$ in a period t, contingent on the event g_t; $a_t(g^{t-1}, g_t, g^s_{t+1})$ in any period $s > t$, contingent on the joint event [g_t and g^s_{t+1}]; and zero in all periods if g_t does not occur.

[Note that this holds for the many-goods case as well. If ${}_0b \equiv 0$, then there is a single security at the beginning of any period t, which is a bond of infinite maturity. The only difference is that the coupon payment on this bond in any period $s \geq t$ is the *vector* of consumption goods, $a_s(g^s)$, defined in (2.20). Thus, with many goods, the single security is a type of indexed bond, where the index weights for each period s are contingent on the event g^s. As in the one-good case, daring each period t, the government issues an array of securities, each contingent on the single event g_{t+1}.]

Values for $(1 - \lambda_0/\lambda_t)$ can then be found by using (2.7), substituting from (2.6), and using (3 4).

$$ \left(1 - \frac{\lambda_0}{\lambda_t}\right)\left[U_c a_t + \sum_{t+1}^{\infty} \beta^{s-t} \int U_c a_s f^s_{t+1} dg^s_{t+1}\right] $$
$$ = U_c\left[c_t - (1-\tau_t)(1-x_t)\right] \quad (3.5) $$
$$ + \sum_{s=t+1}^{\infty} \beta^s \int U_c\left[c_s - (1-\tau_s)(1-x_s)\right] f^s_{t+1} dg^s_{t+1} $$
$$ t = 0, 1, 2, \ldots, \quad \text{all } g^t. $$

EXAMPLE 4. Let ${}_0b \equiv 0$, and $g_T > 0$, and $g_t = 0$ for $t \neq T$. From (2.9), the optimal allocation $(c_t, x_t) = (\bar{c}, \bar{x})$ is constant for all $t \neq T$, and consequently, from (2.5) and (3.4), the tax rate and coupon payment are also constant over these periods, $\tau_t = \bar{\tau}$, and $a_t = \bar{a}$, $t \neq T$. Using (3.2) we can study revenues. For $t \neq T$, $c_t + x_t - 1 - {}_0b_t = 0$, and the last term in (3.2) drops out. Since $\lambda_0 > 0$, the second (quadratic) term is negative, so that the first term must be positive. Since $(1 + \lambda_0) > 0$, this implies

$$0 < \bar{c} + (\bar{x} - 1)U_x/U_c = \bar{c} + (\bar{x} - 1)(1 - \bar{\tau}) = \tau(1 - \bar{x}),$$

so that tax revenue is positive for $t \neq T$. For period T, the last term in (3.2) $\mu_T g_T$, is positive. Therefore, the sign of the first term is indeterminate: labor may be either taxed or subsidized in period T.

Consequently, debt issues are as follows. In each period $t = 0, 1, \ldots, T - 1$, the government runs a surplus, using it to buy bonds issued by the private sector. In period T, the expenditure g_T is met by selling all of these bonds, possibly levying a tax on current labor income, and issuing new consols which have a coupon payment of $\bar{a}$ in every period. From (3.5) we see that

$$(1 - \lambda_0/\lambda_t) = [\bar{c} - (1 - \bar{\tau})(1 - \bar{x})]/\bar{a}, \qquad t = T + 1, T + 2, \ldots.$$

Hence $\lambda_t = \bar{\lambda}$, is a constant for all $t \geq T + 1$, and (3.4) implies that a constant number of consols is outstanding in all periods $t \geq T + 1$. That is, in each period $t = T + 1, T + 2, \ldots$, tax revenue is just sufficient to service the interest on the outstanding consols, and none are ever redeemed.

Example 4 corresponds to a perfectly foreseen war, and is the most pointed possible illustration of the role of optimal fiscal policy in using debt to redistribute tax distortions over time. Note the symmetry over time, previously noted by Barro (1979): consumption is the same in all periods in which government expenditure is zero, regardless of the proximity to the date T at which the positive government expenditure g_T occurs.

EXAMPLE 5. Let ${}_0b \equiv 0$, let $g_t = 0$ for all $t \neq T$, and let $g_T = G > 0$ with probability α and $g_T = 0$ with probability $1 - \alpha$. As in Example 4, $(c_t, x_t) = (\bar{c}, \bar{x})$ (although the optimum values of $\bar{c}$ and $\bar{x}$ will not, in general, be the same) all $t \neq T$. In addition, (2.9) implies that $(c_T, x_T) = (\bar{c}, \bar{x})$ if $g_T = 0$. The argument in Example 4 shows that tax revenue is positive in all these states. Consequently, debt issues are as follows.

In periods $t = 0, 1, \ldots, T - 2$, current tax revenue and interest income of the government are used to buy (infinite-maturity) bonds issued by the consumer. These bonds have a (certain) coupon payment of $\bar{a}$ in each period $t \neq T$; in period T they have a (contingent) coupon payment of $\bar{a}$ if $g_T = 0$, and of $\hat{a} \neq \bar{a}$ if $g_T = G$.

In period $T - 1$, the government collects current tax revenue and interest income, and sells back to the consumer all of its bond holdings. In addition, it issues 'contingent consols'; these have a coupon payment of $\bar{a}$ every period, payable if and only if $g_T = 0$. All of these revenues are used to buy *from* consumers 'contingent bonds' of infinite maturity, which have a coupon payment of $\hat{a}$ in period T and $\bar{a}$ in every period thereafter, payable if and only if $g_T = G$.

In period T, if $g_T = 0$, the consols held by the consumer have value, and the bonds held by the government do not. Tax revenue $\bar{\tau}(1 - \bar{x})$ is just sufficient to meet interest payments on the outstanding consols.

If $g_T = G$, the bonds, held by the government, have value, and the consols held by the consumer do not. The government collects interest on its bonds, sells all of these bonds back to the consumer, and in addition issues (non-contingent) consols with a constant coupon payment of $\bar{a}$ each period. All of these revenues are used to help finance the current expenditure of G.

In periods $T + 1, T + 2, \ldots$, the situation is as in Example 4, regardless of whether $g_T = 0$ or $g_T = G$.

Example 5 corresponds to a situation where there is a probability of war at some specified date in the future. It illustrates the risk-spreading aspects of optimal fiscal policy under uncertainty. In effect, the government in period $T - 1$ buys insurance from the private sector: it promises to pay (the premium) $\bar{a}$ in all subsequent periods with $g_t = 0$, in return for a claim to receive a payment ('damages') in period T, if the (unlucky) event $g_T = G$ occurs.

EXAMPLE 6. Let ${}_0b \equiv 0$, let $g_t = G > 0$, $t = T, T + S, T + 2S, \ldots$, where $0 \leq T \leq S$ (but $S \neq 0$), and let $g_t = 0$, otherwise. From (2.9), the optimal allocation has the form $(c_t, x_t) = (\hat{c}, \hat{x})$, $t = T, T + S, T + 2S, \ldots$, and $(c_t, x_t) = (\bar{c}, \bar{x})$, otherwise. Consequently, from (2.5) it follows that the tax rate also takes on two values, $\hat{\tau}$ and $\bar{\tau}$, in war and peacetime years respectively. As in Example 4, tax revenue is positive during peacetime years, and indeterminate during wartime years. Thus, debt issues are as follows.

In each period $t = 0, 1, \ldots, T - 1$, the government runs a surplus, which it uses to buy bonds issued by the private sector. In period T, the expenditure g_T is met by selling these bonds, possibly levying a tax on current labor income, and issuing new bonds. In periods $t = T + 1, T + 2, \ldots, S - 1$, the government again runs a surplus, which is used to pay interest on and gradually to redeem the outstanding bonds. From (3.5) we see that λ_t is cyclic, with a cycle length of S periods. Thus, at $t = S$ the national debt is zero, and the cycle begins again.

Example 6 corresponds to perfectly foreseen, cyclic wars, with a cycle length of $S > 0$ periods, where a war occurs $T \leq S$ periods into each cycle. It is obvious from Example 5 that with any regular, cyclic expenditure pattern the budget will be balanced over the expenditure cycle.

EXAMPLE 7. Let ${}_0b \equiv 0$ and $g_0 = G > 0$. If $g_t = G$, then $g_{t+1} = G$ with probability α, and $g_{t+1} = 0$ with probability $1 - x$. If $g_t = 0$, then $g_{t+1} = 0$. As in the previous example, it follows from (2.9) that the optimal allocation has the form $(c_t, x_t) = (\hat{c}, \hat{x})$ if $g_t = G$, and $(c_t, x_t) = (\bar{c}, \bar{x})$ if $g_t = 0$, all t, so that the tax rate takes on the values $\hat{\tau}$ and $\bar{\tau}$ during wartime and peacetime years respectively, with net tax revenue positive during peacetime years and indeterminate during wartime years. Let $\hat{a}$ and $\bar{a}$ denote the corresponding values for a_t.

Using (3.5), we can see how the war is financed. First, suppose that the war is still continuing in period $t > 0$. From (3.5) and (3.4), it follows that if $g_t = G$, then $\lambda_t = \bar{\lambda} = \lambda_0$, and ${}_tb \equiv 0$. On the other hand, suppose that the war has ended by period $t > 0$. From (3.5) and (3.4), it follows that if $g_t = 0$, then $\lambda_t = \hat{\lambda} \neq \bar{\lambda}$, and ${}_tb = (1 - \bar{\lambda}/\hat{\lambda})\bar{a}$. Consequently, the debt issues are as follows. While the war is in progress, it is financed at least in part through the issue of 'contingent bonds'. These bonds become consols, with constant coupon payment $\bar{a}$, if the war ends in the following period. If the war continues they become valueless. After the war ends, net tax revenue in each period is just sufficient to cover the current interest on the outstanding consols.

Example 7 corresponds to a war of unknown duration.

EXAMPLE 8. Let ${}_0b \equiv 0$, and let $\{g_t\}$ be a sequence of independently and identically distributed random variables. From (2.17) it follows that the optimal allocation in period t, in state g^t, is a stationary function of g_t, so that the optimal allocation can be written as

$$(c_t(g^t), x_t(g^t)) = (\gamma(g_t), \zeta(g_t)), \quad t = 0, 1, 2, \ldots, \quad \text{all } g^t,$$

with corresponding values $a_t(g^t) = \alpha(g_t)$ for coupon payments on the optimal bond, and $\theta_t(g^t) = \Theta(g_t)$ for the optimal tax rate. It follows, then, using (3.5) and the fact that $\{g_t\}$ is i.i.d., that we can also write $\lambda_t(g^t) = \Lambda(g_t)$. Hence from (3.4), the quantity $(1 - \Lambda(g_0)/\Lambda(g_t))$ of the government security outstanding in period t, in state g^t, depends only on g_0 and g_t. In particular, note that if $g_t = g_0$, then $(1 - \lambda_0/\lambda_t) = 0$, and there are no bonds outstanding.

Hence, debt restructurings occur as follows. In period t, given g_t, the government finds that its predecessor has left it with an obligation to pay $(1 - \Lambda(g_0)/\Lambda(g_t))\alpha(g_t)$ units of goods in the current period and contingent obligations to pay $(1 - \Lambda(g_0)/\Lambda(g_t))\alpha(G)$ units of goods in period s if the event $g_s = G$ occurs, for all $s > t$. Note that the obligation in any period $s > t$ is, at this point, contingent only on the realization of g_s.

Exactly the same statement must hold in period $t + 1$, for every possible value of g_{t+1}. To ensure that this is the case, the government in period t must arrange that its end-of-period debt obligations are as follows:

(i) Contingent obligations to pay $(1 - \Lambda(g_0)/\Lambda(G))\alpha(G)$ units of goods next period if $g_{t+1} = G$, all G.
(ii) Contingent obligations to pay $(1 - \Lambda(g_0)/\Lambda(G))\alpha(G')$ units of goods in period s if the joint event $[g_{t+1} = G$ and $g_s = G']$ occurs, all G, G', all $s > t$.[5]

EXAMPLE 9. Let ${}_0b \equiv 0$, and let $\{g_t\}$ be a stationary Markov process. The arguments and conclusions are exactly as in Example 8.[6]

The examples discussed in this section have not been chosen at random, but rather to illustrate some substantively important aspects of fiscal

5. If U is quadratic, then $\Lambda(G)$ is a monotone increasing function. Thus, under the optimal policy, inherited (contingent) debt obligations are smaller conditional on higher current values for government consumption. This highlights the insurance aspect of optimal debt arrangements in the presence of uncertainty. Outstanding debt obligation are smaller in states with high current government consumption, where any current tax revenue is needed to help finance current government consumption, and excessively high tax rates are to be avoided—work must be encouraged to produce the relatively large quantity of goods $c_t + g_t$. In states with low current expenditure, taxes are used to repay previously incurred debt, or to build up a surplus.

6. If $\{g_t\}$ is a Markov process, the monotonicity of the function Λ, discussed in footnote 5, can be expected only if the higher current levels of government consumption make higher levels in the following period, in some sense, more likely.

policy in practice. The shocks g_t that drive our system are government consumption *relative to* the ability of the economy to produce. In an economy like the United States, the main source of variation in g_t, so interpreted, are wars, brief and infrequent but economically very large when they occur, and business fluctuations, generally much smaller in magnitude but occurring more or less continuously. Examples 4–7 are designed to illustrate the main qualitative aspects of the public finance of wars. Examples 8 and 9, and their special case Example 3, attempt to capture more 'normal' situations.

Of the general lessors one can draw from these examples, three seem to us to be the most important. The first is simply built into the formulation at the outset: budget balance, in some *average* sense, is not something one can argue over in welfare-economic terms. If debt is taken seriously as a binding *real* commitment, then fiscal policies that involve occasional deficits necessarily involve offsetting surpluses at other dates. Thus in all of our examples with erratic government spending, good times are associated with budget surpluses.

Second, our examples illustrate once again the applicability of Ramsey's optimal taxation theory to dynamic situations, as articulated by Pigou (1947) and more recently by Kydland and Prescott (1980) and Barro (1979). In the face of erratic government expenditures, the role of debt issues and retirements is to smooth tax distortions over time, and it is clear that no general, welfare-economic case can be developed for budget balance on a *continuous* basis. Such a case (and nothing in our purely qualitative treatment suggests that it would be a weak one) would have to be based on the 'smoothness' of g_t (Example 3), and on some quantitative argument to the effect that an assumption of perfect smoothness is a useful approximation in some circumstances. Since it is easy to think of situations (Example 4) in which such an approximation would be a very bad one, it is clear that (as seems to be universally recognized) any welfare-improving commitment to budget balance will have to involve 'escape clauses' for exceptional (high g_t) situations.

Third, as is evident from all of the stochastic examples, the contingent-claim character of public debt is not in any sense an incidental feature of an optimal policy. Example 5 makes the insurance character of optimum debt issues clear, as does Example 7, in which a war-financing debt is repeatedly cancelled as long as the war continues, and is paid off only when the war ends. This feature is an entirely novel one in normative analysis of fiscal policy, to the point where even those most sceptical about the efficacy of actual government policy may be led to wonder why governments forego gains in everyone's welfare by issuing only debt that purports to be a *certain* claim on future goods.

Historically, however, nominally denominated debt has been anything but a certain claim on goods, and large-scale debt issues, typically associated with wars, have traditionally been associated with simultaneous and subsequent inflations that have, in effect, converted nominal debt into contingent claims on goods. Perhaps this centuries-old practice may be interpreted as a crude approximation to the kind of debt policies we have found to be optimal. Verifying this would involve going beyond the observation that war debts tend to be inflated away, in part, to establishing that the size of the inflation-induced 'default' on war debt bears some relation to the unanticipated size of the war. Example 7 states this issue about as baldly as it can be stated, but it can hardly be said to resolve it.

4. A Monetary Model

In this section, money, in the form of currency, is introduced into the economy studied in sections 2 and 3. We will first describe and motivate the specific way this will be carried out, paralleling as closely as possible the development of section 2. We consider two kinds of consumption goods, c_{1t} and c_{2t}, in addition to leisure x_t and government consumption g_t, all related by the technology

$$c_{1t} + c_{2t} + x_t + g_t \leq 1, \qquad t = 0, 1, 2, \ldots, \quad \text{all } g^t, \tag{4.1}$$

where, as above, $\{g_t\}$ follows a stochastic process. Preferences are

$$E\left\{\sum_{t=0}^{\infty} \beta^t U(c_{1t}, c_{2t}, x_t)\right\}, \tag{4.2}$$

the expectation in (4.2) being taken with respect to the conditional distribution F_1^∞ of the event $g_1^\infty = (g_1, g_2, \ldots)$, g_0 given.

The distinction between the two types of consumption, c_{1t} and c_{2t}, has to do with available payments arrangements, which we take to be as follows. The first good, c_{1t} ('cash goods'), can be purchased only with fiat currency previously accumulated. The second, c_{2t} ('credit goods'), can be paid for with labor income contemporaneously accrued. To clarify this distinction, consider the following trading scenario [taken in part from Lucas (1980)].

Think of a typical household as consisting of a worker-shopper pair, with one partner engaged each period in producing goods for sale and the other in travelling from store to store, purchasing a variety of consumption goods [all produced under the constant-returns technology (4.1)]. At some stores the shopper is known to the producer, who is willing to sell on trade-credit, the bill to be paid at the beginning of the next period. The total amount purchased on this basis, c_{2t}, we call 'credit goods'. At other stores the shopper is unknown to the seller, and any purchase must be paid for at once in currency. [Presumably the fact that the shopper is 'unknown' to the seller arises because there are resource costs involved in making oneself and one s credit-worthiness 'known' to someone else, but we do not pursue this here. See Prescott (1982).] Purchases made on this basis, c_{1t}, we call 'cash goods'. By postulating a current period utility function $U(c_{1t}, c_{2t}, x_t)$ with a diminishing marginal rate of substitution between cash goods and credit goods, we are assuming that only a limited range of goods is available on a credit basis, so that adding the option to substitute cash goods as well increases utility.

Although one might think of identifying cash and credit goods with observable consumption categories (food, clothing, and so on), we do not wish to do so here. On the contrary, think of one household's credit goods as being another's cash goods just as one can run up a tab at one's own neighborhood bar or grocery but not at others, or as it is worthwhile to establish credit in department stores in the city where one lives, but not in others. This is simply a matter of interpretation, since we offer no analysis of trade credit here, but it will matter in what follows that the 'inflation tax' is not interchangeable with an ordinary excise tax on some specific consumption category.

The *timing* of trading is important and we adopt the following conventions. At the beginning of period *t*, the shock g_t, is realized and known to all. All agents, government included, convene in a centralized securities market. After outstanding debts are cleared, agents trade whatever securities (including currency) they choose. With this trading concluded, shoppers and producers disperse. Shoppers run down their cash holdings and accumulate bills. Producers accumulate cash and issue bills. These activities, together with arrangements entered into in securities trading, determine the household's consumption and leisure mix this period and the circumstances in which it begins the next period.

As in sections 2 and 3, a resource allocation $\{(c_{1t}, c_{2t}, x_t)\}_{t=0}^{\infty}$ is a sequence of contingent claims, the tth term of which is a function of the history g^t of shocks through that date. Price sequences are elements of the same space, as will be various securities to be specified in a moment. To develop the budget constraints faced by a household as of $t = 0$, we use the prices $\{(q_t, p_t)\}$, where $q_t(g^t)$ is the dollar price at time 0 of a dollar at time t, contingent on the history g^t (so that, in particular, $q_0 = 1$), and where $p_t(g^t)$ is the current dollar price at time t of a unit of either type of goods at time t, contingent on g^t. Here 'at time t' means, more precisely, at the time of the 'morning' securities market in period t. Hence the price, in dollars at time 0, of a unit of cash goods in t, is $q_t(g^t)p_t(g^t)$, since the dollars must be acquired in the securities market held *prior* to (on the same day as) the goods purchase. The price at $t = 0$ of a unit of credit goods in t is $q_{t+1}(g^{t+1})p(g^t)$, since bills are paid the day *after* the sale and consumption of such goods.

We imagine the household at $t = 0$ as holding securities of two kinds: contingent claims $\{{}_0B_t\}$ to dollars at times $t = 0, 1, \ldots,$ priced at $\{q_t\}$ and contingent claims $\{{}_0b_{2t}\}$ to credit goods at times $t = 0, 1, \ldots,$ priced at $\{q_{t+1}p_t\}$ to coincide with the timing of payments for such goods. This set of securities is not comprehensive, as households might also wish to trade claims $\{{}_0b_{1t}\}$ to cash goods at times $t = 0, 1, \ldots.$ If such securities were available, however, they could be used by agents to circumvent the use of currency altogether, converting the system directly into the two-good barter economy studied at the end of section 2. This would conflict with our interpretation of cash goods as being anonymously purchased in spot markets only. To maintain the monetary interpretation of the model, then, direct claims to cash goods in 'real' terms will be ruled out.

The household's opportunity set, given prices and initial securities holdings, will then be described in two statements. One, describing options available in the centralized securities market, states that the dollar value of expenditures for all purposes is no greater than the dollar value of receipts from all sources. The other, describing options in decentralized cash goods markets, states that cash goods can only be purchased with currency.

The first of these constraints reads

$$\int q_1 dg_1[p_0c_{10} - M_0 + p_0c_{20} - p_0(1-\tau_0)(1-x_0) - p_0\,{}_0b_{20}]$$
$$+ \sum_{t=1}^{\infty} \int\int q_{t+1}dg_{t+1}[p_tc_{1t} - M_t + p_tc_{2t} - p_t(1-\tau_t)(1-x_t) - p_t\,{}_0b_{2t}]dg_1^t$$
$$+ [M_0 - B_0] + \sum_{t=1}^{\infty} \int q_t[M_t - {}_0B_t]dg_1^t \leq 0, \tag{4.3}$$

where $M_t \geq 0$ denotes wealth held in the form of currency at the close of securities trading in period t. The first terms of (4.3) collect receipts and payments due at the beginning of period $t + 1$, for $t = 0, 1, 2, \ldots$, including unspent currency carried over from t, priced accordingly at q_{t+1}. The second terms collect returns on dollar-denominated securities in t less the amount held in currency. Since (4.3) contains terms of the form $[q_t(g^t) - \int q_{t+1}(g^{t+1})\, dg_{t+1}]M_t(g^t)$, the budget constraint will be binding if and only if

$$q_t(g^{t+1}) - \int q_{t+1}(g^{t+1})dg_{t+1} \geq 0, \quad t = 0,1,2,\ldots, \quad \text{all } g^t. \tag{4.4}$$

If (4.4) is violated for any g^t the consumer can make arbitrarily large profits by holding arbitrarily large quantities of cash in state g^t. Thus, we will assume that (4.4) holds, or that the nominal interest rate is always non-negative.

Since currency must cover spending on cash goods, the second constraint is[7]

$$p_tc_{1t} - M_t \leq 0, \qquad t = 0,1,2,\ldots, \quad \text{all } g^t. \tag{4.5}$$

The consumer's problem is then to maximize (4.2), subject to (4.3) and (4.5), given initial securities holdings $\{({}_0B_t, {}_0b_{2t})\}$, prices $\{(p_t, q_t)\}$ and tax rates $\{\tau_t\}$. Letting γ be the multiplier associated with (4.3), and letting $\rho_t(g^t)$ be the multiplier associated with (4.5) in state g^t, the first-order conditions for this problem are (4.3), (4.5) and

$$\beta^tU_1(c_{1t}, c_{2t}, x_t)f^t(g^t \mid g_0) - \gamma p_t\int q_{t+1}\, dg_{t+1} - \rho_tp_t = 0, \tag{4.6}$$
$$\beta^tU_2(c_{1t}, c_{2t}, x_t)f^t(g^t \mid g_0) - \gamma p_t\int q_{t+1}\, dg_{t+1} = 0, \tag{4.7}$$

7. This is simply the 'Clower constraint' proposed in Clower (1967), but applied to a subset of consumption goods only. Notice that if the function V is defined by $V(c_{1t}, c_{1t} + c_{2t}, x_t) \equiv U(c_{1t}, c_{2t}, x_t)$, and if (4.5) is always binding, current period utility is given by $U(M_t/P_t, c_{2t}, x_t) = V(M_t/P_t, c_{1t} + c_{2t}, x_t)$. So defined, V is the current period utility function used by Sidrauski (1967a, b), and by Turnovsky and Brock (1980). Hence, the imposition of a Clower constraint is not an alternative to Sidrauski's way of formulating the demand for money, but in fact is closely related to it.

$$\beta^t U_x(c_{1t}, c_{2t}, x_t) f^t(g^t \mid g_0) - \gamma p_t \int q_{t+1}\, dg_{t+1}\,(1-\tau_t) = 0, \tag{4.8}$$

$$\gamma[\int q_{t+1}\, dg_{t+1} - q_t] + \rho_t = 0, \quad t = 0, 1, 2, \ldots, \text{all } g^t \tag{4.9}$$

assuming, as we will, that c_{1t}, c_{2t}, x_t, and M_t are all strictly positive.

From (4.9) we see that if $\int q_{t+1}\, dg_{t+1} - q_t < 0$, then $\rho_t > 0$, implying that (4.5) holds with equality. If $\int q_{t+1}\, dg_{t+1} - q_t = 0$, then $\rho_t = 0$. In this case M_t is indeterminate within the constraint imposed by (4.5) (the consumer is indifferent between holding securities and excess cash), and we will assume that (4.5) holds with equality. Bearing in mind that any equilibrium obtained under this hypothesis must satisfy (4.4), (4.3) and (4.5) can be combined to give

$$\begin{aligned} 0 = \int q_1 dg_{t+1} p_0 \left[(c_{20} - {}_0b_{20}) - (1-\tau_0)(1-x_0) \right] + p_0 \left[c_{10} - {}_0B_0/p_0 \right] \\ + \sum_{t=1}^{\infty} \int \Big(\int q_{t+1} dg_{t+1} p_t [(c_{2t} - {}_0b_{2t}) - (1-\tau_t)(1-x_t)] \\ + q_t p_t [c_{1t} - {}_0B_t/p_t] \Big) dg_1^t. \end{aligned} \tag{4.10}$$

Define ${}_0b_{1t} = {}_0B_t/p_t$ (so that ${}_0b_{1t}$ is dollar-denominated debt in 'real' terms). Then multiplying (4.10) through by γ and using (4.5)–(4.8) one obtains

$$\sum_{t=0}^{\infty} \beta^t \int [c_{1t} - {}_0b_{1t}, c_{2t} - {}_0b_{2t}, x_t - 1] \begin{bmatrix} U_1 \\ U_2 \\ U_x \end{bmatrix} dF^t(g^t \mid g_0) = 0. \tag{4.11}$$

Note that (4.11) and the analogous condition (2.16) for the two-good barter economy studied in section 2 are formally identical. It is exactly this parallel that earlier writers have exploited in attempting to analyze the 'inflation tax' through analogy with the theory of excise taxes in barter systems. In the absence of both outstanding debt and government expenditures, efficiency would be attained [cf. (4.6)–(4.8)] if both the labor income lax rate τ_t and the multiplier ρ_t associated with the liquidity constraint (4.5) were set identically equal to zero. From (4.9), the latter requires $\int q_{t+1}\, dg_{t+1} = q_t$, or a nominal interest rate identically zero, brought about by a deflation induced by continuous withdrawals of money from circulation. This is the conclusion Friedman (1969) reached, for the same reasons, but its implementation evidently depends critically on the availability of a non-distorting tax via which currency can be withdrawn.

If, as in Phelps (1973), Calvo (1978) or this paper, non-distorting taxes are assumed to be unavailable and if there are positive government obligations, then the formula (4.11) calls for taxing the two goods c_{1t} and c_{2t}, at rates that depend in Ramsey-like fashion on their relative demand elasticities. Here an income tax τ_t amounts to taxing both goods at the same rate, while an increase of the inflation tax from its 'optimum', zero-nominal-interest-rate level amounts to increasing the tax on cash goods, *relative to* credit goods. This leads to an important qualification to the analogy between (4.11) and (2.16): Since nominal interest rates cannot be negative in this monetary economy, cash goods can feasibly be taxed at a higher rate than credit goods but *not* at a lower one, whatever the relative demand elasticities may be. It leads as well to a substantial difference with Phelps's (1973) argument that 'liquidity' should be viewed as *additional* good, with a presumption that an efficient tax program involves a positive inflation tax. In our framework, 'liquidity' (currency balances) is not a good, but rather the *means* to the acquisition of a subset of ordinary consumption goods. If one wishes to tax this subset at a higher rate than goods generally, the inflation tax is a means for doing so, but a positive interest-elasticity of money demand is clearly not sufficient to make this case.

Whatever the usefulness of these parallels between barter and monetary economies, all share a serious weakness once the issue of time consistency is raised. In the barter economy, we took the government at time 0 to be inheriting sequences, $\{({}_0b_{1t}, {}_0b_{2t})\}_{t=0}^{\infty}$ of binding *real* debt obligations, and to be choosing current excise tax rates, $(\theta_{10}, \theta_{20})$, and a restructuring of the debt, $\{({}_1b_{1t}, {}_1b_{2t})\}_{t=1}^{\infty}$. In the monetary economy, the time 0 government inherits real debt obligations $\{{}_0b_{2t}\}$ and nominal debt obligations $\{{}_0B_t\}$; it chooses the current tax rate τ_0 and, via an open market operation, the money supply M_0 in circulation when time 0 goods trading begins. The fact that (4.11) and (2.16) are formally identical is thus misleading, since $\{{}_0b_{1t}\}$ in (2.16) is a binding obligation, while $\{{}_0b_{1t}\}$ in (4.11) is not. The ability to choose M_0 indirectly gives the time 0 government the ability to affect the initial price level p_0 and all future price levels as well. From (4.10), one can see how this power is optimally used.

If the net value of initial nominal assets is positive [at any given equilibrium pattern $\{q_t\}$ of interest factors], welfare is improved by *any* increase in M_0 and p_0, since any increase reduces the real value of these assets and reduces the need to resort to the distorting tax on labor income to redeem the debt. Hence the optimal price level is 'infinite'. If the net value of initial nominal assets is negative, the best monetary policy is the one that sets the value of these assets equal to the net value of all current and future government spending. In this way, *all* distorting taxation can be avoided. In the first situation, an optimal policy with commitment does not exist. In the second, an optimal policy exists and it is time-consistent (since fully efficient allocations always are so), but it is one based on circumstances bearing little resemblance to those faced by any actual government.

The remaining possibility, and the only one, we think, of potential practical interest, is the situation in which ${}_0B_t \equiv 0$, so that initially there are no outstanding nominal obligations of any kind. In this situation, the ability to manipulate nominal prices through open market operations offers no immediate possibilities for welfare gains. The setting of the initial price level is simply a matter of normalization. For this particular case, then, we will first look for an optimal policy with full commitment by the government at $t = 0$, specifying the tax rates, money supplies, and nominal and real debt issues needed to implement this policy, and the equilibrium prices and interest rates associated with it. With this done, we will try to determine the weakest possible commitments under which the optimal policy might be carried out in a time-consistent way.

An allocation $\{(c_{1t}, c_{2t}, x_t)\}$ satisfying (4.11) with ${}_0b_{1t} \equiv 0$ can be implemented by suitable choices of tax rates and money supplies $\{(\tau_t, M_t)\}$. From (4.7) and (4.8), the required taxes are

$$1 - \tau_t = U_x(c_t, x_t)/U_2(c_t, x_t), \quad t = 0, 1, 2, \ldots, \quad \text{all } g^t. \tag{4.12}$$

From (4.6), (4.7) and (4.9), the required nominal interest factors satisfy

$$\int q_{t+1}\, dg_{t+1} = q_t(U_2(c_t, x_t)/U_1(c_t, x_t)), \quad t = 0, 1, 2, \ldots, \quad \text{all } g^t. \tag{4.13}$$

From (4.4) and (4.6)

$$p_t q_t \gamma = \beta^t U_1(c_t, x_t) f^t(g_1^t \,|\, g_0)$$

so that with $q_0 \equiv 1$,

$$q_t(g^t) = \beta^t \frac{U_1(c_t, x_t) f^t(g_1^t \,|\, g_0)}{U_1(c_0, x_0)} \frac{p_0}{p_t}. \tag{4.14}$$

Thus given a contingent path for prices $\{p_t\}$, (4.14) determines nominal, state-contingent interest rates.

Use the notation $f_{t+1}(g_{t+1} \,|\, g_0^t)$ for the density of g_{t+1} conditional on the history g_0^t. Then $f^{t+1}(g_1^{t+1} \,|\, g_0) = f_{t+1}(g_{t+1} \,|\, g_0^t) f^t(g_1^t \,|\, g_0)$, so integrating (4.14) dated $t + 1$ with respect to g_{t+1} gives

$$\int q_{t+1}\, dg_{t+1} = \beta^{t+1} f^t(g_1^t \mid g_0)[p_0/U_1(c_0, x_0)] \times \int \frac{U_1(c_{t+1}, x_{t+1})}{p_{t+1}} f_{t+1}(g_{t+1} \mid g_0^t)\, dg_{t+1}.$$

Inserting the equation above and (4.14) into (4.13), we find that

$$\frac{U_2(c_t, x_t)}{p_t} = \beta \int \frac{U_1(c_{t+1}, x_{t+1})}{p_{t+1}} f_{t+1}(g_{t+1} \mid g_0^t)\, dg_{t+1}. \tag{4.15}$$

Now any allocation $\{(c_t, x_t)\}$ satisfying (4.11) may be implemented as follows. Tax rates $\{\tau_t\}$ are uniquely given in (4.12). There is much more latitude, however, in the choice of monetary policy. First, note that for any price path $\{p_t\}$ satisfying (4.15), $\{q_t\}$ as given in (4.14) satisfies (4.13). Given *any* such price path, it may be implemented by the associated monetary policy

$$M_t = p_1 c_{1t}.$$

Clearly, there are many such price paths and associated monetary policies, and all are feasible provided (4.4) is not violated. Since all are associated with the same resource allocation, all are equivalent from a welfare point of view.

Since the constraint (4.4) must also hold in equilibrium, (4.13) implies that in addition to satisfying (4.11), feasible allocations must also satisfy

$$U_2(c_t, x_t) - U_1(c_t, x_t) \le 0, \qquad t = 0, 1, 2, \ldots, \quad \text{all } g^t. \tag{4.16}$$

The optimal open-loop allocation for the monetary economy, then, is found by choosing $\{(c_{1t}, c_{2t}, x_t)\}$ to maximize (4.2) subject to (4.1), (4.11) and (4.16).

The first-order conditions for this problem, consolidated in such a way as to parallel condition (2.17) for the n-good barter system, are

$$(1 + \lambda_0)U' + \lambda_0 U'' \begin{bmatrix} c_t - {}_0b_t \\ x_t - 1 \end{bmatrix} - \mu_{0t} 1 - \nu_t \begin{bmatrix} U_{21} - U_{11} \\ U_{22} - U_{12} \\ U_{2x} - U_{1x} \end{bmatrix} = 0, \quad \text{and} \tag{4.17}$$

$$\nu_t(U_2 - U_1) = 0, \quad t = 0, 1, 2, \ldots, \quad \text{all } g^t, \tag{4.18}$$

where $\nu_t f_1^t \beta^t$ is the non-negative multiplier associated with the constraint (4.16), and λ_0 is the multiplier associated with (4.11). It (4.16) is never binding, so that $\nu_t = 0$ for all t, g^t, then (4.17) reduces to (2.17), and the case under consideration reduces exactly to the two-good barter system of section 2.

Let $\{(c_{1t}, c_{2t}, x_t)\}_{t=0}^{\infty}$ be a solution of (4.1), (4.11), and (4.16)–(4.18). Let $\{\tau_t\}_{t=0}^{\infty}$ be given by (4.12), let $\{p_t\}_{t=0}^{\infty}$ be any price path satisfying (4.15), let $\{q_t\}_{t=0}^{\infty}$ satisfy (4.14), and $\{M_t\}_{t=0}^{\infty}$ to be given by $M_t = p_t c_{1t}$. Under what conditions might this optimal policy be time-consistent?

It is clear from the debt-restructuring formulas of section 2 that, in general, the debt issues needed to enforce time-consistency in a two-good economy will involve claims to *both* of the two goods. In the present monetary interpretation of this two-good economy, issuing claims to cash goods, b_{1t}, can be done only through the issue of dollar-denominated assets B_t. Yet we have seen above that any dollar-denominated assets inherited by those governments will be inflated away by them if they are acting in a welfare-maximizing way. Anticipating this, no one would buy such debt at a positive price. There is, in short, no hope that an optimal policy will be time-consistent (will be a closed loop equilibrium policy) with fiscal and monetary policy both determined in an unrestricted, period-by-period way, except under special and uninteresting circumstances.

What is needed for time-consistency in the monetary economy is that nominal debt *always* represent a binding *real* commitment. Since $b_{1t} = B_t/p_t$, a nominal commitment B_t can be equivalent to a real commitment b_{1t} *only* if there is also a commitment to follow a specific price path p_t. Thus the following scenario is the closest imitation the monetary economy can provide to the optimal, time-consistent solution in the barter economy.

Let the initial government take office with no nominal assets in the hands of the public. Let it calculate the optimal (open loop) allocation, as above, along with the corresponding tax and monetary policies and associated prices, with initial money arbitrarily chosen. Let this government choose the initial tax rate τ_0, announce future taxes $\{\tau_t\}_{t=1}^{\infty}$, and *precommit* future monetary policy to enforce *some* price path satisfying (4.15). Finally, let this initial government restructure the initial real debt $\{{}_0b_{2t}\}_{t=0}^{\infty}$ into a new pattern $\{({}_1B_t, {}_1b_2)\}_{t=1}^{\infty}$, of nominal and real debt. Subsequent governments will have full control over future tax rates and over restructurings of debt of both kinds, but no ability to alter the original precommitment on future price level behavior.

Under this scenario, the time-consistency of the optimal policy (in the restricted sense of the paragraph above) follows as a corollary of the time-consistency proof of section 2. The government taking office at $t = 1$, in deciding whether to execute the tax policy announced by its predecessor at $t = 0$, is faced with a severely restricted set of available actions as compared to the government in section 2 (one tax rate to choose instead of two) but the optimal choice of section 2 is in the restricted set. Hence it will be chosen, and time-consistency follows.

Notice that this argument does not go through if the government precommits itself to a monetary path $\{M_t\}$ instead of a price path $\{p_t\}$. For a given money supply, one sees from the condition $M_t \doteq p_t c_{1t}$ that different consumption levels c_{1t} of cash goods will induce different price level behavior, and the income tax rate τ_t can clearly affect c_{1t}. Hence a monetary rule would leave open the possibility of using tax policies to alter the degree to which nominal debt commitments B_t are binding, a possibility that will clearly change the marginal conditions on which our proof of time-consistency in section 2 was based.

The mechanics by which a price precommitment of the sort used above would be carried out are exactly the same as in *any* monetary standard: the government announces (and backs up, if needed) its willingness to exchange any quantities of currency for goods at the state-contingent prices $\{p_t\}$. The amount of currency actually set into circulation is then fully 'demand determined'. In equilibrium, this announcement does not necessitate any government holdings of commodity 'stockpiles' (which is lucky, since we have assumed that all goods are perishable!).

5. Remarks on Scope and Applicability

By considering a closed system with identical consumers, we have abstracted from consideration of conflict between a 'creditor class' and a 'debtor class' a conflict on which historical discussion of national debt policy has been almost exclusively focused. We also denied ourselves the use of the 'small country' device of treating national debt by analogy with the theory of individual debt in a competitive world. We have, in short, restricted attention to situations in which the half-truth 'We only owe it to ourselves' becomes a whole-truth. These abstractions evidently exclude some issues of interest, but they clearly heighten the difficulty of the time-consistency problem. Thus our conclusions as to the necessity and efficacy of government debt obligations being binding in a real sense on successor governments have nothing to do either with maintaining a reputation that impresses outside creditors or with limiting the options open to 'bad' (in the sense of having different objectives from our own) future governments.

The exclusion of capital goods from the model is central, for reasons that are easy enough to see from section 4. In the model of that section, outstanding nominal assets should, from a welfare-maximizing point of view, be taxed away via an immediate inflation in a kind of 'capital levy'. This emerged as a new possibility when money was introduced in section 4 *only* because capital had been excluded from the barter analysis of section 2. Had the taxation of previously accumulated capital been an option in section 2, then it would optimally have been exercised and we would have needed to face this capital levy issue two sections earlier.

Clearly this limitation on the scope of our results is important, and it would be a total misreading of our paper to take its main lesson to be that the time-consistency problem is easy to solve in barter systems and hard only when money is introduced. We stepped around questions about capital not because they are minor or easy, but because they are difficult and basically different from the issues we wanted to address The main difficulty, as Chamley (1982) observes, is that direct capital levies can be imitated to perfection, under same circumstances by combinations of taxes and subsidies that look, superficially, like taxes on current and future decisions only, so that it is hard to devise simple ways to rule them out. However this question may ultimately be resolved, it seems to us different from the ones we have addressed, and it is likely that our main conclusions will be little altered by such a resolution. At present, this opinion is clearly conjecture only.

The assumption that government consumption is determined, perhaps stochastically, by 'nature' (and not by public choice) seems, for our purposes, innocuous. It may be that a deeper look at this issue will reveal a relationship between this assumption and our presumption that while a society can commit itself to an infinite sequence of contingent claim bond payments, it cannot commit itself to a sequence of tax rates, contingent on precisely the same events. Within our formalism, this distinction is inexplicable: the two forms of commitment are describable mathematically as elements of precisely the same space. Why should one represent a practical possibility, the other an impossibility? Yet the idea, that while a government may issue binding debts, the nature of the taxes needed to repay them should be a matter decided by the citizens subject to the tax at the time this decision is taken, is one that we accept almost without question in policy discussion. If a rationale for this presumption is found, it may well be connected to the public choice aspects of government consumption, or to the idea that if our successors are to be free to *choose* to do more or less through government than we anticipate we would do, given their circumstances, then they cannot very well be committed in advance to a pattern of taxes prescribed by us. It seems clear enough that the model utilized here is not well designed to make progress on this class of questions.

Finally, our emphasis on calculating *exact* welfare-maximizing policies may be misleading in a sense worth commenting on. Clearly, a policy or policy rule that is optimal in a theoretical model that is an approximation to reality, can only be approximately optimal applied in reality. This observation suggests that in practice one would probably seek price commitments or bond commitments that are simple and also serviceable approximations to optimal, and perhaps quite complicated, contingent claim commitments, as calculated above. The models we have used, particularly the quadratic examples of appendix A, are well suited to assessing the 'welfare costs' of arbitrary policies relative to optimal ones, and formulae for expected-utility differences of this type could be obtained. At the qualitative, illustrative level at which we are working, we did not find such formulae very revealing, and so did not inflict them on the reader, but with a quantitatively more serious model this line would be well worth developing. Certainly the idea of trying to write bond contracts or set monetary standards in a way that is optimal under *all possible* realizations of shocks would not (even if one knew what that meant) be of any practical interest.

6. Conclusions

This paper has been concerned with the structure and time-consistency of optimal tax policy in two multiperiod economies: a pure barter system and a monetary economy, both without capital goods. In each case, the government had to choose a method of financing an exogenous stochastic sequence of government expenditures. Current consumption goods and a complete set of contingent claim securities were assumed to be traded in each period.

In section 2, we showed that the optimal tax policy is time-consistent, provided that fully binding debt of a sufficiently rich maturity and risk structure can be issued, and that the optimal debt policy is unique. A single debt instrument, a kind of contingent-claim consol, was shown to be the only form of debt needed to enforce time-consistency. In section 3, the optimal tax policy was characterized under a variety of assumptions about the behavior of government consumption. From the examples with stochastic government demand, it was clear that the option to issue state-contingent government debt is important: tax policies that are optimal under uncertainty have an essential 'insurance' aspect to them.

In section 4 money, in the form of currency, was introduced via a transactions demand, along with nominally-denominated debt. The analogy between the monetary economy and a two-good barter system permitted us to apply the analysis of section 2. Our conclusion paralleled familiar results on the 'optimal inflation tax' or 'optimal quantity of money'. However, the analogy with the barter system broke down when time-consistency was considered. The ability to use discretionary monetary policy to levy an 'inflation tax' cannot be disciplined by binding debt issues in the way that ordinary excise taxation can be. Time-consistency can be achieved only if monetary policy is pre-set to maintain a specified path of nominal prices. Somewhat surprisingly, this same effect cannot be achieved through a pre-set path for the quantity of money, since the interaction of fiscal and monetary policy permits tax policies to alter the effects on prices of any given monetary policy.

In a general way, our findings serve to reinforce Kydland and Prescott's (1977) arguments to the effect that some form of institutional commitment is essential for the implementation of fiscal and monetary policies that have desirable effects under the usual welfare-economic criteria. We have tried to make some progress on what seems to us the central task of discovering exactly which forms of commitment are sufficient and what functions they serve.

Appendix A

This appendix describes the calculation of the optimal fiscal policy for the one good model studied in sections 2 and 3, for the case of a quadratic utility function $U(c, x)$. We provide necessary and sufficient conditions for the existence of a unique optimal policy for this case, and give exact formulae for some of the relationships alluded to in the text.

Let $(\bar{c}, \bar{x})$ maximize $U(c, x)$, subject to $c + x \leq 1$, and let δ denote the common value of $U_c(\bar{c}, \bar{x})$ and $U_x(\bar{c}, \bar{x})$. Expanding the marginal utilities of consumption and leisure about $(\bar{c}, \bar{x})$ and using (2.1) to eliminate x, we have

$$U_c(c, x) = \delta + (U_{cc} - U_{cx})(c - \bar{c}) - U_{cx} g, \tag{A.1}$$

$$U_x(c, x) = \delta + (U_{cx} - U_{xx})(c - \bar{c}) - U_{xx} g. \tag{A.2}$$

In this quadratic case, the derivatives U_{cc}, U_{cx} and U_{xx} are constant and (A.1) and (A.2) are exact. We proceed with the construction of an optimal allocation, as sketched in section 2.

For notational convenience, define

$$\Delta = -[U_{cc} - 2U_{cx} + U_{xx}], \quad \text{and} \tag{A.3}$$

$$\nu = -\Delta^{-1}(U_{xx} - U_{cx}). \tag{A.4}$$

Since U is concave, $\Delta > 0$, and since both goods are normal (non-inferior) $0 < \nu < 1$. Note that ν is the derivative of leisure demand with respect to income y in the problem: maximize $U(c, x)$, subject to $c + x \leq y$, and $1 - \nu$ is the derivative of goods demand. In this notation the solution c_t to the first order conditions (2.1) and (2.9) is given explicitly by

$$c_t = \frac{1 + \lambda}{1 + 2\lambda}\bar{c} - \nu g_t + \frac{\lambda}{1 + 2\lambda}(1 - \nu)_0 b_t \tag{A.5}$$

(where the subscript on λ_0 has been dropped). This is the only solution, and it is a local maximum. It is convenient to let $\mu \equiv (1 + 2\lambda)^{-1}\lambda$, so that (A.5) reads

$$c_t = (1 - \mu)\bar{c} - \nu g_t + \mu(1 - \nu)_0 b_t. \tag{A.6}$$

Then the constraint (2.8) reads

$$\sum_{t=0}^{\infty} \beta^t E\{\mu(1 - \mu)\Delta[\bar{c} - (1 - \nu)_0 b_t]^2 - \delta({}_0 b_t + g_t) - \alpha g_t({}_0 b_t + g_t)\} = 0, \tag{A.7}$$

where $E\{\ \}$ denotes an expected value taken with respect to F, given g_0 and α is defined by

$$\alpha = \Delta^{-1}(U_{xx}U_{cc} - U_{cx}^2), \tag{A.8}$$

which is positive for a risk-averse consumer. Then solving (A.7) for μ gives

$$\mu(1-\mu) = \left[\Delta \sum_{t=0}^{\infty} \beta^t E\{[\bar{c} - (1-\nu)_0 b_t]^2\}\right]^{-!} \cdot \sum_{t=0}^{\infty} \beta^t E\{\delta({}_0b_t + g_t) + \alpha g_t({}_0b_t + g_t)\}. \tag{A.9}$$

Provided $g_t \geq 0$ and ${}_0b_t < \bar{c}/(1-\nu)$, the right-hand side of (A.9) is non-negative. It is also increasing in each term of ${}_0b_t$ and g_t. If the right-hand side of (A.9) exceeds 1/4, no real value of μ satisfies (A.9). This is what was meant in section 2 by the looser statement that no optimal policy will exist if ${}_0b$ and g are 'too large'. If, as assumed here, this expression is less than 1/4, (A.9) has two solutions for μ, one in the interval $(-\infty, \frac{1}{2})$, the other in $(\frac{1}{2}, 1)$. The smaller of these two roots corresponds to the welfare-maximizing solution of interest to us. Notice that if ${}_0b_t$ is sufficiently negative, $\mu < 0$ is possible. Thus, the questions of the existence and uniqueness of an optimal allocation are easily resolved in this specific case.

With $\mu \in (0, \frac{1}{2})$, both μ and $1-\mu$ are positive. Thus from (A.6), under an optimal fiscal policy c_t declines as g_t increases, but less than one-for-one unless the income elasticity of leisure demand is zero ($\nu = 0$); c_t increases with debt obligations b_t, unless the income elasticity of consumption demand is zero ($\nu = 1$). When the government budget constraint (A.9) is not binding, $\mu = 0$ and $c_t = \bar{c}$.

In Examples 4–8 of section 3, initial debt commitments ${}_0b$ were taken to be zero. Under this circumstance, in this quadratic case, the bond coupon formula (3.4) becomes

$${}_tb_s = \left(1 - \frac{\lambda_0}{\lambda_t}\right)\frac{\bar{c}}{1-\nu}. \tag{A.10}$$

Since the right-hand side of (A. 10) does not vary with s, only consols are ever issued The formula (A.9) for μ reduces to

$$\mu(1-\mu) = (1-\beta)(\Delta\bar{c}^2)^{-1} \sum_{t=0}^{\infty} \beta^t E\{\delta g_t + \alpha g_t^2\} \tag{A.11}$$

and the optimum consumption formula (A.6) becomes simply

$$c_t = (1-\mu)\bar{c} - \nu g_t. \tag{A.12}$$

It is instructive to apply (A.10)–(A.12) to Examples 4–8, but this exercise is left to the interested reader.

Appendix B

For a broad class of optimal policy problems, if an optimal policy with commitment is time-consistent (as defined in section 2), then that policy corresponds to a set of subgame perfect Nash equilibrium strategies for an appropriately specified game.

A typical policy game can be specified as follows. The set of players is 0, 1, 2, . . . , where player t is the policy-maker in period t. Let Y_t denote the set of possible states of the system in period t, and assume that player t observes (at least) the state $y_t \in Y_t$. Let $A_t(y_t)$, denote the set of actions available to player t if the state is y_t. A strategy for player t is a function σ_t such that $\sigma_t(y_t) \in A_t(y_t)$, all $y_t \in Y_t$. Let S_t denote the set of all such functions, and let S_t be the strategy space for player t. (Mixed strategies could readily be incorporated without altering the rest of the argument.) Define $\sigma_t^\infty \equiv (\sigma_t, \sigma_{t+1}, \ldots)$, and $S_t^\infty \equiv (S_t, S_{t+1}, \ldots)$, all t.

The law of motion for the system is as follows. Let $M_{t+1}(B|(y_t, a_t))$, for all $B \subseteq Y_{t+1}$, all $y_t \in Y_t$, all $a_t \in A_t(y_t)$, be the conditional probability that the state in period $t + 1$ is in the subset B of Y_{t+1}, i.e., that $y_{t+1} \in B \subseteq Y_{t+1}$, given that the state in period t is y_t, and the (feasible) action $a_t \in A_t(y_t)$ was taken.

Next, we must specify a payoff function for each of the players. The payoff for player t will depend only on the current state, y_t, his own strategy σ_t [which specifies his action $\sigma_t(y_t)$], and the strategies of his successors, σ_{t+1}^∞, (which specify, together with the law of motion, a joint probability distribution over future states and actions). Let $\pi_t(\sigma_t^\infty, y_t)$ denote player t's payoff function.

Then under the definition in section 2, a set of strategies (policy) σ_0^∞ is *time consistent* if

$$\pi_t(\sigma_t^\infty, y_t) \geq \pi_t(\hat{\sigma}_t^\infty, y_t), \qquad \text{for all } \hat{\sigma}_t^\infty \in S_t^\infty, \ y_t \in Y_t, \ t \in T,$$

while a set of strategies σ_0^∞ is a *subgame perfect Nash equilibrium* if

$$\pi_t(\sigma_t^\infty, y_t) \geq \pi_t(\hat{\sigma}_t, \sigma_{t+1}^\infty, y_t), \quad \text{for all } \hat{\sigma}_t \in S_t, \ y_t \in Y_t, \ t \in T.$$

Clearly the former condition implies the latter.

For the game in section 2, the state in period t is described by the outstanding debt and the sequence of government consumption to date, $y_t = ({}_tb, g^t)$; the actions available to player t are the choice of a tax rate and debt restructuring, $a_t = (\tau_t, {}_{t+1}b)$; a strategy σ_t for player t maps states $({}_tb, g^t)$ into current policy $(\tau_t, {}_{t+1}b)$; the law of motion is

$$M_{t+1}\left((B_b, B_g) \mid ({}_tb, g^t), (\tau_t, {}_{t+1}b)\right) = \int_{B_g} dF^{t+1}(g^{t+1} \mid g^t) \quad \text{if} \quad {}_{t+1}b \in B_b,$$
$$= 0, \quad \text{otherwise},$$

where $({}_{t+1}b, g^{t+1}) \in (B_b, B_g)$; and the payoff function for player t is

$$\pi_t\left(\sigma_t^\infty, ({}_tb, g^t)\right) = E\left[\sum_{s=t}^{\infty} \beta^{s-t} U(c_s, x_s)\right],$$

where $\{(c_s, x_s)\}_{s=t}^{\infty}$ is the (perfect foresight) equilibrium allocation resulting from the initial state $({}_tb, g^t)$, when the governments in periods $t, t+1, \ldots,$ choose policies according to $\sigma_t, \sigma_{t+1}, \ldots.$

References

Bailey, M.J., 1956, The welfare cost of inflationary finance, Journal of Political Economy 64, 93–110.

Barro, Robert J., 1979, On the determination of the public debt, Journal of Political Economy 87, 940–971.

Calvo, Guillermo A., 1978, On the time consistency of optimal policy in a monetary economy, Econometrica 46, 1411–1428.

Chamley, Christophe, 1982, On optimal taxation in stylized models of intertemporal general equilibrium, Yale University working paper.

Clower, Robert W., 1967, A reconsideration of the microfoundations of monetary theory, Western Economic Journal 6, 1–9.

Friedman, Milton, 1969, The optimum quantity of money, in: The optimum quantity of money and other essays (Aldine Press, Chicago, IL).

Gordon, David, B., 1980, Dynamic equilibria with purposive policy making, University of Chicago working paper.

Hamilton, Alexander, 1795, Second report on the public credit, January 16 and 21, 1795, in: Samuel McKee, ed., Alexander Hamilton's Papers on Public Credit, Commerce and Finance, 1957b (The Liberal Arts Press, New York).

Kydland, Finn E. and Edward C. Prescott, 1977, Rules rather than discretion: The inconsistency of optimal plans, Journal of Political Economy 85, 473–493.

Kydland, Finn E. and Edward C. Prescott, 1980, A competitive theory of fluctuations and the feasibility and desirability of stabilization policy, in: Stanley Fischer, ed., Rational expectations and economic policy (University of Chicago Press, Chicago, IL).

Lucas, Robert E., Jr., 1980, Equilibrium in a pure currency economy, Economic Inquiry 18, 203–220.

Mirrlees, J. A., 1971, An exploration in the theory of optimal income taxation, Review of Economic Studies 38, 175–208.

Phelps, Edmund S., 1973, Inflation in the theory of public finance, Swedish Journal of Economics 75, 67–82.

Pigou, A. C., 1947, A study in public finance, third edition (Macmillan, London).

Prescott, Edward C., 1982, Money as a means of payment, University of Minnesota working paper.

Ramsey, F. P., 1927, A contribution of the theory of taxation, Economic Journal 37, 47–61.

Sidrauski, Miguel, 1967a, Inflation and economic growth, Journal of Political Economy 75, 796–810.

Sidrauski, Miguel, 1967b, Rational choice and patterns of growth in a monetary economy, American Economic Review 57, 534–544.

Strotz, Robert H., 1955–1956, Myopia and inconsistency in dynamic utility maximization, Review of Economic Studies 23, 165–180.

Turnovsky, Stephen J. and William A. Brock, 1980, Time consistency and optimal government policies in perfect foresight equilibrium, Journal of Public Economics 13, 183–212.

— 8 —

Money in a Theory of Finance

I. Introduction

The title of this essay is taken, of course, from the Gurley/Shaw (1960) monograph to remind the reader at the outset that the objective of constructing a unified theory of money and finance is an old one, one that has challenged theorists at least since J. R. Hicks's (1935) "Suggestion." That the attainment of this objective is still regarded as part of an agenda for future research suggests that there must be something difficult about the problem that earlier writers either did not see or did not adequately face. This paper is an attempt to identify this difficulty and to offer one way of dealing with it.*

If it is easier today than it was in 1960 to identify exactly in which respects the theory of finance fails as monetary theory, this is largely due to rapid recent progress in the theory of finance. Theoretical research in finance is now conducted almost entirely within the contingent-claim general equilibrium framework introduced by Arrow (1964) and Debreu (1959). This is not an historical statement, for each of the three pillars of modern financial theory—portfolio theory, the Modigliani-Miller Theorem, and the theory of efficient markets—was discovered within different (and mutually distinct) theoretical frameworks, but all three have since been reformulated in contingent-claim terms, and it was this reformula-

Carnegie-Rochester Conference Series on Public Policy 21, no. 1 (January 1984): 9–46.

*I am grateful to Nancy Stokey for criticism of an earlier draft and for comments by Arthur Kupferman, Allan Meltzer, Bennett McCallum, and Manuel Sanchez.

tion that revealed their essential unity and set the stage for many further theoretical advances.

This paper begins in Section II with a review of a simple version of the Fisherian model of real capital theory in contingent-claim terms and a review of the relationship of this model to various aspects of financial economics. A central feature of this model is that *all* trading occurs in a centralized market, with all agents present. In such a setting, the position of each agent is fully described by a single number: his wealth, or the market value of all the claims he owns. The command any one claim has over goods is fully described by its market value, which is to say all claims are equally "liquid."

If the point of a theory of money, or of "liquidity preference," is to capture the fact that, in some situations in reality, money has a relative command over other goods *in excess of* its relative value in centralized securities trading, then a successful theoretical model must place agents in such situations, at least some of the time. How, as a matter of modeling strategy, might this best be done?

I do not believe we have enough experience with alternative formulations to answer this question now, but the monetary model introduced in Section III employs a device used in Lucas (1982), Townsend (1982), and Lucas and Stokey (1983), in which agents alternate between two different kinds of market situations. Each period, they all attend a securities market in which money and other securities are exchanged. Subsequent to securities trading, agents trade in (implicitly) decentralized goods markets in which the purchase of at least some goods is assumed subject to the cash-in-advance constraint of the form suggested by Clower (1967).

The assumption of this model that agents regularly, if not continuously, trade in a centralized securities market admits a theory of securities pricing that is close to the standard barter theory reviewed in Section II. Yet interesting and fully operational modifications are required for a monetary system, so that pricing formulas differ in important ways from the barter versions that have been subjected to much recent empirical testing. These are reviewed in Section IV.

Section V turns to the question, central to the objectives of monetary theory though traditionally peripheral to the theory of finance, of methods for constructing monetary equilibria under alternative fiscal and monetary regimes. Here a simplified version of the model of Section III is studied to the point where one can begin to see what a full analysis would involve, and various simple examples are fully "solved." Section VI contains concluding comments.

II. The Theory of Finance

The theory of finance, as the term is now generally understood, consists of various specializations and applications of the Arrow-Debreu contingent-claim formulation of a competitive equilibrium for an economy operating through time, subject to stochastic shocks. As background for summarizing several of the main results in the theory of finance, and also for considering how this theory might be extended to include monetary elements, it will be useful to state a highly simplified version.

We consider an economy subject to exogenously given stochastic shocks, $\{s_t\}$, where the realization of the vector s_t is public knowledge prior to any consumption or production activity in t and where the joint density f^t of $(s_1, \ldots, s_t)$ is known to all agents. Use $s^t = (s_1, \ldots, s_t)$ to denote the full history of shocks up to and including time t. A commodity or good in this setting is idealized as a function $c_t(s^t)$, the value of which denotes the quantity of the good to be exchanged (or consumed or produced) at date t contingent on the occurrence of the history s^t. I will confine attention here to two consumption goods: a nonstorable, produced good, c_t, and leisure, x_t. The sequence $\{c_t, x_t\}$ of pairs of functions $c_t(s^t)$, $x_t(s^t)$, each defined over all possible histories s^t, provides a catalogue of an individual consumer's consumption for all dates, under all possible circumstances.[1]

Consumers will be taken to maximize expected utility:

$$\sum_{t=0}^{\infty} \beta^t \int U(c_t(s^t), x_t(s^t)) f^t(s^t) ds^t .$$

The shorthand

$$\sum_{t=0}^{\infty} \beta^t \int U(c_t, x_t) f^t ds^t . \tag{2.1}$$

1. Here and below I am simply setting out a notation useful for discussing technically—elementary aspects of various models. If a mathematically-rigorous exposition were to be provided, it would be necessary to specify the commodity space and functions defined in more detail, and phases like "defined over all possible histories" would need elaboration or replacement.

is taken to mean the same thing and will be used repeatedly below. Firms are assumed to have a technology:

$$c_t + g_t + k_{t+1} = F(k_t, 1 - x_t, s_t) \tag{2.2}$$

describing the combinations of private consumption goods c_t, government consumption goods g_t, and end-of-period capital stocks k_{t+1} that can be produced when beginning-of-period capital stocks are k_t, labor is $1 - x_t$, and the shock history is s^t. At this formal level one could consider many different consumers and firms, but it will economize on subscripts to consider one ("representing" many) of each.

Questions of government finance of the expenditure stream $\{g_t\}$ will be kept simple, here and throughout the paper, by assuming that government has the ability to levy distortion-free, lump-sum taxes on consumers.[2] Let $\theta_t(s^t)$ denote contingent tax obligations of consumers at t. To admit the possibility of deficit finance, let B_0 denote initial, goods-denominated debt obligations owed consumers by government.

To describe the trading possibilities open to these agents, and hence to formulate a definition of equilibrium, it is useful to keep in mind two quite different, but highly complementary scenarios, one of which is standard in general equilibrium theory and the other of which is closer to the traditions of financial and monetary theory. In the first, Arrow-Debreu, scenario, all agents are taken to convene at time 0, knowing s_0 and the distributions $f^1, f^2, \ldots$ of future shocks, to trade in a complete range of sequences $\{c_t, x_t\}$ of contingent claims on goods. In this trading the price $\pi_t(s^t)$ of the contingent consumption claim $c_t(s^t)$ and the price $-\pi_{xt}(s^t)$ of a contingent claim on leisure $x_t(s^t)$ are both dated functions of the shock history s^t, so that, for example, the value of the claim $c_t(s^t)$ is the product $\pi_t(s^t)c_t(s^t)$ and the present value of an entire sequence $\{c_t\}$ is[3]

$$\sum_{t=0}^{\infty} \int \pi_t(s^t)c_t(s^t)ds^t$$

Here prices are quoted in an abstract unit-of-account, so a normalization like $\pi_0 = 1$ is permitted.

2. See Lucas and Stokey (1983) for a normative analysis, in a context similar to this one, of government finance when all taxes distort.

3. Here and below, the normalization $\int ds^t = 1$, all t, is assumed.

In this setting, firms choose $\{c_t + g_t, 1 - x_t, k_{t+1}\}$, given k_0 and $\{\pi_t, \pi_{xt}\}$, to maximize

$$\sum_{t=0}^{\infty} \int [\pi_t(s^t)(c_t(s^t) + g_t(s^t)) - \pi_{xt}(s^t)(1 - x_t(s^t))]\, ds^t, \tag{2.3}$$

subject to (2.2) for all t, s^t. Call the value of this maximized objective function π. Consumers are endowed with one unit of labor-leisure per period, they are liable for taxes, they own the firms, and they hold the outstanding government debt, so their budget constraint is:

$$\begin{aligned}\sum_{t=0}^{\infty} \int [\pi_t(s^t)(c_t(s^t) + \theta_t(s^t)) \\ - \pi_{xt}(s^t)(1 - x_t(s^t))]\, ds^t \leq \Pi + \pi_0 B_0\end{aligned} \tag{2.4}$$

Consumers choose $\{c_t, x_t\}$, given $\{\pi_t, \pi_{xt}\}$, $\{\theta_t\}$, Π, and B_0, to maximize (2.1) subject to (2.4).

This scenario, in which all equilibrium quantities and prices are set at time 0, conflicts (though very superficially) with the observation that in reality trading goes on all the time, concurrent with consumption and production of goods rather than prior to these activities. It also presupposes, though I believe this observation is equally superficial, a "large" number of traded securities. The next, alternative, scenario deals with the first observation or objection fully, sheds some light on the second, and in general permits a reinterpretation of a contingent-claim equilibrium of the sort sketched above that is much closer to traditional capital and monetary theory.

First, imagine that all agents meet at the beginning of *every* period t, trading in contingent claims of exactly the same character as those traded in the Arrow-Debreu, time 0 market. Then, utilizing a notational complication that will shortly be dropped, let $\pi_{0t}(s_0, {}_0s^t)$ denote the original prices ($\pi_t(s^t)$ above) and, in general, use $\pi_{t,\tau}(s^t, {}_ts^\tau)$ to denote the price established at the time-t-market, if s^t has occurred up to that date, for goods dated τ contingent on the history ${}_ts^\tau$ from $t + 1$ through τ. Then these markets at $t > 0$ are simply redundant, for arbitrage will enforce

$$\pi_{0,\tau}(s_0, {}_0s^\tau) = \pi_{0,t}(s_0, {}_0s^\tau)\, \pi_{t,\tau}(s^t, {}_ts^\tau) \tag{2.5}$$

over all dates and histories, and future trading will simply reconfirm trades agreed to at $t = 0$.

In this "sequence economy" reinterpretation of an Arrow-Debreu economy, one is free, without affecting the analysis of equilibria, to think of prices like $\pi_{t,\tau}(s^t, {}_ts^\tau)$, $\tau > t$ not as being *set* at time 0 but rather as being correctly or rationally *expected* (as of $t = 0$) to be set in the time-t market should the history s^t be realized. That is, one thinks of certain prices as being formally established at each date, in light of rational expectations as to how certain other prices will be set later. This reinterpretation evidently permits one to economize drastically on the variety of securities assumed to be traded at any one date. Special assumptions on preferences, technology, and shocks often permit still further economies, as will be seen below. In what follows, the formalism of the timeless Arrow-Debreu scenario will be used to generate equilibrium conditions, but it will be useful to keep this alternative-sequence interpretation in mind and, where possible, to think of these equilibrium conditions as describing the evolution of a competitive system with rational expectations.

The first-order conditions for the consumer's problem: maximize (2.1) subject to (2.4) include:

$$0 = \beta^t U_c(c_t, x_t) f^t - \lambda \pi_t, \text{ all } t, s^t, \tag{2.6}$$

$$0 = \beta^t U_x(c_t, x_t) f^t - \lambda \pi_{xt}, \text{ all } t, s^t \tag{2.7}$$

where the number λ is the multiplier associated with (2.4).

The first-order conditions for the firm's problem: maximize (2.3) subject to (2.2) include:

$$0 = \pi_t - \mu_t, \text{ all } t, s^t, \tag{2.8}$$

$$0 = \pi_{xt} - \mu_t F_x(k_t, 1 - x_t, s^t), \text{ all } t, s^t \tag{2.9}$$

and

$$0 = \int \mu_t F_k(k_t, 1 - x_t, s^t) ds_t - \mu_{t-1}, \tag{2.10}$$
$$\text{all } t \geq 1, s^{t-1},$$

where the functions $\mu_t = \mu_t(s^t)$ are the multipliers associated with the constraints (2.2). In addition, under suitable restrictions, certain boundary or transversality conditions "at infinity" are also necessary.

Equations (2.2) and (2.6)–(2.10) together with boundary conditions implicitly define the set of stochastic processes for quantities and prices that are equilibria for this economy. Eliminating multipliers from (2.6) and (2.7), equilibrium prices are given by:

$$\frac{\pi_{xt}}{\pi_t} = \frac{U_x(c_t, x_t)}{U_c(c_t, x_t)} \tag{2.11}$$

and

$$\frac{\pi_t}{\pi_0} = \beta^t \frac{U_c(c_t, x_t)}{U_c(c_0, x_0)} f^t. \tag{2.12}$$

Eliminating prices as well from (2.6)–(2.10), equilibrium quantities must satisfy:

$$\frac{U_x(c_t, x_t)}{U_c(c_t, x_t)} = F_x(k_t, 1 - x_t, s^t), \tag{2.13}$$

$$U_c(c_{t-1}, x_{t-1}) = \beta \int U_c(c_t, x_t) F_k(k_t, 1 - x_t, s^t) f_{t-1}^t ds_t, \tag{2.14}$$

where $f_{t-1}^t \equiv f^t / f^{t-1}$ is the density of s_t conditional on s^{t-1}. The marginal interpretations of (2.13)–(2.14) and their connections (2.11)–(2.12) to prices are familiar.

Equations (2.13) and (2.14) together with the technology (2.2) and suitable boundary conditions can sometimes be used to construct the equilibrium resource allocation $\{c_t, x_t, k_{t+1}\}_{t=0}^{\infty}$, given the shocks $\{s_t\}_{t=0}^{\infty}$: they are the "stochastic Euler equations" of the system. See Brock (1982) for a useful illustration together with an exposition of their intimate connection to the Capital Asset Pricing Model of the theory of finance. Much of the existing theory of finance is a collection of observations based on these conditions or on more basic properties of the model from which they are obtained. In reviewing the main elements of this theory, in the remainder of this section, it will be convenient to divide these observations into three categories.

One important category of results consists of the various "equivalence theorems" that rest on the linearity of equilibrium price systems and the nature of consumers' budget sets. Thus, the value Π of (2.3) is the equilibrium value of a claim to the entire net receipts stream, $R = \{R_t(s^t)\}$, say, of the firm. Should the firm market this stream in the form of n claims to the receipts streams $R_1, \ldots, R_n$, with $\Sigma_i R_i = R$, each with value (at equilibrium prices) $\Pi_1 \ldots \Pi_n$, it is evident that $\Sigma_i \Pi_i = \Pi$. The proof is simply an observation on the consumer's budget constraint (2.4): if consumers can choose whether the right-hand side of (2.4) is Π or $\Sigma_i \Pi_i$, and if they are indifferent between these choices, these values must be the same. This is Hirshleifer's (1966) proof of the justly-celebrated Modigliani-Miller (1958) Theorem. The fact that the component receipts streams R_i can be arbitrary sequences of contingent claims gives the arbitrage reasoning underlying the Modigliani-Miller Theorem a power, in applications, that may not be apparent, given the simplicity of its proof.

The "Ricardian equivalence theorem" of government finance is another application of the same reasoning.[4] The budget constraint facing the government can be derived from the consumer's constraint (2.4) and the definition (2.3) of the firm's value Π. It is:

$$\pi_0 B_0 = \sum_{t=0}^{\infty} \int \pi_t (g_t - \theta_t) ds^t \tag{2.15}$$

Clearly, for given g_t, any two debt-tax patterns B_0, $\{\theta_t\}$ and B_0', $\{\theta_t'\}$ that satisfy (2.15) will imply the same budget sets for consumers, hence be consistent with the same equilibrium prices and quantities, and hence be "equivalent" economically.

The government budget constraint more frequently appears in the literature in a "flow" form that can be derived from the "stock" form (2.15) as follows. Let the time 0 deficit $\pi_0(g_0 - \theta_0)$ plus retirement of outstanding debt $\pi_0 B_0$ be financed by the issue of new, contingent one-period debt $B_1(s_1)$. Then, for all realizations of s_1

$$\pi_1 B_1 = \sum_{t=1}^{\infty} \int \pi_t (g_t - \theta_t) d({}_1 s^t). \tag{2.16}$$

must hold, analogously to (2.15). Integrating (2.16) with respect to s_1 and subtracting from (2.15) gives:

$$\pi_0(g_0 - \theta_0) + \pi_0 B_0 - \int \pi_1 B_1 ds_1 = 0, \tag{2.17}$$

4. See Barro (1979) for references as well as for a proof that does not rely on the infinitely-lived household device used here.

which states that a current account deficit must be offset by net issues of new debt. The "flow constraint" (2.17) appears more frequently in the literature than does the "stock constraint" (2.15), but it should be clear that the latter is more fundamental and contains more information than does (2.17): a boundary condition is "lost" when (2.15) is differenced.

Notice that these equivalence results do not depend in any detailed way on the nature of technology or consumer preferences. They are simply consequences of the hypothesis that the system is in competitive equilibrium. A second category of results involves the manipulation of the first-order conditions (2.6)–(2.10), similarly taking the existence of equilibrium prices and quantities for granted but involving the technology and/or preferences in an essential way.

Let $\{z_t\}_{t=0}^{\infty}$ be an *arbitrary* sequence contingent-goods claims, and consider the problem of pricing the remaining terms $\{z_\tau\}_{\tau=t}^{\infty}$ in terms of goods at time t. In terms of the sequence economy prices $\pi_{t\tau}$ defined above, this price, $Q_t(z)$ say, is

$$Q_t(z) = \sum_{\tau=t}^{\infty} \int \pi_{t\tau} z_\tau d({}_t s^\tau). \tag{2.18}$$

The time-0 prices π_t are given by (2.12). Similarly, using the normalization on sequence economy prices $\pi_{tt} = 1$, (2.6) implies:

$$\pi_{t\tau} = \beta^{\tau-t} \frac{U_c(c_\tau, x_\tau) f^\tau}{U_c(c_t, x_t) f^t}, \quad \text{all } t,\ \tau \geq t,\ s^\tau . \tag{2.19}$$

Since f^τ / f^t is the density of ${}_t s^\tau$ conditional on s^t, integrating with respect to this density involves applying the operator $E_t(\cdot)$. Therefore, inserting the prices (2.19) into (2.18) gives the pricing formula:

$$Q_t(z) = z_t + \sum_{\tau=t+1}^{\infty} \beta^{\tau-t} E_t \left[\frac{U_c(c_\tau, x_t)}{U_c(c_t, x_t)} z_\tau \right]. \tag{2.20}$$

The formula (2.20) implies, in turn,

$$U_c(c_t, x_t)(Q_t(z) - z_t) = \beta E_t[U_c(c_{t+1}, x_{t+1}) Q_{t+1}(z)] . \tag{2.21}$$

If marginal utility U_c is roughly constant, either because utility is linear or because consumption does not vary much, if the discount factor β is near one, as would be the case if the time unit is short, and if no "dividend" z_t is paid in t, (2.21) reduces to

$$Q_t = E_t(Q_{t+1}). \tag{2.22}$$

This is the famous Martingale property of securities prices that formed the basis for the early tests of "market efficiency."[5] Since the operator $E_t(\cdot)$ is conditional on *all* components of the shock history s^t, a vast variety of specific predictions is implicit in (2.22), so these efficiency tests introduced a degree of empirical stringency without precedent in economic research. Perhaps of even more lasting importance, they introduced a class of statistical tests in which stochastic elements were intrinsic to the economic reasoning underlying the hypothesis, as opposed to being added as an afterthought to a relationship motivated by deterministic theoretical arguments.

More recently it has been recognized that these two virtues do not depend crucially on the accuracy of the narrow conditions under which (2.22) follows from (2.21). Dividends can be measured, whether zero or not, the discount factor can be assigned any value or treated as a parameter to be estimated, and the utility function can be parameterized and its arguments measured from observed time series. Hence, (2.21) as it stands is a statistical hypothesis or can easily be made into one, with implications not appreciably weaker than the original efficiency hypothesis (2.22). A number of studies have pursued this idea in a variety of econometrically sophisticated ways.[6]

It should perhaps be emphasized that the hypothesis (2.22) is merely an example of a variety of conceptually similar hypotheses. The return stream $\{z_t\}$ is arbitrary and can be matched to observed streams in many ways. There are many possible specifications of the set on which $E_t(\cdot)$ is conditioned. Moreover, with many consumers, (2.22) must hold separately for all. Finally, similar tests could as well be based on the firm's first-order conditions (2.10), for each firm separately, and for each type of capital good.

5. See Fama (1970) for a valuable, early survey of a literature that begins with Fama (1965).

6. See, for example, Hall (1978), Grossman and Shiller (1981), and Hansen and Singleton (1983). With the exception of Hall's original paper, the tests reported in these papers, as in Mehra and Prescott (1983), strongly reject the implications of their particular versions of the one-consumer, barter model reviewed in this section.

Neither the equivalence theorems based on the linearity of price systems nor the efficiency tests based on marginal conditions require solving the model for the behavior of economically-determined variables, given the behavior of shocks of various kinds or even the verification that such solutions exist. They are simply implications that follow from the hypothesis that the model (which in practice is typically not even fully specified) has an equilibrium, and they follow from vacuous systems as easily as from internally-consistent ones. A third category of results, perhaps of less interest from the point of view of the theory of finance but obviously of essential importance to monetary theories designed to evaluate the consequences of alternative policies, consists of methods for verifying the existence of, constructing, and characterizing solutions.

Bewley (1972) provides an existence theorem for a class of models much broader than the one discussed in this section, though its usefulness for calculating solutions has not been tested in practice. For an exchange economy with homogeneous agents the question of existence of equilibria is trivially resolved, and the formula (2.20) can be regarded as a *solution* for prices, given the behavior of quantities (and hence of marginal utilities). With production and capital accumulation, one can exploit the equivalence of optimal and equilibrium allocations (again, with homogeneous consumers) together with the possibility of calculating the former by dynamic programming methods to view (2.20) as an operational solution for the price of an arbitrary security. In Lucas and Stokey (1982), a method is provided for constructing optimal allocations with heterogeneous consumers, but with the environment restricted to be deterministic. A recent paper by Mehra and Prescott (1983) uses simulations of an exchange-economy version, adapted for stationarity in rates of growth of output, as the basis for a test on United States time series of output and securities prices.

From the point of view of classical hypothesis testing, nothing is gained in restricting attention to models that have solutions or solutions that can be characterized or simulated. If a first-order condition such as (2.22) is tested and rejected, one can view as rejected all models carrying this equality as an implication, without having to spell out each model or verify its internal consistency. Since there is no doubt that with rich enough data sets any such condition will be rejected, a research program based on purely negative application of first-order conditions has, in a sense, inexhaustible possibilities. Yet I think it is clear that pursuit of this line is at best a useful adjunct in the effort to obtain simulateable, necessarily "false" models that have the potential for shedding light on the questions that lead us to be interested in monetary theory in the first place.

III. Money in a Theory of Finance

Insofar as the model of the preceding section succeeds in capturing the main features of the modern theory of finance, it is surely well-suited to illustrate what I identified in the Introduction as the main difficulty in integrating that theory with monetary theory. Whether trading in this model is viewed as occurring once, at time 0, or repeatedly, all trades occur in centralized markets with all agents simultaneously trading, and no security can enjoy a "liquidity" advantage over any other.

In this section and those following, I will interpret the cash-in-advance constraint suggested by Clower (1967) as capturing the idea that at least some trades are carried out away from centralized markets, so that money can be used to effect purchases that other securities, equally valued in centralized trading, cannot effect. This interpretation, elaborated on below, seems to me consistent with the many earlier applications of this constraint.[7] The present treatment will follow Lucas and Stokey (1983) in applying the cash-in-advance constraint to a subset of consumption goods only, permitting the possibility that consumers can substitute

7. See Kohn (1980), where the idea of a finance constraint is traced to Robertson (1940) and Tsiang (1956). See also Grandmont and Younes (1973); Foley and Hellwig (1975); Lucas (1980), (1982); and Townsend (1982).

The convention adopted in this paper that all traders alternate synchronously between centralized and decentralized markets is only one of many ways of utilizing the cash-in-advance constraint to study situations with incomplete markets. For example, Grossman and Weiss (1982) and Rotemberg (1982) examine models in which some agents are always engaged in securities trading but never all agents at the same time. Comparison of their results with those cited above makes it clear that the characteristics of the equilibrium depend critically on the nature of the assumed trading rules and timing conventions.

The intergenerational models introduced by Samuelson (1958) provide another context for analyzing monetary issues within the general equilibrium framework used in the theory of finance. See Wallace (1980) for a useful description of recent developments.

I do not see any way of judging which of these approaches will prove most useful for which questions that does not involve working out the implications of theories of both types. By pursuing the particular Clower-type approach used here, I do not mean to suggest that I view this question as closed at the present time.

against the holding of money without substituting against consumption in general.

As in Section II, it will be convenient to shift back and forth between the timeless Arrow-Debreu scenario and its sequence-economy interpretation. To motivate the introduction of money, it is easier to think in terms of a sequence of markets, meeting each period. Think of trade in securities—the full range considered in Section II together with fiat currency and contingent claims on future currency—at the beginning of each trading day, say 9:00–9:15 A.M. After securities trading is concluded, production and exchange of current goods is carried out in the remainder of the day, in what I think of as a decentralized fashion.

By "decentralized" I mean firms that are spatially scattered, with workers selling labor to a particular firm going to a specific location, losing contact with other buyers of labor, and shoppers purchasing goods from a particular firm similarly obliged to go to its specific location. Insofar as goods and labor have been contracted for in advance, evidence of such contracts is simply presented by buyers and/or sellers at each location, with the indicated exchange then taking place. Equivalently, under rational expectations and the information structure assumed here, one may think of sellers in these transactions issuing invoices, or trade credit, to be cleared at tomorrow's securities market. In either case, the relevant price and quantity determination is made in the competitive securities market, with only the actual execution of trades taking place elsewhere.

In the complete-markets model of Section II, *all* exchange can be thought of as executed in this way, so that while one may think of much economic activity as occurring in a decentralized way, nothing is lost, and much analytical simplicity is gained, by thinking of all economic *decisions* as arrived at in a single, centralized market. In this section, a subset of consumption goods—"cash goods"—will be thought of as exchanged in circumstances where the buyer is unknown to the seller, so that the latter is unwilling either to accept as payment claims issued in earlier securities trading or to issue trade credit to be discharged later. Such goods, if purchased at all, *must* be paid for with currency acquired in advance: at the securities market of that morning, or earlier.

With trading in securities and in goods assumed to take place at different times *within* a given trading period t, the information structure is complicated somewhat, relative to the last section. As before, let the history of shocks $s^{t-1} = (s_1, \ldots, s_{t-1})$ be public knowledge prior to *all* period t trading. Let period t's shock, s_t, be the *pair* (s_{1t}, s_{2t}), where s_{1t} is realized and publicly known prior to any securities trading in t and where s_{2t} is known prior to any trading in goods and labor, but unknown until securities trading for t is closed. Hence, agents must commit themselves to a portfolio decision on the basis of partial current information. Use f^t as before to denote the density of s^t, f_1^t the density of (s^{t-1}, s_{1t}), and $f_{2t} \equiv f^t/f_1^t$ the conditional density of s_{2t}, given (s^{t-1}, s_{1t}).

Let preferences distinguish between cash goods, c_{1t}, and credit goods, c_{2t}, as follows:

$$\sum_{t=0}^{\infty} \beta^t \int U(c_{1t}, c_{2t}, x_t) f_{20} f^t ds_{20}\, ds^t \tag{3.1}$$

The technology is assumed unchanged from Section II:

$$c_{1t} + c_{2t} + g_t + k_{t+1} = F(k_t, 1 - x_t, s^t). \tag{3.2}$$

It remains to formulate the budget constraints of the household and the objective function of the firm in a way consistent with the trading scenario sketched above.

It is most convenient, as in Section II, to begin by picturing firms and households at 9:00 A.M. at $t = 0$, reviewing the possibilities for $t = 0, 1, 2, \ldots$ under all contingencies $s_{20}, s_1, s_2, \ldots$, with s_{10} being known and k_0 being given. Let us begin with the firm.

In terms of the un-normalized, unit-of-account prices $\{\pi_t, \pi_{xt}\}$, the firms wishes to choose history-contingent plans for total output $\{c_{1t}(s^t) + c_{2t}(s^t) + g_t(s^t)\}$, labor input $\{1 - x_t(s^t)\}$, and capital $\{k_{t+1}(s^t)\}$ to maximize expression (2.3). For the monetary economy, let $p_t(s^t)$ be the dollar spot price of goods in t and $W_t(s^t)$ be the dollar spot wage. Then, net dollar inflow in t is

$$p_t(c_{1t} + c_{2t} + g_t) - W_t(1 - x_t).$$

These dollar receipts are available for distribution as dividends of securities trading in period $t + 1$. This is true whether goods are sold (or labor bought) in t for currency, which is carried into $t + 1$ as overnight balances, or for credit, with payment due at $t + 1$. At this point, $(s^t, s_{1,t+1})$ is known. Let $q_t(s^{t-1}, s_{1t})$ be the price at 0 of a claim to one dollar at t, contingent on (s^{t-1}, s_{1t}). Since this net-receipts expression is a function of s^t but not of

$s_{1,\,t+1}$, each dollar is valued at time 0 at $\int q_{t+1} ds_{1,\,t+1}$. Then, in time-0 dollars, the firm's objective is to maximize:

$$\sum_{t=0}^{\infty} \int \int q_{t+1} ds_{1,t+1} [p_t (c_{1t} + c_{2t} + g_t) - W_t (1 - x_t)] \, ds_{20} \, ds^t = v\Pi \tag{3.3}$$

subject to (3.2).

For the firm to be indifferent between contracting in advance at $\{\pi_t, \pi_{xt}\}$ or at the dollar prices $\{q_t, p_t, W_t\}$, the proportionality conditions

$$\int q_{t+1} ds_{1,\,t+1} \cdot p_t = v\Pi_t \tag{3.4}$$

$$\int q_{t+1} ds_{1,\,t+1} \cdot W_t = v\pi_{xt} \tag{3.5}$$

must hold. Clearly, one may interchangeably think of firms as trading real goods claims in advance or trading claims to dollars. Similarly, one may view $\int q_{t+1} ds_{1,\,t+1} \cdot p_t$ as a future price at 0 for goods in t, or view $p_t(s^t)$ as price *expectation* rationally held at 0 about prices in t, and $\int q_{t+1}\, ds_{1,\,t+1}$ as the price at 0 of one dollar at $t + 1$, contingent on (s^{t-1}, s_{1t}).

The household, in contrast, is not indifferent between purchasing for cash and on trade credit as it is, by convention, obliged to acquire cash in advance:

$$p_t(s^t) c_{1t}(s^t) \leq M_t(s^{t-1}, s_{1t}) \tag{3.6}$$

where $M_t(s^{t-1}, s_{1t})$ is currency holdings at the close of securities trading in t and $p_t c_{1t}$ is cash goods purchases during t. This constraint (3.6) must hold for all realizations of the shock s_{2t}, which is to say that money must be acquired to cover cash goods spending in advance of the realization of information relevant to this spending decision. This formulation is one way (suggested to me by Edwin Burmeister and Robert Flood) of introducing a *precautionary* demand for cash balances.[8]

8. See Svennson (1983) for a useful development of some aspects of this formulation. Though an individual agent would, in this set-up, be willing to pay to observe s_{2t} before committing himself to money holdings, it is the case (as Marianne Baxter pointed out to me) that if *all* agents know s_{2t} at the same time as s_{1t} (as opposed to later, as assumed in the text), the equilibrium resource allocation will not be affected. This is clear from the equation (5.16) derived below, in which the decomposition of s_t into (s_{1t}, s_{2t}) is immaterial.

To develop the household's budget constraint, consider the household's sources of dollars as of 9:00 A.M. in period $t + 1$ and its uses of dollars. Sources of dollars at $t + 1$ include (I assume) wages earned during t, $W_t(1 - x_t)$ and dollars held for cash good purchases in t and carried over unspent, $M_t - p_t c_{1t}$. The time-0 price of these two items, contingent on (s_{20}, s^t), is $\int q_{t+1} ds_{1,\, t+1}$. Uses of dollars at $t + 1$ include payment for goods bought on trade credit in t, $p_t c_{2t}$, for taxes accrued in t, $p_t \theta_t$, and (possibly contingent on $s_{1,\, t+1}$) acquisitions M_{t+1} of cash for spending in $t + 1$ or later. The time-0 price of the first two items is $\int q_{t+1} ds_{1,\, t+1}$; of the third, q_{t+1}.

These sources and uses apply to all times $t = 0, 1, 2, \ldots$. In addition, the household owns the firm, with value at 0 of $v\Pi$, initial cash (prior to securities trading at 0), $\bar{M}$ (say), and initial holdings of dollar denominated government debt, B_0. These considerations motivate, after summing up and collecting terms, the budget constraint:

$$\sum_{t=0}^{\infty} \int \Big\{ \int q_{t+1} s_{1,t+1} \left[p_t (x_{1t} + c_{2t} + \theta_t) - W_t (1 - x_t) - M_t \right] + q_t M_t \Big\} ds_{20} ds^t \leq v\Pi + \bar{M} + B_0 . \tag{3.7}$$

The Lagrangean for the consumer's problem involves a multiplier λ associated with (3.7) and multipliers $\mu_t(s^t)$ associated with the constraints (3.6). It is:

$$\begin{aligned} L = {} & \sum_{t=0}^{\infty} \beta^t \int U(c_t, x_t) f_{20} f^t ds_{20} ds^t \\ & - \lambda \sum_{t=0}^{\infty} \int \{ \int q_{t+1} ds_{1,\, t+1} [p_t (c_{1t} + c_{2t} + \theta_t) - W_t (1 - x_t) - M_t] + q_t M_t \} ds_{20} ds^t \\ & + \lambda [v\Pi + \bar{M} + B_0] + \sum_{t=0}^{\infty} \int \mu_t [M_t - p_t c_{1t}] ds_{20} ds^t . \end{aligned}$$

The first-order conditions for the household's problem include, then,

$$0 = \beta^t U_1(c_t, x_t) f_{20} f^t - \lambda p_t \int q_{t+1} ds_{1,\, t+1} - \mu_t p_t, \quad \text{all } t, s^t, s_{20}, \tag{3.8}$$

$$0 = \beta^t U_2(c_t, x_t) f_{20} f^t - \lambda p_t \int q_{t+1} ds_{1,\, t+1}, \quad \text{all } t, s^t, s_{20}, \tag{3.9}$$

$$0 = \beta^t U_x(c_t, x_t) f_{20} f^t - \lambda W_t \int q_{t+1} ds_{1,\,t+1},$$
$$\text{all } t,\ s^t,\ s_{20}, \tag{3.10}$$

$$0 = \lambda \int q_{t+1} ds_{2,\,t} ds_{1,\,t+1} - \lambda q_t + \int \mu_t ds_{2,\,1},$$
$$\text{all } t,\ s^{t-1},\ s_{1t},\ s_{20}, \tag{3.11}$$

$$M_t \geq p_t c_{1t}, \text{ with equality if } \mu_t > 0,$$
$$\text{all } t,\ s^t,\ s_{20}. \tag{3.12}$$

Here (3.11) sets to zero the derivative of L with respect to M_t, its form reflecting the fact that M_t is a function of $(s_{20}, s^{t-1}, s_{1,\,t})$, not (s_{20}, s^t).

The firm's first-order conditions include

$$0 = p_t F_x(k_t, 1 - x_t, s^t) - W_t, \text{ all } t,\ s^t,\ s_{20} \tag{3.13}$$

$$0 = \int\int q_{t+1} \cdot ds_{1,\,t+1} p_t F_k(k_t, 1 - x_t, s^t) ds_t - \int q_t ds_{1t} p_{t-1},$$
$$\text{all } t \geq 1,\ s^t,\ s_{20} \tag{3.14}$$

together with suitable transversality conditions. An additional equilibrium condition is given by the technology (3.2).

As in Section II, one may eliminate multipliers from (3.8)–(3.14) to obtain various, familiar relationships among marginal rates of substitution, of transformation, and relative prices. Thus, from (3.9), (3.10), and (3.13),

$$\frac{U_x(c_t, x_t)}{U_2(c_t, x_t)} = F_x(k_t, 1 - x_t, s^t) = \frac{W_t}{P_t} \tag{3.15}$$

analogous to (2.11) and (2.13), and from (3.9) and (3.14):

$$U_2(c_{t-1}, x_{t-1}) = \beta \int U_2(c_t, x_t) F_k(k_t, 1 - x_t, s^t) f_{t-1}^t \, ds_t, \tag{3.16}$$

analogous to (2.14). These margins between credit goods and leisure and between credit goods at different dates are not disturbed by the addition of money.

The margin between cash and credit goods is, of course, affected by monetary considerations. From (3.8) and (3.9),

$$\frac{U_2(c_t, x_t)}{U_1(c_t, x_t)} = \frac{\lambda \int q_{t+1} \, ds_{1,t+1}}{\lambda \int q_{t+1} \, ds_{1,t+1} + \mu_t} \tag{3.17}$$

Consider first the case in which all uncertainty in t is resolved prior to securities trading, so that $s_t = s_{1t}$ and $\int x_t ds_{2t} = x_t$ for any variable x_t. Then (3.11) gives:

$$\mu_t = \lambda q_t - \lambda \int q_{t+1} ds_{t+1}$$

and (3.17) becomes

$$\frac{U_2(c_t, x_t)}{U_1(c_t, x_t)} = \frac{\int q_{t+1}\, ds_{1,t+1}}{q_t} = (1 + r_t)^{-1}, \tag{3.18}$$

where r_t is the nominal rate of interest. Here the marginal-transactions benefit to holding cash is determined simultaneously with the one-period nominal bond price, so the latter measures *exactly* the relative price of cash and credit goods.

More generally, in the presence of a precautionary motive s_{2t}, the nominal interest rate at t is given in terms of the time-0 bond prices q_t by

$$(1 + r_t)^{-1} = \frac{\int q_{t+1}\, ds_{2t}\, ds_{1,t+1}}{q_t}. \tag{3.19}$$

Then dividing (3.8) and (3.9) through by p_t, integrating both with respect to s_{2t}, and substituting for $\int \mu_t ds_{2t}$ from (3.11);

$$(1 + r_t)^{-1} = \frac{\int p_t^{-1} U_2(c_t, x_t) f_{2t} ds_{2t}}{\int p_t^{-1} U_1(c_t, x_t) f_{2t} ds_{2t}}. \tag{3.20}$$

Roughly speaking, nominal interest rates must be equated to an *expected* marginal-transactions benefit of holding cash in situations where the money-holding decision must be made before these benefits can be known exactly. Further uses of these marginal conditions will be considered in Section IV and V.

In addition to these first-order conditions, the budget constraints of households and the government must hold in equilibrium. Using (3.3) and (3.7), the government budget constraint is

$$\begin{aligned} \bar{M} + B_0 = \sum_{t=0}^{\infty} \int \{ & M_t (q_t - \textstyle\int q_{t+1}\, ds_{1,t+1}) \\ & - p_t \textstyle\int q_{t+1}\, ds_{1,t+1} (g_t - \theta_t)\}\, ds_{20}\, ds^t \end{aligned} \tag{3.21}$$

or: initial government liabilities $\bar{M} + B_0$ must equal the present value of fiscal surpluses, $\theta_t - g_t$, plus the present value of seigniorage profits, $M_t(q_t - \int q_{t+1}\, ds_{1,\, t+1})$.

A flow version of (3.21), analogous to (2.17), can be derived from the observation that condition (3.21) must hold for all t, s^t, with M_{t-1} playing the role of $\bar{M}$ for $t > 0$. That is, for all t, s^t:

$$q_t(M_{t-1} + B_t) = \sum_{\tau=t}^{\infty} \int M_\tau(q_\tau - \int q_{t+1}\, ds_{1,\tau+1}) - p_\tau\{\int q_{\tau+1}\, ds_{1,\tau+1}(g_\tau - \theta_\tau)\}\, ds_{2t} d(_t s^t). \tag{3.22}$$

Now updating (3.22) from t to $t + 1$, integrating with respect to $s_2 t$ and $s_{1,\, t+1}$ and subtracting from (3.22) gives:

$$\int p_t \int q_{t+1} ds_{1,t+1}(g_t - \theta_t)\, ds_{2t} = \int B_{t+1} q_{t+1}\, ds_{2t}\, ds_{1,t+1} - q_t B_t + q_t(M_t - M_{t-1}) \tag{3.23}$$

That is, a current fiscal deficit, exclusive of debt service, must be financed by net issues of new debt or by issues of money.

For the case, discussed above, in which all uncertainty is resolved prior to the close of securities trading (that is, $s_{1t} \equiv s_t$), the nominal interest rate is defined in (3.18) and (3.23) becomes:

$$(1 + r_t)^{-1} p_t(g_t - \theta_t) = \int \frac{B_{t+1} q_{t+1}}{q_t} ds_{t+1} - B_t + M_t - M_{t-1}.$$

If, in addition, one-period government debt is uncontingent,

$$(1 + r_t)^{-1} p_t(g_t - \theta_t) = (1 + r_t)^{-1} B_{t+1} - B_t + M_t - M_{t-1}.$$

In general, with the government assumed to buy on trade credit, expenditures g_t that depend on s_{2t} involve the implicit issue of s_{2t}-contingent "bonds."

IV. Implications for the Theory of Finance

The incorporation of monetary elements into the real theory of finance as carried out in the last section has no effect on the "equivalence theorems" of private finance: i.e., the Modigliani-Miller Theory and its applications.

The linearity of equilibrium price systems on which they rest is not altered by the addition of monetary complications.

The Ricardian equivalence theorem of public finance requires modification in a monetary setting, as follows. Government policy consists of contingent sequences of government expenditures, taxes, and money supply: $\{g_t, \theta_t, M_t\}$. If there is an equilibrium for a given policy in this sense, so that in particular (3.21) holds, and if $\{g_t, \theta'_t, M_t\}$ is another policy also satisfying (3.21), then the same equilibrium is associated with this second policy. As with the barter version of the theorem, the proof follows from the observation that at given prices the policy change in question does not alter budget sets.

Notice that this equivalence argument does not go through if the policy-change involves $\{M_t\}$ as well as $\{\theta_t\}$, $\{g_t\}$ being held fixed. In general, different M_t paths will be associated with different equilibrium quantities and/or prices, and the seigniorage term

$$\sum_{t=0}^{\infty} \int M_t[q_t - \int q_{t+1}\, ds_{1,\, t+1}]\, ds_{20}\, ds^t$$

on the right-side of (3.21) will not represent the proceeds from a lump-sum tax. One way to interpret this monetary amendment to the Ricardian equivalence theorem is as an "irrelevance theorem" about open-market operations. The path $\{M_t\}$ matters, in this economy, as does the path $\{g_t\}$ of real government consumption, but the route by which money is injected into or withdrawn from the system, changes in $\{\theta_t\}$, or in securities trading is of no independent importance.

Though these modifications for a monetary economy are technically minor, they completely reverse a popular reading of the equivalence theorem for barter economies to the effect that government deficits, being simply announcements of future taxes, do not matter. In a rational-expectations equilibrium, what is "announced" by a change in the current deficit or in the second term in the sum on the right of (3.21) is that something must change in subsequent terms so as to maintain (3.21). In the barter system, this "something" is either $\{g_t\}$ or $\{\theta_t\}$. In the monetary system, it could as well be future monetary policy that changes. One could catalogue various possibilities, but the main lessons are, first, the futility of trying to assess policy changes in terms other than changes in policy processes and, second, the impossibility of analyzing changes in monetary and fiscal processes independently of each other.

The securities-pricing formulas of Section II also require significant modification or reinterpretation for a monetary economy. Let $\{z_t\}$ as before be an arbitrary sequence of claims to credit goods (and hence, in value, to goods-in-general) and let $Q_t(z)$ be the price in terms of time-t goods of the remaining terms $\{z_\tau\}_{\tau=t}^{\infty}$. Then

$$Q_t(z) = [p_t \textstyle\int q_{t+1}\, ds_{1,t+1}]^{-1} \displaystyle\sum_{\tau=t}^{\infty} \int p_\tau \int q_{\tau+1}\, ds_{1,t+1} \cdot z_\tau\, ds({}_t s^\tau)$$

and, using (3.10),

$$Q_t(z) = z_t + \sum_{\tau=t+1}^{\infty} \beta^{\tau-t} \int \frac{U_2(c_\tau, x_\tau)}{U_2(c_t, x_t)} z_\tau f_t d({}_t s^\tau) \tag{4.1}$$

which exactly replicates (2.20) with U_c replaced by U_2. (The notation $E_t(\cdot)$ is no longer useful because uncertainty is resolved at two points within period t.) The analogues to (2.21) and (2.22) then follow from (4.1) as from (2.20).

The marginal utility U_2 of credit goods can be interpreted as the marginal utility of goods-in-general if the function V is defined by:

$$V(c_{1t}, c_{1t} + c_{2t}, x_t) \equiv U(c_{1t}, c_{2t}, x_t)$$

so (4.1) and (2.20) are very close. The *arguments* of these marginal utilities differ in the monetary and real cases, however. For example, in the absence of a precautionary motive ($s_{1t} \equiv s_t$), $c_{1t} = \frac{M_t}{p_t}$ in equilibrium, and

$$U_2(c_t, x_t) = V_2(c_{1t}, c_{1t} + c_{2t}, x_t) = V_2\left(\frac{M_t}{p_t}, c_{1t} + c_{2t}, x_t\right)$$

so that both real balances and leisure affect the marginal utility of total consumption. Clearly one would not wish to impose the hypothesis that V is a separable function of c_{1t} and $c_{1t} + c_{2t}$, so this is not an inessential amendment.

Perhaps more fundamentally, securities in a monetary economy will not in general be claims to streams of real goods. For example, the owner of an equity share in the firm has title to a stream of dollar receipts, payable at the beginning of the period after these receipts are earned. In general, let $\{Z_t\}$ be an arbitrary dollar stream, and assume that Z_t is a function of s^t, including events s_{2t} that are unknown at the time of securities-trading in t. We wish to find the dollar price $R_t(Z)$, as a function of the information

(s^{t-1}, s_{1t}) available at time t securities—trading, of the stochastic stream $Z_t(s^t), Z_{t+1}(s^{t+1}), \ldots$.

Since the dollars Z_τ become available only as of securities-trading at time $\tau + 1$,

$$R_t(Z) = \sum_{\tau=t}^{\infty} q_t^{-1} \int q_{\tau+1} Z_\tau \, ds_{2t} d({}_t s^\tau) \, ds_{1,\tau+1} \tag{4.2}$$

From (3.9),

$$\int q_{\tau+1} \, ds_{1,\tau+1} = \lambda^{-1} p_\tau^{-1} \beta^\tau U_2(c_\tau, x_\tau) f_{20} f^\tau$$

while from (3.8) and (3.10),

$$q_t = \lambda^{-1} \int p_t^{-1} \, U_1(c_t, x_t) f_{20} f^t ds_{2t}.$$

Substituting these values into (4.2) gives:

$$R_t(Z) = \sum_{\tau=t}^{\infty} \beta^{\tau-t} \frac{E[p_\tau^{-1} U_2(c_\tau, x_\tau) Z_\tau \,|\, s^{t-1}, s_{1t}]}{E[p_t^{-1} U_1(c_t, x_t) \,|\, s^{t-1}, s_{1t}]} \tag{4.3}$$

From the interest-rate definition (3.20), (4.3) is equivalent to

$$R_t(Z) = \sum_{\tau=t}^{\infty} \beta^{\tau-t} (1 + r_t)^{-1} \frac{E[U_2(c_\tau, x_\tau) \frac{Z_\tau}{p_\tau} \,|\, s^{t-1}, s_{1t}]}{E[p_t^{-1} U_2(c_t, x_t) \,|\, s^{t-1}, s_{1t}]} \tag{4.4}$$

In general, it is clear that if z_t in (4.1) is identified with $\frac{Z_t}{p_t}$, it will not be the case that $Q_t(z)$ as given by (4.1) will match $\frac{R_t(Z)}{p_t}$ as given by (4.4). The natural deflations do not reduce nominal securities-pricing in a monetary world to the pricing of real securities in a barter world.

Obviously, the predictions of *any* theory will be altered if one introduces into it elements from which the original theory abstracted, so these observations do not amount to serious criticism of the application of a "barter" model to a monetary world. On the contrary, successful empirical applications of financial theory that abstracts from monetary complications testify to the good judgment of financial theorists in leaving such complications aside. The virtue of introducing monetary complications as done here is not to show that they affect the predictions of the theory (how could it be otherwise?) but to show that they do so in a fully operational, testable way.

V. Implications for the Theory of Money

Viewed as examples or prototypes of monetary theories, our interest in models such as that sketched in Section III is not so much in direct testing of first-order conditions as in whether their solutions can be constructed and characterized, given assumed behavior for the various shocks to the system. This section uses simple examples to address this issue.

Constructive proofs that equilibria exist for models as discussed in Section III are even less well-developed than for barter systems. For pure exchange economies equilibrium prices are easily obtained, as in Lucas (1982). With production but without capital, less trivial results can be obtained, as illustrated below. Townsend (1982) has built on earlier work by Bewley (1972) and Heller (1974) to sketch a quite general proof of existence for a model close to that in Section III. The device used by Brock (1982) of exploiting the link between optimally-planned and equilibria allocations is not available in monetary systems, in general, because of the "wedge" which the inflation tax introduces between the marginal rate of substitution in cash and credit goods and their unit marginal rate of transformation.

In this section, the model of Section III will be specialized by (1) excluding capital goods, (2) restricting the technology to the form

$$c_{1t} + c_{2t} + g_t = (1 - x_t)\xi_t, \tag{5.1}$$

where ξ_t is a component of s_t, and (3) assuming that the shocks

$$s_t = (\xi_t, g_t \qquad \text{other variables} \ldots)$$

follow a Markov process with transition density $p(s',s)$ given by

$$\int^{s'} p(u, s)\,du = \Pr\{s_{t+1} \leq s' \mid s_t = s\}. \tag{5.2}$$

That is, the joint density $f^t(s_1, \ldots, s_t)$ takes the form:

$$f^t(s^t) = f^{t-1}(s^{t-1})p(s_t, s_{t-1}) \tag{5.3}$$

Finally, the money-supply process is assumed given by a fixed function m of the current state:

$$M_t = m(s_t)\, M_{t-1}. \tag{5.4}$$

Under these additional assumptions, I will first seek functions c, x and ψ such that the allocations $c_t = (c_{1t}, c_{2t}) = c(s_t)$, $x_t = x(s_t)$ and real balances

$\psi(s_t) = M_t/p_t$ satisfy (3.14)–(3.16) for all t, s^t. Associated with an equilibrium in this stationary sense will be a nominal interest-rate function $r_t = r(s_t)$ and similar recursive expressions for all other equilibrium prices.

As a useful intermediate step, define the functions $v(s)$ and $w(s)$ by

$$v(s) = \xi(s)U_2(c(s), x(s)) \tag{5.5}$$

and

$$v(s) + w(s) = (s)U_1(c(s), x(s)) \tag{5.6}$$

so that from (3.8) and (3.9):

$$v(s_t) = \frac{\lambda \int q_{t+1}\, ds_{1,t+1} M_t}{\beta^t f_{20} f^t} \tag{5.7}$$

and

$$v(s_t) + w(s_t) = \frac{\lambda \int q_{t+1}\, ds_{1,t+1} M_t + \mu_t M_t}{\beta^t f_{20} f^t} \tag{5.8}$$

We are headed for a functional equation in this function $v(s)$.

From (3.9) and (3.10), an additional equilibrium condition is:

$$\frac{U_x(c(s), x(s))}{U_2(c(s), x(s))} = \xi \tag{5.9}$$

From (5.4), (3.12) and the definition of $w(s)$ and $\psi(s)$,

$$\psi(s) \geq c_1(s) \text{ with equality if } w(s) > 0. \tag{5.10}$$

For given $s = s_t$, then, (5.1), (5.5), (5.6), (5.9), and (5.10) provide five "equations" in the six "unknowns" $c_1(s)$, $c_2(s)$, $x(s)$, $\psi(s)$, $w(s)$, and $v(s)$. Alternatively, for given $v(s)$ and (ξ, g) we can think of solving this system for c_1, c_2, x, ψ, and w as functions of (v, ξ, g) or of $(v(s), s)$. For s-values where the constraint (5.10) is binding, (5.1), (5.5), and (5.9) are solved for (c_1, c_2, x) as functions of $(v(s), s)$, $\psi(s)$ equals $c_1(s)$, and $w(s)$ is given by (5.6). For values where (5.10) is slack, $w(s) = 0$, (5.1), (5.9), and the condition $U_1(c, x) = U_2(c, x)$ are solved for (c_1, c_2, x). Then ψ is obtained from (5.5) or (5.6). Let us assume that this static system can be solved uniquely, and denote the solution for w in particular by

$$w(s) = h(v(s), \xi, g) = h(v(s), s) \tag{5.11}$$

This is the first step toward constructing an equilibrium.

Next, note that from (5.7),

$$v(s_{t-1}) = \frac{\lambda \int q_t ds_{1t} M_{t-1}}{\beta^{t-1} f^{t-1}} \tag{5.12}$$

From (3.11), integrated with respect to s_{1t},

$$\begin{aligned} \lambda \int q_t ds_{1t} &= \lambda \int q_{t+1} ds_{1t} ds_{2t} ds_{1,t+1} + \int \mu_t ds_{1t} ds_{2t} \\ &= \int \frac{\beta^t f^t}{M_t} v(s_t) ds_t + \int \frac{\beta^t f^t}{M_t} w(s_t) ds_t \end{aligned} \tag{5.13}$$

where the second equality follows from (5.7) and (5.8). Inserting from (5.13) into (5.12):

$$v(s_{t-1}) = \beta \int \frac{M_{t-1}}{M_t} (v(s_t) + w(s_t)) \frac{f^t}{f^{t-1}} ds_t. \tag{5.14}$$

Since this derivation holds for all states s_{t-1}, we have, using the definitions of $m(s)$ and $p(s', s)$,

$$v(s) = \beta \int \frac{v(s') + w(s')}{m(s')} p(s', s) ds'. \tag{5.15}$$

Using (5.11), (5.15) becomes:

$$v(s) = \beta \int \frac{v(s') + h(v(s'), s')}{m(s')} p(s', s)\, ds'. \tag{5.16}$$

Equation (5.15) arises from the marginal balancing undertaken by an agent in the goods market in state s, deciding whether or not to spend an additional dollar on credit goods. The utility of this marginal expenditure is

$$\frac{1}{p_t} U_2(c_t, x_t) = \frac{1}{M_t} v(s_t).$$

The utility foregone is, from (5.15),

$$\frac{\beta}{M_t} E\left\{ \frac{v(s_{t+1}) + w(s_{t+1})}{M_{t+1}/M_t} \middle| s_t \right\} = \beta E\left\{ \frac{1}{p_{t+1}} U_1(c_{t+1}, x_{t+1}) \middle| s_t \right\}.$$

That is, a dollar spent on credit goods today involves a dollar unavailable for spending on cash goods tomorrow. Since m is a given function, equation (5.16) is a functional equation in the single unknown function $v(s)$. Solving it is the second step toward constructing an equilibrium.

Third and finally, an equilibrium must satisfy the government budget constraint (3.21). Given initial values s_0 of s_t, the transitions $p(s',s)$, the function $m(s)$, and the functions c, x, ψ, w and v just solved, the right side of (3.21) is determined. Substituting from (5.7) and (5.8) into (3.21) gives

$$\lambda(\bar{M} + B_0) = \sum_{t=0}^{\infty} \beta \int \left\{ w(s_t) - v(s_t) \frac{g_t - \theta}{\psi(s_t)} \right\} f_{20} f^t ds_{20} ds^t. \tag{5.17}$$

From (5.7), the multiplier λ is

$$\lambda = \frac{\int v(s_0) f_{20} ds_{20}}{M_0 \int q_1 ds_{20} ds_{11}} = \frac{1 + r_0}{M_0} \int v(s_0) f_{20} ds_{20}. \tag{5.18}$$

Policies $\{g_t, \theta_t\}$, $\bar{M}$, B_0, and $m(s_t)$ are associated with equilibrium allocations only if the implied values of w, v, ψ and λ, calculated as above, satisfy (5.17).

The construction just sketched can be illustrated by examples. To begin with the simplest, consider the deterministic case where s (and hence $m(s)$) is constant. Then (5.15) becomes

$$mv = \beta(v + w)$$

so that (5.5) and (5.6) give

$$\frac{U_1(c, x)}{U_2(c, x)} = \frac{m}{\beta} \tag{5.19}$$

(provided $m \geq \beta$). Then, with (ξ, g) constant as well as m, (5.17), (5.9), and (5.1) are solved for (c, x) as functions of $(\frac{m}{\beta}, \xi, g)$. Real balances ψ are equal to c_1, and the equilibrium values of v and w are, respectively, $c_1 U_2(c, x)$ and $(\frac{m}{\beta} - 1)c_1 U_2(c, x)$. The constant nominal rate of interest r is, from (3.18) and (5.19), given by

$$(1 + r)^{-1} = \frac{\beta}{m}. \tag{5.20}$$

This completes the first two steps in constructing an equilibrium for this deterministic case. For the third, insert the constant values of w, v, g, θ and ψ into (5.17) and use (5.18) and (5.20) to get:

$$\frac{g-\theta}{\psi} = \frac{m}{\beta} - 1 - \frac{m}{\beta}(1-\beta)\frac{M + B_0}{M_0}. \tag{5.21}$$

With a noninflationary monetary policy ($M_0 = \bar{M}$ *and* $m = 1$), and m = 1), the price level is constant at $\psi^{-1}\,\bar{M}$ and (5.21) implies:

$$\beta\theta = \beta g + r\psi\frac{B_0}{\bar{M}}.$$

That is, tax receipts must equal government purchases plus service of the original real debt. (That θ and g are discounted by β reflects the convention that taxes and government spending are carried out on credit, and interest is due in cash.)

Treating M_0 as a free parameter amounts to permitting an initial, arbitrary open-market operation before pursuing the policy m. Thus, if all debt is initially "monetized," $M_0 = \bar{M} + B$, (5.21) gives

$$g - \theta = \psi(m-1)$$

so that real deficits of $g - \theta$ can be perpetually financed by real seigniorage revenues $\psi(m-1)$. As $M_0 \to \infty$, $g - \theta \to \psi\left(\frac{m}{\beta} - 1\right)$, the maximum seigniorage revenue for given m.

In general, it is clear from (5.21) that monetary and fiscal policies cannot be set in an unrestricted way. Equation (5.21) may be read as defining the equilibrium tax rate θ consistent with given m, g, $\bar{M}$, M_0 and B, or as fixing some other "free parameter" of the monetary-fiscal system.

As a second example, let the shocks $[s_t]$ be independent and identically distributed, with $s_{2t} = (\xi_t, g_t)$, with s_{1t} determining monetary shocks, independent of s_{2t}, and with θ_t constant at θ. That is, in each period a monetary shock is realized, securities are traded, real shocks are realized (necessitating government deficits or surpluses on trade credit), and trading is concluded. From (5.16) in this case, $v(s) \equiv k$ for some constant k. Then c, x, ψ and w are functions of k and the real shocks $s_{2t} = (\xi_t, g_t)$. The value of k is implicit in

$$k = \beta E\left\{\frac{k + h(k, s_2)}{m(s_1)}\right\}. \tag{5.22}$$

The nominal interest rate is, from (3.20), (5.5), and (5.6):

$$[1 + r(s_1)]^{-1} = \frac{\displaystyle\int \frac{v(s)}{m(s_1)} p_2(s_2)ds_2}{\displaystyle\int \frac{v(s) + w(s)}{m(s_1)} p_2(s_2)ds_2}$$

$$= \frac{k}{k + \int h(k, s_1)p_2(s_2)ds_2}.$$

Applying (5.22) to the numerator and cancelling:

$$(1 + r)^{-1} = \beta E\left(\frac{1}{m(s_1)}\right) \tag{5.23}$$

which may be compared to (5.20).

As a variation on this last example, retain the assumptions of independence but assume that *all* shocks are realized prior to securities trading. Then again, $v(s)$ is constant at a value k satisfying (5.22). Nominal interest is now given by

$$[1 + r(s)]^{-1} = \frac{k}{h + h(k, \xi, g)},$$

which varies with the real shock (ξ, g). The formula comparable to (5.20) is, in this case.

$$[1 + r(s)]^{-1} = \beta E\left(\frac{1}{m}\right)\frac{k + E(h(k, s))}{k + h(k, s)} \tag{5.24}$$

Inserting this information into (5.20) one finds that the magnitude

$$[1 + r(s_t)]\frac{\bar{M} + B_0}{M_0} - r(s_t) + \frac{g_t - \theta}{\psi(s_t)}$$

must be constant with respect to s_t. Since this condition will hold only coincidentally, the conclusion is that, in general, no equilibrium exists for this case. With taxes fixed at θ and government spending g_t stochastically determined, the fact that interest rates vary with real shocks makes the required value equality (3.20) impossible to maintain under all circumstances. A compensating tax or open-market policy is required for internal consistency.

These three examples all involve serially independent shocks. From (5.16) it is clear that, in general, $v(s_t)$ will vary with s_t due *solely* to the extent that s_t conveys information about future shocks. The corresponding "general" expression for the one-period nominal interest rate is:

$$[1 + r(s_1)]^{-1} = \frac{\int v(s)p_2(s_2, s_1)ds_2}{\int (v(s) + w(s))p_2(s_2, s_1)ds_2}. \tag{5.25}$$

Equation (5.25) is consistent with *any* co-movements of interest rates and real and nominal variables: the kind of single-equation vacuity familiar from other rational-expectations models and, in the case of interest rates, from the financial pages of any newspaper. The content in (5.25) must come from the fact that both $r(s_t)$ and the transition function $p(s_{t+1}, s_t)$ are, at least in part, observable.

The examples just worked through certainly do not constitute a complete analysis of the functional equation (5.16) and of its implications for pricing and resource allocation in a monetary economy. That analysis must await another occasion. They do suggest, however, that an operational theory can be based on (5.16), that such a theory will reproduce familiar results from deterministic theory when specialized to that case, and that its scope can be extended to make predictions under stochastic conditions for which conventional theory is plainly inadequate.

VI. Concluding Remarks

This paper was motivated by reference to earlier research directed at "unifying" the theories of money and finance and by the idea that success in this enterprise will involve capturing in a single model the sense in which securities are traded and priced in centralized "efficient" markets as well as the sense in which other goods are traded outside of these centralized exchanges, in situations where at least one security ("money") is valued higher than it "ought" to be on efficient market grounds alone. I think that this idea, in various forms, is present in most writing on money. One way of developing it was proposed in Sections III–V.

Ultimately, however, financial and monetary theory have quite different objectives, and however desirable theoretical "unity" may be, one can identify strong forces that will continue to pull apart these two bodies of theory. The real capital theory reviewed in Section II can be modified in two distinct directions: toward increasing generality in its assumptions about technology, demography, and preferences or toward the specificity needed to permit the application of constructive solution methods. The empirical failures of the simplest "representative consumer" models indicate that increased generality is required to produce success in the sense of first-order conditions that can pass the modern descendants of the efficiency tests of finance. Such generality is not difficult to obtain, and I expect much additional fruitful work in this direction.

The objective of designing simulatable models, an objective central to monetary theory, necessarily pulls in the opposite direction. The introduction of monetary elements, with the associated "wedge" of inefficiency, renders solution methods that exploit the links between equilibrium and optimality inapplicable and requires new analytical approaches. Sections III and V of this paper outline one possible approach and pursue it to the point where one can begin to get some idea of its potential.

If I am right that the relationship between financial and monetary economics is not, even ideally, one of "unity," it is nevertheless surely the case that there is much to be gained by close interaction. The power in applications of the contingent-claim point of view, so clearly evident in finance, will be as usefully applied to monetary theory. (This is not so much a prediction as it is an observation on the best recent work in the area.) The source of this power, I think, is the ability of this framework to permit the reduction of the study of asset demands to the study of demands for the more fundamental attributes to which assets are claims. If the theory of finance had remained content to postulate preferences over such "goods" as "debt" and "equity," financial textbooks would still be "explaining" corporate capital structure as unique tangency points of indifference curves to budget lines, on the picture that Modigliani and Miller showed to be spurious in 1958.

Postulating preferences or demands for "real balances" together with other "goods" is no more (and no less) useful than postulating a demand for the debt of a particular corporation. To get beyond this point, it is necessary to think more specifically about what it is, exactly, that money gives one access to. The Clower convention, as applied in this paper, is one way to do this. I have tried to illustrate some aspects of the power and flexibility of this approach and, in doing so, I have also revealed some of its limitations. Ultimately, the merits of a particular approach to the theory of money (as to the theory of anything else) will be judged less by its axioms than by whether it seems capable of giving reliable answers to the substantive questions that lead us to be interested in monetary theory in the first place. This is an inquiry that has clearly only just begun.

References

Arrow, K. J. (1964) The Role of Securities in the Optimal Allocation of Risk-Bearing, *Review of Economic Studies,* 31: 91–96.

Barro, R. J. (1979) On the Determination of the Public Debt, *Journal of Political Economy,* 87: 940–71.

Bewley, T. (1972) Existence of Equilibria in Models with Infinitely Many Commodities, *Journal of Economic Theory,* 4: 514–40.

Brock, W. A. (1982) Asset Prices in a Production Economy, (ed.) John J. McCall, *The Economics of Information and Uncertainty,* Chicago: University of Chicago Press.

Clower, R. W. (1967) A Reconsideration of the Microfoundations of Monetary Theory, *Western Economic Journal,* 6: 1–9.

Debreu, G. (1959) *Theory of Value,* New Haven, Connecticut: Yale University Press.

Fama, E. F. (1965) The Behavior of Stock Market Prices, *Journal of Business,* 38: 34–105.

——— (1970) Efficient Capital Markets: A Review of Theory and Empirical Work, *Journal of Finance,* 25: 383–417.

Foley, D. K. and Hellwig, M. F. (1975) Asset Management With Trading Uncertainty, *Review of Economic Studies,* 42: 327–46.

Grandmont, J-M and Younes, Y. (1973) On the Efficiency of a Monetary Equilibrium, *Review of Economic Studies,* 40: 149–65.

Grossman, S. J. and Shiller, R. J. (1981) The Determinants of Variability of Stock Market Prices, *American Economic Review,* 71: 222–27.

——— and Weiss, L. (1982) A Transaction Based Model of the Monetary Transmission Mechanism, University of Chicago Working Paper.

Gurley, J. G. and Shaw, E. S. (1960) *Money in a Theory of Finance,* Washington, D.C.: The Brookings Institution.

Hall, R. E. (1978) Stochastic Implications of the Life Cycle-Permanent Income Hypothesis: Theory and Evidence, *Journal of Political Economy,* 86: 971–88.

Hansen, L. P. and Singleton, K. J. (1983) Stochastic Consumption, Risk Aversion, and the Temporal Behavior of Asset Return, *Journal of Political Economy,* 91: 249–65.

Heller, W. P. (1974) The Holding of Money Balances in General Equilibrium, *Journal of Economic Theory,* 7: 93–108.

Hicks, J. R. (1935) A Suggestion for Simplifying the Theory of Money, *Econometrica,* 2: 1–19.

Hirshleifer, J. (1966) Investment Decision under Uncertainty: Applications of the State-preference Approach, *Quarterly Journal of Economics,* 80: 252–77.

Kohn, M. (1980) In Defense of the Finance Constraint, Dartmouth College Working Paper.

Lucas, R. E., Jr. (1980) Equilibrium in a Pure Currency Economy, *Economic Inquiry,* 18: 203–20.

——— (1982) Interest Rates and Currency Prices in a Two-Country World, *Journal of Monetary Economics,* 10: 335–60.

Lucas, R. E., Jr. and Stokey, N. L. (1982) Optimal Growth with Many Consumers, *Journal of Economic Theory,* 32: 139–71.

——— (1983) Optimal Fiscal and Monetary Policy in an Economy Without Capital, *Journal of Monetary Economics,* 12: 55–93.

Mehra, R. and Prescott, E. C. (1983) The Equity Premium: A Puzzle, Working Paper.

Modigliani, F. and Miller, M. H. (1958) The Cost of Capital, Corporation Finance and the Theory of Investment, *American Economic Review,* 48: 261–97.

Robertson, D. H. (1940) Saving and Hoarding, reprinted in *Essays in Monetary Theory,* London.

Rotemberg, J. J. (1982) A Monetary Equilibrium Model with Transactions Costs, National Bureau of Economic Research Working Paper.

Samuelson, P. A. (1958) An Exact Consumption-Loan Model of Interest With or Without the Social Contrivance of Money, *Journal of Political Economy,* 66: 467–82.

Svensson, L. E. O. (1983) Money and Asset Prices in a Cash-In-Advance Economy, University of Stockholm Working Paper.

Townsend, R. M. (1982) Asset Prices in a Monetary Economy: Explaining Rate of Return Dominance and Other Apparent Anomalies, Working Paper.

Tsiang, S. C. (1956) Liquidity Preferences and Loanable Funds Theories, Multiplier and Velocity Analysis: A Synthesis, *American Economic Review,* 46: 540–64.

Wallace, N. (1980) The Overlapping Generations Model of Fiat Money, (eds.) John H. Karaken and Neil Wallace, *Models of Monetary Economies,* Minneapolis: Federal Reserve Bank of Minneapolis.

— 9 —

Principles of Fiscal and Monetary Policy

1. Introduction

My objective in this lecture will be to spell out in a unified way all of the neoclassical welfare-economic principles that bear on the efficient conduct of national, or aggregative, monetary and fiscal policy.* I use the work *principles,* here and in the title of my talk, to indicate that I will be less concerned with the quantitative specifics of policy—how fast money ought to expand, how large the deficit should be, and so on—than with developing a disciplined way of establishing the connections between particular policy actions and their consequences for resource allocation and individual welfare.

I hope that most of what I have to say will be in the nature of reminding you of things you already know. Insofar as you are familiar with the normative work of Friedman (1969), Phelps (1973), Barro (1979), and Kydland and Prescott (1977, 1980) the chances of this being so are excellent. But it would not be useful for me simply to run through the various writings of these and other economists, taking one principle here and another one there: Major differences in the analytical frameworks they used would make it impossible to see which principles are mutually consistent and which contradictory, and it would be impossible to tell, at the end, whether

---

Journal of Monetary Economics 17, no. 1 (January 1986): 117–134.

*This paper was originally prepared for a Harvard University Political Economy Lecture, which was given on April 20, 1984. I have retained the lecture style in this version, but have added footnotes and references and expanded on a few points in the text at the suggestion of the Editor. I would like to thank Nancy Stokey, Laurence Weiss and Sherwin Rosen for their criticism of an earlier version, without, of course, attempting to shift any responsibility to them.

we had arrived at a complete characterization of an efficient monetary and fiscal policy or only a partial one. Instead, I will begin by considering the dynamics of policy in the context of a specific, necessarily very simple, general equilibrium model. This will occupy most of my time, and when I am finished, we will have arrived at a fully understood consensus as to how monetary and fiscal policy ought to be conducted in this artificial society. Then we can turn to the more difficult question of determining how much of this expertise is transferable to the conduct of policy in the world of today.

2. A Framework

The model I propose as a basis for discussion is taken from a paper by Nancy Stokey and myself, 'Optimal Fiscal and Monetary Policy in an Economy Without Capital', that was published in the Journal of Monetary Economics in 1983. I will use the fact that it is already in print as an excuse to avoid all technical matters today, and simply describe the model economy we constructed and the main facts we learned about it as directly as I can. Though my main purpose today is to discuss what I see as instructive connections between policy in the model and in the United States, it will be best if we can first try to see the issues clearly in the context of the model, without worrying too much about its 'realism'.

The model economy has a constant population of identical agents, all of whom live forever. There is a stable constant returns technology for transforming labor into goods, and goods must be consumed immediately, either by agents individually or by government. There are no capital goods of any kind. Agents' utility is given by the expected, discounted value of current and future utilities, which depend on private consumption (positively) and labor supplied (negatively). Government consumption yields no utility, but simply must be satisfied: Think of periodic wars that *must* be fought for the survival of society. These government demands follow a stochastic process, the distribution of which is exogenously given and known to all agents. There are no other sources of uncertainty inherent in the system (though the government may *create* more by erratic policies).

Business in this economy is carried out in the following way. Each period, agents begin the day by engaging in centralized securities trading of a completely unrestricted, 'Arrow–Debreu' nature. All agents participate in this activity, and if the government wishes to float or retire bonds or engage in open market operations it participates in this market, too. When securities trading is concluded, the real economic activity of the day begins. Each agent splits itself into a pair, a 'worker' and a 'shopper', who will be out of communication with each other until the working day is over. During the day, the shopper acquires consumption goods for the household while the worker produces. [Though the goods look identical to us, as observers, and are produced under an identical technology, they come in a variety of 'colors' (say) and a shopper must visit many production locations to acquire the desired variety.][1]

At some locations, the shopper is known to the seller and may acquire goods on trade credit, to be settled at tomorrow morning's securities market. Call this aggregation of colors 'credit goods'. At other locations, the shopper is unknown to the seller and must pay for goods in fiat currency if he purchases any goods at all. Call goods of this category 'cash goods', with the understanding that one buyer's credit goods will be another's cash goods, so that the distinction between the two will be invisible to national income accountants and hence to econometricians as well. From a seller's viewpoint, credit and cash sales are equivalent since either results in dollar receipts that can be spent tomorrow morning, at the earliest. From a buyer's viewpoint, cash goods require the holding of non-interest bearing currency which must be acquired in that morning's securities trading with funds that would otherwise be invested in interest bearing securities.

If we take the government out of the picture for a moment (by setting government consumption equal to zero in all periods and by assuming that no government securities are outstanding or ever issued, except for a constant supply of circulating currency) it is easy to imagine what a competitive equilibrium looks like for this economy. The marginal rate of substitution between leisure and credit goods will be equated to their technologically given marginal rate of transformation, or marginal product of labor. The marginal rate of substitution between cash and credit goods will be equated to the price of a one-period nominal bond, which will in turn equal the subjective discount factor of consumers. These are two equations in the three current-period unknowns: goods of both categories and leisure. A third equation is given by the technological condition that production equals total consumption.

The nominal price level is given by the quantity-theoretic condition that

1. This scenario is spelled out in a little more detail in Lucas (1982).

all dollars are spent on cash goods each period. With both money supply and real production possibilities constant, the price level will be constant as well. 'Velocity' in this equilibrium depends, of course, on such institutional considerations as the frequency of securities trading (the length of a 'period') and on how well developed the credit system is.

In the economy just described, the economic efficiency of the competitive equilibrium is easy to assess, as long as we restrict ourselves to allocations in which all of the identical agents are treated identically. An allocation that maximizes the utility of the representative consumer must satisfy the same credit goods-leisure marginal condition that the equilibrium I have just described does, and of course it must satisfy the productive feasibility constraint, but unlike this equilibrium, an efficient allocation must also equate the marginal rate of substitution between cash and credit goods to their marginal rate of transformation of unity. In the monetary economy, individuals forego leisure today to acquire, via currency, cash goods tomorrow, but the social tradeoff is contemporaneous: leisure today is foregone to produce goods today.

This wedge of monetary inefficiency must arise whenever the interest yield on currency is below the yield on one-period securities. It can be removed, in principle, by paying interest on currency (though this seems to me to miss the point of what we ordinarily mean by the term 'currency'). It can alternatively be removed, as Friedman pointed out in his 1959 paper on 'The Optimum Quantity of Money', by a monetary policy that withdraws currency from circulation in a lump-sum fashion so as to induce a predictable deflation at precisely the rate of time preference. In the economy we are discussing, such a policy would combine fiscal and monetary elements, with a head tax on individuals used to remove currency at the rate consistent with efficiency. Friedman described this policy as designed to get agents to consume the right amount of 'services of real balances'. In our case, we are able to be a little more explicit about the nature of these services: Money is a *means* to a mix of consumption goods, and the optimal quantity of it is that which directs consumers to the mix that yields maximal utility, given the technology.

To sum up, I have described a family of equilibria, all with constant rates of production and consumption through time but with differing rates of inflation or deflation, and the one member of this family that is economically efficient has been singled out. These equilibria are examples of what Von Mises (1949), in a phrase I have always liked, called an 'evenly rotating economy'. Life goes on, from one period to the next, in a perfectly repetitive fashion. If there are any questions about the nature of these equilibria, this would be a good time to raise them, since I am about to consider complications to this picture in various ways.

3. Static Efficiency

As a first complication, let me reintroduce a pattern of variable and unavoidable government consumptions. Now *provided* we continue to assume that lump-sum or head taxes are feasible, nothing essential is changed in either this positive or normative picture. Neither of the two margins that hold in competitive equilibrium is affected, though the feasible consumption-leisure pairs are, and the quantities that satisfy the required marginal conditions will be altered due to income effects. With lump-sum taxation available, any pattern of required government expenditure is just equivalent analytically to a worsening in the 'technology' by the amount of the expenditure. The only distorting tax is the 'tax' on currency and an efficient allocation is realized when this one distortion is set equal to zero, by Friedman's deflationary proposal or by any other means.

This is one of the many analytical environments in which the result that Buchanan (1976) and Barro (1979) have called the 'Ricardian equivalence theorem' holds: Given a (possibly stochastic) path of government expenditures on goods and given a (possibly stochastic) path of the money supply, changes in the timing of taxes that leave the government's budget constraint satisfied will have no effect on equilibrium allocations or prices (including, of course, interest rates). As the time pattern of taxes is varied, what 'makes up the difference' to keep the government's budget constraint satisfied is, of course, issues and retirements of government debt to the public, so one only slightly misleading way of summarizing this theorem is to say that government debt (its size and its maturity structure) doesn't matter.

In reality government debt and the timing of taxes do matter, so if our purpose is to analyze the consequences of different policies concerning these variables we need to modify the framework so as to get away from this equivalence theorem. The modification that seems to me to bring us closest to a useful kind of realism is to drop the assumption that nondistorting lump-sum taxes can be levied, assuming instead that *only* flat-rate *ad valorem* taxes are available. This modification will bring the normative theory of public debt within the public finance tradition we use for studying other issues involving taxation, which is, I think, exactly where it belongs.[2]

There are three goods in the economy under study: cash goods, credit goods and leisure. The ability to tax all three amounts, we know, to the ability to levy lump-sum taxes on people's endowments, so we consider taxes on two of them only. The 'inflation tax' taxes cash goods relative to credit goods, so we have one flat-rate tax already in the system. This leaves us one more: let us levy a flat-rate tax on labor income, variable from period to period in a possibly state-contingent way. This gives us enough flexibility to study all possible flat-rate tax structures.

Fig. 1 (the only diagram I will use) illustrates the equilibrium if the inflation tax is zero and if the government budget is in balance. The composite consumption good is on the horizontal axis, leisure is on the vertical. The indifference curves represent the current-period preferences of the typical household. The point B would be optimal if there were no government demands; the point E is optimal with a government demand of g. With lump-sum taxation, E can always be attained and society can do no better. With a tax of τ on labor income, the point (0, 1) is available to the consumer, and he is taxed at τ as he moves away from this point. Equilibrium occurs at a point like A, necessarily on a lower indifference curve that E. This is the distortion I am referring to: the *only* objective of fiscal policy is to make it as small as possible.

In a static context, there isn't much to this problem: If there is more than one point like A (and there may well be) the one on the highest indifference curve is best. In a dynamic setting, where g is fluctuating from

2. See Lucas and Stokey (1983) and the references therein. Barro (1979) describes his analysis of debt policy with distorting taxes as positive, not normative, but the main ideas are easily put to either purpose.

An alternative way to 'break' the equivalence results is to use an overlapping generations structure rather than one based on infinitely-lived households. Normatively, this leads to efficiency criteria that assign to 'government' the proxy votes for generations yet unborn, as opposed to assigning them to families or other private sector institutions (churches, professional organizations, and so on). It would be desirable to have frameworks that spread the responsibility for thinking about future generations around in a realistic way, but of the extreme models that are currently available to us, I prefer the infinitely-lived household abstraction. What fraction of the world's population lives under governments as old as the Econometric Society, not to mention the Catholic Church?

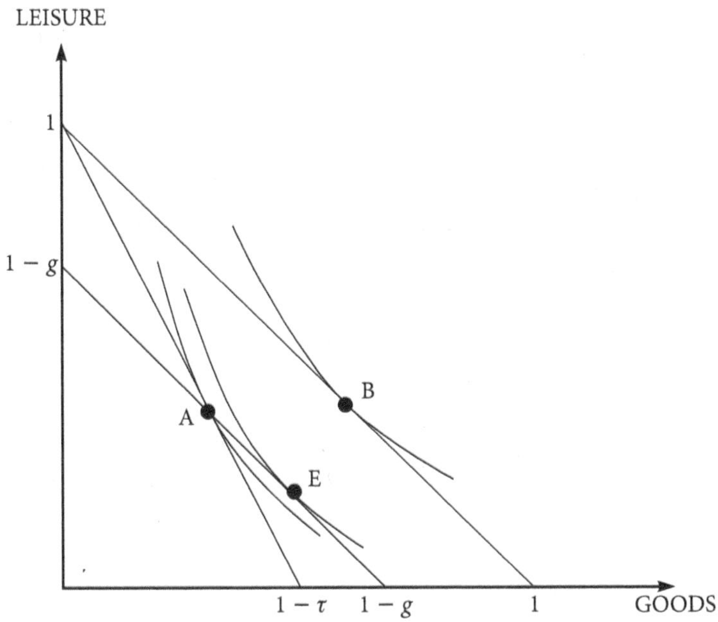

Figure 1

period to period, the problem is more interesting. To state it precisely, an efficient monetary/fiscal authority will choose a history-contingent sequence of income tax rates and money growth rates (inflation tax rates) so as to maximize the expected discounted utility of the typical consumer, subject to the constraints that the system be in competitive equilibrium, given taxes, and that the present value of government obligations (goods consumption plus debt service) not exceed the present value of its revenues (taxes plus seignorage). I am going to argue that (with one or perhaps two important qualifications) *every* useful principle we have for guiding national monetary and fiscal policy comes from the study of this programming problem, so it will be worthwhile to consider its structure with some care.

4. Dynamic Efficiency

The 'givens' in the decision problem I have just described are the distributions of current and future government expenditures and the patterns (possibly state-contingent) of real and nominal coupon payments initially owed the public by the government. If this initial debt can be cancelled or repudiated, it is efficient to do so. More efficient still, each citizen can be declared to owe to the government the pattern of lump-sum obligations that would keep the economy forever at the (now stochastically fluctuating) point E on fig. 1. But we are assuming that such lump-sum tax possibilities are unavailable, not just to make the problem technically interesting but to make it practically relevant as well. I will come back to this, but for the moment, simply take debt obligations to be inviolable.

Given this, the decision problem essentially involves distributing the tax distortions (the point E versus the point A at each date, with g fluctuating) over time so as to maximize consumer utility (or to minimize 'deadweight loss'). The answer takes the form of the famous Ramsey (1927) formulas relating tax rates at each date to the relative demand elasticities for goods and leisure at each date. Solving these conditions for the optimal pattern of taxes sets fiscal and monetary policy both. Debt policy is then determined so as to make up the difference.

As anyone who is familiar with the theory of optimal taxation in static contexts knows, a problem like this has a lot of possibilities: The first-order conditions for an optimal tax structure involve the second derivatives of the utility function, and comparative dynamics, therefore, third derivatives. Moreover, I have so far said nothing about government consumption other than that it is some given stochastic process. The model is special and abstract but not, it seems, special and abstract enough. Keep in mind the general (if imprecise) Ramsey principle of tax spreading, or smoothing, while I try to sort a few things out.

Consider first, monetary policy or inflation taxation. The income tax in this model is a flat-rate tax on the consumption of goods-in-general. The inflation tax is a tax on the consumption of cash goods *relative to* credit goods. Phelps' (1973) famous (and, I once thought, convincing) criticism of Friedman (1969) to the effect that in a world of distorting taxes, Ramsey's principle implies that liquidity ought to be taxed 'just like any other good' is, in the present context, simply incorrect. Liquidity is not 'another good' nor, indeed, a 'good' at all: It is the *means* to a subset of goods that an income tax has already taxed once. Tax spreading at each point in time means an inflation tax fixed at zero, independent of the revenue to be raised. Though evidence on the relative elasticities of cash and credit goods demand could push me off this, let me assume, then, that the best tax spreading is perfect, or that the best inflation tax is zero, or that the efficient nominal rate of interest is zero.[3]

With one set of tax rates, inflation taxes, fixed, then, I will turn to the efficient setting of income taxes, and hence of debt. Four simple examples [all taken from Lucas and Stokey (1983)], each generated by specific assumptions on initial debt and the pattern of government consumption, will illustrate the main ideas.

At first, benchmark, example, consider a system with no government consumption demands and no initial government liabilities (money included) outstanding. With no government action, then, people would have no means to pay for cash goods and hence would be obliged to concentrate their consumption on credit goods only. To prevent this clearly inefficient outcome, the government must somehow put money into the hands of the public and then withdraw it at just the right rate to keep nominal interest pegged at its efficient level of zero. In Friedman's example, this is done via helicopters and vacuum cleaners, but our government does not, by hypothesis, have recourse to such lump-sum fiscal subsidies and taxes. But there is a succession of open-market operations that will accomplish the same end, as follows.[4] Let the government initially sell currency to the public, prior to any goods trading, in exchange for promises, on the part of each household, to pay a stream of real goods in perpetuity. In each subsequent period, the government takes the value equivalent of the coupon payment due from households in the form of currency, which it then retires from circulation. In this benchmark example, the marginal rate of substitution between cash and credit goods is held at its efficient level of unity, and goods and leisure consumption remains forever at point *B* of

3. Roughly speaking, Ramsey's rules require concentrating taxation on goods in relatively inelastic demand or supply, or goods which are close complements to goods that are. Thus if cash goods were inelastically demanded relative to credit goods, and if these elasticity disparities could not be taken advantage of through ordinary differential excise taxes, there would be an efficiency case for positive inflation taxation. This is *not* the case made by Phelps, nor have I seen it made elsewhere.

4. This scenario is due to Nancy Stokey. It seems to me to settle the ancient controversy over whether 'outside money' is 'net wealth' decisively, and in the negative. In this hypothetical move from a barter to a monetary system, the public acquires an asset (currency) in exchange for a liability (a stream of coupon payments owed the government) of equal value. Of course, the public is better off in a welfare sense after this exchange takes place, but this is not reflected in its balance sheet, nor is there any reason to expect it to be.

fig. 1. No distorting taxes or subsidies are ever levied. The initially created, negative government debt is never retired or augmented.

As a second example, differing only slightly from the first, let government consumption be constant at some level *g*. Then monetary policy is efficiently conducted exactly as in example 1, but an income tax must be levied so as to move goods and leisure consumption to the point *A* in fig. 1, and keep it there. Technically (in an accounting sense) the government runs a constant fiscal surplus, but tax revenues and government purchases of goods and services are in perfect balance.

In either of these two examples, the situation is only slightly altered if the government begins as an initial debtor with respect to the public. The effect of this modification is to necessitate an additional distorting tax for debt service, moving the system down from point *B* (in example 1) or from point *A* (in example 2). Such debt is a burden, and society is better off the less of it there is, but it is not an efficient objective of policy to reduce or retire it in situations where government goods demands are constant through time.

Complications to these simple monetary and fiscal policies arise when government demands are erratic, so let us move to a third example that has this feature in extreme form. Let government consumption be zero in all periods except some period *T* in the future, and let it be positive in this period *T*. Take these facts to be known to all decision makers, private and public. Now a *feasible* fiscal response to this situation is to operate at point *A* in period *T* and at point *B* in all other periods, accepting the utility loss from the tax distortion contemporaneously with the loss from the government withdrawal of resources. But while the latter loss cannot (by assumption) be reallocated over time, the first ('second-order') loss can, and in general Ramsey's smoothing principle implies that it is efficient to do so. To do this, the government must levy taxes from time zero on, using the revenues so acquired to purchase bonds from the public. At date *T*, when the real expenditure must be incurred, this ' war chest' is cashed and new bonds are sold to the public. In this way, the tax distortions are spread both backward and forward from the date of the expenditure. After period *T*, society is left with a government debt, but as in the first two examples, it is not an objective of policy to pay it off, unless the government expenditure is expected to recur in the future. (If it *is* recurrent, debt can follow a cyclical pattern, as society pays for the last 'war' and then begins building for the next, but I am trying to keep the number of examples to a minimum and so will not pursue this variation.)

For a fourth and final example, let the situation be exactly as in example 3, except that the positive government demand in period T occurs with probability θ and is zero (as in all periods other than T) with probability $1 - \theta$. This probability is known to all, but no one has advance information on the realization of this one-time shock. Again, tax smoothing will be the guiding fiscal principle, but smoothing must now be over states of nature as well as over dates. The key implication of this principle for present purposes is that the efficient tax rate is the *same* in all peacetime periods: periods 0 through $T - 1$, periods $T + 1$ on, and period T if no war occurs in that period. What is the debt management policy that is consistent with this tax policy and the given behavior of government spending?

From period 0 through $T - 1$, the government uses its budget surplus to purchase bonds from the public. At period $T - 1$ or before those bonds must be made *contingent* on the occurrence of a positive expenditure in T: If the war occurs, the public must owe the government enough to finance it, beyond the funds raised through contemporary taxes and the issue of new bonds. If the war does not occur, this debt must be valueless. In effect, society is using state-contingent public debt to provide itself with distortion-insurance against the contingency that large expenditures must be financed.

It would clarify things to work our general efficiency principles through a few more examples, but I think the general ideas should be clear enough to permit us to proceed to other issues. Public debt in the economy under study serves two purposes. It is the security on the other side of the balance sheet from currency, or outside money. It is, more fundamentally, the device by which tax distortions can be distributed over time and over stochastically determined states of nature. It has no functions other than these two.

5. Time-Consistency

I have been calling the monetary and fiscal principles obtained for this model economy 'Ramsey principles', because they are formally identical to the rules Ramsey derived for setting excise taxes in a multi-good, static economy, if one makes use of the familiar Arrow–Debreu device of treating goods at different dates and states of nature simply as different goods. The parallel between Ramsey's analysis and mine would be exact (except for the technical matter of the dimension of the commodity spaces involved) if it were the case that in the dynamic economy all tax rates and open market operations were set, once and for all, at some initial date. Viewed in this way, what I have been calling 'efficient' monetary and fiscal policies, and the resource allocations associated with them, are Nash equilibria in a static game with a benevolent government and a continuum of private agents as players. (All players, public and private, have the same objective in this game, it is true, but this does not make them a single player: They have very different strategies available to them.)

Alternatively, one could choose to model these same interactions as a sequential game, with an infinity of governmental players, where the date-*t* government inherits a situation from the past, selects a monetary–fiscal move for date-*t*, and passes off stage. The attraction of this alternative formulation is that it seems to match much better the fact that actual governments have very limited abilities to bind their successors to future monetary and fiscal decisions. It also seems much more consistent with the political principle that taxes ought to be set by those who are subject to the tax, not pre-assigned to them by others. This raises the question, then, of whether the efficient policies that are equilibria in a static policy game, or equivalently in a dynamic game with full advance commitment, continue to be equilibria when the game is reformulated sequentially. In general, the answer to this question is: No, they do not. In other, equivalent, terminology: the efficient policies are not, in general, *time-consistent*. Kydland and Prescott (1977) have insisted on the importance of this problem of time-inconsistency for dynamic applications of welfare economics. Some examples will indicate, I think, that they were absolutely right in this insistence.

Suppose, in the model we have just been discussing, that capital goods are added to labor as a factor of production. Then taxing previously accumulated capital—a 'capital levy'—is equivalent to a lump-sum tax, from which it follows that a fully confiscatory tax on capital is part of any efficient tax program. At the same time, taxes on future capital accumulation will clearly result in welfare losses, so an efficient policy must also involve non-confiscatory taxation on new capital. This combination of different tax rates on old and newly accumulated capital is fully consistent with the Ramsey principle (indeed, it follows directly from it) but it is not time-consistent if future governments are free to re-think the optimal tax problem. If they are, then following the same Ramsey reasoning they too will tax the old capital at much higher rates than those that were 'promised' capitalists at the time this capital was accumulated.

This problem of the 'capital levy' is the classic example of a time-inconsistency and it has long been recognized that an efficient tax system must effectively outlaw such taxes. But ruling out capital levies, even if this can effectively be done,[5] does not eliminate the problem of time-inconsistency, because this problem is not limited to the taxation of physical capital goods and the income they produce. It arises, most generally, whenever the private sector must first commit itself to a current decision on the basis of its beliefs about a future action taken by government, and then, with this commitment made, the government is free to select this future action. Two such situations arise in the model I have described, even though capital accumulation was abstracted from. Both are important.

Most obviously, the private sector chooses to hold dollar-denominated government obligations—money and bonds—on the basis of expectations about the future dollar price of goods. This price level is, in turn, determined in part by future monetary policy. Any such nominal asset can be taxed away by a rapid inflation—an exact formal equivalent of the capital levy. As with any time-inconsistency, what makes this possibility so subversive is that, once the private sector is committed, it is *efficient* to do this. Defaulting on nominal debt, currency included, is not simply a problem with gangster government, though it arises there too, but with the ideally beneficent government of welfare economics. There are but two ways to eliminate this kind of capital levy. One is for government policies affecting the general price level to be entirely pre-committed. A second, spelled out in detail by Svensson, Persson and Persson (1985), is for the government to hold nominal bonds issued by the private sector so as to maintain a net *nominal* asset position of zero.

Let us suppose that one of these kinds of pre-commitments is achieved, so that government obligations are equivalent to dated obligations to deliver real goods in the future. Yet another form of time-inconsistency is still present. It arises because government, through its ability to set taxes,

5. It is the equivalences, often hard to see, between apparently different tax structures that make it difficult to rule out any particular tax. For example, Chamley (1982) shows how an investment tax credit can be used, in conjunction with other taxes, to achieve the equivalent of a tax on old capital even if direct capital levies are precluded.

is able to influence equilibrium prices of future goods—interest rates. Even if the previous government has passed on a set of goods commitments, the current one can influence the market value of these commitments. It turns out that this last time-inconsistency is fixable, in roughly the following way: By selecting exactly the right maturity structure for the debt it leaves to its successor, a government can so set the terms of the maximum problem solved by its successor that the latter will choose to continue with an efficient tax policy *and* to restructure the debt it inherits so as to induce its successor in turn to continue efficiently. This normative role for the maturity structure of the debt is spelled out in more detail in Lucas and Stokey (1983). An interesting substantive finding of this analysis is that, starting from an initial position with no outstanding debt obligations, a time-consistent, efficient debt-tax policy involves the issue of consols (infinite maturity bonds) only.

6. Summary

I have been concerned with deriving *efficient* monetary and fiscal policies in a particular context, but in the course of the discussion the term *efficiency* has become stretched to the point where it can no longer bear the weight of multiple meanings I have placed on it. Let me go back over the logic of the argument to clarify this and, in general, to sum up the principles we have arrived at.

Throughout I have been assuming, in the welfare-economic tradition, a government that takes as its objective the maximization of consumer welfare. This narrows the problem of defining efficient government behavior, but it does not resolve it until the strategies available to the government and to private agents are also spelled out. The restriction of fiscal policies to those involving flat-rate taxation only, with the private sector assumed to be in a rational expectations equilibrium, led to an optimal tax problem of the Ramsey type. I have called the policy that solves this *efficient,* and spent some time developing its characteristics.

If we think of a succession of governments taking office through time, each one solving a Ramsey problem of this same structure, it turns out that, in general, a government will not find it efficient, in this sense, to continue with the policy found efficient by its predecessors. One must either permit an initial government to make decisions binding for all time, enforcing the original Ramsey solution, or restrict available strategies still further until this time-inconsistency problem disappears.

I have taken the second of these two courses, imposing two additional, one might call them 'constitutional', rules of game on all governments: That capital levies—taxes on previously accumulated capital and their equivalents—be set at zero, and that monetary policy be pre-committed to the maintenance of a specific path of nominal prices. Under these rules, and if each government manages the maturity structure of the debt it inherits in the right way, the efficient Ramsey taxes—the characteristics of which I have illustrated with examples—are time-consistent. It is *this* tax structure, *together* with the debt policy that enforces its time-consistency, *together* with these two essential monetary and fiscal pre-commitments, that I now want to call an *efficient* policy. If pursued, this policy will permit the citizens of this model economy to attain the highest welfare level they can hope for in the absence of recourse to lump-sum taxes. Moreover, the policy can be implemented by governments with *no* power to set tax rates for their successors (that is, with fiscal authority comparable to existing democratic governments) provided, and *only* provided, that no government can resort to capital levies and none has any discretionary authority over monetary policy.[6]

7. Conclusions

At the beginning of this talk, I said that my main purpose was to discuss connections between policy in the model I was about to set out and policy in the United States, today. My experience is that an economic model, if it is concrete enough really to be visualized, has a life of its own, and people will draw such analogies between it and 'reality' as they find helpful, quite independently of how one might wish or try to direct them. I will sketch

6. What rationalizes the presumption that governments can or ought to precommit future governments to future monetary policies and real debt payments, but not to future taxes? In the framework of Lucas and Stokey (1983) one kind of commitment seems as easy or desirable to enforce as the other. The general idea that future generations ought to be free to determine their own government expenditure and tax rates seems sound to me, but it is not one that can be studied within the infinitely-lived family abstraction. As remarked in footnote 2, it would be good to have a framework within which one could study issues of intergenerational conflict and cooperation.

the connections that seem clearest and most useful to me, but with the understanding that they cannot be established on the same logical level at which we can understand the internal workings of the model itself.

The respect in which policy discussion in the model differs most radically from the way policy is discussed in the United States today is in its dynamic structure. Choice in the model has entirely to do with *timing:* taxes today or taxes tomorrow, deficits now and surpluses later, or the other way around. As soon as the problem of optimal taxation is stated with any care, it is evident that its solution *cannot* take the form of a relationship between the *current* state of the economy and *current* monetary and fiscal policy variables. This observation is, or ought to be, a platitude, but it is very widely ignored in public and even professional discussions of fiscal policy today. In the model, a decision to issue more debt is *equivalent* to a decision to reduce government consumption, increase taxes, or increase the inflation rate at some future date. This equivalence is simply a consequence of the government budget constraint, stated in present value terms, so it obviously does not arise from any special feature of the model. A coherent discussion of fiscal policy would thus require an opponent of deficit-reducing taxes today to indicate specifically which taxes he proposes to increase at future dates or, which comes to the same thing, which future revenues he proposes to sell, today, to the purchasers of new government bonds.[7]

The more specific implications of the model are of two types: implications of the Ramsey efficiency principle and implications concerning time consistency. One implication of the Ramsey principle is that tax rates ought to be smoothed over periods of differing government demands, relative to endowment. In practice, this principle requires deficit spending during wars and depressions, balanced (in a present value sense) by surpluses in times of relative peace and prosperity. This is a principle the common sense of which has long been recognized. One of the attractions of Keynesian theory was that it appeared to give a respectable rationalization of this common sense view, as opposed to the view that budgets ought to be continuously balanced. The present, neoclassical principle implies simi-

7. Indexing debt does not achieve this end. Indexed debt is simply a 'promise' that the government will somehow come up with the real resources to meet coupon payments. A security that entitled its holder to a preassigned share of, say, the excise tax on gasoline would be closer to what I have in mind.

lar fiscal policies over the cycle (at least qualitatively) but does so in a way that respects the budget constraint of governments and is thus also consistent with the common sense view that budgets must, in some sense or other, balance.

On these same Ramsey grounds, inflation taxes do not have a comparable role to play in the intertemporal smoothing of tax distortions. Unless there is a case for varying the mix (as opposed to the level) of private consumption spending as government demands vary, the efficient policy is to keep nominal interest rates low and stable, whatever the state of the system. Though directed at interest rates (for this is the price that matters for monetary efficiency) this policy principle bears no resemblance to the very-short-term (and even there dubious) idea that interest rates can be kept low by monetary expansions. Here the idea is exactly the reverse: to use predictably low rates of monetary growth to keep inflation premia small, or negative.

The rationale for these principles is clear enough, I think, in the model, and seems to me to carry over quite naturally to the more complicated real-world application. The model does not, to be sure, give any help in determining the best *mix* of taxes at each date, but its formulation seems to dovetail very easily with the best neoclassical public finance treatments of this important question. Neither is it useful in considering distributional or social insurance issues, but it does not seem to me likely that the incorporation of these issues would alter in any basic way the model's implications on intertemporal questions.

The model also does not deal with business cycles, so that the rationale it offers for deficit spending during depressions takes the form of an optimal *response* to low-income periods, not a cure for them. I am persuaded by the evidence Friedman and others have marshalled that associates at least major recessions with monetary instability, so that I believe a monetary policy selected on the efficiency grounds I have discussed would, as a kind of by-product, be an adequate counter-recession policy.[8] But, obviously, the model I have described sheds no light on this issue. It may be that some day we will have an operational theory of business cycles that suggests additional, useful principles besides those I have discussed. In the

8. This is exactly the case Friedman (1948) made for the monetary and fiscal framework he proposed.

meantime, it seems sensible to me to take policy guidance from models we can actually understand and work through, not from models we wish we had, or models other people think we have.

A central dilemma of policy in the model is the fact that these intertemporal efficiency principles will *not,* in general, be adhered to by a succession of governments, each of which is free to choose current monetary and fiscal policies as it sees fit, *even if* these governments each fully support the reasoning underlying them. Instead, each government will see the advantage of using monetary policy to relieve some of the very real burdens of current and future taxation, while advising its successor governments not to follow suit. This same dilemma faces actual governments as well, I believe: It is not an issue created artificially by the simplicities of the model.

The term *time-inconsistency* is new to technical macroeconomic analysis, but the general issue of long-term government commitment is an ancient one, and one that has received a great deal of intelligent attention. Certainly the temptation of the capital levy, and the need to preclude recourse to it, has long been recognized by economists and responsible governments. It may be useful to consider briefly some of the other devices governments have adopted in the past to deal with time-inconsistencies that arise in monetary and fiscal policy problems.

The classical gold standard was an explicit mechanism for removing the nominal price level from the influence of national policies. This device has the definite advantage (in contrast to rules fixing the quantity of national currency) of permitting the money supply in each country to fluctuate in response to local real shocks. Its disadvantage, of course, is that the path to which the gold standard pegs prices has no necessary connection to an *efficient* path. Historically, price level behavior under the gold standard did not set inflation and interest rates at or near their efficient levels, nor did it come close to stabilizing either.

On the fiscal side, adherence to the goal of budget balance (or at least peacetime budget balance) has been a traditional and effective device for enforcing time-consistency. Yet like the gold standard, continuous budget balance can come at the expense of efficiency. Though peacetime budget balance, as a principle seriously adhered to, effectively ruled out peacetime inflation for much of U.S. history, the same principle also dictated inefficiently high tax burdens during depressions.

Another form of fiscal discipline, not much in fashion today at the national level, is trust fund accounting, under which revenues from specific taxes are allocated to specific uses. By earmarking gasoline taxes for highway maintenance, say, one is compelled to view this particular form of government spending and its financing as a single decision. The social security system was once, most usefully, on a similar basis. Such linking of specific revenues to specific spending categories need not, of course, be contemporaneous. When Alexander Hamilton successfully committed the U.S. government to retiring the Revolutionary War Debt, he proposed specific excise taxes the proceeds of which were earmarked for bondholders.

Disciplines like these—monetary standards, budget balance, trust fund accounting—formed parts of what James Buchanan and Richard Wagner (1977) have called our unwritten 'fiscal constitution'. In common with written constitutions, each of these disciplines can be amended or evaded, an observation that has led to some skepticism about the usefulness of trying to bind economic policy at all. What is the 'discipline' of a monetary standard if the government always has the option to devalue? This is a difficult question, I think, but it is a poor response to conclude that since the effectiveness of such disciplines is hard to measure, they are unimportant forces. Certainly there are innumerable episodes in U.S. history where disciplines like these appear to have been, for better or worse, binding constraints on policy.

The point of these brief observations is not that these particular institutions served to enforce exactly, or even approximately, the maintenance of economically efficient monetary and fiscal policies. On the contrary, I think that in many cases they served to enforce *in*efficiencies. The point is rather that they illustrate the fact that the need to subject economic policy decisions to constraints or pre-commitments of some kind has long been recognized, and that it is possible to design social institutions that do in fact limit the discretion of future policy makers. The theory of public finance is only now developing the apparatus and vocabulary for thinking about this design problem in a more systematic way. I think this is an important and constructive development.

In Lucas and Stokey (1983), exact formulas are given for the precommitted path of nominal prices and the path, enforced by optimum management of the maturity structure of the debt, of taxes, that will foster efficient resource allocations. These formulas are complex, and their correctness depends, of course, on the correctness of the model within which they were derived. It is hard to imagine an economic constitution, written or unwritten, that spells out its provisions in terms of infinite sequences of contingent claims (as our formulas do). An alternative use of this same formalism would be to quantify the welfare cost of simple (and non-optimal) rules for fiscal and monetary management under realistic assumptions about the nature of the outside shocks to which the economy is subject. I would conjecture, for example, that a Friedman-type four percent rule for money growth, though certainly less efficient than a monetary policy that reacted to real shocks in just the right way, would have welfare consequences differing trivially from the optimum policy and, unlike the latter, would be easy to spell out and monitor. Similarly, I would conjecture (given the smoothness of peacetime government consumption) that a peacetime annual budget balance requirement would have excellent operating characteristics. Research in this quantitative direction would certainly need to go well beyond the purely qualitative considerations I have stressed in this lecture, but its promise in return would be to re-engage macroeconomic research with the policy problems our society actually faces.

If the structure of the 'policy game' faced in reality bears any resemblance to the theoretical situation I have analyzed in this lecture, there is no chance that even the best intentioned governments, operating under these rules, will generate outcomes that even crudely approximate economic efficiency. The tendencies toward permanent deficit finance and inflation that have emerged in our economy in the last fifteen years have much deeper roots that a succession of transient external shocks and internal mistakes. They arose, I believe, because the implicit rules under which monetary and fiscal policy is conducted have undergone a gradual but fundamental change. If this diagnosis is accurate, then the situation will improve only if new rules can be found that bind policy decisions without committing them to permanent inefficiencies.

One of the characteristics that has made Karl Brunner such a stimulating colleague is his steady confidence that doing scientific economics and thinking about practical matters of public policy are one activity, not two. The intellectual span of control required by this attitude is demanding, and for the most part I have been content to admire it in others rather than attempting to maintain it consistently myself. The present paper is an exception, and it does not seem to me unfair to ask Karl to assume some of the responsibility for it.

References

Barro, R. J., 1979, On the determination of the public debt, Journal of Political Economy 87, 940–971.

Buchanan, J. M., 1976, Barro on the Richardian equivalence theorem, Journal of Political Economy 84, 337–342.

Buchanan, J. M. and R. E. Wagner, 1977, Democracy in deficit (Academic Press, New York).

Chamley, C., 1982, On optimal taxation in stylized models of intertemporal general equilibrium, Working paper (Yale University, New Haven, CT).

Friedman, M., 1948, A monetary and fiscal framework for economic stability, American Economic Review 38, 245–264. Reprinted in: 1953, Essays in positive economics (University of Chicago Press, Chicago, IL).

Friedman, M., 1969, The optimum quality of money, in: The optimum quantity of money and other essays (University of Chicago Press, Chicago, IL) 1–50.

Kydland F. E. and E. C. Prescott, 1977, Rules rather than discretion: The inconsistency of optimal plans, Journal of Political Economy 85, 473–93.

Kydland F. E. and E. C. Prescott, 1980, A competitive theory of fluctuations and the feasibility and desirability of stabilization policy, in: Stanley Fischer, ed., Rational expectations and economic policy (University of Chicago Press, Chicago, IL).

Lucas, R. E., Jr., 1982, Interest rates and currency prices in a two-country world, Journal of Monetary Economics 10, 335–360.

Lucas, R. E., Jr. and N. L. Stokey, 1983, Optimal fiscal and monetary policy in an economy without capital, Journal of Monetary Economics 12, 55–93.

Mises, L. von, 1949, Human action (Yale University Press, New Haven, CT).

Phelps, E. S., 1973, Inflation in the theory of public finance, Swedish Journal of Economics 75, 67–82.

Ramsey, F. P., 1927, A contribution to the theory of taxation, Economic Journal 37, 47–61.

Svensson, Lars E. O., Mats Persson and Torsten Persson, 1985, Time consistency of fiscal and monetary policy, Working paper (Institute for International Economic Studies, Stockholm).

— 10 —

Money and Interest in a Cash-in-Advance Economy

ROBERT E. LUCAS, JR. AND NANCY L. STOKEY[1]

I. Introduction

Macroeconomics has traditionally been concerned with the study of a limited set of aggregate variables—GNP, the general price level, "the" interest rate, and so forth—designed to provide a summary description of the economy as a whole. In part this study has involved the statistical description of co-movements in these series, and in part it has involved the analysis of general equilibrium models that are simple enough to permit the construction and characterization of solutions under various assumptions about the way monetary and other policies are conducted. The general idea, of course, is that structural models capable of approximately replicating the actual behavior of these aggregate variables, given policies similar to those actually observed, may be useful in predicting how the behavior of the aggregates would be changed if various alternative policies were to be implemented.

Recently, a number of studies have used the vector autoregression (VAR) methods pioneered by Sims (1972) as a means of summarizing the entire empirical joint distribution of the standard aggregates, under the hypothesis that these series (or suitable transforms of them) form a stationary stochastic process. This method has the advantage of providing a compact

Econometrica 55, no. 3 (May 1987): 491–513.

1. We wish to thank Jean-Michel Grandmont, Rodolfo Manuelli, Edward Prescott, Thomas Sargent, Robert Townsend, and the editor and referees of this journal, for helpful comments. This work was supported by grants from the National Science Foundation, and by the Center for Advanced Studies in Managerial Economics and Decision Sciences at Northwestern University.

summary of the observations in a way that seems theoretically "neutral." Sims (1980), Litterman and Weiss (1985), and others have suggested, beyond this, that these methods are useful as diagnostics in determining which *classes* of structural models may be consistent with observation: certain features of the estimated VARs are described as "Keynesian" (or as inconsistent with Keynesian models), others as "classical," and so on. Thus, Sims' (1972) finding that money "causes" real output (in Granger's sense), was interpreted as "classical" or "monetarist," while his (1980) conclusion that nominal interest rates "cause" output was interpreted as "Keynesian."

If it were in fact the case that VAR (or other purely statistical) methods could perform this diagnostic function, this would obviously be most useful in narrowing the theoretical search for good structural models. The difficulty is that traditional theoretical models, whether Keynesian or classical, typically take the form of deterministic systems that cannot be meaningfully compared to the estimated distribution. Thus, in deciding whether an estimated VAR is or is not consistent with the predictions of, say, an IS/LM model, one is obliged to imagine a stochastic version of the IS/LM model and work out its predictions, all in one's head! It seems clear enough that to interpret empirical distributions of macroeconomic aggregates one needs an explicitly stochastic theoretical model, a model that permits the calculation of a predicted *theoretical* joint distribution of shocks and endogenously determined variables that can be compared to the observed distribution. For comparison with VAR's, stationary models are called for.

Such theories have been developed by Lucas (1982) and Svensson (1985), using recursive models, but in these two papers the equilibrium resource allocations were determined entirely by the exogenously given goods endowments, so the analysis involved determining the behavior of prices *given* quantities. Townsend (1987), on the other hand, has developed a monetary equilibrium model with both production and capital accumulation, so that quantities and prices are simultaneously determined and monetary shocks have the capacity to affect the allocation of resources. The analysis there is directly in terms of sequences, however, so that stationarity (recursivity) is not exploited,

The model presented here is intermediate to these. Agents have possibilities for substituting against money that are not present in Lucas (1982) or Svensson (1987), so that equilibrium quantities and prices must be determined simultaneously. On the other hand, the present model excludes capital formation, and assumes a recursive structure that is much more specific than the one in Townsend (1986). These simplifications permit an existence proof that can be specialized to yield constructive methods for calculating and characterizing equilibrium behavior under alternative assumptions about policy.

In the model, the use of money is motivated by a Clower (1967) type cash-in-advance constraint, applied to purchases of a subset of consumption goods. There are both real and monetary shocks, which are economy wide and observed by all. Agents are infinitely lived and identical in all respects. As we will show later on, under these assumptions equilibrium quantities and goods prices behave *as if* agents were restricted to hold no securities other than currency. Accordingly, we begin by studying recursive equilibria in a simple cash-only model.

In Section 2 we analyze the problem faced by the representative consumer, and in Section 3, we show that solving for the equilibrium is equivalent to finding a solution to a particular functional equation. In Section 4, we use the Schauder fixed point theorem to prove that under certain (not entirely standard) assumptions on preferences, solutions to this functional equation exist. We also show how further restrictions on consumer preferences yield additional information about the multiplicity of equilibria and/or algorithms for constructing them.

In Section 5 we incorporate securities trading into the model. We show that equilibrium consumption allocations in these more general economies coincide with those determined in Sections 2–4, and develop a formula for the equilibrium prices of arbitrary securities. Three examples are then provided to illustrate the predictions of the model for the relationship between interest rates and monetary policy. Section 6 concludes the paper.

2. The Model

The model[2] is formulated in discrete time with an infinite horizon. Shocks to the system in any period, denoted by $s \in S \subset \mathbb{R}^n$, form a first-order Markov process with a stationary transition function. Specifically, let S

2. This model is a special case of the one discussed in Lucas (1984) and is very closely related to Lucas and Stokey (1983) and Townsend (1987); the reader is referred there for further discussion.

denote the family of Borel sets of S, and let $\pi : S \times S \to [0, 1]$ denote the transition function. S and π satisfy the following assumption:

ASSUMPTION 1: *S is compact. For each $s \in S$, $\pi(s, \cdot) : S \to [0, 1]$ is a probability measure, and for each $A \in S$, $\pi(\cdot, A) : S \to [0, 1]$ is S-measurable. Moreover, π is continuous in the weak topology, i.e., for any bounded, continuous function $f: S \to \mathbb{R}$, the function $Tf(s) = \int f(s')\pi(s, ds')$, is also continuous.*

There are two consumption goods available each period: "cash goods," which are subject to a Clower (cash-in-advance) constraint, and "credit goods," which are not.[3] There is a single, infinitely-lived "representative consumer." His consumption of cash and credit goods are c_{1t} and c_{2t} respectively, and his preferences are

$$E\left\{\sum_{t=0}^{\infty} \beta^t U(c_t)\right\},$$

where $0 < \beta < 1$, $c_t = (c_{1t}, c_{2t})$, and the expectation is over realizations of the shocks.

ASSUMPTION 2: *$U : \mathbb{R}^2_+ \to \mathbb{R}$ is bounded, continuously differentiate, strictly increasing, and strictly concave, and for all $\underline{y} > 0$,*

$$\lim_{c \to 0} \frac{U_1(c, y - c)}{U_2(c, y - c)} = \infty, \quad \text{and} \quad \lim_{c \to y} \frac{U_1(c, y - c)}{U_2(c, y - c)} = 0.$$

The two Inada conditions in Assumption 2 are to ensure that the agent will not wish to specialize in either cash or credit goods as long as both have positive prices.

Goods are not storable, and the technology each period is simply $c_1 + c_2 \leq y$, where $y(s)$, the endowment, is a function of the current shock. For sellers, cash goods sales result in currency receipts that simply accumulate during the period and are carried as overnight balances, while credit goods sales result in invoices that are settled in cash at the beginning of the next day. Both overnight balances and invoices become cash available for spending at the same time on the following day. Hence it is clear that in each period cash and credit goods will sell at the same nominal price.

3. One way to interpret "credit goods"—goods which do not need to be paid for in cash—is as non-market goods, such as "leisure." We will make illustrative use of this interpretation in Section 6.

The only activity of the government in this economy is to supply money, injected as lump-sum transfers, and the money growth factor in any period t is a fixed function $g(s)$ of the shock.[4] Therefore, if $\hat{m}_{t-1}$ is per capita money in circulation in $t-1$, an agent who carries overnight balances plus invoices of m_{t-1} will have post-transfer balances in t of $m_t = m_{t-1} + [g(s_t) - 1]\hat{m}_{t-1}$. Throughout the paper, we will normalize per capita money balances to be unity: $\hat{m}_{t-1} = 1$.

ASSUMPTION 3: *$y : S \to \mathbb{R}_+$ and $g : S \to \mathbb{R}_+$ are continuous functions, and both are bounded away from zero.*

Note that under Assumptions 1 and 3, $g(s)$ and $y(s)$ take values in closed intervals $[\underline{g}, \bar{g}]$ and $[\underline{y}, \bar{y}]$, with $\underline{g} > 0$ and $\underline{y} > 0$. Note too that since s is a vector of arbitrary (but finite) length, the specification of the endowment process and monetary "policy" is extremely flexible. In particular, s may include lagged values of the endowment and the rate of money growth, signals about future values of these variables, and pure "noise" components that serve as randomizing devices.

We will motivate a definition of a stationary equilibrium, in which prices and quantities are fixed functions of the state of the system. To do so, we begin with the decision problem facing a single agent, for whom the functions p, g, and y are all fixed and known. Suppose that his cash assets, after the current tax or transfer, are m relative to the economy-wide average, which we normalize to unity. His knowledge about the system consists of the current state, s. He purchases goods (x_1, x_2) at a price $p(s)$ (expressed as a ratio to the current period's money supply) subject to the cash constraint

$$p(s)x_1 - m \leq 0. \tag{2.1}$$

These purchases together with the sale of his endowment $y(s)$, also determine his cash position, x_3, before the tax or transfer next period, so that his budget constraint in the goods market is:

4. With infinitely-lived agents and recourse to lump-sum taxes, the timing of taxes and subsidies is immaterial, and there is no distinction between an injection of money through a fiscal transfer payment and an injection through an "open-market" puchase of government bonds. Hence, this convention will not affect the results. See Lucas and Stokey (1983) for a parallel discussion in which taxes are assumed to distort and this distinction is central.

$$x_3 - m - p(s)[y(s) - x_1 - x_2] \leq 0. \tag{2.2}$$

Given x_3, the agent's post-transfer cash position next period (renormalized by next period's money supply) will be $(x_3 + g(s') - 1)/g(s')$. Finally, since his consumption and money balances must be nonnegative, we have

$$x_1, x_2, x_3 \geq 0. \tag{2.3}$$

For each $(m, s) \in \mathbb{R}_+ \times S$, let $\phi(m, s) \subset \mathbb{R}^3_+$ denote the set of x-values satisfying (2.1)–(2.3). Note that if $p(s)$ is strictly positive the correspondence ϕ is compact- and convex-valued, and is continuous in m. If p is continuous, then under Assumption 3, ϕ is also continuous in s. Finally, for each fixed $s \in S$, $\phi(m, s)$ is convex in m, i.e., if $x \in \phi(m, s)$ and $x' \in \phi(m', s)$, then $\alpha x + (1 - \alpha)x' \in \phi(\alpha m + (1 - \alpha)m', s)$, for all $\alpha \in [0, 1]$.

Let $F(m, s)$ be the value of the maximized objective function for a consumer beginning the period with assets m, when the economy is in state s. Then F must satisfy

$$F(m, s) = \sup_{x \in \phi(m,s)} \left\{ U(x_1, x_2) + \beta \int_S F\left(\frac{x_3 + g(s') - 1}{g(s')}, s' \right) \pi(s, ds') \right\}. \tag{2.4}$$

Let $\mathcal{F}$ be the space of bounded, continuous, real-valued functions $f(m, s)$ on $\mathbb{R}_+ \times S$, with the norm $\|f\| = \sup_{m,s} |f(m, s)|$.

LEMMA 1: *Under Assumptions 1–3, given any continuous, strictly positive price function $p : S \to \mathbb{R}_+$, there exists a unique value function $F \in \mathcal{F}$ satisfying (2.4). F is strictly increasing, strictly concave, and continuously differentiable in its first argument. For each (m, s), the maximum in (2.4) is attained by a unique value $\psi(m, s)$, and the policy function ψ is continuous.*

PROOF: To prove the existence and uniqueness of $F \in \mathcal{F}$, it is sufficient to show that the operator T on $\mathcal{F}$ defined by

$$Tf(m, s) = \sup_{x \in \phi(m, s)} \left\{ U(x_1, x_2) + \beta \int_S f\left(\frac{x_3 + g(s') - 1}{g(s')}, s' \right) \pi(s, ds') \right\}, \tag{2.5}$$

maps $\mathcal{F}$ into itself, and is a contraction. Under Assumption 2, clearly Tf is bounded. Under Assumption 3 the integrand in (2.5) is a continuous function of s', so that under Assumption 1 the integral is a continuous function of s. Clearly the right side of (2.5) is also continuous in x. Then since ϕ *is* compact-valued and continuous, it follows that Tf is continuous and the correspondence $\psi : \mathbb{R}_+ \times S \to \mathbb{R}^3_+$ consisting of the maximizing x-values is nonempty and upper hemicontinuous (see Hildenbrand (1974, p. 30)). Hence $T : \mathcal{F} \to \mathcal{F}$. It then follows directly from a theorem of Blackwell (1965, Theorem 5) that T is a contraction, and so has a unique fixed point $F \in \mathcal{F}$.

Since U is strictly increasing and strictly concave, and ϕ is convex in m, T maps functions that are increasing and concave in m into functions that are strictly increasing arid strictly concave in m. Hence F is strictly increasing and strictly concave in m. Hence for each (m, s), the maximizing value $\psi(m, s)$ is unique, so that ψ is a continuous policy function.

Finally, the theorem of Benveniste and Scheinkman (1979) applies, so that F is continuously differentiable in m. *Q.E.D.*

Lemma 1 summarizes the needed information about the consumer's problem. With that, we can proceed to the study of equilibrium.

DEFINITION: A *stationary equilibrium* for this system consists of a continuous, strictly positive, price function p, a value function $F \in \mathcal{F}$, and a policy function $\psi(m, s)$, such that: (i) the functions F, p satisfy (2.4) and ψ is the associated policy function; (ii) for $m = 1$, the policy function has the form $\psi(1, s) = (c(s), 1)$, for all $s \in S$; and (iii) the function $c(s)$ satisfies

$$c_1(s) + c_2(s) = y(s), \qquad \text{all } s. \tag{2.6}$$

These conditions are standard: at the equilibrium prices, $(c(s), 1)$ must be the demands of a "representative consumer" (that is, one with relative assets equal to unity), and with these demands the goods market must clear.

We turn now to proving the existence of equilibrium, Under Assumption 2, the consumer's problem has an interior solution, characterized by the first-order conditions for (2.4). With the equilibrium conditions $m = x_3 = 1$ imposed, these are:

$$U_1(c(s)) - p(s)[v(s) + w(s)] = 0, \qquad \text{all } s; \tag{2.7}$$

$$U_2(c(s)) - p(s)v(s) = 0, \qquad \text{all } s; \tag{2.8}$$

$$p(s)c_1(s) - 1 \leq 0, \qquad \text{with equality if } w(s) > 0, \qquad \text{all } s; \tag{2.9}$$

$$\beta \int_S F_m(1, s') \frac{1}{g(s')} \pi(s, ds') - v(s) = 0 \quad \textit{all } s; \tag{2.10}$$

where $w(s)$ and $v(s)$ are the multipliers associated with (2.1) and (2.2), respectively. In addition, the envelope condition for (2.4) is

$$F_m(1, s) = v(s) + w(s). \tag{2.11}$$

Then it follows immediately from (2.10) and (2.11) that

$$v(s) = \beta \int_S \frac{[v(s') + w(s')]}{g(s')} \pi(s, ds'). \tag{2.12}$$

Equation (2.12), together with conditions (2.6)–(2.9) form a system of five equations in the five unknown functions, $v(s)$, $w(s)$, $p(s)$, $c_1(s)$, and $c_2(s)$. Continuous, nonnegative solutions to this system, with p strictly positive, are equilibria of the model. In the next two sections we turn our attention to the existence and uniqueness of functions satisfying this system.

3. Existence of Equilibrium: Preliminaries

Our strategy for proving the existence of equilibrium is first to use (2.6)–(2.9) to eliminate $w(s')$ from (2.12), as described in Lemmas 2 and 3. Then (2.12) becomes a functional equation in the single function v, equation (3.7). The latter is then analyzed in Section 4.

For fixed $v \geq 0$ and $y \geq 0$, equations (2.6)–(2.9) are simply four equations in c_1, c_2, w, and p: the values of the equilibrium functions $c(s)$, $w(s)$, and $p(s)$ when $v = v(s)$ and $y = y(s)$. Use (2.8) to eliminate p and (2.6) to eliminate c_2, so that for each $s \in S$, (y, v, w, c_1) must satisfy

$$w = v\left[\frac{U_1(c_1, y - c_1)}{U_2(c_1, y - c_1)} - 1\right] \geq 0, \tag{3.1}$$

$$c_1 U_2(c_1, y - c_1) \leq v, \qquad \text{with equality if } w > 0. \tag{3.2}$$

Therefore, an equilibrium is characterized by continuous functions $v(s)$, $w(s)$, and $c_1(s)$ satisfying (3.1), (3.2), and (2.12).

To further simplify this system we need to make some additional assumptions on preferences.

ASSUMPTION 4: *For all* $y \geq 0$, $cU_2(c, y - c)$ *is strictly increasing in* c, *with*

$$\lim_{c \to 0} cU_2(c, y - c) = 0, \quad \text{and} \quad \lim_{c \to y} cU_2(c, y - c) = \infty;$$

and for some $A < \infty$,

$$cU_1(c, y - c) \leq A, \qquad \text{all } 0 \leq c \leq y, \qquad \text{all } y \geq 0.$$

Define the function $c^* : \mathbb{R}_+ \to \mathbb{R}_+$ by

$$\frac{U_1(c^*(y), y - c^*(y))}{U_2(c^*(y), y - c^*(y))} = 1. \tag{3.3}$$

Thus, $(c^*(y), y - c^*(y))$ is the consumption vector that the consumer chooses if his income is y and the cash constraint is slack ($w = 0$). Under Assumption 2, c^* is well defined and continuous. Next, define v^* by

$$v^*(y) = c^*(y)U_2(c^*(y), y - c^*(y)).$$

Finally, for all $y \geq 0$ and $v \geq 0$, define $\hat{c} : \mathbb{R}^2_+ \to \mathbb{R}_+$ by

$$\hat{c}(v, y)U_2(\hat{c}(v, y), y - \hat{c}(v, y)) = v. \tag{3.4}$$

Under Assumptions 2 and 4, $\hat{c}$ is well defined, continuous, and strictly increasing in v and y. In Figure 1, the curves c_1U_1 and c_1U_2 are shown for fixed y. In Figure 2, the axes are reversed and $\hat{c}(v, y)$ is shown.

We are now ready to prove the following result.

LEMMA 2: *Under Assumptions 2 and 4, for any* $y \geq 0$ *and* $v \geq 0$, *the unique pair of values* (w, c_1) *satisfying* (3.1)–(3.2) *is given by*

$$c_1 = \hat{c}(v, y), \qquad \text{if} \qquad 0 \leq v < v^*(y), \tag{3.5a}$$

$$c_1 = c^*(y), \qquad \text{if} \qquad v \geq v^*(y), \tag{3.5b}$$

and w *given by* (3.1).

PROOF: First note that the requirement $w \geq 0$ in (3.1) implies that $U_1/U_2 \geq 1$, which in turn implies that $c_1 \leq c^*(y)$.

Fix (v, y), and suppose that $0 \leq v < v^*(y)$. Then $c_1 = c^*(y)$ is not a solution, since (3.2) would be violated. Hence $c_1 < c^*(y)$, so that $U_1/U_2 > 1$. Then (3.1) implies $w > 0$, so that (3.2) must hold with equality. Hence the only solution is $c_1 = \hat{c}(v, y)$. Alternatively, suppose that $v > v^*(y)$. Since $c_1 \leq c^*(y)$ is required, (3.2) must hold with inequality. Hence it must be that

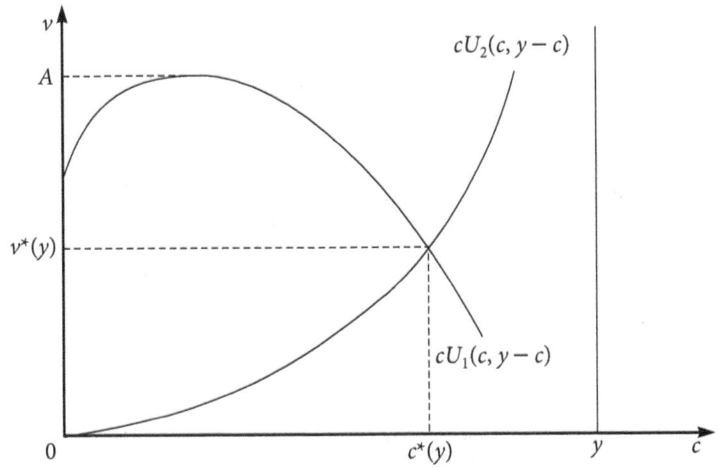

Figure 1

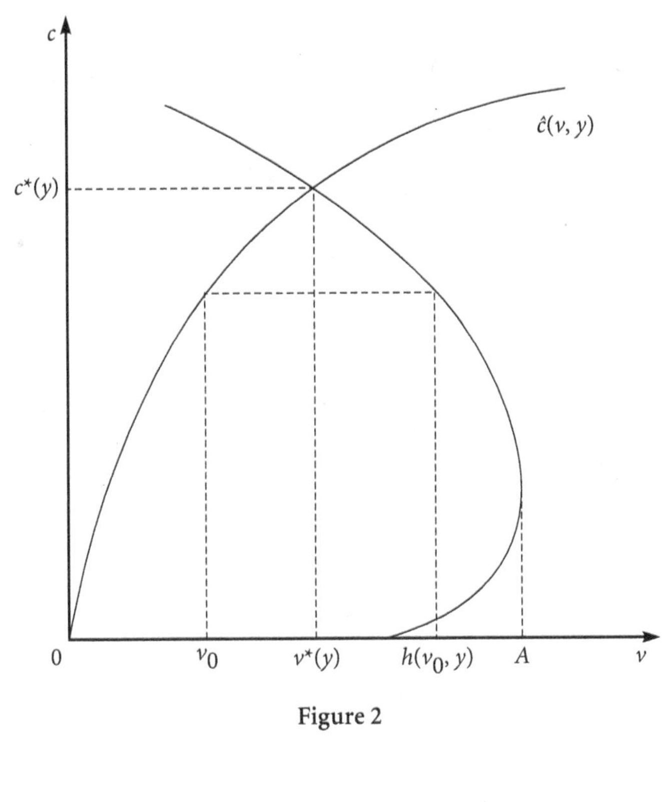

Figure 2

$w = 0$, so that $U_1/U_2 = 1$ and $c_1 = c^*(y)$. Finally, it is clear that if $v = v^*(y)$, then $c^*(y)$ is the only solution. *Q.E.D.*

Next, define $h : \mathbb{R}_+^2 \times \mathbb{R}_+$ by

$$h(v, y) = \hat{c}(v, y)U_1(\hat{c}(v, y), y - \hat{c}(v, y)) \qquad \text{if} \qquad 0 \leq v < v^*(y), \tag{3.6a}$$

$$h(v, y) = v \qquad \text{if} \qquad v \geq v^*(y). \tag{3.6b}$$

To determine h for $0 \leq v < v^*$, refer to Figure 2. Note that h is continuous and for $v < v^*$, h lies between 0 and A, where A is defined in Assumption 4. Using Lemma 2, we can now write (2.12) in terms of the single function v.

LEMMA 3: *Under Assumptions 1–4, the functions v, w, and c_1 satisfy* (2.12), (3.1), *and* (3.2) *if and only if the following hold: v is a continuous function satisfying*

$$v(s) = \int \frac{\beta}{g(s')} h(v(s'), y(s'))\pi(s, ds'), \tag{3.7}$$

c_1 is given by (3.5), *and w is given by* (3.1).

PROOF: From Lemma 2 it follows that we can replace (3.2) with (3.5), and from (3.1) we see that

$$v(s) + w(s) = v(s)\frac{U_1(c_1(s), y(s) - c_1(s))}{U_2(c_1(s), y(s) - c_1(s))}. \tag{3.8}$$

From (3.5a) and (3.4) it follows that

$$\begin{aligned} & 0 \leq v(s) < v^*(y(s)) \\ \Rightarrow \quad & c_1(s) = \hat{c}(v(s), y(s)), \\ \Rightarrow \quad & v(s) = c_1(s)U_2(c_1(s), y(s) - c_1(s)). \end{aligned}$$

It then follows from (3.8) and (3.6a) that

$$\begin{aligned} v(s) + w(s) &= c_1(s)U_1(c_1(s), y(s) - c_1(s)) \\ &= h(v(s), y(s)). \end{aligned}$$

Similarly, we see from (3.5b) and (3.3) that

$$\begin{aligned} & v(s) \geq v^*(y(s)) \\ \Rightarrow \quad & c_1(s) = c^*(y(s)), \end{aligned}$$

$$\Rightarrow \qquad U_1(c_1(s), y(s) - c_1(s))/U_2(c_1(s), y(s) - c_1(s)) = 1,$$

so that (3.8) and (3.6b) imply

$$v(s) + w(s) = v(s) = h(v(s), y(s)).$$

Hence (2.12) can be written as (3.7). *Q.E.D.*

Given a function v satisfying (3.7), we can use (3.5) and (2.6) to find c, (3.1) to find w, and (2.8) to find p. If p is well-defined (finite), continuous, and strictly positive, we can then use Lemma 1 to find F and ψ, and (p, c, F, ψ) is an equilibrium. Under what conditions will the price function have the required properties? If $v > 0$, then we see from (3.4), (3.5), and Assumption 4 that $c_1 > 0$ and hence $U_2 > 0$; and if v is bounded, then (2.8) implies that $p > 0$. Thus, if v is bounded, continuous, and strictly positive, there is a unique corresponding equilibrium. In the next section, we turn to methods for studying (3.7).

4. Existence of Equilibrium: Continued

In this section, we develop a series of results on solutions to (3.7). All of these require additional restrictions on the distribution of the shocks (Assumptions 5 and 6). In Theorem 1 we use Schauder's theorem to establish existence of a solution to (3.7). Theorems 2–5 then impose successively stronger assumptions on preferences to obtain additional results. In Theorem 2, the trivial solution $v(s) \equiv 0$ is ruled out. In Theorem 3 a method for constructing solutions and an operational test for uniqueness are presented. Theorem 4 establiahes the existence of a nontrivial (i.e., strictly positive) solution. Finally, Theorem 5 provides a uniqueness result based on the contraction mapping theorem.

To establish existence of a solution to (3.7), two additional assumptions on the distribution of the shocks are needed.

ASSUMPTION 5: *For each* $s \in S$, $0 < \beta \int_S (1/g(s'))\pi(s, ds') \leq 1$.

ASSUMPTION 6: π *has the following property: for any* $\varepsilon > 0$ *there exists some* $\delta(\varepsilon) > 0$ *such that*

$$\|s - s'\| < \delta(\varepsilon) \Rightarrow \int_S |\Delta(s, s', ds'')| < \varepsilon,$$

where $\Delta : S \times S \times S \to [-1, 1]$ *is defined by*

$$\Delta(s, s', A) = \pi(s, A) - \pi(s', A).$$

Assumption 5 requires that the money supply will never be expected to contract at a rate exceeding the subjective rate of time preference, $\beta^{-1} - 1$. Roughly speaking, this guarantees that nominal interest rates cannot be negative.

Assumption 6 is a strengthening of the continuity requirement of Assumption 1. Assumption 1 states that for each continuous, bounded function $f : S \to \mathbb{R}$, $s \in S$ and $\varepsilon > 0$, there exists $\delta > 0$ such that $s' \in S$ and $|s - s'| \leq \delta$ implies

$$\left|\int f(s'')\pi(s, ds'') - \int f(s'')\pi(s', ds'')\right| \leq \varepsilon \|f\|.$$

Assumption 6 implies that δ can be chosen independently of f and s (so it is a kind of *uniform* continuity requirement).

THEOREM 1: *Under Assumptions* 1–6, *there exists a bounded, continuous function v satisfying* (3.7), *where h is defined in* (3.6). *Moreover, v satisfies* $0 \leq v \leq A$, *where A is defined in Assumption* 4.

PROOF:[5] Let $\mathcal{F}$ be the space of bounded, continuous functions $f : S \to \mathbb{R}$, with the norm $\|f\| = \sup_{s \in S} |f(s)|$. Let $D \subset \mathcal{F}$ be the subset of functions f that have $0 \leq f(s) \leq A$, all $s \in S$, where A is as in Assumption 4. Define the operator T on D by

$$(Tf)(s) = \int_S \frac{\beta}{g(s')} h(f(s'), y(s'))\pi(s, ds').$$

Since $0 \leq h(f(s'), y(s')) \leq A$, all $f \in \mathcal{F}$, and $s' \in S$, it follows from Assumption 5 that $0 \leq Tf(s) \leq A$, all $s \in S$; and since f, g, and h are all continuous, Assumption 1 implies that Tf is continuous. Hence $T : D \to D$.

Moreover, Assumption 6 implies something even stronger. Since the integrand $\beta h/g$ is bounded and π satisfies Assumption 6, it follows that for any $\varepsilon > 0$, there exists $\delta(\varepsilon) > 0$ such that for all $f \in D$ and all $s \in S$,

$$|s - s'| < \delta(\varepsilon) \Rightarrow$$

$$\begin{aligned} |Tf(s) - Tf(s')| &\leq \int_S \left|\frac{\beta}{g(s'')} h(f(s''), s'')\right| |\Delta(s, s', ds'')| \\ &\leq \frac{A\beta}{\underline{g}} \int_S |\Delta(s, s', ds'')| \leq \varepsilon. \end{aligned}$$

5. See Hutson and Pym (1980, Chapter 8), for the terminology used and results cited in this proof.

Since δ does not depend on f or s, this establishes that the family TD is equicontinuous. Clearly this family is also bounded. Then by the Arzela-Ascoli theorem, TD is relatively compact, and consequently every subset of TD is relatively compact.

Finally, T is a continuous operator. To see this note that

$$\begin{aligned}\|Tf - Tf_n\| &= \max_{s\in S} |Tf(s) - Tf_n(s)| \\ &\leq \max_{s\in S} \int_S \frac{\beta}{g(s')} |h(f(s'), y(s)) - h(f_n(s'), y(s'))| \pi(s, ds') \\ &\leq \frac{\beta}{\underline{g}} \max_{s'\in S} |h(f(s'), y(s')) - h(f_n(s'), y(s'))|.\end{aligned}$$

Since h is continuous, $f_n \to f$ implies $Tf_n \to Tf$.

Summing up, D is a nonempty, closed, bounded, convex subset of the Banach space $\mathcal{F}$, and $T: D \to \mathcal{F}$ maps D into itself. Moreover, T is continuous and maps every subset of D into a relatively compact set. Hence, T is a compact operator and, by the Schauder theorem, has a fixed point v in D. Clearly, v satisfies (3.7). *Q.E.D.*

The gist of the proof is to find an appropriate set D, show that $T: D \to D$, with T continuous, and show that TD is equicontinuous. The bound A in Assumption 4 allows us to choose D; Assumption 5 is needed to ensure that $T: D \to D$; and Assumption 6 implies that TD is equicontinuous.

One property of the equilibrium real allocation follows directly from (3.7): current money growth affects the current allocation *only* insofar as it affects expectations about future states, i.e., *only* through its value as a signal. For example, suppose there are two states, s and s', with equal endowments, $y(s) = y(s')$, and the same transition probabilities, $\pi(s, A) = \pi(s', A)$, all $A \in S$, but *different* rates of money growth, $g(s) \neq g(s')$. Then it is clear from (3.7) that $v(s) = v(s')$, so that the real allocation will be the same in both states, $c(s) = c(s')$. Alternatively, suppose that income and money are equal in the two states, $y(s) = y(s')$ and $g(s) = g(s')$, but that they have different implications for the future, $\pi(s, \cdot) \neq \pi(s', \cdot)$. Then it is clear from (3.7) that in general $v(s) \neq v(s')$, so that the real allocations will also differ, $c(s) \neq c(s')$. Thus, the current rate of money growth plays no direct role in determining the current allocation—only income and expectations about money growth matter.

As noted above, a function v satisfying (3.7) corresponds to an equilibrium only if it is strictly positive. Theorem 1 does not rule out the possibility of the solution $v(s) \equiv 0$ to (3.7), nor does it insure that any nontrivial solutions exist. A zero solution, which is consistent with Assumptions 1–6, has an economic interpretation as a "barter" equilibrium. It occurs if

$$\lim_{c \to 0} cU_1(c, y - c) = 0,$$

in which case $\hat{c}(0, y) = 0$, all y, and hence $h(0, y) = 0$.[6] The next result is a sufficient condition to rule this solution out.

THEOREM 2: *Let Assumptions* 1–6 *hold, and assume in addition that for all* $y > 0$,

$$\lim_{c \to 0} cU_1(c, y - c) > 0. \tag{4.1}$$

Then every solution to (3.7) *has* $v > 0$.

PROOF: Under (4.1), $h(v, y)$ is bounded away from zero, so for any $v \in D$, $Tv > 0$. *Q.E.D.*

Theorem 1 guarantees the existence of a solution to (3.7), but says nothing about the number of solutions and/or how to compute them. These questions can be answered, at least in part, by exploiting the fact that under additional hypotheses the operator T defined in the proof of Theorem 1 is monotone. In particular, T is monotone if $h(v, y)$ is weakly increasing in v. To insure this, we add the following assumption.

ASSUMPTION 7: *For each* $y \in [\underline{y}, \bar{y}]$, $cU_1(c, y - c)$ *is weakly increasing in* c.

Since under Assumption 4, $\hat{c}(v, y)$ is strictly increasing in v, the addition of Assumption 7 implies that $h(v, y)$ is weakly increasing in v.

THEOREM 3: *Let Assumptions* 1–7 *hold and define the sequences* $\{\underline{v}_n\}$ *and* $\{\bar{v}_n\}$ *in D by*

$$\underline{v}_0(s) \equiv 0 \quad and \quad \underline{v}_{n+1} = T\underline{v}_n \qquad (n = 0, 1, 2, \ldots),$$

$$\bar{v}_0(s) \equiv A \quad and \quad \bar{v}_{n+1} = T\bar{v}_n \qquad (n = 0, 1, 2, \ldots),$$

6. Since $U_1(0, y)/U_2(0, y) > 1$, the cash-in-advance constraint is binding in this solution, so $p(s)c_1(s) = 1$ and the price level, $p(s)$, is "infinite." A condition like (4.1), below, is used in Brock and Seheinkman (1980) and Scheinkman (1980) to rule out nonstationary equilibria that converge to "barter," as well as stationary barter equilibria in overlapping generations models.

Then $\{\underline{v}_n\}$ *and* $\{\overline{v}_n\}$ *converge pointwise to solutions to* (3.7) *in D, call them* $\underline{v}$ *and* $\overline{v}$, *and for any solution v to* (3.7),

$$\underline{v} \leq v \leq \overline{v}.$$

PROOF: Under Assumptions 4 and 7, the function h is weakly increasing in v, so that the operator T is monotone: $u, v \in D$ and $u \geq v$ imply $Tu \geq Tv$. Moreover, for all $s \in S$

$$\underline{v}_1 = T\underline{v}_0 \geq 0 \equiv \underline{v}_0$$

and

$$\overline{v}_1 = T\overline{v}_0 \leq A \equiv \overline{v}_0.$$

Hence, by induction, $\underline{v}_{n+1} \geq \underline{v}_n$, and $\overline{v}_{n+1} \leq \overline{v}_n$, all n, and since both sequences take values in $[0, A]$, both converge. As shown in the proof of Theorem 1, both $\{\underline{v}_n\}$ and $\{\overline{v}_n\}$ are equicontinuous families, so that the limit functions $\underline{v}$ and $\overline{v}$ are both continuous; hence both are in D.

Finally, if v is any fixed point of T it must satisfy

$$\underline{v}_0 = 0 \leq v \leq A = \overline{v}_0.$$

Then the montonicity of T implies

$$\underline{v}_1 = T\underline{v}_0 \leq Tv = v \leq T\overline{v}_0 = \overline{v}_1,$$

and hence, by induction,

$$\underline{v} = \lim_{n\to\infty} \underline{v}_n \leq v \leq \lim_{n\to\infty} \overline{v}_n = \overline{v}. \qquad \text{Q.E.D.}$$

Theorem 3 is useful computationally because it provides a way of constructing two solutions, $\underline{v}$ and $\overline{v}$, of (3.7) and, if $\underline{v}$ and $\overline{v}$ should coincide, of verifying that their common value is the only solution.

Our next theorem shows that Assumptions 1–7 are also sufficient to ensure that (3.7) has a nontrivial solution.

THEOREM 4: *Let Assumptions* 1–7 *hold. Then* (3.7) *has a solution with* $v(s) > 0$, *all* $s \in S$.

PROOF: By Assumption 1, $\int_S (1/g(s'))\pi(s, ds')$ is continuous in s and since S is compact it attains a minimum value, call it Γ, on S. By Assumptions 3 and 4, we have $0 < \Gamma$ and $\beta\Gamma \leq 1$, and by Assumption 2 there exists $0 < \underline{c} < \underline{y}$ satisfying

$$U_2(\underline{c}, \underline{y} - \underline{c})/U_1(\underline{c}, \underline{y} - \underline{c}) = \beta\Gamma.$$

Since $0 < \beta\Gamma \leq 1$, it follows that $0 < c \leq c^*(y)$ and $\hat{v} \equiv \underline{c}U_2(\underline{c}, \underline{y} - \underline{c}) \leq v^*(\underline{y})$. Then from (3.6a) and Assumption 4, $h(\hat{v}, \underline{y}) = \underline{c}U_1(\underline{c}, \underline{y} - \underline{c}) \leq A$. Note too that

$$\beta\Gamma h(\hat{v}, y) = \beta\Gamma \underline{c}U_1(\underline{c}, \underline{y} - \underline{c}) = \underline{c}U_2(\underline{c}, \underline{y} - \underline{c}) = \hat{v}.$$

We show that the function $\overline{v} = \lim_{n\to\infty} \overline{v}_n$ defined in Theorem 3 is bounded below by $\hat{v}$. For each n, let

$$a_n = \min_{s\in S} \overline{v}_n(s).$$

Hence, $a_{n+1} \geq \beta\Gamma h(a_n, \underline{y})$, all n. Since h is increasing in v and y, it follows that for all n, s

$$\begin{aligned}\overline{v}_{n+1}(s) &= \beta \int_S \frac{h(\overline{v}_n(s'), y(s'))}{g(s')} \pi(s, ds') \\ &\geq \beta \int_S \frac{h(a_n, \underline{y})}{g(s')} \pi(s, ds') \\ &\geq \beta\Gamma h(a_n, \underline{y}).\end{aligned}$$

Hence $a_{n+1} \geq \beta\Gamma h(a_n, \underline{y})$, all n. Since $a_0 \equiv A \geq \hat{v}$, using again the fact that h is increasing in v, it follows by induction that

$$a_{n+1} \geq \beta\Gamma h(a_n, \underline{y}) \geq \beta\Gamma h(\hat{v}, \underline{y}) = \hat{v}, \qquad \textit{all } n,$$

and hence $\overline{v}(s) \geq \hat{v} > 0$, all s. *Q.E.D.*

Theorems 2 and 4 still allow the coëxistence of both zero and strictly positive solutions, as the following example shows. Let

$$U(c_1, c_2) = c_1^{1/2} + c_2^{1/2}.$$

Then

$$\lim_{c\to 0} cU_1(c, y - c) = \lim_{c\to 0} \tfrac{1}{2} c^{1/2} = 0,$$

so that $v(s) \equiv 0$ is a solution. But

$$\beta\Gamma = \frac{U_2(c, y - c)}{U_1(c, y - c)} = \left(\frac{c}{y - c}\right)^{1/2}$$

has a solution c for any $\beta\Gamma$, so that a positive solution also exists.

Our final result gives sufficient conditions for the operator T defined in the proof of Theorem 1 to be a contraction. This will insure the uniqueness of the solution to (3.7). It requires strengthening Assumption 5 as follows.

ASSUMPTION 5′: *For each* $s \in S$,

$$0 < \beta \int \frac{1}{g(s')} \pi(s, ds') < 1.$$

It also requires adding an assumption on preferences that guarantees that the slope of $h(v, y)$ in the v direction is less than unity, i.e., that $h(v, y) - v$ is weakly decreasing in v.

ASSUMPTION 8: *For each* $y \in [\underline{y}, \overline{y}]$,

$$c[U_1(c, y - c) - U_2(c, y - c)] \tag{4.2}$$

is a weakly decreasing function of c.

From (3.4) and (3.6) we see that (4.2), evaluated at $\hat{c}(v, y)$ is just $h(v, y) - v$. Since under Assumptions 2 and 4, $\hat{c}(v, y)$ is strictly increasing in v, the addition of Assumption 8 insures that $h(v, y) - v$ is weakly decreasing in v.

THEOREM 5: *Let Assumptions* 1–4, 5′ *and* 6–8 *hold. Then* (3.7) *has a unique solution* $v \in D$ *and for all* $v_0 \in D$, $\lim_{n\to\infty} \| T^n v_0 - v \| = 0$.

PROOF: We will show that under these additional hypotheses, the operator T defined in the proof of Theorem 1 satisfies Blackwell's (1965, Theorem 5), sufficient conditions for a contraction. As observed in the proof of Theorem 3, under Assumptions 1–7, h is nondecreasing in v, so that T is monotone. We need only to verify that for some $\delta \in (0, 1)$, $T(v + k) \leq Tv + \delta k$, for any $v \in \mathcal{F}$ and constant $k > 0$.

From Assumptions 1, 3, and 5′, it follows that

$$\beta \int_S \frac{1}{g(s')} \pi(s, ds') \leq \delta, \quad \text{for all } s \in S,$$

for some $\delta < 1$. Under Assumption 7, $h(v, y) - v$ is weakly decreasing in v: for any $v \in \mathcal{F}$ and $k > 0$,

$$h(v + k, y) - (v + k) \leq h(v, y) - v$$

or

$$h(v+k, y) \leq h(v, y) + k.$$

Then

$$\begin{aligned} T(v+k)(s) &= \beta \int_S h(v(s')+k, y(s')) \frac{1}{g(s')} \pi(s, ds') \\ &\leq \beta \int_S [h(v(s'), y(s')) + k] \frac{1}{g(s')} \pi(s, ds') \\ &\leq Tv(s) + \delta k, \end{aligned}$$

so that T is a contraction with modulus δ. The conclusion then follows from the contraction mapping theorem. *Q.E.D.*

This completes our analysis of (3.7).[7] In the next section we incorporate securities trading into the economy just studied, and show how arbitrary securities can be priced.

5. Securities Pricing

In Section 2, we developed a definition of a stationary equilibrium for an economy in which currency is the *only* security held by the consumer, and all trade involves either goods for currency or goods for promises to pay currency one period hence. It is not difficult to extend this definition and the subsequent analysis to situations involving trading in a rich variety of securities: The assumption that agents are identical means that in equilibrium, the *quantities* of securities traded are zero, and the consumption levels and good prices are exactly as in the cash-only economy we have just analyzed. But this extension is interesting because it yields formulas for securities *prices*, and in particular for the nominal interest rates that play such an important role in monetary theory.

7. Theorems 1–5 apply to the case in which the state space S consists of a finite number of points and the transition function is described by a Markov matrix

$$\Pi = [\pi_{ij}] \qquad \text{where} \qquad \pi_{ij} = \Pr\{s' = s_j \mid s = s_i\}.$$

In this case (3.7) defines an operator T taking the set $D = \{v \in \mathbb{R}^n \mid 0 \leq v_i \leq A, i = 1, \ldots, n\}$ into itself. Since D is compact and convex, Theorem 1 would in this case be an application of Brouwer's theorem. This is the route taken by Labadie (1984, Theorem 1) in a problem that is technically very similar to ours.

The timing of securities trading and the information available to traders at this time are crucial. We adopt the following conventions. Securities trading at time *t* occurs at the beginning of period *t*, before s_t is known, but after some signal z_t is announced and after monetary injections take place. The signals are generated as follows.

There is a space of possible values for the signal, and for each $s \in S$, there is a conditional probability measure on the signal space. The information available to agents at the time of securities trading in period *t* is the previous period's shock, s_{t-1}, and the signal about the current shock, z_t. It is then straightforward[8] to use the transition function π, together with the family of conditional probability measures on the signal space, to develop the conditional expectation of any function of s_t, given s_{t-1} and z_t. Rather than do this explicitly, however, which requires a considerable investment in notation, we will from this point on simply indicate expected values. But note that since monetary injections occur prior to securities trading, the conditional distribution of $g(s_t)$, given z_t, is always degenerate. Therefore, we may write the monetary injection as $\hat{g}(z)$.

Consider an economy in which only one asset is traded. The single asset may be quite complicated, however. Specifically, we allow an arbitrary, one-period, dollar denominated security,[9] one unit of which pays $b(s, z')$ dollars at the beginning of next period if today's shock is $s_t = s$, and tomorrow's signal is $z_{t+1} = z'$. Thus, the return is a contingent claim that may depend on the current-period state, s_t, and the information about the next period's state that is known at the time the security matures, z_{t+1}. In this notation, then, an ordinary (noncontingent) one-period nominal bond is one with $b(s, z') \equiv 1$.

Let $q(\bar{s}, z)$ be the price of such a security when the last period's state was $\bar{s}$ and the current signal is *z*, and consider the decision problem of a consumer who holds cash balances *m* (after all money transfers and securities redemptions), when available information is $(\bar{s}, z)$. Let $F(m, \bar{s}, z)$ denote

8. Specifically, let $(Z, \mathcal{Z})$ be a measurable space, and let $\eta : S \times \mathcal{Z} \to [0, 1]$. Assume that for each $s \in S$, $\eta(s, \cdot) : \mathcal{Z} \to [0, 1]$ is a probability measure; and that for each $B \in \mathcal{Z}$, $\eta(\cdot, B) : S \to [0, 1]$ is $\mathcal{S}$ measurable. It is then straightforward to define the required conditional expectations.

9. The only restriction is that $b : S \times Z \to \mathbb{R}$ be bounded and measurable. Similarly, when analyzing the consumer's problem below, we assume that the price function $q : S \times Z \to \mathbb{R}$ is measurable. The latter assumption is vindicated by the equilibrium prices so derived, given in (5.12).

his maximized objective function. His objects of choice are contingency plans (elements of $B(S)$, the set of bounded measurable functions on S) for goods purchases $x_1(s)$ and $x_2(s)$ and end-of-period cash holdings $x_3(s)$, and quantities for bond purchases $x_4 \in \mathbb{R}$ and money holdings $x_5 \in \mathbb{R}_+$. These choices must satisfy the constraints:

$$q(\bar{s}, z)x_4 + x_5 - m \leq 0, \tag{5.1}$$

$$p(s)x_1(s) - x_5 \leq 0, \qquad \text{all } s \in S, \tag{5.2}$$

$$p(s)[x_1(s) + x_2(s)] + x_3(s) - x_5 - p(s)y(s) \leq 0, \qquad \text{all } s \in S. \tag{5.3}$$

To rule out "Ponzi schemes," we also require:

$$x_4 \in A \equiv [-a, a] \qquad \text{for some} \qquad 0 < a < \infty. \tag{5.4}$$

Let $\phi(m, \bar{s}, z) \subset (B(S))^3 \times A \times \mathbb{R}_+$ be the set of functions x_1, x_2, x_3 and values x_4 and x_5 satisfying these constraints. Then the value function F must satisfy:

$$F(m, \bar{s}, z) = \max_{x \in \phi(m, \bar{s}, z)} \Big\{ E_s \big[U(x_1(s), x_2(s)) + \beta E_{z'} \Big[F\Big(\frac{x_3(s) + x_4 b(s, z') + g(z') - 1}{g(z')}, s, z' \Big) \Big| s \Big] \Big| [\bar{s}, z] \Big\}. \tag{5.5}$$

As in Section 2, the equilibrium conditions include the market clearing conditions (2.5) and $x_3 = x_5 = 1$. In addition, net securities trades must be zero: $x_4 = 0$. Associating the multipliers $w(s)$ and $v(s)$ with the constraints (5.2) and (5.3), as in Section 2, the necessary conditions for the maximum problem (5.5), evaluated at these market-clearing quantities, include (2.7)–(2.9). The other first-order conditions are:

$$\beta E_{z'} \left[F_m(1, s, z') \frac{1}{g(z')} \middle| s \right] - v(s) = 0, \quad \textit{all } s \in S, \tag{5.6}$$

$$\beta E_{s, z'} \left[F_m(1, s, z') \frac{b(s, z')}{g(z')} \middle| \bar{s}, z \right] - \lambda q(\bar{s}, z) = 0, \tag{5.7}$$

$$\lambda - E_s \left[w(s) + v(s) \middle| \bar{s}, z \right] = 0, \tag{5.8}$$

where λ is the multiplier associated with (5.1). Its value in turn is given by the envelope condition

$$F_m(1, \bar{s}, z) = \lambda. \tag{5.9}$$

Now, substituting for λ and $F_m(1, s, z')$ from (5.9) and (5.8), (5.6) becomes

$$\begin{aligned} v(s) &= \beta E_{z'}\left[E_{s'}[w(s') + v(s') \mid s, z'] \frac{1}{g(z')} \middle| s \right] \\ &= \beta E_{s'}\left[[w(s') + v(s')] \frac{1}{g(s')} \middle| s \right]. \end{aligned} \tag{5.10}$$

This reproduces equation (2.12). Hence the system (2.6)–(2.9) plus (2.12) also describes the equilibrium behavior of $c(s)$, $p(s)$, $w(s)$, and $v(s)$ for the economy with securities trading. It follows that the analysts of Sections 2–4 applies to this economy as well.

To obtain the equilibrium securities price $q(\bar{s}, z)$, substitute from (5.9) and (5.8) into (5.7) to obtain:

$$\begin{aligned} &\beta E_{s,s',z'}\left[(w(s') + v(s')) \frac{b(s, z')}{g(z')} \middle| \bar{s}, z \right] \\ &= q(\bar{s}, z) E_s[w(s) + v(s) \mid \bar{s}, z]. \end{aligned} \tag{5.11}$$

With $v(s)$ and $w(s)$ "solved for" as in Section 2–4, (5.11) prices an arbitrary, one-period security. It is clear that if securities are traded, (5.11) can be used to find the equilibrium price of each, and the equilibrium quantity traded will be zero for each.

If the security is an ordinary one-period bond, then $b(s, z') \equiv 1$, and (5.11) reduces to

$$\begin{aligned} q(\bar{s}, z) &= \frac{\beta E_{s'}[(w(s') + v(s'))/g(s') \mid \bar{s}, z]}{E_s[w(s) + v(s) \mid \bar{s}, z]} \\ &= \frac{E_s[v(s) \mid \bar{s}, z]}{E_s[w(s) + v(s) \mid \bar{s}, z]} \\ &= \frac{E_s[U_2(c(s))/p(s) \mid \bar{s}, z]}{E_s[U_1(c(s))/p(s) \mid \bar{s}, z]}, \end{aligned} \tag{5.12}$$

where the second line uses (5.10) and the third uses (2.7)–(2.8). If in addition the signal z_t is a perfect indicator of the state s_t, then (5.12) implies

$$q(\bar{s}, z) = \frac{v(s)}{v(s) + w(s)} = \frac{U_2(c(s))}{U_1(c(s))}, \tag{5.13}$$

so that the price of a one period nominal bond is equal to the marginal rate of substitution between credit and cash goods.

It is clear from (5.12) that the stochastic behavior of the interest rate $(1/q(\bar{s}, z) - 1)$, will depend critically on the nature of the information available when securities are traded. But from the point of view of resource allocation and welfare, the accuracy of that information is immaterial. Two economies with the same preferences and the same joint stochastic process for income and money growth will allocate resources in the same way, even if their information structures differ.

We next turn to three examples that illustrate the behavior of bond prices (interest rates) under very specific assumptions.

EXAMPLE 1: *A Deterministic Case:* Let the real goods endowment and the rate of money growth be constant; call them y and g, respectively, with $g \geq \beta$. Then (3.7) becomes

$$v = \frac{\beta}{g} h(v, y).$$

If $g = \beta$, (3.6) implies that any constant $v \geq v^*(y)$ is a solution to this equation, and Lemma 2 then implies $w = 0$ and $c_1 = c^*(y)$. This is the efficient equilibrium in which money is withdrawn from circulation at exactly the rate of time preference.

If $g > \beta$, (3.6) implies that $v < v^*(y)$. In this case, the equilibrium allocation is the unique solution to

$$\frac{U_2(c_1, y - c_1)}{U_1(c_1, y - c_1)} = \frac{\beta}{g}.$$

If we let $\beta = 1/(1 + \rho)$ and $g = 1 + \pi$, then (5.13) implies

$$q = \frac{\beta}{g} = \frac{1}{(1 + \rho)(1 + \pi)}$$

so that the price of a one-period nominal bond is the product of the real factor, $1/(1 + \rho)$, and the inflation factor, $1/(1 + \pi)$. It is this price to which the marginal rate of substitution between credit and cash goods is equated. As the rate of money growth π rises, this price falls, and agents substitute against cash goods, which is to say, they economize on the use of money.

EXAMPLE 2: *Serially Uncorrelated and Mutually Independent Shocks:* Let $\pi(s, A) \equiv \pi(A)$, so that s_t is serially uncorrelated and let $y(s_t)$ and $g(s_t)$ be mutually independent. Then (3.7) becomes

$$v(s) = \beta E\left[\frac{1}{g(s')}\right] E[h(v(s'), y(s'))].$$

Since the right side of this equation does not depend on s, the solution is a constant function, $v(s) \equiv \bar{v}$.

Note that the *expected value* $E[1/g(s)]$ will affect v, and hence equilibrium consumption, but all other features of this distribution of $g(s)$ are irrelevant. The *variability* of the rate of money growth is of no allocative importance. This example illustrates a very general feature of the model, which is that many different monetary policies will lead to exactly the same allocation of real resources. Suppose that for a given stochastic process s_t and given functions g and y, we find v satisfying (3.7). Suppose we then change monetary policy by choosing a new function $\hat{g} \neq g$, but choose $\hat{g}$ in such a way that v, y, and $\hat{g}$ satisfy (3.7). Then clearly the equilibrium real allocation remains unchanged. If bond trading takes place with perfect information about the current state, then (5.13) implies that bond prices (interest rates) will also show the same behavior under two regimes.

EXAMPLE 3: *Logarithmic Utility:* Let $U(c_1, c_2) = \alpha \ln(c_1) + (1 - \alpha) \ln(c_2)$. Then $c_1 U_1(c_1, y - c_1) \leq \alpha$, $c^*(y) = \alpha y$, and $v^*(y) = \alpha$. Therefore $h(v, y) = \alpha$ if $v \leq v^*(y) = \alpha$, and $h(v, y) = v$ if $v \geq v^*(y) = \alpha$, so that equation (3.7) becomes

$$v(s) = \beta \int \frac{\max[\alpha, v(s')]}{g(s')} \pi(s, ds').$$

Hence, under Assumption 5,

$$v(s) = \alpha\beta E\left[\frac{1}{g(s')}\middle| s\right] \leq \alpha$$

is a solution, since $v(s) + w(s) = \max[\alpha, v(s)] = \alpha$, for all s.

Then Lemma 2 and (3.4) imply that the equilibrium goods allocation is

$$(c_1(s), c_2(s)) = y(s)\left(\frac{v(s)}{1-\alpha+v(s)}, \frac{1-\alpha}{1-\alpha+v(s)}\right),$$

and (5.13) implies that the price of a one-period nominal bond is

$$q(s) = \frac{v(s)}{\alpha} = \beta E[1/g(s')|s].$$

In this simple example, then, *any* type of correlation between current money growth $g(s)$ and the current nominal interest rate, $1/q(s) - 1$, is possible, depending on the serial correlation properties of the shocks. Thus the model allows the correlation between money growth and the nominal interest rate to be positive or negative, strong or weak. Equation (5.13) suggests that this feature is quite general

6. Conclusions

We motivated this paper, in part, by reference to attempts to use statistical descriptions of lead-lag relationships in aggregate time series as a way of discriminating between broad classes of theoretical models: "classical," "Keynesian," and so on. In one sense, the theoretical direction we have taken is complementary to this line of econometric work, for our model is stochastic and its "predictions" take the form of the entire joint distribution of endogenous and exogenous variables, given preferences, technology, and the distribution of exogenous shocks. Our emphasis, moreover, has been on structures simple enough so that these predicted distributions might be calculated, and on methods of analysis that might assist in such calculations. While we have not computed numerical solutions of the model as yet, many qualitative possibilities are clear enough from the analysis we have presented. Reviewing some of these will be a good way to conclude the paper.

Consider first the joint distribution of real output, the money growth rate, and the inflation rate only. Suppose that y_t in the model is identified with observations on real output and $g_t - 1$ with the observed growth rate of some measure of the money supply, and that the state of the system consists of current and lagged values of these two variables, $s_t = (y_{t-n}, g_{t-n}, \ldots, y_t, g_t)$. Since $p(s_t)$ was expressed as a ratio of the price of goods to the current money supply, the nominal price level in the model is $M_t p(s_t)$. The theoretical counterpart to the rate of change in a general price index—the inflation rate—is thus $M_t p(s_t)/M_{t-1}p(s_{t-1}) - 1 = g_t p(s_t)/p(s_{t-1}) - 1$. What can be said about relationships among these variables?

No statements about "causation" in the statistical sense have been ruled out by our assumptions. However, if y_t were really an exogenous endowment, one would not expect g_t to "cause" y_t, in either the ordinary or the statistical sense of the word. But if the monetary authority reacts to real shocks, y_t *will* in general "cause" g_t. These are simply observations about shocks taken to be exogenous in the theoretical model.

Next consider the inflation rate $g_t p(s_t)/p(s_{t-1}) - 1$. From (2.7) we see that $p(s) = U_1/(v + w)$. Now for concreteness consider Example 3 in Section 5. In that example, $v + w = \alpha$, and $U_1 = \alpha/c_1$, so that $p(s) = 1/c_1(s)$. Therefore, from the solution for $1/c_1$ we see that $p(s_t)$ depends on y_t and $E[1/g_{t+1}|s_t]$. Therefore in this, as in the general case, the inflation rate will depend upon lagged values of the two state variables—money growth and real—income—but *not* on its own lagged value.

In general, in recursive models, lagged values of variables that are not themselves state variables (such as the inflation rate in our model) should not help to predict anything (including their own future values) provided a complete list of state variables is included in the set of variables on which one is conditioning. In practice it is rare to find variables of which *none* of the lagged values contains information useful for prediction. This suggests that in the typical case in practice, there are important state variables that are *not* included in the set of observations one has available. There is a second way to match our theoretical variables with observations that is more consistent with this conclusion, and also with common sense.

Let us think of y_t as an unobservable "productive capacity" or "full income," credit goods c_{2t} as "leisure," and cash goods c_{1t} as measured output. (With three consumption goods we could easily treat intermediate cases, but for the present purposes this extreme example will suffice.) As in the first example, take the state vector to be $s_t = (y_{t-n}, g_{t-n}, \ldots, y_t, g_t)$, but now treat the *observed* series as c_{1t}, g_t and the inflation rate. As in the first example, take information at the time of securities trading to be the money growth rate, g_t, as well as lagged values of all observables. Then observed "output," c_{1t}, and the price level, $p(s_t)$, will depend on expectations about future money growth, g_{t+1}, as well as on the current, unobserved endowment, y_t. Therefore, except by coincidence, the projections of c_{1t}, g_t and the inflation rate $g_t p(s_t)/p(s_{t-1})$ on lagged observables all will now assign weight, or statistical significance, to *all* lagged variables. It is clear from Example 3 that the theory will not place *any* restrictions on individual contemporaneous or lagged correlations.

Including securities, as in Section 5, permits us to consider the likely consequences of adding short term interest rates to the list of observable variables whose empirical joint distribution we are considering. As with the inflation rate, bond prices q_t are not state variables in the model, so that if the full state vector s_t is treated as observable, q_t should not help to predict anything. Empirically, of course, interest rates and other securities exhibit leading or "causal" relationships to many economic variables, strongly suggesting that one wants to think of important components of s_t as being unobserved. In this case, it is clear from Section 5 that q_t will reflect (in the language of efficient market theory) or be affected by early signals about movements in s_t, before these s_t movements affect other date t endogenous variables. Hence it would be surprising if interest rates did not have strong causal properties in the statistical sense, even in a system such as ours in which the securities market plays no allocative role whatever.

The model of this paper is narrowly "classical" in the sense that if changes in the stock of money do not alter the probability distribution of future money growth, then they have an equiproportional effect on goods prices and no other effects. No "rigidities" or informational complexities are present that would attenuate the effects of such a change. Yet even within this severely limited framework, a very wide variety of statistically causal relationships are consistent with the model. It is a kind of converse to this observation that empirical summaries of these relationships are not likely to be useful as diagnostic devices.

This is not to say that models of the type analyzed here are vacuous. On the contrary, with a specific parameterization of preferences the theory would place many restrictions on the behavior of endogenous variables. But these predictions do not take the form of locating blocks of zeros in a VAR description of these variables. While it would clearly be desirable to be able to analyze more complicated models of this general type, it does not seem likely that this particular feature of the equilibria will be reversed.

Department of Economics, University of Chicago, Chicago, Il 60637, U.S.A.
and
J. L. Kellogg Graduate School of Management, Northwestern University, Evanston, Il 60201, U.S.A.

Manuscript received November 1984; final revision received June, 1986.

References

Benveniste, L. M., and J. A. Scheinkman (1979): "On the Differentiability of the Value Function in Dynamic Models of Economics," *Econometrica,* 47, 727–732.

Blackwell, D. (1965): "Discounted Dynamic Programming," *Annals of Mathematical Statistics,* 36, 226–235.

Brock, W. A., and J. A. Scheinkman (1980): "Some Remarks on Monetary Policy in an Overlapping Generations Model," in *Models of Monetary Economies,* ed. by J. H. Karaken and N. Wallace. Minneapolis, Minnesota: Federal Reserve Bank of Minneapolis, pp. 211–232.

Clower, R. W. (1967): "A Reconsideration of the Microfoundations of Monetary Theory," *Western Economic Journal,* 6, 1–9.

Hildenbrand, W. (1974): *Core and Equilibria of a Large Economy.* Princeton, New Jersey: Princeton University Press.

Hutson, V., and J. S. Pym (1980): *Applications of Functional Analysis and Operator Theory.* London: Academic Press.

Labadie, P. (1984): "A Test of Risk Premia Behavior in an Overlapping Generations Model," Columbia University Working Paper.

Litterman, R. B., and L. Weiss (1985): "Money, Real Interest Rates, and Output: A Reinterpretation of Postwar U.S. Data," *Econometrica,* 53, 129–156.

Lucas, R. E., Jr. (1982): "Interest Rates and Currency Prices in a Two-Country World," *Journal of Monetary Economics,* 10, 335–360.

——— (1984): "Money in a Theory of Finance," *Carnegie-Rochester Conference Series on Public Policy,* 21, 9–46.

Lucas, R. E., Jr., and N. L Stokey (1983): "Optimal Fiscal and Monetary Policy in an Economy Without Capital," *Journal of Monetary Economics,* 12, 55–93.

Scheinkman, J. A. (1980): "Discussion," in *Models of Monetary Economies,* ed. by J. H. Karaken and N. Wallace. Minneapolis, Minnesota: Federal Reserve Bank of Minneapolis, pp. 91–96.

Sims, C. A. (1972): "Money, Income and Causality," *American Economic Review,* 62, 540–552.

——— (1980): "Comparison of Interwar and Postwar Cycles: Monetarism Reconsidered," *American Economic Review,* 70, 250–257.

Svensson, L. E. O. (1985): "Money and Asset Prices in a Cash-in-Advance Economy," *Journal of Political Economy,* 93, 919–944.

Townsend, R. M. (1987): "Asset-Return Anomalies in a Monetary Economy," *Journal of Economic Theory,* forthcoming.

Money and Interest in a Cash-in-Advance Economy: A Reply

ROBERT E. LUCAS, JR. AND NANCY L. STOKEY

Teh-Ming Huo is correct in noting that Assumptions 2 and 8 of our 1987 paper are mutually inconsistent. It is an error we should not have made, since Obstfeld and Rogoff (1983) had pointed out exactly this fact.

Huo's Theorem 2 shows how uniqueness can be established for bounded utility functions. Assumptions 7 and 8 are dropped, somewhat different restrictions on the utility function are added, and an additional restriction on the money growth process is added.

An alternative route is to drop the assumption that the utility function is bounded and retain Assumptions 7 and 8. The assumption that the utility function is bounded is used only in Theorem 2, where the existence and properties of the value function are established. Those results can be established even if the utility function is unbounded, however. The basic idea is that *realized* utility each period is bounded above (since resources are finite) and below (since a feasible allocation yielding bounded utility can always be found), even if the utility *function* is unbounded. The proof of this is easy to sketch.

In equilibrium, the household chooses real money balances of unity each period. Therefore, to study the household's decision problem, it is useful to restrict real money balances to a closed interval $[\underline{m}, \bar{m}]$, with $\underline{m} < 1 < \bar{m}$. Any upper bound $\bar{m} > 1$ will do. The lower bound $\underline{m} < 1$ must be chosen so that for any current shock s, a household with beginning-of-period real money balances of at least $\underline{m}$ can choose current consumption and end-of-period money balances so that, for any shock s' next period, its beginning-of-period money balances next period are at least $\underline{m}$. Thus, $\underline{m}$ must satisfy

$$\underline{m} < [p(s)y(s) + \underline{m} + g(s') - 1]/g(s'), \quad \textit{all } s, s'.$$

Econometrica 60, no. 2 (March 1992): 441–442.

If $g(s') > 1$, all s', let $\underline{m} = 0$. Otherwise, choose $0 < \underline{m} < 1$ such that

$$\min_{s \in S} p(s)y(s) > (1 - \underline{g})(1 - \underline{m}).$$

Let $M = [\underline{m}, \bar{m}]$, and for $(m, s) \in M \times S$ define

$$\begin{aligned}\phi(m, s) = \{(x_1, x_2, x_3) \in R^3 : 0 \leq x_1 \leq m/p(s),\\ 0 \leq x_2 \leq y(s) + m/p(s) - x_1,\\ 0 \leq x_3 \leq m + p(s)[y(s) - x_1 - x_2], \text{ and}\\ 1 + (\underline{m} - 1)g(s') \leq x_3 \leq 1 + (\underline{m} - 1)g(s'), \text{ all } s' \in S\}.\end{aligned}$$

$\phi(m, s)$ is the set of feasible choices for consumption and end-of-period money balances. That is, it is the set of choices that satisfy the cash-in-advance and budget constraints, and yield beginning-of-period money balances in the interval M next period.

Drop the assumption that U is bounded, and call the new condition Assumption 2′. We then have the following result.

LEMMA 1′: *Let Assumptions 1, 2′, and 3 hold, and let $p : S \to R_+$ be continuous and strictly positive. Choose $\underline{m}$ and $\bar{m}$ as above, let $M = [\underline{m}, \bar{m}]$, and define $\phi : M \times S \to R^3$ as above. Then there exists a unique continuous function $F : M \times S \to R$ satisfying (2.4). F is bounded, and it is strictly increasing, strictly concave, and continuously differentiable in its first argument. For each (m,s), the maximum in (2.4) is attained by a unique value $\psi(m, s)$, and the policy function ψ is continuous.*

PROOF: Let F be the space of continuous functions $f: M \times S \to R$. Since M and S are compact, every function in F is bounded. Define the operator T on F by (2.5). Clearly, F satisfies (2.4) if and only if it is a fixed point of T. Standard arguments show that T is a contraction on F, and that the other claims hold. (For example, see Stokey, Lucas, and Prescott (1989, Ch. 4).) *Q.E.D.*

It is easy to construct explicit bounds on F. Let $[\underline{p}, \bar{p}]$ be the range for $p(s)$. A feasible strategy for the household is to choose $(x_1, x_2, x_3) = [\varepsilon, \varepsilon, 1 + (\underline{m} - 1)\underline{g}]$ each period, where $0 < \varepsilon < \underline{m}/2\bar{p}$ and

$$\min_{s \in S} p(s)[y(s) - \varepsilon] > (1 - \underline{g})(1 - \underline{m}).$$

In this case utility each period is $\underline{u} = U(\varepsilon, \varepsilon)$. On the other hand, utility in any period cannot exceed $\bar{u} = \max_c U(c, \bar{y} + \bar{m}/\underline{p} - c)$. Hence the value function F satisfying (2.4) is bounded below by $\underline{u}/(1 - \beta)$ and above by $\bar{u}/(1 - \beta)$.

The rest of the results in the 1987 paper then go through without change. A utility function satisfying Assumptions 2′, 4, 7, and 8 is $U(c_1, c_2) = \ln c_1 + \ln c_2$.

It should be emphasized that our approach permits discussion only of stationary equilibria. Thus, Theorem 5 establishes the existence of a unique stationary equilibrium in which money has value in all states. There are, in general, additional equilibria that are nonstationary (so that "sunspots" or "bubbles" are possible), or in which money is valueless in some states. See Woodford (1988) for a full discussion of the entire set of equilibria in this broader sense.

Department of Economics, University of Chicago, 1126 East 59th Street, Chicago, IL 60637, U.S.A.

Manuscript received April, 1990; final revision received April, 1991.

References

Lucas, R. E., Jr., and N. L. Stokey (1987): "Money and Interest in a Cash-in-Advance Economy," *Econometrica*, 55, 491–513.

Obstfeld, M., and K. Rogoff (1983): "Speculative Hyperinflations in Maximizing Models: Can We Rule Them Out?" *Journal of Political Economy*, 91, 675–687.

Stokey, N. L., R. E. Lucas, Jr., and E. C. Prescott (1989): *Recursive Methods in Economic Dynamics*. Cambridge, MA: Harvard University Press.

Woodford, M. (1988): "Monetary Policy and Price Level Indeterminacy in a Cash-in-Advance Economy," Working Paper, University of Chicago.

— 11 —

Money Demand in the United States: A Quantitative Review

I. Introduction

Allan Meltzer's research career has been so productive and so varied that it would be an act of folly, not friendship, to attempt to review it in a single paper. Yet I do want to talk about his research on this occasion, for research is what Allan's career is mainly about, and I want to do so in detail, because details are the way scholarship is carried out. Accordingly, I will focus my attention mainly on a single paper, one that has influenced my own thinking on monetary economics a great deal, Meltzer's "The Demand for Money: The Evidence from Time Series," published in the *Journal of Political Economy* in 1963.

Meltzer's "Demand for Money" was one in a series of his empirical studies in monetary economics, much of which involved joint research with Karl Brunner. It followed earlier work by Latane and others, especially Friedman, and helped to stimulate closely related later contributions by Laidler and others.[1] The shared objective of this research program was, in

---

Carnegie-Rochester Conference Series on Public Policy 29, no. 1 (January 1988): 137–168.

*This paper was prepared for the November, 1987 Carnegie-Rochester Conference. I would like to thank John Cochrane, Thomas Cooley, Milton Friedman, Lars Peter Hansen, Robert King, Leonardo Leiderman, Bennett McCallum, Sherwin Rosen, Thomas Sargent and Lawrence Summers for helpful discussions and/or comments on an earlier draft. I also benefitted from a stimulating discussion at the Conference. P. S. Eswar-Prasad provided excellent research assistance.

1. Two important sequels to this paper are Brunner and Meltzer (1963) and Laidler (1966). Of course, this and other work on money demand was closely related to other contemporary research, especially the earlier contributions of Friedman (1956) and his stu-

Friedman's (1956) terms, to demonstrate that the demand for money is a "highly stable function" of a limited number of variables, to discover the most useful, operational measures of money and these other variables, and (again citing Friedman) to work "toward isolating the numerical 'constants' of monetary behavior." Meltzer's paper was the first to estimate an income (or wealth) elasticity and an interest elasticity simultaneously from time series data from a single country (the U.S.). The objective of the present paper will be to review and replicate these results, to reconsider how they might be interpreted theoretically, and to see how well they stand up to the 25 years of new data that have become available since Meltzer wrote.

An estimated money demand function provides answers to two important questions of economic policy. The income elasticity, in a setting in which long run real output growth is both fairly predictable and insensitive to changes in monetary policy, provides the answer to the question: What rate of growth of money is consistent with long run price stability? The interest elasticity is the key parameter needed to answer the question: What are the welfare costs to society of deviations from long run price stability? Purely qualitative answers to these questions, along the lines of "Inflation rates are significantly related to money growth rates" or "Inflation reduces welfare" are interesting and useful, perhaps, but surely propositions such as "An *M*1 growth rate of 3 percent per year will bring about price stability" or "A ten percent annual inflation rate has a social cost equivalent to a 0.5 percent decline in real income" are more interesting and, if accurate, much more useful.

Though the objective of an economics that provides quantitative answers to important questions of economic policy is now very widely subscribed to, it is remarkable how little attention is paid in many of our discussions to the substance of parameter estimation, and how little honor is paid to those few economists who do it well. All of us have sat through many discussions of econometric work in which the theoretical underpinnings of the relationships estimated and tested and the econometric methods used are subjected to intense scrutiny and yet no one seems to care what the numerical results were! Even in Laidler's (1977) survey of the evidence on money demand, or in McCallum and Goodfriend's (1987) more

---

dents, and Friedman (1959). See Laidler (1977) and, more recently, McCallum and Goodfriend (1987) for some of the relevant background.

recent summary, it is difficult to find clear statements of what the money demand function is. As quantitative economists we often seem to be, in Samuel son's (1947) phrase, "like highly trained athletes who never run a race, and in consequence grow stale."

Meltzer ran this particular race, in 1963, and turned in his two numbers. Much has happened since to monetary theory and to the development of econometric methods, and almost three decades of new data have since become available. In Section II I will summarize the evidence on the income (or wealth) and interest elasticities of money demand from 1900–58 data, essentially identical to those Meltzer used. Section III introduces a utility-theoretic framework for thinking about money demand, from which I will conclude that there is some reason to view these two parameters as structural. Section IV reviews U.S. time series evidence from the 1958–85 period, a period during which nominal interest rates reached levels about twice the highest levels attained in the U.S. in the earlier years of the century. Remarkably, in view of the stringent nature of the experiment, these new data precisely confirm the estimates Meltzer obtained in 1963.

II. Review of the Evidence from 1900–1958

The hypothetical household decision problem underlying the results reported in Meltzer (1963) is that of allocating a given stock of wealth across different assets, given a vector of asset returns. I will come back to this problem in more detail in Section III, but I have said enough to rationalize a demand function for money of the form

$$\frac{M}{P} = f(r, w).$$

Throughout his paper, Meltzer used the log-linear form:

$$\ell n(m_t) = a - b\ell n(r_t) + c\ell n(w_t) + u_t, \tag{1}$$

where m_t is the stock of real balances at t, w_t is real wealth or real income, r_t an interest rate, u_t is an error term, and a, b and c are parameters. Meltzer used a long term interest rate to measure r_t, treated as a stand-in for the entire vector of returns on alternative assets. He experimented with a very wide variety of income and wealth variables as measures of real wealth, and with both $M1$ and $M2$ as measures of the money stock. The sample period was 1900–1958, with results also reported for the two subperiods 1900–1929 and 1930–1958.

The experimental approach Meltzer used for measuring money and wealth is obviously suitable: we do not have theories that single out particular measures as clearly superior to others. One could indeed criticize the paper for reporting too few results, since the single interest rate he used to represent asset returns was arbitrarily chosen. But much of this experimentation indicated that the choice of wealth and money aggregates was not critically important. This finding has been confirmed by much subsequent research, as described in Laidler (1977). I will therefore report and replicate only a small subset of the results reported by Meltzer (1963).

Table 1 transcribes results in Meltzer (1963). Line 1 is equation (3) on p. 225, with R^2 reported instead of R and "standard errors" instead of "*t*-statistics."[2] Lines 2, 3, 5, 6, 7 and 8 are from Table 2, p. 232. Line 4 is from Table 1, p. 229. Of course, all regressions reported in this and all other tables in this paper were estimated with constant terms. Since the units of the dependent variable I used are not meaningful, I will not report these constants.

The central findings in lines 1–3 of Table 1 (these and all subsequent references are to tables in this paper), confirmed by other results in the original paper, are the wealth or income elasticities of about unity and the strong, negative effect of interest rates on real balances demanded. Notice that neither finding shows up very clearly when the period is divided in two, as reported in lines 4–8 of Table 1. For the early period, the income and wealth elasticities diverge, in different directions, from unity and the interest elasticities are much reduced. Meltzer does not report the results with wealth only for 1930–1958. From what is reported, however, it appears that the results for the full period were mainly dictated by events in the latter half.

Table 2 contains my replications of the results in Table 1.[3] I dropped 1958 from the sample because I could not find *w* for that year. Otherwise,

2. The residuals from my replications of Meltzer's equations show very severe autocorrelation, and it is clear from the Durbin-Watson statistics reported in Meltzer (1964) that this is also true of his original regressions. As a result, I do not know how to interpret the "standard errors" reported in these tables. I experimented with a variety of methods for correcting for serial correlation, but obtained only wildly erratic elasticity estimates.

3. For money, I used *M*1 throughout the paper. For 1900–14, this series is taken from Historical Statistics (1960), series X267. From 1914–47, it is from Friedman and Schwartz (1970), pp. 704–718, column 7. For 1948–85, it is the "IMF series 3" from the International Monetary Fund's "International Financial Statistics" tape. (The primary source for these IMF data is the Federal Reserve Bulletin.)

For 1900–49, real wealth is from Goldsmith (1956), Table W-3, column 1 ("total na-

Table 1 Meltzer (1963) Results; dependent variable: $\ell n(M1/P)$

		Coefficients on: (standard errors)			
Line	Years	$\ell n(r)$	$\ell n(W/P)$	$\ell n(Y/P)$	R^2
1	1900–58	−.949 (.044)	1.11 (.026)		.984
2	1900–58	−.79 (.083)		1.05 (.041)	.960
3	1900–58	−.92 (.053)	.97 (.103)	.13 (.093)	.980
4	1900–29	−.32 (.107)	1.84 (.114)		.960
5	1900–29	−.05 (.094)		.70 (.45)	.960
6	1900–29	−.22 (.122)	.48 (.240)	.31 (.194)	.960
7	1930–58	−.69 (.160)		.94 (.094)	.902
8	1930–58	−1.15 (.097)	1.35 (.155)	−.10 (.125)	.980

I attempted to follow the sources and procedures described in Meltzer (1963). One can see that lines 1 and 2 from Tables 1 and 2 are very close, though closer for the income regression than the wealth regression. When both variables are included (line 3) I obtained very different results from his, for reasons I cannot explain. Notice, however, that Meltzer's and my estimates of the sum of these coefficients are very close: I suspect this is all

tional wealth at 1929 prices"). For 1950–57, this series is from Historical Statistics (1960), series F446.

For 1884–1975, real income is real net national product from Friedman and Schwartz (1982), Table 4.8. For 1976–85, it is taken from various July issues of the Survey of Current Business. The price level (used to deflate $M1$) is the implicit NNP deflator from the same sources. Permanent income is the geometrically weighted sum of current and past real NNP's used in Friedman (1957). The weight on current income is .33.

The long term interest rate (used only for 1900–57) is the "basic yield on 20 year corporate bonds" in Historical Statistics (1960), series X346. The short term rate for 1900–75 is the "6 month commercial paper" rate from Friedman and Schwartz (1982), Table 4.8, column 6. For 1976–85 I used Table B-68 in the Economic Report of The President (1987).

either of us is estimating with much precision. The other striking difference is in line 4 of Tables 1 and 2: my wealth elasticity for this subperiod is well below one; Meltzer's is 1.8.

I wanted to use a graphical device to help me see how different a theory one obtains with different wealth or income measures. I know this question is not very well posed, but Figure 1 seems to me helpful. It exhibits three series, all for the full period 1900–1957. They are: actual $M1/P$; the "predicted" $M1/P$ from line 1 of Table 2; and the predicted $M1/P$ from line 2 of Table 2. One can see that real balances followed a different trend from 1930 on than in the earlier years. Both the income and wealth regressions track this well (of course, with the interest rate also included as a regressor). Real balances did not decrease nearly as much as did NNP in the 1930s, but they increased much more than income in the 1940s. I conclude (though this is the sort of issue reasonable people can disagree on) that current income induces "too much" cyclical responsiveness in pre-

Table 2 Replications; dependent variable: $\ell n(M1/P)$

		Coefficients on: (standard errors)			
Line	Years	$\ell n(r)$	$\ell n(W/P)$	$\ell n(Y/P)$	R^2
1	1900–57	−1.32	1.32		.957
		(.09)	(.056)		
2	1900–57	.67		1.04	.971
		(.077)		(.036)	
3	1900–57	.90	.49	.68	.978
		(.089)	(.122)	(.095)	
4	1900–29	−.21	.86		.957
		(.099)	(.051)		
5	1900–29	−.07		.73	.932
		(.119)		(.057)	
6	1900–29	−.20	.65	.19	.960
		(.098)	(.149)	(.132)	
7	1930–57	−1.72	1.53		.901
		(.139)	(.163)		
8	1930–57	−.55		.93	.937
		(.141)		(.075)	
9	1930–57	−.78	.34	.75	.939
		.264	.332	.191	

Table 3 Variations on Table 2 for 1900–1957; dependent variable: $\ell n(M1/P)$

	Coefficients on: (standard errors)				
Line	$\ell n(r)$	$\ell n(r_s)$	r_s	$\ell n(y_p)$	R^2
1	−.77 (.044)			1.03 (.021)	.989
2		−.18 (.025)		1.07 (.039)	.966
3			−.07 (.011)	1.06 (.042)	.963

dicted money demand, relative to wealth, and that wealth or some other "smoothed" income measure is preferred as the regressor. This is also the conclusion reached by Laidler (1977).

In Table 3, I report the consequences of some variations on Meltzer's results. The objective of this experimentation is to locate a version of Meltzer's model that is reasonably faithful, conceptually and quantitatively, to the original and is at the same time inexpensive to test on more recent data.[4]

Line 1 in Table 3 uses permanent income (defined by Friedman's distributed lag on current and past real NNP's) in place of wealth. This change does an excellent job of reproducing line 1 of either Table 1 or 2. From a comparison of Figure 1 with Figure 2, one can see that permanent income behaves more like wealth than like current NNP in the 1930s.

Lines 2 and 3 report two variations on line 1. In line 2, the long interest rate used by Meltzer is replaced by a short rate. I will explain my strong preference for the latter in Section III. The short rate (over this period) varies sympathetically with the long, but with more amplitude: hence its smaller coefficient. Otherwise, this variation doesn't matter much. In line 3, I use an unlogged short rate. The issue between the different functional forms in lines 2 and 3 is mainly aesthetic: the semi-elasticity at the sample mean value of r (3.26 for 1900–57) is, from the estimate of the elasticity in

4. The variations reported in Table 3 are very close to results in Laidler (1966). Laidler used U.S. annual series from 1892–1960, and deflated real balances and permanent income by population. In his counterpart to line 1 of Table 3 (his Table 2, A, p. 548) he obtained permanent income and interest elasticities respectively of 1.51 and .25. His counterpart of my line 2 (also Table 2, A in his paper) are 1.39 and .16. He did not try unlogged interest rates.

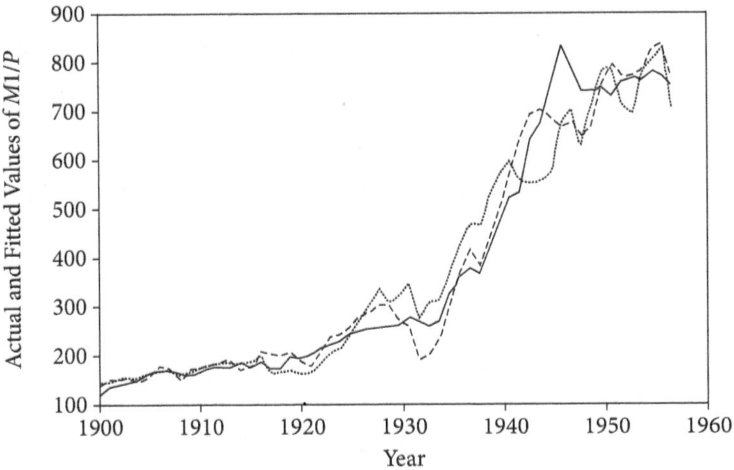

— Actual $M1/P$.
--- Predicted $M1/P$ using current income (line 2, Table 1).
······· Predicted $M1/P$ using wealth (line 1, Table 1).

Figure 1

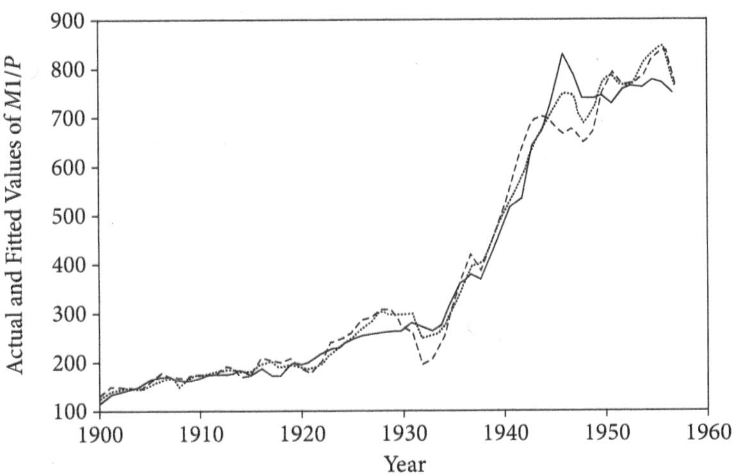

— Actual $M1/P$.
--- Predicted $M1/P$ using current income (line 2, Table 1).
······· Predicted $M1/P$ using wealth (line 1, Table 3).

Figure 2

line 2, (.18)/(3.26) = .055. From line 3, this same semi-elasticity is estimated at .07. (In this, as in all other economic applications with which I am familiar, the choice of functional form is of little substantive consequence.) Thus I will take Table 3 as justifying my referring to the model reported in line 3 as "Meltzer's theory."

Let me conclude this section with a somewhat less formal summary of the information on income and interest elasticities contained in this 1900–57 sample. Over this period, real *M*1 balances grew at the annual rate of .03356 and real permanent income at the rate .03126. Short term interest rates fluctuated between .69 (during World War II) and 7.4 (in 1920) but with a negligible trend. Hence the ratio of the money growth rate to the income growth rate, 1.07, is a good estimate of the income elasticity. This is about the number obtained, under various assumptions, in Table 3. Over long periods, it must always be the case that the trend in the dependent variable must be "explained" by that subset of the regressors that have trends. In this application, real income does and interest rates do not.

Now *imposing* an income elasticity of unity, the semi-elasticity of money demand with respect to the interest rate is just the slope of a plot of $\ln(M1/Py_p)$ against r_s. This plot is displayed in Figure 3. This "estimation method" —get the income elasticity from money and income trends and then get the interest elasticity from a two-variable regression—does not depend very critically on our ability to characterize the residuals accurately, or even on the residuals having a common structure over the entire period. Since we have much more reason, to which I will turn in the next section, for believing these elasticities to be stable than we have reason to believe anything in particular about the residuals, this seems to me a desirable feature.[5]

Of course, no estimation method is satisfactory under all assumptions about the errors, and the critical assumption here is that the errors are trend-free. If there were important technical changes, not occurring in response to interest rate movements, permitting agents to economize on their use of *M*1 balances my method (and Meltzer's too) has understated

5. These informal remarks are not intended as a substitute for econometric theory. One would certainly have a better understanding of the estimates reported here and below if one could write down a believable stochastic model and use it to derive the properties of these estimates explicitly. But I have not done this and so am obliged to follow a second best route and explain why I proceeded as I did in a looser (and hence less informative) way.

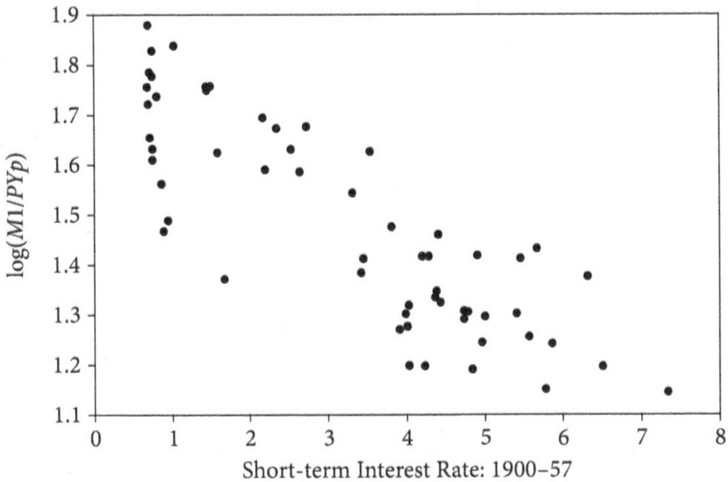

Figure 3

the income elasticity. I do not see how one can learn more about this possibility by examining the series at hand.

III. A Theoretical Framework

As an aid in interpreting the results reported in the last section and the additional results to be reported in Section IV, I will introduce a simple theoretical framework based on the model analyzed in Lucas and Stokey (1987). The framework has the advantage (relative to the framework Meltzer used) of being explicit about the connection between the portfolio and transactions demands for money, and the disadvantage of being unrealistically stylized about the way trading occurs. It will take some care to exploit the explicitness of this model without being led too far astray by its unrealistic features.

We consider an economy in which the representative agent has the ultimate objective of maximizing the discounted expected utility from consumption of goods,

$$E\left\{\sum_{t=0}^{\infty} \beta^t U(c_t)\right\}.$$

This agent lives in a Markovian world, the state of which at t is summarized by a vector s_t. The distribution of s_{t+1}, given s_t, is given by a fixed transition function

$$F(s, A) = Pr\{s_{t+1} \varepsilon A | s = s\}.$$

In this setting, all equilibrium date-t prices and quantities will be fixed (no time subscript) functions of the current state, s_t.

Agents are assumed to alternate between securities trading and goods trading in lockstep fashion. At the beginning of each period, all agents trade in securities, including money, in a single centralized market, all with full knowledge of the current realization of s_t. When securities trading is concluded, all agents disperse either to produce or to purchase consumption goods. Some of these goods can only be purchased with money acquired during the course of securities trad0ing: This transactions requirement is the sole reason for including cash in a portfolio, in preference to interest bearing claims to future cash.

Consider first the decision problem facing an agent who is engaged in securities trading at a time in which the state of the economy is s and his personal wealth in dollar terms is W. (In a centralized securities market all assets are priced, so the single number W summarizes his asset position fully.) Let $v(s, W)$ denote the value of this agent's expected, discounted utility if he proceeds optimally from this point on.

At this point, the agent is faced by a vector $Q(s)$ of securities prices (in dollars, so the price of money is unity). He must choose money holdings M and a vector of securities holdings z, subject to a portfolio constraint:

$$M + Q(s) \cdot z \leq W. \tag{2}$$

Let $G(M, z, s)$ be the indirect utility function he uses to make this choice. (Clearly G will depend on s, since the current state variable includes all the information he has about the returns from these securities.) Then $v(s, W)$ must satisfy:

$$v(s, W) = \max_{M, z} G(M, z, s) \quad \text{subject to (2)}. \tag{3}$$

I call (3) the agent's *portfolio problem.*

Now where does this indirect utility function G come from? Having completed securities trading, the agent is about to engage in purchasing a vector c of consumption goods. He will also receive an endowment $y(s)$ of goods, but this he must sell for cash or future cash: He cannot consume his own endowment. The rules of trading in this goods market are summarized by a vector of constants a, where $a_i \varepsilon [0, 1]$ is the fraction of purchases of good i that must be covered by money. It will be an expositional simplification in what follows to postulate a technology together with a choice of units for measuring goods such that all goods sell for the same nominal price $P(s)$. In this case, the agent's Clower—or cash-in-advance constraint is:

$$P(s)a \cdot c \leq M. \tag{4}$$

The outcome (M, z) of the portfolio decision plus the outcome $(c, y(s))$ of his goods trades plus a given vector $D(s')$ of nominal returns (dividends, interest, principal) on securities will determine this agent's nominal wealth position W' as of tomorrow, conditional on tomorrow's state s'. He begins next period with his dollar holdings as of today, M, plus the dividends and resale value of his securities, $(Q(s') + D(s'))''z$, plus the dollar value of his endowment, $P(s)S\, y\, (s)$, less the dollar value of his goods purchases, $P(s)S\, c$. That is:

$$W' = M + [Q(s') + D(s')] \cdot z + P(s)\Sigma_i[y_i(s) - c_i]. \tag{5}$$

These considerations determine what I call the *transactions problem:*

$$G(M, z, s) = \max_c U(c) + \beta \textstyle\int v(s', W')F(s, ds') \quad \text{subject to (4)}, \tag{6}$$

where W' is defined in (5).

Eliminating the function G between (3) and (6) defines a functional equation in the value function v. See Lucas and Stokey (1987) for an analysis of this equation and its use in constructing an equilibrium for this economy. My purpose here is not so much analysis as it is clarifying what we mean by a "demand function for money," and hence in understanding what an empirical money demand function might mean. Let me begin with what I think Meltzer (1963) and certainly Hamburger (1977) meant by a "demand function for money."

From the portfolio problem (3) one obtains the first order conditions:

$$G_M(M, z, s) = v, \tag{7}$$

$$G_{z_j}(M, z, s) = Q_j v, \; j = 1, \ldots, m, \tag{8}$$

where v is the multiplier associated with the wealth constraint (2) and where j indexes the m available securities. These $m + 1$ equations together with (2) can be solved to obtain the demand functions for the assets (M, z) which have as arguments the prices Q and wealth W. Singling out the demand function (in this sense) for money:

$$M = f(Q, W, s) . \tag{9}$$

Note that the entire vector Q of securities prices enters on the right of (9). In practice, as in any empirical application of demand theory, one would focus on the prices of securities thought to have strong substitution or complementary relationships with money. In this spirit, Meltzer used a long term bond yield in his econometric work. In the same spirit, Hamburger (1977) experimented with equities yields and other securities returns in his.

Certainly (9) is a respectable basis for an empirical study, consistent with what we knew then about monetary theory and, I would say, consistent with what we know now. Yet it does not seem to me that one would have any confidence that the demand function (9), based on portfolio considerations only as in my derivation, would remain stable over time. Included as suppressed arguments in this functions f are all variables s characterizing the current state of the system, including all the information used by agents in forecasting future returns on all securities. Moreover, if the stochastic environment in which agents operate (the "regime," as it is often called) should change from time to time, these changes too will induce shifts in f. Surely shifts in the realizations of informational variables and/or in the processes assumed to generate these realizations must have been substantial over so long a period as 1900–1958.

To decide whether the fact that the functions f are not likely to be structural is an important objection to the empirical application of (9), consider the fact that by exactly the above argument on money demand, we could derive a demand function of the same form as (9) for any portfolio item. Would one, for example, attempt to estimate a demand function for Brazilian government securities, including as arguments only their own current yield and another interest rate standing in for the composite security consisting of all other portfolio items, and expect this relationship to be stable over a 60 year period? I think there is more to Meltzer's money demand theory than portfolio considerations alone.

To see what this is, turn to the transactions problem (6), which also defines the indirect utility function G. The first order conditions for the n consumption goods in this problem are:

$$U_i(c) = \beta \int v_W(s',W')P(s)F(s, ds') + \mu P(s)a_i, \; i = 1, \ldots, n, \tag{10}$$

where μ is the multiplier associated with the cash-in-advance constraint (4). One can also calculate the derivatives of the function G from (6):

$$G_M(M, z, s) = \mu + \beta \int v_W(s', W')F(s, ds'), \tag{11}$$

$$G_{z_j}(M, z, s) = \beta \int v_W(s', W')\left[Q_j(s') + D_j(s')\right]F(s, ds'), \; j = 1, \ldots, m. \tag{12}$$

That is, the value (in utils) of a dollar is its "liquidity" value μ during goods trading plus the marginal value of nominal wealth one period hence. The value of any other security is the value of the increment it provides to future wealth. Equations (11) and (12) thus reduce the values of securities, money included, to the values of their associated "fundamentals."

Now suppose that among the m available securities is a (nominal) risk free, dollar denominated, one period bond. For this security, $Q_j(s') = 0$ and $D_j(s') = 1$. Let its current price be $\frac{1}{1+r(s)}$, so $r(s)$ is the one period nominal interest rate. Then combining (7) and (8) from the portfolio problem and (11) and (12) from the transactions problem (where both (8) and (12) are specialized to this one period bond) and inserting into the first order conditions (10) we obtain:

$$U_i(c) = P(s)\mu\left[a_i + \frac{1}{r(s)}\right], \; i = 1, \ldots, n. \tag{13}$$

That is to say, the relative "prices" of these consumption goods, as seen by consumers (normalized so that the prices of each received by sellers are all equal to $P(s)$) depend on the cash holdings required to purchase them together with the opportunity cost of holding cash, as measured by the nominal interest rate.

In the environment I have been describing, in which no new information reaches agents after they have switched from securities trading to goods trading, agents will plan money holdings so that the cash-in-advance constraint (4) holds with equality: In the theory, as in fact, cash is dominated by nominal bonds as a store of value. In this case (13) and (4) (with equality) form a system of $n + 1$ equations in the consumption vector c and the multiplier μ. It is not quite a demand system (since the "prices" in (13) are not the same as the "prices" in (4)) but it can be treated just as if it were and solved *for the* consumption vector c as a function of $M/P(s)$ and $r(s)$, say:

$$c = g\left(\frac{M}{P}, r\right). \tag{14}$$

Thus we obtain, from transactions considerations, an *exact* relationship between agents' desired consumption mix, their demand for real balances, and the nominal interest rate. Notice that no other securities prices or returns enter into this relationship, nor does the state s (except through the two prices $P(s)$ and $r(s)$).[6] Changes in information or in the information structure of the system will not shift these curves. They will be stable over time provided only that preferences are *and* that the trading technology as summarized in the coefficients $a_1, \ldots, a_n$ is stable.

It seems to me a violation of common usage to call the relationship (14) a "demand function for money." It is a relationship among complementary choice variables that the demand functions must satisfy. Whatever one calls it, however, it is a relationship that must obtain in equilibrium and it seems more likely to be an empirically stable one than does the "true" demand function (9). Why not provide an operational specification of these coefficients a_i and try to estimate it econometrically? This is the approach taken in a recent paper by Mankiw and Summers (1986), with very interesting results that I will come back to in the next section. First, however, it will be useful to go into more detail about the connections between (9) and (14).

Meltzer's estimated income and wealth elasticities are around unity, suggesting (under the utility-theoretic framework I am using here) that

6. This rationale for (14) is essentially the same as that used for a similar purpose by McCallum and Goodfriend (1987). See Ando, Modigliani and Shell (1975) for the earliest derivation of (14) along these lines that I have found. These writers draw the same conclusion I have in the text: that *only* the short rate ought to appear on the right side of a money demand function. Hamburger (1977) views (14) as a "Keynesian" formulation, explicitly contrasting it to the "monetarist" emphasis on portfolio considerations. If he is right, then my use of (14) to derive Meltzer's equation (18) is a very "un-monetarist" argument. But one of the purposes of this section is exactly to argue that portfolio and transactions considerations are *complementary* in thinking about money demand.

the current period utility function U takes the form of a constant relative risk aversion function of a homogeneous of degree one function of consumption. Let us impose this on the model above. Then equation (13) can be solved for the ratios c_i/c of consumption of each good to total consumption $c = \Sigma_i c_i$: $c_i = g_i(r)c$, say. Substituting into the cash constraint gives:

$$\frac{M}{p} = \Sigma_i a_i g_i(r)c = h(r)c, \tag{15}$$

where the second equality defines the function h. This is just a consolidated special case of (14), still not a demand function for money. Under these same assumptions, the "true" demand function for total consumption c takes the form:

$$c = k(Q, s)\frac{W}{P}. \tag{16}$$

Then combining (15) and (16), we have shown that, under this homotheticity assumption, the true demand function for money (9) takes the form:

$$\frac{M}{P} = h(r)k(Q, s)\frac{W}{P}. \tag{17}$$

Now there is no *theoretical* reason to expect (17) to be more stable empirically than (9): They are the same relationship! But empirically, total consumption has been found to be a fairly stable function of permanent income, suggesting that $k(Q, s)/r$ is nearly constant over a wide range of circumstances. If so, then:

$$\frac{M}{P} = \phi(r)y_p, \tag{18}$$

where $\phi'(r) < 0$ should serve as a stable relationship over the same range of circumstances.

I am going to interpret (18) as the relationship Meltzer estimated. This involves using a short term interest rate for r, in contrast to the long term rate Meltzer used. It also precludes adding other yields to the right side of (18), as Hamburger did, unless these other variables can also be shown to affect the propensity to consume out of permanent income. This tighter theoretical rationale will, I hope, give some added insight into why Meltzer's empirical work was so successful.[7]

In the model I have sketched in this section, it is the explicit characterization of transactions demand that leads to a relationship between real balances, short term interest rates and permanent income or wealth that one might want to view as structural. This characterization was made tractable by the assumption that everyone engages in securities trade at the same time, all with the same fixed period. That this assumption is unrealistic is obvious. That it is unrealistic in a way that is critical to the theory of money demand was shown by Grossman and Weiss (1983) and Rotemberg (1984), who examined theoretical settings in which only a subset of agents is engaged in securities trading at any time. This modification alters the way the system responds to open market operations, because when the central bank issues money for bonds, interest rates must move so that the subset of private agents on the other side of this exchange is willing to acquire a disproportionate share of the economy's new money supply. This alteration introduces a Keynesian "liquidity preference" element into money demand that is entirely absent from the formulation I have sketched. Cochrane (1988) appears to have identified these liquidity effects, for periods up to a year, in post-1979 U.S. weekly series on Treasury bill rates and money growth rates. (I say "appears" because the connections between theoretical models of the Grossman-Weiss-Rotemberg type and the estimation methods used by Cochrane have not been worked out in any detail.)

7. It is a perennial subject of debate among monetary economists whether there are advantages to being as explicit about the nature of transactions demand as I have been here, as opposed simply to including real balances as a "good" in agents' utility functions. I do not wish to be doctrinaire about this issue, but surely it cannot be wrong for monetary theorists to think about what people *do* with the money they hold. Economists who study the demand for coffee do not hesitate to use common knowledge about what people do with coffee, and this knowledge leads them to empirically useful ideas about what goods are likely to be close substitutes or complements for coffee, and hence what prices are likely to be useful in coffee demand functions. Why should those who study money demand not do the same thing?

I found Tables 1 and 2 in Mankiw and Summers (1986) of great interest, and of evident use in guiding these authors' thinking about money demand. Researchers confined to thinking of money simply as something people like to hold, without asking *why* they like to hold it, would never have been led to seek out, display and utilize these data.

By using annual data, it seemed possible that Meltzer's results and mine might avoid contamination from these "liquidity preference" effects. We will see in the next section, however, that this hope is not confirmed, at least for post-1958 data. The trick will thus be to get as much as we can out of a money demand theory that is not adequate to account for some short run events.

IV. Money Demand since 1958

Econometric research on money demand has undergone considerable development since the early 1960s. In the main, this work (with the notable exception of Friedman and Schwartz's (1963) and (1982) studies of long U.S. and U.K. time series) has focused on evidence from postwar U.S. quarterly series. Meltzer's work is not cited in Judd and Scadding's (1982) review article (though they do make repeated use of Laidler (1977), which was in turn heavily influenced by Meltzer's work) and, in general, the research cited in this survey is not much concerned with comparison of postwar evidence with evidence from the earlier years of the century.

The pioneering paper in this "modern" era of money demand studies is Goldfeld (1973), which introduced distributed lag methods that seem to be needed to obtain close fits to quarterly data. Subsequent work has, in large part, been devoted to the refinement of Goldfeld's studies and to dealing with the fact (stressed most forcefully by Goldfeld (1976)) that his equations deteriorated in fit on data outside the original sample period.

There is no doubt that recent work is based on a much more sophisticated awareness of econometric issues specific to time series analysis than was the research of the 1950s and 60s. At the same time, the substantive results have been disappointing. Judd and Scadding refer to "the observed instability in the demand for money after 1973," and endorse the conclusion reached earlier by Cooley and LeRoy (1981) "that the negative interest elasticity of money demand reported in the literature represents prior beliefs much more than sample information." The unit income (or wealth) elasticity is no longer regarded as well-established, and most recent work has focused on finding "scale variables" that sharpen short-term forecast errors rather than on estimates of the income elasticity that stand up well over different data sets. In short, one gains the impression that subsequent research has generally failed to support Meltzer's findings, that the income and interest elasticities he estimated are inconsistent with more recent evidence and were even, perhaps, as much the product of his "prior" as they were inferences drawn from the time series he studied.

I think all of these conclusions, or impressions, are incorrect. In this section I will argue that Meltzer's 1963 results are not only qualitatively but *quantitatively* consistent with observations since 1958: that even if one takes the income and interest elasticities estimated, by his methods, from pre-1958 data *alone* one obtains a more useful account of money demand in the 25 year period since than is obtained from more recent distributed lag formulations. Moreover, I will exhibit the information on the interest elasticity of money demand contained in 1900–1985 data in such a way as to concentrate even Cooley and LeRoy's posterior distribution on Meltzer's 1963 conclusion.

At the same time, this application of Meltzer's equation to more recent data will also reveal repeated, systematic patterns in the residuals. These are patterns that are not consistent with the theoretical model reviewed in Section II (and hence not consistent with Meltzer's theory as I have interpreted it). I think it will be easy to see why these patterns motivated Goldfeld and others to resort to distributed lag methods. But I will argue that these methods have served to obscure rather than reveal both the sense in which this theory helps to understand recent events and the sense in which it falls short.

Table 4 provides results for the entire 1900–85 period and for the recent subperiod 1958–85. Line 1 is exactly the same regression as line 3, Table 3 for the full period. Line 3 of Table 4 is the same regression for the period 1958–85 only. One can see that simply adding the later years to the full sample results in virtually no change in the estimated elasticities. However, the results for the later years taken by themselves show a drastic deterioration in fit and large changes in estimated coefficients as compared to the 1900–57 period. In lines 2 and 4 of Table 4, the income elasticity is constrained to be unity (so no "standard error" is reported). Line 2 is, not surprisingly, the same as line 1, but so too is line 4.

Examining trends over the later period (as I did in Section II for the earlier years) helps in interpreting Table 4. In the 27 year period 1958–85, real money balances grew at an annual rate of .004 while real income grew at a rate of .03. Short term interest rates increased (though not at all smoothly) from around 3 percent to around 9 percent, or at a rate of about .22 percentage points per year. To fit these trends, the interest semi-

Table 4 Results from 1900–85; dependent variable: $\ell n(M1/P)$

		Coefficients on: (standard errors)		
Line	Years	r_s	$\ell n(y_p)$	R^2
1	1900–85	−.07	.97	.967
		(.044)	(.019)	
2	1900–85	−.09	1.0	—
		(.005)	—	
3	1958–85	−.01	.21	.328
		(.005)	(.059)	
4	1958–85	−.07	1.0	—
		(.008)	—	

elasticity η_r and the income elasticity η_y have to lie on the line: $\eta_r = -.02 + (.14)\eta_y$. With an income elasticity of unity, this implies an interest semi-elasticity of .12. This pair of estimates is roughly consistent with the estimates 1.06 and .07 reported in line 3 of Table 3. It is also consistent with the estimates .97 and .07 in line 1 of Table 4, and with the constrained estimates in lines 2 and 4 of Table 4. Similarly, the unconstrained estimates .21 and −.01 on line 3 of Table 4 lie roughly on this line. One can account for the divergent trends in income and real balances over the 1958–85 period *either* with the 1900–57 estimated income and interest elasticities *or* with much lower income and interest elasticities.[8]

Figure 4 illustrates, in part, why I prefer the constrained estimates reported on lines 2 and 4 of Table 4 to the unconstrained estimates on line 3. This figure plots the log of $M1/Py_p$ against the short term interest rate for the entire 1900–85 period, with the post 1957 observations indicated by different symbols from the 1900–57 observations. One can see that *if* one constrains the income elasticity for the entire period to be unity, one gets in return a single interest semi-elasticity for the entire period. The most recent points lie exactly or the line defined by the earlier ones and, since interest rates behaved so differently in the recent period, the estimate is greatly sharpened by the new observations.

Let me try to summarize the sense in which Figure 4 confirms both

8. Poole (1970) argued much earlier that one needs to constrain the income elasticity in order to obtain an interest elasticity from post-World War II data that is consistent with pre-war evidence.

Meltzer's hypothesis that real money demand is a stable function of permanent income (or wealth) and interest rates and the numerical estimates he obtained. Meltzer estimated these two parameters by least squares. As Figure 2 shows, the estimated income elasticity is mainly dictated by the common trend of real balances and income. At this estimated value of unity, Figure 3 shows that the interest elasticity is determined by a reasonably tight scatter of $\ell n(M1/Py_p)$ against r_s. If one imposes the same income elasticity of unity on the 1958–85 period, this same scatter, reproduced as Figure 4, confirms the original interest elasticity estimate, and since interest rates were so much higher in the later period, the new experiment is a very good one. Notice that there is nothing arbitrary or experimental about Figure 4: It is precisely the scatter one would want to look at in view of the estimates Meltzer obtained using pre-1958 data only.

However, as line 3 of Table 4 shows, these two elasticity estimates cannot be recovered from the 1958–85 data using least squares (as Meltzer recovered them from the earlier data). There is a reason why these estimates came out as they did, as Figure 5 shows. Interest rates were not only increasing dramatically over the 1958–85 period but were also highly erratic. The relatively high interest semi-elasticity on line 3 reconciles the trends with a high income elasticity, but the cost of this reconciliation is that the "predicted" path of real balances from the constrained estimates is *much* too interest-sensitive to fit observed, year-to-year movements. Actual real balances move in the predicted direction in response to interest rate changes, but by much less than is predicted. These lead to large residuals, which are also strongly correlated with interest rates. This is why the order revealed in Figure 4 cannot be discovered using unconstrained least squares.

Mankiw and Summers (1986) recover *exactly* an income elasticity of unity and an interest semi-elasticity of .05 from least squares applied to 1960–84 U.S. quarterly series. They do so using consumption in place of permanent income (justified in part by the kind of argument I used in Section III) and by using Almon lags to average the independent variables over time. One can conjecture from Figure 5 that averaging interest rates will "work," and Mankiw and Summers's results confirm this. (I suspect that long interest rates worked as well as they did in Meltzer's study for much the same reason: Long rates are a kind of average of short rates.)

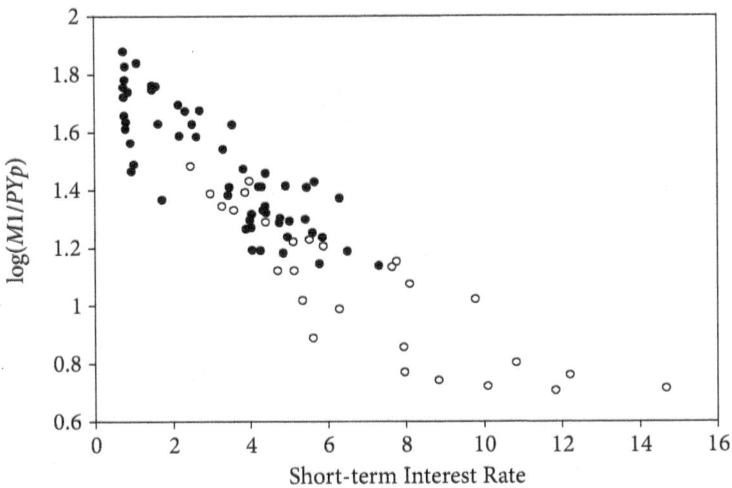

● – denotes observations from 1900 to 1957.
○ – denotes observations from 1958 to 1985.

Figure 4

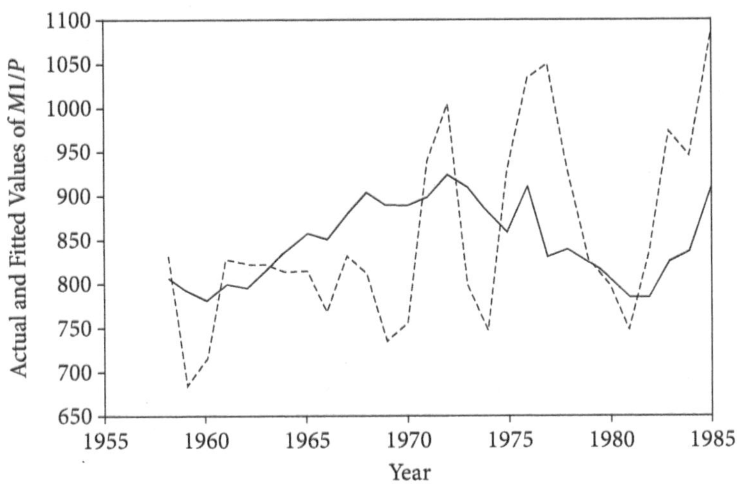

— Actual $M1/P$.
--- Predicted $M1/P$ from line 4, Table 4.

Figure 5

V. Conclusions

This paper has had three main objectives. As reported in Section II, I first replicated some of the results in Meltzer (1963), using his 1900–1957 sample period, and showed that two variations of interest to me are empirically indistinguishable from the model he used. Second, in Section III, I reviewed a theoretical model of money demand in which the two parameters Meltzer estimated could be expected to be "structural." Third, in Section IV, I compared the predictions of Meltzer's model, with his original parameter estimates, to post-1958 data, and concluded that this comparison yields additional confirmation of the theory and of these two estimates.

Meltzer (1963) was criticized (for example, by Courchene and Shapiro (1964)) for, among other things, his failure to correct his estimates for severely serially correlated residuals and his failure, despite great emphasis on the "stability" of the money demand function, to apply standard statistical tests for the stability of parameter estimates across different sample periods. These two criticisms can certainly be applied as well to the present paper, for I share Meltzer's emphasis on the "stability" of the money demand function.

But I agree with Meltzer (1964) that these econometric criticisms are very badly off the economic point. We begin with a simple economic model that suggests a two-parameter description of money demand. When we hypothesize that this relationship is "stable," we mean that we expect these two parameters to reflect relatively stable features of consumer preferences and the way in which business is carried out, and we expect them not to shift around as monetary or other policies are altered over time. This theory does not suggest that the residuals can be characterized in a simple, elegant fashion over a given time period, or even that the stochastic structure of the residuals should be stable over time. Accordingly, there is little point in testing the theory by maintaining an extreme hypothesis on the residuals that is not implied by any theoretical considerations and then performing a Chi-square test for the equality of coefficients over subperiods. One needs a maintained hypothesis in which one has more, not less, confidence than one has in the hypothesis being tested.

Thus Meltzer argued, and I agree, that we can only test the theory by comparing its numerical predictions to as wide a variety of data as we can find. In carrying out such tests, it is of no interest whatever to let the two crucial elasticities isolated by the theory change arbitrarily from one data set to the next. The theory is of no interest or use unless these two parameters are stable under a wide range of circumstances.

Over the time period Meltzer studied, in which income has a strong trend and interest rates had none, the method of least squares isolates an income elasticity of unity, just as does a comparison of income and real balance trends. With this income elasticity, one can see from Figure 3 that there is enough interest variability to trace out a fairly clear demand curve. Over the more recent period, interest rates have a very strong upward trend, as does income, so that there are many combinations of elasticities that are consistent with trends in the holding of real balances. Least squares picks out a combination of elasticities that is very different from the pair that is consistent with earlier evidence. Yet imposing the same elasticities in the later period is also consistent with long term trends and, as Figure 4 shows, traces out a demand function that is consistent with the earlier data, and much clearer than was possible with those data alone.[9] This picture did not arise by chance!

The evidence from the post-1960 years also reveals strong patterns in the residuals from this estimated demand function that did not appear in the earlier years of the century. It is clear that, as investigators since Goldfeld have concluded, the portfolio adjustment process is subject to lags in a way that neither the theory Meltzer had in mind nor the cash-in-advance model I sketched in Section III helps to understand. This fact is hardly surprising: One is, if anything, surprised that this simple model captures as much as it does.

In these circumstances, it seems to me that it is the econometrician's job to display as clearly as he can the respects in which the model he has is a good approximation to reality and the sense in which it is not. This is what Meltzer did in his 1963 paper, and it is what I have tried to do in this one. I hope Figure 4 convinces anyone who sees it that the interest semi-elasticity of money demand has remained stable at something between .05 and .10 for nearly a century in the U.S. I hope Figure 5 helps to stimulate someone, perhaps along the lines suggested by Grossman, Weiss and Rotemberg, to discover the short run dynamics that can reconcile this fact with year-to-year or even quarter-to-quarter movements in observed money holdings.

9. An income elasticity of unity is also consistent with the cross-section evidence reported in Meltzer (1963b). The interest semi-elasticities estimated from U.S. time series are also consistent with the range of estimates Cagan (1956) found in his study of hyperinflations.

References

Ando, A., Modigliani, F., and Shell, K. 1975 Some Reflections on Describing Structures of Financial Sectors, in Gary Fromm and Lawrence R. Klein, (eds.), *Brookings Model Perspective and Recent Developments.* Amsterdam: North-Holland, 524–563.

Brunner, K. and Meltzer, A. H. 1963 Predicting Velocity: Implications for Theory and Policy. *Journal of Finance,* 18: 319–354.

Cagan, P. 1956 The Monetary Dynamics of Hyperinflation, in Milton Friedman, (ed.), *Studies in the Quantity Theory of Money.* Chicago: University of Chicago Press.

Cochrane, J. H. 1988 The Return of the Liquidity Effect: A Study of the Short Run Relation Between Money Growth and Interest Rates. *Journal of Business and Economic Statistics.* Forthcoming.

Cooley, T. F. and LeRoy, S. F. 1981 Identification and Estimation of Money Demand. *American Economic Review,* 71: 825–844.

Courchene, T. J. and Shapiro, H. T. 1964 The Demand for Money: A Note from the Time Series. *Journal of Political Economy,* 72: 498–503.

Economic Report of the President 1987 Washington D.C.

Friedman, M. 1956 The Quantity Theory of Money—A Restatement, in Milton Friedman, (ed.), *Studies in the Quantity Theory of Money.* Chicago: University of Chicago Press.

Friedman, M. 1957 *A Theory of the Consumption Function.* Princeton: Princeton University Press, for the National Bureau of Economic Research.

——— 1959 The Demand for Money—Some Theoretical and Empirical Results. *Journal of Political Economy,* 67: 327–351.

——— and Schwartz, A. J. 1963 *A Monetary History of the United States, 1867–1960.* Princeton: Princeton University Press, for the National Bureau of Economic Research.

——— and ——— (1970) *Monetary Statistics of the United States.* New York: Columbia University Press for the National Bureau of Economic Research.

——— and ——— 1982 *Monetary Trends in the United States and the United Kingdom.* Chicago: University of Chicago Press, for the National Bureau of Economic Research.

Goldfeld, S. M. 1973 The Demand for Money Revisited. *Brookings Papers on Economic Activity,* 577–638.

——— 1976 The Case of the Missing Money. *Brookings Papers on Economic Activity,* 683–730.

Goldsmith, R. W., *et al.* 1956 *A Study of Saving in the United States,* Vol. III. Princeton: Princeton University Press, for the National Bureau of Economic Research.

Grossman, S. and Weiss, L. 1983 A Transactions-Based Model of the Monetary Transmission Mechanism. *American Economic Review*, 73: 871–880.

Hamburger, M. J. 1977 Behavior of the Money Stock: Is There a Puzzle? *Journal of Monetary Economics*, 3: 265–288.

Judd, J. P. and Scadding, J. L. 1982 The Search for a Stable Money Demand Function. *Journal of Economic Literature*, 20: 993–1023.

Laidler, D. E. W. 1966 The Rate of Interest and the Demand for Money — Some Empirical Evidence. *Journal of Political Economy*, 74: 545–555.

——— 1977 *The Demand for Money: Theoretical and Empirical Evidence*. Second Edition. New York: Dun-Donneley.

Lucas, R. E., Jr. and Stokey, N. L. 1987 Money and Interest in a Cash-in-Advance Economy. *Econometrica*, 55: 491–514.

Mankiw, N. G. and Summers, L. H. 1986 Money Demand and the Effects of Fiscal Policies. *Journal of Money, Credit, and Banking*, 18: 415–429.

McCallum, B. T. and Goodfriend, M. S. 1987 Money: Theoretical Analysis of the Demand for Money. Paper prepared for *The New Palgrave: A Dictionary of Economic Theory and Doctrine*.

Meltzer, A. H. 1963 The Demand for Money: The Evidence from the Time Series. *Journal of Political Economy*, 71: 219–246.

Meltzer, A. H. 1963b The Demand for Money: A Cross-Section Study of Business Firms. *Quarterly Journal of Economics*, 77: 405–422.

——— 1964 A Little More Evidence from the Time Series. *Journal of Political Economy*, 72: 504–508.

Poole, W. 1970 Whither Money Demand? *Brookings Papers on Economic Activity*, 485–501.

Rotemberg, J. J. 1984 A Monetary Equilibrium Model with Transactions Costs. *Journal of Political Economy*, 92: 40–58.

Samuelson, P. A. (1947) *Foundations of Economic Analysis*. Cambridge: Harvard University Press.

U.S. Bureau of the Census. 1960 *Historical Statistics of the United States, Colonial Times to 1957.* Washington D.C.

— 12 —

The Effects of Monetary Shocks When Prices Are Set in Advance

1. Introduction

This paper is a theoretical study of the effects of monetary disturbances in an economy in which sellers of goods fix nominal prices in advance and consumers decide how many goods to buy (if available) at these pre-set prices.* It provides another example, in addition to those provided in Lucas (1972), Fischer (1977), Phelps and Taylor (1977) and Taylor (1979), of a monetary economy in which unanticipated changes in nominal spending flows induce less-than-proportional responses in nominal prices, and changes in the same direction in real output. The implications of the theory will thus be consistent with the centuries old observation, documented most recently and comprehensively by Kormendi and Meguire (1984), that increased monetary instability is associated with increased real instability.

Why another example of this monetary non-neutrality, when we already have so many? Because, to paraphrase Tolstoy's observation about happy and unhappy families, complete market economies are all alike, but each incomplete market economy is incomplete in its own individual way. Models of monetary economies necessarily depend on assumed conventions about the way business is conducted in the absence of complete markets, about who does what, when, and what information he has when he does it. Such conventions are necessarily highly specific, relative to the enormous variety of trading practices we observe, so monetary theories can give the impression of basing important conclusions on slender, arbitrary reeds. I

Unpublished manuscript, the University of Chicago (November 1989).

*I am grateful to Nancy L. Stokey for discussions, for comments received in seminars at the University of Iowa and the University of Pennsylvania, and for research support under the National Science Foundation grant number SES-8808835.

think this impression is exactly wrong, that the main implications of theories that attribute real effects to monetary causes by means of some form of price rigidity are largely independent of the way the rigidity is modeled or motivated. The present paper provides additional support for this opinion by offering an example of a rigid-price economy that is very different in structure from earlier ones but very similar in its implications.

In its reliance on nominal prices that are set in advance, the model in this paper is similar to those of Fischer, Phelps and Taylor. In common with these authors, I offer no explanation beyond an appeal to descriptive realism for the assumption that prices are pre-set, or for the assumption that they are set in dollars rather that, say, eggs or pork bellies or yen. I will, however, spell out in detail the maximum problem faced by sellers in their price setting decision, and the nature of the game in which prices and quantities are assumed to be determined. To do so, I adapt a game introduced by Prescott (1975) and Butters (1977), which has the property that sellers are not required to price identical items identically and do not, in equilibrium, choose to do so.[1] This monetary adaptation of the Prescott-Butters structure is the main innovation of the paper.

Section 2 examines a version of a one-shot Prescott-Butters type game, in order to see how prices are set in the simplest possible context. In section 3, the equilibrium of this game is reinterpreted as an equilibrium in an ongoing cash-in-advance type monetary system that is subject to purely transient monetary shocks. Section 4 studies the behavior of this same economy when it is subject to permanent as well as transient shocks, so that Phillips curve effects are mixed with speculative, inflation tax effects. Section 5 works out the main properties of the Phillips curve or money multiplier implied by the theory, and considers several questions of interpretation of these results. Section 6 contains concluding comments.

2. A Price Setting Game

In a theory centered on pre-set nominal prices, it is important to be explicit about exactly who sets prices and why they set them the way they do.[2]

1. Other recent applications of the Prescott-Butters structure include Edens (1990), who also provides an Arrow-Debreu interpretation of the equilibrium, Rotemberg (1988), and Rotemberg and Summers (1988).

2. Lucas (1984) provides an analysis of equilibrium with nominal contracting that is explicit on this issue, but in a way that is very different from this paper.

In this section, I use a simple one-shot game, a straightforward adaption of the games introduced by Prescott (1975) and Butters (1977), to illustrate the mechanism that will be assumed in the rest of the paper.

There are two types of players, producers and consumers, in equal, large numbers. Each producer begins with y units of a single good. Each consumer begins with one dollar. (Though I will use monetary language in referring to this second good in this section, questions about why people value this good should be deferred until the next section, where it will be given as complete an answer as such a question admits. In this section, money is just a good from which some people get utility, in a way I will describe in a moment.) The play proceeds as follows. First, each producer places a dollar price on each unit of his endowment of goods. He need not, and in general will not, choose the same price for all units. Second, each consumer receives a dollar transfer that transforms his money holdings from 1 to θ, where θ is a positive-valued random variable with the distribution function Φ on $\Theta \in \left[\underline{\theta}, \overline{\theta}\right] \subset R_{++}$. I assume that Φ has a continuous density ϕ that is strictly positive on θ. The distribution Φ is known to the producers at the time they price their goods, but the realization θ is not. Third, the shock θ is realized. Fourth, consumers use some or all of their balances θ to purchase goods.

In this situation, I will take a strategy for a producer to be a nondecreasing, right-continuous function $x : R_+ \to R_+$, where $x(u)$, $u \geq 0$, is interpreted as the number of goods offered for sale at a price less than or equal to u. Since the quantity of goods offered is limited by the endowment, it must be the case that:

$$\lim_{u \to \infty} x(u) \leq y. \tag{2.1}$$

Call a value u_0 a *point of increase* of a goods offer schedule x if $x(u_0) > x(u)$ for all $u < u_0$. A point of increase is a price at which positive quantities of goods are placed on sale.

After the monetary transfer θ is realized, consumers select their goods purchases, with the entire priced inventories $x(u)$, $u \geq 0$, of all the producers in full view. Consumers' objectives are to maximize the utility yielded by their total goods purchases plus the utility they receive from their unspent cash balances. Their optimal strategy in buying goods, then, will simply be to buy up goods offered at various prices, starting from the cheapest and working up the price schedule they are faced with. I take as their decision variable the price q of the most expensive item they choose to purchase.

I will define a symmetric equilibrium, in which all producers choose the same strategy $x^0(u)$ and all consumers get the same fraction (also $x^0(u)$) of the goods that are available at prices less than or equal to u.[3] Let $p(\theta)$ denote the equilibrium value of the the highest price paid for goods when the monetary shock is θ. In equilibrium, producers take this function $p : \theta \to R_+$, which summarizes the relevant actions of consumers and all other producers, as given. If a producer chooses the offer schedule $x(u)$ and the realized shock is θ, his dollar revenue is then:

$$\int_0^{p(\theta)} u dx(u),$$

where I use $\int f(u) dx(u)$ to denote the integral of a function f with respect to the (measure defined by the) function x. Each producer's objective is assumed to be the maximization of expected revenues, defined by:

$$\int_\Theta \int_0^{p(\theta)} u dx(u) d\Phi(\theta). \tag{2.2}$$

A consumer choosing a maximum price q when his cash holdings are θ and the goods offer schedule is $x^0(u)$ obtains $x^0(q)$ units of goods and spends $\int_0^q u dx^0(u)$ dollars.[4] I assume this choice yields him the utility value

$$U\left[x^0(q)\right] + \alpha\left[\theta - \int_0^q u dx^0(u)\right] \tag{2.3}$$

3. In order to consider non-symmetric equilibria, I would need to introduce a mathematical framework that would permit adding up goods supplied across a continuum of firms and goods demanded across a continuum of consumers. See, for example, Green (1984). By considering symmetric equilibria only, I avoid even having to provide a definition of the game (in the sense of specifying the outcome under all possible strategy choices by all of the players involved), not to mention an analysis of such a game.

4. A consumer who choose to buy *more* than the equilibrium quantity $x^0(p(\theta))$ does not need to work up the schedule x^0 by offering a price q above $p(\theta)$. Since he is the only buyer, he can have all the additional goods he wants at the price $p(\theta)$. It would be straightforward to modify the statement of the consumer's problem to reflect this correctly (as my statement does not) but also tedious and doing so would clearly not affect the marginal condition (2.5).

The function U is assumed to be twice continuously differentiable, with $U'(c) > 0$ and $U''(c) < 0$ for all c, and $U'(0) = +\infty$. The value α, the marginal utility of money, is a positive constant. The choice of q is subject to the cash constraint:

$$\theta - \int_0^q u dx^0(u) \geq 0. \tag{2.4}$$

Now define an *equilibrium* as a non-decreasing, right-continuous function $x^0 : R_+ \to R_+$ and a non-decreasing, continuous function $p : \Theta \to R_+$ such that (i) x^0 satisfies (2.1), (ii) for all $\theta \in \Theta$, $q = p(\theta)$ maximizes (2.3) subject to (2.4), and (iii) given p, x^0 maximizes (2.2) subject to (2.1).

The first-order conditions for the consumer's problem, evaluated at $q = p(\theta)$, include

$$U'[x^0(p(\theta))] - [\alpha + \mu(\theta)]p(\theta) = 0 \tag{2.5}$$

for all θ such that $p(\theta)$ is a point of increase of x^0, where $\mu(\theta)$ is the multiplier associated with (2.4). A second necessary condition is:

$$\theta \geq \int_0^{p(\theta)} u dx^0(u), \quad \text{with equality if } \mu(\theta) > 0. \tag{2.6}$$

The first order condition for the producer's problem, also at equilibrium values, is:

$$p(\theta)[1 - \Phi(\theta)] \leq \lambda, \qquad \text{all } \theta \in \Theta, \tag{2.7}$$

with equality if $p(\theta)$ is a point of increase of x^0. That is to say, the price of a unit times the probability that that unit will be sold must be equated across all units offered for sale. Since the producer's objective function (2.2) is linear, he is indifferent among the wide variety of goods offer schedules that have this property.

We seek solutions $p : \Theta \to R_+$, $x^0 : R_{++} \to R_+$, $\mu : \Theta \to R_+$ and $\lambda \geq 0$ to the system (2.5)–(2.7). One such solution is p, x^0 and μ all identically zero: no goods are offered for sale, no price other than zero is ever paid, and the constraints (2.1) and (2.4) are always slack. I will simply ignore this possibility, and construct the unique solution that is non-trivial in the sense of having the property that $p(\theta) > 0$ for some $\theta \in \Theta$.

In constructing such a solution it will be convenient to define the total consumption function $c : \Theta \to R_+$ by $c(\theta) = x^0(p(\theta))$. The function c will be non-decreasing and right-continuous on Θ, with $c(\underline{\theta}) \geq 0$ and $c(\overline{\theta}) \leq y$.

In terms of this total consumption function, the equilibrium condition (2.5) becomes:

$$\mu(\theta) = \frac{1}{p(\theta)} U'\left[c(\theta)\right] - \alpha \tag{2.8}$$

if $p(\theta)$ is a point of increase of x^0.

Suppose (x^0, p, μ, λ) is a solution to (2.5)–(2.8) with $p(\theta)$ positive for some $\theta \in \Theta$. From (2.7), this requires that $\lambda > 0$ and thus that $c(\bar{\theta}) = y$. (If any positive quantity can be offered for sale at a positive expected return, the entire endowment will be offered.) Now let A be the subset of Θ consisting of points of increase of $c(\theta)$. From (2.7) and the assumption that $\phi(\theta) > 0$, $p(\theta)$ is strictly increasing on A. Since $c(\theta)$ is non-decreasing and U is concave, (2.8) then implies that $\mu(\theta)$ is strictly decreasing on A. Since $\mu(\theta) \geq 0$, it follows that $\mu(\theta)$ must be strictly positive on A, except at the largest point of this set. Hence the set A either consists of the single point $\underline{\theta}$ or it takes the form of an interval $[\underline{\theta}, \theta^*]$, where $\underline{\theta} < \theta^* \leq \bar{\theta}$.

If A consists of the point $\underline{\theta}$ only, the entire endowment y is placed on sale at the price $p(\underline{\theta})$, and (2.8) implies that

$$p(\underline{\theta}) = \frac{1}{\alpha} U'(y).$$

This is an equilibrium if and only if

$$\frac{1}{\alpha} y U'(y) \leq \underline{\theta}, \tag{2.9}$$

or if cash is so valuable intrinsically that it is never entirely spent on goods.

If the inequality (2.9) does not hold, A is an interval $[\underline{\theta}, \theta^*]$ with $\theta^* > \underline{\theta}$. In this case, $p(\theta)$ is determined by (2.7) on A, up to the constant λ. To determine the latter, note that (2.6) is binding on this interval and, differentiating both sides, this equality implies:

$$p(\theta)x'(p(\theta))p'(\theta) = p(\theta)c'(\theta) = 1, \quad \text{all } \theta \in \left[\underline{\theta}, \theta^*\right]. \tag{2.10}$$

Combined with (2.7), (2.10) implies:

$$1 - \Phi(\theta) = \lambda c'(\theta), \quad \text{all } \theta \in \left[\underline{\theta}, \theta^*\right]. \tag{2.11}$$

Integrating both sides of (2.11) over $[\underline{\theta}, \theta^*]$ yields

$$\int_{\underline{\theta}}^{\theta^*} [1 - \Phi(\theta)]\, d\theta = \lambda \int_{\underline{\theta}}^{\theta^*} dc(\theta) = \lambda y - \underline{\theta}, \tag{2.12}$$

where the second equality uses the facts that $c(\theta^*) = y$, that $p(\underline{\theta}) = \lambda$, and, from the cash constraint, that $p(\underline{\theta})c(\underline{\theta}) = \underline{\theta}$. This equality fixes λ, given θ^*. Inserting this value of λ in (2.7) determines $p(\theta)$ on $[\underline{\theta}, \theta^*]$, given θ^*:

$$p(\theta; \theta^*) = \left[y(1 - \Phi(\theta))\right]^{-1} \left\{ \underline{\theta} + \int_{\underline{\theta}}^{\theta^*} [1 - \Phi(z)] dz \right\}. \tag{2.13}$$

Then (2.6) (with equality) determines $x^0(p(\theta; \theta^*)) = c(\theta; \theta^*)$, given θ^*.

It remains to determine θ^*. Since $c(\theta^*) = y$, (2.8) implies that $U'(y) = \alpha p(\theta^*)$. Using the solution for p on $[\underline{\theta}, \theta^*]$ given in (2.13) this implies that:

$$yU'(y)[1 - \Phi(\theta^*)] = \alpha\underline{\theta} + \alpha \int_{\underline{\theta}}^{\theta^*} [1 - \Phi(z)] dz. \tag{2.14}$$

Provided the inequality (2.9) does not hold, (2.14) has a unique solution θ^* in $(\underline{\theta}, \overline{\theta})$.

Note that $p(\theta^*) = \alpha^{-1} U'(y)$ is just the price at which the marginal utility of money equals the marginal utility of an additional dollar spent on goods. In the equilibrium, no goods are offered for sale at prices above $p(\theta^*)$, since they would never be sold at any value of the shock. (For this reason, $p(\theta)$ will not be uniquely determined at $\theta > \theta^*$.) At shock values below θ^*, consumers spend all their cash on goods. These goods are so priced that the expected revenue from all units offered is equal. At shock values above θ^*, consumers purchase the entire endowment and hold over any cash above the amount needed to purchase y as unspent balances. Of course, if no utility is attached to unspent cash, consumers will always spend the entire amount θ. That is, (2.14) implies that if $\alpha = 0$, $\theta^* = \overline{\theta}$.

It will not have escaped the alert reader that the total consumption function $c(\theta)$ is a kind of Phillips curve: an equilibrium relation between the level of real consumption and the (unanticipated) change in the quantity of money. Over the interval $(\underline{\theta}, \theta^*)$, this function is differentiable, with derivative equal to:

$$c'(\theta) = y \left[\underline{\theta} + \int_{\theta}^{\theta^*} [1 - \Phi(z)] dz \right]^{-1} [1 - \Phi(\theta)]. \tag{2.15}$$

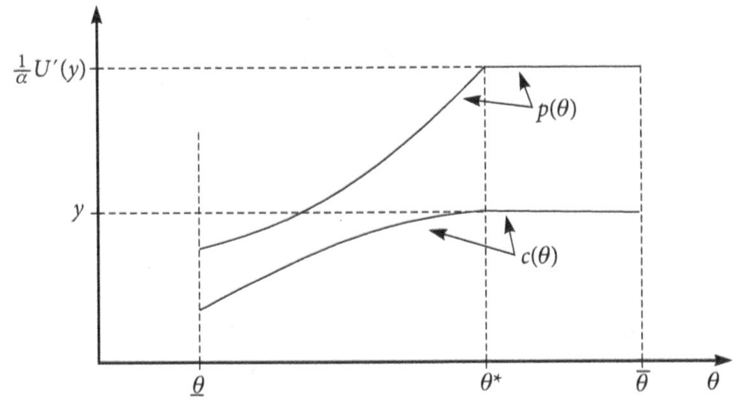

Figure 1

We can think of $c'(\theta)$ as a money multiplier. Figure 1 plots the functions $c(\theta)$ and $p(\theta)$ against θ. Further discussion of these functions will be offered in Section 5.

3. A Monetary Economy with Purely Transient Shocks

The last section considered a game with two player types: producers and consumers. I now want to reinterpret these players as members of producer-consumer families, in a setting in which the cash received by producers in exchange for goods is used later by consumers to purchase goods. This will permit us to replace the assumed objective functions (2.2) and (2.3) in the last section with a household utility function over sequences of consumptions at different dates, and to derive the marginal utility α of unspent balances from more fundamental considerations.

The reader familiar with earlier cash-in-advance models can no doubt guess the nature of many of the conventions under which this reinterpretation is possible.[5] I review them briefly. There is a continuum of households, each with preferences:

$$E\left\{\sum_{t=0}^{\infty}\beta^t U(c_t)\right\},$$

where c_t is consumption of the single good, $\beta \in (0,1)$, and where U has the properties assumed in the last section. Each household consists of a

5. See, for example, Lucas and Stokey (1983), Section 4, and Lucas (1980).

producer-consumer pair. The producer receives the household's endowment y, prices each unit in the manner described in the last section, collects the dollar proceeds from the sale of these units, and brings these proceeds home at the end of the period. Unsold units of the endowment decay immediately. The consumer takes the household's cash holdings and uses them to purchase goods from other households' producers. A household cannot consume its own endowment. Picture the circular flow diagram that used to be a standard feature in beginning economics texts, with cash and goods moving in opposite directions around the circle.

Next I will describe the monetary shocks to which this system is subject, with an eye toward providing a dynamic rationalization of the game described in the last section. These shocks affect the circular flow in two places. First, a consumer with money holdings (relative to average) of m receives a lump sum transfer of size $\theta - 1$, transforming his money holdings from m to $m + \theta - 1$. These shocks θ are serially independent drawings from the distribution Φ, identical for all consumers. Second, after sales are complete, each producer pays a lump sum tax to the government. In this section, this lump sum tax is also given by the *same* realization of the shock θ that determined transfers to consumers earlier in the same period. This is what I mean by the term "purely transient" in the title of this section: a monetary transfer remains in the system only long enough to affect consumers' immediate liquidity. The added cash does not add to anyone's overnight balances. I will consider other possibilities in Section 4, but it will be easiest to begin with a setting in which money shocks have *no* implications for future price levels.

In order to define an equilibrium, I will develop the Bellman equation for the household's decision problem. Let $v(m)$ be the value of the maximized utility function, prior to the realization of the transfer θ, for a household with m units of cash (relative to the economy-wide average of unity) that proceeds optimally. Let $x(u)$ denote the producer's decision variables, interpreted as in the last section, and let $x^0(u)$ denote the equilibrium schedule. Let $p(\theta)$ denote the highest price paid in equilibrium.

Let the consumer's decision variable be q, the highest priced unit of goods he purchases, so that the household's total consumption is $x^0(q)$ and its total dollar outlays are $\int_0^q u dx^0(u)$. The value q is chosen after the transfer θ is received, so spending is subject to the cash constraint:

$$m + \theta - 1 \geq \int_0^q dx^0(u). \tag{3.1}$$

The producer chooses the amounts $x(u)$, $u > 0$, that he will offer for sale at prices less than or equal to u, subject to the endowment constraint:

$$\lim_{u \to \infty} x(u) \le y. \tag{3.2}$$

This choice is made prior to the realization of θ.

Given particular choices q and $x(u)$, the household will begin the next period with balances m', relative to average, of:

$$m' = m - \int_0^q u dx^0(u) + \int_0^{p(\theta)} u dx(u). \tag{3.3}$$

Notice that under the tax and transfer assumptions I am using here, the value of the shock θ does not directly appear in (3.3) .

Under these assumptions, the household's Bellman equation is:

$$v(m) = \max_{x(u)} \int_\Theta \left\{ \max_q \left[U\left[x^0(q)\right] + \beta v(m') \right] \right\} d\Phi(\theta) \tag{3.4}$$

where q is chosen subject to (3.1), $x(u)$ is chosen subject to (3.2), and m' is given by (3.3).

Now define an *equilibrium* for this economy as a continuously differentiable value function $v: R_{++} \to R$, a continuous non-decreasing price function $p: \Theta \to R_+$, and a quantity offer function $x^0 : R_{++} \to R_+$ such that (i) given x^0 and p, v satisfies (3.4), and (ii) given x^0, p and v, for $m = 1$ and for all $\theta \in \Theta$, $q = p(\theta)$ attains the inner maximum on the right side of (3.4) and x^0 attains the outer maximum in (3.4).

As in the last section, there will be a trivial equilibrium in which cash is not valued, no goods are offerred for sale and none are consumed. I will use the first order conditions for (3.4) and the market clearing conditions to characterize the non-trivial equilibrium. The first order condition for q is:

$$U'[x^0(q)] - q[\mu(\theta) + \beta v'(m')] = 0,$$

if q is a point of increase of x^0, where $\mu(\theta)$ is the nonnegative multiplier associated with the cash in advance constraint (3.1). In equilibrium, $m = m' = 1$ and $q = p(\theta)$. As in the last section, it is convenient to write $c(\theta) = x^0(p(\theta))$. Then one equilibrium condition is:

$$U'(c(\theta)) - p(\theta)[\mu(\theta) + \beta v'(1)] = 0, \tag{3.5}$$

whenever $p(\theta)$ is a point of increase of x^0. From (3.1), a second condition is:

$$\theta \geq \int_{\underline{\theta}}^{p(\theta)} u dx^0(u), \quad \text{with equality if } \mu(\theta) > 0. \tag{3.6}$$

The first order condition for the producer's decision, also expressed at equilibrium values, is:

$$p(\theta)[1 - \Phi(\theta)] \leq \lambda, \tag{3.7}$$

with equality if $p(\theta)$ is a point of increase of x^0, where λ is proportional to the multiplier associated with (3.2).[6] That is, the expected real return must be equated across all units of the good offered for sale. If the multiplier λ is positive, the constraint (3.2) must hold with equality.

Notice that if we identify the parameter α in the last section with the quantity $\beta v'(1)$ in this section, equations (3.5)–(3.8) are *exactly* the same system as (2.5)–(2.8). Thus for any given marginal utility of cash $v'(1)$, the system (3.5)–(3.8) has the same two solutions we obtained in Section 2: a trivial solution in which no economic activity takes place, and the solution summarized in Figure 1. To complete the construction, then, we have only to determine $v'(1)$.

For this purpose, we use the envelope condition for the problem (3.4), also evaluated at $m = m' = 1$. It is:

$$v'(1) = \int_{\Theta} \left[\mu(\theta) + \beta v'(1)\right] d\Phi(\theta). \tag{3.8}$$

As shown in the last section, the multiplier $\mu(\theta)$ will equal zero on an interval $[\theta^*, \overline{\theta}]$, while on the interval $[\underline{\theta}, \theta^*]$ it is given by (3.5). Inserting this information into the right side of (3.8) and collecting terms involving $v'(1)$ gives:

$$v'(1)[1 - \beta + \beta\Phi(\theta^*)] = \int_{\underline{\theta}}^{\theta^*} \frac{1}{p(\theta)} U'[c(\theta)] d\theta. \tag{3.9}$$

6. The derivation of (3.7) involves the study of a straightforward variational problem. The multiplier associated with (3.2) is $\beta v'(1)\lambda$, the discounted utility value of the dollar proceeds of an additional unit of endowment. Is it surprising that producers from risk-averse households nonetheless have a first order condition that corresponds to the same linear problem assumed in Section 2? It was to me, but it should not have been. Risk aversion is captured in the concavity of the value function $v(m)$, but in equilibrium $v'(m)$ is always evaluated at the point $m = 1$.

Now $p(\theta;\theta^*)$ is determined, given θ^*, as given by the formula (2.13), and $c(\theta;\theta^*)$ is also determined given θ^* as described in the last section. Inserting the expression for $\beta v'(1)$ given in (3.9) in place of α on the right side of (2.14) gives:

$$U'(y)\left[1-\Phi(\theta^*)\right]\left[1-\beta+\beta\Phi(\theta^*)\right] = \beta\int_{\underline{\theta}}^{\theta^*}\left[1-\Phi(\theta)\right]U'\left[c(\theta;\theta^*)\right]d\Phi(\theta), \tag{3.10}$$

where the function $c(\theta;\theta^*)$ is given by:

$$c(\theta;\theta^*) = x^0(p(\theta;\theta^*)) = c(\underline{\theta};\theta) + \int_{\underline{\theta}}^{\theta}\frac{1}{p(z;\theta)^*}dz. \tag{3.11}$$

If we let $f(\theta^*)$ be the left side of (3.10) minus the right side, solutions θ^* to $f(\theta^*) = 0$ correspond to non-trivial equilibria. One sees that $f(\underline{\theta}) = (1-\beta)U'(y) > 0$ and $f(\overline{\theta}) < 0$, so there is at least one solution θ^* and it must lie in the interior of $[\underline{\theta},\overline{\theta}]$. In this dynamic version of the game, in which the marginal utility of cash α is derived from transactions demand fundamentals, cash cannot be so highly valued that the inequality (2.9) holds. It can also be verified, with some calculation, that $f(\theta^*) = 0$ implies $f'(\theta^*) < 0$. Hence there is a unique solution $\theta^* \in (\underline{\theta},\overline{\theta})$ to (3.10). This completes the construction.

Notice that the non-trivial equilibrium necessarily has the property that consumers carry over unpent cash with the positive probability $1-\Phi(\theta^*)$. One cannot assume that the cash constraint is binding for all values of the monetary shock. For suppose, to the contrary, that $\theta^* = \overline{\theta}$. Then (2.13) would imply that $p(\theta) \to \infty$ as $\theta \to \overline{\theta}$, so that producers would offer goods for sale at arbitrarily high prices. But such goods can be sold with positive probability only if consumers place *no* value on cash carried over. And if consumer-producers do not value cash, why offer goods in exchange for dollars at all? We are back in the trivial, no-activity equilibrium!

4. A Monetary Economy with Permanent and Transitory Shocks

The assumption that monetary shocks are purely transient simplified the analysis in Section 3 by making the monetary equilibria formally equivalent to the equilibria of the one-shot game analyzed in Section 2. In this section, I will dispense with this assumption so that we can examine situations in which the current monetary shock conveys some information about the money supply and the price level in the future.

There are any number of ways in which this might be done. Here I retain *all* of the assumptions of Section 3, with the following exception. When the monetary transfer received by consumers is $\theta - 1$, the lump sum tax paid by producers is assumed to be $(1 - \gamma)(\theta - 1)$, where γ is a parameter between 0 and 1. Thus $\gamma = 0$ gives the purely transitory case studied in Section 3, and $\gamma = 1$ corresponds to the other extreme in which all increases in money are permanent. Other γ values give intermediate cases. Since this modification is notationally very minor, I will just indicate how this alters the system studied in Section 3 rather than re-do the entire exposition from scratch.

For given γ, a household beginning with m dollars and receiving a consumer transfer $\theta - 1$ will pay $(1 - \gamma)(\theta - 1)$ back as a producer tax and begin the following period with $m + \theta - 1 - (1 - \gamma)(\theta - 1) = m + \gamma(\theta - 1)$ dollars (if, as will be the case in equilibrium, it sells as much as it spends). The economy's next period's money supply will be $1 - \gamma + \gamma\theta$. Since we are expressing prices relative to the money supply, and since the function $p(\theta)$ is fixed, this means that $\gamma(\theta - 1)$ is essentially the economy's inflation rate (the rate at which the entire *schedule* of prices shifts up) between this period and the next.

With this modification in the model, the law of motion (3.3) for household balances, relative to average, must be replaced by:

$$m' = [1 - \gamma + \gamma\theta]^{-1}\left[m + \gamma(\theta - 1) - \int_0^q u\,dx^0(u) + \int_0^{p(\theta)} u\,dx(u)\right]. \tag{4.1}$$

The household's Bellman equation continues to be given by (3.4), subject to the constraints (3.1) and (3.2), but with m' given by (4.1) rather than (3.3).

The definition of an equilibrium provided in Section 3 continues to apply to the present case. The system (3.5)–(3.7) of equilibrium conditions is modified, however, as is the envelope condition (3.8). Here I simply restate the modified system. For the consumption decision, we have:

$$U'(c(\theta)) - p(\theta)[\mu(\theta) + \beta(1 - \gamma + \gamma\theta)^{-1}v'(1)] = 0 \tag{4.2}$$

if $p(\theta)$ is a point of increase of x^0, and:

$$\theta - \int_0^{p(\theta)} u\,dx^0(u) \geq 0, \quad \text{with equality if } \mu(\theta) > 0. \tag{4.3}$$

In (4.2), in contrast to (3.5), consumers deflate $v'(1)$ by one plus the inflation rate $1 - \gamma + \gamma\theta$, which they know at the time they make their buying decision.

For the producer's decision, also expressed at equilibrium values, we have:

$$p(\theta)\int_{\theta}^{\bar{\theta}} (1 - \gamma + \gamma z)^{-1} d\Phi(z) \leq \lambda, \tag{4.4}$$

with equality if $p(\theta)$ is a point of increase of x^0. A second condition for producer optimization is:

$$\lim_{u \to \infty} x^0(u) \leq y, \quad \text{with equality if } \lambda > 0. \tag{4.5}$$

It is convenient to define the function $r{:}\Theta \to R_+$ by:

$$r(\theta) = \int_{\theta}^{\bar{\theta}} (1 - \gamma + \gamma z)^{-1} d\Phi(z). \tag{4.6}$$

The term $r(\theta)$ appears on the left in (4.4) rather than the probability of sale $1 - \Phi(\theta)$ as in (3.7). The expression $[1 - \Phi(\theta)]^{-1} r(\theta)$ is the expectation of the inflation factor (one over one plus the inflation rate) *conditional* on the event that the monetary shock exceeds θ. Thus the term $r(\theta)$ is just the product of the probability that an item priced at $p(\theta)$ will be sold and the expected inflation factor conditional on this event occuring. One may think of (4.4), then, as stating that the expected, *real* return per unit must be equated across all units offered for sale.

Finally, the envelope condition, also evaluated at $m = m' = 1$, is:

$$v'(1) = \int_{\underline{\theta}}^{\bar{\theta}} \left[\mu(\theta) + \beta(1 - \gamma + \gamma\theta)^{-1} v'(1) \right] d\Phi(\theta). \tag{4.7}$$

The element of changing inflationary expectations, absent from Section 3 but present here, complicates the use of (4.2)–(4.7) to construct a non-trivial equilibrium, relative to the analysis of (3.5)–(3.9). For a non-trivial equilibrium to exist, we shall need, in the first place, to impose the following condition:

$$\beta r(\underline{\theta}) < 1. \tag{4.8}$$

That is, the product of the consumers' discount factor and the expected inflation factor must be less than one. This condition is familiar from many earlier monetary models.

Even under (4.8), the construction used in Section 3 does not go through in general in the present model. I will proceed with the argument in two steps. First, I add a second restriction on the shock distribution Φ under which a non-trivial equilibrium will take the same form as the equilibrium in Section 3. Second, I will sketch a construction that does not require this additional structure, and discuss the possibilities for equilibrium behavior in general.

For the moment, then, we proceed under the additional hypothesis that:

$$\phi(\theta) - \gamma r(\theta) > 0, \qquad \text{for all } \theta \in \Theta. \tag{4.9}$$

If $\gamma = 0$, as in Section 3, the positivity of the density ϕ ensures that (4.9) holds. To see what kind of behavior is ruled out by (4.9), let $-\eta(\theta)$ denote the *elasticity* of the function r with respect to θ. From (4.4), $\eta(\theta)$ is also the elasticity of the price function $p(\theta)$ at any θ value that is a point of increase of $c(\theta)$. From the definition (4.5) of $r(\theta)$, we have $\eta(\theta) = \frac{\theta}{r(\theta)} \frac{\phi(\theta)}{1-\gamma+\gamma\theta}$. Substituting for $\phi(\theta)$ in (4.9) one sees that (4.9) is equivalent to:

$$\eta(\theta) > \frac{\gamma\theta}{1-\gamma+\gamma\theta}, \qquad \text{for all } \theta \in \Theta. \tag{4.10}$$

Thus (4.9) (or (4.10) is a lower bound on the elasticity of prices with respect to the monetary shock. It is needed, as we will see below, to ensure that the increased producer revenues from higher monetary shocks dominate, in some sense, the losses from holding cash receipts due to increased general inflation.

Under the assumptions (4.8) and (4.9), the use of (4.2)–(4.7) to construct an equilibrium proceeds exactly as in Sections 2 and 3. As in those sections, let $A \subset \Theta$ denote the set of points of increase of $c(\theta)$. From (4.4), $p(\theta) = \lambda^{-1} r(\theta)$ on A. Now consider the function:

$$\lambda^{-1} r(\theta)[1 - \gamma + \gamma\theta] U'[c(\theta)] - 1. \tag{4.11}$$

Its derivative is:

$$\lambda^{-1} U'[c(\theta)] \frac{d}{d\theta}[r(\theta)(1-\gamma+\gamma\theta)] + \lambda^{-1}[r(\theta)(1-\gamma+\gamma\theta)] \frac{d}{d\theta} U'[c(\theta)].$$

The second term is evidently negative. Condition (4.9) implies that the first term is negative. Hence, under (4.9), the expression (4.11) is strictly decreasing on A, in which case it follows from (4.2) that the set A is an interval $[\underline{\theta}, \theta^*]$, that $\mu(\theta) > 0$ is positive on $[\underline{\theta}, \theta^*)$, and that both $c'(\theta)$ and $\mu(\theta)$ are zero on $[\theta^*, \overline{\theta}]$.

With the strict positivity of the function $\mu(\theta)$ on $[\underline{\theta}, \theta^*)$ thus established, under (4.9), we can proceed to construct an equilibrium as in the last section. For any given θ, equation (4.4) determines $p(\theta; \theta^*)$ up to the constant λ. Since (4.3) holds with equality, $c'(\theta) = [p(\theta)]^{-1}$, so integrating and using the boundary conditions $p(\underline{\theta})c(\underline{\theta}) = \underline{\theta}$ and $c(\theta^*) = y$ determines λ. This determines the two functions $p(\theta; \theta^*)$ and $c(\theta; \theta^*)$ on $[\underline{\theta}, \theta^*]$, given θ^*. Inserting this information into (4.2) yields:

$$\mu(\theta; \theta^*) = \frac{1}{p(\theta; \theta^*)} U'[c(\theta; \theta^*)] - \frac{\beta v'(1)}{1 - \gamma + \gamma\theta}. \tag{4.12}$$

Under assumption (4.8), (4.12) and the envelope condition (4.7) imply:

$$v'(1) = [1 - \beta r(\theta^*)]^{-1} \int_{\underline{\theta}}^{\theta^*} \mu(\theta; \theta^*) d\Phi(\theta).$$

These two equations can be solved for $v'(1)$ and $\mu(\theta;\theta^*)$. Finally, inserting all of this information into the boundary condition

$$\frac{1}{p(\theta^*; \theta^*)} U'(y) = \frac{\beta v'(1)}{1 - \gamma + \gamma\theta^*}$$

yields an equation for θ^* of the form $f(\theta^*) = 0$, where f is given by:

$$f(\theta^*) = r(\theta^*)[1 - \beta r(\theta^*)]U'(y) - \frac{\beta}{1 - \gamma + \gamma\theta^*} \int_{\underline{\theta}}^{\theta^*} r(\theta)U'[c(\theta; \theta^*)]\phi(\theta)d\theta.$$

As in Section 3, it can be verified that $f(\underline{\theta}) > 0$ and $f(\overline{\theta}) < 0$, so f has a zero in $(\underline{\theta}, \overline{\theta})$. Under the hypotheses (4.8) and (4.9), it is also true that $f(\theta^*) = 0$ implies $f'(\theta^*) < 0$, so this root is unique.

Under the two restrictions (4.8) and (4.9), then, the construction of a non-trivial equilibrium and the qualitative behavior of the equilibrium functions $p(\theta)$ and $c(\theta)$ are essentially the same as in the case of transient shocks studied in Section 3. The restriction (4.8) is standard in monetary models in which expectations of inflation play a role, so it is not surprising that it is needed here. The restriction (4.9) is new, at least to me, and it is certainly easy enough to think of distributions ϕ and parameters γ such that it will not hold. I will conclude this section, then, with a sketch of an approach to constructing equilibria that does not depend on (4.9), and some conjectures about the economics of equilibrium behavior when (4.9) fails.

To see what the possibilities are when (4.9) does not hold, divide the set A of points of increase of $c(\theta)$ into the set A_1 on which $\mu(\theta) > 0$ and the set A_2 on which $\mu(\theta) = 0$. Let $A_3 = \Theta - A$, the complement of A. We have shown that (4.9) implies that A_2 consists of a single point, but without this assumption this need not be the case. We first consider the problem of finding solutions $(p(\theta), c(\theta))$ to (4.2)–(4.4) treating λ and $v'(1)$ as fixed parameters, reserving (4.6) and (4.7) as boundary conditions to be used later.

Fix λ and $v'(1)$. We first locate $\underline{\theta}$ in one of the sets A_1, A_2 or A_3. Suppose:

$$\lambda^{-1}r(\underline{\theta})[1-\gamma+\gamma\theta]U'[\lambda^{-1}(\beta v'(1)\underline{\theta}r(\underline{\theta}))] > 1. \tag{4.13}$$

In this case, we let $\underline{\theta} \in A_1$, let $p(\underline{\theta})$ be determined by (4.4) with equality, and let $p(\underline{\theta})c(\underline{\theta}) = \underline{\theta}$. If (4.13) does not hold, let $p(\underline{\theta})$ be determined by (4.4) with equality and let $c(\underline{\theta})$ be the solution to:

$$\lambda^{-1}r(\underline{\theta})[1-\gamma+\gamma\theta]U'[c(\underline{\theta})] = 1.$$

Since $U'(0) = +\infty$, there will be a positive $c(\underline{\theta})$ satisfying this equality and since (4.13) does not hold, this value will satisfy the cash constraint (4.3). In this case, $\underline{\theta} \in A_2$.

Next, we show how both these solutions can be continued to the right of $\underline{\theta}$. Suppose $\underline{\theta} \in A_1$. To the right of $\underline{\theta}$, let $p(\theta)$ be given by (4.4) with equality, let $p(\theta)c'(\theta) = 1$, and integrate to get $c(\theta)$ using the initial value determined as in the last paragraph. Continue this solution to the right as long as the quantity (4.11) remains positive. If this is true for all $\theta \in \Theta$, we have found a solution $(p(\theta), c(\theta))$ for this particular $(\lambda, v'(1))$ pair. Otherwise, let $\theta_1 \leq \bar{\theta}$ be the first point at which (4.11) becomes zero. This point θ_1 is in A_2.

Now suppose we have reached a point $\theta_1 \in A_2$, either by the route described in the last paragraph or because $\underline{\theta} \in A_2$ because the inequality (4.13) fails to hold. Let $c(\theta_1)$ be the associated consumption value. Consider the function $c_1(\theta)$ defined for θ to the right of θ_1 as the value of c such that the expression (4.14) remains equal to zero. If this function fails to increase for any $\theta \geq \theta_1$, then that θ is in A_3. If it increases, but not so fast as to violate (4.3), we remain in A_2. If (4.3) binds, we return to A_1.

If the system returns to A_1, we continue as we did when $\underline{\theta} \in A_1$. If the system enters A_3, $c(\theta)$ remains constant at the value c_1 (say) that it had when A_3 was first entered, and the system remains in A_3 as long as the expression

$$\lambda^{-1} r(\theta)[1 - \gamma + \gamma\theta] U'(c_1) - 1 \tag{4.15}$$

is negative. (The quantity (4.15) was negative when A_3 was first entered, since c_1 would have had to decrease to maintain it equal to zero at that point.) When (4.15) becomes zero, the system is back in A_2.

The procedure I have just sketched produces a triple of functions $(p(\theta), c(\theta), \mu(\theta))$ satisfying (4.2)–(4.4) on Θ for any values of $(\lambda, v'(1))$. The two conditions (4.6) and (4.7) then provide two equations in the unknown values of λ and $v'(1)$. Solutions, if they exist, correspond to equilibria of the system (4.2)–(4.7). I have not analyzed this problem, and it would not be trivial to do so, but I have carried the argument far enough to suggest why I think that conditions much weaker than (4.9) would suffice to ensure the existence and the uniqueness of equilibrium in this model.

What would be the economics of such an equilibrium? In the interiors of the sets A_2 and A_3, increases in consumers' money balances θ have no effect on their spending behavior. They prefer to hold cash for future spending and let the constraint (4.3) go slack. Eventually, as θ increases still further, expectations of higher inflation (or less deflation) make cash unattractive to hold, and spending on goods resumes. The behavior of equilibrium consumption and the multiplier $\mu(\theta)$ is thus as shown in Figure 2. One could describe the behavior of these two functions on the intervals $[\theta_1, \theta_2]$ and $[\theta_3, \theta_4]$ shown in Figure 2 as a kind of "liquidity trap." Nominal interest rates are zero on these intervals and issuing more money has no effect on consumer spending.[7]

7. The introduction and pricing of zero net supply securities into this representative agent framework is a standard exercise. See, for example, Stokey, Lucas and Prescott (1989, Section 16.2). If $Q(\theta)$ is the price of a one period nominal bond, set after θ is realized, it must satisfy

$$\beta v'(1)[1 - Q(\theta)] = \mu(\theta) Q(\theta),$$

which justifies the claim in the text. An equivalent formula for this bond price is:

$$Q(\theta) \frac{U'[c(\theta)]}{p(\theta)} = E\left\{ \frac{U'[c(\theta)]}{p(\theta)} \right\}.$$

This looks familiar, but remember that $p(\theta)$ is the *marginal* price, not the average.

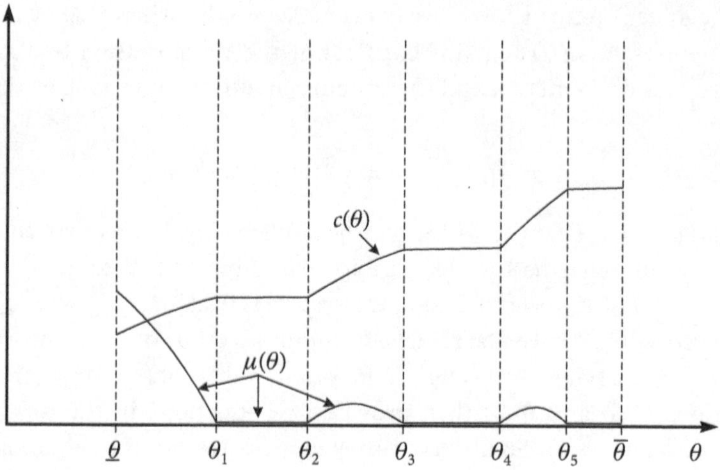

Figure 2

As I interpret this model of price setting behavior, the condition (4.9) that rules out the liquidity-trapped behavior shown in Figure 2 is more reasonable than it may appear to the reader. Let me try to explain this briefly. In the world described in the model, monetary shocks are the *only* unpredictable factor affecting the demand for the goods that each individual seller has to offer. Unless monetary shocks are purely transient, then, each seller reasons (correctly) that conditioning on the event that he sells some high priced goods has a *large* effect on his forecasts of the future value of money. It is as if an impressario reasons: "If I sell those seats in the corners where you can't hear anything except rattling programs, it must be because a big inflation has arrived." Except perhaps in extreme inflationary situations, I do not believe sellers in fact reason in this way, and I think the model would more accurately reflect reality if sellers were assumed to face a large idiosyncratic component to their individual demands, in addition to general monetary instability. Such a modification would introduce a signal-processing element very similar to that used in Lucas (1972). With this modification, the parameter γ would be interpreted as indexing the information content of individual demand shifts for future general prices, and values near zero (the case of Section 3) would be much more plausible.

In this connection, it is interesting to note that in Prescott's original (1975) application of this price-setting model, demand shocks were *entirely* idiosyncratic (in the sense that different demands were not associated with different marginal utilities of money) and setting prices in advance resulted in an efficient resource allocation. If the only consequence of sellers' precommitting to nominal prices were occasional wasting of resources (as in the models of this paper, taken literally) then one would assume that trade would be conducted in some different way. To explain *why* this particular price-setting game is played then, I think one would need to introduce idiosyncratic as well as general demand shocks.

5. Properties of Equilibria

In Sections 2, 3, and 4, price and consumption functions $p(\theta)$ and $c(\theta)$ were constructed that described equilibrium behavior in three different situations as functions of a single monetary shock θ. As remarked at the end of Section 2, the function $c(\theta)$ is a kind of Phillips curve, since it relates real consumption to the unanticipated change in money, and its derivative $c'(\theta)$ is a kind of money multiplier. In this section, I will discuss some of the properties of these equilibria.

The equilibria in Sections 2 and 3 are the same, though the analysis of Section 3 determines endogenously a parameter, the marginal utility of money, that was taken as exogenously given in Section 2. My interest, of course, is in the dynamic monetary interpretation given to this equilibrium in Section 3, so I confine my discussion to that case. Figure 1 exhibits the only possible (non-trivial) equilibrium in this case.

The equilibrium for the model of Section 4, that admits the possibility of an expected inflation or deflation, may also look like that shown in Figure 1. I have provided a sufficient condition (4.9) for this to be the case. But there may also be equilibria such as that shown in Figure 2, in which intervals of cash-constrained behavior alternate with intervals on which the system is liquidity-trapped. As the importance of inflationary expectations, indexed by the parameter γ, increases, this kind of behavior becomes more likely (condition (4.9) becomes less likely to hold).

The simpler case of Section 3 corresponds to a situation where a monetary shock induces a pure Phillips effect in exactly the same sense as the situation analyzed in Lucas (1972). In that earlier paper, inflation tax effects were removed from the discussion by an assumption that monetary transfers were proportional, as opposed to lump sum. In Section 3 of this paper, the same effect is achieved by the different device of assuming that the monetary shocks are purely transient. I will focus on this case first.

We are interested in questions of two types. Given a shock distribution Φ, what time series behavior of prices and quantities is predicted by the theory? How is this behavior affected by changes in the shock distribution? I address these in turn, and then discuss the relation between these theoretical variables and time series we observe.

Figure 1 displays the functions $c(\theta)$ and $p(\theta)$. Real consumption $c(\theta)$ is an increasing, concave function of θ, up to the shock value θ^*, and constant thereafter at y. The dollar value of consumption—nominal GNP in this economy—is equal to θ if $\theta \leq \theta^*$, and to $p(\theta^*)y$ if $\theta \geq \theta^*$. The implicit price deflator at shocks below θ^* is therefore $\theta/c(\theta)$. The elasticities of $c(\theta)$ and $\theta/c(\theta)$ sum to one. The elasticity of consumption with respect to the shock is:

$$\frac{\theta c'(\theta)}{c(\theta)} = \frac{\theta}{p(\theta)c(\theta)} \leq 1, \tag{5.1}$$

with equality only if $\theta = \underline{\theta}$, since if $\theta > \underline{\theta}$ the marginal price $p(\theta)$ exceeds the average price $\theta/c(\theta)$. Thus monetary shocks induce less than proportional changes in both real output and the implicit price deflator, provided the shock is less than θ^*. Notice that the price level in this model is rigid upward! Increasing the purely transient monetary shock beyond the level that induces capacity output has no inflationary effect.

These are the main features of the equilibrium of Section 3 for a fixed shock distribution Φ. Under the restriction (4.9) on the shock distribution, the equilibrium of Section 4 has these same features. As Inflation rates increase, however, this Phillips-like relationship can break down. There can be intervals of shock values on which increases in θ do not affect either consumption or prices.

I next turn to the way in which changes in Φ affect equilibrium behavior. The main result is that as the distribution of θ is concentrated—for the model of Section 3, it does not matter on what value—the distribution of equilibrium consumption $c(\theta)$ becomes concentrated on the efficient, capacity level y. The simplest way to show this is to examine the behavior of consumption as the length of the interval $[\underline{\theta}, \bar{\theta}]$ which is the support of Φ decreases.

In Section 3, we located the value θ^* of the shock at which capacity consumption is reached in $[\underline{\theta}, \bar{\theta}]$. Obviously if the endpoints of this interval are close to each other, both are close to θ^*. Consumption is an increasing function of θ, so its smallest value is $c(\underline{\theta})$. As shown in Section 2 (in an argument that applies equally to the model of Section 3),

$$c(\theta) = \left[p(\underline{\theta})\right]^{-1}\underline{\theta} = y\left[\underline{\theta} + \int_{\underline{\theta}}^{\theta^*}[1-\Phi(\theta)]d\theta\right]^{-1}\underline{\theta}.$$

Since Φ is a cdf, $\int_{\underline{\theta}}^{\theta^*}[1-\Phi(\theta)]d\theta \le \theta^* - \underline{\theta}$, so

$$c(\theta) \ge c(\underline{\theta}) \ge y\underline{\theta}/\theta^*.$$

Thus as $\theta^* \to \underline{\theta}$, $c(\theta) \to y$. In the transient shock model of Section 3, then, reducing the variability of the shocks (at least in the way I have done) reduces real instability and improves efficiency. With a perfectly predictable monetary policy, the allocation is always efficient.

Since this argument is based only on the range of the shock, it seems clear that the same inequalities must hold in the equilibrium of the more complex model of Section 4 as well, provided one exists at all. It is clear that a necessary condition for this to be so is (4.8): the distribution of θ cannot be concentrated on too deflationary a monetary policy. But so long as (4.8) holds, any predictable policy is a good as any other. It should be stressed, however, that since the model of Section 4 excludes many possibilities for substituting against cash that are available in reality, it is bound to understate the effects of changes in the expected rate of inflation.

How is the *slope* of the Phillips curve, or of the money multiplier, affected by changes in the variability of the monetary shocks? The prediction of a negative relationship was a key implication of my (1972) model, and this prediction has received a remarkable amount of empirical confirmation, most recently and convincingly in Kormendi and Meguire (1984). The right way to pose this question, I think, would be to postulate a parametric family $\Phi(\theta;\sigma)$ on $[\underline{\theta}(\sigma), \overline{\theta}(\sigma)]$, let $c(\theta;\sigma)$ denote equilibrium consumption at each σ, and then to examine the way the average value

$$\int_{\underline{\theta}(\sigma)}^{\theta^*(\sigma)} [c(\theta;\sigma)]^{-1}\theta c'(\theta;\sigma)d\Phi(\theta;\sigma) \tag{5.2}$$

of the (log) money multiplier varies as σ changes. If σ is identified with the variance of unanticipated money growth, the expression (5.2) is pretty close (distributed lag complications aside) to the curve Kormendi and

Meguire (1984) plot in their Figure 5, p. 900. For the parametric families I have tried, the calculations required to characterize the expression (5.2) are tedious and uniformative. This is probably a question best addressed numerically, with a variety of parameterizations. However, the following example is simple and suggestive.

Let Φ be the rectangular distribution

$$\Phi(\theta) = \frac{1}{2\varepsilon}[\theta - (1 - \varepsilon)]$$

on the interval $[\underline{\theta}, \overline{\theta}] = [1 - \varepsilon, 1 + \varepsilon]$. For this particular case, the elasticity formula (5.1) takes the form:

$$\frac{\theta}{c(\theta)}c'(\theta) = \left[(1+\varepsilon)\theta - \frac{1}{2}\theta^2 - \frac{1}{2}(1-\varepsilon)^2\right]^{-1}\left[(1+\varepsilon)\theta - \theta^2\right]. \quad (5.3)$$

This formula holds only on $[1 - \varepsilon, \theta^*]$, but I do not know the value of θ^*. The right side of (5.3) equals 1 at $\theta = 1 - \varepsilon$, and 0 at $\theta = 1 + \varepsilon$. At $\theta = 1$, it takes the value $\left[2 - \frac{1}{2}\varepsilon\right]^{-1}$, an increasing function of ε.

Figure 3 plots the right side of (5.3) against θ for various ε values. At θ values less than unity, the elasticity of $c(\theta)$—the money multiplier in elasticity form—decreases as the range ε of the shock increases. This suggests (though does not prove, even for this example) that the same flattening of

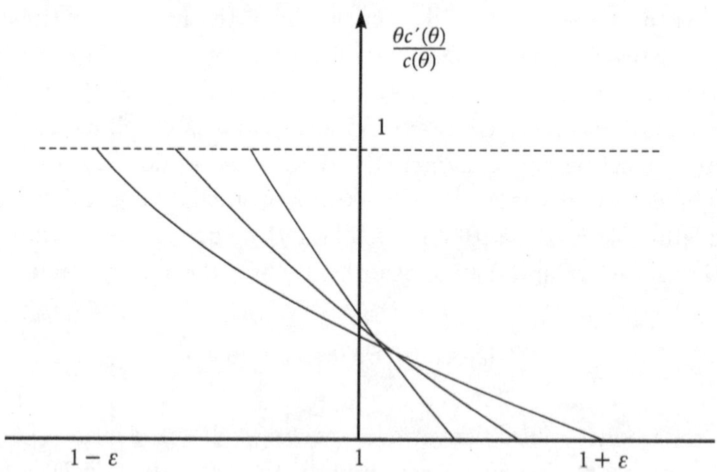

Figure 3

the Phillips curve as monetary variability increases that was predicted in Lucas (1972) is also an implication of the present, quite different, model of the Phillips curve.

The models in this paper are so stylized that there is a good deal of latitude as to how one might identify the variables involved with observed magnitudes. If we think of each household as endowed with one unit of labor that can be used, with no disutility attached, to produce y units of goods, then we could think of the ratio $c(\theta)/y$ as the employment rate. Alternatively, if we think of each seller as spending a full period selling his endowment no matter how much he sells, like a clerk in a store, then employment is constant at unity and movements in the ratio $c(\theta)/y$ would appear as a fluctuating level of productivity.[8] Both interpretations seem quite reasonable to me.

On either interpretation, there is a precise notion of *capacity* output in this model. The economy spends the fraction $1 - \Phi(\theta^*)$ of the time at full capacity y and the rest of the time at varying levels of less-than-capacity consumption. Since no disutility is attached to the production of goods, full capacity is the efficient output level. The possibility of producing too much, present in the model of Lucas (1972), is absent here. If one wished, one could even call the ratio $(y - c(\theta))/y$ "involuntary unemployment," since at each realized price θ, every seller would, if he could, sell all his remaining endowment units at any positive price. Of course, any individual seller could always have chosen to price his endowment at $p(\underline{\theta})$, ensuring the sale of all units. After the fact, of course, all sellers wish they had priced all units at $p(\theta)$.

6. Conclusions

The models analyzed in Sections 3–5 of this paper are additions to the list of theoretical examples that illustrate possible mechanisms through which monetary instability may induce inefficient fluctuations in economic activity. As did the older Keynesian and monetarist theories, these examples focus on a form of nominal price rigidity as the fundamental source of this inefficiency. In contrast to these theories, but in common with the theoretical examples cited in the introduction, it is only unanticipated move-

8. The implications of the second interpretation are taken much further in Rotemberg and Summers (1988).

ments in money that are predicted to result in inefficient levels of production and consumption.

Each of these models that trace real pathologies to a combination of rigid prices and monetary unpredictability focuses on one specific source of the crucial rigidity: nominal contracting (Fischer (1977), Phelps and Taylor (1977)), incomplete information about the current state of the system (Lucas (1972)), a game that obliges sellers of goods to commit in advance to nominal prices (the present paper). All of these assumed sources of price rigidity have the important virtue of descriptive realism: people really do sign nominal contracts, people really do have seriously incomplete information about the state of the economy in general and the quantity of money (and where it is located) in particular, people really do put dollar prices on the goods they sell and live with these pricing decisions for non-negligible time periods. All of the models we have that incorporate any one of these facts have the common implication that unanticipated monetary shocks have non-neutral, multiplier effects that are quite different in character from the real distortions that result from anticipated inflations. It is hard for me to imagine, and I see no empirical reason for making the effort to do so, that similar multiplier effects are not also present in any modern economy.

But there are several harder and more important questions than this one. What can be said about the importance of monetary instability, relative to shifts in technology and preferences, in accounting for movements in real output? Do the various rigid price models have enough in common to have useful empirical or policy implications, or does everything hinge on the accuracy of the assumptions used in constructing each specific example? How can we know or determine whether the key parameters in any of these models of price rigidity are structural? I will conclude by indicating how, if at all, the analysis of this paper bears on these three questions.

Since Kydland and Prescott's surprising (1982) demonstration that productivity shocks with realistic statistical properties can account for *all* real output variability in the post-World War II U.S. economy, the need for an adequate theory of monetary sources of instability has come to seem much less pressing. This important finding has been buttressed by much subsequent research, but it is an "R^2" finding that does not bear directly on the size of the money multiplier. Nothing in the recent volume of real business cycle research shows, or even suggests, that a sudden monetary contraction would have negligible output and employment effects, and that monetary policy is therefore of little real importance.

The model of this paper bears on this issue of the sources of real fluctuations in an illustrative way. It provides an example of an economy with a constant resource endowment, in which output $c(\theta)$ varies as a function of a stochastic shock θ. I have called this shock "unanticipated money," but to an outside observer looking at the real time series $c(\theta_t)$ only, it could as well be called a "technology shock." Only by looking at the associated series on money and nominal prices could one begin to discriminate between these possible sources of real instability. I think this same problem of identification arises in post-war U.S. time series, and I do not see how it can be resolved by looking at real series only.

The models that have been advanced to explain, or at least to embody, price rigidity, all have very special structures that attach great importance to magnitudes (for example, the length of a period) on which there is no agreed-upon method of measurement. Do these models, as a class, have any useful implications? Much macroeconomic writing in the past decade emphasizes differences in the implications of various rationalizations of price rigidity—some models imply policy "irrelevance," others are "activist," and so forth—but this emphasis seems false to me. A comparison of the implications of the models of this paper, in which prices are pre-set and misinformation plays no role, and the model in Lucas (1972), in which prices are flexibly determined in Walrasian markets and all rigidity is attributed to incomplete information, is helpful in explaining what I mean by this. Both models have an irrelevance or neutrality theorem, in the sense that if inflation tax effects are removed, monetary changes that are announced sufficiently far in advance affect the price level but not real variables. Both rationalize activist policy, in what seems to me the trivial sense that a monetary authority with information or flexibility or both that are not available to private agents can act so as to improve resource allocation. Both models imply that noisy monetary policy reduces welfare. Both predict a positive money-real output multiplier, and a money-price level multiplier that is less than unity. Both predict that the size of the money multiplier (the slope of the Phillips curve) will decline as monetary variability increases. Would anything essential in a serious policy analysis based on a modern view of price rigidity (Sargent's analyses (1986, Chs. 3 and 4), of historical disinflations, say) be altered depending on which of these specific rationalizations, or a contract rationalization, one has in mind? I do not see what.

But is a money multiplier a structural parameter? No, of course it isn't. One purpose of models such as those in this paper is to understand the ways in which changes in policy parameters affect this multiplier, but even to do this one needs to take as fixed other parameters—the length of the period over which prices are fixed, say, or the length of information lags or labor contracts—which must in fact react to sufficiently large changes in policy. Sometimes one can check on the sensitivity of key lags empirically (as Taylor (1983) did with labor contract lengths), but a money multiplier is *never* going to be recognized by the American Kennel Club. I think if we are to use economic theory to improve monetary policy and institutions, we are just going to have to get used to this.

References

Butters, Gerard. "Equilibrium Distributions of Sales and Advertising Prices." *Review of Economic Studies* 44 (July 1977): 465–491.

Eden, Benjamin. "Marginal Cost Pricing When Spot Markets are Complete." *Journal of Political Economy.* Forthcoming, 1990.

Fischer, Stanley. "Long-Term Contracts, Rational Expectations, and the Optimal Money Supply Rule." *Journal of Political Economy* 85 (February 1977): 191–206.

Green, Edward J. "Continuum and Finite-Player Noncooperative Models of Competition." *Econometrica* 52 (July 1984): 975–994.

Kormendi, Roger C., and Meguire, Philip G. "Evidence of Macroeconomic Rationality." *Journal of Political Economy* 92 (October 1984): 875–908.

Lucas, Deborah J. "Price and Interest Rate Dynamics Induced by Multiperiod Contracts in a Cash-in-Advance Economy." University of Chicago Working Paper. 1984.

Lucas, Robert E., Jr. "Expectations and the Neutrality of Money." *Journal of Economic Theory* 4 (April 1972): 103–124.

Lucas, Robert E., Jr. "Equilibrium in a Pure Currency Economy." *Economic Inquiry* 18 (1980): 203–220.

Lucas, Robert E., Jr. and Stokey, Nancy L. "Optimal Fiscal and Monetary Policy in an Economy without Capital." *Journal of Monetary Economics* 12 (1983): 55–93.

Lucas, Robert E., Jr., Stokey, Nancy L. and Prescott, Edward C. *Recursive Methods in Economic Dynamics.* Cambridge: Harvard University Press. 1989.

Phelps, Edmund S., and Taylor, John B. "Stabilizing Powers of Monetary Policy under Rational Expectations." *Journal of Political Economy* 85 (February 1977): 163–190.

Prescott, Edward C. "Efficiency of the Natural Rate." *Journal of Political Economy* 83 (December 1975): 1229–1236.

Rotemberg, Julio J. "Rationing in Centrally Planned Economies." MIT Working Paper. 1988.

Rotemberg, Julio J. and Summers, Lawrence H. "Labor Hoarding, Inflexible Prices and Procyclical Productivity." NBER Working Paper. 1988.

Sargent, Thomas J. *Rational Expectations and Inflation*. New York: Harper and Row. 1986.

Taylor, John B. "Estimation and Control of a Macroeconomic Model with Rational Expectations." *Econometrica* 47 (September 1979): 1267–1286.

Taylor, John B. "Union Wage Settlements During a Disinflation." *American Economic Review* 73 (December 1983): 981–993.

— 13 —

Liquidity and Interest Rates

1. Introduction

This paper analyzes a series of models in which money is required for asset transactions as well as for transactions on goods.* This modification to more familar cash-in-advance models of monetary economies is a step toward realism: According to the *Federal Reserve Bulletin,* about 11% of all demand deposits in the United States are held by financial businesses, and financial businesses hold about twice as many deposits per employee as do other businesses. One can imagine societies in which at least the most sophisticated financial markets clear, Arrow-Debreu style, without the use of non-interest-bearing reserves, but this is not the way U.S. financial markets operate today, nor do they show any trend toward operating in such a way.

If cash is required for trading in securities, then the quantity of cash—of "liquidity"—available for this purpose at any time will in general influence the prices of securities traded at that time. That is, the price of a security will in general depend not only on the properties of the income stream to which it is a claim—its "fundamentals"—but also on the liquidity in the market at the time is traded. In view of the mounting evidence that theories of asset pricing based solely on fundamentals cannot adequately account for observed movements in securities prices, there should be no

Journal of Economic Theory 50, no. 2 (April 1990): 237–264.

*Lars Peter Hansen, Robert Hodrick, Nancy Stokey, and Neil Wallace provided very helpful criticism. Chi-Wa Yuen carried out all the calculations. I am also grateful for the comments of seminar participants at U.C.L.A., Yale, the Money and Banking Workshop at Chicago, and the 1988 Summer Research Workshop at Northwestern, and for research support provided by NSF Grant SES 8420420.

difficulty in motivating a theoretical study of a non-fundamental influence on asset prices.[1] Since the paper is frankly exploratory, however, I will defer discussion of the particular observations the theory may help to explain until the concluding section of the paper.

The term "liquidity" is used here in exactly the sense of recent papers by Grossman and Weiss [2] and Rotemberg [13].[2] These papers worked out the effects of open market operations on interest rate behavior in settings in which the agents on the opposite side of a government sale (or purchase) of bonds hold only a fraction of the economy's money supply, and have no ability to obtain more money—more liquidity—in time to affect their ability to purchase bonds. In this situation, these authors show, a bond issue will raise interest rates, for reasons having nothing to do with changes in expected inflation or in marginal rates of substitution—the Fisherian fundamentals of interest rate determination. These papers were the first to isolate such an effect, long thought by monetary and financial theorists to be present in reality, in a model of economic equilibrium. This paper is thus a sequel to their analyses.

In [2] and [13], an open market operation that induces a liquidity effect will also alter the distribution of wealth, since agents who participate in the trade will have different post-trade portfolios than those who were absent. These distributional effects linger on indefinitely (as they no doubt do in reality), a fact that vastly complicates the analysis, effectively limiting both papers to the study of a one-time, unanticipated bond issue in an otherwise deterministic setting. This paper studies this same liquidity effect using a simple device that abstracts from these distributional effects.

1. A long line of econometric research from Sargent [14] through Hansen and Singleton [5] has failed to confirm a relationship between short-term interest rates and their Fisherian fundamentals, real interest rate movements and expected inflation. An equally long line of work stimulated by the research of LeRoy and Porter [8] and Shiller [15] identifies movements in stock prices that cannot be accounted for by their fundamentals. Though this work has been forcefully challenged, for example by Kleidon [7] and Marsh and Merton [11], I interpret West [16] as confirming these authors' original conclusions. There is, of course, a vast literature bearing on this issue in addition to these few papers.

2. Helpman and Razin [6] also apply a cash-in-advance constraint to securities purchases, with different analytical objectives in mind.

The term "liquidity" is also used in an entirely different sense, to refer to a quality of "moneyness" that different, non-money securities are supposed to possess in differing degrees. In this paper, as in [2, 6, 13], this second sense of liquidity is entirely absent. There are assumed payment functions that can be served by money and for these purposes all other securities are assumed to be equally useless or "illiquid."

The idea is to view agents trading in securities and agents engaging in other activities as members of a single "family" that meets periodically to pool resources and information. This device serves the purpose of permitting us to study situations in which different people face different trading opportunities while still retaining the convenience of the representative household fiction.[3] As we will see, it permits us to analyze in a stochastic setting the effects of a very wide variety of monetary policies.

The paper consists of a series of examples, with an emphasis on special cases that can be solved by pencil-and-paper methods. When a new effect is introduced it is useful to experiment with many variations before investing much in any one of them. In the next section a benchmark example, taken from Lucas and Stokey [9], will be used to introduce the liquidity effect in its simplest form. In this example, inflation and liquidity effects determine the interest rate on one period bonds. Section 3 introduces a more general formulation that can accommodate a wide variety of bonds and other securities. Section 4 then specializes to the case in which shocks to the system are serially independent and liquidity effects are transient. Section 5 studies a logically inconsistent case in which goods prices are held fixed, an analysis that will, I hope, provide a useful introduction to the full treatment of the case of Markovian shocks (with a finite number of states) in Section 6. Section 7 describes some numerical simulations designed to give a sharper picture of the effects of serially correlated shocks. Section 8 contains concluding remarks.

2. A Benchmark Example

Throughout the paper, I will consider a representative agent economy, in which the typical housefold has preferences

$$E\left\{\sum_{t=0}^{\infty} \beta^t U(c_t)\right\},$$

where $\{c_t\}$ is a stochastic stream of consumption of a single good, β is a discount factor between zero and one, and U is a bounded, twice-differentiable function with $U'(c) > 0$, $U'(0) = \infty$, and $U''(c) < 0$. The household has a constant, non-storable goods endowment y, and in equi-

3. Grossman [3] shows that distributional effects are not *necessary* for the occurrence of liquidity effects, using a perfect insurance argument that serves the same function as this "family" construct.

librium, $c_t = y$ for all t and all realizations of shocks that I will specify in a moment. Hence the sole concern of the analysis will be the determination of goods and securities prices under a particular set of trading conventions.

Trading is assumed to proceed in the following way. Think of the typical household as consisting of three members, each of whom goes his own way during a period, the three regrouping at the end of a day to pool goods, assets, and information. One member of the household collects the endowment y, which he must sell to other households on a cash-in-advance basis. A household *cannot* consume any of its own endowment. Cash receipts from the sale of date-t endowment cannot be used for any purpose during period t. A second member of the household takes an amount $N_t - Z_t \geq 0$ of the household's initial cash balances N_t and uses it to purchase goods from other households. If the dollar price of goods is P_t, and if this member spends all of his balances, his household thus consumes the amount $c_t = (N_t - Z_t)/P_t$. A third member of the household takes the remaining cash balances, $Z_t \geq 0$, and engages in securities trading.

This construction of a multiple-member household that pools its resources at the end of each day is the device the permits us to study situations in which different individuals have different trading opportunities during a period, while retaining the simplicity of the representative household. It will be retained in all the examples I consider. It is very similar in its effect to the perfect insurance assumptions used by Rogerson [12] and Hansen [4] to achieve the same analytical end in different contexts.

These features are common to all the examples considered in the paper. The examples differ with respect to the securities that are assumed to be traded and the nature of the policies affecting the supplies of these securities. In the initial example considered in this section, the *only* security we consider is a one period, dollar denominated government bond that entitles its purchaser to one dollar at the beginning of the following period, prior to any trading. These bonds are auctioned off in the securities market at a price q_t. Thus a household beginning with N_t dollars that chooses the division Z_t of these balances can acquire $B_t \leq Z_t/q_t$ bonds. This household will begin the following period with cash balances given by[4]

$$N_{t+1} = P_t y + Z_t + (1 - q_t)B_t. \tag{2.1}$$

4. Neil Wallace suggested the following alternative conventions about timing. Require the household to attend securities trading at date $t + 1$ to obtain—in cash—the face value B_t of the bonds it purchased at date t (as opposed to getting B_t dollars in cash mailed to the

The size of the government bond issue, expressed relative to the economy's beginning-of-period money stock, will be taken to be an i.i.d. random variable x_t, with a probability distribution λ on a compact set $X \subset (0, \infty)$. That is, if there are M_t dollars outstanding, the government auctions off claims to $x_t M_t$ dollars payable one period hence. A bond issue of size x_t thus withdraws $q_t x_t M_t$ dollars from private circulation today and returns $x_t M_t$ tomorrow. The ratio M_{t+1}/M_t is then the random variable $1 + (1 - q_t)x_t$. Aside from these stochastic open market operations there are no other shocks to this economy.

For this model, a critical issue will be whether the open market shock x_t is taken to be realized before agents commit themselves to a cash division Z_t or after this decision is made. Throughout the paper, attention is restricted to the case where x_t is announced *after* households have made their decisions on the allocation of cash between its two uses. I assume as well that only agents present in the securities market observe the current shock; agents in goods markets do not. With i.i.d. shocks, this will mean that neither the division of cash balances nor the price of goods will depend on the open market shock x_t. The price of one period bonds will be the only variable responding to these shocks.

It will be convenient to use a normalization employed in [9]. Let $m_t = N_t/M_t$ denote a household's money holdings *relative to* the economy-wide average beginning-of-period money holdings (so that $m_t = 1$ in equilibrium). Similarly, let $z_t = Z_t/M_t$, $b_t = B_t/M_t$, and $p_t = P_t/M_t$. In terms of these normalized variables, (2.1) becomes

$$m_{t+1} = [1 + (1 - q_t)x_t]^{-1} [p_t y + z_t + (1 - q_t)b_t]. \tag{2.2}$$

I will define a stationary equilibrium consisting of a constant (normalized) price level $p > 0$, a constant division of money balances $0 \leq z < 1$, and a bond price $q(x)$ consistent with utility maximizing behavior and market clearing. Let $v(m)$ be the maximized objective function for a house-

house, as I am assuming). Under this assumption, a dollar unspent in securities trading is a different security from a zero-interest bond, since the dollar can be spent on goods next period while the bond cannot. This assumption gives a kind of "liquidity" (in a different sense from the way I am using the term in this paper) advantage to cash over bonds that is, I think, a step toward realism from the present model. On the other side, it complicates the analysis by necessitating the use of *two* variables to describe the state of a household, one to describe its cash holdings and another to describe where these holdings are located. I have analyzed this interesting variation in [10].

hold beginning a period with (normalized) balances m. The above description of the household's decision problem motivates the Bellman equation,

$$v(m) = \max_{0 \leq z \leq m} \left\{ U\left[(m - z)/p\right] + \beta \int_X \max_{0 \leq q(x) b \leq z} \left[v(m')\right] \lambda(dx) \right\}, \quad (2.3)$$

where m' is defined by

$$m' = [1 + (1 - q(x))x]^{-1} [py + z + (1 - q(x))b]. \quad (2.4)$$

Then an equilibrium is defined as a value function $v : \mathbf{R}_+ \to \mathbf{R}$, a number $z \in [0, 1)$, a number $p > 0$, a bond purchase function $b : X \to \mathbf{R}$, and a bond price function $q : X \to (0, 1]$ such that (i) given p and $q(x)$, $v(m)$ satisfies (2.3); (ii) z and b attain the right side of (2.3) at $m = 1$; (iii) $1 - z = py$; and (iv) $b(x) = x$ for all $x \in X$. Conditions (i) and (ii) describe utility maximization at equilibrium prices. Conditions (iii) and (iv) require cleared goods and bonds markets.[5]

Here and in later sections, I will proceed to use first order and envelope conditions for the problem (2.3) to characterize equilibrium behavior, assuming that value functions exist and are increasing, differentiable, and concave. For the inner maximization in (2.3), the possibilities are $q(x) = 1$ and any feasible value of b, $q(x) < 1$ and $b = z/q(x)$, or $q(x) > 1$ and $b = 0$. This last is not an equilibrium possibility, since $x > 0$ and (iv) must hold.

For any m, the unique maximizing value of z in the outer maximization in (2.3) satisfies the first-order condition

$$\frac{1}{p} U'\left(\frac{m - z}{p}\right) = \beta \int_X v'(m') \frac{1}{q(x)[1 - xq(x) + x]} \lambda(dx),$$

where m' is given in (2.4). The envelope condition for m is

$$v'(m) = \frac{1}{p} U'\left(\frac{m - z}{p}\right).$$

5. Of course, this narrow definition of equilibrium rules out many possibilities characterized by optimal consumer behavior and cleared markets that one might well want to call equilibria. For example, I have no reason to believe that the assumptions I am using preclude the existence of nonstationary equilibria or sunspot equilibria. On the contrary, on the basis of Woodford's analysis [17] of a version of the model in [9], I would conjecture that the present model does have sunspot equilibria, in addition to the stationary equilibrium I will characterize.

In equilibrium, $m = m' = 1$ and $(1 - z)/p = y$. Thus we can cancel the term $(1/p)\ U'(y)$ and obtain the equilibrium condition

$$1 = \beta \int_X \frac{1}{q(x)[1 - xq(x) + x]} \lambda(dx). \tag{2.5}$$

Since $q(x) = \min[1, z/x]$, we can eliminate $q(x)$ from (2.5) to obtain

$$z = \beta \int_X \max\left\{z, \frac{x}{1 + x - z}\right\} \lambda(dx). \tag{2.6}$$

The right side of (2.6) is positive at $z = 0$ and equal to β at $z = 1$; it is a continuous and strictly increasing function of z, with a slope strictly less than one if $z < 1$. Hence (2.6) has a unique solution $z^* \in (0, 1)$. Then $p = (1 - z^*)/y$ is the equilibrium price level, and $q(x) = \min[1, z^*/x]$ is the equilibrium bond price function.

This example can be used to illustrate the potential force of the liquidity effect on the stochastic behavior of interest rates. Consider the case when $q(x) < 1$ for all $x \in X$ so that $q(x) = z^*/x$.[6] Then the interest rate is the i.i.d. random variable

$$r_t \simeq -\ln[q(x_t)] = -\ln(z^*) + \ln(x_t).$$

The Fisherian fundamentals for the interest rate are the real rate, constant in this example at $-\ln(\beta)$, plus the expected inflation rate, $\ln(P_{t+1}/P_t) = \ln(M_{t+1}/M_t) \simeq -x_t q(x_t) + x_t = -z^* + x_t$. (Here I am assuming that the expectation of inflation is formed after x_t is realized.) The variance of the interest rate is thus $\text{Var}[\ln(x_t)]$ while the variance one would predict on the basis of the variability of fundamentals is $\text{Var}(x_t)$. Since x_t is a small fraction (the short-term bond issue in period t divided by the total money supply), the interest rate in this example is *much* more variable than one would predict on the usual Fisherian grounds.

In the rest of the paper, I will work through a number of variations on this example, in an attempt to get a better idea of which aspects of this liquidity effect are due to the peculiarities of the example and which obtain more generally. One possibility would be to examine the liquidity effect in a context, such as that used in [9], in which real and monetary fundamen-

6. This is a logical possibility. For example, let $\beta = \frac{1}{2}$, let $x = \frac{1}{4}$ with probability $\frac{1}{2}$ and let $x = \frac{1}{2}$ with probability $\frac{1}{2}$. Then $z^* = 0.149$, so that $q(x) = z^*/x < 1$ for both possible values of x.

tals follow a much more generally specified stochastic process. It is clear from the example just discussed that liquidity effects and fundamentals can interact, and introducing a more general process for the fundamentals would enable us to study these interactions more fully. But trying to study too many complicated things at once carries the risk of misunderstanding any one of them, so instead I will turn in the opposite direction and analyze examples of what might be called a "pure" liquidity effect. I will use the present example to explain what I mean by this.

In the example above endowments and real consumption are constant, so marginal rates of substitution and hence real interest rates are constant. Changes in interest rates result from a mix of expected inflation effects and liquidity effects, both driven by the same random variable x_t. Now suppose we introduce into the model a lump sum tax of the magnitude $\pi(x_t)M_t$, payable at the beginning of period $t+1$, prior to any trading. With this modification, the ratio M_{t+1}/M_t in the model becomes $1 + (1 - q(x_t))x_t - \pi(x_t)$. Given any equilibrium bond price function q it is clearly possible to choose this transfer function π so as to maintain money growth at zero, $M_{t+1}/M_t = 1$, for all realizations x_t. Under the assumption that π is so chosen, the factor $1 + (1 - q(x))x$ drops out of equation (2.4) and the equilibrium condition (2.6) becomes

$$z = \beta \int_X \max(z, x)\, \lambda(dx). \tag{2.7}$$

The right side of (2.7) is a continuous function of z, positive at $z = 0$, with a slope between zero and one. Thus (2.7) has a unique solution $z^* > 0$. This solution will be less than one (and hence be interpretable as an equilibrium) if and only if:

$$\frac{\beta}{1-\beta} \int_1^\infty (x-1)\lambda(dx) < 1. \tag{2.8}$$

What does condition (2.8) mean, and why was nothing like it required for existence of a solution to the original Eq. (2.6)? Roughly speaking, if (2.8) is violated, it is because there is enough probability on the contingency that a large bond issue may make bonds such a bargain that, at constant goods prices, consumers gain by putting more cash into securities than any fraction $z < 1$. Technically, this means that no stationary equilibrium exists (though an equilibrium with rising prices, ruled out by definition in my analysis , might exist). In the formulation leading to (2.6), large bond issues are always associated with the prospect of a large influx of money, so low bond prices are needed to compensate for expected inflation and are not a bargain in this sense. In future sections, where only pure liquidity effects are studied in constant-money environments, some analogue to (2.8) will always be needed to guarantee the existence of a stationary equilibrium.

3. Pure Liquidity Effects: A General Framework

The remainder of the paper will deal with variations on the second of the two examples in the last section, generalizing it to accommodate a wider variety of securities and more generally specified shocks to the supplies of these securities. Preferences and technology will be exactly as in the last section, as will the timing and nature of trading. I will assume that lump sum transfers maintain the money supply at a constant level, and normalize this level at unity. Hence all values will be expressed as relative to the existing quantity of money. In this section I will set up a general notation and work out some issues that are common to all the examples that are worked through later in the paper.

As in Section 2, the only shocks to the economy will be changes in the supplies of securities. This suggests taking stocks of securities as the state variables of the system, but it turns out to be more convenient to specify the motion of the state more abstractly and to use functions defined on the state space to define various aspects of securities. Let $s_t \in S$, where $(S, \mathbf{S})$ is a measurable space, be a complete description of the state of the economy at the beginning of date t. Assume that the state follows a Markov process with the transition function P:

$$P(s, A) = \Pr\{s_{t+1} \in A \mid s_t = s\}, \qquad s \in S, \qquad A \in \mathbf{S}.$$

A given state s_t determines, via a given function $a : S \to D \subset \mathbf{R}^n$, a vector $a(s_t)$ of the supplies of n securities that are available prior to trading at date t. Think of s_{t+1} as being realized after cash is divided in period t, but before securities are traded. The states s_t and s_{t+1} together determine, via a function $\phi : S \times S \to D$, the stocks $\phi(s_t, s_{t+1})$ held at the end of trading on date t. I assume that end-of-t and beginning-of-$(t + 1)$ holdings are linearly related, so that there is an $n \times n$ matrix B such that

$$a(s_{t+1}) = B\phi(s_t, s_{t+1}) \qquad \text{for all} \quad (s_t, s_{t+1}).$$

Finally, a holder of the vector $u \in D$ at the end of t receives the inner product $\pi(s_t, s_{t+1}) \cdot u$ in cash at the beginning of $t + 1$, where $\pi : S \times S \rightarrow R^n$ is another given function. This function π specifies the dollar payment the holder of the security is entitled to receive from the issuer at each state–date (s_t, s_{t+1}) combination. It represents a contractual obligation, not a market price. These three given functions a, ϕ, and π, together with the matrix B, define the set of securities assumed to be traded.

The purpose of this notation is to capture at the same time fixed maturity and infinite maturity securities. Thus if the only security in existence is a consol with a unit coupon, we would let $s_t \in \mathbf{R}$ be the stock of such consols, and define $a(s_t) = s_t$, $\phi(s_t, s_{t+1}) = s_{t+1}$, $\pi(s_t, s_{t+1}) = 1$, and let B be the 1×1 matrix [1]. But with fixed maturity securities, an end-of-t n-period security becomes a beginning-of-$(t + 1)$ $(n - 1)$-period security or, if $n = 1$, passes out of existence entirely. Thus in the one-period bond example studied in the last section, we would let $s_t = x_{t-1}$, $a(s_t) = 0$, $\phi(s_t, s_{t+1}) = s_{t+1} = x_t$, $\pi(s_t, s_{t+1}) = 1$ and let $B = [0]$. Later sections will provide other examples of particular specifications of these functions. For all the securities I will consider, B will be block-diagonal, with blocks equal to identity matrices or else having ones on the diagonal above the main diagonal and zeroes elsewhere ($b_{i,\,i+1} = 1$ for $i = 1, \ldots, n - 1$ and $b_{ij} = 0$ for $j \neq i + 1$), but imposing this structure here would not simplify the discussion in this sec tion.

In this setting, let $q(s, s')$ be the vector of securities prices when the current and next period states are (s, s'). Then the liquidity constraint for a household that carries z units of cash into securities trading and trades from the portfolio a to the portfolio u takes the form

$$z \geq q(s, s') \cdot (u - a). \tag{3.1}$$

(Cash must cover net purchases.) This household will begin next period with cash balances of

$$m' = \pi_0(s, s') + z - q(s, s') \cdot (u - a) + \pi(s, s') \cdot u, \tag{3.2}$$

where $\pi_0(s, s')$ denotes net cash inflow from sources other than securities (uncapitalized endowment income plus subsides less taxes).

The household's functional equation is

$$v(m, a, s) = \max_{0 \leq z \leq m} \left\{ U\left(\frac{m - z}{p(s)}\right) + \beta \int_S [\max_u v(m', Bu, s')] P(s, ds') \right\}, \tag{3.3}$$

where m' is defined by (3.2) and where the inner maximization is subject to the constraint (3.1).

An equilibrium is defined, then, as a value function $v: \mathbf{R}_+ \times D \times S \to \mathbf{R}$, a cash allocation function $z: S \to [0, 1)$, a securities purchase function $u: S \times S \to D$, a goods price function $p: S \to \mathbf{R}_{++}$, a securities price function $q: S \times S \to R^n_{+}$, and a transfer function $\pi_0: S \times S \to \mathbf{R}$ such that

(i) given p and q, v satisfies (3.3);
(ii) z and u attain the right side of (3.3) at $(m, a, s) = (1, a(s), s)$;
(iii) $1 - z(s) = p(s)\,y$ for all $s \in S$;
(iv) $u(s, s') = \phi(s, s')$ for all $(s, s') \in S \times S$; and
(v) $\pi_0(s, s') + z(s) - q(s, s') \cdot [\phi(s, s') - a(s)] + \pi(s, s') \cdot \phi(s, s') = 1$

for all $(s, s') \in S \times S$.

As in the last section, I will use the first-order and envelope conditions for problem (3.3) to characterize equilibria. The first-order conditions for the inner maximization in (3.3) are

$$\begin{aligned}\sum_{j=1}^{n} b_{ji} v_{a_j}(m', Bu, s') &= v_m(m', Bu, s')[q_i(s, s') - \pi_i(s, s')] \\ &\quad + \mu(s, s')q_i(s, s'), \qquad i = 1, 2, \ldots, n,\end{aligned} \tag{3.4}$$

where $\mu(s, s')$ is the non-negative multiplier associated with (3.1). If $\mu(s, s') > 0$, then (3.1) must hold with equality. (Note that if the matrix B has the near-diagonal form that it will assume in all the examples later in the paper, at most one of the coefficients b_{ji} in the sum on the left of (3.4) will be non-zero.)

The first-order condition for the outer problem is

$$U'\left(\frac{m - z}{p(s)}\right)\frac{1}{p(s)} \geq \beta \int_S [v_m(m', Bu, s') + \mu(s, s')]P(s, ds'), \tag{3.5}$$

with equality if $z > 0$.

The envelope conditions are

$$v_m(m, a, s) = U'\left(\frac{m - z}{p(s)}\right)\frac{1}{p(s)} \tag{3.6}$$

and

$$v_{a_i}(m, a, s) = \beta \int_S [v_m(m', Bu, s') + \mu(s, s')] q_i(s, s') P(s, ds'), \qquad i = 1, \dots, n. \tag{3.7}$$

In an equilibrium, it must be the case that $m = m' = 1$, $a = a(s)$, $Bu = a(s')$, $u = \phi(s, s')$, and $p(s)y = 1 - z(s)$. Then (3.6) implies that

$$v_m(1, a(s), s) = yU'(y)\frac{1}{1 - z(s)}.$$

Define the functions $\varphi_i : S \rightarrow \mathbf{R}$, $i = 1, \dots, n$ by $\varphi_i(s) = [yU'(y)]^{-1} v_{a_i}(1, a(s), s)$ and define $\theta : S \times S \rightarrow \mathbf{R}$ by $\theta(s, s') = [yU'(y)]^{-1} \mu(s, s')$. Making these substitutions in (3.4), (3.5), and (3.7) we obtain

$$\sum_{j=1}^{n} b_{ji}\varphi_j(s') = \frac{1}{1 - z(s')}[q_i(s, s') - \pi_i(s, s')] + \theta(s, s')q_i(s, s'), \quad i = 1, \dots, n, \tag{3.8}$$

$$\frac{1}{1 - z(s)} \geq \beta \int_S \left[\frac{1}{1 - z(s')} + \theta(s, s')\right] P(s, ds'), \tag{3.9}$$

with equality if $z(s) > 0$, and

$$\varphi_i(s) = \beta \int_S \left[\frac{1}{1 - z(s')} + \theta(s, s')\right] q_i(s, s') P(s, ds'), \qquad i = 1, \dots, n. \tag{3.10}$$

The constraint (3.1) becomes, in equilibrium,

$$z(s) + q(s, s') \cdot (a(s) - \phi(s, s')) \geq 0, \tag{3.11}$$

with equality if $\theta(s, s') > 0$.

If we let $\varphi(s) = (\varphi_1(s), \dots, \varphi_n(s))$ then Eqs. (3.8) and (3.10) can be written more compactly as

$$\frac{1}{1 - z(s')}[q(s, s') - \pi(s, s')] + \theta(s, s')q(s, s') = B^{\mathrm{T}}\varphi(s') \tag{3.12}$$

and

$$\varphi(s) = \beta \int_S \left[\frac{1}{1 - z(s')}\pi(s, s') + B^{\mathrm{T}}\varphi(s')\right] P(s, ds'), \tag{3.13}$$

where B^{T} denotes the transpose of the matrix B.

Now using (3.12) to solve for the vector $q(s, s')$, inserting this expression into (3.11), and rearranging gives

$$\frac{1}{1-z(s')}+\theta(s,s')\geq\frac{1}{z(s)}\left[B^{\mathrm{T}}\varphi(s')+\frac{1}{1-z(s')}\pi(s,s')\cdot\left[\phi(s,s')-a(s)\right]\right] \tag{3.14}$$

with equality if $\theta(s, s') > 0$. Hence (3.9) can be written

$$\frac{z(s)}{1-z(s)}=\beta\int_S\left\{\max\left[\frac{z(s)}{1-z(s')},\left[B^{\mathrm{T}}\varphi(s')+\frac{1}{1-z(s')}\pi(s,s')\right]\right.\right. \tag{3.15}$$
$$\left.\left.\cdot\left[\phi(s,s')-a(s)\right]\right]\right\}P(s,ds').$$

(Note that (3.15) must hold with equality even if $z(s) = 0$, since the right side is non-negative.)

We can view (3.13) and (3.15) as $n + 1$ equations in the unknown functions $z(s), \varphi_1(s), \ldots, \varphi_n(s)$. If they can be solved, then equilibrium asset prices are given, using (3.12), by

$$q(s,s')=\left[\frac{1}{1-z(s')}+\theta(s,s')\right]^{-1}\left[B^{\mathrm{T}}\varphi(s')+\frac{1}{1-z(s')}\right], \tag{3.16}$$

where

$$\frac{1}{1-z(s')}+\theta(s,s')$$
$$=\max\left\{\frac{1}{1-z(s')},\frac{1}{z(s)}\left[B^{\mathrm{T}}\varphi(s')+\frac{1}{1-z(s')}\right]\cdot\left[\phi(s,s')-a(s)\right]\right\}. \tag{3.17}$$

The rest of this paper is concerned with using Eqs. (3.13) and (3.15) to characterize solutions for $z(s)$ and $\varphi(s)$ under various assumptions about the nature of the securities being traded, and then using (3.16) and (3.17) to characterize equilibrium securities prices. The case of shocks with serially independent increments is treated in the next section, while Sections 5, 6, and 7 consider serially correlated shocks.

4. The Case of Independent Shocks

Consider the special case in which $a(s_t) = s_t$, so the state is just the stock of outstanding securities. Let $\phi(s_t, s_{t+1}) = s_t + x_t$, where $\{x_t\}$ is a sequence of independent shocks with common distribution λ on $X \subset \mathbf{R}^n$. Thus x_t has the interpretation as new issues at date t. Assume that the cash payout function π is constant. This is the case in which current issues give *no* information about the distribution of issues or cash payouts in the future. Intuition suggests that under this assumption the system (3.13) and (3.15) will have a constant solution (z^*, φ^*). Why? Because this is a Modigliani–Miller–Ricardian-equivalence world, except for liquidity effects, so the outstanding stocks of securities should not matter unless they help to predict future liquidity effects.

Under these assumptions, and if the conjecture of a constant solution is correct, Eqs. (3.13) and (3.15) become

$$\varphi = \beta \int_X \left[\frac{1}{1-z} \pi + B^{\mathrm{T}} \varphi \right] \lambda(dx), \tag{4.1}$$

$$\frac{z}{1-z} = \beta \int_X \left\{ \max \left[\frac{z}{1-z}, \left[\frac{\pi}{1-z} + B^{\mathrm{T}} \varphi \right] \cdot x \right] \right\} \lambda(dx). \tag{4.2}$$

Assume that the matrix

$$[I - \beta B]^{-1} = \lim_{k \to \infty} [I + \beta B + \beta^2 B^2 + \cdots + \beta^k B^k]$$

exists (as it will when B has the near-diagonal form used in all the examples studied below). Then (4.1) has the solution

$$\varphi = \beta \frac{1}{1-z} [I - \beta B^{\mathrm{T}}]^{-1} \pi.$$

Substituting into (4.2) and cancelling the factor $(1 - z)^{-1}$, we obtain

$$z = \beta \textstyle\int_X \{\max[z, [(I - \beta B^{\mathrm{T}})^{-1} \pi] \cdot x]\} \lambda(dx), \tag{4.3}$$

where the fact that $I + \beta B^{\mathrm{T}} [I - \beta B^{\mathrm{T}}]^{-1} = [I - \beta B^{\mathrm{T}}]^{-1}$ has been applied. Solutions $z \in [0, 1)$ to (4.3) correspond to equilibria.

Define the function $\eta : X \to \mathbf{R}$ by $\eta(x) = [(I - \beta B')^{-1} \pi] \cdot x$. Then the scalar random variable $\omega = \eta(x)$ may be interpreted as a kind of total "value" of the vector x of new issues. Let μ denote the probability distribution of this random variable ω. Then (4.3) can be written

$$z = \beta \textstyle\int \max(z, \omega)\, \mu(d\omega). \tag{4.4}$$

Equation (4.4) will have a unique solution $z^* \in [0, 1)$ if and only if

$$\int_1 [\omega - 1]\mu(d\omega) < \frac{1-\beta}{\beta}, \tag{4.5}$$

which may be compared to (2.8). If $\int_0^\infty \omega\mu(d\omega) > 0$ (that is, if bonds are ever issued) then $z^* > 0$. We have shown, then, that if (4.5) holds a constant solution exists for this case of independent shocks. I do not know if there are other solutions to (3.13) and (3.15) for this case.

Let us characterize the constant solution for some even more specific sub-cases.

EXAMPLE 4.1: Consols. Let there be only one security in the system: a consol with the coupon payment $\pi = 1$. Then x_t is just the issue (possibly negative) of new consols at t and B is the matrix [1]. The random variable ω_t is equal to $(1 - \beta)^{-1}x_t$, which is of the order of the *value* of new consol issues at t. Hence the existence criterion (4.5) will be satisfied if the value of new issues cannot exceed the existing money supply.

As a check on units, suppose x_t is constant at the positive level x^*. Then the liquidity constraint is always just binding, so that (3.11) implies that $q = z^*/x^*$. Equation (4.4) implies $z^* = (1 - \beta)^{-1}\beta x^*$. When these facts are combined, the equilibrium price of a consol is $q^* = (1 - \beta)^{-1}\beta$. If we define the rate of time preference ρ in the usual way by $\beta = (1 + \rho)^{-1}$, then $q^* = 1/\rho$, which is just right as the price of a stream of \$1 payments starting one period hence, under my assumption that \$1 is not risky in real terms.

More generally, if (4.5) holds, so that (4.4) determines a unique equilibrium $z^* \in [0, 1)$, then the equilibrium bond price function $q(x)$ can be obtained from (3.12) and (3.14). Specialized to this example, these imply

$$q(x) = \left[\frac{1}{1-z} + \theta(x)\right]^{-1}\left(\frac{1}{1-z}\right)\left(\frac{1}{1-\beta}\right),$$

where

$$\frac{1}{1-z} + \theta(x) = \max\left\{\frac{1}{1-z}, \left(\frac{1}{1-z}\right)\left(\frac{1}{1-\beta}\right)\frac{x}{z}\right\}.$$

We conclude that

$$q(x) = \begin{cases} z/x & \text{if } x > (1-\beta)z \\ \dfrac{1}{1-\beta} & \text{if } x \leq (1-\beta)z. \end{cases}$$

Note that in the case where the liquidity constraint is slack, $x \leq (1 - \beta)z$, the consol price is $(1 + \rho)\rho^{-1}$, not ρ^{-1}. It is as if the current one period rate is zero and all forward rates are ρ.

EXAMPLE 4.2: Fixed Maturity Bonds. As a second example, suppose that (pure discount) bonds are issued maturing in 1, 2, . . . , n periods, each bond entitling its holder to \$1 at maturity and nothing until then. Let $x_t = (x_{1t}, \ldots, x_{nt})$ describe new issues at t, where $\{x_t\}$ are independent random variables with the common distribution λ on X. In this example, B is an $n \times n$ matrix with ones on the diagonal above the main diagonal and zeroes elsewhere: as n-period bond purchased at t becomes an $(n - 1)$-period bond at $t + 1$ or, if $n = 1$, it becomes a dollar at $t + 1$. The payout function π is the vector $(1, 0, \ldots, 0)$.

In this case, (4.1) becomes $\varphi_1 = \beta(1 - z)^{-1}$ and $\varphi_{i+1} = \beta\phi_i$, $i = 1, \ldots, n - 1$. This difference equation can be solved to obtain $\varphi_i = \beta^i(1 - z)^{-1}$, $i = 1, \ldots, n$. Then the inner product appearing on the right of (4.2) is

$$\left[\frac{1}{1-z}\pi + B^{\mathrm{T}}\varphi\right] \cdot x = \frac{1}{1-z}\sum_{i=1}^{n} \beta^{i-1}x_i = \frac{1}{1-z}\omega,$$

where the second equality defines the random variable $\omega = \eta(x)$. Cancelling the factor $(1 - z)^{-1}$, (4.2) implies

$$z = \beta \int_X \max(z, \omega)\, \mu(d\omega). \tag{4.6}$$

Then again, (4.5) is a sufficient condition for there to exist an equilibrium $z^* \in [0, 1)$.

Note that the consol example 4.1 is just the limiting case of this example as $n \to \infty$ when the random variables $x_1, x_2, \ldots$ are all equal to a common value. The second example of Section 2 is obtained if $x_i = 0$ for $i \geq 2$.

When (3.12) and (3.14) are specialized to this case, equilibrium bond prices must satisfy

$$q_i(x) = \left[\frac{1}{1-z} + \theta(x)\right]^{-1}\left(\frac{1}{1-z}\right)\beta^{i-1}, \qquad i = 1, \ldots, n,$$

where

$$\frac{1}{1-z} + \theta(x) = \max\left\{\frac{1}{1-z}, \left(\frac{1}{1-z}\right)\frac{1}{z}\sum_{i=1}^{n}\beta^{i-1}x_i\right\}.$$

These equations imply

$$q_i(\omega) = \begin{cases} \beta^{i-1}(z/\omega) & \text{if } z < \omega \\ \beta^{i-1} & \text{if } z \geq \omega. \end{cases}$$

Note that forward interest rates for $i \geq 2$ are always ρ (forward one period bond prices are always β) whatever the value of $\omega = \sum_{i=1}^{n} \beta^{i-1} x_i$. Moreover, it is immaterial what maturities of bonds are issued: only the "value-weighted" sum ω matters.

EXAMPLE 4.3: Equities. The two examples 4.1 and 4.2 can readily be combined, or other securities can be added, or both. Consider, for example, the situation where n-period bonds are traded and where an equity claim to the (normalized) dollar income stream $p(s)y$ is also traded. With independent shocks, $p(s)y = 1 - z$, so $\pi_e(x) = 1 - z$ for this added security. We consider the effect of this modification on the system (4.1)–(4.2).

Adding equities to the system alters the matrix B simply by adding another row and column with a one on the diagonal and zeroes elsewhere. This adds an independent equation to (4.1), which may be solved for the added marginal value term φ_e, say

$$\varphi_e = \frac{\beta}{1-\beta}.$$

The price of equities is, from (3.16), then

$$q_e(x) = \left[\frac{1}{1-z} + \theta(x)\right]^{-1} \left(\frac{1}{1-\beta}\right).$$

If the government does not trade in equities, the addition of this security does not affect the liquidity constraint and the determination of z and $\theta(x)$ is exactly as in example 4.2. In this case, equity prices are given by

$$q_e(x) = \begin{cases} \dfrac{1-z}{1-\beta}\dfrac{z}{\omega} & \text{if } \omega > z \\ \dfrac{1-z}{1-\beta} & \text{if } \omega \geq z. \end{cases}$$

Thus a large bond issue depresses equity prices, as it does bond prices. If the government does trade in equities (and this case is as easily imagined as the one discussed) then one would need to characterize these trades in terms of an additional component in the vector x.

5. A Pseudo-Case with Constant Goods Prices

The case studied in the last section is simple because the assumption of independent shocks keeps the information structure simple: securities prices are subject to liquidity effects but are not affected by speculation about future liquidity effects. Now return to the more complicated situation described by Eqs. (3.13) and (3.15). The function $z(s)$ enters into these two equations in two ways: the factor $[1 - z(s)]^{-1}$ appears on the right side of (3.13) and on both sides of (3.15). In both cases, it represents the inverse of the equilibrium goods price level $p(s) = [1 - z(s)]/y$. If $z(s)$ is constant, as in the last section, these factors cancel from both sides of (3.15). In addition $z(s)$ appears on the right of (3.15), in its role as the amount of money, or of liquidity, in the securities market. This is the only role played by $z(s)$ in the last section.

In this section, we are interested in the case in which the current state of the system conveys information about future bond issues, so that money moves in or out of securities markets in response to changes in s. But if this is the case then cash spent on goods has to fluctuate as well: all the money in the system has to go somewhere. With a constant endowment of goods, this means the price level fluctuates, and these fluctuations imply changes in expected inflation rates that will affect interest rates for fundamental, Fisherian reasons. For present purposes, I think these price effects are just a nuisance, getting in the way of analyzing the more interesting and direct liquidity effects. Why not just assume them away by taking prices to be fixed and analyze the interest rate movements that result? That is exactly what I will do in this section. It leads to a very tractable system of equations that do not, unfortunately, exactly describe any economic equilibrium.

By the system (3.13) and (3.15) with constant prices I mean the equations

$$\psi(s) = \beta \int_S [\pi(s, s') + B^{\mathrm{T}}\psi(s')]\, P(s, ds'), \tag{5.1}$$

$$z(s) = \beta \int_S \{\max[z(s), [\pi(s, s') + B^{\mathrm{T}}\psi(s')] \cdot [\phi(s, s') - a(s)]]\}\, P(s, ds'). \tag{5.2}$$

The function ψ is related to φ by $\psi(s) = (1 - z)\,\varphi(s)$, where $1 - z$ is the fixed price. The level at which it is fixed does not matter: this system has a kind of homogeneity property, corresponding to the fact that it is rates of inflation that affect interest rates, not price levels.

We have

LEMMA 1. *Let S be a metric space. Let* π *be continuous and bounded. Let the transition function P have the Feller property* ($g: S \to \mathrm{R}$ *is continuous implies* $\int g(s')\,P(s, ds')$ *is continuous*). *Let B be a matrix with entries either* 0 *or* 1, *with no column having more than one entry* 1. *Then* (5.1) *has a unique continuous bounded solution* $\psi : S \to R^n_+$.

PROOF. Let the right side of (5.1) define an operator V on the space C_n of continuous, bounded functions $f : S \to R^n_+$. Norm C_n by $\|f\| = \max_i \sup_{s \in S} |f_i(s)|$. Then under the given assumptions $V: C_n \to C_n$ and V is a contraction with modulus β. Since C_n is a complete metric space, the conclusion follows.

Indeed, since (5.1) is linear, one can write out a formula for the unique solution ψ, just as we did for the solution to (4.1).

Given a solution ψ to (5.1), let $\eta(s, s')$ be the real-valued random variable defined by $\eta(s, s') = [\pi(s, s') + B^{\mathrm{T}}\psi(s')] \cdot [\phi(s, s') - a(s)]$. Now define the operator T on C_1 by

$$(Tz)(s) = \beta \int_S \{\max[z(s), \eta(s, s')]\}\,P(s, ds'). \tag{5.3}$$

Then fixed points of this operator T coincide with solutions to (5.2). We have

LEMMA 2. *Let the hypotheses of Lemma* 1 *hold, and assume that* ϕ *and a are continuous and bounded. Then* (5.3) *has a unique continuous bounded solution z.*

PROOF. Under the stated assumptions, $\eta(s, s')$ is bounded and continuous. Hence if z has these properties, so does $\max[z(s), \eta(s, s')]$. Then since P has the Feller property, Tz is continuous. Thus $T: C_1 \to C_1$. Since T is evidently a contradiction with modulus β, the conclusion follows.

To interpret the fixed point z of T as a cash allocation function, we need $z: S \to [0, 1)$. Clearly $z(s) \geq 0$ implies $(Tz)(s) \geq 0$. A sufficient condition for $z(s) \leq 1$ to imply $(Tz)(s) < 1$ is that

$$\int_A [\eta(s, s') - 1]P(s, ds') < \frac{1-\beta}{\beta} \quad \text{for all} \quad s \in S, \tag{5.4}$$

where the set A is defined by

$$A = \{s' \in S : \eta(s, s') \geq 1\}.$$

Compare to (4.5).

If the function $\pi(s, s')$ is constant, as in the examples of Sections 2 and 4, then the solution ψ to (5.1) is constant, equal except for the factor $1 - z$ to the solutions for φ given in Section 4. Thus the determination of interest rates is not much altered if serial correlation is added the way I have done it here. If the only security is a consol, as in Example 4.1, with s_t interpreted as the stock and $s_{t+1} - s_t$ as new issues, the consol price is

$$q(s, s') = \begin{cases} z(s)/(s' - s) & \text{if } s' - s > (1 - \beta)z(s) \\ (1 - \beta)^{-1} & \text{if } s' - s \leq (1 - \beta)z(s). \end{cases}$$

If there are bonds of n different maturities, as in Example 4.2, where $s_t \in R^n$ is the vector of outstanding stocks, let $\eta(s, s') = \sum_{i=1}^{n} \beta^{i-1}(s_i' - s_i)$. Then the price of a bond maturating in i periods is

$$q_i(s, s') = \begin{cases} \beta^{i-1} z(s)/\eta(s, s') & \text{if } z(s) < \eta(s, s') \\ \beta^{i-1} & \text{if } z(s) \geq \eta(s, s'), \end{cases}$$

where $z(s)$ is the fixed point of T.

The forward interest rate at maturity i is just $-\ln[q_i(s, s')/q_{i-1}(s, s')]$, which equals the constant $-\ln(\beta) = \rho$ for all states (s, s'). Hence the theory, even with serially correlated shocks, does not offer the possibility of accounting for term structure fluctuations. On the other hand, complicated intertemporal patterns in interest rates generally, due to liquidity effects and the anticipation of such effects in the future, are possible.

6. The Case of Serially Correlated Shocks: Finite State Space

The analysis of the last section was greatly simplified by the assumption of constant prices. Since this assumption is not tenable in the context of this model (except when shocks are independent in the sense of Section 4), the results of that analysis can be, at best, an approximation. Nevertheless, we will see that the methods used to arrive at these results are suggestive for the more general case introduced in Section 3. This analysis will be conducted under the assumption that the state space S is finite.

We return to (3.13) and (3.15). The givens in these equations are the characteristics of the securities being traded, defined by π, B, ϕ, a, S, and P. We impose the following assumptions on these characteristics.

(A1) S is finite.
(A2) The functions π, ϕ, and a are non-negative.
(A3) B has entries 0 or 1, with no more than one entry 1 in any column.

Under (A1), the coupon payments $\pi_i(s, s')$ are bounded. Let $\alpha = \max_i \max_{s, s' \in S} \pi_i(s, s')$. The last assumption serves the function of (2.8), (4.5), and (5.4).

(A4) There exists a number D with $(1 - \beta)D > 1$ such that for all $s \in S$

$$\int_{A(s)} \{D\alpha\mathbf{1} \cdot [\phi(s, s') - a(s)] - 1\} P(s, ds') \le \frac{1-\beta}{\beta},$$

where $A(s) = \{s' \in S : D\alpha\mathbf{1} \cdot [\phi(s, s') - a(s)] \ge 1\}$, where $\mathbf{1}$ denotes an n-vector of ones.

We will show (Theorem 1) that under (A1)–(A4) there exists an equilibrium cash allocation function $z(s)$ that is non-negative and strictly less than one. Our strategy, as in Sections 4 and 5, will be to solve (3.13) for φ in terms of z, substitute this solution into (3.15), and then to study the latter. We begin with

LEMMA 3. *Let z be a function on S with range $[0, 1 - 1/M]$ for some number $1 < M < \infty$. Let* (A1)–(A3) *hold. Then* (3.13) *has a unique solution φ_z with*

$$0 \le \varphi_z(s) \le \frac{\alpha\beta M}{1-\beta}\mathbf{1}, \quad \text{all} \quad s \in S. \tag{6.1}$$

PROOF. The existence of a unique solution is an application of the Contraction Mapping Theorem, as in Lemma 1. To prove that the bounds (6.1) are satisfied, use an induction on the sequence $\{\varphi_n\}$ defined by $\varphi_{n+1} = V\varphi_n$, where V is the operator defined in the proof of Lemma 1 and where φ_0 is the zero vector. Every term in this sequence satisfies (6.1), and it converges to the unique solution to (3.13).

In view of Lemma 3, there is a solution φ_z to (3.13) corresponding to any function z on S with $1 \le [1 - z(s)]^{-1} \le M < \infty$. Let z be such a function, and consider the equation in the single variable γ

$$\frac{\gamma}{1-\gamma} = \beta \int_S \left\{ \max\left[\frac{z(s)}{1 - z(s')}, K(s, s') \right] \right\} P(s, ds'), \tag{6.2}$$

where the real-valued function K is defined on $S \times S$ by

$$K(s, s') = \left[\frac{1}{1 - z(s')} \pi(s, s') + B^{\mathrm{T}} \varphi_z(s') \right] \cdot [\phi(s, s') - a(s)].$$

We want to define an operator T on functions z by setting $(Tz)(s)$ equal to the unique γ-value satisfying (6.2). The next lemma justifies this.

LEMMA 4. *Let* (A1)–(A3) *hold. Let* $z : S \to [0, 1 - 1/M]$ *for some* $M > 1$. *Then for each* $s \in S$ *there is a unique* $\gamma \in [0, 1)$ *satisfying* (6.2).

PROOF. For each fixed s and z let $B_z(s)$ denote the right side of (6.2). Since $0 \le z(s) < 1$ for all s, $B_z(s) \ge 0$ for all s. Then $\gamma = [1 + B_z(s)]^{-1} B_z(s) \in [0, 1)$ is the unique solution to (6.2).

Call the solution to (6.2) $(Tz)(s)$. For any $M > 1$, this defines an operator on the set C_M of functions (n-vectors) $z : S \to [0, 1 - 1/M]$. The next result shows that M can be chosen so that T takes C_M into itself.

LEMMA 5. *Let* (A1)–(A4) *hold. Then there exists* $M > 1$ *such that* $T : C_M \to C_M$.

PROOF. We need to find $M > 1$ such that if $z \in C_M$, then $(Tz)(s) = [1 + B_z(s)]^{-1} B_z(s) \le 1 - 1/M$, where $B_z(s)$ is the right side of (6.2), as in the proof of the last lemma. Equivalently, we seek an M such that $z \in C_M$ implies $B_z(s) \le M - 1$ or

$$\beta \int_S \left\{ \max\left[\frac{z(s)}{1 - z(s')}, K(s, s') \right] \right\} P(s, ds') \le M - 1 \tag{6.3}$$

for all $s \in S$.

If $z \in C_M$, then $[1 - z(s')]^{-1}z(s) \leq M - 1$ for all s, s'. By Lemma 3 and (A3)

$$K(s, s') \leq \left(M\alpha + \frac{M\alpha\beta}{1-\beta} \right) 1 \cdot [\phi(s, s') - a(s)] \leq M \frac{\alpha}{1-\beta} 1 \cdot [\phi(s, s') - a(s)].$$

Thus (6.3) will hold for all $z \in C_M$ provided

$$\beta \int_S \max \left\{ 1, \frac{M}{M-1} \frac{\alpha}{1-\beta} 1 \cdot [\phi(s, s') - a(s)] \right\} P(s, ds') \leq 1. \quad (6.4)$$

Now let D be as in (A4). Then if $M = [1 - 1/(1 - \beta)D]^{-1}$, (6.4) holds and the proof is complete.

We summarize the results of this section in:

THEOREM 1. *Under* (A1)–(A4), *there is a solution* $(\varphi(s), z(s))$ *to* (3.13) *and* (3.15) *with* $0 \leq z(s) < 1$ *for all* $s \in S$.

PROOF. Choose D as in (A4) and M as in the proof of Lemma 5. By Lemmas 3 and 4, the operator T defines a function on the subset $C_M = [0, 1 - 1/M]^n$ of $\mathbf{R}^n$ into $\mathbf{R}^n$. This function is evidently continuous. By Lemma 5, T takes $[0, 1 - 1/M]^n$ into itself. By Brouwer's Theorem, T has a fixed point z in this set and this z together with the function φ constructed from z in Lemma 3 satisfy (3.13) and (3.15).

7. Numerical Illustrations

The examples in Section 4 provide, I hope, a good idea of the possibilities of the theory when shocks are independent. When shocks are serially correlated, as in the analysis of Sections 5 and 6, pencil-and-paper methods are of more limited usefulness. Accordingly, this section reports the results of some illustrative calculations on an example in which the only security priced is a one-period bond (as in Section 2).

In all the illustrations, the state of the system x takes on a finite number of values $x_1, \ldots, x_n$, and these values are interpreted as the size of an issue of one period government bonds. There are no other securities. The transition matrix is $P = [p_{ij}]$, where p_{ij} is the probability that $x_{t+1} = x_j$ conditional on $x_t = x_i$. I will deal with the two equations

$$z_i = \beta \sum_{j=1}^{n} \max(z_i, k_j) p_{ij}, \quad i = 1, \ldots, n \tag{7.1}$$

and

$$\frac{z_i}{1 - z_i} = \beta \sum_{j=1}^{n} \frac{1}{1 - z_j} \max(z_i, x_j) p_{ij}, \quad i = 1, \ldots, n. \tag{7.2}$$

Equation (7.1) is a specialization of the system (5.1)–(5.2) that holds for the pseudo-case described in Section 5. Equation (7.2) is a specialization of the system studied in Section 6.

Let T_1 be the operator on $\mathbf{R}^n$ such that $(T_1 z)_i$ is the right side of (7.1), so that solutions to (7.1) coincide with fixed points of T_1, and fixed points with all coordinates in $[0, 1)$ can be interpreted as equilibria. The solutions of (7.1) tabulated below were obtained by iterating the operator T_1 on the indicated initial vector z_0. As in Section 5, T_1 is a contraction, so this method locates the unique fixed point. Choosing the number of iterates m so that $\left\| T_1^{m+1} - T_1^{m} \right\| \leq (1 - \beta)(.001)$ will yield answers accurate to the third decimal place.

Let T_2 be the operator on the subset of $\mathbf{R}^n$ with coordinates less than one defined by $(T_2 z)_i = [1 + R_i(z)]^{-1} R_i(z)$, where $\mathbf{R}_i(z)$ is the right side of (7.2). Then fixed points of T_2 coincide with solutions to (7.2), and solutions with coordinates in $[0, 1)$ have interpretations as equilibria. I calculated fixed points of T_2 by the method described in the preceding paragraph for T_1. Theorem 1 in Section 6 gives sufficient condition for T_2 to satisfy the conditions of Brouwer's Theorem, but these conditions played no role in the calculations. In all cases, this iterative method located a fixed point, but Theorem 1 gives no assurance that this must always be the case, nor does it guarantee uniqueness of the fixed point when one is found.

The results from some of these calculations are reported in Tables 1 and 2. I used $\beta = 0.995$, thinking of a *monthly* discount rate of 0.5 percent. The bond issue x takes on two values, .02 and .08, which are of the right order of magnitude for monthly U.S. government bond issues, relative to total reserves. Beyond selecting numbers of realistic orders of magnitude, I made no attempt to be realistic. To experiment with different degrees of positive and negative serial correlation, I used the transition matrix

$$P = \begin{pmatrix} \theta & 1 - \theta \\ 1 - \theta & \theta \end{pmatrix}.$$

Values of 0.001, 0.01, 0.1, 0.3, 0.5, 0.7, 0.9, 0.99, and 0.999 were used for θ. For all these values, P has the unique stationary distribution (0.5, 0.5) over the two issue-states 0.02 and 0.08, with an average issue of 0.05.

For $\theta = 0.5$, the shocks are independent and the solution can be obtained by hand as in Sections 2 or 4. The fixed point (z_1, z_2) has equal coordinates, with the common value 0.079. For the other θ-values, this vector z was taken as the initial value to which the operators T_1 and T_2 were applied.

Table 1 reports the fixed points of T_1 in the first two columns, and the iterations needed to meet the tolerance level $\left\| T_1^{m+1} - T_1^m \right\| = (0.005)(0.001) = 0.000005$ for the θ-values listed on the left. The next three columns in the table give the fixed points of T_2 and the iterations required to give the same tolerance level.

Table 2 describes the properties of equilibrium interest rates associated with the fixed points of T_2, again for each θ-value. With serial correlation, bond prices and hence interest rates are functions of the current state, which determines x_i, and last period's state, which can affect z_i. Hence if x follows an n-state Markov process, interest rates follow an n^2-state Markov process. The transition function for this latter process can be calculated from P alone. The values of the interest rate in each state are calculated using the fixed point z. The table reports the mean interest rate, the standard deviation, the probability of a zero rate, and the first four autocorrelation coefficients, with all moments taken with respect to the unique stationary

Table 1 Solutions to (7.1) and (7.2)

	Equation (7.1)			Equation (7.2)		
θ	z_1	z_2	m	z_1	z_2	m
0.001	0.080	0.020	381	0.079	0.075	58
0.01	0.080	0.054	289	0.079	0.075	51
0.1	0.080	0.076	37	0.079	0.078	23
0.3	0.079	0.079	9	0.079	0.079	6
0.5	0.079	0.079	6	0.079	0.079	6
0.7	0.079	0.079	9	0.079	0.079	8
0.9	0.076	0.080	37	0.076	0.080	37
0.99	0.054	0.080	289	0.055	0.080	287
0.999	0.020	0.080	381	0.020	0.080	414

Note. Two states; $\beta = 0.995$; $(x_1, x_2) = (0.02, 0.08)$; $\left(z_1^0, z_2^0\right) = (0.079, 0.079)$.

Table 2 Monthly Interest Rate Behavior Implied by (7.2)

θ	$E(r)$	StD(r)	Pr{$r = 0$}	ρ_1	ρ_2	ρ_3	ρ_4
0.001	0.005	0.005	0.500	−0.922	0.920	−0.919	0.917
0.01	0.005	0.006	0.500	−0.567	0.556	−0.545	0.534
0.1	0.005	0.007	0.500	−0.185	0.148	−0.118	0.095
0.3	0.005	0.006	0.500	−0.076	0.030	−0.012	0.005
0.5	0.005	0.005	0.500	0.000	0.000	0.000	0.000
0.7	0.005	0.006	0.500	0.038	0.015	0.006	0.002
0.9	0.005	0.010	0.500	0.022	0.017	0.014	0.011
0.99	0.005	0.026	0.500	0.005	0.005	0.005	0.005
0.999	0.004	0.031	0.001	0.002	0.002	0.002	0.002

distribution of the process. Again, the row corresponding to $\theta = 0.5$ is readily calculated by hand.

Table 1 is mainly interesting for the information it contains about the differences between (7.1) and (7.2). The solution (z_1, z_2) to (7.1) is a continuous function of the parameter θ on the interval [0, 1]. At $\theta = 1$ (the current state is always maintained), the solution is $z = \beta x = (0.995)(0.02, 0.08)$, which is equal to three decimals to the solution for $\theta = 0.999$ given in the table. Similarly, the solution given for $\theta = 0.001$ equals the solution at $\theta = 0$ (the current state is never maintained). But away from these extremes, the solution to (7.1) is insensitive to changes in the degree of serial correlation, remaining almost constant on the interval [0.1, 0.9].

The solution to (7.2) behaves in a very similar way, except at very low θ values where the second coordinates of the solutions z to (7.1) and (7.2) are very different. At this extreme, the price effects reflected in the terms $(1 - z)^{-1}$ have an important influence. When θ is very low, a system in state 2 will almost certainly move to state 1 next period, which means that unless z_2 falls below $x_2 = 0.02$, interest rates will almost certainly be zero. With no price effect (that is, if (7.1) holds), z_2 does fall, for just this reason. Suppose the same z_2 value were to occur when a price effect is operating (that is, if (7.2) holds). Then the price level in state 1 will rise (since less cash held for securities trading means more cash is spent on goods), but then the system almost certainly will return to state 2 the period after, with a return to a lower price level. Hence state 1 would be associated with a large expected deflation, and cash is an excellent security to hold. It is this expected deflation effect that keeps z_2 from falling to (0.995)(0.02) near $\theta = 0$ in (7.2). Indeed, the solution for z_2 to (7.2) at $\theta = 0$ can be calculated theoretically: It is also 0.075.

Table 2 describes the interest rate behavior implied by Eq. (7.2). Obviously, except for very low θ values, Eq. (7.1) implies about the same behavior. Average interest rates are essentially given by consumers' rate of time preference. Recall that I have set the rate of money growth equal to zero, so one would expect nominal and real rates to be equal. Attitudes toward risk play no role in these liquidity effects, so interest rates do not change as the risk situation changes. The variability of interest rates is fairly stable, too, as well as fairly high: rates fluctuate between zero and very high levels. Serial correlation patterns are negligible, except at very low θ values where they reflect the assumed serial correlation pattern of the shocks in an obvious way.

I found these simulations informative, in an unexpected direction. If one were to apply a model of this type to explaining or predicting actual short-term interest rate series, one would do very well simply by calculating the constant equilibrium z-value for the i.i.d. case studied in Section 4, and assuming it holds for *any* time pattern of the shocks. The cash allocation is so insensitive to advance information on bond issues, even when this information is very sharp compared to what one would ever see in practice, that these information effects can as well be ignored. Perhaps one can think of shock processes where this would not be the case, but I was not able to do so. Another way of stating this conclusion is to say that Section 4 contains about 99% of what this paper has to say about the behavior of interest rates!

I carried out a number of calculations to check the sensitivity of the results in Tables 1 and 2 to changes in assumptions. There were no surprises, so I will just summarize them briefly. Changes in the discount factor β had no systematic effects on the speed of convergence of the algorithm. Apparently the bounds implied by the Contraction Mapping Theorem are not approached in practice in (7.1). Changes in the initial guess z^0 in some cases increased the iterations required to over 1000 (in (7.2)) but the algorithm always converged and in no case was a fixed point found that differed from those reported in Table 1. Increasing the number of shock-states to three, while retaining the symmetry of the two-state example, did not affect much the first two moments of the implied interest rate series.

8. Conclusions

The premise of this paper, as of the earlier contributions of Grossman and Weiss [2] and Rotemberg [13], is that at any time an economy's money is distributed over distinct locations, or markets, and that it takes time to move funds from one location to another. One implication of this premise is that an unanticipated change in the excess demand for cash in any one market will have different effects on prices and interested rates, depending on the way cash is distributed when the change occurs. To predict the consequences of such a change, one needs to know *where* money is as well as *how much* there is.

In order to model such effects in a tractable way, I followed [2] and [13] and imposed separate cash-in-advance or liquidity constraints on agents trading in distinct goods and securities markets. I departed from these earlier papers by taking these agents as being members of a single family, sharing a household utility function. This latter device greatly simplifies much of the analysis, permitting the analysis of a wide variety of stochastic (much wider, indeed, than I have explored here). It is also, in a sense, realistic. When we apply general equilibrium theory in the study of asset pricing, we typically consolidate accounts and impute as wealth to households the assets held by corporations in which they own shares, pension funds, and other institutions. This means that a given household's cash includes its own currency and bank accounts, plus the currency and bank accounts of its pension fund, of the financial intermediaries with which it deals, of the businesses of which it is part owner, and so on. All of this cash is properly viewed as included in the household's wealth, but it obviously cannot all be viewed as serving a common transactions purpose. I can pay for a cab ride with the currency I hold, but not with the money that TIAA-CREF holds on my behalf and, symmetrically, TIAA-CREF cannot use my demand deposits to acquire securities on my account, even when it would be in my interest for it to do so.

An immediate consequence of a financial liquidity constraint is that, at any time, there is a fixed demand curve for government securities along which the monetary authority can "peg" interest rates in a very literal sense. In this world, issuers of bonds can pick an interest rate at the beginning of a period and then conduct open market operations in such a way as to make it happen. This is the feature that the models of Grossman and

Weiss and Rotemberg were designed to capture, and by building on their work, the models of this paper capture it too.

Beyond this, I have shown that there liquidity effects can induce a serially correlated stochastic component to equilibrium interest rates that need not bear any definite relationship to fundamentals in the sense of Irving Fisher. These liquidity shocks have the capacity to induce sudden, large drops in the prices of bonds and other securities. The right image is not a bubble popping, but getting one's wind knocked out: The return to fundamental levels should be quick. In the examples I have developed, these shocks are tightly linked to government bond issues that can be directly observed. In practice, I think shifts in the private sector's demand for cash balances are also an important source of liquidity effects, as I am using that term, so I would not be optimistic about an econometric test that treats the state of the system as fully observable.[7]

A more central prediction of the theory arises from its "one factor" character. Since the liquidity effect works through a single cash constraint, it has to affect all centrally traded securities at once, in more or less the same way. Thus the theory has no ability to account for changes in the term structure of interest rates or in the relative prices of bonds and equities. Technically, this prediction could be relaxed by assuming segmentation of securities markets, but I think this would move us farther from the kind of realism I am seeking.

One feature of the theory that I find most unattractive is the fact that traders in securities will carry cash balances over only if short-term interest rates are zero. The set-up does not get us far enough away from rate-of-return dominance. The example in the paper that comes closest to facing this issue is the case of consols (Example 4.1). Here, there is no maturity as short as one "period," so no security exactly dominates cash. Even so, the implicit short rate is zero if cash is carried over in this example too.[8]

There is a wealth of interesting data on flow of funds, turnover rates of various kinds of accounts, and so on that monetary theory ought to deal with but generally has not. To do so, we will need to get farther away from

7. Atkeson[1] analyzes a model similar to those in this paper in which private sector "churning" is the source of liquidity fluctuations.

8. See note 4. The modification Wallace suggested would imply that money need not be dominated by one-period interest-bearing bonds. In calculations based on the model in [10], however, I found that even with this modification interest rates equal zero with a non-negligible probability.

complete markets in our theory, just as labor economists have had to in their attempts to account for their interesting turnover series. If the theory of transactions demand for money is to move in this direction, it is clear that we will need formulations that place a smaller burden on the idea of a fixed period than do the models of this paper. I have in mind not so much explaining the crucial time lags in the monetary system (though that would be nice, too) but just describing them with free parameters that can be more easily varied to fit data than the period length in the usual discrete-time formulations.

References

1. A. Atkeson, "On the Effect of Liquidity Constraints," University of Chicago working paper, 1989.
2. S. J. Grossman and L. Weiss, A transactions-based model of the monetary transmission mechanism, *Amer. Econ. Rev.* **73** (1983), 871–880.
3. S. J. Grossman, Monetary dynamics with proportional transaction costs and fixed payment periods, *in* "New Approaches to Monetary Economics: Proceedings of the Second International Symposium in Economic Theory and Econometrics" (W. A. Barnett and K. J. Singleton, Eds.), Cambridge University Press, Cambridge, England, 1987.
4. G. D. Hansen, Indivisible labor and the business cycle, *J. Monet. Econ.* **16** (1985), 309–328.
5. L. P. Hansen and K. J. Singleton, Stochastic consumption, risk aversion, and the temporal behavior of asset returns, *J. Polit. Econ.* **91** (1983), 249–265.
6. E. Helpman and A. Razin, Floating exchange rates with liquidity constraints in financial markets, *J. Int. Econ.* **19** (1985), 99–117.
7. A. W. Kleidon, Variance bounds tests and stock price valuation models, *J. Polit. Econ.* **94** (1986), 953–1001.
8. S. F. LeRoy and R. D. Porter, The present-value relation: Tests based on implied variance bounds. *Econometrica* **49** (1981), 555–574.
9. R. E. Lucas, Jr., and N. L. Stokey, Money and interest in a cash-in-advance economy, *Econometrica* **55** (1987), 491–514.
10. R. E. Lucas, Jr., "Notes on Wallace Reformulation: Liquidity and Interest Rates," University of Chicago working paper, 1988.
11. T. A. Marsh and R. C. Merton, Dividend variability and variance bounds tests for the rationality of stock market prices, *Amer. Econ. Rev.* **76** (1986), 483–498.
12. R. Rogerson, "Nonconvexities and the Aggregate Labor Market," University of Rochester working paper, 1985.

13. J. J. Rotemberg, A monetary equilibrium model with transactions costs, *J. Polit. Econ.* **92** (1984), 40–58.
14. T. J. Sargent, Interest rates and prices in the long run, *J. Money, Credit, Banking* **5** (1973), 385–449.
15. R. J. Shiller, Do stock prices move too much to be justified by subsequent changes in dividends? *Amer. Econ. Rev.* **71** (1981), 421–436.
16. K. D. West, Dividend innovations and stock price volatility, *Econometrica* **56** (1988), 37–61.
17. M. Woodford, "Monetary Policy and Price Level Indeterminacy in a Cash-in-Advance Economy," University of Chicago working paper, 1988.

— 14 —

Supply-Side Economics: An Analytical Review

1. Introduction

When I left graduate school, in 1963, I believed that the single most desirable change in the U.S. tax structure would be the taxation of capital gains as ordinary income.* I now believe that neither capital gains nor any of the income from capital should be taxed at all. My earlier view was based on what I viewed as the best available economic analysis, but of course I think my current view is based on better analysis. I thought the story of this transformation, which is by no means mine alone, would make an interesting subject for a lecture. Indeed, I think it makes a particularly suitable subject for the Hicks Lecture, for the theoretical point of view advanced in *Value and Capital* plays the central role in this story, as it has in so many other chapters of our intellectual history.

The framework most of us used, or at least had in the back of our minds, for thinking about taxation, capital accumulation and economic growth in the 1960s was the Solow (1956)–Swan (1956) model in which an economy's

Oxford Economic Papers 42, no. 2 (April 1990): 293–316.

*This paper is a version of the Hicks Lecture, which I had the honor to give in March, 1989. I would like to thank Peter Sinclair for his hospitality on that occasion.

With respect to the analysis of taxation, I am originally a student of Arnold Harberger, and I am grateful for his comments an this paper as well. More recently, I have benefitted from instruction, comments and criticism from Christophe Chamley, Kenneth Judd, Laurence Kotlikoff, Kevin M. Murphy, Edward Prescott, Sherwin Rosen, Nancy Stokey and Lawrence Summers. Peter Sinclair and James Mirrlees provided useful comments after the Hicks Lecture, as did Costas Azariadis and Joan Esteban at the June, 1989 Conference in Santander, Spain. Finally, I thank Chi-Wa Yuen both for his comments and his expert assistance.

savings rate was assumed to be a fixed fraction of income. In this framework, returns to capital are pure rents, so taxing these returns should have no allocative consequences.[1] With progressive schedules and without preferential treatment of returns arbitrarily classified as capital gains, wealthier capitalists could be singled out for the heaviest taxation. Who could ask for a better tax base than this?

The view that an economy's total stock of capital could safely be taken as approximately fixed in tax analysis was forcefully challenged in the 1970s by Feldstein (1978) and Boskin (1978), who argued that the tax treatment of capital and other income in fact had major effects on accumulation and growth. Boskin and others pursued this issue empirically within the Solow–Swan framework, by framing it as a question about the magnitude of the interest elasticity of savings. But it is clear enough from the modern theory of consumer behavior that there is no reason to hope that aggregate savings can be represented as a stable function of the contemporaneous return on capital. A savings function will necessarily depend on a whole list of current and expected future returns, and demand functions on infinite dimensional spaces are awkward objects to manipulate theoretically or to estimate econometrically. The Solow–Swan framework, even modified to permit elastic savings behavior along the lines Solow had outlined in his original paper, was simply not suitable for making progress on the questions Feldstein and Boskin raised.

Contributions by Brock and Turnovsky (1981), Chamley (1981) and Summers (1981) provided the framework—really, two frameworks—that proved suitable for this purpose.[2] Each of these papers replaced the savings function of the household with a preference function, the discounted sum of utilities from consumption of goods at different dates. Each used the assumption of perfect foresight, or rational expectations, to deal with the

1. Of course, differential taxation of different kinds of capital has allocative consequences, even when savings are inelastic. Thus the analysis in Harberger (1966) focused on tax-induced misallocation of a fixed total capital stock. Chamley (1981) argues that misallocations due to differential capital taxation are larger than misallocations due to an inappropriate average rate. Jorgenson and Yun (1990) also report estimates of the effects of differential as well as average capital taxation. I will focus here exclusively on the effects of taxation on the total stock of capital, but my doing so should not be interpreted as expressing a position on the relative importance of these two kinds of misallocations.

2. Summers and others acknowledge the stimulus of earlier contributions by Hall (1968) and Miller and Upton (1974).

effects of future taxes on current decisions. Each went directly from the first-order conditions for optimal household behavior to the construction of equilibrium, without any need to construct the savings function. In short, all three contributions recast the problem of capital taxation in a Hicksian general equilibrium framework with a commodity space of dated goods. As we will see, this recasting was not a matter of aesthetics, of finding an elegant foundation for things our common sense had already told us. It was a 180 degree turn in the way we think about policy issues of great importance.

The objective of this lecture is to provide a quantitative review of the research on capital taxation that has followed from these contributions. In this attempt, I draw on the contributions of many others, notably Bernheim (1981), Auerbach and Kotlikoff (1987), Judd (1985), (1987) and, especially, Chamley's (1986) normative analysis. But rather than try to mix-and-match conclusions from a variety of different, mutually inconsistent models I will begin by stating a fairly typical example of my own to serve as the basis for a more unified discussion. In Section 3 I follow Chamley (1986) in characterizing the efficient, in the sense of Ramsey (1927), tax structure for this economy. Section 4 uses figures for the U.S. economy to compare long-run behavior under Ramsey taxes to the allocation induced by the existing U.S. tax structure. Section 5 offers some conjectures on transitional dynamics for this model, based on results that have been obtained by others for closely related models.

The result will not be a set of definitive answers, for I will be reviewing an ongoing and active body of research. In any case, the personal experience I have described has led me to a certain suspicion of definitive answers to tax questions. But I hope it will be a fair summary of what the best recent research tells us about capital taxation. I hope as well that my story will serve as illustration of the way in which the search for theory at a more fundamental level can revolutionalize our thinking about important practical questions, and hence of the way in which progress at the most purely technical, abstract end of economics serves as the fuel for what Alfred Marshall called our "engine for the discovery of truth."

2. A Theoretical Framework

As a basis for discussion, I will propose a model suitable for assessing changes in a tax structure consisting of flat-rate taxes on capital and labor income. The model focuses on three margins: the division of production between consumption and investment, the division of time between income-directed activities and all other activities (which I call *leisure*), and the division of income-directed time between the production of goods and the accumulation of human capital (which I will call *learning*). Our interest will be in determining how each of these three margins is affected by changes in the tax structure.

Focusing on some margins means neglecting some others. Thus I will not be studying the division of goods production into private and public goods: government goods consumption and transfer payment obligations will be taken as unalterable givens. I will not analyze the choice of country to invest in, or to acquire capital or consumption goods from: the discussion will be confined to a closed system. Population growth will be mechanically treated, with all demographic choices abstracted from.

By restricting attention to flat-rate taxes (with a small exception to be noted later), in a setting in which, taken literally, lump sum taxes would be both feasible and ideal, I will be evading the fundamental questions on the nature of the tax structure studied in Mirrlees (1971). I consider only tax rates to which the government is fully and credibly committed, though they need not be constant over time, so I am also evading (or at least postponing) the equally fundamental issue of time-consistency raised in Kydland and Prescott (1977) and, in a context very close to the one I will use, in Fischer (1980).

Recent fiscal research based on models with these general features is about evenly divided between work that follows Chamley (1981) in postulating an infinitely-lived typical consumer, interpreted as in Barro (1974) as a family or dynasty, and research that follows Summers (1981) in assuming a succession of finitely-lived overlapping generations. These two classes of models have very different theoretical structures, yet in practice, for the kind of tax problem under study here, seem to yield quite similar results.[3] Nevertheless, a choice must be made, and I will base all of the

3. Diamond (1965) demonstrated the possibility of inefficiently large capital accumulation, of a nature that cannot arise in a dynasty structure, in an overlapping generations formulation. Recent work by Kehoe and Levine (1985) and Muller and Woodford (1988) has shown that overlapping generations models can have a continuum of equilibria, and has made some progress in characterizing the circumstances under which this can arise. On the other hand, Laitner (1990) has shown that the overlapping generations equilibria

analysis in this lecture on the relatively simpler dynasty structure. As we will see, many of the ideas and techniques that have been introduced in an overlapping generations context can usefully be adapted to the dynasty context.

In this setting, then, I ask two questions. The first is Ramsey's (1927) normative question: What choice of tax rates will lead to maximal consumer utility, consistent with given government consumption and with market determination of quantities and prices? The second is positive and quantitative: How much difference does it make? To make progress on either question, it will be useful to set out the notation for the model the main feature of which I have just sketched.

There is a single household (representing many) whose objective is to maximize the discounted sum of utilities from the consumption of a single produced good and of leisure, over an infinity of periods:

$$\int_0^\infty e^{-(\rho-\lambda)t} U[c(t), x(t)]\, dt. \tag{2.1}$$

Here $c(t)$ and $x(t)$ stand for per capita consumption of goods and leisure, ρ is the subjective rate of discount, and λ is the rate of population growth. The household is endowed with one unit of time per person per unit of time, so $1 - x(t)$ is time spent in income-directed activities.

The production technology is equally simple. Total production of goods (which I will identify with net national product) is a constant returns to scale function of the stock of the per capita capital stock $k(t)$ and effective hours per worker. The latter is just the product of the fraction of time $u(t)$ that each worker devotes to goods production, and his average skill level $h(t)$. Production is divided among consumption, net investment, and government purchases of goods and services, so the technology is described by:

$$c(t) + \frac{dk(t)}{dt} + \lambda k(t) + g(t) = F[k(t), u(t)h(t)]. \tag{2.2}$$

We may think of the average skill level $h(t)$ as growing at an exogenously given rate: Harrod neutral technical change. But I want also to allow for

calculated by Auerbach and Kotlikoff (1987) are at least locally unique, for the particular parameter values Auerbach and Kotlikoff assumed.

the possibility that human capital accumulation can be affected by the way people allocate their time. Accordingly, let $v(t)$ be the fraction of time people spend improving their skills, and assume:

$$\frac{dh(t)}{dt} = h(t)G[v(t)]. \tag{2.3}$$

Of course,

$$u(t) + v(t) + x(t) = 1. \tag{2.4}$$

In this situation, then, we can define a *first-best* allocation as a choice of paths $c(t)$, $u(t)$, $v(t)$, $x(t)$, $k(t)$ and $h(t)$ that maximizes utility (2.1) subject to the feasibility constraints (2.2)–(2.4), given the initial stocks of the two kinds of capital, $k(0)$ and $h(0)$, and the path $g(t)$ *of* government consumption.[4]

If government activity must be financed by flat-rate taxes, then of course this first-best allocation cannot be attained. To examine the allocations that will arise under flat-rate taxes, we will need explicit statements of the three key marginal conditions.

In a market equilibrium with taxes, households face a budget constraint of the form:

$$\int_0^\infty \exp\left[-\int_0^t (r(s) - \lambda)\, ds\right] [c(t) - b(t) - w(t)u(t)h(t)]\, dt \leq k(0), \tag{2.5}$$

where $r(t)$ is the interest rate and $w(t)$ the real wage, both expressed net of taxes, and $b(t)$ denotes transfer payments (including coupon payments on government debt) due to households at date t. (Here w is the wage of a worker with a unit skill level, so a worker with skill level h receives wh per unit of time worked.) The right side of this constraint, $k(0)$, is the value (in units of date-0 consumption) of the household's initial capital holdings. In

4. The functions U, F and G are assumed to be twice differentiable, U is strictly increasing in both arguments and strictly concave. F is strictly increasing in both arguments and strictly quasi-concave. G will be assumed either to be a constant function (when I want to treat human capital growth as exogenous) or strictly increasing and strictly concave. These restrictions are sufficient to ensure the uniqueness of the first-best allocation (if one exists) but not to ensure uniqueness of the taxed equilibria I will discuss below. They are not, in general, adequate to ensure existence of first- or second-best allocations. I will not offer a rigorous treatment of these issues in this lecture.

an equilibrium, competition among profit-maximizing firms ensures that both factors are paid their marginal products. Hence:

$$w = (1 - \theta)F_n(k, uh), \tag{2.6}$$

$$r = (1 - \tau)F_k(k, uh), \tag{2.7}$$

where θ is the tax rate on labor income and τ is the tax rate on capital income. Then a competitive equilibrium consists of paths for quantities (c, u, v, x, b, g, k, h), prices (r, w), and taxes (θ, τ) such that (c, u, v, x, h) maximizes (2.1) subject to the constraints (2.3)–(2.5) and $(k, uh, r, w, \theta, \tau)$ satisfy (2.2), (2.6) and (2.7). Note that (2.2) and (2.5)–(2.7) together imply that the government's present value budget constraint is satisfied.

The consumer's problem involves three margins. The marginal rate of substitution between consumption at dates 0 and t must equal the relative prices of these two goods:

$$e^{-(\rho-\lambda)t}U_c\left(c(t), x(t)\right)/U_c\left(c(0), x(0)\right) = \exp\left\{-\int_0^t \left(r(s) - \lambda\right) ds\right\}. \tag{2.8}$$

The marginal rate of substitution between leisure and consumption must be equal to the real wage:

$$wh = U_x(c, x)/U_c(c, x). \tag{2.9}$$

The allocation of non-leisure time between the two income-directed activities, producing goods and learning new skills, must be such that the value of a unit of time spent producing (and earning) at each date is equal, on the margin, to the value of spending that unit of time accumulating skills that will enhance earnings in the future:

$$w(t)h(t) = G'[v(t)]\int_t^\infty \exp\left\{-\int_t^s \left(r(\xi) - \lambda\right) d\xi\right\} u(s)w(s)h(s)\, ds. \tag{2.10}$$

The left side is just earnings per unit of time for a worker at skill level $h(t)$. The right side is the product of the percentage increment $G'(v)$ to human capital if v units of time are spent in learning and the discounted value of the increased earnings flow that these additional skills will yield. The latter flow depends, of course, on the amount of work effort $u(t)$ one intends to supply in the future.

The marginal conditions (2.6)–(2.10), together with the equations of motion (2.2) and (2.3) for the two kinds of capital, form a system of Euler equations that can be solved for the full dynamics of this model economy given the initial stocks of human and physical capital. I will appeal to them at various points in the argument that follows. By setting the tax rates τ and θ equal to zero, these same equalities also serve to characterize the first-best allocation, a fact I will also cite later on.

With this apparatus in place, I return to the questions I raised a moment ago. What can be said about an optimal tax structure, in Ramsey's second-best sense? This is the subject of the next section. After dealing with it, we will turn to the issues involved in quantifying the gap between current fiscal policy and an ideal one.

3. Efficient Taxes

It will provide a useful benchmark for the quantitative analysis to follow to ask first: What is the *best* tax structure for the economy I have just described? One way to frame this Ramsey problem, used in Lucas and Stokey's (1983) analysis of an economy without capital, is to think of the government as directly choosing a feasible resource allocation, subject to constraints that express the assumption that it is possible to find prices such that price-taking households will be willing to consume their part of this allocation. We can then work backward from such an *implementable* allocation to the set of taxes that will implement it.[5]

In an implementable allocation, the household budget constraint (2.5) must be satisfied, and so must the marginal conditions (2.8) and (2.9). Using these marginal conditions to express prices in terms of quantities and substituting back into the budget constraint (2.5) we obtain:

$$\int_0^\infty e^{-(\rho-\lambda)t}[(c-b)U_c(c,x) - uU_x(c,x)]\,dt = k(0)U_c[c(0),x(0)]. \quad (3.1)$$

Proceeding in exactly the same way to eliminate prices from the marginal condition (2.10) for human capital accumulation, this condition can be expressed in terms of quantities as:

$$U_x[c(t),x(t)] = G'[v(t)]\int_t^\infty e^{-(\rho-\lambda)(s-t)}u(s)\,U_x[c(t),x(s)]\,ds. \quad (3.2)$$

5. This is, I am taking what Atkinson and Stiglitz (1980), ch. 12, call a *primal* approach, as opposed to the *dual* approach in which tax rates are viewed as governmental decision variables and an indirect utility function is maximized.

A feasible allocation (one that satisfies (2.2)–(2.4)) can be implemented by flat rate taxes on capital and labor income if and only if it satisfies the constraints (3.1) and (3.2). Thus choosing time paths of quantities so as to maximize consumer utility subject to these additional constraints determines the Ramsey, second-best allocation. The two associated tax rates can then be read off the marginal conditions provided in the last section. It would be a useful but difficult task to provide a full characterization of solutions to this maximum problem. I have not done so. What I will do instead is to make some observations about the Ramsey taxation of capital income, based on what we know about Ramsey taxes in general and on Chamley's more specific (1986) analysis of a very similar problem.

The nature of efficient capital taxation arises out of the tension between two principles, both of which are familiar from Ramsey's original static analysis. One principle is that factors of production in inelastic supply—factors whose income is a pure rent—should be taxed at confiscatory rates. In the present application, if the value $k(0)$ of consumers' initial capital holdings can be taxed directly via a capital levy, this eases the constraint (3.1) and reduces (or possibly eliminates entirely) the need to resort to distorting taxes. In the same way, defaulting on initial government debt and reducing promised transfer payments from government to households (both summarized in the path $b(t)$ in (2.5) and (3.1)) will reduce the need to resort to distorting taxes and improve welfare. Insofar as the government's ability to obtain capital levies in this general sense is left unrestricted—insofar as $k(0)$ and $b(t)$, $t \geq 0$, are regarded as choice variables in formulating the Ramsey problem—it will increase utility to use these tax sources fully. Moreover, insofar as other taxes can imitate such a capital levy, it will be efficient to resort to them. (For example, it is known that a tax on capital income combined with an investment tax credit can imitate a capital levy perfectly.) In my analysis, I will assume that all such capital levy possibilities are already captured in the path $b(t)$ of transfers, so that $b(t)$ and $k(0)$ are taken as givens in the formulation of the Ramsey problem.

A second principle in Ramsey's analysis is that goods that appear symmetrically in consumer preferences should be taxed at the same rate—taxes should be spread evenly over similar goods. In this application, this principle means that taxes should be spread evenly over consumption at different dates. Since capital taxation applied to new investment involves taxing later consumption at heavier rates than early consumption, this second principle implies that capital is a bad thing to tax.

In my formulation there is but one tax rate applied to income from old and new capital alike, so these two principles cannot simultaneously be obeyed. The full solution to the Ramsey problem, then, must involve heavy initial capital taxation followed by lower and ultimately zero taxation.[6] Chamley (1986) provides a very sharp characterization of Ramsey taxes in a model very close to this one that exhibits this tension in a very clear way. In one of his two main results, he showed that if the Ramsey allocation converges to a constant or a balanced growth path, then the tax rate on capital must be zero on this path. It will be illuminating to sketch a proof of this result for our model.

This implication can be developed by examination of the marginal condition for capital only. For a taxed economy with the capital tax rate $\tau(t)$ arbitrarily chosen, this marginal condition is:

$$(1-\tau)F_k(k, uh) = \rho - \frac{d}{dt}\ln[U_c(c, x)]. \tag{3.3}$$

(This equality is obtained by differentiating (2.8) with respect to time and substituting for $r(t)$ from (2.7).) To characterize the Ramsey taxation of capital, then, we simply obtain the analogue of (3.3) for the Ramsey problem and compare the two.

It is easiest to begin with the special case in which the rate of human capital growth is given (the function G is constant with respect to v) so that no time is spent accumulating human capital ($v = 0$) and the time spent producing goods, u, is equal to one minus leisure. In this case, the rate of human capital growth ν, say, is an exogeneously given constant. Then we can set aside condition (3.2) and the equality (3.1) completely characterizes the set of allocations that can be implemented with flat-

6. Roughly speaking, reducing the right side of the constraint (3.1) eases the excess burden of taxation. If this cannot be achieved by a capital levy that reduces $k(0)$, the next best thing is to reduce the relative *value* of consumers' initial wealth by reducing the initial marginal utility of consumption, $U_c(c(0), x(0))$ and then increasing it rapidly. Since τ cannot exceed unity (no one can be compelled to use his capital in production), the rate of increase in the marginal utility of consumption is (see (3.3) below) bounded by ρ. Chamley shows that on a Ramsey path, this constraint will initially bind, which is to say that $\tau(t) = 1$ for t sufficiently small.

rate taxes. Under these assumptions, the Ramsey problem is: maximize (2.1) subject to (2.2), (2.4) and (3.1). The Lagrangean for the government's maximum problem, in this case, involves the discounted value of the function:

$$W(c, x, \Phi) = U(c, x) + \Phi[(c - b)U_c(c, x) - (1 - x)U_x(c, x)],$$

where Φ is a non-negative multiplier, constant over time, and strictly positive if it is necessary to use any distorting taxes. This problem has exactly the form of the first-best planning problem, except that the current period utility function U is replaced by this pseudo-utility function W. The term multiplied by Φ gives a "bonus" to date-t allocations (c, x) that bring tax revenues in to the government, hence relieving other periods of some of their "excess burden," and assigns a penalty to allocations that have the reverse effect.

It is straightforward to show that among the necessary conditions that a solution to the Ramsey problem must satisfy is the equality:

$$F_k(k, uh) - \rho - \frac{d}{dt}\ln[W(c, x, \Phi)]. \tag{3.4}$$

It is an immediate consequence of (3.3) and (3.4) that if the Ramsey allocation converges to a steady state—an allocation in which quantities are constant—then the Ramsey tax on capital is zero in that steady state. In this case, the time derivative on the right of (3.4) is zero, and the marginal product of capital is just ρ. From (3.3), this requires $\tau = 0$.

For studying a growing economy, models that converge to steady states are not useful, and the appropriate analogue to a steady state is a balanced growth path, defined in this case as an allocation in which consumption, government spending and both kinds of capital grow at the rate ν of technical progress, and the time allocation (u, x) is constant. To ensure that such a path exists for this model, it is necessary to assume that the current period utility function U has the constant elasticity form:

$$U(c, x) = \frac{1}{1-\sigma}[c\varphi(x)]^{1-\sigma}, \tag{3.5}$$

where the coefficient of risk aversion σ is positive. When U takes the form (3.5), then with x constant (as on a balanced path) the growth rate of marginal utility is just the product of σ and the growth rate ν of consumption, and the right side of (3.3) is just $\rho + \sigma v$. Moreover, if U has the constant elasticity form (3.5), then a simple calculation shows that for fixed x and Φ, W is also a constant elasticity function with the *same* elasticity σ. Hence along a balanced Ramsey path, (3.4) implies:

$$F_k(k, uh) = \rho + \sigma v. \tag{3.6}$$

Comparing (3.3), which holds for any taxed balanced path, to (3.6), we have shown that if the Ramsey path converges to a balanced path, the tax rate on capital must converge to zero.

This proof of Chamley's result requires modification if human capital growth is assumed to be endogenous, for in that case the government's Lagrangean must incorporate the constraint (3.2) as well as the budget constraint (3.1). But it is not hard to show that (3.6) continues to characterize a Ramsey balanced path even in this more general case. The common sense of this result is clear enough from (2.10): the net-of-tax wage rate appears on both sides of this constraint and it is constant along a balanced path. Thus changes in the labor income tax rate do not distort the learning decision on such a path, except through their effects on leisure demand, and these effects are already taken into account in the constraint (3.1).

Even without working out the details of the Ramsey problem, then, some of the general features of efficient capital taxation are fairly clear. Capital income taxation will initially be high, imitating a capital levy on the initial stock. If the system converges to a balanced path, capital taxation will converge to zero. Chamley (1986) verifies both features for an economy that is very similar to this one. His proof of the long-run result applies to the present model, while the short-run conclusion seems a necessary consequence of the efficiency of capital levies.

The implication that capital should be untaxed in the long run is not sufficient to define the efficient long run fiscal policy, even in a setting in which government spending is given and there is only one other good to tax. This is because the level of debt to be serviced in the long run, which along with the level of government spending will determine what labor income taxes will have to be, will depend on the entire time path of taxes and spending: it cannot be inferred on the basis of balanced-path reasoning alone. Auerbach and Kotlikoff (1987) have emphasized this point in a life cycle context. It is equally important in the kind of dynasty framework I am using here.

4. A Balanced Growth Analysis

According to the analysis of the last section, the best structure of income taxation—for an economy growing smoothly along a balanced path—is to raise all revenues from the taxation of labor income and none at all from capital. To evaluate how interesting a result that is, we need to know just how far away from efficiency, in Ramsey's sense, we now are. I will turn to this issue next, taking the U.S. economy as the case under study. Since I am somewhat familiar with, though by no means an expert on, the U.S. tax structure and national accounts, this will reduce—though not entirely eliminate—the chances of major quantitative blunders.

The general idea will be to view the U.S. economy in the postwar period as though it were a closed economy on a balanced growth path. Then I assume that Ramsey taxes are introduced at some date—I will use 1985—and try to characterize the dynamics of the system from then on. As we have just seen, if this system converges to a balanced path, as I will assume it does, capital will not be taxed on this path. Since the Ramsey path is maximal, consumer utility after this hypothetical reform will exceed what it would have been had the economy continued along the original path. To put the welfare gain in comprehensible units, I would like to calculate the lump-sum, permanent supplement to consumption, expressed as a constant percentage, that would leave consumers indifferent between following the original path and switching to the Ramsey path. In this section, I will work out a rough answer to this question based *only* on a comparison of old and new balanced paths. Transitional dynamics are then discussed in Section 5.

To describe behavior along a balanced path, defined as in the last section, I assume that U is the constant elasticity function (3.5) and that the fiscal variables θ, τ, g/h and b/h are constant. It is convenient to let $z = k/uh$ denote the constant value of the capital to effective labor ratio, and to let $F(z, 1) = f(z)$. Then a balanced path is described by the values of z, c/h, u, v, x and ν that satisfy:

$$u[f(z) - (\nu + \lambda)z] = \frac{c}{h} + \frac{g}{h}, \tag{4.1}$$

$$\nu = G(v), \tag{4.2}$$

$$\rho + \sigma\nu = (1 - \tau)f'(z), \tag{4.3}$$

$$\frac{\varphi'(x)}{\varphi(x)}\frac{c}{h} = (1-\theta)[f(x) - xf'(z)], \tag{4.4}$$

$$\rho - \lambda + (\sigma - 1)\nu = uG'(v), \tag{4.5}$$

together with the time budget constraint (2.4).

These equations are just specializations of the technology description (2.2) and (2.3) and the marginal conditions (2.6)–(2.10) to the kind of balanced path I have described. One can think of solving them for the balanced path resource allocation, including the endogenously determined growth rate along this path, given the two tax rates τ and θ and the level of government consumption g/h. This procedure would leave the government budget deficit (or surplus) free. A more sensible alternative is to add an equation requiring budget balance along the balanced path:

$$\theta u[f(z) - zf'(z)] + \tau uf'(z) = \frac{g}{h} + \frac{b}{h}. \tag{4.6}$$

The left side of (4.6) is the revenue from the taxes on the two factors of production (deflated by the growing stock of human capital). The right side is government consumption g/h, similarly deflated, plus direct transfers b/h, defined to include debt service payments.[7] With equation (4.6) added to the system, we must treat one of the four fiscal variables as endogenous, given the values of the other three.

Tables 2–4 describe numerical solutions to the system (4.1)–(4.6) under various assumptions, based on parameter estimates summarized in Table 1. Let me first describe, very briefly, where these numbers come from. From 1955 to 1985, real output in the U.S. grew at an annual rate of 0.029. (This figure, and all others I cite unless explicitly mentioned, is from the supplemental tables at the back of the 1988 *Economic Report of the President.*) This is also the U.S. growth rate over the entire century: U.S. real growth is amazingly stable, which is why it is attractive to model the system as a balanced path. The population growth rate from 1955 to 1985 was 0.012; employment grew at 0.018, and employed manhours at 0.014. Take the latter figure as an estimate of the parameter λ. Then since I have *defined* all growth in output per person to be human capital growth, the

7. As remarked at the end of the last section, it is not possible to know the balanced path value of b/h without calculating the transitional dynamics. The provisional assumption used here is that debt is neither accumulated nor decumulated along the transitional path.

Table 1 Initial Values and Benchmark Parameter Values

Initial output	$F(k, uh)$	1
Initial private consumption	c	0.72
Initial government consumption	g	0.21
Initial government transfers	b	0.18
Initial capital stock	k	2.4
Initial human capital	h	1
Initial employment	u	1
Labor's share		0.76
Capital/labor substitution elasticity	σ_p	0.6
Coefficient of Risk Aversion	σ	2.0
Leisure elasticity	α	0.5
Learning elasticity	γ	0.8
Human Capital Growth Rate	ν	0.015
Population Growth Rate	λ	0.014
Labor Income Tax Rate	θ	0.40

value $0.015 = 0.029 - 0.014$ must be assigned to ν. Neglecting imports and exports, net national product was divided in the fractions 0.07 to net investment, 0.72 to private consumption, and 0.21 to government purchases of goods and services. The capital-output ratio consistent with these numbers is 2.4. I normalized initial production (NNP), initial human capital, and initial employment all at unity. These are the sources for the first seven figures in Table 1 (excepting transfer payments, to which I return shortly) and the two growth rates ν and λ.

For the production technology, I used a CES function with a substitution elasticity $\sigma_p = 0.6$, a value consistent with time series estimates in Lucas (1969). Auerbach and Kotlikoff (1987) and most other recent taxation studies use the Cobb-Douglas assumption $\sigma_p = 1$. In Table 4 I will report results based on this higher value for comparison. The share and intercept parameters were then fit to U.S. averages, using a labor share of 0.76.

The utility function has already been assumed to take the form (3.5). I used $\sigma = 2.0$ for the coefficient of risk aversion. Auerbach and Kotlikoff use $\sigma = 4.0$, and even higher estimated values have been reported. But from equation (4.3), one can see that if two countries have consumption growth rates ν differing by one percentage point, their interest rates must differ by G percentage points (assuming similar discount rates ρ). A value

Table 2 Long-Run Per Capita Capital as a Function of the Capital Tax Rate Expressed as Percentage Change from Benchmark Value

Tax Rate	(A) Inelastic Labor Exogenous v	(B) Elastic Labor Exogenous v	(C) Elastic Labor Endogenous v	v
0.36	0.0	0.0	0.0	0.0150
0.30	7.0	6.8	7.0	0.0150
0.25	12.4	12.0	12.3	0.0149
0.20	17.4	16.7	17.2	0.0149
0.15	22.0	21.0	21.7	0.0149
0.10	26.4	25.1	26.0	0.0148
0.05	30.5	28.8	30.0	0.0148
0	34.3	32.3	33.7	0.0147

Table 3 Long-Run Allocation as a Function of the Capital Tax Rate Expressed as Percentage Change from Benchmark Values

	Case (A)	Case (B): Elastic Labor; Exogenous v			
Capital Tax Rate	Consumption	Consumption	Labor Supply	Welfare	Labor Tax Rate
0.36	0.0	0.0	0.0	0.0	0.40
0.30	1.6	1.4	−0.2	1.5	0.41
0.25	2.7	2.2	−0.5	2.5	0.42
0.20	3.7	2.9	−0.7	3.3	0.43
0.15	4.6	3.4	−1.0	4.0	0.44
0.10	5.4	3.8	−1.3	4.6	0.45
0.05	6.1	4.1	−1.6	5.1	0.45
0	6.7	4.2	−2.0	5.5	0.46

of σ as high as 4 would thus produce cross-country interest differentials much higher than anything we observe, and from this viewpoint even $\sigma = 2$ seems high. (I owe this observation to Kevin M. Murphy.) As Table 4 shows, this parameter is not critical for long-run comparisons.

I assumed that φ is the constant elasticity function $\varphi(x) = x^{\alpha}$. The elasticity of substitution between goods and leisure implied by this parameterization is unity, as compared to the elasticity of 0.8 used by Auerbach and Kotlikoff (1987). I assumed that $\alpha = 0.5$, which implies an (uncompen-

Table 4 Sensitivity of Long-Run Capital, Consumption, Employment, and Welfare to Changes in Benchmark Parameter Values Case (B), Capital Tax Rate Equal to Zero; Entries Are Percentage Changes from Initial Values

Parameter	Value	Capital	Consumption	Employment	Welfare
σ_p	0.6	32.3	4.2	−2.0	5.5
σ_p	1.0	54.9	7.6	−3.9	10.0
σ	1.0	32.3	4.2	−2.0	5.5
σ	2.0	32.3	4.2	−2.0	5.5
σ	4.0	32.3	4.2	−2.0	5.5
α	0.5	32.3	4.2	−2.0	5.5
α	5	28.1	−1.3	−6.3	2.5
α	50	26.2	−3.8	−8.2	1.2

sated) labor supply elasticity of 0.11 at benchmark values. Most studies estimate this elasticity to be zero or slightly negative (see Borjas and Heckman (1978)), so this value may be viewed as high. Nevertheless, Table 4 reports results with much higher α values for comparison. I used a time endowment of B (not unity), so that $x = B - u - v$, and chose B so that (4.4) holds at 1985 values. The parameterization and estimation of preferences for goods and leisure, obviously critical for tax problems, is a controversial issue that deserves much more careful treatment.

The learning function $G(v)$ was also assigned a constant elasticity form: $G(v) = Dv^{\gamma}$. I used $\gamma = 0.8$, and chose D and the initial learning time allocation v so that (4.2) and (4.5) hold. The elasticity estimate 0.8 is slightly higher that the value 0.65 that is implicit in the estimates reported in Rosen (1976).

I am imagining that the allocation described in Table 1 arose under a tax structure with two constant flat-rate taxes on labor and capital income. The actual tax structure involves thousands of taxes, many of them with nonlinear schedules, at the federal, state, and local levels of government. Viewed at close range, the U.S. tax structure is not a pretty sight. Rather than take you through all the details, I will indicate what the main issues are and how I resolved them, and end up with two numbers: a rate of 0.36 on capital income and 0.40 on labor.

First, I consolidated government at all levels into a single fiscal authority. This matches the share of 0.21 I use for government spending. It should be understood, then, that by eliminating capital taxation I do not mean something that could be brought about by a single piece of legislation, like eliminating the federal tax on corporate profits. I mean the far more utopian experiment of eliminating capital taxes at *all* levels. To arrive at these two national tax rates, under this assumption, I calculated the total revenues at all levels from capital taxation in 1985 and divided by total capital income. This produced an estimate of $\theta = 0.36$ for the tax rate, assumed constant, on capital. I imputed all other taxes to labor, an assumption suited to a balanced path, where consumption and labor income taxes are equivalent. Since total tax receipts were 0.36 times NNP, this implies an average tax rate of 0.36 on labor as well.

This flat rate assumption is about right—the U.S. tax structure has never been nearly as progressive as people think. But there is some progressivity in the personal income tax, due mainly to the personal exemption: one is permitted to deduct a fixed dollar amount from one's income in calculating one's tax base. A crude way to take this kind of progressivity into account is to think of all labor income as being taxed at a higher rate and then to treat the difference between labor income tax revenues at this higher rate and actual revenues and a lump-sum rebated back to consumers. I will take the labor tax rate to be $\tau = 0.40$, so that the implicit transfer as a fraction of NNP is $(0.40\text{–}0.36)(0.76) = 0.03$ (where 0.76 is labor's share).[8] Since explicit transfers are 0.15 times NNP, the transfers I assume are $b = 0.18$.

To summarize this discussion, we think of an economy in which real output and the stock of physical capital are growing at an annual rate of 0.029, 0.014 due to population growth and 0.015 to human capital accumulation. Fiscal policy in this system is described by four numbers: government consumption is 0.21 and lump-sum consumption transfers to households are 0.18, both expressed as fractions of NNP. The tax rates on labor and capital income are 0.4 and 0.36 respectively. In this situation, we think of reducing the tax rate on capital and keeping both government activity variables g/h and b/h fixed, as ratios to human capital. Let the system adjust to the new balanced path, with the labor tax rate adjusting so as to maintain budget balance in the sense of (4.6).

The long-run consequences of this change are displayed in Table 2, for the capital stock, and Table 3, for other variables. (In all of these tables,

8. Joines (1981), Sealer (1982) and Barro and Sahasakul (1983) provide careful studies of average marginal federal tax rates in the U.S. My figure of 0.40 for the marginal overall labor income tax rate is loosely based on these.

"percentage change" means a log difference times 100.) The columns of Table 2 refer to different assumptions about labor supply. The first column (case (A)) refers to a case in which human capital growth is exogenous (so $v = 0$ and equations (4.2) and (4.5) can be discarded) and labor is inelastically supplied, so u and x are constant and equation (4.4) can be discarded. Then the tax rate τ determines, via (4.3), the capital-effective-labor ratio z on the balanced path. Given g, one can determine the necessary tax θ on labor given any tax τ on capital. Under these assumptions, labor income is a pure rent, and can be taxed at any level without allocative consequences. This is exactly the first case studied in Chamley (1981).

To calculate the second column of Table 2 (case (B)), I retain the assumption that the growth rate ν is given exogeneously (so (4.2) and (4.5) will again not be used) but let labor supply be elastic. Then (4.3) again determines the capital-effective-labor ratio, but the marginal condition (4.4) must be used to determine capital k and labor supply u separately. In this case, the determination of the labor income tax rate θ that will maintain budget balance will not be trivial, and as this tax is varied there will be consequences for resource allocation and welfare that cannot be determined from the marginal condition for capital alone.

For case (C), the last columns of Table 2, I let the growth rate of human capital be endogenously determined, so that the full system (4.1)–(4.6) is needed. In this case neither the growth rate ν of the economy nor the capital-labor ratio z can be determined from the marginal condition (4.3) alone. The growth rate ν implied by each capital tax rate is given in the last column of the table.[9]

9. For comparison, Summers (1981) estimates that the replacement of a tax rate of 0.5 on capital income and 0.2 on labor with a consumption tax would induce a 23 percent increase in the long-run capital stock, using a substitution elasticity of $\sigma_p = 0.5$. (See the last column of Table 2, p. 541.) Auerbach and Kotlikoff (1987) estimate that the replacement of a tax rate of 0.15 on all income with a consumption tax would induce a 19 percent increase in the long-run capital stock, with $\sigma_p = 0.8$. (See Table 5.4, p. 69.) Roughly speaking, Summers' estimate is the overlapping generations counterpart to my Table 2, column (A) estimate, and Auerbach and Kotlikoff's can be compared to my Table 2, column (B). I say "roughly speaking" because there are so many ways in which these models differ from mine (and from each other), but even rough comparisons are useful in making the point that the estimated effects of capital tax reductions ace of the same order of magnitude in overlapping generations models and in dynasty models when the technology is parameterized is similar ways. Of course, the dynasty models of Chamley (1981) and Judd (1987) would produce estimates identical to mine if parameterized in the same way, as my formulation is adapted directly from theirs.

The capital accumulation effects listed under case (A) in Table 2 can just be read off the production function: none of the other equations is needed. Under case (B), there are labor supply effects of the tax changes as well, but they do not much affect the results on capital accumulation. Under case (C), the system's growth rate becomes endogenous, but one can see that the effects of this change are quantitatively trivial. For this reason, Table 3 reports allocation effects for cases (A) and (B) only.

The consumption effects in Table 3 reflect the importance of diminishing returns. In case (B), about half of the potential increase of 4.2 percent is achieved if capital tax rates are reduced from the current 0.36 to 0.25. The required increases in the labor tax rate are modest: Even the complete elimination of capital taxation increases the labor tax rate only to 0.46. Of course, this reflects the much larger share of labor as well as the assumed leisure elasticity.

Table 4 indicates the sensitivity of these results to changes in the assumed values of the critical elasticities. Substitution in production is evidently crucial. With a Cobb-Douglas technology ($\sigma_p = 1$) the capital accumulation effects are far greater than under my assumption of $\sigma_p = 0.6$. The coefficient of risk aversion σ, in constrast, matters not at all in determining the balanced path allocation. The leisure elasticity α is also important. As this elasticity increases, so does the distortion entailed in shifting taxes to labor and the welfare effects are correspondingly reduced. Though the Table does not show this, for $\alpha = 5$ or 50, balanced path welfare is not maximized at $\tau = 0$. This does not, of course, contradict Chamley's theorem, but it does illustrate the fact that one cannot give tax regimes a welfare ranking on the basis of their balanced path rankings alone.

To sum up these results, Table 2 certainly provides a resounding confirmation of Feldstein's and Boskin's original intuition. Changes in the tax structure can have enormous effects on capital accumulation. Even under my conservative assumption on capital-labor substitution, capital stock after this hypothetical reform is 32 percent larger than it would have been without any tax change. With a Cobb-Douglas technology, the increase would be 55 percent.

The effects on consumption and welfare reported in Table 3 are also substantial. The consumption effects in case (A) exceed 6 percent—an enormous gain in welfare. With elastic labor supply, the consumption effects are smaller, but increased leisure makes up most of the difference: the welfare effects under case (B) are close to those in case (A). Consumption and capital accumulation effects of similar magnitude have been reported in every study of the last ten years: They do not depend on the details of the particular formulation I am using.

Indeed, they do not depend on anything much beyond the marginal productivity for capital condition (4.3) and the curvature of the production function. Though I have explored other possibilities on the labor side of the model, neither leads to substantial modification of the conclusions one reaches from the simplest model I have called case (A). One could have worked out the key features of these results with pencil and paper in a few minutes!

5. Transitional Dynamics

The balanced growth analysis of the last section gives a good description of the long run allocative consequences of a shift to the efficient tax rate of zero on income from capital, but there is a good deal more to the story than can be told on the basis of balanced path comparisons alone. First, the implication that the efficient long-run capital tax is zero does not uniquely define long-run fiscal policy, since one needs to know the efficient long-run debt level. The comparisons of the last section finesse this issue by taking long run debt service to be unchanged from its original value. Second, and I think quantitatively more crucial, the passage from the current balanced path to an efficient one, since it involves a large increase in the level of physical relative to human capital, will involve a long period of reduced consumption or reduced leisure or both, partially offsetting the welfare gains enjoyed on the new balanced path. How can these considerations be quantified?

I will set up a notation for explaining what I think a sharp answer to this question would be, which will then serve as well for discussing various approximations. Let τ denote a complete description of a tax structure, implying some path $(c_\tau(t), x_\tau(t))$ for consumption of goods and leisure. Let ζ be a fraction that will serve as a compensating consumption supplement, and define the indirect utility function V by:

$$V(\zeta, \tau) = \int_0^\infty e^{-(\rho-\lambda)t} U[(1+\zeta)c_\tau(t), x_\tau(t)]\,dt.$$

Then $V(\zeta, \tau)$ is interpreted as the utility the consumer enjoys under the tax structure τ if he receives, in addition, a non-tradeable consumption supplement $\zeta c_\tau(t)$ at each date t. Then if τ_r denotes the Ramsey tax structure and τ_0 the existing one, I will define the unique, positive value of ζ that satisfies $V(\zeta, \tau_0) = V(0, \tau_t)$ as the welfare gain of moving from the existing structure to the Ramsey structure.

Neither I nor anyone else has calculated this number ζ for the model I am using (though all the ingredients for doing so are in Table 1). But from calculations that have been carried out with closely related models, I think we can get a good idea of what ζ has to be. I will begin with the inelastic labor supply version of the model, the version I called case (A) in the last section, which corresponds very closely to a model studied in Chamley (1981). In this model, the labor income tax is effectively a lump sum tax, so the timing of debt does not matter and the only distortion arises from capital income taxation. In this situation, both the existing and Ramsey tax structures can be characterized by a single number τ, interpreted as the *constant* tax rate on capital, where the Ramsey case corresponds to $\tau = 0$ and the existing case to $\tau = 0.36$. The welfare estimate we seek is then the solution ζ to $V(\zeta, \tau) = V(0, 0)$ when $\tau = 0.36$. Or, if we think of solving this equation for the welfare gain as a function of the tax rate, $\zeta = g(\tau)$, we seek $g(0.36)$.

In dealing with approximations to this welfare gain, I will assume without proof that with fiscal variables constant, or eventually constant, the system converges to a balanced path satisfying conditions (4.1)–(4.6) of the last section. Uzawa (1965) shows that the first-best allocation in a very similar model has this property, provided the learning technology G is so restricted as to keep the system from growing too fast. Under this assumption, Tables 2 and 3 describe the long-run behavior of the economy.

For stable systems, Bernheim (1981) provides a very useful formula for the derivative $V_\tau(0, 0)$ of utility with respect to the tax rate. The derivative $V_\zeta(0, 0)$ is readily calculated, so we can use

$$g(\tau) \approx g'(0)\,\tau = -V_\tau(0, 0)/V_\zeta(0, 0)\tau$$

as an approximation to the welfare cost $g(\tau)$, valid for small distortions.

Applying Bernheim's formula to the problem at hand yields:

$$g(\tau) \approx \left(\frac{\xi}{\xi + \delta}\right) \Delta \ln\left(c(0)\right) + \left(\frac{\delta}{\xi + \delta}\right) \Delta \ln\left(c(\infty)\right), \qquad (5.1)$$

where $\xi = \rho + \sigma\nu - (\lambda + \nu)$, δ is the annual rate of convergence of capital to its post-tax-reform steady state, $\Delta \ln (c(0))$ is the initial percentage change in consumption, and $\Delta \ln (c(\infty))$ is the percentage difference in long-run consumption. The latter difference, for $\tau = 0.36$, is just the last row of Table 3, the long-run welfare measure we have already calculated. Thus Bernheim's formula expresses the overall welfare gain as a simple weighted average of the immediate welfare effect and the ultimate, long-run effect.

To use this formula, we need an estimate of the immediate effect $\Delta \ln(c(0))$. From Table 2, when τ goes from 0.36 to zero, capital will expand by 34 percent, or $(0.34)k_0$. If the fraction δ of this adjustment occurs in the first year, then $\delta(0.34)k_0$ must be added to net investment, which is to say, this amount must be subtracted from initial consumption. The percentage effect on consumption is therefore approximately $\Delta \ln(c(0)) = -\delta(0.34)k_0/c_0 = -(1.14)\delta$, using Table 1 benchmark values. Inserting all of this information into (5.1), we find:

$$g(0.36) = \frac{\delta}{\xi + \delta}[0.067 - (1.14)\xi] = \frac{\delta}{\xi + \delta}(0.027),$$

where the second equality uses the estimate $\xi = 0.035$ which is implied by Table 1 values.

According to this estimate, then, the welfare gain from eliminating capital taxation has a *maximal* value of 2.7 percent of consumption, occurring when the adjustment to the new balanced path is very rapid. Of course, the adjustment implied by very large δ implies infeasibly low initial consumption levels; this experiment strains this local approximation beyond its limits. Chamley (1981) provides an estimate of $\delta = 0.09$ for the actual adjustment rate, using Table 1 parameter values. With $\xi = 0.035$, this implies a welfare estimate of $g(0.36) = 0.019$, or 1.9 percent of consumption.

The Bernheim formula is useful, I think, because it provides such a clear picture both of the way long-run gains and short-run costs are traded off against each other in the kind of tax reform we are assessing, and of the factors on which the terms of this tradeoff depend. Chamley (1981) provides an alternative expansion which, for Table 1 parameter values, yields the estimate $g(\tau) = (0.0322)\tau^2$, so that $g(0.36) = 0.00417$, or only about one-fourth of the estimate obtained using the Berheim formula. Chamley also provides a correction factor for large tax changes, which modifies this estimate to $g(0.36) = (1.76)(0.00417) = 0.0073$, or seven-tenths of a percentage point. I do not have sufficient understanding of the two expansion methods to reconcile these differences, though it would appear to me that

Bernheim's formula as I have applied it overstates the welfare gain for large tax changes (by understating the initial cost).[10] In summary, in the inelastic labor supply case (A), it appears that the welfare gains reported for balanced paths in Table 3 overstate the actual gains by a factor of five, or perhaps more.

As soon as one admits an elastic labor supply, the situation becomes much more complex. From Table 3, one can see that long-run consumption increases are smaller with elastic labor supply, and while this is partially offset by an increased consumption of leisure, the long-run gain in welfare is about 18 percent less. *If* the system were to move to the long-run Ramsey structure at once, increasing θ to 0.46 and decreasing τ to zero, and *if* the present value of tax receipts under both structures were the same, I would expect the overall welfare gain to be reduced about 18 percent as well.

But neither of these two hypotheses is at all likely to be satisfied. From the discussion in Section 3, based on Chamley (1986), the Ramsey structure will surely involve initial heavy taxation of capital combined with an announcement of a future shift to zero taxation. Hence the initial tax on labor income will not have to be raised to anything like its long-run level immediately, and might even be reduced to ease the burden during the transition. The expansions introduced in Judd (1985), (1987) provide an ideal method for assessing the welfare consequences of announcement effects of this kind. By experimenting with different timing possibilities using Judd's method, I think one could find transitional dynamics for the elastic labor case with welfare gains that are closer to the gains in the inelastic labor case than the 18 percent figure implied by Table 3. This would be a much simpler exercise than fully characterizing the Ramsey structure, but I have not carried it out.

Solving for the Ramsey structure would also guarantee that the government's present value budget constraint is satisfied, but this is not ensured in any of the approximations I have discussed or proposed, all of which

10. Chamley uses a second-order expansion taken about a steady state in which capital is untaxed, so that the coefficient of the first-order term τ vanishes. Bernheim uses a first-order expansion taken about the original, taxed steady state. The approximations used by Judd (1985), (1987) and by Laitner (1990) are conceptually the same as Bernheim's. Of course, there is no reason to expect these different approximations to yield the same answer, especially for the enormous change in the tax rate τ that I am analyzing here.

work by first constructing a tax structure for the balanced path and then piecing this structure together with some transitional dynamics. This issue is addressed computationally in a satisfactory and inexpensive way in Auerbach and Kotlikoff (1987). Their method involves proposing a long-run structure, working out the transitional dynamics, and calculating the resulting government debt (or surplus) that will need to be serviced on the balanced path. This debt service is then used to construct a new long-run tax structure, new transitional dynamics are calculated, and so on. Iterating in this way, Auerbach and Kotlikoff arrive at a mutually consistent characterization of a complete, feasible time path of taxes and spending, where the latter is defined to include debt service. Applied to the present model, this would involve iterating on the value of transfer payments, b/h in Table 1. Again, I have not carried this calculation out.

In summary, there is much to be done to obtain a precise estimate of the overall gain in welfare that would result from a switch from the present U.S. tax structure to an efficient, Ramsey structure. On the other hand, there is available a wealth of analytical and computational methods, all developed and applied in realistic settings in the last ten years, for carrying this estimation out. My summary has been limited to crude pencil and paper calculations and extrapolations from existing studies, and so is little more than an advertisement for the more powerful tools that are now at our disposal. Yet I would be most surprised if the application of these methods to the particular problem I have been discussing should produce estimated welfare gains much outside the range 0.75–1.25 percent of consumption.

6. Conclusions

It is impossible to finish an exercise of this sort without accumulating a long list of issues one would like to address more thoroughly. I will mention just two of these, and then sum up.

I introduced human capital accumulation and endogenous growth into the framework used by Chamley (1981) and others because I thought that, as suggested by Rebelo (1987) and Jones and Manuelli (1988), tax changes might alter long-run growth rates as well as long-run equilibrium levels. For the tax changes I considered, this turned out to be true but quantitatively trivial. Roughly speaking, this is because changes in labor taxation affect equally both the cost and the benefit side of the marginal condition governing the learning decision.[11] Certainly one can think of other fiscal changes, for example increased subsidies to schooling, that would affect this margin directly and have potentially large effects on human capital accumulation and long-term growth rates. This was not the subject of my lecture, but it might well be an interesting subject for future research within the framework I have used here.

Second, I have referred to the "efficiency" of such fiscal measures as capital levies and default on government obligations. Within the Ramsey framework as I have applied it, I have no choice: such measures *do* increase efficiency in the sense of reducing the excess burden of taxation. But the time-consistency issue is a very real one, even though I have not addressed it, and there is no point in pretending that, as a practical matter, governments have the ability simultaneously to default on past promises and to issue credible new ones. Serious discussion of the efficient taxation of capital income presupposes a society that is able to commit itself to honoring debt and transfer obligations, and to the avoidance of capital levies, however disguised. This issue is much more important than getting the details of the Ramsey structure just right, and I certainly do not wish my attention to the latter question to suggest otherwise.

I have called this paper an analytical review of "supply-side economics," a term associated in the United States with extravagent claims about the effects of changes in the tax structure on capital accumulation. In a sense, the analysis I have reviewed supports these claims: Under what I view as conservative assumptions, I estimated that eliminating capital income taxation would increase capital stock by about 35 percent. Achieved over a ten-year period, such an increase would more than double the annual growth rate of the U.S. capital stock. Translated into an effect on welfare, this change is much less dramatic, for two main reasons. First, diminishing returns to capital implies that a long-run capital increase of 35 percent translates into a long-run consumption increase of something like 7 percent. Second, such an enormous capital expansion requires a long period of severely reduced consumption before this long-run gain can be enjoyed.

11. King and Rebelo (1989) report somewhat larger effects of income tax rate changes on endogenous growth rates, in a setting in which capital as well as labor is used in the accumulation of human capital.

Taking both these factors into account, I estimated the overall gain in welfare to be around one percent of consumption, or perhaps slightly less.

Now one percent of U.S. consumption is about $30 billion, and we are discussing a flow starting at this level and growing at 3 percent per year in perpetuity. It is about twice the welfare gain that I have elsewhere estimated would result from eliminating a 10 percent inflation, and something like 20 times the gain from eliminating post-war-sized business fluctuations.[12] It is about 10 times the gain Arnold Harberger (1954) once estimated from eliminating all product-market monopolies in the U.S. Quantitative welfare economics, seriously practiced, can be a discouraging business. The supply-side economists, if that is the right term for those whose research I have been discussing, have delivered the largest genuinely free lunch I have seen in 25 years in this business, and I believe we would have a better society if we followed their advice. But capital taxation at the levels we have been discussing is not an issue that can make or break a society, and to understand the main discrepancies in the wealth of nations I think we have to look elsewhere.

As a practicing macroeconomist, I must say that I have greatly enjoyed this excursion into public finance. In my area, those of us who advocate structural modeling of aggregate behavior—accounting for observed behavior in terms of preferences and technology—remain very much on the defensive, accused of scientific utopianism and an excessive fascination with mathematical technique. How refreshing it is to spend some time in the company of a group of applied economists who simply take for granted the desirability of using (and extending) the powerful methods of dynamic general equilibrium theory to gain a deeper understanding of policy issues. This research demonstrates its respect for the achievements of past economists by building on these achievements, not by preserving them in the amber of methodological and substantive orthodoxy. The result is not conflict between those interested in new techniques and those interested in issues of policy but a unity that delivers the kind of hard, productively debatable results on real questions that traditional macroeconomics has so clearly failed to deliver. The attraction of neoclassical economies is not that it is pretty—though it can be—but that, given half a chance, it works.

12. See Lucas (1981) and Lucas (1987), ch. 3.

References

Atkinson, Anthony B. and Joseph E. Stiglitz. (1980). *Lectures on Public Economics*, New York: McGraw-Hill.

Auerbach, Alan J. and Laurence J. Kotlikoff. (1987). *Dynamic Fiscal Policy*. Cambridge, England; Cambridge University Press.

Barro, Robert J. (1974), "Are Government Bonds Net Wealth?" *Journal of Political Economy* 82, 1095–1117.

Barro, Robert J. and Chaipat Sahasakul. (1983). "Measuring the Average Marginal Tax Rate from the Individual Income Tax." *Journal of Business* 56, 419–452.

Bernheim, B. Douglas. (1981). "A Note on Dynamic Tax Incidence." *Quarterly Journal of Economics* 96, 705–723.

Borjas, George J. and James J. Heckman. (1978). "Labor Supply Estimates for Public Policy Evaluation." *Proceedings of the Thirty-first Annual Meeting of the I. R. R. A.* 320–331.

Boskin Michael J. (1978). "Taxation, Saving, and the Rate of Interest." *Journal of Political Economy* 86, S3–S27.

Brock, William A. and Stephen J. Turnovsky. (1981). "The Analysis of Macroeconomic Policies in Perfect Foresight Equilibrium." *International Economic Review* 22, 179–209.

Chamley, Christophe P. (1981). "The Welfare Cost of Capital Income Taxation in a Growing Economy." *Journal of Political Economy* 89, 468–496.

Chamley, Christophe P. (1986). "Optimal Taxation of Capital Income in General Equilibrium with Infinite Lives." *Econometrica* 54, 607–622.

Diamond, Peter A. (1965). "National Debt in a Neoclassical Growth Model." *American Economic Review* 55, 1126–1150.

Feldstein, Martin S. (1978). "The Welfare Cost of Capital Income Taxation." *Journal of Political Economy* 86, S29–S51.

Fischer, Stanley. (1980). "Dynamic Inconsistency, Cooperation, and the Benevolent Dissembling Government." *Journal of Economic Dynamics and Control* 2, 93–107.

Hall, Robert E. (1971). "The Dynamic Effects of Fiscal Policy in an Economy with Foresight." *Review of Economic Studies* 38, 229–244.

Harberger, Arnold C. (1954). "Monopoly and Resource Allocation." *American Economic Review* 44, 77–87.

Harberger, Arnold C. (1966). "Efficiency Effects of Taxes on Income from Capital," in Marian Krzyzaniak, ed., *Effects of the Corporate Income Tax*. Detroit: Wayne State University Press.

Joines, Douglas H. (1981). "Estimates of Effective Marginal Tax Rates on Factor Incomes." *Journal of Business* 54, 191–226.

Jones, Larry E. and Rodolfo Manuelli. (1988). "A Model of Optimum Equilibrium Growth." Northwestern University working paper.

Jorgenson, Dale W. and Kun-Young Yun. (1990). "Tax Reform and U.S. Economic Growth." *Journal of Political Economy* (forthcoming).

Judd, Kenneth L. (1985). "Short-Run Analysis of Fiscal Policy in a Simple Perfect Foresight Model." *Journal of Political Economy* 93, 298–319.

Judd, Kenneth L. (1987). "The Welfare Cost of Factor Taxation in a Perfect Foresight Model." *Journal of Political Economy* 95, 675–709.

Kehoe, Timothy J. and David K. Levine. (1985). "Comparative Statics and Perfect Foresight in Infinite Horizon Economies." *Econometrica* 53, 433–453.

King, Robert G. and Sergio Rebelo. (1989). "Public Policy and Economic Growth: Developing Neoclassical Implications." University of Rochester working paper.

Kydland, Finn E. and Edward C. Prescott. (1977). "Rules Rather than Discretion: The Inconsistency of Optimal Plans." *Journal of Political Economy* 85, 473–491.

Laitner, John. (1990). "Tax Changes and Phase Diagrams for an Overlapping Generations Model," *Journal of Political Economy* (forthcoming).

Lucas, Robert E., Jr. (1969). "Labor-Capital Substitution in U.S. Manufacturing," in Arnold C. Harberger and Martin J. Bailey, eds., *The Taxation of Income from Capital*. Washington: The Brookings Institution.

Lucas, Robert E., Jr. (1981). "Discussion of: Stanley Fischer, 'Towards an Understanding of the Costs of Inflation: II'." *Carnegie-Rochester Conference Series on Public Policy* 15, 43–51.

Lucas, Robert E., Jr. (1987). *Models of Business Cycles*. Oxford: Basil Blackwell.

Lucas, Robert E., Jr. and Nancy L. Stokey. (1983). "Optimal Fiscal and Monetary Policy in an Economy Without Capital." *Journal of Monetary Economics* 12, 55–93.

Miller, Merton H. and Charles W. Upton. (1974). *Macroeconomics: A Neoclassical Introduction*. Homewood, Illinois: Irwin.

Mirrlees, James A. (1971). "An Exploration in the Theory of Optimal Income Taxation." *Review of Economic Studies* 38, 175–208.

Muller, Walter J., III and Michael Woodford. (1988). "Determinacy of Equilibrium in Stationary Economies with Both Finite and Infinite Lived Consumers." *Journal of Economic Theory* 46, 255–290.

Ramsey, Frank P. (1927). "A Contribution to the Theory of Taxation." *Economic Journal* 37, 47–61.

Rebelo, Sergio. (1987). "Long Run Policy Analysis and Long Run Growth." University of Rochester working paper.

Rosen, Sherwin. (1976). "A Theory of Life Earnings." *Journal of Political Economy* 84, S45–S67.

Seater, John J. (1982). "Marginal Federal Personal and Corporate Income Tax Rates in the U.S., 1909–1975." *Journal of Monetary Economics* 10, 361–381.

Solow, Robert M. (1956). "A Contribution to the Theory of Economic Growth." *Quarterly Journal of Economics* 70, 65–94.

Summers, Lawrence H. (1981). "Capital Taxation and Accumulation in a Life Cycle Growth Model." *American Economic Review* 71, 533–544.

Swan, Trevor W. (1956). "Economic Growth and Capital Accumulation." *Economic Record* 66, 334–361.

Uzawa, Hirofumi. (1965). "Optimum Technical Change in an Aggregative Model of Economic Growth." *International Economic Review* 6, 18–31.

— 15 —

Review of Milton Friedman and Anna J. Schwartz, *A Monetary History of the United States, 1867–1960*

1.

A contribution to monetary economics reviewed again after 30 years—quite an occasion! Keynes's *General Theory* has certainly had reappraisals on many anniversaries, and perhaps Patinkin's *Money, Interest and Prices.* I cannot think of any others. Milton Friedman and Anna Schwartz's *A Monetary History of the United States* has become a classic. People are even beginning to quote from it out of context in support of views entirely different from any advanced in the book, echoing the compliment—if that is what it is—so often paid to Keynes.

Why do people still read and cite *A Monetary History*? One reason, certainly, is its beautiful time series on the money supply and its components, extended back to 1867, painstakingly documented and conveniently presented. Such a gift to the profession merits a long life, perhaps even immortality. But I think it is clear that *A Monetary History* is much more than a collection of useful time series. The book played an important—perhaps even decisive—role in the 1960s' debates over stabilization policy between Keynesians and monetarists. It organized nearly a century of U.S. macroeconomic evidence in a way that has had great influence on subsequent statistical and theoretical research. Perhaps most of all, *A Monetary History* served the purpose that any narrative history must serve: It told a coherent story of important events, and told it well.

Journal of Monetary Economics 34, no. 1 (August 1994): 5–16.

2.

A Monetary History has a very simple structure. There is a brief introductory chapter, announcing the aim of providing an account of 'the stock of money in the United States' and of 'the reflex influence that the stock of money exerted on the course of events'. There follow eleven chronologically ordered chapters, each of which treats a subperiod of the 1867–1960 period covered by the book. In each of these chapters, the behavior of the money supply (*M*2) and of its proximate determinants is described. Contemporary movements in real income and the general price level are also described in each chapter. These facts are set out in a similar verbal and graphic format each time, and then the main economic and political events that determined their behavior are discussed in a straightforward narrative. Chapter 13 concludes with a brief summary of the empirical generalizations that emerge from the study. (Some of these generalizations might better have been announced in Chapter 1, as the organizing principles that underlie the narrative.)

If the reader has not already anticipated it, he learns in this summing up that the history of the U.S. money stock and its effects on other variables is, for Friedman and Schwartz, a complete macroeconomic history of the United States over these nine decades. Every major depression and movement of prices and interest rates has been accounted for, every policy decision seen by the authors as important has been reviewed, and where policies have been found deficient, alternatives have been proposed and their likely consequences assessed. In place of a ninety-year period that in fact included many depressions and episodes of both deflation and inflation, one is given a vision of the way this portion of our history might have evolved, with stable prices and smoothly growing real output, and of the policies—well within the limits of the powers given to the monetary authority by the Federal Reserve Act of 1914—that would have achieved this outcome.

A Monetary History constructs this vision through the consistent application to specific historical events of two simple principles. The first of these is the hypothesis of long-run monetary neutrality. It is implicit in Friedman and Schwartz's account that there is a trend path of real output, governed by forces that are not examined in the book, which has the property that neither its level nor its growth rate is affected by monetary policies. This secular path is stable: the economy returns to its trend behavior after displacements. The second central hypothesis is a short-run nonneutrality of money. Fluctuations in *M*2 induce spending fluctuations and these, in the face of nominal price rigidities, induce real output fluctuations. Again, no effort is made to elucidate or explain the nature of these price rigidities, except to say that they are transient (and so reconcilable with long-run neutrality). Little is said about the details of the economy's response to money changes, beyond the repeated insistence that monetary tightness and ease cannot be gauged by looking at interest rates. The empirical connection one observes is between *M*2 and nominal and real spending directly, with neither interest rates nor the composition of expenditures playing important roles.

All the aggregative positive and normative analysis in the book is a direct and simple consequence of these two principles. On the positive side, every depression is accounted for, as much as it can be, by prior and contemporary contractions in money. Of course, other sources of short-run instability are also active, and indeed many such possibilities are discussed in some detail, but monetary shocks form the consistent thread in the story, and it is an explicit conclusion that such shocks play the key role in all major fluctuations.

In arriving at this conclusion, no claim is made that *M*2 fluctuations are exogenous (a term never used in the book), although it is argued in specific instances that particular *M*2 movements cannot be seen as response to real events. On the contrary, a main theme of the book is the examination of the way governmental and private forces interact to determine the broad money supply. A few contractions are directly attributable to decisions by the monetary authority. Others are attributed to banking panics and flights to currency. The only consistent claim is that in every case the monetary authority *could* have prevented the contraction from occurring, either by avoiding its own mistake or by the timely offsetting of events in the private banking system, and that such action would have prevented or greatly mitigated the associated depression.

Given this account of observed depressions, the normative analysis is straightforward: The monetary authority has always had the ability to eliminate *M*2 instability, and it should have done so. In every instance, Friedman and Schwartz provide a detailed, operational account of how and when actions could have been taken that would have achieved this outcome. They do not discuss the possibility that monetary variability might have had a constructive role to play in offsetting nonmonetary sources of real instability. Whether this is because they believe that such active stabilization policies would be welfare-reducing, or that we do not have the knowledge to carry such policies out, or simply that they viewed this question as outside the scope of the study, they do not say.

3.

One level on which one can try to evaluate *A Monetary History*—and it is a level on which the book clearly invites a response—is to ask oneself whether one would follow its normative advice if one were in a position of monetary authority. On this level, I will say that I find the argument of *A Monetary History* wholly convincing. I think Friedman and Schwartz are right to focus on the avoidance of the really major macroeconomic disasters of the past as the main responsibility of current monetary policy. I find their diagnosis of the 1929–33 downturn persuasive and indeed, uncontested by serious alternative diagnoses, and remain deeply impressed with their success in explaining the remarkable events of these four years by applying the same principles they apply to lesser contractions. I do not believe our understanding of business cycle dynamics is adequate to guide any subtler monetary policy than the smoothing of the money supply (and disregard of interest rate movements) that Friedman and Schwartz argue would have avoided past disasters. If I ever go to Washington for some reason other than viewing cherry blossoms, I will pack my copy of *A Monetary History* and leave the rest of my library—well, most of it—at home.

These are my opinions on *A Monetary History* as a manual on the use of U.S. monetary history as a guide to macroeconomic policy-making. They are certainly opinions on which reasonable and competent economists may disagree: These are not issues resolved by theorems or hypothesis tests. To persuade me to change my opinions, however, a competitor to Friedman and Schwartz will need to apply his preferred principles to U.S. monetary history—certainly including the 1930s—and show that they yield an equally coherent analysis of past events and equally operational guidelines for policies likely to improve on past performance. This is a tall order.

A Monetary History is full of numbers, but there are many quantitative questions to which its model-free approach cannot provide answers. On the Great Contraction, for example, Friedman and Schwartz conclude (p. 301):

> Prevention or moderation of the decline in the stock of money, let alone the substitution of monetary expansion, would have reduced the contraction's severity and almost as certainly its duration. The contraction might still have been relatively severe. But it is hardly conceivable that money income could have declined by over one-half and prices by over one-third in the course of four years if there had been no decline in the stock of money.

This is not a verbal summary of tables describing the results of a numerical simulation; it *is* the simulation. Certainly Friedman and Schwartz are to be commended, not criticized, for the scholarly caution that marks this passage and the entire book. On the other hand, such conclusions obviously leave a good deal of room for disagreement over the sufficiency of smooth money growth as an antidepression policy.

One may be convinced by Friedman and Schwartz's account that it was well within the abilities of U.S. monetary authorities to prevent the occurence of contractions in the money supply, and that had this been done, depressions would have been much less severe. But by *how much* would the decline in real output to 1933 have been reduced had such a monetary policy been pursued? In general, what would the variance in real output growth have been over the 90-year period under study had money growth been smooth? What would the variance in real output growth have been over this period if resources had been allocated efficiently, in the face of unavoidable real shocks of various kinds? In order to conclude that smooth monetary policy is all the stabilization policy we need to have, we want to know the answers to quantitative questions like these.

There is, then, a second level on which the contribution of *A Monetary History* can be assessed. The book does not offer an explicit model of the economy, but its narrative account rests on the rigorous application of few simple economic principles. Are these principles useful as a starting point or guide to the development of a model that could provide answers to questions like those I have raised in the last paragraph? Or is it more promising to start from scratch, on some other basis? (Either answer to this question is obviously consistent with the opinion that familiarity with *A Monetary History* would come in handy in Washington.) Nothing in *A Monetary History* suggests that Friedman and Schwartz had any interest in explicit macroeconomic modeling, but I think it is clear that they viewed their work as providing a scientific foundation on which future economists could build [as they themselves did in Friedman and Schwartz (1982)]. The extent to which they succeeded in doing so has been controversial from the beginning.

4.

At the time *A Monetary History* appeared, many macroeconomists believed that simulations of Keynesian macroeconometric models were capable of providing accurate, quantitative answers to questions about the effects of alternative stabilization policies, or that improved versions of these models would soon be able to do so. All of these models incorporated price rigidities of one sort or another, and so were consistent with the short-run nonneutrality of money that is at the center of Friedman and Schwartz's account. But monetary shocks were assigned no special importance by these models (or, as the authors of the models would have put it, by the data). Thus the Adelman and Adelman (1959) simulations of the early Klein–Goldberger (1955) model showed that income fluctuations in that model were almost entirely attributable to shocks to various components of private spending or, as we would say today, to preference and technology shocks. I have no doubt that this feature continued to obtain in all later Keynesian models.

Within the Keynesian tradition, then, the presumption was that an economy could drift into depression for all kinds of reasons. No emphasis was placed on identifying a single causal factor in depressions, and in any case there would be little hope of reducing the impact of changes in factors like 'consumer confidence' at their source. From this point of view, the appropriate stabilizing response did not depend crucially on the exact nature of the disturbance that set off a particular downturn: Massive open market operations would have been useful in 1930; so, too, would have been a large-scale program of public works.

When *A Monetary History* was published, in 1963, it did not stimulate a useful debate over the relative merits of these different approaches to stabilization policy. Friedman and Schwartz simply ignored contemporary econometric developments (although I take the reference on p. 102 to 'the absence of a tested theory of cyclical movements' as oblique criticism) and, in general, treated what they termed 'the Keynesian Revolution in academic economic thought' (p. 626) as a minor event, responsible mainly for a temporary lapse of attention to monetary policy. Keynesian model builders returned the compliment and ignored *A Monetary History.* [James Tobin's thoughtful (1965) review article is an exception, but Tobin accepted *A Monetary History* on its own terms, and avoided comparing Friedman and Schwartz's approach to that of contemporary model builders. His dissatisfaction with Friedman and Schwartz's treatment of the interest elasticity of money demand, for example, was shared by monetarists like Allan Meltzer and Karl Brunner, and did not raise more general issues of method that divided Keynesians and monetarists at that time.] At about the same time, of course, Friedman and Meiselman (1963) articulated their skepticism about models based on 'autonomous spending' shocks. Later, Friedman (1968) emphasized the inconsistency of these models with long-run monetary neutrality, and explained why he believed neutrality must obtain in any reasonable general equilibrium view of the long-run behavior of the economy. These direct attacks demanded (and got) a response from the opposition, but *A Monetary History* is content to stand on its own merits and leave it to others to draw comparisons with alternative approaches.

As everyone knows, the Keynesian macroeconometric models fell on hard times in the 1970s, when inflation exposed the deficiencies in their treatment of monetary neutrality. This research line has permanently altered our view of what macroeconomics can hope to achieve, but the models themselves now seem hopelessly crude and dated. As Fair (1992) observes, modern neo-Keynesians steer very clear of the Keynesian econometric tradition and of quantitative issues in general, contenting themselves with small-scale, qualitative models that illustrate various logical possibilities. The narrative approach taken by Friedman and Schwartz has proved more durable: In a two-volume collection of recent papers entitled *New Keynesian Economics* [Mankiw and Romer (1991)], Keynes's name does not appear in an index that contains 17 references to Friedman!

5.

In the 1970s, a number of explicit models were developed that were designed to reconcile the two neutrality principles on which Friedman and Schwartz built and to capture the central importance Friedman and Schwartz assigned to monetary instability. These models all assumed some form of nominal price rigidity, in order to obtain monetary non-neutrality in the short run, but did so in such a way that, using the principle of rational expectations, neutrality in the long run was preserved. All of these models were consistent, in a general way, with Friedman and Schwartz's accounts of depressions in the period they studied. Moreover, because of the long-run neutrality they embodied, all of them were consistent with the breakdown of empirical inflation–unemployment tradeoffs that occurred during the inflation of the 1970s. Thus it seemed that the principles underlying the analysis in *A Monetary History* could be used as the basis for econometric models that were as explicit as the Keynesian alternatives and empirically superior as well.

Though these rational expectations models all are consistent with the Friedman and Schwartz neutrality principles and with monetary shocks as the central factor in business cycles, not all of them carry the normative implication that the best monetary policy is perfectly smooth growth. This conclusion depends critically on the details of the way price rigidities are modeled. In the illustrative model of Lucas (1972), all exchange occurs in competitive markets and the *only* source of price rigidity is the limited information available to goods suppliers. In this context, smooth monetary policy leads to efficient resource allocation, even in the face of nonmonetary shocks. On the other hand, in models such as Fischer (1977), Phelps and Taylor (1977), Taylor (1979), and Mankiw (1985), in which the rigidity of prices is attributed to nominally set contracts or to costly price setting by firms, there is no presumption that simply removing monetary variability will result in a system that responds efficiently to other shocks. Though it is now clear that the two neutrality principles used by Friedman and Schwartz can be reconciled, the question of the appropriate conduct of monetary policy remains unresolved. I do not see how it can be resolved without better theories of price rigidity than we now have available to us.

The new element introduced in these rational expectations models was the distinction between anticipated changes in money, predicted to be neutral, and unanticipated changes that were predicted to have real effects. Of course, the particular conditional expectation to be identified with 'anticipated' varies with the nature of the assumed price rigidity. The distinction adds little to Friedman and Schwartz's account of the 1867–1960 period in the U.S., where every large monetary contraction can reasonably be viewed as unanticipated, but its power in interpreting historical events received striking demonstrations in Sargent's (1986) studies of the disinflations that ended the European hyperinflations and the moderate French inflation of the 1920s. An unqualified association between monetary contractions (in the sense of reductions in the growth rate of money) and real activity would lead one to expect these disinflations to have been associated with major depressions. Sargent's analysis of the political context within which these contractions occurred shows that one can interpret them as anticipated, even though sudden and drastic, and hence reconcile their magnitude with the modesty of the real effects they induced.

Sims (1972) took a very different approach to the study of monetary influences on real activity, also explicitly in debt to Friedman and Schwartz, in his 'Money, Income, and Causality'. Rather than attempting to construct an *economic* model consistent with the principles applied in *A Monetary History,* Sims developed a purely statistical definition of *cause,* related to Granger (1969), in terms of lead–lag relations among variables. Sims's methods provide a test of the hypothesis that movements in money cause (in his sense) real output movements, estimates of a kind of dynamic money multiplier, and estimates of the fraction of output variance, by frequency, that can be accounted for by monetary instability. Sims also argues convincingly that lead–lag considerations play a very similar role, though not formalized in the same way, in Friedman and Schwartz's discussion of what they term the 'independence' of money changes.

More recently, Romer and Romer (1989) have drawn on Friedman and Schwartz's discussion of the independence of monetary changes in a related way, arguing for the use of historical evidence to establish that particular money movements—'natural experiments'—did not occur in response to real events. They credit this method to Friedman and Schwartz, though they do not believe Friedman and Schwartz were successful in applying it, and they, too, argue convincingly that its roots can be traced to *A Monetary History.* For Romer and Romer, exogeneity is a property of a particular realization, while for Sims it is a property of a distribution: the two approaches are not the same. Friedman and Schwartz's discussion of independence is sufficiently unclear that both interpretations are defensible. So, too, is a third, which I prefer, which is that independence as Friedman and Schwartz use the term has nothing to do with statistical exogeneity, but means rather that whatever the sources of monetary contractions may have been, on average or in particular instances, the monetary authorities *could* have maintained *M*2 growth had they chosen to do so. It is independence in this sense that is, I think, conclusively defended by Friedman and Schwartz in detailed analysis of episode after episode.

I do not see any possibility of obtaining answers to normative questions of economic policy by atheoretical, purely statistical means. But the attempt to estimate the fraction of real variability (over a particular period) that can be attributed to monetary instability by atheoretical (Sims) or similar methods that use very little theory [e.g., Shapiro and Watson (1988)] is certainly worth pursuing, and success in this effort would obviously be immensely useful in guiding future theorizing. Certainly admirers of Friedman and Schwartz do not want to be drawn into arguments over whether theory or facts should come first!

6.

If the 1970s were a time of prosperity for the influence of *A Monetary History*, the 1980s must be viewed as at least a mild recession. With Kydland and Prescott's (1982) development of a purely real stochastic growth model that is operational enough to stand comparison to postwar U.S. time series, the role of monetary shocks has faded into the background of professional discussion. The idea that 'money doesn't matter', attributed (unfairly, I think) to Keynesians by Friedman and Schwartz, is now embraced even by many former monetarists. As a result, the last ten years have yielded little ostensible progress in our understanding of the appropriateness of different kinds of monetary policies. Kydland and Prescott showed, and much subsequent research has confirmed, that with the variance of productivity shocks matched to the variance of total factor productivity growth measured as in Solow (1957), such shocks can induce output variability of about the same magnitude as observed in the U.S. in the postwar period, as well as realistic behavior of other variables.

Viewed as positive theory, real business cycle models do not offer a serious alternative to Friedman and Schwartz's monetary account of the early 1930s. The Solow (1957) residuals for the years 1928 through 1933 were: 0.020, −0.043, 0.024, 0.023, 0.011, 0.072! There is no real business cycle model that can map these shocks into anything like the 40% decline in real output and employment that occurred between 1929 and 1933 (nor, indeed, does anyone claim that there is). Even if there were, imagine trying to rewrite the Great Contraction chapter of *A Monetary History* with shocks of this kind playing the role Friedman and Schwartz assign to monetary contractions. What technological or psychological events could have induced such behavior in a large, diversified economy? How could such events have gone unremarked at the time, and remain invisible even to hindsight? It is surely no accident that no one has attempted to apply real business cycle theory to the 90-year period that Friedman and Schwartz studied.

In Kydland and Prescott's original model, and in many (though not all) of its descendants, the equilibrium allocation coincides with the optimal allocation: Fluctuations generated by the model represent an efficient response to unavoidable shocks to productivity. One may thus think of the model not as a positive theory suited to all historical time periods but as a normative benchmark providing a good approximation to events when monetary policy is conducted well and a bad approximation when it is not. Viewed in this way, the theory's relative success in accounting for postwar experience can be interpreted as evidence that postwar monetary policy has resulted in near-efficient behavior, not as evidence that money doesn't matter.

Indeed, the discipline of real business cycle theory has made it more difficult to defend real alternatives to a monetary account of the 1930s than it was 30 years ago. It would be a term-paper-size exercise, for example, to work out the possible effects of the 1930 Smoot–Hawley Tariff in a suitably adapted real business cycle model. By now, we have accumulated enough quantitative experience with such models to be sure that the aggregate effects of such a policy (in an economy with a 5% foreign trade sector before the Act and perhaps a percentage point less after) would be trivial.

Whatever one's views on the potential of real business cycle theory as positive economics, it has taken normative discussion in macroeconomics to a new level, where the efficiency of fluctuating time paths of real variables can be assessed in the same terms we routinely apply to welfare analysis in other areas of economics. Once one *states* the question of efficiency the way Kydland and Prescott did, it is evident that the perfect smoothing of real output growth is not a sensible objective of policy, and that attempts to attain it would entail large welfare costs. (Indeed, with hindsight one wonders why this question was not raised in the context of the old Keynesian models, in which fluctuations are largely driven by shocks to private spending.) Beyond this qualitative observation, it appears that *quantitatively* efficient output fluctuations are of the same order of magnitude as observed fluctuations in the postwar period.

Of course, research on the cyclical role of money has also continued in the last decade. The models in Taylor's (1993) recent monograph capture the effects of monetary forces in an operational, quantitative way. McCallum's (1988, 1990) analyses of base control rules, while not based on any specific economic model, are grounded in a sophisticated understanding of what is useful in recent theoretical research. Models in the style of Kydland and Prescott are now being adapted to the study of nonneutral monetary influences, though it is far from clear how this might best be done and to what extent such modifications will improve empirical performance. The reward from success in this enterprise is very high, since these models admit meaningful normative comparisons of alternative monetary policy rules in a way that earlier models did not. The prospects for success depend, I think, on our willingness to leave the placid and familiar world of postwar quarterly time series and test our ideas against the events of the interwar period.

7.

A Monetary History of the United States is a remarkable and durable achievement of historical and economic scholarship. Friedman and Schwartz used a few basic economic principles to organize nine decades of tremendously varied economic history into a coherent picture, in which the main events become understandable as the effects of identifiable causes. It is a picture that is consistent with our instinct that the depression of the 1930s was an event that should not have happened, a preventable disaster. The role of the Federal Reserve System, the institution that was created to prevent such disasters and that had ample power to do so, is described in enough detail that one can see how disaster can follow from arrangements that grant wide discretion to well-intentioned managers, secure in their business-world sophistication, ignorant of economics and of economic history.

This thirtieth anniversary review has focused on subsequent research that seems to me to have the promise of sharpening the picture provided by *A Monetary History* to the point where questions passed over or given only qualitative answers by Friedman and Schwartz might be answered quantitatively with some reliability. This focus has taken me far into what Tobin (1965) called 'the parochial disputes of monetary theorists'. That is what I get paid to do but, as was Tobin, I find myself relieved to agree with Friedman and Schwartz that we already know enough, and knew enough in 1963, to avoid the major policy mistakes of the interwar period. Whatever may be the influence of *A Monetary History of the United States* on future research, it will stand as the classic statement of these important lessons from our past.

References

Adelman, Irma and Frank L. Adelman, 1959, The dynamic properties of the Klein-Goldberger model, Econometrica 27, 596–625.

Fair, Ray C., 1992, The Cowles Commission approach, real business cycle theories, and new Keynesian economics, National Bureau of Economic Research working paper.

Fischer, Stanley, 1977, Long-term contracts, rational expectations, and the optimal money supply rule, Journal of Political Economy 85, 191–206.

Friedman, Milton, 1968, The role of monetary policy, American Economic Review 58, 1–17.

Friedman, Milton and David Meiselman, 1963, The relative stability of monetary velocity and the investment multiplier in the United States, 1897–1958, in: Commission on Money and Credit, ed., Stabilization policies (Prentice-Hall, Englewood Cliffs, NJ).

Friedman, Milton and Anna J. Schwartz, 1982, Monetary trends in the United States and the United Kingdom (University of Chicago Press for the National Bureau of Economic Research, Chicago, IL).

Granger, Clive W. J., 1969, Investigating causal relations by econometric models and cross-spectral methods, Econometrica 37, 424–438.

Klein, Lawrence A. and Arthur S. Goldberger, 1955, An econometric model of the United States (North-Holland, Amsterdam).

Kydland, Finn E. and Edward C. Prescott, 1982, Time to build and aggregate fluctuations, Econometrica 50, 1345–1370.

Lucas, Robert E., Jr., 1972, Expectations and the neutrality of money, Journal of Economic Theory 4, 103–124.

Mankiw, N. Gregory, 1985, Small menu costs and large business cycles, Quarterly Journal of Economics 100, 529–537.

Mankiw, N. Gregory and David Romer, eds., 1991, New Keynesian economics (MIT Press, Cambridge, MA).

McCallum, Bennett T., 1988, Robustness properties of a rule for monetary policy, Carnegie-Rochester Conference Series on Public Policy 29, 173–203.

McCallum, Bennett T., 1990, Could a monetary base rule have prevented the great depression?, Journal of Monetary Economics 26, 3–26.

Phelps, Edmund S. and John B. Taylor, Stabilizing powers of monetary policy under rational expectations, Journal of Political Economy 85, 163–189.

Romer, Christina D. and David H. Romer, 1989, Does monetary policy matter? A new test in the spirit of Friedman and Schwartz, in Olivier Jean Blanchard and Stanley Fischer, eds., NBER macroeconomics annual 1989 (MIT Press, Cambridge, MA).

Sargent, Thomas J., 1986, Rational expectations and inflation (Harper and Row, New York, NY).

Shapiro, Matthew D. and Mark W. Watson, 1988, Sources of business cycle fluctuations, in: Stanley Fischer, ed., NBER macroeconomics annual 1988 (MIT Press, Cambridge, MA).

Sims, Christopher A., 1972, Money, income, and causality, American Economic Review 62, 540–552.

Solow, Robert M., 1957, Technical change and the aggregate production function, Review of Economics and Statistics 39, 312–320.

Taylor, John B., 1979, Estimation and control of a macroeconomic model with rational expectations, Econometrica 47, 1267–1286.

Taylor, John B., 1993, Macroeconomic policy in a world economy (Norton, New York, NY).

Tobin, James, 1965, The monetary interpretation of history: A review article, American Economic Review 55, 462–485.

— 16 —

Nobel Lecture: Monetary Neutrality

I. Introduction

The work for which I have received the Nobel Prize was part of an effort to understand how changes in the conduct of monetary policy can influence inflation, employment, and production.* So much thought has been devoted to this question and so much evidence is available that one might reasonably assume that it had been solved long ago. But this is not the case: It had not been solved in the 1970s when I began my work on it, and even now this question has not been given anything like a fully satisfactory answer. In this lecture I shall try to clarify what it is about the problem of bringing available evidence to bear on the assessment of different monetary policies that makes it so difficult and to review the progress that has been made toward solving it in the last two decades.

From the beginnings of modern monetary theory, in David Hume's marvelous essays of 1752, *Of Money* and *Of Interest,* conclusions about the effect of changes in money have seemed to depend critically on the way in which the change is effected. In formulating the doctrine that we now call the quantity theory of money, Hume stressed the units-change aspect of changes in the money stock and the irrelevance of such changes to the behavior of rational people.

Journal of Political Economy 104, no. 4 (August 1996): 661–682.

*I thank Nancy Stokey for invaluable discussion and criticism. I am also very grateful for comments from William Brock, John Cochrane, Milton Friedman, Lars Hansen, Anil Kashyap, Randall Kroszner, Bennett McCallum, Casey Mulligan, Sherwin Rosen, Allen Sanderson, Thomas Sargent, John Taylor, Neil Wallace, Warren Weber, and Jörgen Weibull.

> It is indeed evident that money is nothing but the representation of labour and commodities, and serves only as a method of rating or estimating them. Where coin is in greater plenty, as a greater quantity of it is required to represent the same quantity of goods, it can have no effect, either good or bad . . . any more than it would make an alteration on a merchant's books, if, instead of the Arabian method of notation, which requires few characters, he should make use of the Roman, which requires a great many. [*Of Money*, p. 32][1]

Hume returns to this idea that changes in the quantity of money are just units changes in *Of Interest:*

> Were all the gold in England annihilated at once, and one and twenty shillings substituted in the place of every guinea, would money be more plentiful or interest lower? No surely: We should only use silver instead of gold. Were gold rendered as common as silver, and silver as common as copper, would money be more plentiful or interest lower? We may assuredly give the same answer. Our shillings would then be yellow, and our halfpence white, and we should have no guineas. No other difference would ever be observed, no alteration on commerce, manufactures, navigation, or interest, unless we imagine that the colour of the metal is of any consequence. [p. 47]

These are two of Hume's statements of what we now call the quantity theory of money: the doctrine that changes in the number of units of money in circulation will have proportional effects on all prices that are stated in money terms, and no effect at all on anything real, on how much people work or on the goods they produce or consume. Notice, though, that there is something a little magical about the way in which changes in money come about in Hume's examples. All the gold in England gets "annihilated." Elsewhere he asks us to "suppose that, by miracle, every man in Great Britain should have five pounds slipt into his pocket in one night" (p. 51). Money changes in reality do not occur by such means. Is this just a matter of exposition, or should we be concerned about it? This turns out to be a crucial question. In fact, Hume writes as follows:

> When any quantity of money is imported into a nation, it is not at first dispersed into many hands but is confined to the coffers of a few persons,

1. All page references to Hume's essays are taken from Hume (1970). I have left the spelling as in the original and modernized the punctuation.

> who immediately seek to employ it to advantage. Here are a set of manufacturers or merchants, we shall suppose, who have received returns of gold and silver for goods which they sent to Cadiz. They are thereby enabled to employ more workmen than formerly, who never dream of demanding higher wages, but are glad of employment from such good paymasters. . . . [The artisan] carries his money to market, where he finds every thing at the same price as formerly, but returns with greater quantity and of better kinds for the use of his family. The farmer and gardener, finding that all their commodities are taken off, apply themselves with alacrity to raising more. . . . It is easy to trace the money in its progress through the whole commonwealth, where we shall find that it must first quicken the diligence of every individual before it encrease the price of labour. [p. 38]

Symmetrically, Hume believes that a monetary contraction could induce depression:

> There is always an interval before matters be adjusted to their new situation, and this interval is as pernicious to industry when gold and silver are diminishing as it is advantageous when these metals are encreasing. The workman has not the same employment from the manufacturer and merchant, though he pays the same price for everything in the market. The farmer cannot dispose of his corn and cattle, though he must pay the same rent to his landlord. The poverty, and beggary, and sloth which must ensue are easily foreseen. [p. 40]

Hume makes it clear that he does not view his opinions about the initial effects of monetary expansions as major qualifications to the quantity theory, to his view that "it is of no manner of consequence, with regard to the domestic happiness of a state, whether money be in a greater or less quantity" (p. 39). Perhaps he simply did not see that the irrelevance of units changes from which he deduces the long-run neutrality of money has similar implications for the initial reaction to money changes as well. Why, for example, does an early recipient of the new money "find every thing at the same price as formerly"? If everyone understands that prices will ultimately increase in proportion to the increase in money, what force stops this from happening right away? Are people committed, perhaps even contractually, to continue to offer goods at the old prices for a time? If so, Hume does not mention it. Are sellers ignorant of the fact that money has increased and a general inflation is inevitable? But Hume claims that the real consequences of money changes are "easy to trace" and "easily foreseen." If so, why do these consequences occur at all?

These questions do not involve mere matters of detail. Hume has deduced the quantity theory of money by purely theoretical reasoning from "that principle of reason" that people act rationally and that this fact is reflected in market-determined quantities and prices. Consistency surely requires at least an attempt to apply these same principles to the analysis of the *initial* effects of a monetary expansion or contraction. I think the fact is that this is just too difficult a problem for an economist equipped with only verbal methods, even someone of Hume's remarkable powers.

This tension between two incompatible ideas—that changes in money are neutral units changes and that they induce movements in employment and production in the same direction—has been at the center of monetary theory at least since Hume wrote. Though it has not, in my opinion, been fully resolved, important progress has been made on at least two dimensions. The first is a purely theoretical question: Under what assumptions and for what kinds of changes can we expect monetary changes to be *neutral*? (I take this terminology from Don Patinkin's *Money, Interest, and Prices* [1965], the book that introduced so many economists of my cohort to these theoretical issues.) The theoretical equipment we have for sharpening and addressing such questions has been vastly improved since Hume's day, and I shall draw on these improvements below. Of at least equal importance, an enormous amount of evidence on money, prices, and production has been accumulated over the past two centuries, and much fruitful thought has been applied to issues of measurement. In the next section, I shall examine some of this evidence.

II. Evidence

It is hard to tell from the essays what evidence Hume actually had in front of him. Certainly he wrote before systematic data on money supplies were collected anywhere in the world, before the invention of price indexes, and long before the invention of national income and product accounting. His development of the quantity theory was based largely on purely theoretical reasoning, though tested informally against his vast historical knowledge, and his belief in short-run correlations between changes in money and changes in production was apparently based mainly on his everyday knowledge. (He cites one Mons. du Tot for the assertion that "in the last year of Louis XIV, money was raised three-sevenths but prices augmented only one" [p. 39]. In a footnote he characterizes his source as "an author of reputation," but feels obliged to "confess that the facts which he advances on other occasions are often so suspicious as to make his authority less in this matter." Even in the eighteenth century, it seems, there were tensions between theorists and econometricians!)

The central predictions of the quantity theory are that, in the long run, money growth should be neutral in its effects on the growth rate of production and should affect the inflation rate on a one-for-one basis. The modifier "long run" is not free of ambiguity, but by any definition the use of data that are heavily averaged over time should isolate only long-run effects. Figure 1, taken from McCandless and Weber (1995), plots 30-year (1960–90) average annual inflation rates against average annual growth rates of *M2* over the same 30-year period, for a total of 110 countries. One can see that the points lie roughly on the 45-degree line, as predicted by

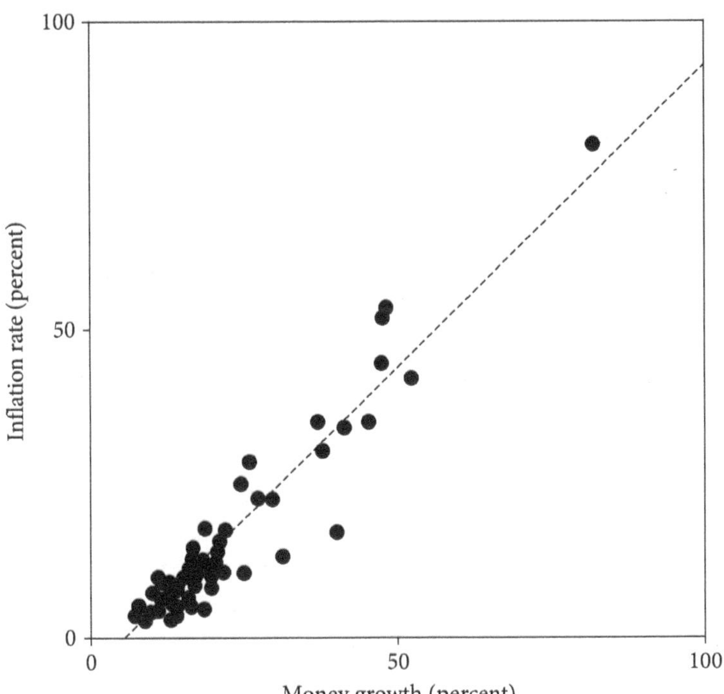

Figure 1

the quantity theory. The simple correlation between inflation and money growth is .95. The monetary aggregate used in constructing figure 1 is *M*2, but nothing important depends on this choice. McCandless and Weber report a simple correlation of .96 if *M*1 is used and .92 if *M*0 (the monetary base) is used. They also report correlations for subsets of their 110-country data set: .96 (with *M*2) with only OECD countries and .99 with 14 Latin American countries.

It is clear from these data (and from the many other studies that have reached similar conclusions) that the applicability of the quantity theory of money is not limited to currency reforms and magical thought experiments. It applies, with remarkable success, to comovements in money and prices generated in complicated, real-world circumstances. Indeed, how many specific economic theories can claim empirical success at the level exhibited in figure 1? Central bankers and even some monetary economists talk knowledgeably of using high interest rates to control inflation, but I know of no evidence from even one economy linking these variables in a useful way, let alone evidence as sharp as that displayed in figure 1. The kind of monetary neutrality shown in this figure needs to be a central feature of any monetary or macroeconomic theory that claims empirical seriousness.

McCandless and Weber also provide evidence on correlations between money growth and growth in real output, averaged over the 1960–90 period. Figure 2 is their plot for the full 100-country data set from the International Monetary Fund. Evidently, there is no relation between these 30-year averages.[2] For examining short-term trade-offs, of course, one does not want to use such time-averaged data. Figure 3, taken from Stockman (1996), provides six plots of annual inflation rates against unemployment rates for various subperiods of the years 1950–94, for the United States. Panel *f* plots the Phillips curve (after A. W. Phillips [1958]) for the entire period. In this panel, the two variables appear to be completely unrelated. On the other hand, the five panels for subperiods (or at least for the subperiods since 1960) seem to show a clear, negative relation. But then look at the axes in these six panels! In order to see inflation and unemployment as lying on a negatively sloped curve, one needs to keep shifting the curve.

2. It must be said that the evidence of long-run links between money growth and output growth is more mixed than one would infer from fig. 2. McCandless and Weber find a weak positive relation for the OECD economies. Both positive and negative correlations have been found by other investigators on other data sets.

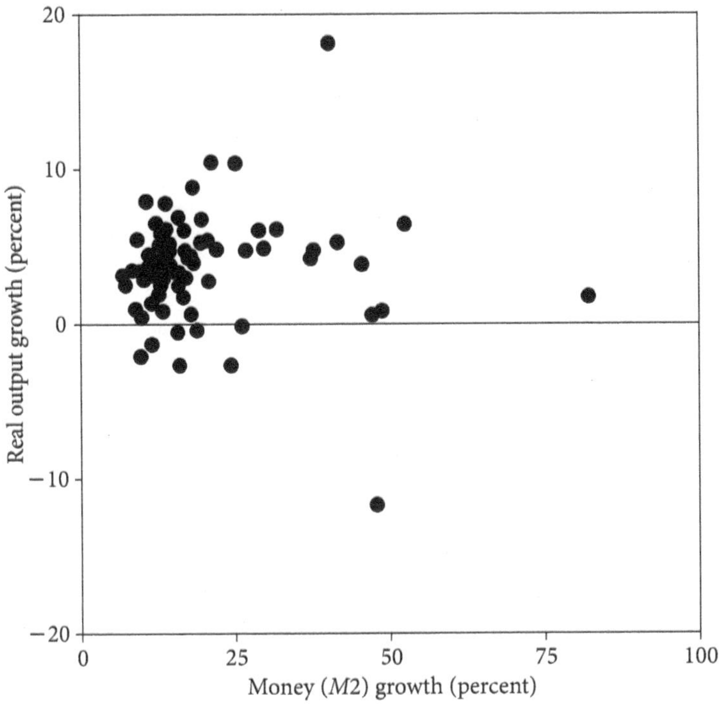

Figure 2

Evidence on trade-offs is also marshaled, though in a very different way, in Friedman and Schwartz's (1963) monograph *A Monetary History of the United States.* These authors show that every major depression in the United States over the period 1867–1960 was associated with a large contraction in the money supply and that every large contraction was associated with a depression. These observations are correlations of a sort, too, but they gain force from the size of the largest contractions. In a period such as the post–World War II years in the United States, real output fluctuations are modest enough to be attributable, possibly, to real sources. There is no need to appeal to money shocks to account for these movements. But an event such as the Great Depression of 1929–33 is far beyond anything that can be attributed to shocks to tastes and technology. One needs some other possibilities. Monetary contractions are attractive as the key shocks in the 1929–33 years, and in other severe depressions, because there do not seem to be any other candidates.

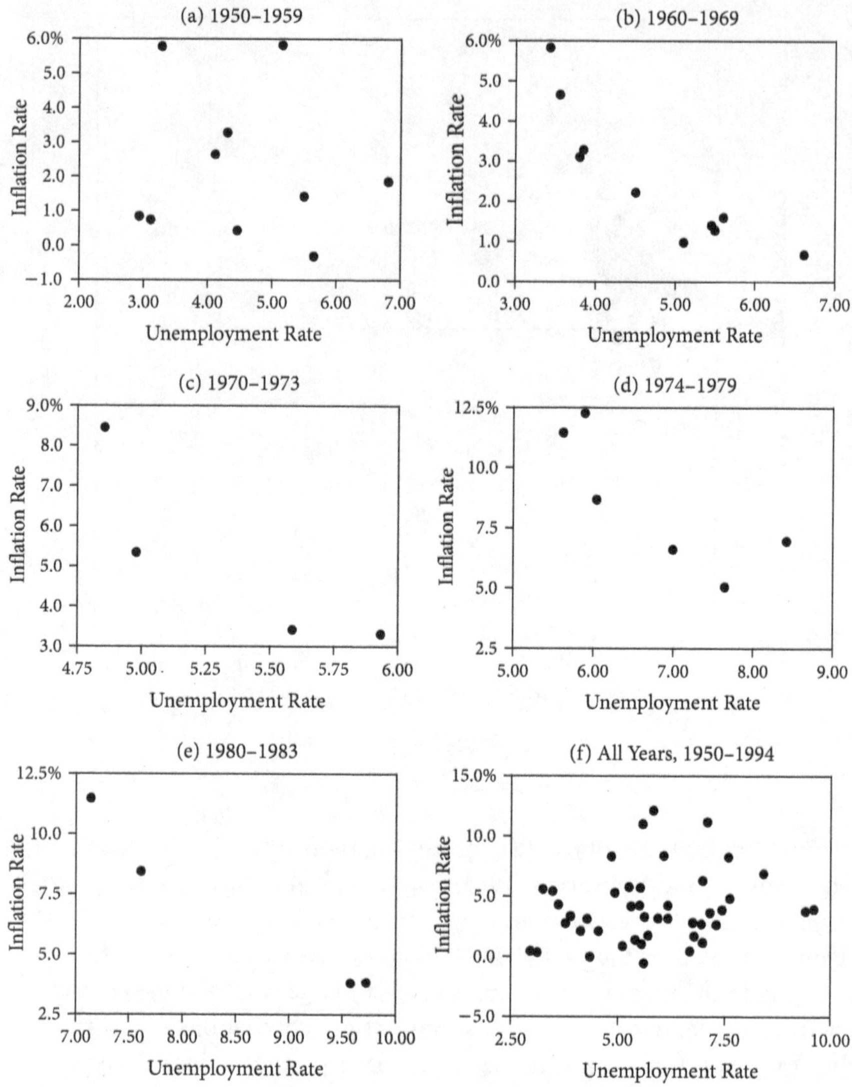

Figure 3

Sargent (1986) also examines large, sudden reductions in rates of money growth (though not reductions in the *levels* of money stocks). In his case, these are the monetary and fiscal reforms that ended four of the post–World War I European hyperinflations. These dramatic reductions in growth rates of the money supply dwarf anything in Friedman and

Schwartz or in the postwar data used by McCandless and Weber. Yet as Sargent shows, they were not associated with output reductions that were large by historical standards, or possibly by any depressions at all. Sargent goes on to demonstrate the likelihood that these reductions in money growth rates were well anticipated by the people they affected and, because of visible and suitable fiscal reforms, were expected by them to be sustained.

In summary, the prediction that prices respond proportionally to changes in money in the long run, deduced by Hume in 1752 (and by many other theorists, by many different routes, since), has received ample—I would say decisive—confirmation, in data from many times and places. The observation that money changes induce output changes in the same direction receives confirmation in some data sets but is hard to see in others. Large-scale reductions in money growth can be associated with large-scale depressions or, if carried out in the form of a credible reform, with no depression at all.

III. Theoretical Responses

Hume was able to theorize rigorously, and, as we have seen, with great empirical success, about comparisons of long-run average behavior across economies with different average rates of money growth. For short-run purposes, on the other hand, he was obliged to rely on much looser reasoning and rough empirical generalizations. As economic theory evolved in the last century and most of this one, the double standard that characterized Hume's argument was perpetuated. The quantity-theoretic "neutrality theorems" were stated with increasing precision and worked through rigorously, using the latest equipment of static general equilibrium theory. The dynamics had a kind of patched-in quality, fitting the facts, but only in a manner that suggests they could equally well fit *any* facts. Patinkin interprets all of monetary theory from Wicksell's *Interest and Prices* (1898) through his own *Money, Interest, and Prices* as concerned with processes of adjustment between one quantity-theoretic equilibrium position and another, conceived as outside the framework of general equilibrium theory in a way that seems to me very much at the level of Hume's analysis. The passages on dynamics that I cited from Hume in Section I could be slipped into Keynes's *Treatise on Money* (1930) or Hayek's *Monetary Theory and the Trade Cycle* (1933) without inducing any sense of anachronism.

Yet all these theorists *want* to think in general equilibrium terms, to think of people as maximizing over time, as substituting intertemporally. They resort to disequilibrium dynamics only because the analytical equipment available to them offers no alternative. Even in Hume's scenario, the motives and expectations of economic actors during the transition are described, even rationalized: The adjustment to a new equilibrium is not seen as a purely mechanical *tâtonnement* process, the character of which is determined by forces apart from the producers and consumers of the system. Certainly Wicksell and, I would say, Patinkin, too, are trying to think through the way the dynamic adjustment process appears to people as it occurs, to see the actions people take as rational responses to their situations. Though the theoretical formalism on which they draw involves a static equilibrium combined with a mechanical process to describe dynamic adjustments, their verbal descriptions of periods of transition, like Hume's before them, show that they are in fact thinking of people solving intertemporal decision problems.

The intelligence of these attempts to deal theoretically with the real effects of changes in money is still impressive to the modern reader, but serves only to underscore the futility of attempting to talk through hard dynamic problems without any of the equipment of modern mathematical economics. Hayek and Keynes and their contemporaries were willing to make assumptions and to set out something like a model, but they were simply not able to work out the predictions of their own theories.

The depression of the 1930s shifted attention away from the subtle problems of monetary neutrality and toward the potential of monetary policy for short-run stimulus. Keynes's *General Theory* (1936) was one product of this change of focus. Another was Tinbergen's (1939) development of an explicit statistical model of the U.S. economy. Tinbergen's model and its immediate successors made little or no contact with earlier traditions in monetary theory; but in the atmosphere of the 1930s and 1940s this was perhaps an advantage, and it fit well with the revolutionary rhetoric of Keynes's book. Economic theory aside, the macroeconometric models that evolved from Tinbergen's work had two important advantages over all earlier macroeconomic theory. They were mathematically explicit and so could be estimated from and tested against data in a much more disciplined way than earlier theories could. Moreover, they could be simulated to yield quantitative answers to policy questions. It was these features that excited younger researchers and had such a dramatic influence on future developments in the field.

By the 1960s, then, two very different styles of macroeconomic theory, both claiming the title of Keynesian economics, coexisted. There were attempts at a unified monetary and value theory, like Patinkin's, based on extensions of static general equilibrium theory to accommodate money, combined with some kind of *tâtonnement* process to provide some dynamics. These theories were developed with great attention to earlier monetary theory and to developments in economic theory more generally, but they lacked the operational character of the macroeconometric models: No one could tell exactly what their predictions were or what normative implications they carried. On the other hand, there were macroeconometric models that could be fit to data and simulated to yield quantitative answers to policy questions but whose relation to microeconomic theory and classical monetary theory was unclear.

Virtually no one at the time regarded this situation as healthy. Everyone paid lip service to the idea of unification of micro- and macroeconomics or of discovering the microeconomic "foundations" of macroeconomic theories, and a vast amount of creative and valuable economics, focused on intertemporal decision problems, was inspired by this goal. The work of Modigliani and Brumberg (1954) and Friedman (1957) on consumption; Eisner and Strotz (1963) and Jorgenson (1963) on investment in physical capital; Becker (1962) and Ben-Porath (1967) on investment in human capital; and Baumol (1952), Tobin (1956), Brunner and Meltzer (1963), and Meltzer (1963) on money demand all contributed. Mathematically inclined economists who entered the profession in the 1960s were drawn to methods for studying intertemporal decision problems, the calculus of variations, the theory of optimal control, and Bellman's (1957) dynamic programming. Work on optimal growth by Uzawa (1964) and Cass (1965) was followed by applications of similar methods to a variety of problems in all subfields of economics. In these applications, the dynamics were an integral part of the theory, not tacked-on *tâtonnement* processes. When Leonard Rapping and I began our collaboration on the study of labor markets over the business cycle (Lucas and Rapping 1969), we thought of these studies of individual intertemporal decision problems as models of what we wanted to do.[3]

The prevailing strategy for macroeconomic modeling in the early 1960s held that the individual or sectoral models arising out of this intertemporal theorizing could then simply be combined in a single model, the way

3. See Phelps et al. (1970) for several similarly motivated studies.

Keynes and Tinbergen and their successors assembled a consumption function, an investment function, and so on into a model of an entire economy. But models of individual decisions over time necessarily involve expected, future prices. Some microeconomic analyses treated these prices as known; others imputed adaptive forecasting rules to maximizing firms and households. However it was done, though, the "church supper" models assembled from such individual components implied behavior of *actual* equilibrium prices and incomes that bore no relation to, and were in general grossly inconsistent with, the price expectations that the theory imputed to individual agents.

As intertemporal elements and expectations came to play an increasingly explicit and important role, this modeling inconsistency became more and more glaring. John Muth's (1961) "Rational Expectations and the Theory of Price Movements" focused on this inconsistency and showed how it could be removed by taking into account the influences of prices, including *future* prices, on quantities and *simultaneously* the effects of quantities on equilibrium prices.[4] The principle of rational expectations he proposed thus forces the modeler toward a market equilibrium point of view, although it took some time before a style of thinking that recognized this fact had a major effect on macroeconomic modeling.

Other considerations reinforced a move in the same direction. In the late 1960s, Friedman (1968) and Phelps (1968) saw, by thinking through the issue at a general equilibrium level, that there could be no long-run Phillips curve trade-off between inflation and real output. But such long-run trade-offs were implicit in all the macroeconometric models of the day, and the econometric methods that were in standard use at that time seemed to reject the Friedman-Phelps natural rate hypothesis. This conflict led to a rethinking of the theoretical basis of these statistical tests, and the discovery of serious difficulties with them. Sargent (1971) and Lucas (1972*a*, 1976) showed that the conventional rejections of the natural rate hypothesis depended critically on *irrational* expectations or, to put the same point backward, that if one assumed rational expectations these tests settled nothing. It seemed clear that it was necessary to put macroeconomics on a general equilibrium basis that incorporated rational expectations.

4. Eugene Fama's (1965) theory of efficient markets was another direct application of economic reasoning to the behavior of *equilibrium* prices, in a setting in which stochastic shocks were an intrinsic part of the economic model.

IV. General Equilibrium Macroeconomics

By the 1960s, two closely related general equilibrium frameworks were in fact already available for thinking about economic dynamics. One was the mathematical model of general equilibrium, developed by Hicks (1939), Arrow (1951), McKenzie (1954), and Debreu (1959), in which the commodity vector is defined to include dated claims to goods, possibly made contingent on random events. Prescott and I (Lucas and Prescott 1971) adopted this framework for the construction of a rational expectations model of investment in a competitive industry, taking a stochastically shifting demand curve (rather than prices) as given. And, in a paper that was to set the research agenda for the next decade, Kydland and Prescott (1982) utilized a version of the stochastic growth optimal growth model of Brock and Mirman (1972) as an operational model of a competitive economy undergoing recurrent business cycles, induced by shifts in the technology. This turned out to be a tremendously fruitful idea, whose potential is still being realized. But such a model without money is obviously not suited to the study of Hume's problem. Economists who believed that monetary forces were at the center of the business cycle needed to look elsewhere.

A second general equilibrium framework, due to Samuelson (1958), was also available and seemed better suited to the study of monetary questions. That paper introduced a deceptively simple example of an economy in which money with no direct use in either consumption or production nonetheless plays an essential role in economic life. I used this model (Lucas 1972*b*) in an attempt to show how monetary neutrality might be reconciled with the appearance of a short-term stimulus from a monetary expansion. The model is so simple and flexible that it can be used to illustrate many issues. I shall introduce a version of it here, along with enough notation to permit discussion of some interesting details.

In Samuelson's model, people live for two periods only, so that the ongoing economy is always populated by two age cohorts, one young and the other old. Here I assume a constant population, so that per capita and economywide magnitudes can be used interchangeably. At each year's end, the old die, the young become old, and a new young group arrives. It is important for my purposes (as it was for Samuelson's) to assume that there is no family structure in this economy: no inheritances and no financial support by one cohort for another. Suppose that a young person in this economy can work and produce goods, whereas an old person likes to consume goods but has no ability to produce them. Denote a person's two objects of choice by the pair (c, n), where n is units of labor supplied when young and c is units of the good consumed when old. Assume that everyone's preferences over these two goods are given by $U(c) - n$. Assume a labor-only technology in which one unit of labor yields one unit of goods.

If the good were storable, everyone would produce in his youth and carry the production over for his own later consumption, solving the problem

$$\max_{n}[U(n) - n]. \tag{1}$$

Call the solution to this problem n^*. But I shall assume that the good cannot be stored, so that any individual acting purely on his own *cannot* produce for his own pleasure.[5] The best one acting alone can do is to enjoy leisure when young and never consume anything. Clearly society as a whole should be able to do *much* better than that, by somehow inducing the young to produce for the consumption of their *contemporary* old. Some institution is needed to achieve this.

A social security system may be one real-world instance of such an institution. (Or it may not: Everything hinges on the realism of the assumption of no family structure.) As Samuelson noted, a monetary system may be another such institution, for one can view the failure of the autarchic allocation as arising from the absence of the double coincidence of wants that barter exchange requires. Those who wish to consume goods, the old, have nothing to offer in return to those who are able to produce, the young. But suppose that there were some paper money in circulation, initially in the hands of the old. The old would offer this cash to the young in exchange for goods, establishing a market price of some kind. Would the young accept these tokens—intrinsically useless, in Wallace's (1980) terms—and hence keep the value of tokens in terms of goods at any level above zero? Maybe not: This possibility can certainly not be ruled out. If the young were willing to produce goods in exchange for fiat money, the reason would have to be that they hoped to be able to trade the money they received for goods in their own old age.

The interesting thing about Samuelson's example is that this second

5. In fact, Cass and Yaari (1966) show that even if storage is possible, the autarchic allocation can be improved on since it ties up goods in inventory permanently and unnecessarily.

scenario cannot be ruled out. It is possible, though by no means necessary, that the money in this economy will circulate forever, being exchanged over and over again for goods. If this exchange takes place in a single competitive spot market and the price p is established, then a young person who begins with no money and works n units will acquire pn units of cash. If he spends it all on goods next period, this yields $pn/p = n$ units of consumption. Thus everyone solves the problem (1). If the money supply is constant and evenly distributed over the old in the amount m per person, the equilibrium price will also be constant, at the level $p = m/n^*$. Evidently, this equilibrium is quantity-theoretic in Hume's sense: if m is (somehow) increased, the equilibrium price level will be increased in the same proportion, and quantities of labor and production will not be affected at all.

When we consider monetary changes that differ from once-and-for-all changes in the money *stock*, however, the issue of neutrality becomes more complicated. To see this, suppose that we replace the assumption of a constant money supply with the assumption that the quantity of money grows at a constant percentage rate. We need to be explicit (another point in favor of Samuelson's model) about the way the new money gets into the system, and it matters how this is done. Assume, to begin with, that each young person receives an equal share of the newly created money, in between his youth and old age, and that the size of this addition to his cash is independent of the amount he has earned by working. Then if the money supply is m and is to be augmented by the lump-sum transfer $m(x - 1)$, each young person now solves

$$\max_n \left[U\left(\frac{pn + (x-1)m}{p'} \right) - n \right], \tag{2}$$

where p is the price at which he sells goods, today, and p' is the price at which he buys goods, tomorrow. The first-order condition for this problem is

$$U'\left(\frac{pn + (x-1)m}{p'} \right) \frac{p}{p'} = 1. \tag{3}$$

In order to work out a rational expectations equilibrium for this model, we exploit the observation that the only thing that changes over time in this situation is the money supply, which is simply multiplied by the known factor x in every period. It seems natural, then, to seek an equilibrium in which the price level is proportional to the money stock, $p = km$ for some constant k, and in which labor is constant at some value $\hat{n}$. In such an equilibrium, the constant k will evidently be $1/\hat{n}$. Tomorrow's price is then $p' = kmx = mx/\hat{n}$. Inserting all this information into the first-order condition (3), one obtains

$$U'(\hat{n}) = x. \tag{4}$$

In this circumstance, then, the price level will increase between periods at exactly the rate of growth of the money supply. The equilibrium level of employment $\hat{n}$, from (4), will be a decreasing function of the rate of money growth.[6]

The quantity-theoretic predictions we saw confirmed in figures 1 and 2 would also be confirmed in this hypothetical world. But note that this does *not* mean that the rate of money growth and the equal rate of price inflation are merely units changes, of no consequence to anyone. The faster money grows, the more important the overnight transfer is, relative to the cash accumulated through working. The monetary transfers dilute the return from working. Goods production declines as the inflation rate rises, and everyone is made worse off. This is a nonneutrality of money, a real effect of a money change (some would prefer to call it a real effect of the fiscal transfer that is used to bring the money change about), but this effect is obviously not the stimulating effect of a monetary expansion that Hume discusses. In this example, inflation does not "quicken the diligence of every individual." It is a kind of tax that deadens diligence by reducing its real return.

This inflation tax is an issue of the first importance, I think, and its effects are captured in a useful way by the theoretical example I have just worked through. But further study of the inflation tax is not going to bring us any closer to an understanding of the trade-off that Hume thought he observed, and that so many others have seen since. Let us then get the inflation tax out of the picture by assuming that the fiscal transfers through which the money supply expands are made in proportion to the balances

6. Jörgen Weibull pointed out to me that one could obtain a version of this example in which equilibrium employment is an *increasing* function of the money shock x by assuming that only some of the young receive the entire transfer and by making the right assumptions about the curvature of the function U.

one has earned through working. That is, if one works n units, one receives the transfer $pn(x - 1)$, not $m(x - 1)$, and thus has pnx to spend next period. In this situation, the first-order condition (4) becomes $U'(\hat{n}) = 1$, independent of x, and $\hat{n}$ is always at its efficient level n^*: there is no inflation tax. These proportional transfers are just an assumption of convenience, but one that will simplify the discussion of some hard questions.

Now how might this overlapping generations economy be modified so that a monetary expansion will act as a stimulus to production? One might think that this could be achieved by replacing the assumption that the transfer variable x is constant with the assumption that it is drawn independently each period from some fixed probability distribution. Evidently, if the current-period realization is known to everyone, this will not change anything. What is perhaps less obvious, but equally true, is that even if the transfer realization is known directly only to the old, it will be revealed perfectly to the young by the equilibrium price that it induces. As in the constant money growth example we worked through above, prices are determined by m and x. What else is there in this context? If m is known and p is observed, as of course it must be in competitive trading, then one can infer the value of x.

In order to get an output effect from a monetary shock, then, it is not enough simply to introduce uncertainty. We need to imagine that the exchange of money for goods takes place in some manner other than in a centralized Walrasian market. In Lucas (1972*b*), I assumed that exchange occurs in two markets, each with a different number of goods suppliers. In this circumstance, a given price increase can signal a supplier that the money transfer x is large, in which case he wants to treat it like a units change and not respond; or it can mean that there are only a few suppliers in his market, in which case he wants to treat it like a real shift in his favor and respond by producing more. The best the individual can do, given his limited information, is to hedge. On average, then, labor supply and production are an increasing function $\varphi(x)$ of the monetary transfer. Equilibrium prices, $mx/\varphi(x)$, move in proportion to m, which is known to all traders, but increase less than proportionally with the transfer x. By next period, the transfer x is known, and prices complete their proportional increase, but not without a transition during which production is increased.

The resemblance of this scenario to the one I quoted from Hume in my Introduction seems clear. In an important sense the new scenario is an improvement since in place of the unexplained errors of judgment or ignorance that lie at the center of Hume's account, this one rests on an assumption that people lack complete information. But perhaps this only pushes the question back one step: *Why is it* that people cannot obtain that last bit of information that would enable them to diagnose price movements accurately? In reality, up-to-date information on the money supply does not seem all that hard to come by.

Let us step back from the specifics of this particular, information-based version of Hume's scenario and consider the possibilities more abstractly. Assume simply that old and young engage in some kind of trading game, to which the old bring the cash m obtained in the previous period's trading.[7] Either before or perhaps during the play of this game, the old receive a proportional transfer that totals x. Let each young person and each old person select a trading strategy. Notice that the strategy of a young person can depend on m, and the strategy of an old person can depend on m and x. On the basis of these choices, suppose that a Nash equilibrium is reached under which each young person supplies some amount of labor and ends up with some amount of cash. I shall restrict attention to symmetric equilibria, so that in equilibrium each young person ends up with mx dollars. Each young person also ends up supplying $f(m, x)$ units of labor, and this quantity is also the equilibrium consumption of each old person (the notation is chosen to emphasize that m and x are the only state variables in this model). Different specifications of the trading game will have different implications for this *outcome function* f.

Now assume that before the play of such a game begins, the money stock m is evenly distributed over the old; that everyone, young and old, knows what it is; and that everyone knows how transfers occur—the rules of this trading game. In these circumstances, changes in m must be neutral units changes, so that f is constant with respect to m and can be written $f(m, x) = \varphi(x)$ for some function φ. Given this function φ, the average price of goods is just the money stock divided by production, or $p = mx/\varphi(x)$. In competitive trading, φ is a constant function, so price is proportional to mx, where x is known; but in many other trading games, the function φ will vary with the value x. In this notation, rationalizing a trade-off of the type described by Hume translates into constructing a game that rationalizes an increasing function $\varphi(x)$.

7. This point of departure has long been advocated by Shubik (see, e.g., Shubik 1980).

One such game (though that equilibrium was not quite symmetric) was described in Lucas (1972*b*). There, the response in output was based on suppliers' imperfect information about the transfer x. But at this level of abstraction there are many other noncompetitive trading games that have outcomes with these same features. Some of them achieve this end by assuming that some nominal prices are set in advance, as in Fischer (1977), Phelps and Taylor (1977), Taylor (1979), or Svensson (1986). Others postulate games in which the transfer is only gradually revealed, as in Eden (1994), Lucas and Woodford (1994), or Williamson (1995). All these papers offer rationalizations of a short-run monetary nonneutrality in the sense of an increasing function $\varphi(x)$, though of course in quite different ways. In an important sense, then, Hume's paradox has been resolved: We have a wide variety of theories that reconcile long-run monetary neutrality with a short-run trade-off. They all (and any other game that fits into the formalism above) carry the implication that anticipated money changes will not stimulate production and that at least some unanticipated changes can do so.[8]

Does it matter which of these rationales is appealed to? The answer to this harder question must depend on what our purposes are. Any of these models leads to the distinction between anticipated and unanticipated changes in money, the distinction that seems to me the central lesson of the theoretical work of the 1970s. On the other hand, none of these models deduces the function φ from assumptions on technology and preferences alone, Of course φ depends on such factors, but it also depends on the specific assumptions one makes about the strategies available to the players, the timing of moves, the way in which information is revealed, and so on. Moreover, these specifics are all, for the sake of tractability, highly unrealistic and stylized: We cannot choose among them on the basis of descriptive realism. Consequently, we have no reason to believe that the function φ is invariant under changes in monetary policy—it is just a kind of Phillips curve, after all—and no reliable way to break it down into well-understood components,

Theories that emphasized the distinction between anticipated and unanticipated money shocks led to a variety of statistical tests. Sargent (1976) interpreted the prediction that anticipated money would have no real effects as the hypothesis that money would not "cause," in the sense of

8. Of course, this conclusion requires the usual caveat about the inflation tax.

Granger (1969) and Sims (1972), changes in unemployment rates, and he found that this prediction was confirmed for U.S. time series. Barro (1977) used residuals from regressions of M1 on its own lagged values as measures of unanticipated money shocks and concluded that the unemployment rate responded to these shocks but did not respond to current and lagged M1.[9] The signal-processing feature of the model of Lucas (1972*b*) implied that the magnitude of a money multiplier should decline as the variance of money changes increased. This prediction was confirmed in the cross-country comparisons reported in Lucas (1973) and Alberro (1981) and by the much more extensive results reported in Kormendi and Meguire (1984).

In the models in Lucas (1972*b*, 1973), trade takes place in competitive markets, though these markets are incomplete; so any real effects of monetary policy need to work through movements in prices. The tests described in the last paragraph do not use data on prices and so do not test this prediction. Other econometric work that did require money shocks to be transmitted through price movements was much less favorable. Estimates in Sargent (1976) and in Leiderman (1979) indicated that only small fractions of output variability can be accounted for by unexpected price movements. Though the evidence seems to show that monetary surprises have real effects, they do not seem to be transmitted through price surprises, as in Lucas (1972*b*).[10]

V. Conclusions

The main finding that emerged from the research of the 1970s is that anticipated changes and unanticipated changes in money growth have very different effects. Anticipated monetary expansions have inflation tax effects and induce an inflation premium on nominal interest rates, but they are not associated with the kind of stimulus to employment and production that Hume described. Unanticipated monetary expansions, on the

9. Whether this work in fact tests implications of the model in Lucas (1972*b*) is questioned in King (1981).

10. Wallace (1992) develops a variation of the Lucas (1972*b*) model in which real shocks need not be perfectly negatively correlated across markets (so that real shocks can be positive in the aggregate). In this more general model, money shocks can induce output movements in the same direction (but not perfectly correlated) and the inflation-output correlation can have either sign. The evidence in Sargent (1976) and Leiderman (1979) is not decisive against such a variation.

other hand, can stimulate production as, symmetrically, unanticipated contractions can induce depression. The importance of this distinction between anticipated and unanticipated monetary changes is an implication of every one of the many different models, all using rational expectations, that were developed during the 1970s to account for short-term trade-offs. This distinction is consistent with the long-run evidence displayed in Figures 1 and 2, with the year-to-year changes displayed in Figure 3, with Friedman and Schwartz's account of depressions in the United States, and with Sargent's account of the ending of the European hyperinflations.

The discovery of the central role of the distinction between anticipated and unanticipated money shocks resulted from the attempts, on the part of many researchers, to formulate mathematically explicit models that were capable of addressing the issues raised by Hume. But I think it is clear that none of the specific models that captured this distinction in the 1970s can now be viewed as a satisfactory theory of business cycles. Perhaps in part as a response to the difficulties with the monetary-based business cycle models of the 1970s, much recent research has followed the lead of Kydland and Prescott (1982) and emphasized the effects of purely real forces on employment and production.[11] This research has shown how general equilibrium reasoning can add discipline to the study of an economy's distributed lag response to shocks, as well as to the study of the nature of the shocks themselves. More recently, many have tried to reintroduce monetary features into these models, and I expect much future work in this direction.

But who can say how the macroeconomic theory of the future will develop, any more than anyone in 1960 could have foreseen the developments I have described in this lecture? All one can be sure of is that progress will result from the continued effort to formulate explicit theories that fit the facts, and that the best and most practical macroeconomics will make use of developments in basic economic theory.

References

Alberro, José. "The Lucas Hypothesis on the Phillips Curve: Further International Evidence." *J. Monetary Econ.* 7 (March 1981): 239–50.

Arrow, Kenneth J. "An Extension of the Basic Theorems of Classical Welfare Eco-

11. The approach of directly testing the implications of Euler equations, initiated in Hall (1978) and advanced by methods described in Hansen (1982), has also been productively pursued.

nomics." In *Proceedings of the Second Berkeley Symposium on Mathematical Statistics and Probability,* edited by Jerzy Neyman. Berkeley: Univ. California Press, 1951.

Barro, Robert J. "Unanticipated Money Growth and Unemployment in the United States." *A.E.R.* 67 (March 1977): 101–15.

Baumol, William J. "The Transactions Demand for Cash: An Inventory Theoretic Approach." *Q.J.E.* 66 (November 1952): 545–56.

Becker, Gary S. "Investment in Human Capital: A Theoretical Analysis." *J.P.E.* 70, no. 5, pt. 2 (October 1962): 9–49.

Bellman, Richard E. *Dynamic Programming.* Princeton, NJ.: Princeton Univ. Press, 1957.

Ben-Porath, Yoram. "The Production of Human Capital and the Life Cycle of Earnings." *J.P.E.* 75, no. 4, pt. 1 (August 1967): 352–65.

Brock, William A., and Mirman, Leonard J. "Optimal Economic Growth and Uncertainty: The Discounted Case." *J. Econ. Theory* 4 (June 1972): 479–513.

Brunner, Karl, and Meltzer, Allan H. "Predicting Velocity: Implications for Theory and Policy." *J. Finance* 18 (May 1963): 319–54.

Cass, David. "Optimum Growth in an Aggregative Model of Capital Accumulation." *Rev. Econ. Studies* 32 (July 1965): 233–40.

Cass, David, and Yaari, Menahem E. "A Re-examination of the Pure Consumption Loans Model." *J.P.E.* 74 (August 1966): 353–67.

Debreu, Gerard, *Theory of Value: An Axiomatic Analysis of Economic Equilibrium.* New Haven, Conn.: Yale Univ, Press, 1959.

Eden, Benjamin. "The Adjustment of Prices to Monetary Shocks When Trade Is Uncertain and Sequential." *J.P.E.* 102 (June 1994): 493–509.

Eisner, Robert, and Strotz, Robert H. "Determinants of Business Investment." In *Impacts of Monetary Policy,* by the Commission on Money and Credit, Englewood Cliffs, NJ.: Prentice-Hall, 1963.

Fama, Eugene F. "The Behavior of Stock-Market Prices," *J. Bus.* 38 (January 1965): 34–105.

Fischer, Stanley, "Long-Term Contracts, Rational Expectations, and the Optimal Money Supply Rule." *J.P.E.* 85 (February 1977): 191–205.

Friedman, Milton. *A Theory of the Consumption Function.* Princeton, N.J.: Princeton Univ. Press (for NBER), 1957.

———. "The Role of Monetary Policy," *A.E.R.* 58 (March 1968): 1–17.

Friedman, Milton, and Schwartz, Anna J. *A Monetary History of the United States, 1867–1960.* Princeton, N.J.: Princeton Univ. Press (for NBER), 1963.

Granger, Clive W. J. "Investigating Causal Relations by Econometric Models and Cross-Spectral Methods." *Econometrics* 37 (July 1969): 424–38.

Hall, Robert E. "Stochastic Implications of the Life Cycle—Permanent Income Hypothesis: Theory and Evidence." *J.P.E.* 86 (December 1978): 971–88.

Hansen, Lars Peter. "Large Sample Properties of Generalized Method of Moments Estimators," *Econometrica* 50 (July 1982): 1029–54.

Hayek, Friedrich A. von. *Monetary Theory and the Trade Cycle.* London: Jonathan Cape, 1933.

Hicks, John R. *Value and Capital.* Oxford: Clarendon, 1939.

Hume, David. *Writings on Economics,* edited by Eugene Rotwein, Madison: Univ. Wisconsin Press, 1970.

Jorgenson, Dale W. "Capital Theory and Investment Behavior." *A.E.R. Papers and Proc.* 53 (May 1963): 247–59.

Keynes, John Maynard. *A Treatise an Money.* London: Macmillan, 1930.

———. *The General Theory of Employment, Interest, and Money.* London: Macmillan, 1936.

King, Robert G. "Monetary Information and Monetary Neutrality." *J. Monetary Econ.* 7 (March 1981): 195–206.

Kormendi, Roger C., and Meguire, Philip G. "Cross-Regime Evidence of Macroeconomic Rationality." *J.P.E.* 92 (October 1984): 875–908.

Kydland, Finn E., and Prescott, Edward C. "Time to Build and Aggregate Fluctuations." *Econometrics* 50 (November 1982): 1345–70.

Leiderman, Leonardo. "Expectations and Output-Inflation Tradeoffs in a Fixed-Exchange-Rate Economy." *J.P.E.* 87 (December 1979): 1285–1306.

Lucas, Robert E., Jr. "Econometric Testing of the Natural Rate Hypothesis." In *The Econometrics of Price Determination: Conference, October 30–31, 1970, Washington, D.C.,* edited by Otto Eckstein. Washington: Board of Governors, Fed. Reserve System, 1972. (*a*)

———. "Expectations and the Neutrality of Money." *J. Econ. Theory* 4 (April 1972): 103–24. (*b*)

———. "Some International Evidence on Output-Inflation Tradeoffs." *A.E.R.* 63 (June 1973): 326–34.

———. "Econometric Policy Evaluation: A Critique." *Carnegie-Rochester Conf. Ser. Public Policy,* no. 1 (1976): 19–46.

Lucas, Robert E., Jr., and Prescott, Edward C. "Investment under Uncertainty," *Econometric* 39 (September 1971): 659–81.

Lucas, Robert E., Jr., and Rapping, Leonard A, "Real Wages, Employment, and Inflation." *J.P.E.* 77 (September/October 1969): 721–54.

Lucas, Robert E., Jr., and Woodford, Michael. "Real Effects of Monetary Shocks in an Economy with Sequential Purchases." Working paper. Chicago: Univ. Chicago, 1994.

McCandless, George T., Jr., and Weber, Warren E. "Some Monetary Facts." *Fed. Reserve Bank Minneapolis Q. Rev.* 19 (Summer 1995): 2–11.

McKenzie, Lionel W. "On Equilibrium in Graham's Model of World Trade and Other Competitive Systems." *Econotmtrica* 22 (April 1954): 147–61.

Meltzer, Allan H. "The Demand for Money: The Evidence from the Time Series." *J.P.E.* 71 (June 1963): 219–46.

Modigliani, Franco, and Brumberg, Richard. "Utility Analysis and the Consumption Function: An Interpretation of Cross-Section Data." In *Post-Keynesian Economics,* edited by Kenneth K. Kurihara. New Brunswick, N.J.: Rutgers Univ. Press, 1954.

Muth, John F. "Rational Expectations and the Theory of Price Movements." *Econometrica* 29 (July 1961): 315–35.

Patinkin, Don. *Money, Interest, and Prices: An Integration of Monetary and Value Theory.* 2d ed. New York: Harper and Row, 1965.

Phelps, Edmund S. "Money-Wage Dynamics and Labor-Market Equilibrium." *J.P.E.* 76, no, 4, pt. 2 (July/August 1968): 678–711.

Phelps, Edmund S., et al. *Microeconomic Foundations of Employment and Inflation Theory,* New York: Norton, 1970.

Phelps, Edmund S., and Taylor, John B. "Stabilizing Powers of Monetary Policy under Rational Expectations." *J.P.E.* 85 (February 1977): 163–90.

Phillips, A. W. "The Relation between Unemployment and the Rate of Change of Money Wage Rates in the United Kingdom, 1861–1957." *Economica* 25 (November 1958): 283–99.

Samuelson, Paul A. "An Exact Consumption-Loan Model of Interest with or without the Social Contrivance of Money," *J.P.E.* 66 (December 1958): 467–82.

Sargent, Thomas J. "A Note on the 'Accelerationist' Controversy." *J. Money, Credit and Banking* 3 (August 1971): 721–25.

———. "A Classical Macroeconometric Model for the United States." *J.P.E.* 84 (April 1976): 207–37.

———. "The Ends of Four Big Inflations." In *Rational Expectations and Inflation.* New York: Harper and Row, 1986.

Shubik, Martin. "The Capital Stock Modified Competitive Equilibrium." In *Models of Monetary Economies,* edited by John H. Kareken and Neil Wallace. Minneapolis: Fed. Reserve Bank, 1980.

Sims, Christopher A. "Money, Income, and Causality." *A.E.R.* 62 (September 1972): 540–52.

Stockman, Alan C. *Introduction to Economics.* Fort Worth, Texas: Dryden, 1996.

Svensson, Lars E. O. "Sticky Goods Prices, Flexible Asset Prices, Monopolistic Competition, and Monetary Policy," *Rev. Econ. Studies* 53 (July 1986): 385–405.

Taylor, John B. "Estimation and Control of a Macroeconomic Model with Rational Expectations." *Econometrica* 47 (September 1979): 1267–86.

Tinbergen, Jan. *Business Cycles in the United States of America, 1919–1932.* Geneva: League of Nations, 1939.

Tobin, James. "The Interest-Elasticity of Transactions Demand for Cash." *Rev. Econ. and Statis.* 38 (August 1956): 241–47.

Uzawa, Hirofumi. "Optimal Growth in a Two-Sector Model of Capital Accumulation." *Rev, Econ. Studies* 31 (January 1964): 1–24.

Wallace, Neil. "The Overlapping Generations Model of Fiat Money." In *Models of Monetary Economies,* edited by John H. Kareken and Neil Wallace. Minneapolis: Fed. Reserve Bank, 1980.

———. "Lucas's Signal-Extraction Model: A Finite State Exposition with Aggregate Real Shocks." *J. Monetary Econ.* 30 (December 1992): 433–47.

Wicksell, Knut. *Interest and Prices: A Study of the Causes Regulating the Value of Money,* 1898. Translated by R. F. Kahn. London: Macmillan (for Royal Econ. Soc.), 1936.

Williamson, Stephen D. "Optimal Monetary Policy in an Economy with Sequential Service." Working paper. Iowa City: Univ. Iowa, 1995.

— 17 —

Inflation and Welfare

1. Introduction

In a monetary economy, it is in everyone's private interest to try to get someone else to hold non-interest-bearing cash and reserves.[1] But someone has to hold it all, so all of these efforts must simply cancel out. All of us spend several hours per year in this effort, and we employ thousands of talented and highly-trained people to help us. These person-hours are simply thrown away, wasted on a task that should not have to be performed at all.

Since the opportunity cost of holding non-interest-bearing money is the nominal rate of interest, we would expect that the time people spend trying to economize on cash holdings should be an increasing function of the interest rate. This observation is consistent with much evidence, and suggests that as long as interest rates are positive people could be made better off if money growth, and hence the average inflation rate and the interest rate, were reduced. The problems of working out the details of this theoretical idea and of applying it to estimate the potential gains in welfare

---

Econometrica 68, no. 2 (March 2000): 247–274.

1. This paper was prepared for the 1997 summer meetings of the Econometric Society in Pasadena, Hong Kong, and Toulouse. Earlier versions, entitled "On the Welfare Cost of Inflation," were given at the 1993 Hitotsubashi International Symposium on Financial Markets in the Changing World, and at conferences in Bergen and the Federal Reserve Bank of San Francisco. I am grateful to many colleagues and discussants, but particularly to Martin Bailey, Lars Hansen, Bennett McCallum, Casey Mulligan, and Nancy Stokey, for helpful discussion and criticism. Michael Beveridge, Vimut Vanitcharearnthum, Tomoyuki Nakajima, and Esteban Rossi-Hansberg provided able research assistance. The National Science Foundation provided research support.

from the adoption of the monetary policies that reduce inflation and interest rates are classic questions of monetary economics, addressed in a long line of research stemming from the contributions of Bailey (1956) and Friedman (1969). The goal of this paper is to provide a substantive summary of where this line of research stands today.

The way the analysis of inflation and its consequences has developed over the years is also interesting from a methodological point of view, as an illustration of the extent to which the quantitative, mathematical vision shared by the founders of the Econometric Society has succeeded in transforming the practice of economics. An applied economist today uses explicit theoretical modelling to organize data from a variety of sources and brings this information to bear on quantitative questions of policy in a way that is almost entirely a development of the last 50 years. As compared to older, more literary methods, the explicit theoretical style of postwar economics can lead to sharper questions and better answers, and at the same time expose the limits of current knowledge in ways that can stimulate improvements in both theory and data. I would like the present paper to exemplify these virtues as well.

In the next section, I will display and discuss evidence on money, prices, production, and interest rates for the 20th century United States. Using this evidence, I replicate essentially Meltzer's (1963a) estimated money demand function, and then use these estimates to replicate Bailey's (1956) welfare cost calculations. The rest of the paper deals with the theoretical interpretation of these calculations.

Section 3 provides one possible general equilibrium rationale for the welfare estimates reported in Section 2, based on a simplified version of Sidrauski's (1967a, b) model. Section 4 then uses the Sidrauski framework to consider the consequences of dropping the assumption, used in Section 3, that the monetary policy that implements any given interest rate can be carried out with lump-sum fiscal transfers. It re-examines the estimation under the alternate assumption that only flat rate income taxes can be used, and that a government sector of given size must be financed either with inflation taxation or with income taxation. This modification introduces theoretical complications but does not, I argue, lead to major quantitative differences from the conclusions of Section 2.

Section 5 provides a second general equilibrium rationale for the welfare estimates of Section 2, using as context a model of a transactions technology proposed by McCallum and Goodfriend (1987). This model provides another theoretical justification of the consumers' surplus formulas used in Section 2, one that turns out to be closely related to Baumol's (1952) inventory-theoretic analysis. Section 6 contains concluding remarks.

2. Money Demand and Consumers' Surplus

Figure 1 shows plots of annual time series of a short-term nominal interest rate, r_t, and of the ratio of M1 to nominal GDP, $m_t = M_t/(P_t y_t)$, for the United States, for the period 1900–1994.[2] Over this 95-year period, real GDP grew at an average annual rate of 3 percent, M1 grew at 5.6 percent, and the GDP deflator grew at 3.2 percent. The money-income ratio is thus essentially trendless over the entire century, although there has been a strong downward trend since World War II. Technical change in the provision of transactions services would, other things equal, produce a downward trend in the money-income ratio m_t. An income elasticity of money demand exceeding one would produce an upward trend. Neither trend appears in the data, though of course both might have been present in an offsetting way.

In this section, I will interpret these two time series as points on a demand function for real balances of the form $M_t/P_t = L(r_t, y_t)$, where this function L takes the form $L(r, y) = m(r)y$.[3] Figure 2 displays a plot of observations (the circles in the figure) on the money-income ratio m_t and the interest rate r_t for the years 1900–1994. The figure also plots the curves

2. The interest rate is the short-term commercial paper rate. For 1900–75, it is from Friedman and Schwartz (1982, Table 4.8, Column 6). For 1976–94, it is from the *Economic Report of the President* (1996, Table B-69).

The money supply is *M1* in billions of dollars, December of each year, not seasonally adjusted. For 1900–14, it is from *Historical Statistics of the United States* (1960, Series X-267). From 1915–1947, it is from Friedman and Schwartz (1982, pp. 708–718, Column 7). For 1948–85, it is from the *International Financial Statistics Tape*. From 1986–94, it is from the Federal Reserve Bank of St. Louis *FRED Database.*

Real GDP is in billions of 1987 dollars. From 1900–28, it is from Kendrick (1961, Table A-III). From 1929–58, it is from the *National Income and Product Accounts of the U.S., 1929–1958,* Table 1.2. From 1929–94, it is from *Citibase,* Series GDPQ.

The GDP deflator equals 1.0 in 1987. For 1900–1928, it is from *Historical Statistics of the United States* (1960, Series F-5). For 1929–58, it is from the *National Income and Product Accounts of the U.S., 1929–1958,* Table 7.13. For 1959–94, it is from *Citibase,* Series GDPD.

3. Estimates of the income or wealth elasticity of money (MI or M2) demand obtained from long U.S. time series tend to be around unity: Meltzer (1963a), Laidler (1977), Lucas (1988), Stock and Watson (1993). Ball (1998), using methods simitar to Stock and Watson's but applied to data through 1996, obtains an income elasticity near 0.5. Meltzer (1963b)

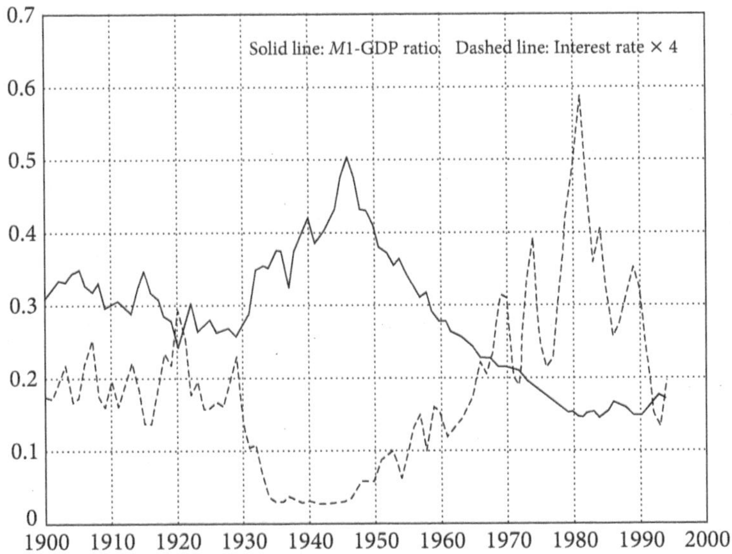

U.S. money, income, and interest rates

Figure 1

$m = Ar^{-\eta}$ for the η-values 0.3, 0.5, and 0.7, where A is selected so the curve passes through the geometric means of the data pairs. Within this parametric family, it is evident that $\eta = 0.5$ gives the best fit. Figure 3 presents the same data, this time alongside the curves $m = Be^{-\xi r}$ for the ξ-values 5, 7, and 9. Again, all three curves pass through the geometric means. Within this parametric family, $\xi = 7$ appears to give the best fit. It is also clear, I think, that the semi-log function plotted here provides a description of the data that is much inferior to the log-log curve in Figure 2.[4]

In order to provide some perspective on these estimates, Figure 4 plots actual U.S. real balances (not deflated by income) against the real balances predicted by the log-log demand curve: $Ar_t^{-0.5}y_t$. One sees that the fitted values successfully track the secular increase in the money-income ratio

reports estimates near one for sales elasticities in a cross-section sample of firms. Estimates from post-war quarterly data are generally below one: Goldfeld (1987). Recent estimates by Mulligan and Sala-i-Martin (1992) from panel data on U.S. states are higher, around 1.3.

4. Cagan (1956) used the semi-log form in his classic study of the European hyperinflations. It is interesting that the paradox that Cagan noted, of inflation rates during hyperinflations that exceeded the revenue-maximizing levels, is specific to semi-log money demand. With, log-log demand, seigniorage is always an increasing function of the money growth rate.

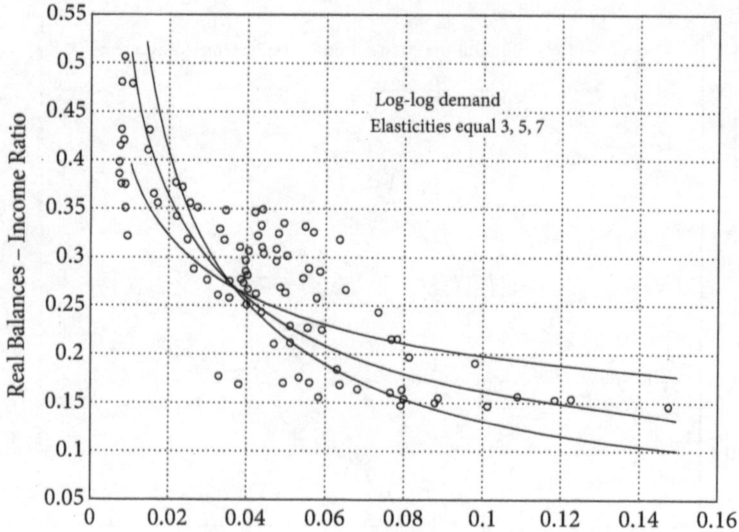

Interest Rate

U.S. money demand, 1900–1994

Figure 2

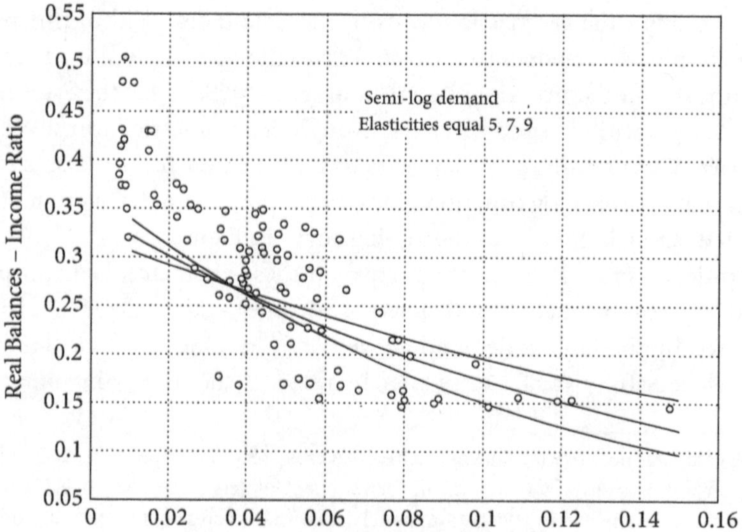

Interest Rate

U.S. money demand, 1900–1994

Figure 3

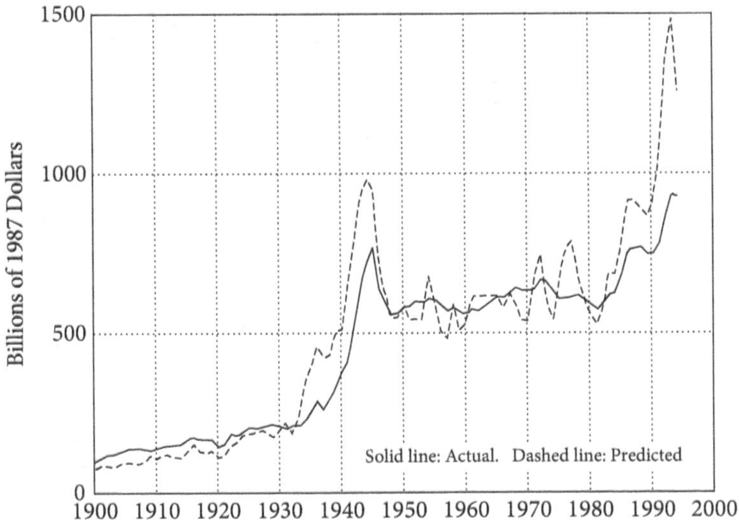

Actual and predicted real balances, 1900–1994

Figure 4

prior to World War II, including the acceleration of this increase in the 1930s and 40s. They also track the decrease in m_t, as interest rates rose in the postwar period (though they miss the 1990s, when interest rates declined and velocity did not). One also sees, however, that the fitted series exhibits some large, shorter-term, fluctuations that do not appear in the actual series. The interest elasticity needed to fit the long-term trends (and very sharply estimated by these trends) is much too high to permit a good fit on a year-to-year basis. Of course, it is precisely this difficulty that has motivated much of the money demand research of the last 30 years, and has led to distributed lag formulations of money demand that attempt to reconcile the evidence at different frequencies. In my opinion, this reconciliation has not yet been achieved, but in any case, it is clear that the functions plotted in Figures 2 and 3 contribute nothing toward the resolution of this problem.

To translate the evidence on money demand into a welfare cost estimate, we first apply the method of Bailey (1956), defining the welfare cost of inflation as the area under the inverse demand function—the *consumers' surplus*—that could be gained by reducing the interest rate from r to zero. That is, let $m(r)$ be the estimated function, let $\psi(m)$ be the inverse function, and define the welfare cost function $w(r)$ by

$$w(r) = \int_{m(r)}^{m(0)} \psi(x)\,dx = \int_0^r m(x)\,dx - rm(r). \tag{2.1}$$

Since the function m has the dimensions of a ratio to income, so does the function w. Its value $w(r)$ has the interpretation, to be made more precise in later sections, as the fraction of income people would require as compensation in order to make them indifferent between living in a steady state with an interest rate constant at r and an otherwise identical steady state with an interest rate of (or near) zero.

For the log-log demand function $m(r) = Ar^{-\eta}$, (2.1) implies

$$w(r) = A\frac{\eta}{1-\eta}r^{1-\eta}.$$

For $\eta = 0.5$, this is just a square root function. It is plotted in Figure 5. For the semi-log function $m(r) = Be^{-\xi r}$, (2.1) implies

$$w(r) = \frac{B}{\xi}[1 - (1 + \xi r)e^{-\xi r}].$$

This curve is also plotted, for $\xi = 7$, in Figure 5. This is the parameterization used by Bailey.

Note that the two demand curves imply very different estimates for the

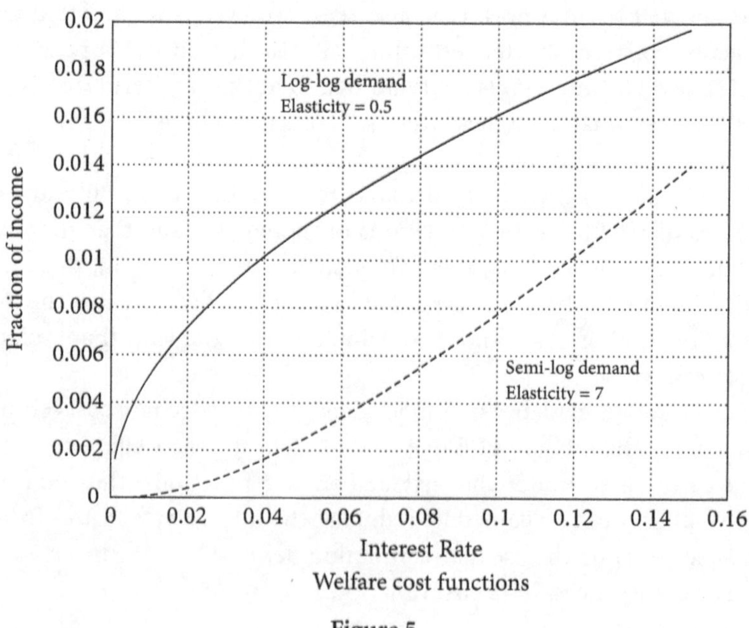

Figure 5

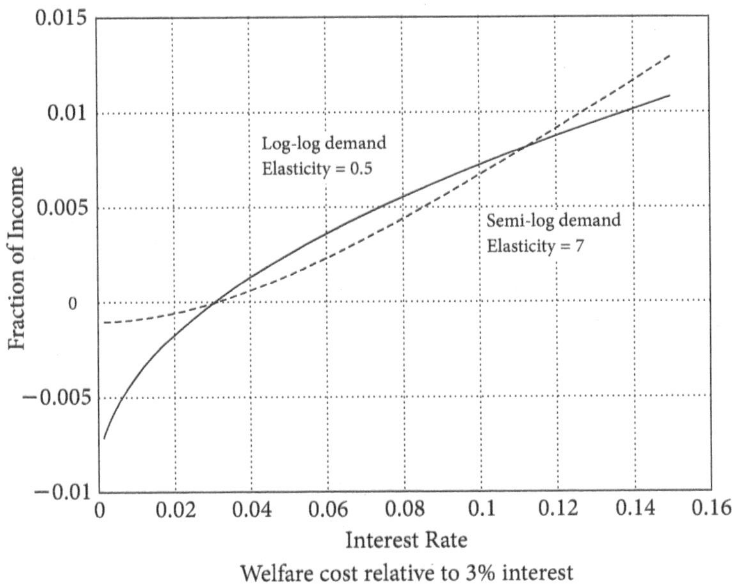

Figure 6

welfare cost of moderate inflations. At a six percent interest rate, for example, the log-log curve implies a welfare cost of about one percent of income, while the semi-log curve implies a cost of less than 0.3 percent. But much of this difference is due to the difference in behavior at very low interest rates predicted by these two curves. Figure 6 plots the curves $w(r) - w(0.03)$ for both fitted demand curves, where $r = 0.03$ is chosen as the interest rate that would be associated with an inflation rate of zero. Since the two curves on Figure 5 are nearly parallel between interest rates of 3 and 10 percent, the two curves on Figure 6 imply very similar estimates of the cost of exceeding an inflation rate of zero by moderate amounts. The main difference, then, is that log-log demand implies a substantial gain in moving from zero inflation to the deflation rate needed to reduce nominal interest rates to zero, while under semi-log demand this gain is trivial.

3. The Sidrauski Framework

In order to decide whether we want to view either of the curves plotted in Figure 5 as describing the consequences of policy changes in the actual U.S. economy, we need to be clear on the nature of the thought experiment the outcome of which is traced out by these curves. For this purpose, we need a model of the entire economy that can let us see what changes in monetary policy might generate the curve $m(r)$ and the associated welfare costs $w(r)$. Simply labelling the points plotted in Figure 2 a "demand function" does not tell us anything about what we are estimating or how accurate these estimates are: Giving colorful names to statistical relationships is not a substitute for economic theory.

The following simplified version of the general equilibrium model of Sidrauski (1967a, b) provides one framework that can provide an explicit rationale for the consumers' surplus formula (2.1).[5] Consider a deterministic, representative agent model, in which households gain utility from the consumption c of a single, nonstorable good, and from their holdings $z = M/P$ of real balances. Household preferences are

$$\sum_{t=0}^{\infty} (1+\rho)^{-t} U(c_t, z_t), \tag{3.1}$$

where the current period utility function U is given by

$$U(c, z) = \frac{1}{1-\sigma}\left[c\varphi\left(\frac{z}{c}\right)\right]^{1-\sigma}, \tag{3.2}$$

provided $\sigma \neq 1$. These homothetic preferences are consistent with the absence of trend in the ratio of real balances to income in U.S. data, and the constant relative risk aversion form is consistent with balanced growth.

Each household is endowed with one unit of time, which is inelastically supplied to the market and which produces $y_t = y_0(1+\gamma)^t$ units of the consumption good in period t.[6] Hence one equilibrium condition is

$$c_t = y_t = y_0(1+\gamma)^t.$$

Households begin period t with M_t units of money, out of which they pay a lump sum tax H_t (or, if $H_t < 0$, receive a lump sum transfer). The price level is P_t, so the cash flow constraint for households is

$$M_{t+1} = M_t - H_t + P_t y_t - P_t c_t$$

in nominal terms. In real terms, it is

5. Here I follow Brock's (1974) perfect-foresight version of the Sidrauski model.

6. Throughout this paper I take the real growth rate γ to be independent of monetary policy. The role of inflation when real growth is endogenously determined is examined in De Gregorio (1993), Gomme (1993), Jones and Manuelli (1995), Chari, Jones, and Manuelli (1995), and Dotsey and Ireland (1996).

$$(1 + \pi_{t+1})z_{t+1} = z_t - h_t + y_t - c_t, \tag{3.3}$$

where $h_t = H_t/P_t$ and $1 + \pi_t = P_t/P_{t-1}$.

We consider the decision problem of a household in an economy on a balanced growth equilibrium path, on which the money growth rate is constant at μ, maintained by a constant ratio $v = h/y$ of transfers to income. In this case, the ratio of money to income will be constant, and the inflation factor $1 + \pi_t$ will be constant at the value $(1 + \mu)/(1 + \gamma)$. Let $\tilde{v}(z, y)$ be the value of the maximized objective function (3.1) for a household in such an equilibrium that has real balances z when the economy-wide income level has reached y. This function $\tilde{v}$ satisfies the Bellman equation:

$$\tilde{v}(z, y) = \max_c \left\{ \frac{1}{1-\sigma}\left[c\varphi\left(\frac{z}{c}\right)\right]^{1-\sigma} + \frac{1}{1+\rho}\tilde{v}\left(z', y(1+\gamma)\right)\right\}, \tag{3.4}$$

where next period's real balances z' are

$$z' = \frac{z - h + y - c}{1 + \pi}.$$

Under the homogeneity assumptions I have imposed, the problem (3.4) can be simplified to a single state variable problem as follows. Define the function $v(m)$ by

$$\tilde{v}(z, y) = v(m)y^{1-\sigma},$$

where $m = z/y$ is the money-income ratio. If we view $\omega = c/y$ as the household's choice variable, we can see that the function $v(m)$ will satisfy:[7]

$$v(m) = \max_\omega \left\{ \frac{1}{1-\sigma}\left[\omega\varphi\left(\frac{m}{\omega}\right)\right]^{1-\sigma} + \frac{(1+\gamma)^{1-\sigma}}{1+\rho} v(m')\right\} \tag{3.5}$$

where

$$m' = \frac{z'}{y(1+\gamma)} = \frac{z - h + y - c}{y(1+\gamma)(1+\pi)} = \frac{m - v + 1 - \omega}{1 + \mu}.$$

The first-order and envelope conditions for the problem (3.5), evaluated at $\omega = 1$ (which will hold along any equilibrium path) are:

7. If a function v satisfies (3.5), then it is easy to see that the function $\tilde{v}(m, y) = y^{1-\sigma}v(m/y)$ satisfies (3.4). Ruling out other solutions to (3.4) is mote difficult. In general, I will not provide a rigorous treatment of the Bellman equations that arise in this paper.

$$[\varphi(m)]^{-\sigma}[\varphi(m) - m\varphi'(m)] = \frac{1}{1+r} v'\left(\frac{m-\nu}{1+\mu}\right),$$

and

$$v'(m) = [\varphi(m)]^{-\sigma}\varphi'(m) + \frac{1}{1+r} v'\left(\frac{m-\nu}{1+\mu}\right),$$

where the nominal interest rate r is defined by

$$\frac{1}{1+r} = \frac{(1+\gamma)^{1-\sigma}}{(1+\rho)(1+\mu)}. \tag{3.6}$$

(Note that this nominal interest r approximately equals $\rho + \sigma\gamma + \mu - \gamma$, the familiar sum of the real rate and the inflation premium.) Along the balanced path, m is constant, and eliminating $v'(m)$ between these two equations and simplifying yields

$$\frac{\varphi'(m)}{\varphi(m) - m\varphi'(m)} = r. \tag{3.7}$$

Let $m(r)$ denote the m value that satisfies (3.7), expressed as a function of the interest rate. Throughout the paper, it is this kind of steady state equilibrium relation $m(r)$ that I call a "money demand function," and that I identify with the curves shown in Figures 2 and 3.

The flow utility enjoyed by the household on the balanced path is $U(y, m(r)y)$, where y is growing at the constant rate γ. Provided $m'(r) < 0$, this utility is maximized over nonnegative nominal interest rates at $r = 0$: the Friedman (1969) rule of a deflation equal to the real rate of interest.[8] In this section, I define the welfare cost $w(r)$ of a nominal rate r to be the percentage income compensation needed to leave the household indifferent between r and 0. That is, $w(r)$ is defined as the solution to

$$U[(1 + w(r))y, m(r)y] = U[y, m(0)y].$$

With the assumed functional form (3.2), this definition is equivalent to

8. Depending on the way the holding of real balances is motivated, the equilibrium in the limiting economy where $r = 0$ may be ill-defined, or there may be equilibria with $r = 0$ that are not close to equilibria with r positive but arbitrarily small. I will confine attention here to economies with $r > 0$. By referring to 0 as the optimal rate in this context I mean that reducing r is welfare-improving for any $r > 0$.

$$(1+w(r))\varphi\left(\frac{m(r)}{1+w(r)}\right)=\varphi[m(0)]. \tag{3.8}$$

An estimated function $m(r)$ can be used to calculate the function $w(r)$ as follows. Let $m(r)$ be given and let $\psi(m)$ be the inverse function. Then (3.7) implies that the function φ satisfies the differential equation

$$\varphi'(m)=\frac{\psi(m)}{1+m\psi(m)}\varphi(m). \tag{3.9}$$

Differentiating (3.8) through with respect to r, we obtain

$$0=w'(r)\varphi\left(\frac{m(r)}{1+w(r)}\right)+\varphi'\left(\frac{m(r)}{1+w(r)}\right)\left[m'(r)-\frac{m(r)w'(r)}{1+w(r)}\right]. \tag{3.10}$$

Now apply (3.9) with $m=m(r)/(1+w(r))$ to (3.10) and cancel, to obtain the differential equation

$$w'(r)=-\psi\left(\frac{m(r)}{1+w(r)}\right)m'(r) \tag{3.11}$$

in the welfare cost function w, which has the natural initial condition $w(0)=0$.

Given any money demand function m (and inverse ψ), (3.11) is readily solved numerically for an exact welfare cost function $w(r)$. But comparing (3.11) and (2.1), one can guess that for small values of r—and hence of $w(r)$—the solution to (3.11) must be very close to the value implied by the consumers' surplus formula. In fact, on a plot such as Figure 5 the exact and the approximate solutions cannot be distinguished by the eye. (See also Figure 8 in Section 5.)

We can also solve the differential equation (3.9) for the function φ, reconstructing the utility function. For the particular demand function $m(r)=A/\sqrt{r}$, for example, (3.9) has the solution

$$\varphi(m)=\left[1+\frac{A^2}{m}\right]^{-1}$$

with the boundary condition $\varphi(0)=0$, Since the value of A in the U.S. is empirically about 0.05 (see Figure 2), the Sidrauski utility function takes the form

$$U(c,z) = \frac{1}{1-\sigma}\left(\left[\frac{1}{c} + \frac{0.0025}{z}\right]^{\sigma-1} - 1\right).$$

The implied elasticity of substitution between goods and real balances is 0.5. The estimated money demand function gives no information on the intertemporal substitution parameter σ.[9]

To interpret the welfare cost functions plotted in Figure 5, then, we think of these curves as tracing out different steady states of deterministic economies subjected to different, constant rates of money growth. The differences in interest rates across these economies are attributed *solely* to differences in inflation premia. This interpretation seems to me to rationalize a focus on low-frequency evidence on money demand in the 20th century U.S. time series, and suggests the possibility that accurate estimates of welfare costs, in the sense of across-steady-state comparisons, can be obtained without a good understanding of the behavior of velocity at high frequencies.

Using a general equilibrium framework to interpret the welfare estimates of the last section, even one as simple as my version of Sidrauski's, is helpful—essential, really—in exploring the effects of changes in assumptions on these estimates. Many economists, for example, believe that a deterministic framework like Bailey's or mine misses important costs of inflation that are thought to arise from price or inflation rate *variability*. It would be a straightforward exercise, today, to add stochastic shocks of realistic magnitude and behavior to both real productivity and money supply behavior in this model, and to re-examine the welfare calculations in this new context. Based on the Cooley and Hansen (1989) study of a similar model of the U.S. economy, I am very confident that the effects of such a modification on the welfare costs estimated in Section 2 would be negligible.[10] In the next section, I will illustrate in another way this process of modifying the model in order to examine the importance of its simplifying assumptions.

9. The irrelevance of the intertemporal substitution parameter for money demand reflects the fact that, in this model, money is dominated as a store of value by nominal bonds.

10. Burdick (1997) contains an interesting analysis of transition dynamics in a model closely related to Cooley and Hansen's.

4. Fiscal Considerations

In the analysis to this point the nominal interest rate r has been treated as a policy variable, and the welfare cost of inflation has been defined by a comparison of resource allocations when $r > 0$ to a benchmark case of $r = 0$, In fact, of course, any particular interest rate policy must be implemented by a specific money supply policy, and this monetary policy must in turn be implemented by a policy of fiscal transfers, open market operations, or both. This fact raises no difficulties as long as the necessary transfers can be effected through lump-sum payments or assessments, but if this is not possible the optimality of the Friedman rule can cease to obtain. Aspects of this question have been examined by Phelps (1973), Bewley (1983), Kimbrough (1986a, b), Lucas and Stokey (1983a), Woodford (1990), Cooley and Hansen (1991), Eckstein and Leiderman (1992), Miller (1995), and most recently by Guidotti and Vegh (1993), Chari, Christiano, and Kehoe (1993), Correia and Teles (1997), and Mulligan and Sala-i-Martin (1997). This section addresses some of these fiscal questions in the contexts of the Sidrauski model of the last section.

Let $m(r)$ be steady state real balances. Define the parameter δ by $1 + \delta = (1 + \rho)/(1 + \gamma)^{1-\sigma}$, so that $\delta \approx \rho + \sigma\gamma - \gamma$ is the amount by which the real interest rate exceeds the growth rate of output. Recall that $r = \delta + \mu$ and $\nu = -\mu m(r)$. Then the consumer budget constraint and the resource constraint together imply that to implement a nominal interest rate r, the fraction

$$\nu = -\mu m(r) = (\delta - r)m(r) \tag{4.1}$$

of income y_t must be transferred from the private sector to the government in a steady state, in the form of real balances withdrawn from circulation. (If $\delta < r$, the negative of this magnitude is seigniorage revenue, relative to income.)

For the function $m(r) = A/\sqrt{r}$ that fits U.S. data, $m(r) \to \infty$ as $r \to 0$, so if the flow (4.1) must be withdrawn using a fractional tax on income, the policy $r = 0$ is not feasible. The need to resort to income taxation thus places a positive lower bound on r. But with $\delta = 0.02$ and $A = 0.05$, an income tax rate of 0.03 would implement an interest rate of 0.001 (that is, one-tenth of one percent). The Friedman rule requires qualification in this case, but the qualification is of no quantitative interest.

The cases considered by most of the authors cited above, however, have the additional complications that labor is elastically supplied, so an income tax distorts resource allocation, and there is a positive amount of government consumption, necessitating a resort to distorting taxation of some kind. In these circumstances, it is not impossible that a positive inflation tax might have a useful role to play in the overall tax structure. In this section, these two features will be added to the model of Section 3, and the welfare cost calculations described there will be redone. The results of these calculations are given in Figure 7.

We modify the current period preferences (3.1) to include the consumption of leisure, x:

$$U(c, m, x) = \frac{1}{1-\sigma}\left[c\varphi\left(\frac{z}{c}\right)\phi(x)\right]^{1-\sigma}.$$

Modify the resource constraint to include government consumption, g_t:

$$c_t + g_t = (1 - x_t)y_t = (1 - x_t)y_0(1 + \gamma)^t.$$

Modify consumers' budget constraints to reflect income taxation at a flat rate τ:

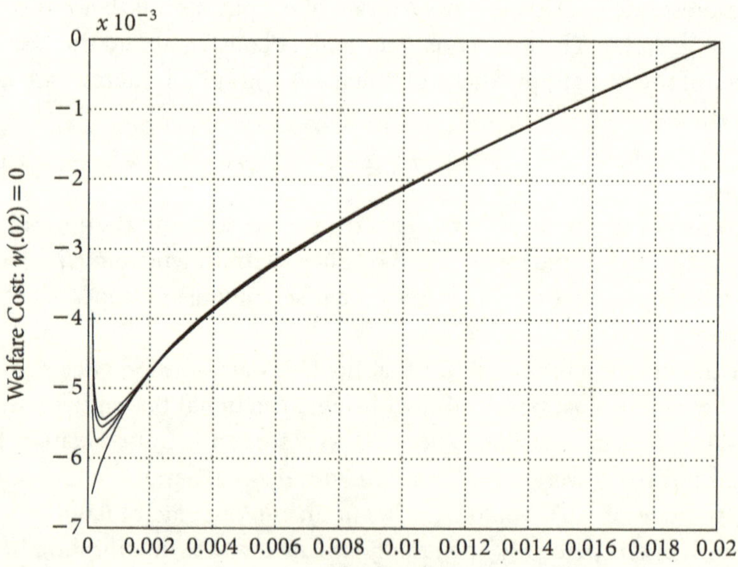

Welfare cost with income taxation

Figure 7

$$(1+\mu)m_{t+1} = m_t + (1-\tau)(1-x_t) - \omega_t,$$

where $m_t = z_t/y_t$ is the ratio of money to full income, and $\omega_t = c_t/y_t$.

If government consumption is a constant ratio g to full income y_t, this model has an equilibrium path with constant ratios of consumption and real balances to income and with leisure constant as well. Using the same normalization employed in Section 3, an individual household's Bellman equation on such a path is

$$v(m) = \max_{\omega, x}\left\{\frac{1}{1-\sigma}\left[\omega\varphi\left(\frac{m}{\omega}\right)\phi(x)\right]^{1-\sigma} + \frac{(1+\gamma)^{1-\sigma}}{1+\rho}v(m')\right\}$$

where

$$(1+\mu)m' = m + (1-\tau)(1-x) - \omega.$$

The first order and envelope conditions for this problem are

$$\left[\omega\phi\left(\frac{m}{\omega}\right)\phi(x)\right]^{-\sigma}\left[\varphi\left(\frac{m}{\omega}\right) - \frac{m}{\omega}\varphi'\left(\frac{m}{\omega}\right)\right]\phi(x) = \frac{1}{1+r}v'(m'),$$

$$\left[\omega\varphi\left(\frac{m}{\omega}\right)\phi(x)\right]^{-\sigma}\omega\varphi\left(\frac{m}{\omega}\right)\phi'(x) = \frac{1}{1+r}v'(m')(1-\tau),$$

and

$$v'(m) = \left[\omega\varphi\left(\frac{m}{\omega}\right)\phi(x)\right]^{-\sigma}\varphi'\left(\frac{m}{\omega}\right)\phi(x) + \frac{1}{1+r}v'(m'),$$

where again the nominal interest rate r is defined by (3.6). Along the balanced path, m is constant, and eliminating $u'(m)$ from these equations and simplifying yields

$$r\left[\varphi\left(\frac{m}{\omega}\right) - \frac{m}{\omega}\varphi'\left(\frac{m}{\omega}\right)\right] = \varphi'\left(\frac{m}{\omega}\right), \tag{4.2}$$

$$\omega\varphi\left(\frac{m}{\omega}\right)\phi'(x) = \left[\varphi\left(\frac{m}{\omega}\right) - \frac{m}{\omega}\varphi'\left(\frac{m}{\omega}\right)\right]\phi(x)(1-\tau). \tag{4.3}$$

Additional steady state equilibrium conditions are

$$\omega + g + x = 1, \tag{4.4}$$

$$\mu m = (1 - \tau)(1 - x) - \omega. \tag{4.5}$$

Condition (4.2) just repeats (3.6). Condition (4.3) equates the marginal rate of substitution between goods and leisure to the after-tax real wage, $1 - \tau$. Conditions (4.4) and (4.5) are the resource and consumer budget constraints; together, they imply the government budget constraint. For any given nominal interest rate r and government consumption rate g, (4.2)–(4.5) are four equations that can be solved for the steady state allocation (ω, x, m) and the income tax rate τ. Any monetary policy dictates a tax policy, depending on the extent to which seigniorage revenues help to finance g, or the extent to which the need to withdraw cash from the public adds to the burden on the tax system.

Figure 7 tabulates a welfare cost function $w(r)$, defined as

$$U[(1 + w(r))c(r), m(r), x(r)] = U[c(\delta), m(\delta), x(\delta)]. \tag{4.6}$$

I use $r = \delta$ as a benchmark rather than $r = 0$ because, depending on the assumed functions φ and ϕ, the system (4.2)–(4.5) may not have a solution at $r = 0$.

The figure is based on the following parameterization. For the function φ, I used $\varphi(m) = (1 + 1/(km))^{-1}$, which follows from the money demand function $m(r) = A\sqrt{1/r}$; A was set equal to 0.05, to fit the U.S. data. For the function ϕ, I used $\phi(x) = x^{\beta}$. With these assumptions, the definition (4.6) of the function $w(r)$ implies

$$(1 + w(r))\frac{m(r)}{1 + k\left(m(r)/\omega(r)\right)}x(r)^{\beta} = \frac{m(\delta)}{1 + k\left(m(\delta)/\omega(\delta)\right)}x(\delta)^{\beta}.$$

I let the elasticity β range over the values 0.0001, 0.3, 0.6, and 0.9. Reading from bottom to top, these are the four curves plotted in Figure 7. I set $1 - g = 0.35$, so that if $x = 0$, $\omega = 1$. Finally, I set $\delta = 0.02$.

One can see from Figure 7 that above about half a percent, estimated welfare costs are the same as in the inelastic labor supply, lump sum tax case studied in earlier sections. The effects of distorting taxation appear only at extremely low interest rates. Thus for a leisure elasticity of $\beta = 0.3$, the optimal interest rate is about 0.03 percent, while at $\beta = 0.9$, it is about 0.04 percent. For any $\beta > 0$, the optimal r is strictly positive, but the deviations from $r = 0$ are minute. The differences in welfare are small too. The minimized welfare costs are in all cases less than -0.0045, while the intercept of the benchmark curve, $-w(\delta)$, is -0.006, a difference of 0.0015 times income.

These second-best tax problems have so many logical possibilities that I thought it would be useful to work one case through, quantitatively, to see what kind of magnitudes are at stake. But the case I selected for study is, in some respects, arbitrary, and the literature cited above is helpful in isolating crucial assumptions. The model underlying Figure 7 is a special case of the model analyzed in Section 2 of Chari, Christiano, and Kehoe (1993), where it is shown that the Friedman $r = 0$ policy is optimal in the sense of Ramsey, provided that the private sector begins with a net nominal position (money plus nominal debt) of zero. If, on the other hand, the net nominal position of the private sector is positive, a monetary-fiscal policy that is efficient in Ramsey's sense entails an initial hyperinflation to exploit the capital levy possibilities. In my analysis, there is no government debt and the public holds a positive initial nominal position (its cash), but I have constrained the money growth rate and the tax rate to be constant, precluding a capital levy. Under these assumptions, Woodford (1990) shows that $r = 0$ is not optimal, a fact that Figure 7 reflects.

In short, the optimality of the Friedman rule can be studied in a very wide variety of second-best frameworks, with a wide variety of different qualitative conclusions. In the specific context I have used, the Friedman rule needs qualification, but the magnitude of the needed amendment is trivially small. The fact is that real balances are a very minor "good" in the U.S. economy, so the fiscal consequences of even sizeable changes in the rate at which this good is taxed—the inflation rate—are just not likely to be large.[11]

5. The McCallum-Goodfriend Framework

The Sidrauski theory takes us behind the estimated money demand function to possible underlying preferences and technology, and by so doing certainly clarifies the welfare interpretation of Figure 5. It is also a convenient framework for exploring the consequences of different assumptions that may affect welfare cost estimates, such as the fiscal considerations examined in the last section. It is less helpful in thinking about cash management behavior at very low interest rates. The same criticism can be raised about Friedman's (1969) argument: What does it mean, exactly, to satiate

11. In the U.S. tax structure, inflation also has an indirect effect on the effective tax rates on income from capital (due to its effects on allowable deductions for depreciation, for example). These effects, if not offset by indexing or legislative changes, can be sizeable. See Feldstein (1996) and Bullard and Russell (1997).

an economy with cash? To make progress on this question, one needs to think more concretely about what people *do* with their money holdings.

The cash-in-advance formulation used in Lucas and Stokey (1983b) provides a specific image of a cash-using society that could be useful for this purpose. In this section, though, I will use a version of McCallum and Goodfriend's (1987) proposed variation on the Sidrauski model. In their model, the use of cash is motivated by an assumed transactions technology, rather than by an assumption that real balances yield utility directly. One can also see useful connections between this assumed technology and earlier inventory-theoretic studies of money demand.

In the McCallum-Goodfriend model, household preferences depend on goods consumption only:

$$\sum_{t=0}^{\infty} (1+\rho)^{-t} \frac{1}{1-\sigma} c_t^{1-\sigma}, \qquad \sigma \neq 1. \tag{5.1}$$

Each household is endowed with one unit of time, which can be used either to produce goods or to carry out transactions. Call s the fraction devoted to transacting. The goods production technology is assumed to be

$$c_t = (1 - s_t)y_t = (1 - s_t)y_0(1+\gamma)^t. \tag{5.2}$$

The cash flow constraint in real terms is

$$(1 + \pi_{t+1})z_{t+1} = z_t - h_t + (1 - s_t)y_t - c_t,$$

where $z_t = M_t/P_t$. In terms of the money-income ratio m_t, this constraint reads

$$(1 + \mu_{t+1})m_{t+1} = m_t - v_t + 1 - s_t - \omega_t,$$

where $v_t = h_t/y_t$ and $\omega_t = c_t/y_t$.

The new element in the model is a transactions constraint, relating household holdings of real balances and the amount of household time devoted to transacting to the spending flow the household carries out. I assume that in real terms this constraint takes the form

$$c_t = z_t f(s_t), \tag{5.3}$$

which will be consistent with a unit income elasticity of money demand.[12]

12. Brock (1974) proposes a similar formulation, and shows that it is equivalent to a utility-based formulation in which utility depends on leisure as well as goods and real balances.

As in the last section, I consider the decision problem of a household in an economy on a balanced growth equilibrium in which the money growth rate is constant at μ, maintained by a constant ratio $\nu = h/y$ of transfers to income, the ratio of money to income is a constant m, and the inflation factor $1 + \pi_t$ is constant at the value $(1 + \mu)/(1 + \gamma)$. Think of the household's choice variables as the time allocation s and the consumption-income ratio ω. Let $y^{1-\sigma}v(m)$ be the value of the maximized objective function (5.1) for a household in this balanced path equilibrium that has a ratio of money balances to income of $m = M_t/(P_t y)$ when the economy-wide income level has reached y. Then the function v satisfies the Bellman equation

$$v(m) = \max_{\omega, s} \left\{ \frac{1}{1-\sigma} \omega^{1-\sigma} + \frac{(1+\gamma)^{1-\sigma}}{1+\rho} v(m') \right\}$$

subject to

$$\omega = mf(s),$$

where

$$m' = \frac{m - \nu + 1 - s - \omega}{1 + \mu}. \tag{5.4}$$

We use the transactions constraint to eliminate ω as a decision variable:

$$\begin{aligned} v(m) = \max_{s} \Bigg\{ & \frac{1}{1-\sigma} [mf(s)]^{1-\sigma} \\ & + \frac{(1+\gamma)^{1-\sigma}}{1+\rho} v\left(\frac{m - \nu + 1 - s - mf(s)}{1 + \mu} \right) \Bigg\}. \end{aligned} \tag{5.5}$$

The value function that satisfies (5.5) need not be concave, so one cannot use standard arguments to show that a time allocation that satisfies the first-order condition for (5.5) is in fact optimal. Even so, I will begin, as in Sections 3 and 4, by using the first-order and envelope conditions to characterize a balanced path equilibrium. Then I will carry out a numerical analysis of (5.5) to determine the conditions under which consumer utility is maximal along this balanced path.

The first-order and envelope conditions for (5.5) are

$$[mf(s)]^{-\sigma} mf'(s) = \frac{1}{1+r} v'(m')[1 + mf'(s)]$$

and

$$v'(m) = [mf(s)]^{-\sigma} f(s) + \frac{1}{1+r} v'(m')[1 - f(s)],$$

where as in Section 3, the nominal interest rate r is given by (3.6). Along the balanced path, $m = m'$, and eliminating $v'(m)$ and simplifying yields

$$f(s) = rmf'(s). \tag{5.6}$$

A second equilibrium condition follows from the transactions constraint and the fact that $\omega = c/y = 1 - s$ on a balanced path:

$$1 - s = mf(s). \tag{5.7}$$

Given f, we can solve (5.6) and (5.7) for s and m as functions of r.

In this model, the time spent economizing on cash use, $s(r)$, has the dimensions of a percentage reduction in production and consumption, and hence is itself a direct measure of the welfare cost of inflation, interpreted as wasted time. To estimate this function $s(r)$, we work backward from the function $m(r)$ as estimated in Section 2 to the transactions technology function f. As in Section 3, we do this by finding a first order differential equation in the welfare cost $s(r)$.

Given f, let $m(r)$ and $s(r)$ satisfy (5.6) and (5.7). Then differentiating (5.7) through with respect to r and using (5.6) and (5.7) to eliminate $f(s)$ and $f'(s)$ yields

$$s'(r) = -\frac{rm'(r)\big(1 - s(r)\big)}{1 - s(r) + rm(r)}. \tag{5.8}$$

Comparing (5.8) and (2.1), one can see that for small r—and hence small $s(r)$—solutions to (5.8) and the area under the inverse money demand function will be very close. Figure 8 plots the solution $s(r)$ with initial condition $s(0) = 0$ for the log-log and semi-log demand cases, for interest rates ranging from 0 to 2 (200%). Also plotted are the areas under the two demand curves, as in Figure 5. For the semi-log case, the exact and approximate welfare cost estimates cannot be distinguished. For the log-log case, the two curves are also virtually identical at interest rates below 20%. Thus the McCallum-Goodfriend model yields simply a new interpretation of estimates already obtained.

For the log-log case with interest elasticity of 0.5, the implied transactions time function is simply a straight line through the origin, $f(s) = ks$, for some constant k. This case is of particular interest, since a multiplica-

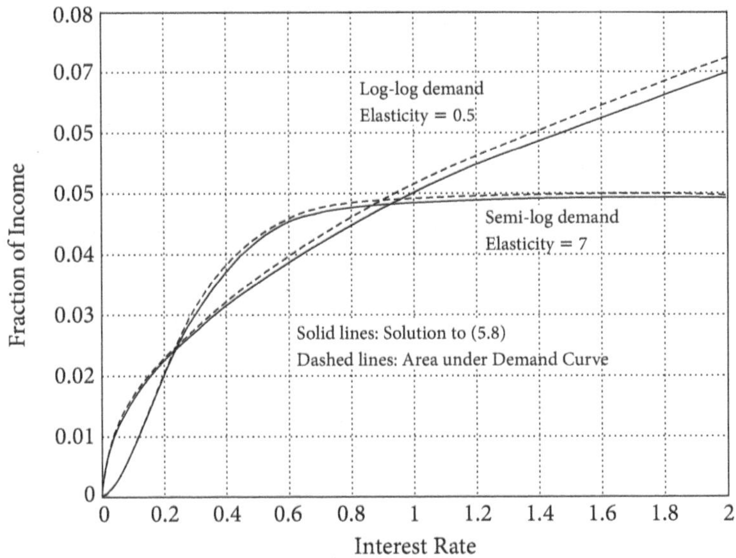

Approximate and exact welfare cost functions

Figure 8

tive transactions technology *kms* corresponds to the celebrated inventory-theoretic model introduced by Baumol (1952), and developed by Tobin (1956), Miller and Orr (1966), Dvoretsky and Patinkin (1965), Frenkel and Jovanovic(1980), and Chang (1992).[13] If one can sustain a given pattern of transactions with average balances m and s units of time in trips to the bank, then the same pattern can be sustained by halving average cash and doubling the number of trips. In this special case, the two steady state equations (5.6) and (5.7) become

$$s = rm$$

and

$$1 - s = kms,$$

13. Karni (1973), Kimbrough (1986a, b), Den Haan (1990), Cole and Stockman (1992), and Gillman (1993) have also used monetary models featuring a time-using technology for transactions. Karni is explicit about the links with the inventory-theoretic literature that I am here using to motivate a specific form for this technology. The construction of an explicit general equilibrium model in which agents solve Baumol-like cash management problems has not been carried out in any of these papers, nor is it in this one. See Fusselman and Grossman (1989) or Grossman (1987) for interesting results along this line. A useful recent contribution is Rodriguez (1996).

and eliminating the money-income ratio m between the two yields a quadratic in the steady state value of s:

$$\frac{k}{r}s^2 = 1 - s. \tag{5.9}$$

For large values of the ratio k/r, the unique positive solution to (5.9) is very well approximated by the square root rule[14]

$$s(r) = \sqrt{\frac{r}{k}},$$

and the money-income ratio by

$$m(r) = \sqrt{\frac{1}{rk}}. \tag{5.10}$$

The parameter k can be calibrated from the intercept $A = 0.05$ of the money demand function: $k = (0.05)^{-2} = 400$.

Could it be simply coincidence that the interest elasticity predicted by Baumol's theory—one-half—is the value that best fits U.S. time series evidence? This is a possibility, certainly, but attributing striking results to coincidence is not the way science tends to move forward![15]

Figures 9 and 10 report results of numerical calculations designed to check whether consumer utility is in fact maximized along the balanced path that I have constructed from the first-order conditions for the dynamic program (5.5). In all calculations, the technology $f(s) = ks$ is assumed, with $k = 400$. I assumed the real growth rate $\gamma = 0.02$ and a subjective discount rate of $\rho = 0.05$. The coefficient of risk aversion σ and the nominal interest rate r were varied over several values, as indicated. For

14. Jovanovic (1982) contains another derivation of the square root formula from an aggregative general equilibrium model.

15. Depending on the way one interprets the Baumol theory, one may take it as also predicting that the *income* elasticity of money demand is one-half. If this is right, the theory fails badly on U.S. time series evidence. The issue is whether we interpret the growth in the economy's aggregate production as growth in the size of the cash flows to be managed, or in the number of flows, or somewhere in between. The constant returns, unit income elasticity that I have built into the aggregate theory requires the assumption that it is the *number* of cash flows to be managed that doubles whenever real GDP doubles, not their average size.

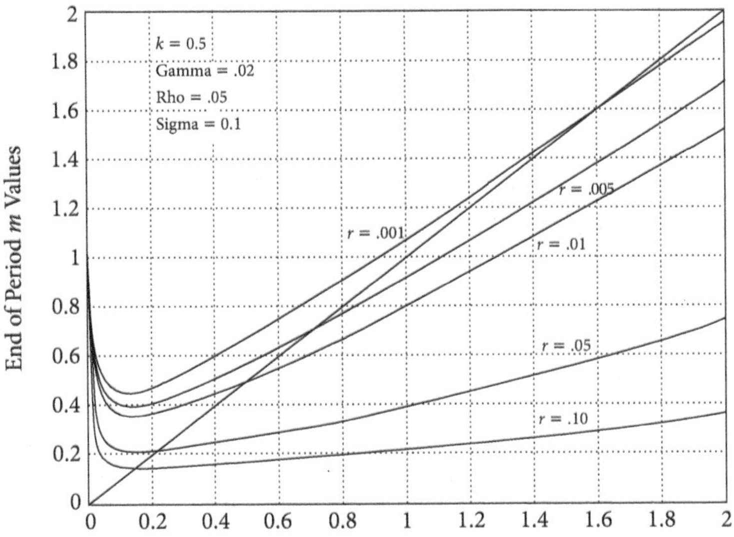

Policy functions for different interest rates

Figure 9

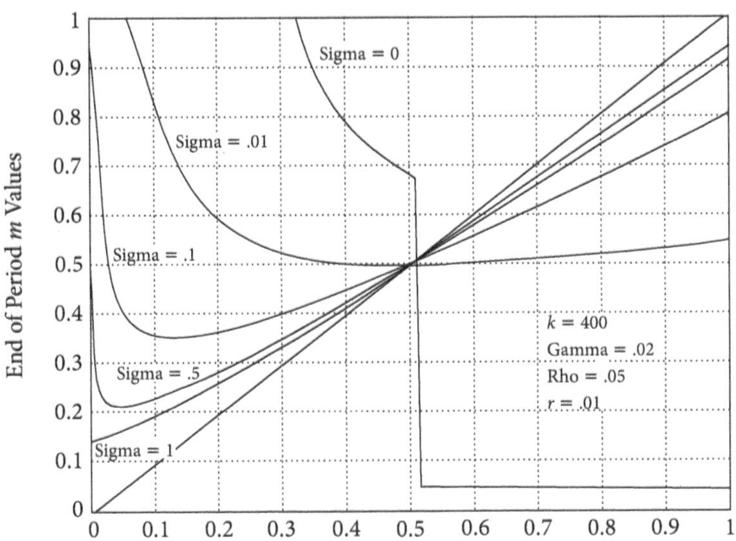

Policy functions for different sigma values

Figure 10

each (σ, r) pair, I used (3.6) to calculate the rate of money growth μ that is implied by given values of γ, ρ, σ, and r. Then I used the condition $\mu m = -v$, with m at the balanced path value given in (5.10), to calculate the implied fiscal policy. These parameter values completely specify the consumer's problem, (5.5).

To calculate the optimal value and policy functions for (5.5), the values of m and m' were restricted to a grid of 1000 values ranging from 0 to 2 in Figure 9 and 0 to 1 in Figure 10. Maximization was carried out by comparing values at all points of the grid: No first-order conditions were used. Each figure plots a different family of policy functions (the optimal m' as a function of m) for (5.5).

In Figure 9, σ is set at the low value of 0.1, and the nominal interest rate is varied from 0.001 (one-tenth of one percent) up to 0.10, In all cases, the cash holdings of a single consumer with arbitrary initial balances converges to the steady state value given by (5.10). As the interest rate increases above 0.10, the policy function continues to flatten above balanced path values, reflecting the fact that at high interest rates, consumers very quickly reduce cash holdings to long-run levels. Similar results are obtained at higher values of σ.

In Figure 10, the interest rate is held fixed at 0.01 and the parameter σ is varied from the linear case $\sigma = 0$ through the log utility case $\sigma = 1$. For $\sigma > 0$, all of these policy functions have a fixed point at $m = 0.5 = 1/\sqrt{rk} = 1/\sqrt{(400)(0.01)}$, consistent with the analysis based on first-order conditions that leads to (5.10). For linear utility, however, the policy function has a discontinuity at $m = 0.5$: The optimal policy in this case is to set $s = 0$ for a while, consuming nothing, earning maximum income, and accumulating cash, and then to enjoy a consumption orgy in which all cash is spent at once. The consumer then returns to the cash-accumulation phase, and the cycle is repeated. Similar behavior emerges at positive but very small (smaller than 0.01) values of σ.

In summary, then, it *is* possible that in this nonconvex problem the first-order conditions can fail to hold under optimal behavior. In such cases, the McCallum-Goodfriend theory cannot be used to rationalize the money demand function (5.10). But these difficulties arise only under near-linear utility, with values of σ far below any available estimates. For realistic values of the risk aversion parameter, and in particular even for very low interest rates, (5.10) is an implication of the theory.

6. Conclusions and Further Directions

There are several research developments that hold promise for sharpening our knowledge on the cost of inflation that I have not yet mentioned. I will discuss these briefly, and then offer some conclusions.

I have emphasized that money-holding behavior at very low interest rates is central for estimating welfare costs. In this paper, I have pursued the idea that models parameterized to fit time series behavior under interest rates as low as two percent could be used to predict behavior at interest rates in the zero to two percent range. Recent work by Mulligan and Sala-i-Martin (1996) provides reason to believe that this extrapolation will not be reliable, and proposes a quite different empirical approach to the problem. They begin from the hypothesis that there is a fixed cost (renewable annually, say) of holding positive amounts of interest-bearing securities, and that households who hold only cash do not incur this cost. In this case, if a monetary policy driving interest rates to zero were implemented, more and more households would decide not to incur this fixed cost, which is to say that fewer and fewer households would be using resources to economize on cash holdings. The presence of such a cost might be undetectable in aggregate time series, yet important enough to completely negate any welfare gain from reducing interest rates from, say, 1.5 percent to zero.

Mulligan and Sala-i-Martin then observe that in deciding whether to incur the fixed cost, a household will compare it to something like the *product* rA of the interest rate r and asset holdings A. If so, then the portfolio behavior of people with low asset holdings should resemble behavior at low interest rates, and we should be able to see the effects of the fixed cost by looking at people with low financial wealth in a cross section. According to the Survey of Consumer Finances, as described in Avery et al. (1984), about 59% of American households in 1989 hold no financial assets beside cash and their checking account. Mulligan and Sala-i-Martin interpret this fact as evidence that the fixed cost described in the last paragraph is sizeable. I think this interpretation is right, and conclude that the construction of models that can utilize cross-section and time series evidence together has real promise for learning about behavior under very low interest rates. If so, then there is good reason to doubt that accurate estimates of cash holding at very low interest rates can be obtained from aggregate U.S. time series evidence alone.

Another set of questions about the time series estimates concerns the fact that *M*1—the measure of money that I have used—is a sum of currency holdings that do not pay interest and demand deposits that (in some circumstances) do. Moreover, other interest-bearing assets beside these may serve as means of payment. One response to these observations is to formulate a model of the banking system in which currency, reserves, and deposits play distinct roles. Such a model seems essential if one wants to consider policies like reserve requirements, interest on deposits, and other measures that affect different components of the money stock differently. See Yoshino (1993) for a promising start in this direction.[16]

A second response to the arbitrariness of *M*1, more fully developed so far than the first, is to replace *M*1 with an aggregate in which different monetary assets are given different weights. The basic idea, as proposed in Barnett (1978, 1980), and Poterba and Rotemberg (1987), is that if a treasury bill yielding 6 percent is assumed to yield no monetary services, then a bank deposit yielding 3 percent can be thought of as yielding half the monetary services of a zero-interest currency holding of equal dollar value. Implementing this idea avoids the awkward necessity of classifying financial assets as either entirely money or not monetary at all, and lets the data do most of the work in deciding how monetary aggregates should be revised over time as interest rates change and new instruments are introduced. The Divisia monetary aggregates constructed by Barnett and others can behave quite differently from "simple sum" aggregates like *M*1 or *M*2.[17] For most of the U.S. time series data used in this paper, though, demand deposits were required by law not to pay interest. I doubt that this issue is of much importance for Meltzer's (1963a) estimates, nor do I think it is of much importance for my extension of Meltzer's estimation to later years. But one can see from Figure 4 that my estimated money demand functions do very badly in the 1990s. I share the widely held opinion that Ml is too narrow an aggregate for this period, and I think that the Divisia approach offers much the best prospects for resolving the difficulty.

As in any active research area, then, there are many interesting avenues left to pursue. But I began this paper with the substantive question of estimation of the welfare gains available to a society that reduces the long-run

16. Other recent work that treats components of M1 separately includes Dotsey (1988) and Marty (1993).

17. See, for example, Belongia (1996).

growth rates of money and prices, and I owe the reader a summary of what is known, now, on this question.

In all of the models I have reviewed, the estimated gains of reducing inflation and interest rates are positive, starting from any interest rate above, say, one tenth of one percent. Even when fiscal considerations make a strictly positive interest rate optimal, the necessary qualification to the Friedman (1969) rule is quantitatively trivial. According to Figure 5 (or 6) reducing interest rates from 14 percent to 3 percent would yield a benefit equivalent to an increase in real income of about 0.008, eight tenths of one percent. This estimate is about the same whether one uses the fitted log-log demand curve for money or the semi-log version. It is based on observations that contain a great deal of information on behavior over this entire range of interest rates. I have argued that this estimate is not at all sensitive to assumptions about the fiscal policy used to effect the interest rate reduction, and that adding realistic productivity or money supply shocks to the model of Section 3 or to that of Section 5 will not alter the estimated welfare cost by much. I regard all of these conclusions as solidly, though of course not conclusively, established.

A 3 percent interest rate is about the rate that would arise in the U.S. economy under a policy of zero inflation. The optimal monetary policy, within the class of theories discussed in this paper, entails a *deflation* consistent with interest rates at or near *zero*. Based on the theory and evidence I have reviewed, the estimated welfare gain of a reduction in interest rates to near zero levels can vary considerably, depending on the specific model one uses. According to the estimates based on a log-log demand curve, as reported in Figure 5, the welfare gain from a monetary policy that reduces interest rates from 3 percent to zero, measured as a fraction of real GDP, is about 0.009, which is to say slightly larger than the gain from reducing rates from 14 to 3 percent! Using the semi-log estimates, however, the estimated gain from reducing interest rates from 3 percent to zero is less than 0.001. Insofar as the fixed costs postulated by Mulligan and Sala-i-Martin are important, even this figure may be an overstatement.

Successful applied science is done at many levels, sometimes close to its foundations, sometimes far away from them or without them altogether. As Simon (1969) observes, "This is lucky, else the safety of bridges and airplanes might depend on the correctness of the 'Eightfold Way' of looking at elementary particles." The analysis of sustained inflation illustrates this observation, I think: Though monetary theory notoriously lacks a generally accepted "microeconomic foundation," the quantity theory of money has attained considerable empirical success as a positive theory of inflation. Beyond this, I have argued in this survey that we also have a normative theory that is quantitatively reliable over a wide range of interest rates. There are indications, however, that theory at the level of the models I have reviewed in this paper is not adequate to let us see how people would manage their cash holdings at very low interest rates. Perhaps for this purpose theories that take us farther on the search for foundations, such as the matching models introduced by Kiyotaki and Wright (1989), are needed.

References

Avery, Robert B., Gregory E. Elliekausen, Arthur B. Kennickell, and Glenn Canner (1984): "Survey of Consumer Finances, 1983," *Federal Reserve Bulletin,* 70, 679–692.

Bailey, Martin J. (1956): "The Welfare Cost of Inflationary Finance," *Journal of Political Economy,* 64, 93–110.

Ball, Laurence (1998): "Another Look at Long-Run Money Demand," Johns Hopkins University Working Paper.

Barnett, William A. (1978): "The User Cost of Money," *Economics Letters,* 1, 145–149.

——— (1980): "Economic Monetary Aggregates: An Application of Index Number and Aggregation Theory," *Journal of Econometrics,* 14, 11–48.

Baumol, William J. (1952): "The Transactions Demand for Cash: An Inventory Theoretic Approach," *Quarterly Journal of Economics,* 66, 545–556.

Belongia, Michael T. (1996): "Measurement Matters: Recent Results from Monetary Economics Reexainined," *Journal of Political Economy,* 104, 1065–1083.

Bewley, Truman (1983): "A Difficulty with the Optimum Quantity of Money," *Econometrica,* 51, 1485–1504.

Brock, William A. (1974): "Money and Growth: The Case of Long Run Perfect Foresight," *International Economic Review,* 15, 750–777.

Bullard, James, and Steven Russell (1997): "How Costly Is Sustained Low Inflation for the U.S. Economy?" Federal Reserve Bank of St. Louis Working Paper.

Burdick, Clark A. (1997): "A Transitional Analysis of the Welfare Cost of Inflation," Federal Reserve Bank of Atlanta Working Paper.

Cagan, Phillip (1956): "The Monetary Dynamics of Hyperinflation," in *Studies in the Quantity Theory of Money,* ed. by Milton Friedman. Chicago: The University of Chicago Press.

Caplin, Andrew, and John Leahy (1991): "State-Dependent Pricing and the Dynamics of Money and Output," *Quarterly Journal of Economics,* 106, 683–708.

Chang, Fwu-Ranq (1992): "Homogeneity and the Transactions Demand for Money," Indiana University Working Paper.

Chari, V. V., Lawrence J. Christiano, and Patrick J. Kehoe (1993): "Optimality of the Friedrnan Rule in Economies with Distorting Taxes," Federal Reserve Bank of Minneapolis Working Paper.

Chari, V. V., Larry E. Jones, and Rodolfo E. Manuelli (1995): "The Growth Effects of Monetary Policy," *Federal Reserve Bank of Minneapolis Quarterly Review,* 19, 18–32.

Cole, Harold L., and Alan C. Stockman (1992): "Specialization, Transactions Technologies, and Money Growth," *International Economic Review,* 33, 283–298.

Cooley, Thomas F., and Gary D. Hansen (1989): "The Inflation Tax in a Real Business Cycle Model," *American Economic Review,* 79, 733–748.

——— (1991): "The Welfare Costs of Moderate Inflations," *Journal of Money, Credit, and Banking,* 23, 483–503.

Correia, Isabel, and Pedro Teles (1997): "The Optimal Inflation Tax," Federal Reserve Bank of Minneapolis Working Paper.

De Gregorio, Jose (1993): "Inflation, Taxation, and Long-run Growth," *Journal of Monetary Economics,* 31, 271–298.

Den Haan, Wouter J. (1990): "The Optimal Inflation Path in a Sidrauski-Type Model with Uncertainty," *Journal of Monetary Economics,* 25, 389–409.

Dotsey, Michael (1988): "The Demand for Currency in the United States," *Journal of Money, Credit, and Banking,* 20, 22–40.

Dotsey, Michael, and Peter Ireland (1996): "The Welfare Cost of Inflation in General Equilibrium," *Journal of Monetary Economics,* 37, 29–47.

Dvoretzky, Aryeh (1965): "The Probability Distribution Generated by the Random Payments Process," Special Appendix to Chapter V in Patinkin (1965).

Eckstein, Zvi, and Leonardo Leiderman (1992): "Seigniorage and the Welfare Cost of Inflation," *Journal of Monetary Economics,* 29, 389–410.

Economic Report of the President (1996): Washington DC: Govt. Printing Office.

Feldstein, Martin (1996): "The Costs and Benefits of Going from Low Inflation to Price Stability," National Bureau of Economic Research Working Paper.

Frenkel, Jacob, and Boyan Jovanovic (1980): "On Transactions and Precautionary Demand for Money," *Quarterly Journal of Economics,* 95, 25–43.

Friedman, Milton (1969): *The Optimum Quantity of Money and Other Essays.* Chicago: Aldine.

Friedman, Milton, and Anna J. Schwartz (1982): *Monetary Trends in the United*

States and the United Kingdom, 1867–1975. Chicago: University of Chicago Press, for the National Bureau of Economic Research.

Fusselman, Jerry, and Sanford J. Grossman (1989): "Monetary Dynamics with Fixed Transactions Costs," Princeton University Working Paper.

Gillman, Max (1993): "The Welfare Cost of Inflation in a Cash-in-Advance Economy with Costly Credit," *Journal of Monetary Economics,* 31, 97–115.

Goldfeld, Stephen M. (1987): "Demand for Money: Empirical Studies," in *The New Palgrave: A Dictionary of Economics,* ed. by John Eatwell, Murray Milgate, and Peter Newman. London: Macmillan; New York: Stockton Press, 770–775.

Gomme, Paul (1993): "Money and Growth Revisited," *Journal of Monetary Economics,* 32, 51–77.

Grossman, Sanford J. (1987): "Monetary Dynamics with Proportional Transactions Costs and Fixed Payment Periods," in *New Approaches to Monetary Dynamics,* ed. by William A. Barnett and Kenneth J. Singleton. Cambridge, England: Cambridge University Press.

Guidotti, Pablo E., and Carlos A. Vegh (1993): "The Optimal Inflation Tax When Money Reduces Transactions Costs: A Reconsideration," *Journal of Monetary Economics,* 31, 189–206.

Jones, Larry E., and Rodolfo E. Manuelli (1995): "Growth and the Effects of Inflation," *Journal of Economic Dynamics and Control,* 19, 1405–1428.

Jovanovic, Boyan (1982): "Inflation and Welfare in the Steady State," *Journal of Political Economy,* 90, 561–577.

Karni, Edi (1973): "The Transactions Demand for Cash: Incorporation of the Value of Time into the Inventory Approach," *Journal of Political Economy,* 81, 1216–1225.

Kendrick, John W. (1961): *Productivity Trends in the United States.* Princeton: Princeton University Press, for the National Bureau of Economic Research.

Kimbrough, Kent P. (1986a): "Inflation, Employment, and Welfare in the Presence of Transactions Costs," *Journal of Money, Credit, and Banking,* 18, 127–140.

——— (1986b): "The Optimum Quantity of Money Rule in the Theory of Public Finance," *Journal of Monetary Economics,* 18, 277–284.

Kiyotaki, Nobuhiro, and Randall Wright (1989): "Money as a Medium of Exchange," *Journal of Political Economy,* 97, 927–954.

Laidler, David E. W. (1977): "The Rate of Interest and the Demand for Money," *Journal of Political Economy,* 74, 545–555.

Lucas, Robert E., Jr., and Nancy L. Stokey (1983a): "Optimal Fiscal and Monetary

Policy in an Economy without Capital," *Journal of Monetary Economics,* 12, 55–93.

——— (1983b): "Money and Interest in a Cash-in-Advance Economy," *Econometrica,* 55, 491–513.

Lucas, Robert E., Jr. (1988): "Money Demand in the United States: A Quantitative Review," *Carnegie-Rochester Conference Series on Public Policy,* 29, 137–168.

Marty, Alvin L. (1993): "The Inflation Tax, and the Marginal Welfare Cost in a World of Currency and Deposits," City University of New York Working Paper.

McCallum, Bennett T., and Marvin S. Goodfriend (1987): "Demand for Money: Theoretical Studies," in *The New Palgrave: A Dictionary of Economics,* ed. by John Eatwell, Murray Milgate, and Peter Newman. London: Macmillan; New York: Stockton Press, 775–781.

Meltzer, Allan H. (1963a): "The Demand for Money: The Evidence from Time Series," *Journal of Political Economy,* 71, 219–246.

——— (1963b): "The Demand for Money: A Cross-Section Study of Business Firms," *Quarterly Journal of Economics,* 77, 405–422.

Miller, Merton H., and Daniel Orr (1966): "A Model of the Demand for Money by Firms," *Quarterly Journal of Economics,* 80, 413–435.

Miller, Preston J. (1995): "The Jointly Optimal Inflation Tax, Income Tax Structure, and Transfer," Federal Reserve Bank of Minneapolis Working Paper.

Mulligan, Casey B., and Xavier Sala-i-Martin (1992): "U.S. Money Demand: Surprising Cross-Sectional Estimates," *Brookings Papers on Economic Activity,* 2, 285–343.

——— (1996): "Adoption of Financial Technologies: Technologies and Implications for Money Demand and Monetary Policy," National Bureau of Economic Research Working Paper.

——— (1997): "The Optimum Quantity of Money: Theory and Evidence," National Bureau of Economic Research Working Paper.

Patinkin, Don (1965): *Money, Interest, and Prices,* Second edition. New York: Harper and Row.

Phelps, Edmund S. (1973): "Inflation in the Theory of Public Finance," *Swedish Journal of Economics,* 75, 67–82.

Poterba, James M., and Julio J. Rotemberg (1987): "Money in the Utility Function: An Empirical Implementation," in *New Approaches to Monetary Dynamics,* ed. by William A. Barnett and Kenneth J. Singleton. Cambridge, England: Cambridge University Press.

Rodríguez Mendezibál, Hugo (1996): "The Variability of Money Velocity in a Modified Cash-in-Advance Model," University of Chicago Working Paper.

Sidrauski, Miguel (1967a): "Rational Choice and Patterns of Growth in a Monetary Economy," *American Economic Review,* 57, 534–544.

——— (1967b): "Inflation and Economic Growth," *Journal of Political Economy,* 75, 796–810.

Simon, Herbert A. (1969): *The Sciences of the Artificial.* Cambridge: The MIT Press.

Stock, James H., and Mark W. Watson (1993): "A Simple Estimator of Cointegrating Vectors in Higher Order Integrated Systems," *Econometrica,* 61, 783–820.

Tobin, James (1956): "The Interest Elasticity of the Transactions Demand for Cash," *Review of Economics and Statistics,* 38, 241–247.

U.S. Bureau of the Census (1960): *Historical Statistics of the United Slates, Colonial Times to 1957.* Washington, D.C.: Govt. Printing Office.

U.S. Office of Business Economics: *The National Income and Product Accounts of the United States.* Washington, D.C.: Govt. Printing Office.

Woodford, Michael (1990): "The Optimum Quantity of Money," in *Handbook of Monetary Economics,* v.ii, ed. by Benjamin M. Friedman and Frank H. Hahn. Amsterdam: North Holland.

Yoshino, Joe A. (1993): "Money and Banking Regulation: The Welfare Costs of Inflation," University of Chicago Doctoral Dissertation.

— 18 —

Interest Rates and Inflation

FERNANDO ALVAREZ, ROBERT E. LUCAS, JR., AND WARREN E. WEBER

A consensus has emerged among practitioners that the instrument of monetary policy ought to be the short-term interest rate, that policy should be focused on the control of inflation, and that inflation can be reduced by increasing short-term interest rates.* At the center of this consensus is a rejection of the quantity theory. Such a rejection is a difficult step to take, given the mass of evidence linking money growth, inflation, and interest rates: increases in average rates of money growth are associated with equal increases in average inflation rates and interest rates.

These observations need not rule out a constructive role for the use of short-term interest rates as a monetary instrument. One possibility is that increasing short-term rates in the face of increases in inflation is just an indirect way of reducing money growth: sell bonds and take money out of the system. Another possibility is that, while control of monetary aggregates is the key to low long-run average inflation rates, an interest-rate policy can improve the short-run behavior of interest rates and prices. The short-run connections among money growth, inflation, and interest rates are very unreliable, so there is much room for improvement. These possibilities are surely worth exploring, but doing so requires new theory. The

American Economic Review 91, no. 2 (May 2001): 219–225.

*Recent Advances in Monetary-Policy Rules. *Discussants:* Lars Svensson, Institute for International Economic Studies, Sweden; James Stock, Harvard University; John Williams, Federal Reserve Board. We thank Lars Svensson for his discussion, Nurlan Turdaliev for his assistance, and seminar participants at the Federal Reserve Bank of Minneapolis for their comments and suggestions. Alvarez thanks the National Science Foundation and the Alfred P. Sloan Foundation for support. The views expressed herein are those of the authors and not necessarily those of the Federal Reserve Bank of Minneapolis or the Federal Reserve System.

analysis needed to reconcile interest-rate policies with the evidence on which the quantity theory of money is grounded cannot be found in old textbook diagrams.

I. An Economy with Segmented Markets

Much recent discussion of monetary policy is centered on a class of policies known as "Taylor rules," rules that specify the interest rate set by the central bank as an increasing function of the inflation rate (or perhaps of a forecast of the inflation rate) (see John Taylor, 1993). The properties of Taylor rules can be studied within a Keynesian framework.[1] Here we examine the properties of Taylor rules using a neoclassical framework that is also consistent with the quantity theory of money and the body of evidence that confirms this theory. An essential assumption in this inquiry is that markets are incomplete, or *segmented,* in a way that is consistent with the existence of a *liquidity effect*: a downward-sloping demand for nominal bonds. The segmented-market model we use is adapted from Alvarez et al. (2001), where references to earlier work on these models can be found.

The model we develop is an exchange economy: There is no Phillips curve and no effect of monetary-policy changes on production.[2]

Think, then, of an exchange economy with many agents, all with the preferences

$$\sum_{t=0}^{\infty}\left(\frac{1}{1+\rho}\right)^{t} U(c_t)$$

where

$$U(c_t) = \frac{c_t^{1-\gamma}}{1-\gamma}$$

over sequences $\{c_t\}$ of a single, non-storable consumption good. All of these agents attend a goods market every period. A fraction λ of agents also attend a bond market. We call these agents "traders." The remaining $1-\lambda$

1. See Richard Clarida et al. (1999) for a helpful review.

2. Segmented market models that have such effects include contributions by Lawrence Christiano and Martin Eichenbaum (1992) and Charles T. Carlstrom and Timothy S. Fuerst (1995). Our simpler model permits a discussion of inflation, but not of all of inflation's possible consequences.

agents (we call them "non-traders") never attend the bond market. We assume that no one ever changes status between being a trader and a non-trader.

Agents of both types have the same constant endowment of y units of the consumption good. The economy's resource constraint is thus

$$y = \lambda c_t^{\mathrm{T}} + (1 - \lambda)c_t^{\mathrm{N}} \tag{1}$$

where c_t^{T} and c_t^{N} are the consumptions of the two agent types. We ensure that money is held in equilibrium by assuming that no one consumes his own endowment. Each household consists of a shopper–seller pair, where the seller sells the household's endowment for cash in the goods market, while the shopper uses cash to buy the consumption good from others in the same market. Prior to the opening of this goods market, money and one-period government bonds are traded in another market, attended only by traders.

Purchases are subject to a cash-in-advance constraint, modified to incorporate shocks to velocity. Assume, to be specific, that goods purchases P_tc_t are constrained to be less than the sum of cash brought into goods trading by the household and a variable fraction v_t of *current-period* sales receipts. Think of the shopper as visiting the seller's store at some time during the trading day, emptying the cash register, and returning to shop some more.

Thus, every non-trader carries his unspent receipts from period-$(t - 1)$ sales, $(1 - v_{t-1})P_{t-1}y$, into period-t trading. He adds to these balances v_tP_ty from period-t sales, giving him a total of $(1 - v_{t-1})\, P_{t-1}y + v_tP_ty$ to spend on goods in period t. In order to keep the determination of the price level as simple as possible, we assume that every household spends all of its cash, every period.[3] Then every non-trader spends

$$P_tc_t^{\mathrm{N}} = (1 - v_{t-1})P_{t-1}y + v_tP_ty \tag{2}$$

in period t.

Traders, who attend both bond and goods markets, have more options. Like the non-traders, each trader has available the amount on the right of

3. After solving for equilibrium prices and quantities under the assumption that cash constraints always bind, one can go back to individual maximum problems to find the set of parameter values under which this provisional assumption will hold (see Alvarez et al., 2001 appendix A).

(2) to spend on goods in period t, but each trader also absorbs his share of the increase in the per capita money supply that occurs in the open-market operation in t. If the per capita increase in money is $M_t - M_{t-1} = \mu_t M_{t-1}$, then each trader leaves the date-t bond market with an additional $\mu_t M_{t-1}/\lambda$ dollars.[4] Consumption spending per trader is thus given by

$$P_t c_t^{\mathrm{T}} = (1 - v_{t-1})P_{t-1}y + v_t P_t y + (M_t - M_{t-1}) / \lambda. \tag{3}$$

Now, using the cash flow equations (2) and (3) and the market-clearing condition (1) we obtain

$$P_t y = (1 - v_{t-1})P_{t-1}y + v_t P_t y + M_t - M_{t-1} = M_{t-1} + v_t P_t y + M_t - M_{t-1}$$

since $M_{t-1} = (1 - v_{t-1})\ P_{t-1} y$ is total dollars carried forward from $t - 1$. Thus, a version

$$M_t \left(\frac{1}{1 - v_t} \right) = P_t y \tag{4}$$

of the equation of exchange must hold in equilibrium, and the fraction v_t can be interpreted (approximately) as the log of velocity.

Introducing shocks to velocity captures the short-run instability in the empirical relationship between money and prices. In addition, it allows us to study the way interest rates react to news about inflation for different specifications of monetary policy. In the formulation of the segmented-markets model that we use here, there are no possibilities for substituting against cash, so the interest rate does not appear in the money demand function [in (4)], and velocity is simply given. Given the behavior of the

4. If B_t is the value of bonds maturing at date t and if T_t is the value of lump-sum tax receipts at t, the market-clearing condition for this bond market becomes

$$B_t - \left(\frac{1}{1 + r_t} \right) B_{t+1} - T_t = M_t - M_{t-1}.$$

We assume that all taxes are paid by the traders, so Ricardian equivalence will apply, and the timing of taxes will be immaterial. These taxes play no role in our discussion, except to give us a second way to change the money supply besides open-market operations. With this flexibility, any monetary policy can be made consistent with the real debt remaining bounded. The arithmetic that follows will be both monetarist and pleasant in the sense of Thomas J. Sargent and Neil Wallace (1985).

money supply, then prices are entirely determined by (4). This is the quantity theory of money in its very simplest form.

The exogeneity of velocity in the model is, of course, easily relaxed without altering the essentials of the model, but at the cost of complicating the solution method. In the version we study here, the two cash-flow equations (2) and (3) describe the way the fixed endowment is distributed to the two consumer types. The three equations (1)–(3) thus completely determine the equilibrium resource allocation and the behavior of the price level. No maximum problem has been studied, and no derivatives have been taken!

To study the related behavior of interest rates, however, we need to examine bond-market equilibrium, and there the real interest rate will depend on the current and expected future consumption of the traders only. Solving (1), (2), and (4), we derive the formula for c_t^{T}:

$$c_t^{\mathrm{T}} = \left[\frac{1 + \mu_t v_t + \mu_t(1 - v_t)/\lambda}{1 + \mu_t}\right] y = c(v_t, \mu_t) y$$

where the second equality defines the relative consumption function $c(v_t, \mu_t)$. Then the equilibrium nominal interest rate must satisfy the familiar marginal condition,

$$\frac{1}{1 + r_t} = \left(\frac{1}{1 + \rho}\right) E_t \left[\frac{U'(c(v_{t+1}, \mu_{t+1})y)}{U'(c(v_t, \mu_t)y)} \left(\frac{1}{1 + \mu_{t+1}}\right)\left(\frac{1 - v_{t+1}}{1 - v_t}\right)\right] \quad (5)$$

where $E_t(\cdot)$ means an expectation conditional on events dated t and earlier.

We use two approximations to simplify equation (5). The first involves expanding the function $\log[c(v_t, \mu_t)]$ around the point $(\bar{v}, 0)$ to obtain the first-order approximation

$$\log\left[c(v_t, \mu_t)\right] \simeq (1 - \bar{v})\left(\frac{1 - \lambda}{\lambda}\right)\mu_t.$$

(Note that the first-order effect of velocity changes on consumption is zero.) With the constant-relative-risk-aversion (CRRA) preferences we have assumed, the marginal utility of traders is then approximated by

$$U'(c(v_t, \mu_t)y) = \exp(-\phi\mu_t)y^{-\gamma}$$

where

$$\phi = \gamma(1 - \bar{v})\left(\frac{1-\lambda}{\lambda}\right) > 0.$$

Taking logs of both sides of (5), we have

$$r_t = \rho - \log\left(E_t\left[\exp\{-\phi(\mu_{t+1} - \mu_t)\}\left(\frac{1}{1+\mu_{t+1}}\right)\left(\frac{1-v_{t+1}}{1-v_t}\right)\right]\right).$$

We apply a second approximation to the right-hand side to obtain

$$r_t = \hat{\rho} + \phi\left(E_t\left[\mu_{t+1}\right] - \mu_t\right) + E_t\left[\mu_{t+1}\right] + E_t\left[v_{t+1}\right] - v_t \qquad (6)$$

where $\hat{\rho} - \rho > 0$ is a risk correction factor.[5]

From equation (6) one can see that the immediate effect of an open-market-operation bond purchase, $\mu_t > 0$, is to reduce interest rates by $\phi\mu_t$. This is the liquidity effect that the segmented-market models are designed to capture. If we drop the segmentation and let everyone trade in bonds, then $\lambda = 1$, $\phi = 0$, and the liquidity effect vanishes. In this case, open-market operations can only affect interest rates through information effects on the inflation premium. Interest-rate increases can only reflect expected inflation: monetary ease. With $\phi > 0$, the model combines quantity-theoretic predictions for the long-run behavior of money growth, inflation, and interest rates, with a *potential* role for interest rates as an instrument of inflation control in the short run. We explore this potential in the next section.

II. Inflation Control with Segmented Markets

In this section, we work through a series of thought experiments based on the equilibrium condition (6) that illuminate various aspects of monetary policy. These examples all draw on the fact, obtained by differencing the equation of exchange (4), that the inflation rate is the sum of the money growth rate and the rate of change in velocity:

$$\pi_t = \mu_t + v_t - v_{t-1}. \qquad (7)$$

5. The risk correction $p - \hat{p}$ depends on conditional variances, which are constant in the following applications.

EXAMPLE 1 (Constant Velocity and Money Growth): Let v_t be constant at $\overline{v}$, and let μ_t be constant at μ. Then (6) becomes

$$r = \rho + \mu.$$

We can view this equation interchangeably as fixing money growth, given the interest rate, or as fixing the interest rate given money growth and inflation. This Fisher equation must always characterize long-run average money growth, inflation, and interest rates.

EXAMPLE 2 (Constant Money Growth and i.i.d. Shocks): Let the velocity shocks be independently and identically distributed (i.i.d.) random variables, with mean $\overline{v}$ and variance σ_v^2. Let μ_t be constant at μ. Under these conditions, (6) implies

$$r_t = \hat{\rho} + \mu - (v_t - \overline{v}).$$

A transient increase in velocity raises the current price level, reducing expected inflation. This induces a transient decrease in interest rates. In this example, r_t is i.i.d., with mean $\hat{\rho} + \mu$ and variance σ_v^2; the inflation rate has mean μ and variance $2\sigma_v^2$.

EXAMPLE 3 (Exact Inflation-Targeting): It is always possible to attain a target inflation rate $\overline{\pi}$ exactly. Just set the money growth rate according to

$$\mu_t = \overline{\pi} - v_t + v_{t-1}.$$

Then interest rates will be given by

$$r_t = \hat{\rho} + \phi(-E_t[v_{t+1}] + 2v_t - v_{t-1}) + \overline{\pi}.$$

If the velocity shocks are i.i.d., as in Example 2, then $\mathrm{Var}(\mu_t) = 2\sigma_v^2$, and r_t has mean $\hat{\rho} + \overline{\pi}$ and variance $5\phi^2\sigma_v^2$.

EXAMPLE 4 (An Interest-Rate Peg): Assume i.i.d. v_t, with mean $\overline{v}$ and variance σ_v^2. Let μ_t satisfy

$$\mu_t - \mu = B(v_t - \overline{v})$$

where the constant B is chosen to make r_t constant at $\hat{\rho} + \mu$. Then (6) implies

$$\hat{\rho} + \mu = \hat{\rho} - B\phi(v_t - \bar{v}) + \mu - (v_t - \bar{v}).$$

If this equality holds for all realizations of v_t, it follows that $B = -1/\phi$. In this case, $\text{Var}(\mu_t) = (\sigma_v/\phi)^2$. Using (7), the variance of the inflation rate is,

$$\sigma_\pi^2 = \text{Var}(\mu_{t+1} + v_{t+1} - v_t) = \left[1 + \left(\frac{\phi - 1}{\phi}\right)^2\right]\sigma_v^2.$$

Comparing this case to Example 2, one sees that pegging the interest rate is inflation-stabilizing, relative to constant money growth, if and only if $\phi > ½$.

In Examples 2, 3, and 4, the economy is subjected to unavoidable velocity shocks. The variability of these shocks must show up somewhere, either in interest rates, money-growth rates, or inflation rates. The way it is distributed over these three variables can, in the presence of a liquidity effect, be determined by policy. However this is done, the long-run connections between money growth, inflation, and interest rates are entirely quantity-theoretic.

Our next two examples consider versions of Taylor rules. Suppose, to be specific, that interest rates are set according to the formula

$$r_t = \hat{\rho} + \bar{\pi} + \theta(\pi_t - \bar{\pi}) \tag{8}$$

where $\theta > 0$ means that if the current inflation rate π_t is to exceed the target rate $\bar{\pi}$, we raise this period's interest rate above its target level, $\hat{\rho} + \bar{\pi}$. To study the dynamics implied by the rule (8), we eliminate r_t and π_t between (6), (7), and (8) to obtain the difference equation

$$\mu_t - \bar{\pi} = \left(\frac{1+\phi}{\theta+\phi}\right)(E_t[\mu_{t+1}] - \bar{\pi}) + \left(\frac{1}{\theta+\phi}\right)[E_t[v_{t+1}] - v_t - \theta(v_t - v_{t-1})]. \tag{9}$$

We can solve this difference equation "forward" to get

$$\mu_t - \bar{\pi} = \sum_{i=0}^{\infty}\left(\frac{1+\phi}{\theta+\phi}\right)^i E_t[s_{t+i}] \tag{10}$$

where

$$s_t = \frac{1}{\theta+\phi}[v_{t+1} - v_t - \theta(v_t - v_{t-1})]$$

provided that the series on the right-hand side of (10) converges.[6] We now use (10) to study two more examples.

EXAMPLE 5 (A Taylor Rule with i.i.d. Velocity): Let v_t be i.i.d., with mean $\bar{v}$ and variance σ_v^2. Inserting the corresponding values of $E_t[s_{t+j}]$ into (10) gives

$$\mu_t - \bar{\pi} = -\left(\frac{\phi + \theta^2}{(\theta + \phi)^2}\right)(v_t - \bar{v}) + \left(\frac{\theta}{\theta + \phi}\right)(v_{t-1} - \bar{v}). \tag{11}$$

The interest-rate consequences of these open-market operations can then be calculated from the Taylor rule, (8):

$$r_t = \hat{\rho} + \bar{\pi} + \left(\frac{\theta\phi}{(\theta + \phi)^2}\right)(2\theta + \phi - 1)(v_t - \bar{v}) - \left(\frac{\theta\phi}{\theta + \phi}\right)(v_{t-1} - \bar{v}). \tag{12}$$

The money-supply response to a temporary increase in velocity, described in (11), is to reduce money growth initially, increase it in the next period, and return to the target growth rate thereafter. This will smooth the inflationary impact of the velocity increase, whether or not there is a positive liquidity effect ϕ. If $\phi > 0$ and $2\theta + \phi > 1$, (12) implies that these open-market operations will raise the interest rate initially in response to a velocity increase, then reduce it below the target, and then return it to $\hat{\rho} + \bar{\pi}$.

EXAMPLE 6 (A Taylor Rule with Random-Walk Velocity): Assume that the changes, $v_t - v_{t-1}$, in velocity are i.i.d. random variables with mean 0 and variance σ_v^2. Then, for any t, calculating the terms $E_t[s_{t+k}]$ and substituting (10) yields

$$\mu_t - \bar{\pi} = \left(\frac{\theta}{\theta + \phi}\right)(v_t - v_{t-1}).$$

Again, the interest-rate consequences can be calculated from the Taylor rule, (8):

$$r_t = \hat{\rho} + \bar{\pi} + \left(\frac{\theta\phi}{\theta + \phi}\right)(v_t - v_{t-1}). \tag{13}$$

6. If $\theta > 1$, the right-hand side of (10) is the only solution to (9) with bounded expected values. This case is referred to as an "active" Taylor rule. If $\theta < 1$ (a "passive" Taylor rule) and the series in (10) converges, (10) gives one solution to (9), but there will be others (which we do not examine here) as well.

As in the case of i.i.d. shocks in Example 5, (13) implies that open-market bond sales in response to a velocity increase will increase interest rates only if $\phi > 0$.

EXAMPLE 7 (A Change in the Inflation Target): Holding the distribution of velocity shocks fixed, suppose that the inflation target is moved permanently from $\bar{\pi}$ to $\hat{\pi}$. This re-targeting changes nothing on the right-hand side of (10), so (10) implies simply an immediate, permanent change in the money-growth rate from $\bar{\pi}$ to $\hat{\pi}$. Of course, this implies an immediate, permanent change in the interest rate of $\hat{\pi} - \bar{\pi}$. Neither the size ϕ of the liquidity effect nor the responsiveness θ of the Taylor rule has any bearing on these changes.

III. Conclusions

Using a model of segmented markets, we have shown that a policy of increasing short-term interest rates to reduce inflation can be rationalized with essentially quantity-theoretic models of monetary equilibrium. In the model we used to generate all of our specific examples, production is a given constant, velocity is an exogenous random shock, and the equation of exchange determines the equilibrium price level, given the money supply. In this theory of inflation, consistent with much of the evidence, interest rates play no role whatsoever.

To this simple model we have added segmented markets. With this added feature, we can describe a monetary policy action interchangeably as a change in the money supply or as a change in interest rates. In this context, we considered a series of examples under different assumptions on the behavior of velocity shocks and on the specification of a policy rule.

In the first two stochastic examples, Examples 2 and 3, a policy at any date is set in advance of the realization of the velocity shock in that period: One can commit to a given rate of money growth, leaving interest rates free to vary with the velocity shock (Example 2), or one can commit to an interest rate, leaving money growth to be adjusted later to maintain this rate (Example 3). Neither policy can reduce the variance of inflation to zero. The larger is the liquidity effect, the higher is the relative effectiveness of the interest-rate rule in stabilizing inflation rates about a target rate.

In the remaining examples we consider, policy (however specified) is permitted to respond to contemporaneous velocity shocks. In Example 4, we show that under this assumption an inflation target can be hit *exactly* by a money-supply rule that is conditioned on the shock, and that this is true whatever is the shock process. In our context, inflation-targeting cannot be done any better than this.

The remaining examples in the paper consider Taylor rules: policies in which the interest rate is set so as to deviate from its long-run (Fisherian) target in proportion to the deviation of the inflation rate from its target. Such rules use the same information as the rule in Example 4 that attains the inflation target perfectly. From the viewpoint of inflation-targeting, then, committing to a Taylor rule amounts to tying the hands of the monetary authority in a way that can only limit its effectiveness. As our examples illustrate, the importance of this limitation varies with assumptions on the time-series character of the velocity shocks.

To rationalize the use of any of the interest-rate rules we have examined, it would be necessary to use an objective function that assigns weight to some other objective besides the attainment of an inflation target. We have in fact considered variations on the model presented here in which relative endowments of agents fluctuate, giving rise to gains from pooling endowment risk. In the absence of a monetary-policy design to offset these shocks, they will increase interest-rate variability. In a model with segmented markets where such pooling cannot take place, there can be real gains from policies that smooth real interest rates. We leave the analysis of this question, the issue of what the founders of the Federal Reserve System called an "elastic currency," to another paper.

References

Alvarez, Fernando; Atkeson, Andrew, and Kehoe, Patrick. "Money, Interest Rates, and Exchange Rates with Endogenously Segmented Asset Markets." *Journal of Political Economy*, 2001 (forthcoming).

Carlstrom, Charles T., and Fuerst, Timothy S. "Interest Rate Rules vs. Money Growth Rules: A Welfare Comparison in a Cash-in-Advance Economy." *Journal of Monetary Economics*, November 1995, *36*(2), pp. 246–67.

Christiano, Lawrence J., and Eichenbaum, Martin. "Liquidity Effects and the Monetary Transmission Mechanism." *American Economic Review*, May 1992 (*Papers and Proceedings*), *82*(2), pp. 346–53.

Clarida, Richard; Galí, Jordi, and Gertler, Mark. "The Science of Monetary Policy: A New Keynesian Perspective." *Journal of Economic Literature,* December 1999, *37*(4), pp. 1661–1707.

Sargent, Thomas J., and Wallace, Neil. "Some Unpleasant Monetarist Arithmetic." *Federal Reserve Bank of Minneapolis Quarterly Review,* Winter 1985, *9*(1), pp. 15–31.

Taylor, John B. "Discretion versus Policy Rules in Practice." *Carnegie-Rochester Conference Series on Public Policy,* December 1993, *39*(0), pp. 195–214.

— 19 —

Macroeconomic Priorities

Macroeconomics was born as a distinct field in the 1940's, as a part of the intellectual response to the Great Depression.* The term then referred to the body of knowledge and expertise that we hoped would prevent the recurrence of that economic disaster. My thesis in this lecture is that macroeconomics in this original sense has succeeded: Its central problem of depression prevention has been solved, for all practical purposes, and has in fact been solved for many decades. There remain important gains in welfare from better fiscal policies, but I argue that these are gains from providing people with better incentives to work and to save, not from better fine-tuning of spending flows. Taking U.S. performance over the past 50 years as a benchmark, the potential for welfare gains from better long-run, supply-side policies exceeds *by far* the potential from further improvements in short-run demand management.

My plan is to review the theory and evidence leading to this conclusion. Section I outlines the general logic of quantitative welfare analysis, in which policy comparisons are reduced to differences perceived and valued by individuals. It also provides a brief review of some examples—examples that will be familiar to many—of changes in long-run monetary and fiscal

---

American Economic Review 93, no. 1 (March 2003): 1–14.

*Presidential Address delivered at the one-hundred-fifteenth meeting of the American Economic Association, January 4, 2003, Washington, DC. I am grateful for discussions with Fernando Alvarez, Gadi Barlevy, Lars Hansen, Per Krusell, Ellen McGrattan, Chris Phelan, Edward Prescott, Esteban Rossi-Hansberg, Tom Sargent, Matthew Shapiro, Tony Smith, Nancy Stokey, Kjetil Storesletten, and Tom Tallarini, and for the able assistance of Adrian Kats and Mikhail Golosov.

policies that consumers would view as equivalent to increases of 5–15 percent in their overall consumption levels.

Section II describes a thought-experiment in which a single consumer is magically relieved of all consumption variability about trend. How much average consumption would he be willing to give up in return? About one-half of one-tenth of a percent, I calculate. I will defend this estimate as giving the right order of magnitude of the potential gain to society from improved stabilization policies, but to do this, many questions need to be addressed.

How much of aggregate consumption variability should be viewed as pathological? How much can or should be removed by monetary and fiscal means? Section III reviews evidence bearing on these questions. Section IV considers attitudes toward risk: How much do people dislike consumption uncertainty? How much would they pay to have it reduced? We also know that business-cycle risk is not evenly distributed or easily diversified, so welfare cost estimates that ignore this fact may badly understate the costs of fluctuations. Section V reviews recently developed models that let us explore this possibility systematically. These are hard questions, and definitive answers are too much to ask for. But I argue in the end that, based on what we know now, it is unrealistic to hope for gains larger than a tenth of a percent from better countercyclical policies.

I. Welfare Analysis of Public Policies: Logic and Results

Suppose we want to compare the effects of two policies, A and B say, on a single consumer. Under policy A the consumer's welfare is $U(c_A)$, where c_A is the consumption level he enjoys under that policy, and under policy B it is $U(c_B)$. Suppose that he prefers $c_B : U(c_A) < U(c_B)$. Let $\lambda > 0$ solve

$$U((1 + \lambda)c_A) = U(c_B).$$

We call this number λ—in units of a percentage of all consumption goods—the *welfare gain* of a change in policy from A to B. To evaluate the effects of policy change on many different consumers, we can calculate welfare gains (perhaps losses, for some) for all of them, one at a time, and add the needed compensations to obtain the welfare gain for the group. We can also specify the compensation in terms of one or a subset of goods, rather than all of them: There is no single, right way to carry these comparisons out. However it is done, we obtain a method for evaluating policies that has comprehensible units and is built up from individual preferences.

There is a great tradition of quantitative public finance that applies this general framework using well-chosen Taylor expansions to calculate estimates of the compensation parameter λ, "welfare triangles" as Arnold C. Harberger called them. Today we use numerical simulation of general-equilibrium models, often dynamic and subject to unpredictable shocks, to carry out welfare analysis with the general logic that I have just sketched. Some examples will, I hope, convey the applicability of this approach and some of the estimates that have emerged.

Martin J. Bailey's (1956) thought-experiment of a perfectly predictable inflation at a constant rate, induced by sustained growth in the money supply, was a pioneering example of the quantitative evaluation of policy. In a replication of the Bailey study, I estimated the welfare gain from reducing the annual inflation rate from 10 to 0 percent to be a perpetual consumption flow of 1 percent of income.[1] Some economists take estimates like this to imply that inflation is a relatively modest problem, but 1 percent of income is a serious amount of money, and in any case, the gain depends on how much inflation there is. The gain from eliminating a 200-percent annual inflation—well within the range of recent experience in several South American economies—is about 7 percent of income.

The development of growth theory, in which the evolution of an economy over time is traced to its sources in consumer preferences, technology, and government policies, opened the way for extending general-equilibrium policy analysis to a much wider class of dynamic settings. In the 1980's, a number of economists used versions of neoclassical growth theory to examine the effects of taxation on the *total* stock of capital, not just the composition of that stock.[2] The models used in these studies differ in their details, but all were variations on a one-good growth model in which consumers (either an infinitely lived dynasty or a succession of generations) maximize the utility of consumption and leisure over time, firms maximize profit, and markets are continuously cleared.

In general, these studies found that reducing capital income taxation

1. Lucas (2000). My estimates are based on the money demand estimates in Allan H. Meltzer (1963).

2. For example, William A. Brock and Stephen J. Turnovsky (1981), Christophe P. Chamley (1981), Lawrence H. Summers (1981), Alan J. Auerbach and Laurence J. Kotlikoff (1987), and Kenneth L. Judd (1987).

from its current U.S. level to zero (using other taxes to support an unchanged rate of government spending) would increase the balanced-growth capital stock by 30 to 60 percent. With a capital share of around 0.3, these numbers imply an increase of consumption along a balanced growth path of 7.5 to 15 percent. Of course, reaching such a balanced path involves a period of high investment rates and low consumption. Taking these transition costs into account, overall welfare gains amount to perhaps 2 to 4 percent of annual consumption, in perpetuity.

Production per adult in France is about 70 percent of production per adult in the United States. Edward C. Prescott (2002) observes that hours worked per adult in France, measured as a fraction of available hours, are also about 70 percent of the comparable U.S. figure. Using estimates for France and the United States of the ratio $(1 + \tau_c)/(1 - \tau_h)$ that equals the marginal rate of substitution between consumption and leisure in the neoclassical growth model, he shows that tax differences can account for the entire difference in hours worked and, amplified by the indirect effect on capital accumulation, for the entire difference in production. The steady-state welfare gain to French households of adopting American tax rates on labor and consumption would be the equivalent of a consumption increase of about 20 percent. The conclusion is not simply that if the French were to work American hours, they could produce as much as Americans do. It is that the utility consequences of doing so would be equivalent to a 20-percent increase in consumption with *no* increase in work effort!

The gain from reducing French taxes to U.S. levels can in part be viewed as the gain from adopting a flat tax on incomes,[3] but it is doubtful that all of it can be obtained simply by rearranging the tax structure. It entails a reduction in government spending as well, which Prescott interprets as a reduction in the level of transfer payments, or in the government provision of goods that most people would buy anyway, financed by distorting taxes. Think of elementary schooling or day care. The gains from eliminating such fiscal "cross-hauling" (as Sherwin Rosen [1996] called the Swedish day-care system) involve more than eliminating "excess burden," but they may well be large.

The stakes in choosing the right monetary and fiscal policies are high. Sustained inflation, tax structures that penalize capital accumulation and

3. See also Robert E. Hall and Alvin Rabushka (1995).

work effort, and tax-financed government provision of private goods all have uncompensated costs amounting to sizeable fractions of income. We can see these costs in differences in economic performance across different countries and time periods. Even in the United States, which visibly benefits from the lowest excess burdens in the modern world, economic analysis has identified large potential gains from further improvements in long-run fiscal policy.

II. Gains from Stabilization: A Baseline Calculation

In the rest of the lecture, I want to apply the public finance framework just outlined to the assessment of gains from improved stabilization policy. Such an exercise presupposes a view of the workings of the economy in which short-run monetary and fiscal policies affect resource allocation in ways that are different from the supply side effects I have just been discussing.

One possibility is that instability in the quantity of money or its rate of growth, arising from government or private sources, induces inefficient real variability. If that were all there was to it, the ideal stabilization policy would be to fix the money growth rate. (Of course, such a policy would require the Federal Reserve to take an active role in preventing or offsetting instabilities in the private banking system.) But this cannot be all there is to it, because an economy in which monetary fluctuations induce real inefficiencies—indeed, any economy in which money has value—must be one that operates under missing markets and nominal rigidities that make changes in money into something other than mere units changes. Then it must also be the case that these same rigidities prevent the economy from responding efficiently to real shocks, raising the possibility that a monetary policy that reacts to real shocks in some way can improve efficiency.

If we had a theory that could let us sort these issues out, we could use it to work out the details of an ideal stabilization policy and to evaluate the effects on welfare of adopting it. This seems to me an entirely reasonable research goal—I have been thinking success is just around the corner for 30 years—but it has not yet been attained. In lieu of such a theory, I will try to get quantitative sense of the answer to the thought-experiment I have posed by studying a series of simpler thought-experiments.

In the rest of this section, I ask what the effect on welfare would be if *all* consumption variability could be eliminated.[4] To this end, consider a single consumer, endowed with the stochastic consumption stream

$$c_t = Ae^{\mu t}e^{-(1/2)\sigma^2}\varepsilon_t, \tag{1}$$

where $\log(\varepsilon_t)$ is a normally distributed random variable with mean 0 and variance σ^2. Under these assumptions

$$E(e^{-(1/2)\sigma^2}\varepsilon_t) = 1$$

and mean consumption at t is $Ae^{\mu t}$. Preferences over such consumption paths are assumed to be

$$E\left\{\sum_{t=0}^{\infty}\left(\frac{1}{1+\rho}\right)^t \frac{c_t^{1-\gamma}}{1-\gamma}\right\}, \tag{2}$$

where ρ is a subjective discount rate, γ is the coefficient of risk aversion, and the expectation is taken with respect to the common distribution of the shocks $\varepsilon_0, \varepsilon_1, \ldots$.

Such a risk-averse consumer would obviously prefer a deterministic consumption path to a risky path with the same mean. We quantify this utility difference by multiplying the risky path by the constant factor $1 + \lambda$ in all dates and states, choosing λ so that the household is indifferent between the deterministic stream and the compensated, risky stream. That is, λ is chosen to solve

$$E\left\{\sum_{t=0}^{\infty}\beta^t \frac{((1+\lambda)c_t)^{1-\gamma}}{1-\gamma}\right\} = \sum_{t=0}^{\infty}\beta^t \frac{(Ae^{\mu t})^{1-\gamma}}{1-\gamma}, \tag{3}$$

where c_t is given by (1). Canceling, taking logs, and collecting terms gives

$$\lambda \simeq \frac{1}{2}\gamma\sigma^2. \tag{4}$$

This compensation parameter λ—the *welfare gain* from eliminating consumption risk—depends, naturally enough, on the amount of risk that is present, σ^2, and the aversion people have for this risk, γ.

4. This calculation replicates the one I carried out in Lucas (1987, Ch. III).

We can get an initial idea of the value to the economy as a whole of removing aggregate risk by viewing this agent as representative of U.S. consumers in general. In this case, to estimate λ we need estimates of the variance σ^2 of the log of consumption about its trend, and of the coefficient γ of risk aversion. Using annual U.S. data for the period 1947–2001, the standard deviation of the log of real, per capita consumption about a linear trend is 0.032.[5] Estimates of the parameter γ in use in macroeconomics and public finance applications today range from 1 (log utility) to 4. Using log utility, for example, the formula (4) yields the welfare cost estimate

$$\lambda = \frac{1}{2}(0.032)^2 = 0.0005, \tag{5}$$

about one-twentieth of 1 percent of consumption.

Compared to the examples of welfare gains from fiscal and monetary policy changes that I cited above, this estimate seems trivially small: more than an order of magnitude smaller than the gain from ending a 10-percent inflation! Many questions have been raised about this estimate, and subsequent research on this issue has pursued many of them, taking the discussion deep into new scientific territory. In the next four sections, I will review some of the main findings.

III. Removeable Variance: Two Estimates

Even if we do not know exactly how much consumption risk would be removed by an optimal monetary and fiscal policy, it is clear that it would fall far short of the removal of *all* variability. The major empirical finding in macroeconomics over the past 25 years was the demonstration by Finn E. Kydland and Prescott (1982), replicated and refined by Gary D. Hansen (1985) and by many others since then, that technology shocks measured by the method of Robert M. Solow (1957) can induce a reasonably parameterized stochastic growth model to exhibit nearly the same variability in production and consumption as we see in postwar U.S. time series. In the basic growth model, equilibrium and optimal growth are equivalent, so that if technology shocks are all there is to postwar business cycles, resources

5. The comparable figure using a Hodrick-Prescott trend with the smoothing parameter 400 is 0.022.

are already being allocated efficiently and a variance-reducing monetary-fiscal policy would be welfare *reducing*. Even if the equilibrium is inefficient, due to distorting taxes, missing markets or the like, in the face of unavoidable technology and preference shocks an optimal monetary and fiscal policy will surely be associated with a positive level of consumption variance. We need to estimate the size of that part and remove it from the estimate of σ^2 used in (4).

Matthew D. Shapiro and Mark W. Watson's (1988) study is one of several relatively atheoretical attempts to break down the variance of production and other variables into a fraction due to what these authors call "demand" shocks (and which I will call "nominal" shocks) and fractions due to technology and other sources. Their study represents quarterly U.S. time series over the period 1951–1985 as distributed lags of serially independent shocks. The observables include first differences of a measure of hours worked, a log real GDP measure, and the corresponding implicit price deflator. To these three rates of change are added an *ex post* real interest rate (the three-month Treasury bill rate minus the inflation rate) and the change in the relative price of oil. The coefficients of an invertible vector autoregression are estimated, subject to several restrictions. This procedure yields time series of estimated shocks $\hat{\varepsilon}_t$ and decompositions of the variance of each of the five variables into the fractions "explained" by the most recent k values of each of the five shocks.

Shapiro and Watson apply a variety of theoretical principles to the interpretation of their estimates. They do not consistently follow the general-equilibrium practice of interpreting *all* shocks as shifts in preferences, technologies, or the behavior of policy variables, but they have in mind some kind of monetary growth model that does not have a long-run Phillips curve.[6] Real variables, in the long run, are determined by real factors only. Nominal shocks can affect real variables and relative prices in the short run but not in the long run. This idea is not tested: Long-run neutrality is *imposed* on the statistical model. In return it becomes possible to estimate separately the importance of nominal shocks to the short- and medium-run variability of output, hours, and real interest rates.[7]

6. To remove any doubt on the latter point, they quote from Milton Friedman's (1968) Presidential Address.

7. A similar, and similarly motivated, identification procedure was used in Olivier J. Blanchard and Danny Quah (1989). Thomas J. Sargent and Christopher A. Sims (1977) is a predecessor in spirit, if not in detail.

Table 1 Percentage of Variance Due to Nominal Shocks at Different Forecast Horizons

Quarter	Output	Hours	Inflation	Interest rate
1	28	36	89	83
4	28	40	82	71
8	20	31	82	72
12	17	27	84	74
20	12	20	86	79
36	8	12	89	85
∞	0	0	94	94

In the five-variable scheme that Shapiro and Watson use, there are two nominal variables—the inflation rate and the nominal interest rate—and three real ones—output, hours, and the relative price of oil. They assume as well five shocks, two of which are nominal in the sense of having no effect on real variables in the long run. They are not able to measure the effects of the two dimensions of nominal instability separately. The other three shocks are taken to be real. The assumed exogeneity of oil price shocks plus a long-run neutrality hypothesis on hours are used to estimate the importance of three distinct real shocks. This aspect of their identification seems to me questionable, and in any case it is of an entirely different nature from the neutrality of nominal shocks. I will just lump the effects of the real shocks together, as Shapiro and Watson do with the two nominal shocks, and interpret their paper as partitioning the variance of output and hours into nominal and real sources. The resulting Table 1 is a condensation of their Table 2.

The two zeroes for output and hours in the last, long-run, row of Table 1 are there by the *definition* of a nominal shock. But the two 94-percent entries in this row for inflation and the nominal interest rate could have come out any way. I take the fact that these values are so close to 1 as a confirmation of Shapiro and Watson's procedure for identifying nominal shocks. According to Table 1, these nominal shocks have accounted for something less than 30 percent of short-run production variability in the postwar United States. This effect decays slowly, with no change after one year, a reduction to 20 percent after two years, and so on.

One can ask whether a better estimate of the importance of nominal shocks could have been obtained by using *M*1 or some other observable measure of monetary shocks. Many studies have proceeded in this more direct way,[8] and much has been learned, but in the end one does not know whether the importance of monetary shocks has been estimated or just the importance of a particular, possibly very defective, measure of them. Information on future prices is conveyed to people by changes in monetary aggregates, of course, but it is also conveyed by interest-rate and exchange-rate movements, by changes in the fiscal situation that may lead to tighter or easier money later on, by changes in financial regulations, by statements of influential people, and by many other factors. Shapiro and Watson's method bypasses these hard measurement questions and goes directly to an estimation of the importance of nominal shocks in general, those we know how to measure and those we do not, whatever they may be.

A second reason for preferring the procedure Shapiro and Watson used is that the effects of nominal shocks as they estimate them include the effects of real shocks that could have been offset by monetary policy but were not. Whatever it is that keeps prices from rising in proportion to a given increase in money must also keep relative prices from adjusting as neoclassical theory would predict they should to, say, an increase in the OPEC-set price of oil. Effects of either kind—those initiated by monetary changes and those initiated by real shocks—will last only as long as the rigidity or glitch that gives rise to them lasts, vanishing in the long run, and will be identified as arising from the "nominal," or "demand," shock under the Shapiro and Watson identification procedure. Thus I want to interpret the estimates in columns 2 and 3 of Table 1 as *upper bounds* on the variance that could have been removed from output and hours at different horizons under some monetary policy other than the one actually pursued. The table gives no information on what this variance-minimizing monetary policy might have been, and there is no presumption that it would have been a policy that does not respond to real shocks.

Shapiro and Watson applied the theoretical idea that nominal shocks should be neutral in the long run to obtain an estimate of the fraction of short-run output variability that can be attributed to such shocks. Prescott (1986a) proceeded in a quite different way to arrive at an estimate of the fraction of output variability that can be attributed to technology shocks. He used actual Solow residuals to estimate the variance and serial correla-

8. For example, Lawrence J. Christiano et al. (1996).

tion of the underlying technology shocks. Feeding shocks with these properties into a fully calibrated real-business-cycle model resulted in output variability that was about 84 percent of actual variability.[9] In a complementary study, S. Rao Aiyagari (1994) arrived at an estimate of 79 percent for the contribution of technology shocks, based on comovements of production and labor input over the cycle.

Shapiro and Watson find that at most 30 percent of cyclical output variability can be attributed to nominal shocks. Working from the opposite direction, Prescott and Aiyagari conclude that at least 75 percent of cyclical output variability must be due to technology shocks. These findings are not as consistent as they may appear, because there are important real factors besides technological shocks—shocks to the tax system, to the terms of trade, to household technology, or to preferences—that are cyclically important but not captured in either of the categories I have considered so far.[10] Even so, on the basis of this evidence I find it hard to imagine that more than 30 percent of the cyclical variability observed in the postwar United States could or should be removed by changes in the way monetary and fiscal policy is conducted.

IV. Risk Aversion

The estimate of the potential gains from stabilization reviewed in Section II rests on assumed consumer preferences of the constant relative risk aversion (CRRA) family, using but two parameters—the subjective discount rate ρ and the risk-aversion coefficient γ—to characterize all households. This preference family is almost universally used in macroeconomic and public finance applications. The familiar formula for an economy's average return on capital under CRRA preferences,

$$r = \rho + \gamma g, \tag{6}$$

9. Questions of measurement errors are discussed in the paper and by Summers (1986) in the same volume. In Prescott (1986b), estimates of 0.5 to 0.75 for the contribution of technology shocks to output variance are proposed.

10. For example, Shapiro and Watson attribute a large share of output variance to a shock which they call "labor supply" [and which I would call "household technology," following Jess Benhabib et al. (1991) and Jeremy Greenwood and Zvi Hercowitz (1991)].

where g is the growth rate of consumption, makes it clear why fairly low γ values must be used. Per capita consumption growth in the United States is about 0.02 and the after-tax return on capital is around 0.05, so the fact that ρ must be positive requires that γ in (6) be at most 2.5. Moreover, a value as high as 2.5 would imply much larger interest rate differentials than those we see between fast-growing economies like Taiwan and mature economies like the United States. This is the kind of evidence that leads to the use of γ values at or near 1 in applications.

But the CRRA model has problems. Rajnish Mehra and Prescott (1985) showed that if one wants to use a stochastic growth model with CRRA preferences to account for the entire return differential between stocks and bonds—historically about 6 percent—as a premium for risk, the parameter γ must be enormous, perhaps 50 or 100.[11] Such values obviously cannot be squared with (6). This "equity premium puzzle" remains unsolved, and has given rise to a vast literature that is clearly closely related to the question of assessing the costs of instability.[12]

One response to the puzzle is to adopt a three- rather than two-parameter description of preferences. Larry G. Epstein and Stanley E. Zin (1989, 1991) and Philippe Weil (1990) proposed different forms of *recursive utility*, preference families in which there is one parameter to determine intertemporal substitutability and a second one to describe risk aversion. The first corresponds to the parameter γ in (6), and can be assigned a small value to fit estimated average returns to capital. Then the risk-aversion parameter can be chosen as large as necessary to account for the equity premium.

Thomas D. Tallarini, Jr. (2000) uses preferences of the Epstein-Zin type, with an intertemporal substitution elasticity of 1, to construct a real-business-cycle model of the U.S. economy. He finds an astonishing separation of quantity and asset price determination: The behavior of aggregate quantities depends hardly at all on attitudes toward risk, so the coefficient of risk aversion is left free to account for the equity premium *perfectly*.[13] Tallarini estimates a welfare cost of aggregate consumption risk of 10 percent of consumption, comparable to some of the supply-side gains cited in Section I, and two orders of magnitude larger than the estimate I proposed

11. See also Lars Peter Hansen and Kenneth J. Singleton (1983).

12. Two especially informative surveys are John H. Cochrane and Hansen (1992) and Narayana R. Kocherlakota (1996).

13. Similar results, obtained in a closely related context, were reported by Hansen et al. (1999).

in Section II.[14] As Maurice Obstfeld (1994) shows, this result is basically the formula (4) with a coefficient of risk aversion two orders of magnitude larger than the one I used.

Fernando Alvarez and Urban J. Jermann (2000) take a nonparametric approach to the evaluation of the potential gains from stabilization policy, relating the marginal cost of business-cycle risk to observed market prices without ever committing to a utility function. Their estimation procedure is based on the observation that consumption streams with a wide variety of different risk characteristics—or something very nearly equivalent to them—are available for sale in securities markets. They use a mix of asset-pricing theory and statistical methods to infer the prices of a claim to the actual, average consumption path and alternative consumption paths with some of the uncertainty removed. They call the price differentials so estimated *marginal* welfare costs, and show that they will be upper bounds to the corresponding total cost: my compensation parameter λ. The basic underlying hypotheses are that asset markets are complete and that asset-price differences reflect risk and timing differences *and nothing else.*

The gain from the removal of *all* consumption variability about trend, estimated in this way, is large—around 30 percent of consumption.[15] This is a reflection of the high risk aversion needed to match the 6-percent equity premium, and can be compared to Tallarini's estimate of 10 percent. But the gain from removing risk at what Alvarez and Jermann call business-cycle frequencies—cycles of eight years or less—is two orders of magnitude smaller, around 0.3 percent. Most of the high return on equity is estimated to be compensation for long-term risk only, risk that could not be much reduced by short-run policies that are neutral in the long run.

Accepting Shapiro and Watson's finding that less that 30 percent of output variance at business-cycle frequencies can be attributed to nominal

14. James Dolmas (1998) uses still another preference family, obtaining much higher cost estimates than mine. Like Tallarini, Christopher Otrok (1999) develops and analyzes a complete real-business-cycle model. He uses a preference family proposed by John Heaton (1995). His cost estimates are close to mine. A recent paper by Anne Epaulard and Aude Pommeret (2001) contains further results along this line, and provides a very useful quantitative comparison to earlier findings.

15. Alvarez and Jermann offer many estimates in their Tables 2A–2D. My summary is based on Table 2D, which uses postwar (1954–1997) data and requires that consumption and dividends be cointegrated. From this table, I follow the authors and cite averages over the columns headed "8 years" and "inf."

shocks, the lower Alvarez and Jermann estimate of 0.3 should be reduced to 0.1 if it is to serve my purpose as an estimate of the value of potential improvements in stabilization policy. But it is important to keep in mind that this estimate is not smaller than Tallarini's because of a different estimate of risk aversion. Tallarini's estimate of $\gamma = 100$ is the parametric analogue of Alvarez and Jermann's "market price of risk," based on exactly the same resolution of the equity premium puzzle. The different cost estimate is entirely due to differences in the consumption paths being compared.

Resolving empirical difficulties by adding new parameters always works, but often only by raising more problems. The risk-aversion levels needed to match the equity premium, under the assumption that asset markets are complete, ought to show up somewhere besides securities prices, but they do not seem to do so. No one has found risk-aversion parameters of 50 or 100 in the diversification of individual portfolios, in the level of insurance deductibles, in the wage premiums associated with occupations with high earnings risk, or in the revenues raised by state-operated lotteries. It would be good to have the equity premium resolved, but I think we need to look beyond high estimates of risk aversion to do it. The great contribution of Alvarez and Jermann is to show that even using the highest available estimate of risk aversion, the gain from further reductions in business-cycle risk is below one-tenth of 1 percent of consumption. The evidence also leaves one free to believe—as I do—that the gain is in fact one or two orders of magnitude smaller.

V. Incomplete Markets and Distribution Effects

The calculations I have described so far treat households as identical and individual risks as diversifiable. But as Per Krusell and Anthony A. Smith, Jr. (1999) observe, "it is quite plausible that the welfare costs of cycles are not so high on average, but may be very high for, say, the very poor or currently unemployed members of society." Several recent studies have pursued this possibility.[16] Doing so evidently requires models with incomplete risk sharing and differently situated agents.

Krusell and Smith (1999, 2002) study a model economy in which indi-

16. For example, Ayse Imrohoroğlu (1989), Andrew Atkeson and Christopher Phelan (1994), Krusell and Smith (1999, 2002), Kjetil Storesletten et al. (2001), and Tom Krebs (2002).

vidual families are subject to three kinds of stochastic shocks. There is an aggregate productivity shock that affects everyone, and employment shocks that differ from person to person. Families are infinitely lived dynasties, but every 40 years or so a family draws a new head, whose subjective discount rate is drawn from a fixed distribution. Dynasties with patient heads will accumulate wealth while others will run their wealth down.[17] The sizes of these shocks are chosen so that the model economy experiences realistic GDP fluctuations, unemployment spells have realistic properties, and the overall wealth distribution matches the U.S. distribution: In the model, the wealthiest 5 percent of households own 54 percent of total wealth; in reality, they hold 51 percent.

It is essential to the substantive question that motivates this study that neither the employment shocks nor the uncertainty about the character of the household head can be diversified away. Otherwise, the individual effects of the aggregate productivity shocks would be the same as in the representative agent models I have already discussed. One may argue over why it is that markets do not permit such diversification, but it seems clear enough that they do not: Where is the market where people can be insured against the risk of having irresponsible or incompetent parents or children?

These exogenous forces acting differentially across households induce different individual choices, which in turn lead to differences in individual capital holdings. The state space in this economy is very large, much larger than anything people were working with numerically 15 years ago, and without the method developed in Krusell and Smith (1998) it would not have been possible to work out the predictions of this model. A key simplification comes from the fact that the impact on any one family of the shocks that hit others has to work through two prices, the real wage and the rental price of capital. These prices in turn depend only on the total stock of capital, regardless of the way it is distributed, and total employment, regardless of who has a job and who does not. By exploiting these features, solutions can be calculated using an iterative procedure that works like a dream: For determining the behavior of aggregates, they discovered, realistically modeled household heterogeneity just does not matter very much.

17. This way of modeling wealth changes within a fixed distribution across families was introduced in John Laitner (1992).

For *individual* behavior and welfare, of course, heterogeneity is everything. In the thought-experiments that Krusell and Smith run with their model, removal of the business cycle is defined to be equivalent to setting the aggregate productivity shock equal to a constant. It is important to be clear on what the effect of such a change would be on the behavior of the employment shocks to which individuals are subject, but the magical character of the experiment makes it hard to know how this question is best resolved. I will describe what Krusell and Smith did, and deal with some other possibilities later on.

Suppose that a shock $y = az + \varepsilon$ affects an individual's behavior, where z is the aggregate shock and ε is idiosyncratic. We project the individual shock on the aggregate, $\varepsilon = cz + \eta$, where the residual η is uncorrelated with z, and then think of an ideal stabilization policy as one that replaces

$$y = az + \varepsilon = (a + c)z + \eta$$

with

$$\hat{y} = (a + c)E(z) + \eta.$$

Not only is the direct effect of the productivity shock z removed but also the indirect effects of z on the individual employment shocks ε.[18] In this particular application, removing the variance of the aggregate shock is estimated to reduce the standard deviation of the individual employment shocks by 16 percent.[19]

The first such thought-experiment Krusell and Smith describe involves a comparison between the expected utility drawn from the steady state of the economy with aggregate shocks and the expected utility from the steady state of the economy with aggregate shocks and their indirect effects removed in the way I have just described. The welfare gain from eliminating cycles in this sense turns out to be negative! In a model, like this one, in which markets for risk pooling are incomplete, people will engage in precautionary savings, overaccumulating capital in the effort to self-insure. This implies larger average consumption in the more risky economy. Of course, there are costs to accumulating the higher capital stock, but these costs are not fully counted in a steady-state comparison.

18. This is a linear illustration of the more generally defined procedure described in Krusell and Smith (1999).

19. Here and below, the numbers I cite are taken from Krusell and Smith (2002).

In any case, as Krusell and Smith emphasize, there is nothing really distributional about a steady-state comparison: Every infinitely lived dynasty is assigned a place in the wealth distribution at random, and no one of them can be identified as permanently rich or poor. The whole motivation of the paper is to focus on the situation of people described as "hand-to-mouth consumers," but a steady-state comparison misses them. This observation motivates a second thought-experiment—one with much more complicated dynamics than the first—in which an economy is permitted to reach its steady-state wealth distribution with realistic aggregate shocks, and then is relieved of aggregate risk. The full transition to a new steady state is then worked out and taken into account in the utility comparisons. In this experiment, we can identify individuals as "rich" or "poor" by their position in the initial wealth distribution, and discuss the effects of risk removal category by category.

The average welfare gain in this second experiment is about 0.1 of 1 percent of consumption, about twice the estimate in Section II of this paper. (Krusell and Smith also assume log utility.) But this figure masks a lot of diversity. Low-wealth, unemployed people—people who would borrow against future labor income if they could—enjoy a utility gain equivalent to a 4-percent perpetual increase in consumption. Oddly, the very wealthy can also gain, as much as 2 percent. Krusell and Smith conjecture that this is due to the higher interest rates implied by the overall decrease in precautionary savings and capital. Finally, there is a large group of middle-wealth households that are made worse off by eliminating aggregate risk.

These calculations are sensitive—especially at the poor end of the distribution—to what is assumed about the incomes of unemployed people. Krusell and Smith calibrate this, roughly, to current U.S. unemployment insurance replacement rates. If one were estimating the costs of the depression of the 1930's, before the current welfare system was in place, lower rates would be used and the cost estimates would increase sharply.[20] It would also be interesting to use a model like this to examine the trade-offs between reductions in aggregate risk and an improved welfare system.

Storesletten et al. (2001) study distributional influences on welfare cost estimates with methods that are closely related to Krusell and Smith's, but they obtain larger estimates of the gains from removing all aggregate shocks. They use an overlapping generations setup with 43 working-age

20. See Satyajit Chatterjee and Dean Corbae (2000).

generations, in which the youngest cohort is always credit constrained. In such a setting, the young are helpless in the face of shocks of all kinds and reductions in variance can yield large welfare gains. But if the age effects are averaged out to reflect the importance of intrafamily lending (as I think they should be) the gains estimated by Storesletten et al. under log utility are no larger than Krusell and Smith's.[21] In contrast to earlier studies, however, the Storesletten et al. model implies that estimated welfare gains rise faster than proportionately as risk aversion is increased: From Exhibit 2, for example, the average gain increases from 0.6 of a percent to 2.5 as γ is increased from 2 to 4.

Two features of the theory interact to bring this about.[22] First, and most crucial, is a difference in the way reductions in the variance of aggregate shocks affect risks faced at the individual level. In the Storesletten et al. simulations, a bad realization of the aggregate productivity shock increases the conditional *variance* of the idiosyncratic risk that people face, so aggregate and individual risks are compounded in a way that Krusell and Smith rule out. A second difference is that idiosyncratic shocks are assumed to have a random walk component, so their effects are long lasting. A bad aggregate shock increases the chances that a young worker will draw a bad individual shock, and if he does he will suffer its effects throughout his prime working years.

The effects of these two assumptions are clear: They convert small, transient shocks at the aggregate level into large, persistent shocks to the earnings of a small fraction of households. Whether they are realistic is question of fact. That individual earnings differences are highly persistent has been clear since Lee Lillard and Robert Willis's pioneering (1978) study. The fanning out over time of the earnings and consumption distributions within a cohort that Angus Deaton and Christina Paxson (1994) document is striking evidence of a sizeable, uninsurable random walk component in earnings. The relation of the variance of earnings shocks to the aggregate state of the economy, also emphasized by N. Gregory Mankiw (1986) in connection with the equity premium puzzle, has only recently been studied empirically. Storesletten et al. find a negative relation over time between cross-section earnings means and standard deviations in

21. Based on Exhibits 2 and A.3.1.

22. Storesletten et al. do a good job of breaking the differences into intelligible pieces. I also found the example explicitly solved in Krebs (2002) very helpful in this regard.

Panel Studies of Income Dynamics data. Costas Meghir and Luigi Pistaferri (2001) obtain smaller estimates, but also conclude that "the unemployment rate and the variance of permanent [earnings] shocks appear to be quite synchronized" in the 1970's and 1980's.

These issues are central to an accurate description of the risk situation that individual agents face, and hence to the assessment of welfare gains from policies that alter this situation. The development of tractable equilibrium models capable of bringing cross-section and panel evidence to bear on this and other macroeconomic questions is an enormous step forward. But Krusell and Smith find only modest effects of heterogeneity on the estimates of welfare gains from the elimination of aggregate risk, and even accepting the Storesletten et al. view entails an upward revision of a factor of only about 5.

The real promise of the Krusell-Smith model and related formulations, I think, will be in the study of the relation of policies that reduce the impact of risk by reducing the variance of shocks (like aggregate stabilization policies) to those that act by reallocating risks (like social insurance policies). Traditionally, these two kinds of policies have been studied by different economists, using unrelated models and different data sets. But both appear explicitly in the models I have reviewed here, and it is clear that it will soon be possible to provide a unified analysis of their costs and benefits.

VI. Other Directions

My plan was to go down a list of all the things that could have gone wrong with my 1987 calculations but, as I should have anticipated, possibilities were added to the list faster than I could eliminate them. I will just note some of the more interesting of these possibilities, and then conclude. The level of consumption risk in a society is, in part, subject to choice. When in an economy that is subject to larger shocks, people will live with more consumption variability and the associated loss in welfare, but they may also substitute into risk-avoiding technologies, accepting reduced *average* levels of production. This possibility shows up in the precautionary savings—overaccumulation of capital—that Krusell and Smith (1999, 2002) found. As Garey Ramey and Valerie A. Ramey (1991) suggested, this kind of substitution surely shows up in other forms as well.

In an endogenous growth framework, substitution against risky technologies can affect rates of growth as well as output levels. Larry E. Jones et al. (1999) and Epaulard and Pommeret (2001) explore some of these possibilities, though neither study attributes large welfare gains to volatility-induced reductions in growth rates. Gadi Barlevy (2001) proposes a convex adjustment cost that makes an erratic path of investment in knowledge less effective than a smooth path at the same average level. In such a setting, reducing shock variability can lead to higher growth even without an effect on the average level of investment. He obtains welfare gains as large as 7 percent of consumption in models based on this idea, but everything hinges on a curvature parameter on which there is little evidence. This is a promising frontier on which there is much to be done. Surely there are others.

VII. Conclusions

If business cycles were simply efficient responses of quantities and prices to unpredictable shifts in technology and preferences, there would be no need for distinct stabilization or demand management policies and certainly no point to such legislation as the Employment Act of 1946. If, on the other hand, rigidities of some kind prevent the economy from reacting efficiently to nominal or real shocks, or both, there is a need to design suitable policies and to assess their performance. In my opinion, this is the case: I think the stability of monetary aggregates and nominal spending in the postwar United States is a major reason for the stability of aggregate production and consumption during these years, relative to the experience of the interwar period and the contemporary experience of other economies. If so, this stability must be seen in part as an achievement of the economists, Keynesian and monetarist, who guided economic policy over these years.

The question I have addressed in this lecture is whether stabilization policies that go beyond the general stabilization of spending that characterizes the last 50 years, whatever form they might take, promise important increases in welfare. The answer to this question is "No": The potential gains from improved stabilization policies are on the order of hundredths of a percent of consumption, perhaps two orders of magnitude smaller than the potential benefits of available "supply-side" fiscal reforms. This answer does depend, certainly, on the degree of risk aversion. It does not appear to be very sensitive to the way distribution effects are dealt with, though it does presuppose a system of unemployment insurance at postwar U.S. levels. I have been as explicit as I can be on the way theory and evidence bear on these conclusions.

When Don Patinkin gave his *Money, Interest, and Prices* the subtitle "An Integration of Monetary and Value Theory," value theory meant, to him, a purely static theory of general equilibrium. Fluctuations in production and employment, due to monetary disturbances or to shocks of any other kind, were viewed as inducing disequilibrium adjustments, unrelated to anyone's purposeful behavior, modeled with vast numbers of free parameters. For us, today, value theory refers to models of dynamic economies subject to unpredictable shocks, populated by agents who are good at processing information and making choices over time. The macroeconomic research I have discussed today makes essential use of value theory in this modern sense: formulating explicit models, computing solutions, comparing their behavior quantitatively to observed time series and other data sets. As a result, we are able to form a much sharper quantitative view of the potential of changes in policy to improve peoples' lives than was possible a generation ago.

References

Aiyagari, S. Rao. "On the Contribution of Technology Shocks to Business Cycles." *Federal Reserve Bank of Minneapolis Quarterly Review*, Summer 1994, *18*(3), pp. 22–34.

Alvarez, Fernando and Jermann, Urban J. "Using Asset Prices to Measure the Cost of Business Cycles." Working paper, University of Chicago, 2000.

Atkeson, Andrew and Phelan, Christopher. "Reconsidering the Costs of Business Cycles with Incomplete Markets." *NBER macroeconomics annual, 1994*. Cambridge, MA: MIT Press, 1994, pp. 187–207.

Auerbach, Alan J. and Kotlikoff, Laurence J. *Dynamic fiscal policy*. Cambridge: Cambridge University Press, 1987.

Bailey, Martin J. "The Welfare Cost of Inflationary Finance." *Journal of Political Economy*, April 1956, *64*(2), pp. 93–110.

Barlevy, Gadi. "The Cost of Business Cycles Under Endogenous Growth." Working paper, Northwestern University, 2001.

Benhabib, Jess; Rogerson, Richard and Wright, Randall. "Homework in Macroeconomics: Household Production and Aggregate Fluctuations." *Journal of Political Economy*, December 1991, *99*(6), pp. 1166–87.

Blanchard, Olivier J. and Quah, Danny. "The Dynamic Effects of Aggregate Demand and Supply Disturbances." *American Economic Review,* September 1989, *79*(4), pp. 655–73.

Brock, William A. and Turnovsky, Stephen J. "The Analysis of Macroeconomic Policies in Perfect Foresight Equilibrium." *International Economic Review,* February 1981, *22*(1), pp. 179–209.

Chamley, Christophe P. "The Welfare Cost of Capital Income Taxation in a Growing Economy." *Journal of Political Economy,* June 1981, *89*(3), pp. 468–96.

Chatterjee, Satyajit and Corbae, Dean. "On the Welfare Gains of Reducing the Likelihood of Economic Crises." Federal Reserve Bank of Philadelphia Research Working Paper No. 00/14, November 2000.

Christiano, Lawrence J.; Eichenbaum, Martin and Evans, Charles. "The Effects of Monetary Policy Shocks: Evidence from the Flow of Funds." *Review of Economics and Statistics,* February 1996, *78*(1), pp. 16–34.

Cochrane, John H. and Hansen, Lars Peter. "Asset Pricing Explorations for Macroeconomics." *NBER macroeconomics annual, 1992.* Cambridge, MA: MIT Press, 1992, pp. 115–65.

Deaton, Angus and Paxson, Christina. "Intertemporal Choice and Inequality." *Journal of Political Economy,* June 1994, *102*(3), pp. 437– 67.

Dolmas, James. "Risk Preferences and the Welfare Cost of Business Cycles." *Review of Economic Dynamics,* July 1998, *1*(3), pp. 646–76.

Epaulard, Anne and Pommeret, Aude. "Recursive Utility, Endogenous Growth, and the Welfare Cost of Volatility." International Monetary Fund Working Paper No. WP/01/05, 2001.

Epstein, Larry G., and Zin, Stanley E. "Substitution, Risk Aversion, and the Temporal Behavior of Consumption Growth and Asset Returns I: A Theoretical Framework." *Econometrica,* July 1989, *57*(4), pp. 937–69.

———. "Substitution, Risk Aversion, and the Temporal Behavior of Consumption Growth and Asset Returns II: An Empirical Analysis." *Journal of Political Economy,* April 1991, *99*(2), pp. 263–86.

Friedman, Milton. "The Role of Monetary Policy." *American Economic Review,* March 1968, *58*(1), pp. 1–17.

Greenwood, Jeremy and Hercowitz, Zvi. "The Allocation of Capital and Time over the Business Cycle." *Journal of Political Economy,* December 1991, *99*(6), pp. 1188–214.

Hall, Robert E. and Rabushka, Alvin. *The flat tax,* 2nd Ed. Stanford, CA: Hoover Institution Press. 1995.

Hansen, Gary D. "Indivisible Labor and the Business Cycle." *Journal of Monetary Economics,* November 1985, *16*(3), pp. 309–27.

Hansen, Lars Peter; Sargent, Thomas J. and Tallarini, Thomas D., Jr. "Robust

Permanent Income and Pricing." *Review of Economic Studies,* October 1999, *66*(4), pp. 873–908.

Hansen, Lars Peter and Singleton, Kenneth J. "Stochastic Consumption, Risk Aversion, and the Temporal Behavior of Asset Returns." *Journal of Political Economy,* April 1983, *91*(2), pp. 249–65.

Heaton, John. "An Empirical Investigation of Asset Pricing with Temporally Dependent Preference Specifications." *Econometrica,* May 1995, *63*(3), pp. 681–717.

Imrohoroğlu, Ayse. "The Cost of Business Cycles with Indivisibilities and Liquidity Constraints." *Journal of Political Economy,* December 1989, *97*(6), pp. 1364–83.

Jones, Larry E.; Manuelli, Rodolfo E. and Stacchetti, Ennio. "Technology (and Policy) Shocks in Models of Endogenous Growth." National Bureau of Economic Research (Cambridge, MA) Working Paper No. 7063, April 1999.

Judd, Kenneth L. "The Welfare Cost of Factor Taxation in a Perfect Foresight Model." *Journal of Political Economy,* August 1987, *95*(4), pp. 675–709.

Kocherlakota, Narayana R. "The Equity Premium: It's Still a Puzzle." *Journal of Economic Literature,* March 1996, *34*(1), pp. 42–71.

Krebs, Tom. "Growth and Welfare Effects of Business Cycles in Economies with Idiosyncratic Human Capital Risk." Working paper, Brown University, 2002.

Krusell, Per, and Smith, Anthony A., Jr. "Income and Wealth Heterogeneity in the Macroeconomy." *Journal of Political Economy,* October 1998, *106*(5), pp. 867–96.

———. "On the Welfare Effects of Eliminating Business Cycles." *Review of Economic Dynamics,* January 1999, *2*(2), pp. 245–72.

———. "Revisiting the Welfare Effects of Eliminating Business Cycles." Working paper, Carnegie Mellon University, 2002.

Kydland, Finn E. and Prescott, Edward C. "Time to Build and Aggregate Fluctuations." *Econometrica,* November 1982, *50*(6), pp. 1345–70.

Laitner, John. "Random Earnings Differences, Lifetime Liquidity Constraints, and Altruistic Intergenerational Transfers." *Journal of Economic Theory,* December 1992, *58*(2), pp. 135–70.

Lillard, Lee and Willis, Robert. "Dynamic Aspects of Earnings Mobility." *Econometrica,* September 1978, *46*(5), pp. 985–1012.

Lucas, Robert E., Jr. *Models of business cycles.* New York: Basil Blackwell, 1987.

———. "Inflation and Welfare." *Econometrica,* March 2000, *68*(2), pp. 247–74.

Mankiw, N. Gregory. "The Equity Premium and the Concentration of Aggregate Shocks." *Journal of Financial Economics,* September 1986, *17*(1), pp. 211–19.

Meghir, Costas and Pistaferri, Luigi. "Income Variance Dynamics and Heterogeneity." Working paper, Institute for Fiscal Studies, 2001.

Mehra, Rajnish and Prescott, Edward C. "The Equity Premium: A Puzzle." *Journal of Monetary Economics,* March 1985, *15*(2), pp. 145–61.

Meltzer, Allan H. "The Demand for Money: The Evidence from Time Series." *Journal of Political Economy,* June 1963, *71*(3), pp. 219–46.

Obstfeld, Maurice. "Evaluating Risky Consumption Paths: The Role of Intertemporal Substitutability." *European Economic Review,* August 1994, *38*(7), pp. 1471–86.

Otrok, Christopher. "On Measuring the Welfare Cost of Business Cycles." Working paper, University of Virginia, 1999.

Prescott, Edward C. "Theory Ahead of Business Cycle Measurement." *Federal Reserve Bank of Minneapolis Quarterly Review,* Fall 1986a, *10*(4), pp. 9–21.

———. "Response to a Skeptic." *Federal Reserve Bank of Minneapolis Quarterly Review,* Fall 1986b, *10*(4), pp. 28–33.

———. "Richard T. Ely Lecture: Prosperity and Depression." *American Economic Review,* May 2002 *(Papers and Proceedings), 92*(2), pp. 1–15.

Ramey, Garey and Ramey, Valerie A. "Technology Commitment and the Cost of Economic Fluctuation." National Bureau of Economic Research (Cambridge, MA) Working Paper No. 3755, June 1991.

Rosen, Sherwin. "Public Employment and the Welfare State in Sweden." *Journal of Economic Literature,* June 1996, *34*(2), pp. 729–40.

Sargent, Thomas J. and Sims, Christopher A. "Business Cycle Modeling without Pretending to Have Too Much A-Priori Economic Theory," in *New methods in business cycle research.* Proceedings from a Conference, Federal Reserve Bank of Minneapolis, 1977, pp. 45–109.

Shapiro, Matthew D. and Watson, Mark W. "Sources of Business Cycle Fluctuations." *NBER macroeconomics annual, 1988.* Cambridge, MA: MIT Press, 1988, pp. 111–48.

Solow, Robert M. "Technical Change and the Aggregate Production Function." *Review of Economics and Statistics,* August 1957, *39*(3), pp. 312–20.

Storesletten, Kjetil; Telmer, Chris I. and Yaron, Amir. "The Welfare Cost of Business Cycles Revisited: Finite Lives and Cyclical Variation in Idiosyncratic Risk." *European Economic Review,* June 2001, *45*(7), pp. 1311–39.

Summers, Lawrence H. "Capital Taxation and Accumulation in a Life Cycle Growth Model." *American Economic Review,* September 1981, *71*(4), pp. 533–44.

———. "Some Skeptical Observations on Real Business Cycle Theory." *Federal Reserve Bank of Minneapolis Quarterly Review,* Fall 1986, *10*(4), pp. 22–27.

Tallarini, Thomas D., Jr. "Risk-Sensitive Real Business Cycles." *Journal of Monetary Economics,* June 2000, *45*(3), pp. 507–32.

Weil, Philippe. "Non-Expected Utility in Macroeconomics." *Quarterly Journal of Economics,* February 1990, *105*(1), pp. 27–42.

— 20 —

Menu Costs and Phillips Curves

MIKHAIL GOLOSOV
ROBERT E. LUCAS JR.

I. Introduction

This paper develops a model of a monetary economy in which firms must pay a fixed cost—a "menu cost"—in order to change nominal prices.* Menu costs are interesting to macroeconomists because they are often cited as a microeconomic foundation for a form of "price stickiness" assumed in many New Keynesian models. Without sticky prices these models would not exhibit the real effects of monetary shocks—Phillips curves —that they are designed to analyze.

Under menu costs, any individual price will be constant most of the time and then occasionally jump to a new level. Thus the center of the model will be the firm's pricing decision to reprice or not to do so. Many New Keynesian models do not examine this decision but instead rely on a simplifying assumption proposed by Calvo (1983) that the waiting time between repricing dates is selected at random from an exponential distribution: Firms choose the size of price changes but not their timing.

As many others are, we are skeptical that the Calvo model provides a serviceable approximation to behavior under menu costs.[1] One reason is

Journal of Political Economy 115, no. 2 (April 2007): 171–199.

*We have benefitted from discussions with Ariel Burstein, Ricardo Caballero, V. V. Chari, Larry Christiano, Lars Hansen, Larry Jones, Boyan Jovanovic, Patrick Kehoe, Timothy Kehoe, Bob King, Pete Klenow, Oleksiy Kryvtsov, Ellen McGrattan, Thomas Philippon, Thomas Sargent, Nancy Stokey, Julia Thomas, and Aleh Tsyvinski. Seminar participants at many universities and research centers provided helpful comments. We thank the editors and referees of this *Journal* for their criticism.

1. Another common basis for price stickiness is nominal contracting. Chari, Kehoe, and McGrattan (2000) showed that rational expectations equilibrium models in which firms

that the assumption of a constant repricing rate cannot fit the fact that repricing is more frequent in high-inflation environments. But a second, more important, reason was discovered by Caplin and Spulber (1987), who constructed a theoretical example of an economy with menu costs in which only a small fraction of firms reprice yet changes in money growth are neutral. In their example, there is a stationary distribution of firms' *relative* prices, and as a monetary expansion proceeds, the firms at the low end of this distribution reprice to the high end. The repricing rate is very low—prices are very "sticky"—but no price stickiness can be seen at the aggregate level. The key to the example is that the firms that change price are not selected at random but are rather those firms whose prices are most out of line.

The Caplin and Spulber example is well designed to exhibit this selection effect, but it is unrealistic in too many respects to be implemented quantitatively. In this paper we capture the selection effect in a new model of menu cost pricing, designed so that it can be realistically calibrated using a new data set on prices, assembled and described by Bils and Klenow (2004) and Klenow and Kryvtsov (2005). This estimation makes use of both cross-section and time-series evidence on the prices of narrowly defined individual goods and summary statistics on the frequency of individual price changes.

The average annual inflation rate in these data is about 2.5 percent and on average 22 percent of prices were changed each month, yet the average price change conditional on a price increase was 9.5 percent. These numbers cannot be understood with a model in which sellers react to aggregate inflation shocks only. We introduce a second, idiosyncratic shock chosen to rationalize the magnitude of the price changes that do occur at the individual market level. In order to keep the variances of *relative* prices from growing over time, we require this second shock to be mean-reverting. A model with these features is described in detail in Sections II and III, and the calibration is described in Section IV.

Our main finding is that even though monetary shocks have almost no impact on the rate at which firms change prices, the shocks' real effects are

---

sign long-term nominal price contracts cannot rationalize the impulse-response functions implied by macroeconomic sticky price models: They do not exhibit nearly enough persistence. Our paper is complementary to theirs.

dramatically less persistent than in an otherwise comparable economy with time-dependent price adjustment. Simulations of the model's responses to a one-time impulse of inflation show small and transient effects on real output and employment (figs. 4*a* and *b* in Sec. V), in contrast to much larger and more persistent responses of the same model with Calvo pricing. Figure 6 compares before and after distributions of individual prices to illustrate the reason for these different responses. In the menu cost model, a positive aggregate shock induces the lowest-priced firms to increase prices. At the same time, it offsets negative idiosyncratic shocks, and some firms that would otherwise have decreased prices choose to wait. As a result, the lowest-priced firms do most of the adjusting, their adjustments are large and positive, and the economywide price level increases quickly to reflect the aggregate shock. In the Calvo setting, in contrast, firms get the opportunity to reprice randomly, many firms reprice even though they were already close to their desired price, and the average response of prices to the shock is much smaller. It takes longer for the monetary shock to be reflected in prices, and impulse responses become more persistent.

The paper is organized as follows. In Section II we set out the general model. Section III contains the benchmark specification of the model with a constant inflation rate. Section IV describes the data we used and the calibration procedure. We also compare the predictions of the model, as estimated from data from the low-inflation U.S. economy of 1988–97, to international evidence on the frequency of price changes for several countries and time periods, and for the entire Euro area for the period 1995–2000. Although these studies differ in many details and cover a wide range of inflation rates, we found that our model can account extremely well for most of the episodes (see fig. 3 below). Section V then calculates some impulse-response functions. Section VI reintroduces a stochastic shock to the inflation rate and proposes an approximation to the firm's pricing policy. This approximation is then used to examine the behavior of Phillips curves, in the sense of correlations between inflation rates and levels of production and employment. Estimates of the fraction of the variability in these variables that can be accounted for by monetary shocks in the presence of menu costs are also provided.

The model we describe in the next section builds on the original formulations of the pricing problem of a single firm by Barro (1972) and Sheshinski and Weiss (1977) and on the long literature of other papers that apply (S, s) type inventory theory to pricing problems.[2] It has proved difficult to situate these pricing models in equilibrium models, but several precedents have been influential and valuable. Lach and Tsiddon (1992) look at individual price distributions in Israel, finding them not to be rectangular and the changes not to be synchronized, even for firms with the same initial price. They suggest that a successful model would need to have idiosyncratic shocks as well as economywide shocks. Bertola and Caballero (1990) and Danziger (1999) also consider models with idiosyncratic as well as aggregate shocks. Dotsey, King, and Wolman (1999) propose a monetary equilibrium model in which the synchronization of price changes is broken by a transient, random shock to the menu cost itself: Firms that draw a high cost have an incentive to postpone repricing. They explore a number of issues numerically using a log-linear approximation. Further developments are described in Willis (2000) and Burstein (2006).

Although several of these earlier papers introduce idiosyncratic as well as aggregate shocks, none does so in a way that quite serves the empirical objectives of this study. In the Dotsey et al. (1999) model and its successors, the idiosyncratic shock affects an individual firm's menu cost and thus influences which firms will reprice at a given time. All firms that do reprice move to the same new price, and that new price is determined entirely by the general inflation shock. To fit the data we use, heterogeneity has to show up in observed prices too. The models of Bertola and Caballero (1990), Danziger (1999), and Gertler and Leahy (2005) are closer to ours and have some of the same qualitative implications. But in these models, all the multiple shocks are random walks, so the variances of relative prices grow linearly over time. Thus these models do not provide theoretical counterparts to the sample moments we use in our calibration.

II. A Model of Monetary Equilibrium

The theory that we calibrate and simulate in this paper is a Bellman equation for a single price-setting firm that hires labor at a given nominal wage, produces a consumption good with a stochastically varying technology,

2. Sheshinski and Weiss (1977) analyzed the pricing decision of an individual seller facing a deterministic trend in the desired price level. Versions of this problem, many of them stochastic, have been studied by Frenkel and Jovanovic (1980), Sheshinski and Weiss (1983), Mankiw (1985), Caplin and Leahy (1991), Chang (1999), and Stokey (2002).

and sets product price subject to a menu cost of repricing. We situate our model of a firm in a model of a monetary economy so as to be able to relate its predictions to aggregative evidence. In this economy, there is a continuum of infinitely lived households, each of which consumes a continuum of goods. A Spence-Dixit-Stiglitz utility function is used to aggregate across goods to form current-period utility. Each household also supplies labor on a competitive labor market. Firms hire labor, used to produce the consumption good and to reset nominal prices for the good, and sell goods to consumers. Each firm produces only one of the continuum of consumption goods.

The economy is subject to two kinds of shocks: a monetary shock, which we summarize in the money supply m_t, and a firm-specific productivity shock v_t. The log of the money supply is assumed to follow a Brownian motion with drift parameter μ and variance σ_m^2,

$$d\log(m_t) = \mu dt + \sigma_m dZ_m, \tag{1}$$

where Z_m denotes a standard Brownian motion with zero drift and unit variance. In the absence of the real menu costs associated with changing prices, the evolution of m_t would have no effect on resource allocation.

There are also firm-specific productivity shocks v_t, which are assumed to be independent across firms. We assume that log (v_t) follows the mean-reverting process:

$$d\log(v_t) = -\eta \log(v_t) dt + \sigma_v dZ_v, \qquad \eta > 0, \tag{2}$$

where Z_v is a standard Brownian motion with zero drift and unit variance, distributed independently of Z_m.

There is an economywide labor market on which firms hire labor from households at a nominal wage w_t. The model will be constructed so as to ensure that the log of w_t also follows the process (1). There is a capital market on which claims to the monetary unit are traded. We adopt the convention that $E[\int_0^\infty Q_t y_t dt]$ is the value at date 0 of a dollar earnings stream $\{y_t\}_0^\infty$, also a stochastic process defined in terms of m_t.[3]

The *state* of the economy at date t includes the levels m_t and w_t of the money supply and the nominal wage rate. The situation of an individual firm depends also on the price p that it carries into t from earlier dates and

3. Thus Q_t must be multiplied by the appropriate probabilities to obtain the Arrow-Debreu prices.

its idiosyncratic productivity shock v_t. There is a continuum of firms, so the state of the economy also depends on the joint distribution $\phi_t(p, v)$ of these pairs (p_t, v_t).

We describe the decision problem of consumers in this environment. At each date t, each household buys from every seller, and each seller is characterized by a pair (p, v), distributed according to a measure $\phi_t(p, v)$. The household chooses a buying strategy $\{C_t(\cdot)\}$, where $C_t(p)$ is the number of units of the consumption good that it buys from a seller who charges price p at date t. It also chooses a labor supply strategy $\{l_t\}$ and a money-holding strategy $\{\hat{m}_t\}$, where l_t is the units of labor supplied and $\hat{m}_t$ is dollar balances held.

For any buying strategy $C_t(p)$, let c_t be the implied Spence-Dixit-Stiglitz consumption aggregate

$$c_t = \left[\int C_t(p)^{1-(1/\varepsilon)} \phi_t(dp, dv)\right]^{\varepsilon/(\varepsilon-1)}. \tag{3}$$

Current-period utility depends on c_t and also on labor supply l_t and cash holdings $\hat{m}_t$, deflated by a price index P_t. Preferences over time are

$$E\left[\int_0^\infty e^{-\rho t}\left[\frac{1}{1-\gamma} c_t^{1-\gamma} - \alpha l_t + \log\left(\frac{\hat{m}_t}{P_t}\right)\right] dt\right]. \tag{4}$$

(It is obvious that the price deflator P_t will not affect consumer decisions, and it plays no role in the analysis that follows.) The operator $E(\cdot)$ is defined by the shock processes (1) and (2).[4]

We write the consumer's budget constraint as

$$E\left[\int_0^\infty Q_t\left[\int pC_t(p)\phi_t(dp, dv) + R_t\hat{m}_t - W_t l_t - \Pi_t\right] dt\right] \leq m_0, \tag{5}$$

4. Equilibrium prices and quantities will be modeled as stochastic processes, defined in terms of an initial joint distribution $\phi_0(p, v)$ of firms by their inherited price p and productivity level v and by the evolution of the exogenous processes v_t and m_t. Specifically, each firm chooses a pricing strategy that takes the form of a right-continuous step function whose date t value depends on the histories of its own productivity shocks $\{v_s\}_0^t$, the monetary shocks $\{m_s\}_0^t$, the initial distribution $\phi_0(p, v)$, and its inherited initial price p_0. Consumer strategies depend on the monetary history only. For given firm behavior the initial joint distribution of (p_0, v_0), the initial money supply m_0, and the probabilities implied by (1) and (2) induce a family of probability measures ϕ_t for the prices facing consumers at all dates t. For any Borel set $A \subset \mathrm{R}^2$,

$$\phi_t(A) = \int \Pr\{(p_t(p_0), v_t)(\omega) \in A \mid v_0\}\phi_0(dp_0, dv_0).$$

where Π_t is profit income, obtained from the household's holdings of a fully diversified portfolio of claims on the individual firms, plus any lump-sum cash transfers. The term $R_t\hat{m}_t$, where R_t is the nominal interest rate, represents the opportunity cost of holding cash. The household chooses goods demand, labor supply, and money-holding strategies $\{C_t(\cdot)\}$, $\{l_t\}$, and $\{\hat{m}_t\}$ so as to maximize (4), subject to (5), taking $\{Q_t\}$, $\{R_t\}$, $\{w_t\}$, $\{\Pi_t\}$, $\{\phi_t\}$, and m_0 as given.

We will use the first-order conditions for consumers to state the problem solved by firms. These include the first-order condition for money holdings

$$e^{-\rho t}\frac{1}{m_t} = \lambda Q_t R_t, \tag{6}$$

where the equilibrium condition $\hat{m}_t = m_t$ is imposed. They also include the first-order conditions for consumption choices and labor supply

$$e^{-\rho t}c_t^{-\gamma}c_t^{-1/\varepsilon}C_t(p)^{-1/\varepsilon} = \lambda Q_t p, \tag{7}$$

where the multiplier λ does not depend on time, and

$$e^{-\rho t}\alpha = \lambda Q_t w_t. \tag{8}$$

One can show that there is an equilibrium in which the nominal rate is constant at the level

$$R_t = R = \rho + \mu \tag{9}$$

for all realizations of the two shock processes. In such an equilibrium, (6), (8), and (9) imply

$$w_t = \alpha R m_t, \tag{10}$$

from which it is evident that log (w_t) follows a Brownian motion with drift μ and variance σ_m^2. We emphasize that the derivation of (10) depends crucially on the assumptions (i) that utility is separable, (ii) that the disutility of labor is linear, and (iii) that the utility of money is logarithmic. Dropping any one of these opens the door to technical complications.

With these facts about equilibrium prices established, we turn to the problem facing an individual firm. At each date, a firm faces consumer demand $C_t(\cdot)$, a nominal wage rate w_t, and a stochastically determined productivity parameter (goods per hour worked) v_t. The firm enters the period with a price level p carried over from the past. If it leaves price unchanged, its current profit level is

$$C_t(p)\left(p - \frac{w_t}{v_t}\right).$$

If it chooses any price $q \neq p$, its current profit level is

$$C_t(q)\left(q - \frac{w_t}{v_t}\right) - kw_t,$$

where the parameter k is the hours of labor needed to change price, the real menu cost.

Let $\varphi(p, v, w, \phi_t)$ denote the present value of a firm that begins at any date t with the price p when the productivity and wage shocks take the values v and w, and in which the current, joint distribution of (p, v) across firms is ϕ_t. This firm chooses a shock-contingent repricing time $T \geq 0$ and a shock-contingent price q to be chosen at $t + T$ so as to solve

$$\varphi(p, v, w, \phi_t) = \max_T E_t\left[\int_t^{t+T} Q_s C_s(p)\left(p - \frac{w_s}{v_s}\right) ds \right.$$
$$\left. + Q_T \cdot \max_q [\varphi(q, v_{t+T}, w_{t+T}, \phi_{t+T}) - kw_{t+T}]\right]. \tag{11}$$

Eliminating the multiplier between (7) and (8) and simplifying using (3) yields the demand function facing each firm:

$$C_t(p) = c_t^{1-\varepsilon\gamma}\left(\frac{\alpha p}{w_t}\right)^{-\varepsilon}. \tag{12}$$

Applying the natural normalization $Q_0 = 1$ to (8), we obtain

$$Q_{t+s} = e^{-\rho s}\frac{w_t}{w_{t+s}}. \tag{13}$$

Using (12) and (13), we can express the Bellman equation (11) as

$$\varphi(p, v, w, \phi_t) = \max_T E_t\left[\int_t^{t+T} e^{-\rho(s-t)}\frac{w}{w_s} c_s^{1-\varepsilon\gamma}\left(\frac{\alpha p}{w_s}\right)^{-\varepsilon}\left(p - \frac{w_s}{v_s}\right) ds \right.$$
$$\left. + e^{-\rho T}\frac{w}{w_T} \cdot \max_q [\varphi(q, v_{t+T}, w_{t+T}, \phi_{t+T}) - kw_{t+T}]\right]. \tag{14}$$

We call the choices of stopping times T and prices q that attain the right side of (14) a firm's *pricing strategy.* We note the simultaneous determination of firms' pricing strategies: For given joint distributions $\{\phi_t\}$ of prices and productivity levels at current and future dates, each firm's pricing strategy is determined by (14). Conversely, the pricing strategies adopted by all sellers define the distributions $\{\phi_t\}$ at future dates, given the initial distribution ϕ_0. There is a Nash equilibrium of pricing strategies over a continuum of monopolistically competitive firms.

Finally, a process $\{Y_t\}$ with the interpretation that $Y_t dt$ is the number of firms that reprice during the time interval $(t, t + dt)$ is also defined in equilibrium. The labor market-clearing condition for this economy is then

$$l_t = \int \frac{C_t(p)}{v} \phi_t(dp, dv) + kY_t. \tag{15}$$

The equality of goods consumed and goods produced is incorporated in (14).

III. Special Case: Constant Monetary Growth

Most previous work on menu costs has been simplified by eliminating or avoiding the idiosyncratic shocks, $\{v_t\}$ in our setup, and focusing on aggregate inflation shocks only. We will initially go in the opposite direction, treating the special case in which the variance σ_m^2 of the money growth and wage processes is zero, so that the drift parameter μ is simply the constant rate of wage inflation. In this situation, we will seek an invariant joint distribution $\tilde{\phi}$ for *real* prices p/w_t and idiosyncratic shocks v. In this section we formulate, calibrate, and study a Bellman equation for this case of a stationary equilibrium with constant inflation.

The feature of our general equilibrium formulation that makes the firm's Bellman equation (14) hard to analyze is the presence of the distribution ϕ_t as a state variable. Unless we can provide or construct a law of motion for ϕ_t, (14) is just a suggestive formalism. But note that ϕ_t enters (14) only as a determinant of the consumption aggregate c_t, which acts as a shifter in the demand function facing the individual firm. This feature of the problem can be exploited.

Using (3) and (12), we can express the consumption aggregate in terms of the distributions ϕ_t in general:

$$c_t = \left[\int \left(\frac{\alpha p}{w_t} \right)^{1-\varepsilon} \phi_t(dp, dv) \right]^{1/[\gamma(\varepsilon-1)]} . \quad (16)$$

In the case of deterministic money growth, where both the money supply and the nominal wage rate follow a Brownian motion with drift μ and variance zero, we can use the change of variable $x = p/w_t$ and restate (16) as

$$c_t = \left[\alpha^{1-\varepsilon} \int x^{1-\varepsilon} \tilde{\phi}_t(dx, dv) \right]^{1/[\gamma(\varepsilon-1)]} . \quad (17)$$

In these circumstances, we will conjecture an equilibrium in which the distributions $\tilde{\phi}_t$ are all equal to an invariant measure $\tilde{\phi}$, and the corresponding consumption aggregate, given by (17), is constant, at some level $\bar{c}$. Then we can write (14) as

$$\varphi(p, v, w) = \max_T E \left[\int_0^T e^{-\rho s} \frac{w}{w_s} c^{-1-\varepsilon\gamma} \left(\frac{\alpha p}{w_s} \right)^{-\varepsilon} \left(p - \frac{w_s}{v_s} \right) ds \right.$$
$$\left. + e^{-\rho T} \frac{w}{w_T} \cdot \max_q [\varphi(q, v_T, w_T) - k w_T] \right]. \quad (18)$$

With the change of variable p/w, over intervals $[0, T)$ between repricings, $\log(x)$ follows a Brownian motion with drift $-\mu$ and variance zero. Then (18) can be restated, after we cancel and collect terms, as

$$\frac{1}{w} \varphi(wx, v, w) = \max_T E \left[\int_0^T e^{-\rho s} c^{-1-\varepsilon\gamma} (\alpha x_s)^{-\varepsilon} \left(x_s - \frac{1}{v_s} \right) ds \right.$$
$$\left. + e^{-\rho T} \frac{1}{w_T} \cdot \max_{x'} [\varphi(w_T x', v_T, w_T) - k w_T] \right]. \quad (19)$$

Finally, we seek a solution to (19) of the form

$$\varphi(p, v, w) = w\psi(x, v),$$

where the function ψ satisfies

$$\psi(x, v) = \max_T E \left[\int_0^T e^{-\rho t} c^{-1-\varepsilon\gamma} (\alpha x_t)^{-\varepsilon} \left(x_t - \frac{1}{v_t} \right) dt \right.$$
$$\left. + e^{-\rho T} \cdot \max_{x'} [\psi(x', v(T)) - k] \right]. \quad (20)$$

The time-invariant Bellman equation (20) can be studied with familiar methods. The value and policy functions will evidently depend on the parameter $\overline{c}$. It is clear that the policy functions will be consistent with an invariant distribution $\tilde{\phi}$ for (x, v), which will also depend on $\overline{c}$. Then we find the value of $\overline{c}$ by solving the fixed-point problem:

$$\overline{c} = \left[\alpha^{1-\varepsilon} \int x^{1-\varepsilon} \tilde{\phi}_t(dx, dv;\ \overline{c}\right]^{1/[\gamma(\varepsilon-1)]}. \tag{21}$$

This completes the construction of the equilibrium.

We studied the problem (20) using a discrete time and state approximation—a Markov chain—following Kushner and Dupuis's (2001) description of finite-element methods. That is, we studied the Bellman equation

$$\begin{aligned}\psi(x, v) = \max\Bigg\{ & \Pi(x, v)\Delta t + e^{-r\Delta t} \sum_{x',v'} \pi(x', v' \,|x, v)\psi(x', v'), \\ & \max_{\xi}\left[\Pi(\xi, v)\Delta t + e^{-r\Delta t} \sum_{x',v'} \pi(x', v' \,|\xi, v)\psi(x', v')\right] - k\Bigg\},\end{aligned} \tag{22}$$

under the assumption that

$$\Pi(x, v) = c^{-1-\varepsilon\gamma}(\alpha x)^{-\varepsilon}\left(x - \frac{1}{v}\right).$$

The details are given in the Appendix.

Figure 1 illustrates some qualitative features of the optimal pricing policy. It is based on the benchmark parameter values described in the next section, and in particular on the assumption that the aggregate shock is deterministic: $\sigma_m^2 = 0$. To construct the figure, we define the function $\Omega(v)$ of the productivity shock as

$$\Omega(v) = \max_x[\psi(x, v)],$$

so $\Omega(v)$ is the value the firm *would* have if it could move costlessly to a new price xw when the wage is w and the productivity level is v. (After this costless move, the menu cost k is again in force.) The two curves on the figure are the boundaries of the set $D(v)$ defined by

$$D(v) = \{x > 0 : \psi(x, v) > \Omega(v) - k\},$$

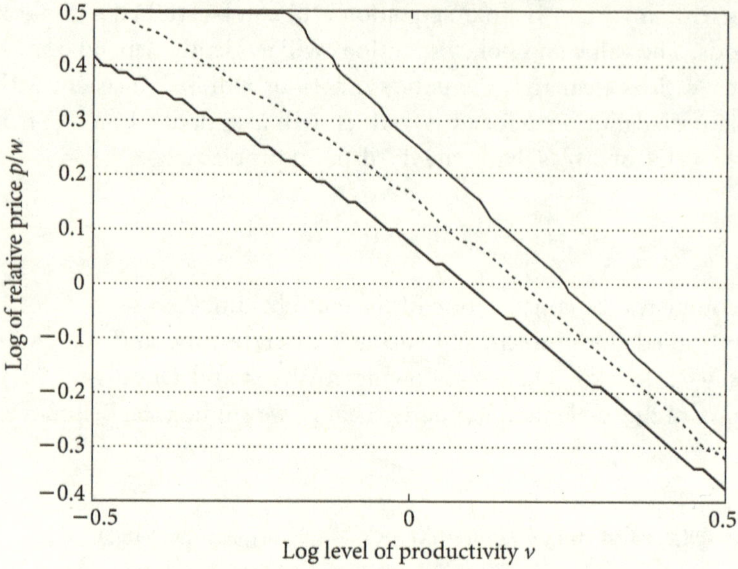

Pricing bounds for 0.64 percent quarterly inflation. Solid lines: upper and lower bounds $U(\nu)$ and $L(\nu)$. Dotted line: $g(\nu)$.

Figure 1

the "region of inaction" on which the firm leaves its price unchanged. Within this region, the firm's relative price $x = p/w$ declines at the rate μ because of deterministic wage growth, and its productivity level ν moves stochastically as described in (2). When the upper boundary is reached, price is reduced to a point in the interior, indicated as the dotted line on the figure. At the lower boundary, price is raised to the dotted line. Once in the set between the curves, a firm will never leave. The functions defining the boundary of this region are decreasing: high productivity shocks imply price decreases. Note that the inaction intervals $D(\nu)$ are wider for low ν values: Getting prices "right" is more important when productivity shocks—and hence quantities sold—are high. Notice too that the firm will occasionally reduce its price, even in an inflationary environment implied by $\mu > 0$.

IV. Data, Calibration, and a Test

Our basic model lacks many features that a business cycle model needs—it has no capital and no aggregate shocks—but we drew on that literature for

Table 1 Calibrated Parameter Values

	Baseline Values: $(\eta, \sigma_V^2, k) = (.55, .011, .0025)$				
Moment	Data (1)	Model (2)	$\eta = .65$ (3)	$\sigma_V^2 = .015$ (4)	$k = .002$ (5)
Quarterly inflation rate	.0064	.0064	.0064	.0064	.0064
Standard deviation of inflation	.0062	0	0	0	0
Frequency of change	.219	.239	.232	.273	.269
Mean price increase	.095	.097	.094	.104	.092
Standard deviation of new prices	.087	.090	.080	.108	.091

Note.—Col. 2 is based on the baseline values. Cols. 3–5 are based on the same values, except for the changes indicated at the head of each column.

the values of the preference parameters ρ, γ, α, and ε. We used the annual discount rate $\rho = .04$, the risk aversion parameter $\gamma = 2$, the elasticity of substitution parameter $\varepsilon = 7$, and the disutility of labor $\alpha = 6$. These ρ and γ values are conventional. The value of ε is related to the degree of monopoly power firms have. The elasticity of substitution implies that a firm's markup—defined as the percentage by which price exceeds marginal cost—is about 16 percent. Estimates of markups typically fall in the 10–20 percent range, implying values of ε in the 6–10 range.[5] Our results are not sensitive to changes in ε within that range. We interpreted our linear labor disutility as indivisible labor with lotteries, following Hansen (1985). The value $\alpha = 6$ implies that 37 percent of the unit time endowment is allocated to work.

For the menu cost parameter k, the drift parameter μ, and the two parameters σ_v^2 and η that characterize the idiosyncratic productivity shocks, we used new information on individual prices due to Klenow and Kryvtsov (2005). This price data set is based on the Bureau of Labor Statistics (BLS) survey and contains about 80,000 time series of individual price quotes in 88 geographical locations. The series are either monthly or bimonthly, depending on the location, for the years 1988–97. The individual price quotes pertain to 123 narrowly defined goods categories. The data set also pro-

5. See, e.g., Rotemberg and Woodford (1995) and Basu and Fernald (1997). It is not clear to us, we should add, that the estimates reported in these studies are best interpreted as markups in the sense used in this paper.

vides the weights that are used to form the consumer price index from the individual prices. We used the prices and weights for the New York metropolitan area only to calibrate the parameters $(\mu, \sigma_m^2, \eta, \sigma_v^2)$ and the fixed cost k of the model described in the previous sections.

For calibrating the model under the assumption of a deterministic trend, we set the variance σ_m^2 equal to zero. The actual value, shown in table 1, is .0062. To estimate the inflation rate μ, we used the appropriately weighted average (over goods and time) of the observed first differences.

To calibrate the three parameters (η, σ_v^2, k), we calculate three additional sample moments that intuition suggests will convey information. The results are given in the last three rows of the table. The first is the frequency of price change: the average over all months in the data of the fraction of prices that were changed in that month. As shown in the table, this fraction is .219.[6]

Second, we calculated the average log price increase over all prices that increased from any date to the next date: .095 in the data. Finally, from among all prices that were increased, we calculated the standard deviation of the new prices. To do that we calculated log deviations from the average, $z_i(t) = p_i(t) - \bar{p}(t)$, for each good i and then computed the standard deviation of $z_i(t)$ over time for each good i. Then we averaged over goods i. This yielded the number .087.

For any values of $(\mu, 0, \eta, \sigma_v^2, k)$, we can calculate the corresponding moments predicted by the theory, under the assumption that the probability distribution of (x, v) is the invariant distribution $\tilde{\phi}(x, v)$, say, and that prices are given by the optimal policy function for the dynamic program (18). We then simulated the model of Section III under the parameter values given in the first paragraph of this section plus the "baseline values" indicated in the table to calculate the theoretical moments. These produced the estimates reported in column 2 in the table, headed Model.

This value, .239, shown in the appropriate row of column 2 of the table, is calculated with $(\mu, \sigma_m^2, \eta, \sigma_v^2, k)$ set equal to (.0064, 0, .55, .011, .0025). Columns 3–5 of the table indicate how the calculated moments change as

6. There is substantial heterogeneity in the frequency of price changes across different sectors: Airline prices are much more flexible than prices of postage stamps. We considered an alternative version of the model with goods divided into categories with different menu costs and calibrated those costs to the evidence in Bils and Klenow (2004). This multisector model has predictions almost identical to those of the experiments that we report in the paper.

(η, σ_v^2, k) are changed one at a time from these benchmark values. That is, column 3 shows the computed statistics when the parameter vector $(\mu, \sigma_m^2, \eta, \sigma_v^2, k) = (.0064, 0, .55, .011, .0025)$ is replaced by $(.0064, 0, .65, .011, .0025)$. Thus the table shows that the frequency of price changes is insensitive to changes in the rate of mean reversion in the idiosyncratic shock, that it increases with the variance of these shocks, and that it decreases with increases in the menu cost.

There are many studies that try to estimate or calibrate menu costs for particular products. For example, Levy et al. (1997) estimate that the cost of changing prices in supermarkets is about 0.7 percent of firms' revenue. In our baseline model with $k = .0025$, menu costs are about 0.5 percent of revenues. The labor required to adjust prices is equal to 0.5 percent of overall employment.

The treatment of sale pricing is important in microeconomic pricing studies. The BLS flags observations that it regards as sale prices, and the Klenow-Kryvstov data we used had such sale observations removed. Figure 2, taken from Chevalier, Kashyap, and Rossi (2000), shows the time series of actual prices for Triscuits, based on scanner data from a Chicago supermarket chain. On figure 2, temporary sales are evident in the many times the price of Triscuits is reduced for a short time and returned to exactly the former price soon thereafter. Such patterns are of course common to many price series. To obtain a good match between theory and data, then, sales must be either removed from the data or added to the model. As discussed above, we took the first course.[7]

We solved the model, calibrated as just described, for quarterly inflation rates μ ranging from zero to 20 percent, calculated the invariant distribution λ in each case, and calculated the fraction of firms that change price each month in this stationary equilibrium. For comparison, we carried out the same calculations for the deterministic Sheshinski-Weiss case in which the variance of the idiosyncratic shocks is set equal to zero. These are the solid and dashed lines shown in figure 3.

7. A recent study by Midrigan (2006) uses the Chicago scanner data to calibrate a menu cost model that is similar to ours. He finds too many small price changes to be consistent with our model and argues for a version in which menu costs apply to *groups* of goods. When the menu cost is incurred for a given group, items that are only slightly mispriced are repriced along with the group members that are badly mispriced. Kashyap (1995) also reports a large number of small price changes in a context, catalogue sales, in which prices change infrequently.

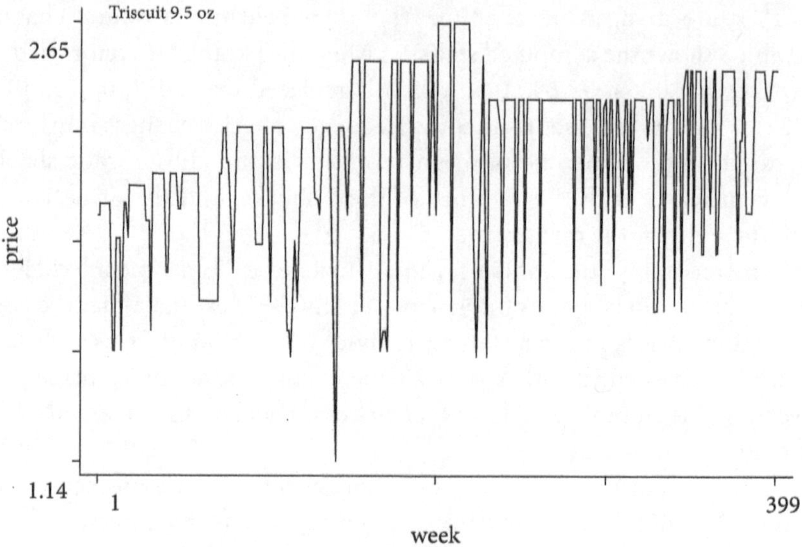

Price of Triscuits (9.5 oz.) in Dominick's Finer Foods supermarket in Chicago. Source: Chevalier et al. (2000).

Figure 2

The individual points on figure 3 are taken from seven empirical studies of pricing behavior, in addition to the U.S. studies we used in our calibration. These include the studies of Lach and Tsiddon (1992) on Israeli inflations of 1978–79 and 1981–82, Baharad and Eden's (2004) study of the Israeli inflation of 1991–92, Konieczny and Skrzypacz's (2005) analysis of Poland's experience in 1990–96, Gagnon's (2005) study of the frequency of price changes in Mexico during various periods from the late 1990s to 2000, and the Dhyne et al. (2005) study of a variety of countries in the Euro area over the years 1995–2000. The inflation-repricing pair (.64, 21.9) from the Klenow-Kryvtsov data for the United States is also shown. This pair lies very close to the upper curve, reflecting the fact that we used the Klenow-Kryvtsov data to calibrate our model. The model so calibrated fits the international evidence well, too, in spite of the fact that these studies are based on quite different samples of individual prices and differ in many other details. Our model and the Sheshinski-Weiss model both make the correct, qualitative prediction that the repricing frequency should increase as the rate of inflation increases, but ours gets the magnitude about right at both high and low inflation rates. Since we used only low-

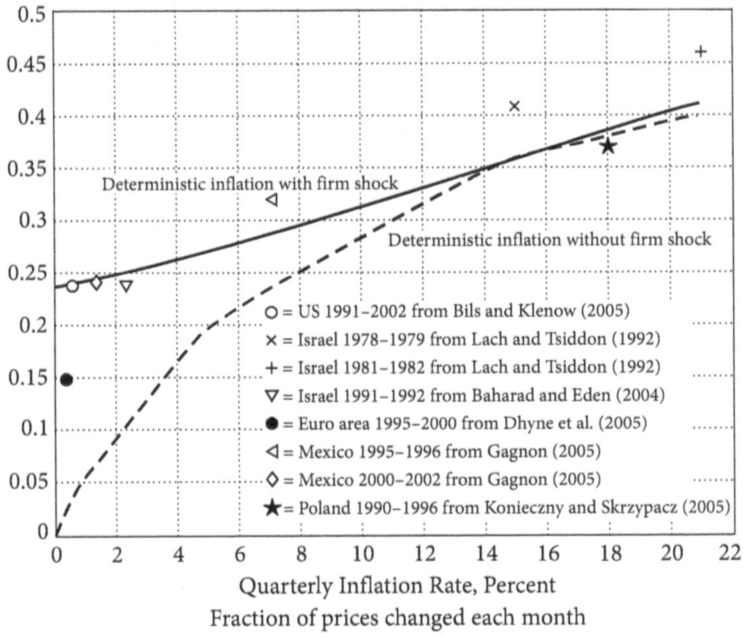

Figure 3

inflation data to calibrate the model, this is a genuine out-of-sample test of the theory.

Figure 3 also confirms the necessity of including idiosyncratic shocks if the model is to fit the evidence from low-inflation economies. As inflation rates are reduced, a lot of "price stickiness" remains in the data. Of course, this evidence does not bear on our interpretation of the idiosyncratic shocks as productivity differences, as opposed to shifts in preferences, responses to inventory buildups, or other factors.

V. Impulse-Response Functions

In this section we consider a thought experiment using the benchmark model with the variance σ_m^2 of the inflation rate equal to zero. We subject this economy, assumed to be in the stationary equilibrium corresponding to money growth rate constant at μ, to an unanticipated jump from m to $(1 + h)m$ in the level of money, after which money growth resumes its original rate μ. (By [10] this experiment corresponds to an unanticipated jump in nominal wages from w to $[1 + h]w$.) This experiment will provide intuition for the small effects of monetary policy that we will show in the following section with stochastic inflation.

A monetary disturbance of a one-time shock will take the economy out of the stationary equilibrium we studied in Section III. This fact raises new computational problems, which we deal with as follows. Let $c(\mu)$ denote the constant value of the consumption aggregate defined in (3) in a stationary equilibrium under the original policy. We construct an equilibrium response in which the original stationary distribution is restored and in which the time path $\{c_t\}$, $c_0 = c(\mu)$, and $c_t \rightarrow c(\mu')$ induced by the shock is perfectly foreseen by firms. Details are provided in the Appendix.

Figures 4*a* and *b* plot the impulse-response functions calculated in this way when μ equals 1 percent per quarter and $h = .0125$. First, note that the initial response in output is less than the size of the monetary shock. Since aggregate output is

$$\begin{aligned} y_t &= \int C_t(p)\,\phi_t(dp, dv) \\ &= \alpha^{-1/\gamma}\left[\int\left(\frac{p}{w}\right)^{1-\varepsilon}\phi_t(dp, dv)\right]^{(1-\gamma\varepsilon)/(\gamma\varepsilon-\gamma)} \times \int\left(\frac{p}{w}\right)^{-\varepsilon}\phi_t(dp, dv), \end{aligned}$$

the increase of w to $(1 + h)w$ can increase total output by at most $(1 + h)^{1-\gamma\varepsilon)/\gamma} \times (1 + h)^{\varepsilon} = (1 + h)^{1/\gamma}$.[8]

The increase in w leads to a temporary increase in the number of the firms changing their prices. This effect is over very quickly, occurring right after the jump in wages, after which the frequency of price changes reverts to its steady-state level. The effect on real output lasts longer, but it also declines to zero by the middle of the first quarter. The decline is fast because many of the firms that do not initially react to the aggregate shock will soon reprice as a result of idiosyncratic shocks. Once a firm decides to reprice for any reason, it will take the higher level of nominal wages into account in choosing the new price.

The impulse responses are much more transient than a standard time-dependent model would predict. The two heavy curves in figure 5 compare the output response to the monetary shock described in figure 4*a* to the output response that would occur in a Calvo (1983) type model, otherwise identical to ours, in which a firm is permitted to reprice in any period with

8. Also, note that (12) and (3) imply that $c_t = (w_t/\alpha P_t)^{1/\gamma}$, where P_t is the price aggregate defined as $P_t = [\int p^{1-\varepsilon}\phi_t(dp, dv)]^{1/(1-\varepsilon)}$. This relationship shows that the maximum impact of an h percent shock on the consumption aggregate c_t is $(1 + h)^{1/\gamma}$.

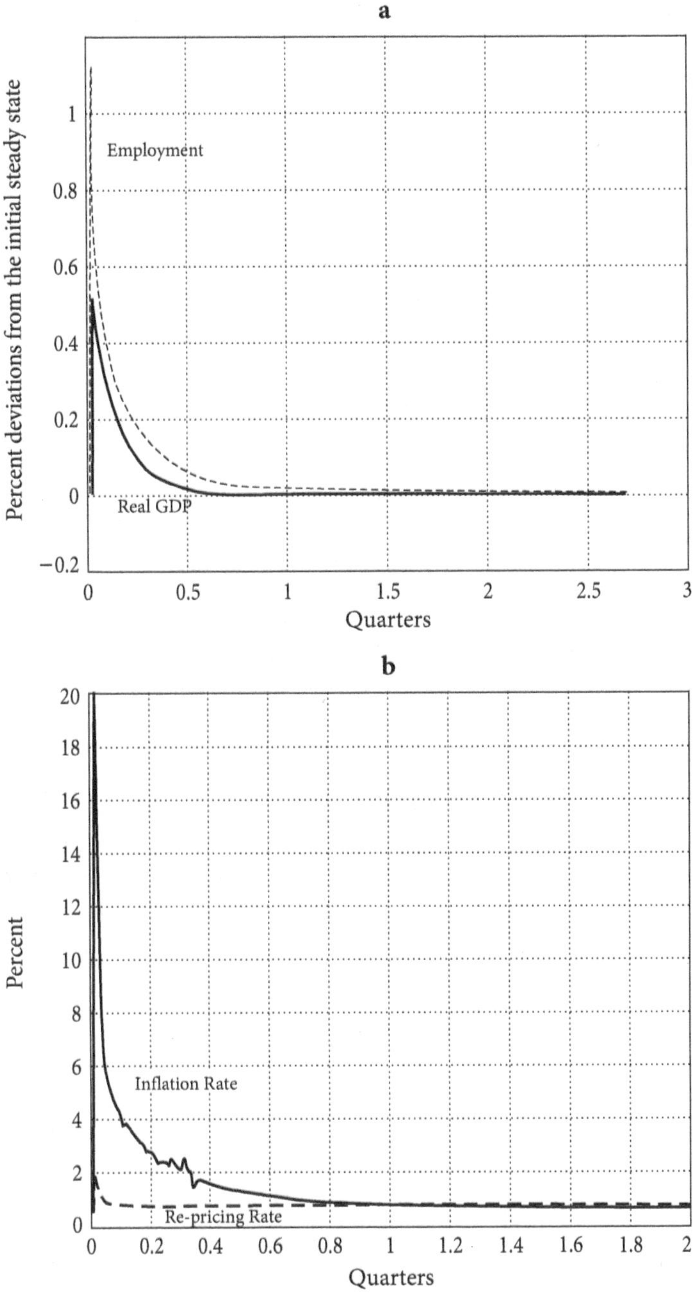

Responses to a transient monetary shock. *a*, Responses of employment and output to a one-time increase (impulse) in the level of money of 1.25 percent. The initial level is normalized to one. *b*, Responses of the quarterly inflation rate (percentage) and repricing rate (percentage of firms per day) to a one-time increase (impulse) in the level of money of 1.25 percent.

Figure 4

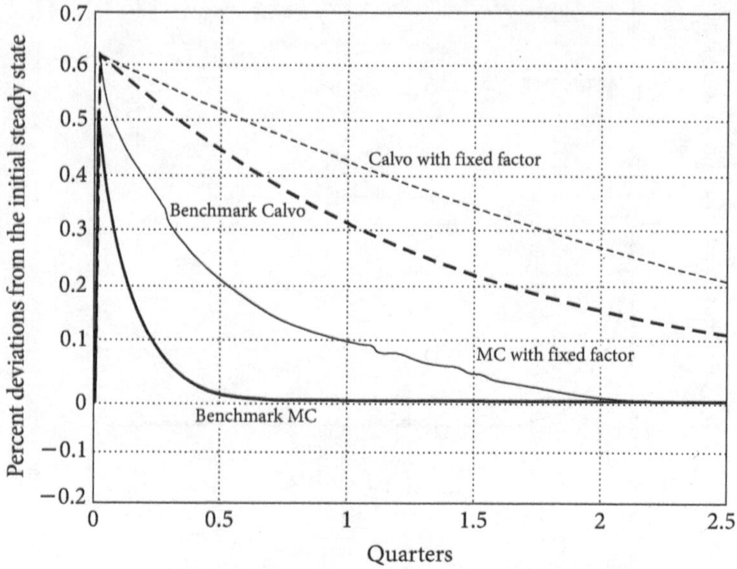

Output responses in menu cost and Calvo models

Figure 5

a fixed probability that is independent of its own state and the state of the economy. (The two light, "fixed-factor," curves are discussed below.) In both simulations we set this fixed repricing probability equal to .23 per month, the frequency predicted by our model. The two curves are very different. The initial response is much larger with "time-dependent" repricing, as compared to our "state-dependent" pricing. Time-dependent pricing also implies a much more persistent effect.

Figure 6 compares before and after distributions of individual prices to illustrate the reason for these different responses. Figure 6*a* shows repricing behavior in the absence of any aggregate shock. Firms in the menu cost model reprice when idiosyncratic shocks are large enough, and then they reprice to p^*. The average size of these price adjustments is large. In the Calvo model the firms that adjust prices are chosen randomly, and since many such firms are not far from their desired prices, the average size of the price adjustment is smaller. Increases and decreases of prices in both models are roughly symmetric.

In figure 6*b*, a positive aggregate shock shifts the distribution of the relative prices to the left. In the menu cost environment, this implies that many firms will be outside of the lower bound of their inaction region (see

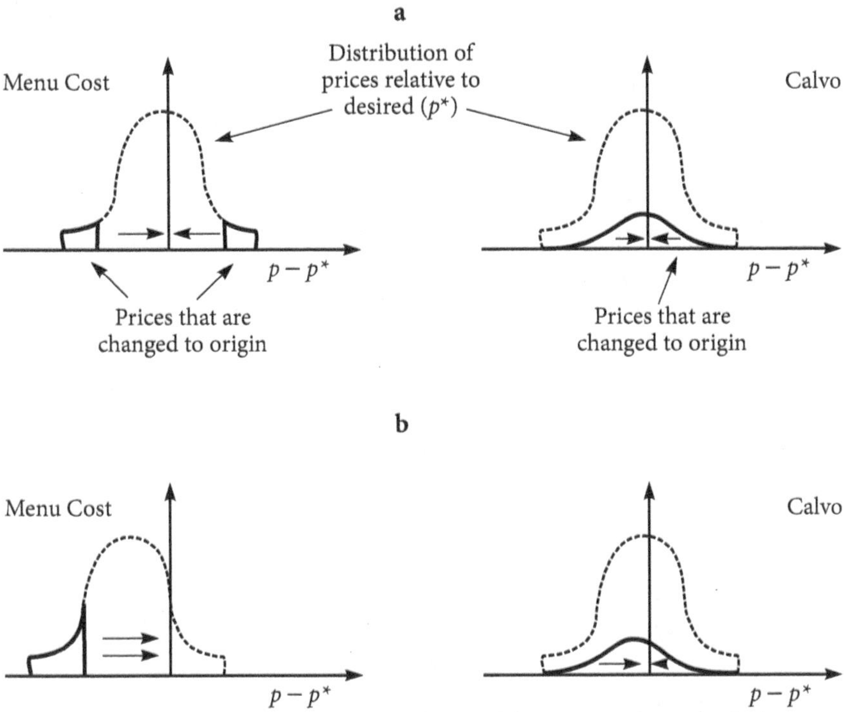

Price adjustment in menu cost and Calvo models. *a*, Price adjustment before aggregate shock. *b*, Price adjustment after aggregate shock.

Figure 6

fig. 1) and they increase prices. At the same time, the positive aggregate shock offsets negative idiosyncratic shocks, and firms that would otherwise have decreased prices choose to wait. As a result, the firms in the left-hand tail of the distribution do most of the adjustments, these adjustment are large and positive, and the economywide price level increases quickly to reflect the aggregate shock. In the Calvo setting, in contrast, firms get the opportunity to reprice randomly, the average firm that changes price remains very close to its desired level, and the average response of prices to the shock is much smaller. It takes longer for the monetary shock to be reflected in prices, and impulse responses become more persistent.[9]

9. Klenow and Kryvtsov (2005) provide an empirical decomposition of average inflation into components they label as "time dependent" and "state dependent." They find that in the BLS data the time-dependent component accounts for 88–96 percent of inflation variability. We carried out the same decomposition using simulated series from our menu cost model, in which all price variability is in fact state dependent, and found that the Klenow-

These results can be compared to the previous menu cost literature. In the absence of idiosyncratic shocks, the log-linear approximation of our firms' problem would be equivalent to the setup of Caplin and Spulber (1987). Their result that aggregate shocks are completely neutral would then hold in ours: In a stationary equilibrium the distribution of firms' relative prices would be uniform, and a κ percent increase in w would cause κ percent of the firms to adjust their prices. The resulting distribution of the relative prices would then be the same as the stationary distribution, and so total output would remain unchanged. The presence of idiosyncratic shocks introduces more complicated distributions of the relative prices, so in our case the shock to nominal wages leads to a real response. However, the main lesson is similar to Caplin and Spulber's: What matters is not so much *how many* prices are changed but *which* prices are changed.

This self-selection effect would lead to a smaller effect of monetary policy relative to time-dependent models in a variety of environments, even though the number of prices that are being changed may appear to be similar. To illustrate this point, we relax the assumptions that labor is fully mobile and enters linearly in both the production and utility functions, and instead introduce a fixed factor so that the production function exhibits decreasing returns. It is known (see, e.g., Chari et al. 2000) that such fixed factors cause monetary shocks to be more persistent in the time-dependent models. We then compare the responses of our benchmark Calvo and menu cost models to a model in which the production function takes the form $y = (Vl)^{\theta}$ with $\theta = .8$. We keep all other parameters the same. These comparisons are shown in figure 5. One can see that both the menu cost and Calvo models do have more persistent impulse responses in the fixed-factor version of the models. However, persistence in the Calvo model (measured by a half-life of a shock) is still five times larger than persistence in a corresponding menu cost model.

VI. Approximations to a Two-Shock Equilibrium

The analysis so far has been based only on the model with a constant inflation or the same model subjected to a one-time shock. In this section we consider the model with stochastic inflation: $\sigma_m^2 > 0$. In calculating the

---

Kryvtsov method would attribute 85 percent of inflation variability to the time-dependent component.

impulse-response functions reported in the previous section, we found that the effects of monetary shocks on the consumption aggregate were extremely small. This suggests that there may be little loss in accuracy if we hold c_t constant at $\bar{c}$, say, and simulate a two-shock model with $\sigma_m^2 > 0$. The Bellman equation suited for this continues to be (20). The policy function is dependent on this constant $\bar{c}$, and again we assume that the implied (x, v) process has a unique invariant distribution $\tilde{\phi}(x, v; c)$ (not, of course, the same distribution as when the money shock is deterministic). As before, we obtain the equilibrium (or pseudo-equilibrium) value of c as the solution to (21). We calculated this solution iteratively. The policy function computed in this way is the policy of a firm that correctly observes the mean level of c_t but ignores all the fluctuations about this level. We propose this function as an approximation to the true behavior of the firms in a two-shock equilibrium.

To get some idea of the likely accuracy of this approximation, we recalculated the impulse-response functions displayed in figures 4*a* and *b* in Section V (which display a rational expectations equilibrium in which c_t varies over time) using the constant-c approximation just described. We also increased the size of the initial shock by a factor of four. Figure 7 shows the results for real GDP. Evidently, the approximation works very well for the effects of a one-time shock, even a large one. We take this as an indication that it will also be accurate for stochastic shocks of the same order of magnitude.

We conduct two thought experiments using this approximation. First, we will study the effect of the volatility of inflation on the volatility of the real output by simulating 40 quarters of data.[10] For these simulations we chose $\sigma_m^2 = (.0062)^2$, which corresponds to the .0062 standard deviation of quarterly inflation in the Klenow-Kryvtsov data set. The standard deviation of the log level of output is equal to .0006 in our simulation. The standard deviation of actual U.S. quarterly consumption for the same period (1989–98) around linear trend is equal to .015. Thus monetary fluctuations in this model can account for less than 10 percent of the observed fluctuations in output. This estimate is consistent with estimates from other sources (see Lucas's [2003] survey).

In the second experiment we regress the log level of real output on the

10. Since the model is in continuous time (actually, about 40 discrete periods per quarter) and the economic data come in discrete intervals, we aggregate the output of the model into quarterly values by taking the means of the relevant variables over the quarter. Thus the level v_T^Q at quarter T of any function of time $v(t)$ is defined as $v_T^Q = \int_T^{T+1} v(t)dt$.

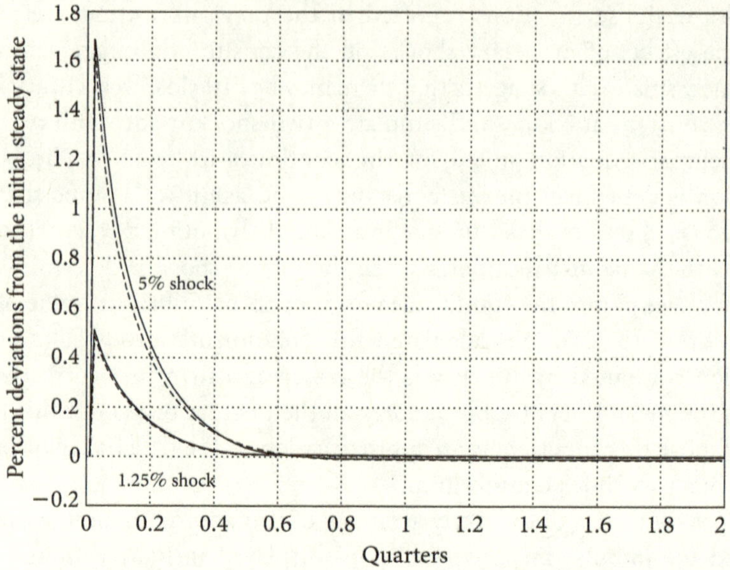

Approximate (dashed lines) and exact (solid lines) impulse-response functions; responses of output to a one-time increase (impulse) in the level of money. Initial levels are normalized to one.

Figure 7

log difference of the nominal wages, using the simulated series generated by the model:

$$\log(y_t^Q) = \alpha + \beta[\log(w_t^Q) - \log(w_{t-1}^Q)].$$

In this regression, we obtain the estimate $\beta = .049$ with the standard error .008. Thus an increase in nominal wage rates leads to an increase in real output, as in standard Phillips curve regressions, but the effect is very small. This conclusion is not sensitive to different specifications of the parameters (μ, σ_m).

VII. Conclusions

We have constructed a model of a monetary economy in which repricing of goods is subject to a menu cost and studied the behavior of this economy numerically. The model is distinguished from its many predecessors by the presence of idiosyncratic shocks in addition to general inflation. We used a data set on individual U.S. prices recently compiled by Klenow and Kryvtsov to calibrate the menu cost and the variance and autocorrelation of the idiosyncratic shocks. We conducted several experiments with the model.

A key prediction of any menu cost model is that the fraction of firms that reprice in a given time interval will increase with increases in the inflation rate. We simulated our model at inflation rates varying from zero to 20 percent per quarter. The results, shown in figure 3, trace out a curve that passes through the inflation rate–repricing rate pair estimated using data from the low-inflation U.S. economy of the 1990s. The same curve also fits very well the low-inflation periods in Mexico and Israel and high-inflation periods in Mexico, Israel, and Poland and reasonably well the low-inflation experience in the Euro area. We note that a model without idiosyncratic shocks could not fit any except the very highest inflations.

We next used the model to calculate the responses of output, employment, and prices to an unanticipated increase in money, equivalent in our setup to an impulse in the nominal wage. The predicted output responses were small and transient, bearing little resemblance to the response characteristics of New Keynesian models based on time-dependent pricing.

These results all refer to a special case in which inflation is deterministic. We also solved an approximation to a more realistic two-shock model. With a realistic inflation variance, this model can account for perhaps one-tenth of the observed variance of U.S. real consumption about trend. A Phillips curve estimated from data generated by the model implies that a one-percentage-point reduction in the inflation rate will depress production by 0.05 percent.

In summary, the model we proposed and calibrated to microeconomic evidence on U.S. pricing behavior does a remarkably good job of accounting for behavior differences between countries with very different inflation rates. It does not appear to be consistent with large real effects of monetary instability. These results seem to us another confirmation of the insight provided by the much simpler example of Caplin and Spulber (1987) that even when most prices remain unchanged from one day to the next, nominal shocks can be nearly neutral: The prices that stay fixed are those for which stickiness matters least, and the prices that are far out of line are the ones that change. Figure 5 substantiates the quantitative importance of this effect.

Appendix

The construction of approximating Markov chains for the one-shock model of Sections III–V and the two-shock model of Section VI is based on Kushner and Dupuis (2001). This appendix provides the details, based on the two-shock model of Section VI. For the most part, the specialization to the one-shock case is obvious.

In the calculations described below, we fix the grid size h and define the state space $S = X \times V$. To economize on notation, we define $\tilde{x} = \log(p/w)$ and $\tilde{v} = \log(v)$. To find an approximate solution to the two-shock firm's Bellman equation, we fix c_t at $\bar{c}$ as described in Section VI, so that the firm's Bellman equation becomes

$$\psi(\tilde{x}, \tilde{v}) = \max_T E\left[\int_0^T e^{-\rho t}\Pi(\tilde{x}_t, \tilde{v}_t)dt + e^{-\rho T} \max_{\tilde{x}'}[\psi(\tilde{x}', \tilde{v}(T)) - k]\right], \quad \text{(Al)}$$

where

$$\Pi(\tilde{x}, \tilde{v}) = c^{-1-\varepsilon\gamma}\alpha^{-\varepsilon}e^{-\varepsilon\tilde{x}}(e^{\tilde{x}} - e^{-\tilde{v}}). \quad \text{(A2)}$$

The processes $(\tilde{x}, \tilde{v})$ are assumed to follow

$$d\tilde{x} = -\mu dt + \sigma_m dZ_m \quad \text{(A3)}$$

and

$$d\tilde{v} = -\eta\tilde{v}dt + \sigma_v dZ_v. \quad \text{(A4)}$$

Then we approximate the continuous problem (Al) with a discrete problem

$$\psi(\tilde{x}, \tilde{v}) = \max\Bigg\{ \Pi(\tilde{x}, \tilde{v})\Delta t + e^{-r\Delta t} \sum_{\tilde{x}', \tilde{v}'} \pi(\tilde{x}', \tilde{v}' | \tilde{x}, \tilde{v})\psi(\tilde{x}', \tilde{v}'),$$
$$\max_{\xi}\left[\Pi(\xi, \tilde{v})\Delta t + e^{-r\Delta t} \sum_{\tilde{x}', \tilde{v}'} \pi(\tilde{x}', \tilde{v}' | \xi, \tilde{v})\psi(\tilde{x}', \tilde{v}')\right] - k\Bigg\}, \quad \text{(A5)}$$

where π is a transition function defined on $S \times S$ that we define in a moment. The time interval Δt is related to the grid size and other parameters by

$$\Delta t = \frac{h^2}{D}, \quad \text{(A6)}$$

where

$$D = \sigma_m^2 + \mu h + \sigma_v^2 + \eta \bar{v} h. \tag{A7}$$

We assume that in a given time interval Δt, at most one of the variables $\tilde{x}$ and $\tilde{v}$ changes.[11] Provided that neither $\tilde{x}$ nor $\tilde{v}$ is at its upper or lower bound, we assume that if $\tilde{x}$ changes, it moves either to $\tilde{x} + h$ or to $\tilde{x} - h$; if $\tilde{v}$ changes, it moves either to $\tilde{v} + h$ or to $\tilde{v} - h$. The final possibility is that neither of the variables changes and the state remains at $(\tilde{x}, \tilde{v})$. The probability of all other transitions is zero. Away from the boundaries of S, the five nonzero transition probabilities will then be defined by

$$\pi(\tilde{x} + h, \tilde{v}, \tilde{x}, \tilde{v}) = \frac{\sigma_m^2/2}{D}, \tag{A8}$$

$$\pi(\tilde{x} - \tilde{h}, \tilde{v}, \tilde{x}, \tilde{v}) = \frac{(\sigma_m^2/2) + \mu h}{D}, \tag{A9}$$

$$\pi(\tilde{x}, \tilde{v} + h, \tilde{x}, \tilde{v}) = \frac{\sigma_v^2/2}{D} \quad (\textit{if } \tilde{v} \geq 0), \tag{A10}$$

$$\pi(\tilde{x}, \tilde{v} - h, \tilde{x}, \tilde{v}) = \frac{(\sigma_v^2/2) + \eta \tilde{v} h}{D} \quad (\textit{if } \tilde{v} \geq 0), \tag{A11}$$

and

$$\pi(\tilde{x}, \tilde{v}, \tilde{x}, \tilde{v}) = 1 - \frac{\sigma_m^2 + \sigma_v^2 + \eta \tilde{v} h + \mu h}{D} \quad (\textit{if } \tilde{v} \geq 0). \tag{A12}$$

(The $\tilde{v}(t)$ process is symmetric about zero, so the adaptations of [A10] and [A11] for the case $\tilde{v} < 0$ are obvious.) Transitions at the boundaries are handled by assuming that if, for example, $\tilde{x}$ hits its upper bound $\bar{x}$, then $\tilde{x}$ goes one step down to $\bar{x} - h$ with probability $\pi(\bar{x} - h, \tilde{v}, \bar{x}, \tilde{v})$ and stays at $\bar{x}$ with probability $\pi(\bar{x} + h, \tilde{v}, \bar{x}, \tilde{v}) + \pi(\bar{x}, \tilde{v}, \bar{x}, \tilde{v})$ as given by the formulas (A8) and (A12). It is evident that the five probabilities (A8)–(A12) add to one and that the probabilities (A8)–(A11) are positive. That (A12) is nonnegative follows from the fact that $|\tilde{v}| \leq \tilde{v}$.

11. This means that the Markov chains approximating $\tilde{v}(t)$ and $\tilde{x}(t)$ will not be independent for $h > 0$, even though the continuous processes are. But independence will hold in the limit as $h \to 0$.

The first and second moments of the Markov chain we have just defined, conditional on the current state $(\tilde{x}, \tilde{v})$ (assumed not be a boundary point of S), are readily calculated from (A8)–(A12). They are

$$\frac{E\{\tilde{x}(t+\Delta t)|\tilde{x}(t)=\tilde{x}, \tilde{v}(t)=\tilde{v}\}-\tilde{x}}{\Delta t}=-\mu,$$

$$\frac{E\{\tilde{v}(t+\Delta t)|\tilde{x}, \tilde{v}\}-\tilde{v}}{\Delta t}=-\eta\tilde{v} \quad (if\ \tilde{v}\geq 0),$$

$$\frac{\text{Var}\{\tilde{x}(t+\Delta t)|\tilde{x}, \tilde{v}\}}{\Delta t}=\sigma_m^2+\mu h-\mu^2\Delta t,$$

$$\frac{\text{Var}\{\tilde{v}(t+\Delta t)|\tilde{x}, \tilde{v}\}}{\Delta t}=\sigma_v^2+h|\eta\tilde{v}|-(\eta\tilde{v})^2\Delta t,$$

and

$$\frac{\text{Cov}\{\tilde{x}(t+\Delta t), \tilde{v}(t+\Delta t)|\tilde{x}, \tilde{v}\}}{\Delta t}=-\eta\tilde{v}\mu\Delta t \quad (if\ \tilde{v}\geq 0).$$

From (A6) and (A7),

$$\frac{\Delta t}{h}=\frac{h}{\sigma_m^2+\mu h+\sigma_v^2+n\bar{v}h}\to 0 \quad as\ h\to 0.$$

This is the sense in which the conditional, local moments of the approximating chain approximate the conditional, local moments of the continuous-time $(\tilde{x}(t), \tilde{v}(t))$ process defined by (A3) and (A4). See Kushner and Dupuis (2001, chap. 9) for a proof that this approximation converges in distribution to the continuous-time diffusion process when $h\to 0$.

Computations of impulse responses.—It is easiest to describe this construction in terms of the discrete approximation (22). Initially, we set a limit n on the number of transition periods and begin with an assumed finite sequence $c^n=(c_1, c_2, \ldots, c_n)$ of values of the consumption aggregate. Then we define the sequence $\{\psi_i(x, v, c^n)\}_{i=1}^n$ of value functions recursively by

$$\psi_n(x, v, c^n)=\psi(x, v), \tag{A13}$$

where $\psi(x, v)$ is the solution to (22) at a stationary equilibrium with c_t constant at $\bar{c}$, and

$$\psi_i(x, v, c^n) = \max\left\{ \Pi(x, v, c_i)\Delta t + e^{-\rho\Delta t} \sum_{v'} \pi(v' | v) \psi_{i+1}(xe^{\mu\Delta t}, v', c^n), \right.$$
$$\left. \max_{x'} \left[\Pi(x', v, c_i)\Delta t + e^{-\rho\Delta t} \sum_{v'} \pi(v' | v) \psi_{i+1}(x'e^{\mu\Delta t}, v', c^n) \right] - k \right\} \tag{A14}$$

for $i = 1, 2, \ldots, n-1$. Let $\{f_i(x, v, c^n)\}_{i=1}^n$ be the sequence of policy functions corresponding to the value functions $\{\psi_i(x, v, c^n)\}_{i=1}^n$ so defined. For given behavior c^n of the consumption aggregate, these functions can be calculated by the usual backward induction.

The pricing behavior $\{f_i(x, v, c^n)\}_{i=1}^n$ in turn implies a sequence $\{\tilde{\phi}_i(x, v, c^n)\}_{i=1}^n$ of joint distributions of real prices and productivity shocks, taking the original invariant distribution $\tilde{\phi}$ as the initial condition. Individual firm sales are given by (12), and then new values of the consumption aggregate by (3):

$$(\Gamma c)_i = \left\{ \int c_i^{(1-\varepsilon\gamma)[1-(1/\varepsilon)]} (\alpha x)^{1-\varepsilon} \tilde{\phi}_i(dx, dv) \right\}^{\varepsilon/(\varepsilon-1)}. \tag{A15}$$

The construction described in equations (A13)–(A15) thus defines a function Γ taking an n-vector c into Γc.

In our calculations we used the policy functions from the stationary equilibrium with money growth equal to μ to generate $c(\mu)$ and then iterated using Γ until a fixed point was found. This procedure requires a choice of the length n of the transition period. We chose n large enough that the last few terms of the fixed point c^n were close to the value $c(\mu)$ associated with the new stationary equilibrium. The resulting description of the transition is thus a rational expectations equilibrium in which agents have perfect foresight about the evolution of aggregate variables.

References

Baharad, Eyal, and Benjamin Eden. 2004. "Price Rigidity and Price Dispersion: Evidence from Micro Data." *Rev. Econ. Dynamics* 7 (July): 613–41.

Barro, Robert J. 1972. "A Theory of Monopolistic Price Adjustment." *Rev. Econ. Studies* 39 (January): 17–26.

Basu, Susanto, and John G. Fernald. 1997. "Returns to Scale in U.S. Production: Estimates and Implications." *J.P.E.* 105 (April): 249–83.

Bertola, Giuseppe, and Ricardo J. Caballero. 1990. "Kinked Adjustment Costs and Aggregate Dynamics." In *NBER Macroeconomics Annual 1990,* edited by Olivier J. Blanchard and Stanley Fischer. Cambridge, MA: MIT Press.

Bils, Mark, and Peter J. Klenow. 2004. "Some Evidence on the Importance of Sticky Prices." *J.P.E.* 112 (October): 947–85.

Burstein, Ariel T. 2006. "Inflation and Output Dynamics with State-Dependent Pricing Decisions." *J. Monetary Econ.* 53 (October): 1235–57.

Calvo, Guillermo A. 1983. "Staggered Prices in a Utility-Maximizing Framework." *J. Monetary Econ.* 12 (September): 383–98.

Caplin, Andrew S., and John Leahy. 1991. "State-Dependent Pricing and the Dynamics of Money and Output." *Q.J.E.* 106 (August): 683–708.

Caplin, Andrew S., and Daniel F. Spulber. 1987. "Menu Costs and the Neutrality of Money." *Q.J.E.* 102 (November): 703–25.

Chang, Fwu-Ranq. 1999. "Homogeneity and the Transactions Demand for Money." *J. Money, Credit, and Banking* 31 (November): 720–30

Chari, V. V., Patrick J. Kehoe, and Ellen R. McGrattan. 2000. "Sticky Price Models of the Business Cycle: Can the Contract Multiplier Solve the Persistence Problem?" *Econometrica* 68 (September): 1151–79.

Chevalier, Judith A., Anil K. Kashyap, and Peter E. Rossi. 2000. "Why Don't Prices Rise during Periods of Peak Demand? Evidence from Scanner Data." Working Paper no. 7981 (October), NBER, Cambridge, MA.

Danziger, Leif. 1999. "A Dynamic Economy with Costly Price Adjustments." *A.E.R.* 89 (September): 878–901.

Dhyne, Emmanuel, et al. 2005. "Price Setting in the Euro Area: Some Stylized Facts from Individual Consumer Price Data." Working Paper no. 524 (September), European Central Bank, Frankfurt am Main.

Dotsey, Michael, Robert G. King, and Alexander L. Wolman. 1999. "State-Dependent Pricing and the General Equilibrium Dynamics of Money and Output." *Q.J.E.* 114 (May): 655–90.

Frenkel, Jacob A., and Boyan Jovanovic. 1980. "On Transactions and Precautionary Demand for Money." *Q.J.E.* 95 (August): 25–43.

Gagnon, Etienne. 2005. "Price Setting during Low and High Inflation: Evidence from Mexico." Manuscript, Northwestern Univ.

Gertler, Mark, and John Leahy. 2005. "A Phillips Curve with an Ss Foundation." Manuscript, New York Univ.

Hansen, Gary D. 1985. "Indivisible Labor and the Business Cycle." *J. Monetary Econ.* 16 (November): 309–27.

Kashyap, Anil K. 1995. "Sticky Prices: New Evidence from Retail Catalogs." *Q.J.E.* 110 (February): 245–74.

Klenow, Peter J., and Oleksiy Kryvtsov. 2005. "State-Dependent or Time-Dependent Pricing: Does It Matter for Recent U.S. Inflation?" Manuscript, Stanford Univ.

Konieczny, Jerzy D., and Andrzej Skrzypacz. 2005. "Inflation and Price Setting in a Natural Experiment." *J. Monetary Econ.* 52 (April): 621–32.

Kushner, Harold J., and Paul G. Dupuis. 2001. *Numerical Methods for Stochastic Control Problems in Continuous Time.* 2nd ed. New York: Springer-Verlag.

Lach, Saul, and Daniel Tsiddon. 1992. "The Behavior of Prices and Inflation: An Empirical Analysis of Disaggregated Price Data." *J.P.E.* 100 (April): 349–89.

Levy, Daniel, Mark Bergen, Shantanu Dutta, and Robert Venable. 1997. "The Magnitude of Menu Costs: Direct Evidence from Large U.S. Supermarket Chains." *Q.J.E.* 112 (August): 791–825.

Lucas, Robert E., Jr. 2003. "Macroeconomic Priorities." *A.E.R.* 93 (March): 1–14.

Mankiw, N. Gregory. 1985. "Small Menu Costs and Large Business Cycles: A Macroeconomic Model of Monopoly." *Q.J.E.* 100 (May): 529–38.

Midrigan, Virgiliu. 2006. "Menu Costs, Multi-product Firms, and Aggregate Fluctuation." Working paper, Ohio State Univ.

Rotemberg, Julio J., and Michael Woodford. 1995. "Dynamic General Equilibrium Models with Imperfectly Competitive Product Markets." In *Frontiers of Business Cycle Research,* edited by Thomas F. Cooley. Princeton, NJ: Princeton Univ. Press.

Sheshinski, Eytan, and Yoram Weiss. 1977. "Inflation and Costs of Price Adjustment." *Rev. Econ. Studies* 44 (June): 287–303.

———. 1983. "Optimum Pricing Policy under Stochastic Inflation." *Rev. Econ. Studies* 50 (July): 513–29.

Stokey, Nancy L. 2002. "Brownian Models in Economics." Manuscript, Univ. Chicago.

Willis, Jonathan L. 2000. "General Equilibrium of a Monetary Model with State-Dependent Pricing." Working paper, Fed. Reserve Bank Kansas City.

— 21 —

Occasional Pieces

The Death of Keynesian Economics*

I intend to duck both questions put to the panel. I will not tell you where the economy is headed or what the President ought to do about it. I'm sure that other panel members have wrapped these questions up for you. Instead I will try to tell you where I think economics is going—with emphasis on macro- or monetary economics. This is a question of interest to me—I'm an economist and everyone is interested in developments in his own industry. But occasionally developments in economics matter for non-economists, and I hope the developments I will discuss will be of some interest to you.

The main development I want to discuss has already occurred: Keynesian economics is dead [maybe 'disappeared' is a better term]. I don't know exactly when this happened but it is true today and it wasn't true two years ago. This is a sociological not an economic observation, so the evidence for it is sociological. For example, you cannot find a good, under 40 economist who identifies himself and his work as 'Keynesian'. Indeed, people even take offense if referred to in this way. At research seminars, people don't take Keynesian theorizing seriously any more—the audience starts to whisper and giggle to one another. Leading journals aren't getting Keynesian papers submitted any more.

I suppose that I, along with many others, was in on the kill in an intellectual sense, but I don't say this as any kind of boast, or even with much

---

**Issues and Ideas* (Winter 1980): 18–19.

pleasure. It is just a fact. True, there are still leading Keynesians in academics and government circles—so Keynesian economics is alive in this sense—but this is transient because there is no fresh source of supply. The only way to produce a 60 year old Keynesian is to produce a 30 year old Keynesian, and wait 30 years. So the implications for policy will take a while to be evident—but can be very accurately predicted.

This disappearance of Keynesian economics is more than just industry gossip because Keynesianism *mattered*—it filled a very central ideological function. Now that it is gone, something is going to have to take its place—and we need to think about what that something is likely to be. To start on this, I want to recall what the function of Keynesian economics was.

The central lesson of economic theory is the proposition that a competitive economy, left to its own devices, will do a good job of allocating resources. Of course, I need to make this proposition more precise, add necessary qualifications, etc.—there is no shortage of work for professional economists—but this is the basic message of 19th century economics, continued in into 20th century. Recurrent recessions and occasional inflations were something of an embarrassment to this theory but these tended to be brief and it seemed not unreasonable to hope that *some* reform of monetary institutions could be found. These beliefs were *very* widely shared in pre-1929 capitalistic economies—not just by a few economists, but the public at large. The main dissenters were Marxists, who stressed depressions as a central problem of capitalism.

Now in the 1930s, all this went out the window. The next time you go to a cocktail party, try asking people "Do you think our private economy, left to its own devices, could be trusted to do a good job at maintaining full employment?" If you ask an economist, he will probably ask you to spell out what you mean by "left to its own devices" but if you ask a normal, literate person, he will say "Of course, not. Just think of the 1930s." Try it. This is still the central political fact governing discussions of economic policy—50 years after 1929. As a result, the view that the economy needs to be managed on a year in, year out basis is almost universal. Indeed, this session could be called—"how should the economy be managed in 1979–80?"—given its advance billing.

But what do we mean by "managing" an economy? Prior to Keynes, "managing" was taken to involve a good deal of governmental intervention at the individual market level—socialism in Russia, fascism in Italy and Germany, the confusion of early New Deal programs in the United States.

It meant a fundamental shift away from market allocation and towards centralized direction.

The central message of Keynes was that there existed a middle ground between these extremes of socialism and laissez faire capitalism. (Actually, there is some confusion as to what Keynes really said—largely Keynes's own fault. Did you ever actually try to read the General Theory? I am giving you Keynes as interpreted by Alvin Hansen and Paul Samuelson.) It is true (Keynes argued) that an economy cannot be left to its own devices, but *all* that we need to do to manage it is to manipulate the general level of fiscal and monetary policy. If this is done right, all that elegant 19th century economics will be valid and individual markets can be left to take care of themselves.

In effect, Samuelson told his colleagues: "Face it—you live in a world where virtually nobody has any faith in this laissez faire religion of yours. I am offering a substitute ideology which concedes the inability of a competitive economy to take care of itself, but which also offers a management system which is, say, 95% consistent with laissez faire". These were hard times, and this was too good a deal to pass up. We took it. So did society as a whole. (Conservatives were a little grumpy, but how bad off could we be in a country where Paul Samuelson is viewed as a leftist?)

What I meant by saying that Keynesian economics is dead at the beginning of my talk is just that this middle ground is dead. Not because people don't *like* the middle ground any more but because its intellectual rationale has eroded to the point where it is no longer serviceable. There are many reasons for this. It is a difficult technical problem to spell it out. I think the problem in a nutshell was that the Keynes-Samuelson view involved *two* distinct, mutually inconsistent theoretical explanations of the determinants of employment. For a time, we thought that we could find a new theory that would unify or reconcile these two—but the more progress was made the more difficulties came into view, dragging us further under. By now, it is fairly clear that the attempt is hopeless—that, with hindsight, it was misleading from the beginning. As a result, new talent is not attracted to refining, developing Keynesian economics. This is what we mean by the "death" of a scientific idea.

So, what happens now? In academic circles, it is total chaos. Everyone has his own theories and since orthodoxy has no way of discriminating all get a fair hearing. It's a great time to be a macroeconomist. For social policy, the outlook is not so cheerful. The collapse of the center means the end of consensus economics—crackpot proposals like Humphrey-Hawkins or Roth-Kemp will get attention along serious ones. There is no 'establishment' with influence to align the profession against them. I expect public debate to grow increasingly more ideological, a reversion to pre-Keynesian lines of laissez faire types versus socialist/fascist detailed interventionists. (Presumably both types will select fresher labels.)

What will the outcome be? Who knows? But it is certain that it won't be settled by a few dozen academic experts. If the general reading of the 30s as the 'failure of capitalism' continues to prevail, I see one outcome. If some combination of counter-arguments or perhaps just the passage of time overcomes this, I see brighter prospects.

Keynote Address to the 2003 *HOPE* Conference: My Keynesian Education*

I have mixed feelings about Bob Byrd[1] saying he's looking forward to receiving my papers. He's probably only going to get them when I'm gone: I don't seem to be able to give up anything out of my file drawers. But when that does happen, my papers will be in the best library for the history of economic thought they can find anywhere, so they will have a happy home.

Well, I'm not here to tell people in this group about the history of monetary thought. I guess I'm here as a kind of witness from a vanished culture, the heyday of Keynesian economics. It's like historians rushing to interview the last former slaves before they died, or the last of the people who remembered growing up in a Polish shtetl. I am going to tell you what it was like growing up in a day when Keynesian economics was taught as a solid basis on which macroeconomics could proceed.

My credentials? Was I a Keynesian myself? Absolutely. And does my Chicago training disqualify me for that? No, not at all. David Laidler [who was present at the conference] will agree with me on this, and I will explain in some detail when I talk about my education. Our Keynesian credentials, if we wanted to claim them, were as good as could be obtained in any graduate school in the country in 1963.

*History of Political Economy 36, Supplement 1 (2004): 12–24.

1. Director of Duke University's Rare Book, Manuscript, and Special Collections Library.

I thought when I was trying to prepare some notes for this talk that people attending the conference might be arguing about Axel Leijonhufvud's thesis that IS-LM was a distortion of Keynes, but I didn't really hear any of this in the discussions this afternoon. So I'm going to think about IS-LM and Keynesian economics as being synonyms. I remember when Leijonhufvud's book[2] came out and I asked my colleague Gary Becker if he thought Hicks had got the *General Theory* right with his IS-LM diagram. Gary said, "Well, I don't know, but I hope he did, because if it wasn't for Hicks I never would have made *any* sense out of that damn book." That's kind of the way I feel, too, so I'm hoping Hicks got it right.

Today I'm going to reminisce about my macro courses at Chicago and a little bit about what I learned teaching macroeconomics at Carnegie Mellon, which is where the Keynesian phase of my career ended. And then I would like to talk about what I now think, not as a graduate student but as an adult, about Keynesian economics, both as a political force in the years during and after the Depression and as a scientific influence. But I do think those are two different questions. And then, since I love the reference to the "strange persistence" of IS-LM in the conference title, in the end I'm going to take a crack at that, too. Because it *has* persisted.

I started graduate school in the history department at Berkeley in the fall of 1959. As a Chicago undergraduate in history, I had been excited by writings like Marx and Engels's *Communist Manifesto* and the work of the Belgian historian Henri Pirenne. I was interested in ancient history in those days, and Pirenne had an economic interpretation of the end of the Roman Empire in Western Europe and the advent of the Dark Ages that was exciting for me. So I wanted to learn some economics, but hadn't got around to actually doing so.

In those days, Keynes's standing was kind of like Einstein's—everyone knew he was important—this was among undergraduates, but I suppose it was true everywhere; but no one understood what he meant. In high school, they told us that only six people in the world understood the theory of relativity. So I don't know—the *General Theory* maybe would have had sixteen or something. I remember Alvin Hansen had actually written a watered-down version—you had to have an intermediary to get close to

2. *On Keynesian Economics and the Economics of Keynes: A Study in Monetary Theory* (New York, 1968).

the *General Theory.* Somebody had to help you get at it. But I had no idea what was actually in Keynes's book.

At Berkeley, I took economic history courses from Carlo Cipolla and David Landes, which in hindsight was amazing good luck. Landes taught a seminar course for first-year graduate students that was sort of a bibliographical boot camp where you had to pick a topic off a list of his and go to the library and find out everything that was known on this topic and come back and report to the seminar. One student came into the seminar with a single piece of paper that he just unfolded and unfolded until it covered the whole seminar table; we were all lost in admiration for this guy! It was a fun seminar; people were having a lot of fun. For me, history courses had been other people handing me things and saying, "Read this," so it was a new experience to be in a seminar where our job was to find out what was worth reading and to tell other people about it.

One of the topics on Landes's list was nineteenth-century British business cycles. I chose this one, since I wanted an excuse to learn some economics. That's where I met Anna Schwartz, although she doesn't know this. I read the monograph by Gayer, Rostow, and Schwartz[3]—yes, that's *Anna* Schwartz and *W. W.* Rostow—I mean this is really a team, right? And they were the *junior* authors in this book! The senior author was A. D. Gayer at Queen's College. This book was a mix: it went over British economic history in the first part of the nineteenth century. It included a kind of a year-by-year history. There was NBER Mitchell-type stuff, and then there was a sort of Keynesian diagnosis, episode by episode. It was an amazingly ambitious and exciting mix of history and theory. Anna [also at the conference] later told me she was embarrassed by the Keynesian theory in the book, but as a student I thought it was very exciting.

I decided I had to take some real economics courses or I was always going to be on the sideline even of economic history, and Landes encouraged me in this view. But Berkeley wasn't going to support me to study economics. At Christmas break I moved back to Chicago: I had passed an exam as a history undergraduate at a high enough level that I was automatically admitted as a graduate student in social science. So I just showed up at the economics department and said, "Here I am."

3. *The Growth and Fluctuation of the British Economy, 1790–1850: An Historical, Statistical, and Theoretical Study of Britain's Economic Development* (Oxford, 1953).

I started by taking remedial courses, like undergraduate courses in economics. I took some price theory. At Chicago price theory—micro—is always at the center, but my first macro course was from Carl Christ, who introduced me to Patinkin's work. We never used Patinkin in a course. And then I had a fabulous course from Martin Bailey. Christ's course was a step-by-step model-building course, making sure you had the same number of equations and unknowns. Just what I needed. We read some of the Keynesian classics. That's where I first read Hicks's "Mr. Keynes and the 'Classics'" and Modigliani's 1944 paper.[4] I think this was the basis for IS-LM theory, those two papers. Christ also assigned us Klein's book *The Keynesian Revolution*, which is a pretty nice little book.[5] Another book that influenced me a lot was Samuelson's *Foundations*—I'm part of the Samuelson generation that Mark Blaug [who had been mentioned in the introduction to this talk] talked about—which I started reading on my own.

After class one day, I asked Christ about what Hicks thought was going on in labor markets, because there's not much on it in "Mr. Keynes and the 'Classics.'" That's when Christ told me to read Patinkin's *Money, Interest, and Prices*,[6] and I tried to do it. It's such a beautiful book physically, even the pictures. I just loved looking at that book. It made me feel like I was in touch with something elevated. Also, Patinkin's scholarly style, his erudition, I liked that, too. I still do. But the main thing I liked about Patinkin's book was that it was full of supply and demand, of people maximizing, of markets. There's a lot of micro in the book. That was the objective Patinkin had stated in his subtitle: to unify value theory and monetary theory. I liked his high aspirations. They were inspiring to me. But the book doesn't quite come off, does it? I mean, the theory is never really solved. What are the predictions of Patinkin's model? The model is too complicated to work them out. All the dynamics are the mechanical auctioneer dynamics that Samuelson introduced, where *anything* can happen.

There's an interesting footnote in Patinkin's book. Milton Friedman had told him that the rate of change of price in any one market ought to depend on excess demand and supply in all markets in the system. Patinkin

4. "Liquidity Preference and the Theory of Interest and Money," which appeared in the January 1944 issue of *Econometrica*. Hicks's article appeared in the April 1937 issue of that same journal.

5. Published in 1947 by Macmillan.

6. Published in 1956 by Row, Peterson of Evanston, Ill. The book was subtitled *An Integration of Monetary and Value Theory.*

is happy about this suggestion because he loves more generality, but if you think about Friedman's review of Lange, of Lange's book,[7] what Friedman must have been trying to tell Patinkin is that he thinks the theory is empty, that anything can happen in this model. And I think he's got a point.

If you look at Rapping's and my paper on labor markets[8]—which I'll come back to, because that's a Keynesian paper—we have a cleared labor market at every point in time, and we were a little self-conscious about that because people didn't think that was the right way to do things. Going back to Patinkin's book, and even though Patinkin says that all the dynamics is some auctioneer moving prices, you can see from his verbal discussion that he's reading a lot of economics into these dynamics. What are people thinking? What are they expecting? He's too good an economist to take the Samuelsonian dynamics literally. He's really thinking about intertemporal substitution. He doesn't know *how* to think about it well, but he's trying to. So in some sense Patinkin's book is less mechanical than it looks.

I think Patinkin was absolutely right to try and use general equilibrium theory to think about macroeconomic problems. Patinkin and I are both Walrasians, whatever that means. I don't see how anybody can not be. It's pure hindsight, but now I think that Patinkin's problem was that he was a student of Lange's, and Lange's version of the Walrasian model was already archaic by the end of the 1950s. Arrow and Debreu and McKenzie had redone the whole theory in a clearer, more rigorous, and more flexible way. Patinkin's book was a reworking of his Chicago thesis from the middle 1940s and had not benefited from this more recent work.

In the spring quarter that year, I took Martin Bailey's course. He was then writing his book *National Income and the Price Level.*[9] It wasn't out then, but it was in draft and this was the basis for the course. Bailey's book moves right along. He's got a Keynesian cross in nine pages. He's got a well-motivated IS-LM diagram by page 20. He's got a production sector and a labor market by page 35. It took Patinkin to page 343 to get to that point! So, Bailey is speeding things up by a factor of ten. And he's getting the mathematical structure of the model clear. You can count equations and

7. *Price Flexibility and Employment* (Bloomington, Ind., 1944). Friedman's review appeared in the September 1946 regular issue of the *American Economic Review.*

8. "Real Wages, Employment, and Inflation," which appeared in the September-October issue of the *Journal of Political Economy.*

9. Published in 1962 by McGraw-Hill.

unknowns. You can see what the predictions of Bailey's model are. You have to make some assumptions, but you can work with the model.

When I think of IS-LM, I think of what I learned from Bailey, where you have IS-LM and then this production sector that he took from Modigliani's paper and put them all together with some additions. For example, Bailey put us on to the fact that it's a *nominal* interest rate in the LM curve and a *real* interest rate in the IS curve. You are making use of the vertical axis for two different things. You have to do something about that. So Bailey's book was good training and was the basis for preparing for the core exam at Chicago and Carnegie Mellon for ten or fifteen more years after that.

I mentioned Samuelson's book [*Foundations*]. You'll see the IS-LM model in Samuelson's chapter when he introduces the correspondence principle: the idea that you can learn about comparative statics by looking at the stability properties of a model. Example 1 is the IS-LM model. (Maybe that's example 2. Maybe supply and demand is example 1.) That's an example of how standard IS-LM was at that point.

So that's my first year [1959–60] of graduate school, as an unsuccessful history student and then as a student in remedial courses in economics. And then by the next fall, I was ready to take Friedman's course, which was the high point of everyone's education at Chicago.

But in my day, Friedman taught price theory; he didn't teach macro. I don't know if Mike Bordo [also at the conference] may have had him—["I had him for money and macro," Bordo said]. I had a neighbor in Chicago, Sue Freehling, who was an MBA student at Chicago and had taken Friedman's course in money and macro. Sue was an active liberal Democrat, and I wondered how she liked the course. She said, "Oh, I loved Friedman. He's such a wonderful guy. But he had us read this awful book by Keynes." I don't know if that's how it was for you [speaking to Bordo], but Sue thought Friedman took that book way too seriously and she wished he'd just talked more about his own ideas.

Anyway, I didn't have any macro from Friedman. What I had that was exciting in macro in my first year was Harry Johnson's first course at Chicago. He had just arrived in Chicago, and he was full of the controversy stemming from Patinkin's book, Archibald and Lipsey's criticism,[10] and so

10. "Monetary and Value Theory: A Critique of Lange and Patinkin," published in the October 1958 issue of the *Review of Economic Studies*.

on. This stuff was *way* over the heads of anyone in the class as far as I could tell. Except for Neil Wallace. I remember Neil asking him—I can't imitate his voice but he just calls out without raising his hand: "Wait a minute, Harry! *That's* not what you want to say." Things didn't happen this way in England, and nobody called him Harry. [*Laughter.*] Somehow I got nothing out of the course. Too much detail. I think I thought I knew everything after Bailey's class, so I basically bailed out and got a C in the course. Which was probably an overstatement of what I actually learned. And Harry never really had a high opinion of me after that.

Johnson's heyday as a teacher at Chicago came when Mundell arrived a few years later, and then he and Mundell trained Frenkel, Dornbusch, Mussa, Razin—people who just transformed and kind of Keynesianized international macro. That was a great period, but it hadn't even started when we were students, and I missed out on that.

Johnson's was the last macro class I took at Chicago. My fields were econometrics and public finance, so I didn't take any advanced macro, I just took the core courses. But public finance in those days was half macro. If you remember, Musgrave's book[11] was divided about equally into a macro part and a micro part. Sort of a Ramsey part and a Keynesian part. Arnold Harberger taught a course—a public finance course on macro policy, and this was really a nice thing. It was based on a multiplier-accelerator model he had calibrated to U.S. national income and product accounts. He really got into the nitty-gritty of all the leakages and the multipliers. It was the only place at Chicago where I saw a dynamic model, I mean with time subscripts, and he actually ran a system of difference equations out, trying to see what kind of shocks it would take to produce a recession. That was an exciting course. In terms of dynamics, until Uzawa showed up—again, after I left—Chicago was a backwater then. The growth theory that was starting at MIT and Stanford and Yale at that point had not yet got under way at Chicago, even though all the students had read Solow's paper[12] and were excited about it.

So what about Milton Friedman and the monetarist counterrevolution? That's what you think of when you think of Chicago in the 1960s. I was even the draftsman for Friedman and Meiselman's paper for the Commis-

11. *The Theory of Public Finance: A Study in Public Economy* (New York, 1959).

12. "A Contribution to the Theory of Economic Growth," which appeared in the February 1956 issue of the *Quarterly Journal of Economics.*

sion on Money and Credit where they criticized Keynesian models.[13] But I thought of it as just drafting—it was a job. I didn't really know what was going on in the paper. His consumption book was published in 1957.[14] His project with Anna Schwartz on monetary history was just getting going.[15] There were a lot of things that Friedman was doing in macroeconomics in my day, but he didn't talk about any of this in his price theory courses. In fact, Friedman didn't spend much time plugging his past work or talking about it. The only way you would have been in on this monetarist counter-revolution was to be writing your thesis with Friedman and be a member of the money and banking workshop, but that was an invitation-only thing. I was not working with him. The first money and banking workshop I went to was in 1974 when I was a visiting faculty member. I remember learning about the consumption study from my classmate Glen Cain, who was using it in his thesis and saw how important it was going to be, but I can't remember Friedman mentioning that book. It would not have been out of place to talk about it in his price theory course, but I can't remember his doing it. Maybe David's memory differs from mine. He was there.

["I'm trying to remember; I don't remember," said Laidler.

"You were probably more with it than I was," said Lucas.

"He did Archibald and Lipseyian price theory, though," said Laidler.

"He did?" asked Lucas.

"Yeah, he did," said Laidler.

"God, I missed it. I had two shots at Archibald and Lipsey and whiffed both times," said Lucas.]

Everyone from Chicago is a Friedman student in some very basic sense, but in terms of macro, I claim that the credentials I'm describing are true-blue Keynesian.

When I was done with my graduate education, how did I think of Keynesian economics? I didn't think about it very deeply, to tell you the truth. It wasn't my field. I didn't picture myself as doing research in the area. But I certainly thought of myself as a Keynesian. Kennedy was elected in 1960. I remember the Kennedy tax cut. We, meaning students, were excited with the Council of Economic Advisors that Kennedy appointed, the

13. "The Relative Stability of Monetary Velocity and the Investment Multiplier in the United States, 1897–1958," which was published in the commission's *Stabilization Policies* (Englewood Cliffs, N.J., 1963).

14. *A Theory of the Consumption Function* (Princeton, N.J., 1957).

15. The results of which were published in 1963 by Princeton University Press as *A Monetary History of the United States, 1867–1960.*

tax cut—it seemed like the theory we were learning about in class was being put in place. We were definitely excited about that. I also remember that the cost-benefit analysis was explicitly introduced in the Department of Defense back in the Kennedy administration when McNamara became secretary—and that was another exciting thing for economics. It seemed like everything we were learning in class, micro and macro, was being put to work in U.S. economic policy. It all went down the drain in Vietnam, so all we remember now about McNamara is how he got us into that awful war, but, at the beginning, it was much more promising.

When I began to teach at Carnegie, I took Bailey's book [*National Income and the Price Level*], his version of IS-LM, as kind of standard stuff. This is the theory, the accepted theory that everyone should know, that it was my job to teach to graduate students, and did. I also held on to Patinkin's ambition somehow, that the theory ought to be microeconomically founded, unified with price theory. I think this was a very common view. Ed Burmeister. [Burmeister attended the talk.] Where's Ed? Ed can remember this, I'm sure. Nobody was satisfied with IS-LM as the end of macroeconomic theorizing. The idea was we were going to tie it together with microeconomics and that was the job of our generation. Or to continue doing that. That wasn't an *anti*-Keynesian view. You can see the same ambition in Klein's work or Modigliani's.

The first macroeconomics work I ever did was my work with Leonard Rapping on Phillips curves and labor markets.[16] This was an ambitious move for us. We wanted to contribute to Keynesian economics, and in particular to the econometric models that were being based on Keynesian economics. Our models—the examples we wanted to follow—were Friedman and Modigliani's work on consumption or Jorgensen and Eisner's work on investment or Meltzer's and Friedman's work on money demand.[17]

16. See Lucas and Rapping, "Real Wages" (cited in footnote 8) and "Price Expectations and the Phillips Curve," published in the June 1969 issue of the *American Economic Review.*

17. See Friedman, *A Theory of the Consumption Function*; Modigliani and Richard Brumberg, "Utility Analysis and the Consumption Function: An Interpretation of Cross-Section Data," in *Post-Keynesian Economics*, edited by Kenneth K. Kurihara (New Brunswick, N.J., 1954); Dale W. Jorgenson, "Capital Theory and Investment Behavior," in the May 1963 "Papers and Proceedings" issue of the *American Economic Review*; Robert Eisner and Robert H. Strotz, "Determinants of Business Investment," in *Impacts of Monetary Policy* (Englewood Cliffs, N.J., 1963); Allan H. Meltzer, "The Demand for Money: The Evidence from the Time Series," in the June 1963 issue of the *Journal of Political Economy*; and Friedman and Schwartz, *A Monetary History of the United States.*

These were the people who staked out an important equation for macroeconomics and were trying to estimate its parameters. We were going to go after the production and labor side of that model. There was a lot of really bad work being done on labor unions: people regressing wages in this industry on wages in some other industry and getting R-squares of .99. Really junk. There was a paper by George Perry that had a respectable theory of wage determination with a Phillips curve in it, but it was all based on labor unions.[18] Rapping and I knew that something like a fifth of the U.S. labor force was in labor unions. It didn't make any sense to have a model of the whole labor market that pretended everybody was a union member. So we thought we'd write down a competitive model.

If you look back at Rapping's and my *JPE* paper, the introduction to that paper, it's a Keynesian introduction, very much so. It's an IS-LM introduction, not that we have an IS-LM sector—somebody else had worked that stuff out—but we were going to try and work out a compatible production side and then put it all together. That was the general idea. Remember the Brookings model from those days? It was like a church supper, the way I think about it, where somebody's bringing the consumption function and somebody else is bringing the investment function. It's like Mrs. Smith is bringing the potato salad and Mrs. Jones is bringing the ribs. Somehow—you just trusted dumb luck that there was going to be the right balance of desserts and salads and God knows what. It's not a good way to design a menu, and it's a completely crazy way to put together a general equilibrium model of the whole economy. Nobody's thinking about the whole thing.

Well, that takes me up to the end of the Keynesian phase of my career. What went wrong? I'm not going to talk about this. It's a complicated story, the story of what's happened in macroeconomics since the late 1960s. It's pretty interesting. I've written about it elsewhere and so have lots of other people. So I'm just going to fast forward. This is complete hindsight. It has nothing to do with what I thought in '63 or '68, but how I think about it now. What happened? What did in Keynesian economics? I'm just going to sketch an outrageously simple view of how I think economic thought evolves, and then I'm going to try and apply it to the models that I've been talking about.

18. "The Determinants of Wage Rate Changes and the Infiation-Unemployment Trade-Off for the United States," published in the October 1964 issue of the *Review of Economic Studies.*

I think the basic view of economics that Hume and Smith and Ricardo introduced, taking people as basically alike, pursuing simple goals in a pretty direct way, given their preferences, where you are trying to explain differences in behavior by differences in the situation people are finding themselves in rather than differences in their culture, their inner wiring, inner workings, their race, whatever, their class, just thinking about people as people and then trying to account for their behavior in terms of how they are responding to their environment, that this is it for economics. We got that view from Smith and Ricardo, and there have never been any new paradigms or paradigm changes or shifts. Maybe there will be, but in two hundred years it hasn't happened yet. So you've got this kind of basic line of economic theory.

And then I see the progressive—I don't want to say that everything is in Smith and Ricardo—the progressive element in economics as entirely technical: better mathematics, better mathematical formulation, better data, better data-processing methods, better statistical methods, better computational methods. I think of all progress in economic thinking, in the kind of basic core of economic theory, as developing entirely as learning how to do what Hume and Smith and Ricardo wanted to do, only better: more empirically founded, more powerful solution methods, and so on. So I don't think there *was* a Keynesian revolution in a scientific sense, in the sense of a new paradigm or a bifurcation of economic theory into two different directions. I'll tell you what I think did happen, but it wasn't that.

In the twentieth century, which I think was a pretty good century for economics, important technical developments included mathematically rigorous general equilibrium theory, which can be analyzed in modern mathematical terms in a rigorous and clear way, and a language for talking about dynamics, difference equations, differential equations, shocks. The latter tradition I think of as due to Slutsky, Frisch, Tinbergen. It's sort of a statistical language, not an economic language. You think of Slutsky's paper on stochastic difference equations, it's just a purely statistical model that he simulates using results from some Russian lottery and then generates a time series and says, "Hey, this thing looks like pictures I saw in Mitchell's book."[19] People started putting the economics into it, and I think

19. Slutsky's paper, "The Summation of Random Causes as the Source of Cyclic Processes," appeared in the April 1937 issue of *Econometrica*.

of Keynesian theory as having this excitement because it breathes some economic life into these difference equation systems. So when I think of Keynesian economics or at least the Keynesian economics *I* signed on for, it was part of this econometric model-building tradition. We didn't really treat much of this when I was a student at Chicago, but I certainly moved into it at Carnegie Mellon.

Now what happened is that this statistical way of thinking about dynamics failed. It got replaced by the Arrow-Debreu model, which shows how you can take what seems to be a static general equilibrium model and talk about markets for contingent claims, talk about any kind of dynamics you'd like, coming right out of the economics. No auctioneer, or the auctioneer works very quickly. Everything is accounted for in terms of preferences and technology in this model, and everything can include as much dynamics as you can get from a Tinbergen model or Slutsky's model. Patinkin or Bailey or their students, we didn't know this theory existed back in 1960, although it did. But now its potential is getting realized. It has completely succeeded in taking over growth theory, most of public finance, financial economics. Now it's coming in use in macroeconomics with real business cycle theory; certain kinds of monetary variations have been introduced with success. So when I teach macro now, that's all that I teach: variations on these models. Of course, I specialize them and try to apply them to particular economic questions: I'm not a mathematician. But I don't teach any IS-LM. I don't even mention it. I tell them to go somewhere else. Take the course from somebody else. In that sense, for me, it's over.

But I want to come to this persistence of the IS-LM model, because it *isn't* over.

The problem is that the new theories, the theories embedded in general equilibrium dynamics of the sort that we know how to use pretty well now—there's a residue of things they don't let us think about. They don't let us think about the U.S. experience in the 1930s or about financial crises and their real consequences in Asia and Latin America. They don't let us think, I don't think, very well about Japan in the 1990s. We may be disillusioned with the Keynesian apparatus for thinking about these things, but it doesn't mean that this replacement apparatus can do it either. It can't. In terms of the theory that researchers are developing as a cumulative body of knowledge—no one has figured out how to take that theory to successful answers to the real effects of monetary instability. Some people just deny that there are real effects of monetary instability, but I think that is just a mistake. I don't think that argument can be sustained. I do think that most of the post–World War II fluctuations of GDP about trend can be accounted for in real terms. I've estimated that would be something on the order of 80 percent. People can argue with that. But that's not because money doesn't matter. That's because monetary policy in the postwar United States has been so good.

So that's I think where Keynes's real contribution is. It's not Einstein-level theory, new paradigm, all this. I am in agreement with my neighbor Sue Freehling, that's just so much hot air. I think that in writing the *General Theory,* Keynes was viewing himself as a spokesman for a discredited profession. That's why he doesn't cite anyone but crazies like Hobson. He knows about Wicksell and all the "classics," but he is at pains to disassociate his views from theirs, to overemphasize the differences. He's writing in a situation where people are ready to throw in the towel on capitalism and liberal democracy and go with fascism or corporatism, protectionism, socialist planning. Keynes's first objective is to say, "Look, there's got to be a way to respond to depressions that's consistent with capitalist democracy." What he hits on is that the government should take some new responsibilities, but the responsibilities are for stabilizing overall spending flows. You don't have to plan the economy in detail in order to meet this objective. And in that sense, I think for everybody in the postwar period—I'm talking about Keynesians and monetarists both—that's the agreed-upon view: We should stabilize spending flows, and the question is really one of the details about how best to do it. Friedman's approach involved slightly less government involvement than a Keynesian approach, but I say slightly.

So I think this was a great political achievement. It gave us a lasting image of what we need economists for. I've been talking about the internal mainstream of economics, that's what we researchers live on, but as a group we have to earn our living by helping people diagnose situations that arise and helping them understand what is going on and what we can do about it. That was Keynes's whole life. He was a political activist from beginning to end. What he was concerned about when he wrote the *General Theory* was convincing people that there was a way to deal with the Depression that was forceful and effective but didn't involve scrapping the capitalist system. Maybe we could have done it without him, but I'm glad we didn't have to try. Thank you.

Review of Robert Skidelsky, *John Maynard Keynes*, Volumes 1 and 2*

Each of the two available volumes of Robert Skidelsky's biography of John Maynard Keynes concludes with the publication of a book. The first ends with *The Economic Consequences of the Peace*, the attack on the Treaty of Versailles that made Keynes a celebrity and public figure. The second ends with the publication of *The General Theory of Employment, Interest, and Money*, the book on which Keynes's reputation as an economic theorist now rests. A planned third volume, to cover the decade to Keynes's death in 1946, will not end in this way: *The General Theory* was his last important book. But it will describe Keynes's role in setting up the economic institutions of the post–World War II world, institutions under which an ever-widening set of liberal democracies has enjoyed unprecedented economic growth, free of depressions, for nearly fifty years now. This will be fitting, for *The Economic Consequences of the Peace* set out the vision of a postwar Europe of interdependent economies that Versailles, for a crucial time, precluded, and *The General Theory* set out a rationale for a government role in maintaining high employment that was consistent with capitalism and free institutions. It is to these accomplishments that Skidelsky refers when he calls Keynes a "savior."

Maynard Keynes (the first name John was used only by his mother) is a marvelous subject for a biography, a tremendously interesting and attractive personality, actively and, in some cases centrally, involved in several spheres of British life. As the son of a leading don and then as an influential student, teacher, journal editor, and administrator, he was involved with Cambridge University life from birth to death. Through his classmate Lytton Strachey he became a part of what came to be known as the Bloomsbury group, on which a parallel London life was centered. Through his economic writings, political activism, magazine editing, and economic advising he was engaged in every important political issue of the interwar period. And he had a passionate and varied sex life, beginning as a com-

**Journal of Modern History* 67, no. 4 (December 1995): 914–917.

mitted homosexual and then, around age forty, entering into a long and loving marriage with the ballerina Lydia Lopokova.

All of these involvements are massively and literately documented through diaries and correspondence. Though not a diarist himself, Keynes wrote to and received letters from parents, friends, and lovers on a nearly daily basis. These letters are remarkably revealing: as did others in the Bloomsbury circle, Keynes prided himself on his frankness and lack of hypocrisy. Skidelsky develops his account of Keynes's life from these materials as an endlessly interesting story.

Above all, Keynes was an intellectual, and Skidelsky is a skillful enough intellectual historian to provide a rich context for the origins of his thinking. *Hopes Betrayed* introduces the "Cambridge civilization" dominated by Henry Sidgwick and Keynes's economics teacher Alfred Marshall and treats the philosophy of G. E. Moore, who was as important for Keynes as for the rest of the Bloomsbury group. Skidelsky is also a good economist, well equipped to explicate even the more abstruse of Keynes's writings and to understand the critical reactions they stimulated among contemporaries. He does a serious and respectful job even with writings such as the *Treatise on Probability* and the *Treatise on Money,* with which he has little sympathy, and an inspired (though not uncritical) job with works he admires: *The Economic Consequences of the Peace* and *The General Theory.*

It is, of course, *The General Theory,* Keynes's masterwork, that is the climax of these two volumes. Though Keynes wrote three earlier books on economics, these are now almost universally viewed as way stations on the road to *The General Theory,* preliminaries to the long "struggle of escape from habitual modes of thought and expression" that the writing of this book was for its author.[20] Any modern reference to "Keynesian economics" is a reference to *The General Theory* and its wide influence.

Something over one-third of the text of *The Economist as Savior* is devoted to the writing and the reception of *The General Theory.* There are chapters on Keynes's mature intellectual style, on influences while he was formulating the theory, and on some precursive statements. One chapter is a masterful chapter-by-chapter summary of the book itself, and the next is an invaluable discussion of initial reactions to and interpretations of its contents, most notably that of John R. Hicks. But for Skidelsky, I think, all

20. John Maynard Keynes, *The General Theory of Employment, Interest, and Money* (New York, 1935), p. viii.

of this volume—and its predecessor volume, too—are about *The General Theory,* about the events and the people that formed the author of this central work of the twentieth century.

Certainly Keynes himself had no doubts about the book's central importance. The view he advanced in the introduction was that it provided a new theory that subsumed "classical" economics, his term for the tradition from Adam Smith to Alfred Marshall in which he and all his English contemporaries had been trained, as a special case. As Skidelsky notes in discussing this chapter (2:487), Keynes's language invokes a conscious parallel between his own contribution and Albert Einstein's: "Keynes's identification with Einstein is also too clear to miss. Keynes was writing a 'General Theory' of employment, in which he called classical economics a 'special case' and classical economists 'Euclidean geometers in a non-Euclidean world.'"

The subject matter of *The General Theory* is, of course, the determination of an economy's *overall* level of employment and production (as opposed to employment in the production of particular goods or services), with special emphasis on the influence of monetary factors, such as interest rates, on this level. The topic of *The Wealth of Nations* was hardly a new one, but Adam Smith's original treatment, as well as still earlier essays by David Hume, had deemphasized the importance of monetary influences on a nation's living standards. Throughout the nineteenth century, economists refined the idea—called the "quantity theory of money"—that changes in an economy's overall money supply induced one-for-one changes in prices but (in the long run, anyway) had no effect on its employment and production level. It was as a spokesman for this established position that Keynes wrote in 1923 that "[the quantity theory's] correspondence with fact is not open to question" (2:156).

Skidelsky writes: "The history of the Keynesian revolution is largely a story of Keynes's escape from the quantity theory of money" (1:214). This is an attempt to put intellectual discovery at the center of the story, but I did not find the attempt a successful one. The difficulty is that escape from the quantity theory is so easy! Even Hume, its original formulator, viewed the theory as referring to long-run average behavior only and recorded his view that monetary expansions were a stimulus to production in the short run. Certainly all of Keynes's contemporaries had "escaped from the quantity theory" in the sense that they believed that monetary instability played a causal role in the real events we call the business cycle, and all agreed that finding a theoretical framework that could capture this cause-effect relation in a useful way was an important objective. Indeed, this had been the explicit objective of *The Treatise on Money,* of much of the work of Keynes's friends Dennis Robertson and Ralph Hawtrey, and of Friedrich Hayek's London School of Economics lectures of 1931, published as *Prices and Production.*[21] If Keynes found escape from the quantity theory a struggle, he at least had the consolation that virtually all of his "classical" teachers and contemporaries were engaged in it too!

It would have been a great achievement, one that would have lived up to the pretensions of the introduction to the *General Theory,* to have formulated a more general theory that captured both the quantity theory of money as a special case describing long-run average behavior and also the real effects of monetary changes that seem to be so important in the short run. This is what Hayek attempted, intelligently though unsuccessfully, in the 1930s, what Don Patinkin's *Money, Interest, and Prices* attempted in the 1950s, and what many others have attempted since.[22] But this is *not* what the *General Theory* does, or even what it tries to do. The *General Theory* escapes from the quantity theory simply by forgetting about it, and about long run behavior in general, and focusing on a situation in which prices do not adjust. This was why J. R. Hicks called the theory "slump economics" in his contemporary review, and why he questioned its originality relative to what "classical" economists had long believed.

Hicks and later Franco Modigliani worked out simple equation systems that captured what can be made precise in *The General Theory.* These systems turned out to be useful in the construction of statistical models of the economy, and their influence was no doubt enhanced by their origins in Keynes's book. But if Hicks's and Modigliani's interpretations were right, a Keynesian theory can be constructed from a "classical" one by simply freezing one of the variables in the latter (the price level or the level of wages) and discarding one of the equations! Many would credit Keynes's instincts for seeing that such an exercise could be useful in thinking about certain economic policy questions, but the parallels that Keynes and others drew between the economics of *The General Theory* and Einstein's theory of relativity can now be read only with embarrassment.

As a systematic thinker, Maynard Keynes was not a success. Two of his

21. Friedrich A. Hayek, *Prices and Production* (London, 1931).

22. Don Patinkin, *Money, Interest, and Prices* (Evanston, Ill., 1950).

three ambitious attempts to formulate systematic theory, *A Treatise on Probability* and *A Treatise on Money*, were failures, without even transient influence on specialists. The third, *The General Theory*, was a central ideological event of this century, the book that helped many to interpret that terrible economic failure of the 1930s, the Great Depression, as a kind of mistake that was fixable by bold but not revolutionary policies within the general framework of capitalist democracy. Perhaps at one time it served a useful ideological end to treat *The General Theory* as though it were an Einsteinian-level revolution in economic theory. But it was not, and as the years have passed and as economic theory has moved on, such a view has become increasingly irrelevant and difficult to defend.

Yet many economists of the first rank continue to describe themselves as "Keynesians," and many interesting new research ideas are motivated as addressing "Keynesian questions" or as taking a "Keynesian approach." (For a physicist to identify himself as an "Einsteinian" would be redundant: Einstein's theory succeeded!) These modern economists do not, I think, claim detailed precedent in Keynes for their ideas or method, and many have not even read him. In adopting the label "Keynesian" they are identifying themselves not so much with particular economic theories as with an activist, freewheeling spirit in applying economics to practical problems. They (rightly) associate with Keynes, and wish to associate with themselves, a sense that it is legitimate to advocate policies that promise immediate relief from economic distress, and to worry about possible long-run consequences of such policies later on, if ever.

Robert Skidelsky would disagree strongly with my assessment of *The General Theory*, but one of the reasons I found this biography so valuable is that Keynes's enormous influence is so difficult to understand on the basis of his theoretical writings alone. Skidelsky makes it clear that it was an entirely different matter to be subject in person to the force of his personality and his intelligence. According to Hayek, who knew Keynes and liked and admired him personally (but whose view of Keynes as a theorist was the same as mine), "[Keynes] was so convinced that he was cleverer than all the other people that he thought his instinct told him what ought to be done, and he would invent a theory to convince people to do it. That was really his approach."[23] Skidelsky provides many, many illustrations, not all

23. Friedrich A. Hayek, *Hayek on Hayek*, ed. Stephen Krege and Leif Wenar (Chicago, 1994), p. 97.

from economics, of the boundless intellectual and managerial confidence that Hayek remarked on in Keynes, and of the intensity of Keynes's engagement in the world around him.

Maynard Keynes was fully committed to the idea that a system of capitalism and liberal democracy was workable, but his image of workability was not that of a machine that could be set into operation and then left to run on its own. For Keynes, workability meant a continued application of open-minded intelligence and decency to the diagnosis of new situations and to the modification of institutions to deal with them. This view of society and of the role of economic ideas in society is hard to see amid the complications and confusions of Keynes's theoretical writings. Skidelsky has used Keynes's life to make it clear.

Panel Discussion: Is Science Replacing Art?*

Congratulations to Otmar Issing for his leadership during the first years of the Euro and the European Central Bank! An important and valuable international institution has been founded and set on course, earning the confidence of the world. It is a great pleasure and honor for me to be included in the celebration of this achievement.

As an economist I take a special pleasure in the central role that economic analysis has played in the design and operation of the ECB. Since 1999, Otmar Issing and his coauthors have published a flow of books and articles articulating the specifics and underlying principles of the ECB's monetary policy. These publications are distinguished by their clarity, their directness, and their sophisticated and up-date use of statistics and monetary theory. They are inspiring examples of economics in the service of a better world.

The ECB, in common with central banks everywhere today, has adopted the "primary objective of maintaining price stability." A distinctive feature of the ECB approach to inflation control is the emphasis on the "two pillars" of monetary policy. In addition to the ongoing readjustment of the money market interest rate in response to real and nominal information on inflationary pressures, the ECB is also committed to the systematic use of information in monetary aggregates.

**Monetary Policy: A Journey from Theory to Practice;* an ECB Colloquium in Honor of Otmar Issing, 16–17 March 2006, European Central Bank (2007b): 168–171.

Events since 1999 have not tested the importance of this second, monetary, pillar, and central banks that do not make explicit use of money supply data have recent histories of inflation control that are quite as good as the record of the ECB. I am concerned that this encouraging but brief period of success will foster the opinion, already widely held, that the monetary pillar is superfluous, and lead monetary policy analysis back to the kind of muddled eclecticism that brought us the 1970s inflation.

One source of this concern is the increasing reliance of central bank research on New Keynesian modeling. New Keynesian models define monetary policy in terms of a choice of a money market rate, and so make direct contact with central banking practice. Money supply measures play no role in the estimation, testing, or policy simulation of these models. A role for money in the long run is sometimes verbally acknowledged, but the models themselves are formulated in terms of deviations from trends that are themselves determined somewhere off stage. It seems likely that these models could be reformulated to give a unified account of trends, including trends in monetary aggregates, and deviations about trend but so far they have not been. This remains an unresolved issue on the frontier of macroeconomic theory. Until it is resolved, monetary information should continue be used as a kind of add-on or cross-check, just as it is in ECB policy formulation today.

It would be simpler, I suppose, to ignore monetary information altogether. But this would entail ignoring the only explanation we have for the inflation of the 1970s, the only major macroeconomic policy mistake of the OCED economies in the last 60 years. It would entail as well ignoring the only principle that proved useful in bringing that inflation to an end. I will elaborate briefly on both these assertions.

Figure 1, taken from McCandless and Weber (1995), plots average rates of *M*2 growth and CPI inflation for 110 countries over the years 1960–1990. They lie roughly on a line of slope one as predicted by the simplest, constant-velocity form of the quantity theory of money. When Otmar Issing (2005, p. 8) writes of a "fundamental and robust result of monetary economics," this is the kind of theory and evidence he is referring to.

But what does this have to do with the 1970s inflation? Figure 2, taken from Benati (2005) is one way to answer this question. The figure plots annual growth rates of *M*2 and the GDP deflator against time for more than a century of U.S. data, but obviously the series shown are not simply the originally published data. In order to reveal the long term connections between money and inflation, Benati has used a standard statistical for-

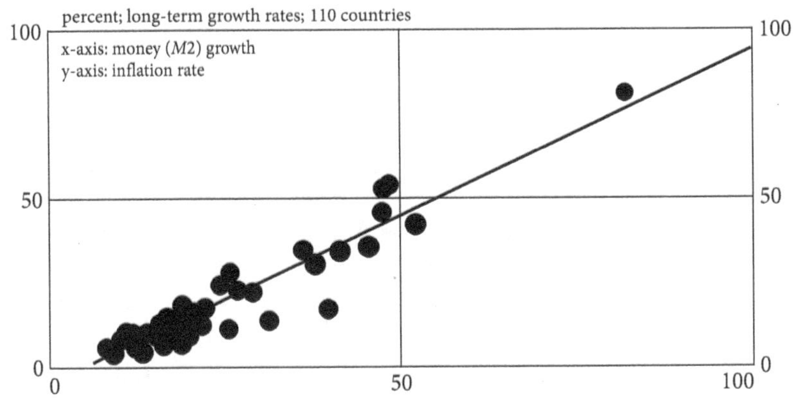

Money Growth and Inflation

Figure 1

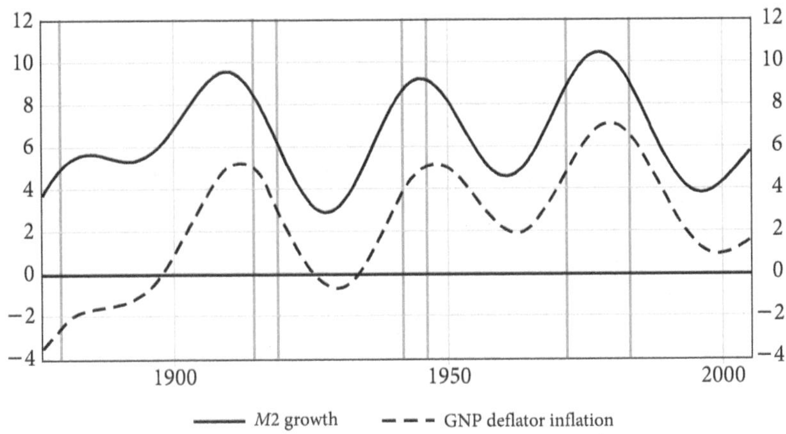

Figure 2

mula—a "filter"—to remove all but the most slowly moving components in the two series. A lot of information is lost in applying such a procedure, but what remains is a demonstration that the same simple version of the quantity theory of money that accounts for cross-country differences in the postwar period accounts as well for the three major 20th century U.S. inflations: the two world wars and the 1970s. In particular, the 1970s inflation in the United States is fully accounted for as a one-for-one response to increased money growth.

I want to emphasize that there is no Keynesian—old or New—counterpart to these two figures. Whatever its limitations, and there are many, the quantity theory of money gives a useful account of the main features of the major historical inflations. The New Keynesian theory and the conventional banking wisdom with which it was designed to be compatible accounts for none.

The first central banks to deal effectively with the 1970s inflation were the Bundesbank and the Swiss National Bank, and both did so in the mid-70s by deliberate reductions in money growth rates. In October, 1979 the U.S. Federal Reserve followed suit, with new operating procedures defined in terms of the monetary base and with the federal funds rate left up to market forces. Figure 3 plots the funds rate against time (in weeks) for a few years before and after October, 1979.

The change in Fed operating procedure was announced and explained at the time, but even if it had not been, one can see the abrupt change in the behavior of the funds rate in the figure. In the period before 1979 the week-to-week changes in the funds rate are tiny: The little high frequency variation we see reflects only the fact that the old (like the current) interest rate policy is not an exact peg. After October, a large high frequency component appears in the series and continues to be visible for several years. New Keynesian theorists describe these movements in the funds rate in terms of the "Taylor rule" used to describe deliberate open market committee decisions. One often sees references to Paul Volcker's "use" of high

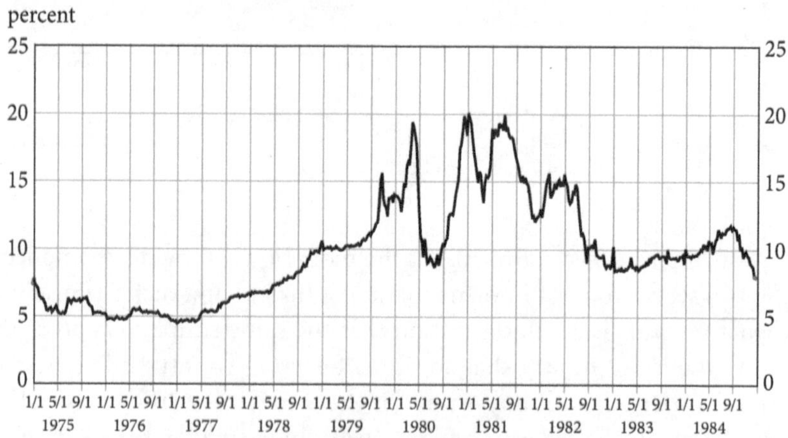

Federal Funds Rates — Weekly, 1975–1984

Figure 3

interest rates to curb the inflation. But can anyone seriously argue that the fluctuations after October, 1979 represent the deliberations of the Open Market Committee? If so, they must have been meeting every week and been ridiculously undecisive when they did!

Anyone familiar with financial time series will recognize these funds rate movements as fluctuations in an uncontrolled market price. In particular, they reflect the large amount of uncertainty about future inflation that prevailed in 1979, and the resulting high sensitivity of the inflation premium to new price information. The peaks in the figure are Fisherian market responses to inflation announcements, not applications of a Taylor rule. All of this was completely understood at the time: Volcker had been explicit that open market operations would no longer be used to stabilize the funds rate. The inflation in the United States was brought to an end by a focus on money growth, just as it was in Germany and Switzerland.

To sum up, neither the occurence of the inflation of the 1970s nor the policies that brought it to an end can be understood without emphasis on the second, monetary pillar of central bank policy. To let the success of inflation control of the last 20 years lead us to forget this fact would be a very foolish mistake.

At the same time—and this is not easy for an old monetarist to say—the use of interest rate control to target inflation rates in the short run has succeeded far beyond the possibilities suggested by the quantity theory of money. Relative to what we knew 20 years ago, inflation targeting is a genuine practical breakthrough. The New Keynesian program to develop a useful theoretical understanding of this success is a well-motivated and valuable enterprise.

References

Benati, L. (2005), Long-run Evidence on Money Growth and Inflation, *Bank of England Quarterly Bulletin.*

Issing, O. and Gaspar V. (2005), *Imperfect Knowledge and Monetary Policy: The Stone Lectures in Economics.*

McCandless, G. T. Jr. and Weber, W. E. (1995), Some Monetary Facts, *Federal Reserve Bank of Minneapolis Quarterly Review.*

Index

www.ingramcontent.com/pod-product-compliance
Lightning Source LLC
LaVergne TN
LVHW091518200926
848483LV00005B/448/J
* 9 7 8 0 6 7 4 0 6 6 8 7 8 *